MUSIC CONTRACTS IN THE STREAMING AGE

This book focuses on music industry contracts and the contractual dynamics between composing and/or performing musicians and their primary partners in the digitised music industry, namely music publishers and record companies, taking account of the ubiquitous nature of music streaming. It focuses on the question of how the legal framework intervenes and should intervene in such contracts, both in theory and in practice. Its objective is to contribute to a level playing field that counteracts the imbalance in bargaining power between musicians and their corporate partners in a proportionate way. The book draws upon an analysis of copyright contract law at the European Union and national level, as well as relevant principles of general contract law, competition law and related applicable rules that curb business-to-business contract terms and trade practices characterised as unreasonable. The book studies the applicable legal framework in Belgium, France, Germany, the Netherlands and the United Kingdom. This title is part of the Flip it Open Programme and may also be available Open Access. Check our website Cambridge Core for details.

Jozefien Vanherpe is Assistant Professor at the KU Leuven Centre for IT and IP law (CiTiP) in Belgium. She studied law at KU Leuven and the University of Cambridge. After working as an attorney for several years, she successfully defended her PhD at KU Leuven in 2022.

CAMBRIDGE INTELLECTUAL PROPERTY AND INFORMATION LAW

As its economic potential has rapidly expanded, intellectual property has become a subject of front-rank legal importance. Cambridge Intellectual Property and Information Law is a series of monograph studies of major current issues in intellectual property. Each volume contains a mix of international, European, comparative and national law, making this a highly significant series for practitioners, judges and academic researchers in many countries.

A list of books in the series can be found at the end of this volume.

Music Contracts in the Streaming Age

LAW AND POLICY IN THE EUROPEAN UNION AND THE UNITED KINGDOM

JOZEFIEN VANHERPE
KU Leuven

CAMBRIDGE
UNIVERSITY PRESS

CAMBRIDGE
UNIVERSITY PRESS

Shaftesbury Road, Cambridge CB2 8EA, United Kingdom

One Liberty Plaza, 20th Floor, New York, NY 10006, USA

477 Williamstown Road, Port Melbourne, VIC 3207, Australia

314–321, 3rd Floor, Plot 3, Splendor Forum, Jasola District Centre, New Delhi – 110025, India

103 Penang Road, #05-06/07, Visioncrest Commercial, Singapore 238467

Cambridge University Press is part of Cambridge University Press & Assessment, a department of the University of Cambridge.

We share the University's mission to contribute to society through the pursuit of education, learning and research at the highest international levels of excellence.

www.cambridge.org
Information on this title: www.cambridge.org/9781009394703

DOI: 10.1017/9781009394666

When citing this work, please include a reference to the DOI 10.1017/9781009394666

First published 2024

A catalogue record for this publication is available from the British Library.

A Cataloging-in-Publication data record for this book is available from the Library of Congress

ISBN 978-1-009-39470-3 Hardback

ISBN 978-1-009-39467-3 Paperback

Contents

Figures and Tables

FIGURES

TABLES

Acknowledgements

To achieve great things, two things are needed:
a plan and not quite enough time.

—Leonard Bernstein

On a sunny day in May 2018, I got a phone call, out of the blue. Would I be interested in pursuing a PhD in law at KU Leuven? asked the voice at the other side of the phone. I was slightly taken aback, and momentarily – some might say uncharacteristically – lost for words. At the time, I had been an intellectual property (IP) attorney for almost four years and felt quite comfortable in my professional life. Regardless, the seed planted during that brief conversation quickly grew, to such an extent that, after just a few days, it could no longer be ignored. I eventually took the leap, and started my PhD trajectory at the beginning of 2019. Fast forward a few years, and that brings us here today – to me thanking everyone that has provided me with abundant support, love and laughter along the way.

First, I would like to thank my PhD supervisor, Professor Dr Evelyne Terryn. Thank you for writing me a letter of recommendation for the Cambridge LLM, which expanded my world; for the ample opportunities you gave me to write, teach and grow in an independent way; and for showing me what to aspire to, on both a professional and a personal level. My heartfelt thanks also go out to my co-supervisor, Professor Dr Marie-Christine Janssens. Thank you for being a beacon of integrity, intelligence and vision at the Faculty of Law and Criminology at KU Leuven (and beyond) and for challenging me to always do and be better. Thank you, also, to Professors Dr Hendrik Vanhees and Dr Fabienne Brison, for being members of my supervisory committee and PhD jury. I will admit that, ever since I read both of your PhD theses in full, I have unashamedly been a fangirl to you both. Without a doubt, the same is true for Professors Dr Lionel Bently and Dr Séverine Dusollier, whom I thank not only for agreeing to be members of my PhD jury but also for the seminal contributions that they have both made – and are still making – to an inclusive intellectual property law framework that is fit not only for the digital age but also for the artists that live, create and perform in it. I feel truly honoured to have you on my side.

To the immensely diverse group of people that I get to call my friends, whether met through school in Belgium or abroad, via travel, work, sports or – especially – music: thank you for bringing me joy and ensuring that I always have a place to stay across the globe. I hope you realise how much you inspire me.

Most of all, however, my thanks go out to my family. The Vanherpe name may very well be close to extinction on a global level, but my parents' legacy on that front is undeniable – in both quantity and quality. My parents and all of my siblings give me something to aim for, ranging from an incredible resilience in the face of adversity, over the impressive ability to stay calm and pragmatic when confronted with insurmountable chaos, to the incredible strength of always taking the high road. I am very lucky, and I know it. The greatest luck of all, however, is seeing and experiencing the expansion of our family, with mini versions of the people I love the most. While the past few years have forced us to say an untimely goodbye to a number of valued family members, the future looks bright.

And with that, I close the journey of my PhD research, which started in February 2019, hit a high note with my public defence in March 2022 and has now culminated in this volume. No dazzling grand finale, no encores, no snazzy 500-days-of-Summer-style wrap-up musical number, no mic drop – only my sincere, heartfelt gratitude. As ABBA would say: thank you for the music.

Abbreviations

A&R	Artist & Repertoire
ACM	*Autoriteit Consument en Markt* (Authority for Consumers and Markets)
ADAMI	*Administration des Droits des Artistes et Musiciens Interprètes* (Administration of the Rights of Performing Artists and Musicians)
ADR	alternative dispute resolution
AEPO-ARTIS	Association of European Performers' Organisations
AHRC	Arts and Humanities Research Council
AIE	*Artistas Interpretes o Ejecutantes de España* (Performing Artists of Spain)
AIMP	Association of Independent Music Publishers
AIPPI	*Association Internationale pour la Protection de la Propriété Intellectuelle* (Association for the Protection of Intellectual Property)
ALS	artist and label services
AREC	Artists Rights Enforcement Corporation
ARPU	average revenue per user
B2B	business-to-business
B2C	business-to-consumer
BAM	*Beroepsvereniging voor Auteur-Muzikanten* (Professional Association for Author-Musicians)
BEUC	*Bureau Européen des Unions de Consommateurs* (European Bureau of Consumer Unions)
BGB	*Bürgerliches Gesetzbuch*
BGBl	*Bundesgesetzblatt*
BGH	*Bundesgerichtshof*
BMAC	Black Music Action Coalition

BRMA	Belgian Recorded Music Association
BS	*Belgisch Staatsblad*
BSCG	Belgian Screen Composers Guild
BUMA	*Bureau voor Muziek-Auteursrechten* (Bureau for Music Copyrights)
BVerfG	*Bundesverfassungsgericht*
BVMI	*Bundesverband Musikindustrie* (Federal Music Industry Association)
CC	Creative Commons
CCFG	Cultural Creators Friendship Group
CCIs	cultural and creative industries
CEL	Code on Economic Law
CIS	Common Information System
CISAC	*Confédération Internationale des Sociétés d'Auteurs et Compositeurs* (International Confederation of Societies of Authors and Composers)
CJEU	Court of Justice of the European Union
CMA	Competition and Markets Authority
CMO	collective management organisation
CNM	*Centre National de la Musique* (National Centre for Music)
CPI	*Code de la Propriété Intellectuelle*
CRM	collective rights management
CSPLA	*Conseil Supérieur de la Propriété Littéraire et Artistique* (High Council for Literary and Artistic Property)
D2C	direct-to-consumer
D2F	direct-to-fan
DCFR	Draft Common Frame of Reference
DCMS	Department for Digital, Culture, Media & Sport
DIY	do-it-yourself
DKV	*Deutscher Komponistenverband* (German Composer Association)
DRM	digital rights management
DSM	Digital Single Market DSP digital service provider
EC	European Commission
ECJ	European Court of Justice
ECHR	European Convention on Human Rights
ECtHR	European Court of Human Rights
ECSA	European Composer and Songwriter Alliance
EDM	electronic dance music
EEA	European Economic Area
EEC	European Economic Community

EMMA	European Music Managers Alliance
ER	equitable remuneration
EU	European Union
FAC	Featured Artists Coalition
FACIR	*Fédération des Auteur·rices, Compositeur·rices et Interprètes Réuni·es* (Federation of Authors, Composers and Performers United)
FIM	*Fédération Internationale des Musiciens* (International Federation of Musicians)
GALM	*Genootschap Artiesten Lichte Muziek* (Society of Light Music Artists, now 'de Muziekgilde')
GDPR	General Data Protection Regulation
GEMA	*Gesellschaft für musikalische Aufführungs- und mechanische Vervielfältigungsrechte* (Society for Musical Performance and Mechanical Reproduction Rights)
GESAC	*Groupement Européen des Sociétés d'Auteurs et Compositeurs* (European Grouping of Societies of Authors and Composers)
GRD	Global Repertoire Database
GVL	*Gesellschaft zur Verwertung von Leistungsschutzrechten* (Society for the Exploitation of Neighbouring Rights)
IAO	International Artists Organisation
ICMP	International Confederation of Music Publishers
IFPI	International Federation of the Phonographic Industry
ILO	International Labour Organization
IMMF	International Music Managers Forum
IMPEL	Independent Music Publishers European Licensing
IMPF	Independent Music Publishers International Forum
IMPALA	Independent Music Companies Association (originally: Independent Music Publishers and Labels Association)
INA	*Institut national de l'audiovisuel* (National Audio-Visual Institute)
IP	intellectual property
IPRs	intellectual property rights
IPRED	Intellectual Property Rights Enforcement Directive
ISPs	internet service providers
ISRC	International Standard Recording Code
ISWC	International Standard Musical Work Code
JORF	*Journal Officiel de la République Française*
M&A	mergers and acquisitions
MLC	Mechanical Licensing Collective

MMA	Music Modernization Act
MME	Music Moves Europe
MMF	Music Managers Forum
NDA	non-disclosure agreement
NMPA	National Music Publishers Association
NMUV	*Nederlandse Muziek Uitgevers Vereniging* (Dutch Music Publishers Association)
NORMA	*Naburige Rechtenorganisatie voor Musici en Acteurs* (Neighbouring Rights Organisation for Musicians and Actors)
NVPI	*Nederlandse Vereniging van Producenten en Importeurs van beeld- en geluidsdragers* (Dutch Association of Producers and Importers of Image and Sound Carriers)
OCSSP	online content-sharing service provider
OECD	Organisation for Economic Co-operation and Development
P2P	peer-to-peer
PALM	*Professionele Auteurs Lichte Muziek* (Professional Authors Light Music)
PEC	AHRC Creative Industries Policy & Evidence Centre
PECL	Principles of European Contract Law
PICC	Principles of International Commercial Contracts
PPD	published price to dealer
PPL	Phonographic Performance Limited
RAAP	Recorded Artists Actors Performers
RIAA	Recording Industry Association of America
RRP	recommended retail price
SABAM	*Société d'Auteurs Belge – Belgische Auteurs Maatschappij* (Belgian Authors Society)
SACEM	*Société des Auteurs, Compositeurs et Éditeurs de Musique* (Society of Authors, Composers and Music Publishers)
SAI	*Société des Artistes Interprètes* (Society of Performing Artists)
SENA	*Stichting ter Exploitatie van Naburige Rechten* (Foundation for the Exploitation of Neighbouring Rights)
SLRP	suggested retail list price
SMEs	small and medium-sized enterprises
SNEP	*Syndicat National de l'Édition Phonographique* (National Union of Phonographic Publishing)

SPEDIDAM	*Société de Perception et de Distribution des Droits des Artistes-Interprètes* (Collecting and Distributing Society for the Rights of Performing Artists)
Stb	*Staatsblad*
STEMRA	*Stichting tot Exploitatie van Mechanische Reproduktierechten voor Auteurs* (Union for the Exploitation of Reproduction Rights for Authors)
TEU	Treaty on European Union
TFEU	Treaty on the Functioning of the European Union
TRIPS	Trade-Related Aspects of Intellectual Property Rights
UrhG	*Urheberrechtsgesetz*
UCC	Universal Copyright Convention
UCPS	User-Centric Payment System
UDHR	Universal Declaration of Human Rights
UGC	user-generated content
UKIPO	UK Intellectual Property Office
UNAC	*Union Nationale des Auteurs et des Compositeurs* (National Union of Authors and Composers)
UNESCO	United Nations Educational, Scientific and Cultural Organization
UrhDaG	*Urheberrechts-Diensteanbieter-Gesetz*
UWG	*Gesetz gegen den unlauteren Wettbewerb*
VAT	value-added tax
VGG	*Verwertungsgesellschaftengesetz*
WIN	Worldwide Independent Network
WIPO	World Intellectual Property Organization
WPPT	WIPO Performances and Phonograms Treaty
WTO	World Trade Organization

1

Prelude

We have no idea what we are signing,
in an act of legendary mental deficiency.

—Morrissey[1]

1.1 INTRO

Music forms the soundtrack that accompanies and brightens our daily lives. It is one of the very few endeavours that unites us all. Its intrinsic value is undeniable. However, this often does not translate into economic value. In the streaming age, the instantaneous accessibility of music is the norm. It is deceptively easy to forget the artistic and commercial journey a melody must travel before reaching an audience. A fruitful collaboration between a wealth of individuals and companies is required to ensure successful completion of the artistic and commercial process of 'making music'. This process constitutes the common thread of this book, which focuses on the legal aspects of contractual dynamics in the music industry.

A structural difference in relative bargaining power between musicians and their primary corporate business partners characterises the wide array of contractual relationships in the music value chain.[2] This rings especially true at the beginning

[1] Morrissey, *Autobiography* (Penguin Classics 2013) 156.

[2] Séverine Dusollier and others, 'Contractual Arrangements Applicable to Creators: Law and Practice of Selected Member States' (Publications Office of the EU 2014) <https://op.europa.eu/s/zIba> 6, 16; Europe Economics and others, 'Remuneration of Authors and Performers for the Use of Their Works and the Fixations of Their Performances. Final Report' (Publications Office of the EU 2015) <https://op.europa.eu/s/zIa9> 138–39; Isabelle De Voldere and others, 'Mapping the Creative Value Chains. A Study on the Economy of Culture in the Digital Age. Final Report' (Publications Office of the EU 2017) <https://op.europa.eu/s/zIa8> 77; Ananay Aguilar, '"We Want Artists to Be Fully and Fairly Paid for Their Work". Discourses on Fairness in the Neoliberal European Copyright Reform' [2018] JIPITEC 160, 161; Séverine Dusollier, 'EU Contractual Protection of Creators: Blind Spots and Shortcomings' [2018] Colum J L & Arts, 436, 444; Abbe EL Brown and others, *Contemporary Intellectual Property: Law and Policy* (5th edn, Oxford University Press 2019) 222.

of musicians' musical careers. Parties' bargaining power is not only affected by their negotiating abilities, but also by their prior success, the availability of alternative options and their patience in holding out for a better deal.[3] The imbalance in relative bargaining power is not only affected by the characterisation of the music industry as a winner-takes-all superstar economy, but also by a tenacious information asymmetry, whereby relevant knowledge of corporate partners surpasses that of musicians.[4]

The flexibility of the legal framework, based on the freedom of contract, combined with an oversupply of musicians with low bargaining power, may prevent Coasean bargaining in practice.[5] Put simply, it makes commercial sense for corporate players in the music industry to lean towards exercising their market power in a way that is disadvantageous to musicians.[6] Over the years, moreover, there have been many examples of one-sided, industry-friendly music industry contracts, often leading to dire situations for musicians.[7] Until at least the turn of the century, contracts between musicians and their corporate partners were almost exclusively contracts of adhesion of a 'take it or leave it' nature, with boilerplate language and a list of standard terms which many aspiring superstars were nevertheless eager to sign.[8] Possible sources of unfairness in such contracts include (1) excessive rights granted to and (2) limited obligations on the part of the record company/music

[3] Martin Kretschmer and others, 'The Relationship between Copyright and Contract Law' (2010) <https://ssrn.com/abstract=2624945> 28–32; Europe Economics and others (n 2) 111–12, 120–21.

[4] Cf Europe Economics and others (n 2) 136; De Voldere and others, 'Mapping the Creative Value Chains' (n 2) 143–44; Agnès Lucas-Schloetter, 'The Remuneration of Authors and Performers in Copyright Contract Law' in Paul Torremans (ed), *Research Handbook on Copyright Law* (Research Handbooks in Intellectual Property, 2nd edn, Edward Elgar 2017) 268–69; Morten Hviid and others, 'Digitalisation and Intermediaries in the Music Industry: The Rise of the Entrepreneur?' (2018) 15 SCRIPTed 242, 271; Alan B Krueger, *Rockonomics* (John Murray 2019) 161.

[5] Cf De Voldere and others, 'Mapping the Creative Value Chains' (n 2) 74; Rebecca Giblin and Cory Doctorow, *Chokepoint Capitalism: How Big Tech and Big Content Captured Creative Labor Markets and How We'll Win Them Back* (Beacon Press 2022) 16; Richard Osborne and Hyojung Sun, 'Economics of Streaming: Contract Adjustment and Rights Reversion' (6 February 2023) ch 1.

[6] Cf Phillip W Hall Jr, 'Smells Like Slavery: Unconscionability in Recording Industry Contracts' [2002] Hastings Comm & Ent LJ 189, 190; Krueger, *Rockonomics* (n 4) 160.

[7] Nancy K Baym, *Playing to the Crowd. Musicians, Audiences, and the Intimate Work of Connection* (New York University Press 2018) 65; Krueger, *Rockonomics* (n 4) 164, 170.

[8] Ruth Towse, 'Copyright and Economic Incentives: An Application to Performers' Rights in the Music Industry' (1999) 52 Kyklos 369, 372–73; Hall Jr, 'Smells Like Slavery' (n 6) 201; Abhinay Muthoo, 'Bargaining Theory and Royalty Contract Negotiations' (2006) 3 RERCI 19, 19; Jean-Christophe Lardinois, *Les Contrats Commentés de l'Industrie de La Musique 2.0: Cadre Général et Pratique Contractuelle* (Création Information Communication Pratique 1, 2nd edn, Larcier 2009) 7; Dusollier and others, 'Contractual Arrangements Applicable to Creators' (n 2) 16; Dusollier, 'EU Contractual Protection of Creators' (n 2) 436; Hviid and others, 'Digitalisation and Intermediaries in the Music Industry' (n 4) 260; Bruno Racine, 'L'Auteur et l'Acte de Création' (January 2020) 33; Yannos Paramythiotis, 'Fairness in Copyright Contract Law: Remuneration for Authors and Performers under the Copyright in

publisher in terms of both the exploitation of the musical content and the remuneration therefor, as well as (3) issues concerning the termination of a contract.

Musicians who seek to enter into a commercial relationship in the recorded music and/or music publishing sector now have a vast array of options at their disposal, much more than a few decades ago. This has led to a markedly more artist-friendly environment, whereby some rules that used to be set in stone, such as a full transfer of rights against a modest flat fee, have become more malleable and open to contractual modulation. However, some corporate music industry habits have proven rather hard to break and, in many cases, the traditional power relationships still seemingly prevail.

This book seeks to address the consequences of this perceived difference in relative bargaining power. Particular focus lies with the contractual relationships between musicians and record companies and/or music publishers. The oversupply of musicians may lead to unfair situations whereby musicians draw the short straw. The digitisation wave and the rise of music streaming add an additional layer of complexity. While musicians may now in theory reach and build their audience in a fully independent way, significant barriers to entry remain. Moreover, analogue contracts have proven to be a difficult fit with technological opportunities in the music market. Music industry professionals are faced with constantly evolving business models to which the principles of past contracts are tough to apply.

Regulating the music industry may be compared to hitting a moving target. The law inherently lags behind technological and economic developments. This should not be cause for despair. Instead, concerted efforts are required to construct a legal framework that is fair, fit for the digital age and sufficiently flexible in the long run. This book seeks to contribute to such a legal framework, that serves as a real and tangible instrument towards achieving a fair(er) balance between the interests of the primary stakeholders in the streaming age. It aims to develop a holistic regulatory approach, seeking an appropriate, fair(er) balance between the interests of musicians and the main corporate actors, while taking account of the interests of users. Thus, the book envisages an application of copyright that enhances musician welfare and is aligned with its original objective, while at the same time ensuring a healthy investment climate and appropriate access to content. The methodology applied in order to achieve this goal is fleshed out below.

1.2 METHODOLOGY

This book analyses the extent to which the law intervenes in the contractual relationship between musicians and corporate partners and the extent to which it

the Digital Single Market Directive' in Tatiana-Eleni Synodinou and others (eds), *EU Internet Law in the Digital Single Market* (Springer International 2021) 78.

should do so: where the line should be drawn between freedom of contract and the desirability of protecting parties with weaker bargaining power in business-to-business (B2B) situations in the streaming age. The tools available to stakeholders faced with unfair contractual situations as well as legislative developments in Belgium, France, Germany, the Netherlands and the United Kingdom are analysed and evaluated. The book accords attention to both the substantive content of the applicable legal framework and its application in practice.

The central research question is formulated as follows: how can the legal framework contribute to achieving a fair(er) balance between the interests of musicians and the main corporate partners in the music industry in the context of the streaming age? This question is addressed through the following sub-questions:

1. What are the main interests involved in the music industry, how do these interests converge/conflict in practice and how should the goal of achieving a fair(er) balance between those interests be understood, particularly in the streaming age?
2. How does the relevant legal framework in Belgium, France, Germany, the Netherlands and the United Kingdom, consisting primarily of copyright contract law and secondarily of the law of unfair B2B contract terms and trade practices and general contract law, seek to contribute to achieving such a balance?
3. Does the legal framework actually achieve a fair balance in practice?
4. How may the existing legal framework be improved in order to ensure a fair(er) balance in the music industry in the streaming age?

The research method consists of a critical literature review and content analysis, applying an integrated intradisciplinary, interdisciplinary and comparative approach. First, as to the separate sub-questions, several fields of law are analysed. Second, the complexity of the music industry and the many interests involved require the book to be interdisciplinary. Moreover, this book aims higher than a merely descriptive outcome. To the extent it is useful and relevant, in addition to authoritative positivistic legal sources, non-legal research is included. Third, a comparative analysis between five different national jurisdictions constitutes one of the main building blocks of this book. Below, the methodological choices made in the context of each sub-question are explained further.

The first sub-question is defining, descriptive and explanatory and, importantly, specifies the normative framework. This question entails an analysis of the dynamic power structures in and the effects of digitisation on the music industry. Given the legal focus of this book, it presents these industry developments in the context of the copyright framework in the broad sense. Finally, the normative aspect of this first sub-question asks how the concept of a ‘fair balance’ should be interpreted in the music industry, particularly in the age of streaming. As this book focuses on music, it does not treat the debate surrounding the exploitation of music in audio-visual form and, in particular, the issue of buyouts in the audio-visual sector.[9]

The relevant sources for all aspects of this first sub-question include authoritative legal sources such as legislation and legal doctrine as well as non-legal research, with a focus on cultural economics literature, cultural music studies and reports on the structure and functioning of the music industry.[10] In addition, popular literature has been sourced, including blogs, interviews and news items.

The second sub-question is descriptive and explanatory. It focuses on how the legal framework in Belgium, France, Germany, the Netherlands and the United Kingdom seeks to contribute to achieving a fair(er) balance between artistic and commercial interests in the streaming age.

The third sub-question evaluates the existing framework in the selected jurisdictions, with the objective of achieving a fair(er) balance as defined in the normative aspect of the first sub-question.

The fourth, normative sub-question treats whether and how the existing legal framework, as analysed and evaluated in the context of the second and third sub-questions, may be improved in light of the objective of achieving a fair(er) balance, both in theory and in practice.

The relevant legal framework includes authoritative legal sources such as legislation, legal doctrine and case law of higher courts relating to the fields of copyright contract law, principles of general contract law, competition law and related applicable rules that curb B2B contract terms and trade practices characterised as unreasonable. Focus lies with copyright contract law as the pertinent *lex specialis*.

9 See ia Jean-Christophe Lardinois, *Les Contrats Commentés de l'Industrie Audiovisuelle: Cadre Général et Pratique Contractuelle* (Création Information Communication Pratique 3, Larcier 2007); Cécile Despringre and others, 'Audiovisual Authors' Rights and Remuneration in Europe' (SAA White Paper, 2015); Raquel Xalabarder, 'International Legal Study on the Implementation of an Unwaivable Right of Audiovisual Authors to Obtain Equitable Remuneration for the Exploitation of Their Works' (2018); Raquel Xalabarder, 'The Equitable Remuneration of Audiovisual Authors: A Proposal of Unwaivable Remuneration Rights under Collective Management' [2018] RIDA 5; Stéphanie Carre, Stéphanie Le Cam and Franck Macrez, 'Buyout Contracts Imposed by Platforms in the Cultural and Creative Sector' (Publications Office of the EU 2023) <https://shorturl.at/bhsNR>; Amélie Lacourt, Justine Radel-Cormann and Sophie Valais, 'Fair Remuneration for Creators in Exploitation Contracts' (European Audiovisual Observatory 2023) <https://shorturl.at/dwT68>.

10 See ia Jim Rogers, *The Death & Life of the Music Industry in the Digital Age* (Bloomsbury 2013); Mark Mulligan, *Awakening: The Music Industry in the Digital Age* (Createspace 2015); Kenneth W Barr, 'Music Copyright in the Digital Age. Creators, Commerce and Copyright. An Empirical Study of the UK Music Copyright Industries' (University of Glasgow 2016); Ananay Aguilar, 'Distributed Ownership in Music: Between Authorship and Performance' (2018) 27 Social & Legal Studies 776; Aguilar, 'We Want Artists' (n 2); Chris Cooke, *Dissecting the Digital Dollar* (3rd edn, Music Managers Forum and CMU Insights 2020); Stef van Gompel and others, 'Evaluatie Wet Auteurscontractenrecht: Eindrapport' (2020) <https://bit.ly/3UBZrh4>. See also <www.copyrightevidence.org>.

As UK law does not expressly contain a copyright contract law framework, the applicable rules of contract law bear particular relevance for this jurisdiction.

The national level retains importance in the field of copyright law, in view of the essentially territorial nature of copyright law, which means that its application is limited to the confines of a certain country.[11] In view of the digitised, globalised nature of our present-day society, many – if not all – of the contracts under review have a link with several national legal systems. This gives rise to questions as to the court having jurisdiction for a certain dispute and the law applicable to a given situation. Associated issues of private international law fall outside the scope of this book.[12]

The book analyses the pertinent national legislation as applicable and amended since the turning of the millennium in 2000. In Belgium, the copyright framework is included in the general *Wetboek van economisch recht*[13]/*Code de droit économique* (in English: Code on Economic Law), in particular in Book XI, Title 5, entitled *Auteursrecht en naburige rechten* (in English: Copyright and Neighbouring Rights). This book refers to that code as the Belgian CEL. While France's *Code de la Propriété Intellectuelle*[14] (in English: Code of Intellectual Property) brings together the various IP rights in one act, both Germany and the Netherlands have legislation that is uniquely devoted to copyright law. Hereinafter, the French CPI, of which Part I contains the legal regime on copyright and neighbouring rights, is referred to as the French IP Code. The German national framework contains two separate relevant acts on copyright law. The main substantive act is the *Gesetz über Urheberrecht und verwandte Schutzrechte (Urheberrechtsgesetz)*[15] (abbreviated as UrhG, in English: Act on Copyright and Neighbouring Rights (Copyright Act). In this book, it is referred to as the German Copyright Act. There is also a specific act concerning collective management, entitled *Gesetz über die Wahrnehmung von Urheberrechten und verwandten Schutzrechten durch Verwertungsgesellschaften (Verwertungsgesellschaftengesetz)*[16] (abbreviated as VGG, in English: Act on the Management of Copyright and Neighbouring Rights by Collective Management Organisations). This text is referred to below as the German CMO Act. The relevant acts of German law are subdivided into parts (*Teile*), subsections (*Abschnitte*) and

[11] Paul Goldstein and P Bernt Hugenholtz, *International Copyright. Principles, Law and Practice* (2nd edn, Oxford University Press 2010) 95–99.

[12] See Jozefien Vanherpe, 'Copyright Contracts at the Frontiers: A Closer Consideration from a Conflict of Laws Perspective' in Simon Geiregat and Hendrik Vanhees (eds), *Copyright Contracts Tomorrow* (LeA 2023).

[13] Full text at <www.ejustice.just.fgov.be>.

[14] Text at <https://bit.ly/3mMpIs5>.

[15] *Gesetz über Urheberrecht und verwandte Schutzrechte*, text at <www.gesetze-im-internet.de/urhg>.

[16] *Gesetz über die Wahrnehmung von Urheberrechten und verwandten Schutzrechten durch Verwertungsgesellschaften*, text at <www.gesetze-im-internet.de/vgg>.

paragraphs (§). For the sake of uniformity, this book refers to the relevant paragraphs as 'Articles'.

The Netherlands has three copyright-specific acts. First, the *Auteurswet*[17] (in English: Copyright Act) contains the substantive provisions of copyright law *sensu stricto*. It is referred to below as the Dutch Copyright Act. Second, the *Wet op de naburige rechten*[18] (in English: Act on Neighbouring Rights) is specific to neighbouring rights protection. It is referred to as the Dutch Neighbouring Rights Act. Third, Dutch law comprises an act specific to collective management, namely the *Wet toezicht en geschillenbeslechting collectieve beheersorganisaties auteurs- en naburige rechten*[19] (in English: Act on Management and Dispute Resolution regarding Collective Management organisations of copyright and neighbouring rights). It is referred to below as the Dutch CMO Act.

Finally, in the United Kingdom, the copyright framework is included in the Copyright, Designs and Patents Act 1988 (CDPA). This book refers to this code as the UK CDPA. The UK CDPA is subdivided into Parts, Chapters and Sections. As for German law, this book refers to the relevant sections as 'Articles'.

Further, since the chosen jurisdictions include four Member States of the European Union, the EU regulatory level is integrated into the analysis. The EU legislator has drafted a significant number of harmonising legal texts in the field of copyright law.[20] As of yet, the *acquis communautaire* consists of twelve directives, two regulations and a significant body of ECJ case law.[21] The primary directive that recurs throughout this book is the Digital Single Market (DSM) Directive.[22]

On the international level, several relevant international conventions apply in all five chosen jurisdictions. These conventions primarily contain general principles and minimum standards.[23] This overarching legal framework leaves a significant

[17] *Auteurswet*, text at <https://wetten.overheid.nl/BWBR0001886>.

[18] *Wet op de naburige rechten*, text at <https://wetten.overheid.nl/BWBR0005921>.

[19] Text at <https://wetten.overheid.nl/BWBR0014779>.

[20] Lionel Bently and others, *Intellectual Property Law* (5th edn, Oxford University Press 2018) 51–54, 56–57; Justine Pila and Paul Torremans, *European Intellectual Property Law* (2nd edn, Oxford University Press 2019) 229–39. Cf Rec 2 DSM Directive.

[21] See <https://bit.ly/30U8ITq>. See Michel M Walter and Silke von Lewinski (eds), *European Copyright Law. A Commentary* (Oxford University Press 2010); Thomas Dreier and P Bernt Hugenholtz (eds), *Concise European Copyright Law* (2nd edn, Kluwer Law International 2016); Irini Stamatoudi and Paul Torremans (eds), *EU Copyright Law. A Commentary* (Elgar Commentaries, 2nd edn, Edward Elgar 2021). See as to the ECJ Eleonora Rosati, *Copyright and the Court of Justice of the European Union*, vol 2 (Oxford University Press 2023).

[22] Directive (EU) 2019/790 of the European Parliament and of the Council of 17 April 2019 on copyright and related rights in the Digital Single Market and amending Directives 96/9/EC and 2001/29/EC [2019] OJ L130/92 (DSM Directive).

[23] See Sam Ricketson and Jane Ginsburg, *International Copyright and Neighbouring Rights. The Berne Convention and Beyond* (2nd edn, Oxford University Press 2006); Silke von Lewinski, *International Copyright Law and Policy* (Oxford University Press 2008); Goldstein and Hugenholtz, *International Copyright* (n 11).

margin for regional and national differences. Applicable provisions of international copyright law are referenced throughout this book where deemed relevant.

1.3 OUTRO

This book is structured in eight chapters, including the present 'Prelude'. Chapter 2 analyses the structure and functioning of the music industry value chain in the streaming age and explores several different avenues for industry-led change. The book then goes on to analyse the protective legal regimes that are aimed at securing a fair(er) balance in contractual situations, applied in particular to the contracts entered into between musicians and record companies and/or music publishers.

Chapter 3 explores the role of the law in the regulation of the music industry in the streaming age and provides a typology of the relevant substantive legal regimes. It analyses their scope in substance, place and time, as well as the interplay between them. It also discusses various options to shape future policy initiatives that may contribute to a fair(er) balance in the streaming age.

In the subsequent three chapters, focus shifts to the substantive content of the relevant legal framework. The division into three chapters is based on the three stages of the 'life' of a contract, namely its formation, its performance and, ultimately, its termination. Chapter 4 treats the negotiation and formation stage of the contract. It analyses limitations on the scope of rights granted at the outset of the contractual relationship and the regulatory framework applicable to the determination of this scope in practice. Chapter 5 analyses the performance phase of the contract, focusing on the extent of corporate partners' duty to exploit the music at issue and fairly remunerate the musician(s). Chapter 6 inquires further regarding the end of the contracts under review, assessing the potential grounds for and consequences of contract termination in the streaming age.

Chapter 7 discusses the tools that are available to enforce the substantive provisions discussed in Chapters 3–6 in practice, both in a judicial and extra-judicial context. Chapter 8 brings together the research findings in a concluding 'Coda'.

2

The Music Industry in the Streaming Age

We don't like their sound,
and guitar music is on the way out.

—Executive at Decca Recording Co,
on the Beatles (1962)

2.1 INTRO

The shift from analogue to digital has revolutionised the music industry. The constant rise and fall of new methods of exploitation and associated evolving business models ensure that any researcher only has one certainty, namely that the results of their research will become outdated. Specialised volumes on the ever-changing structure of the music industry require almost yearly updates.[1]

This chapter nevertheless takes up the gauntlet. It first analyses the rights and interests of the primary stakeholders and introduces the various contracts entered into between musicians and their corporate partners (Section 2.2). It then discusses the music value chain that results from such contracts in the streaming age (Section 2.3). Two separate sections are dedicated to, respectively, the division of revenues (Section 2.4) and the ongoing quest towards enhanced transparency (Section 2.5). A concluding 'Bridge' (Section 2.6) brings together the most relevant findings that lead into the analysis of the relevant legal framework in the subsequent chapters.

2.2 RIGHTS AND INTERESTS OF THE PRIMARY STAKEHOLDERS

2.2.1 *Overview*

The basic structure of the music industry may be presented on the basis of the distinction between composition, performance and phonogram. First, on an abstract

[1] See eg Ann Harrison, *Music: The Business* (8th edn, Ebury 2021); Donald Passman, *All You Need to Know about the Music Business* (11th edn, Simon & Schuster 2023).

level, there is a musical 'composition'. This is an intangible work that consists of a melody, chord progressions and a certain instrumentation; is structured in a certain way; and is often accompanied by specific lyrics. However, music is more than notation alone. A 'performance' brings a composition to life. Performers are the driving force of this activity. They transform paper notes into real-life action on stage. A performance may be recorded in one way or another, resulting in a 'sound recording',[2] referred to throughout this book as a 'phonogram'.

A distinction thus arises between a composition, a performance and a phonogram. This distinction results in a three-way division of the music industry into (1) music publishing, (2) live performances and (3) recorded music sectors. The music publishing sector revolves around the exploitation of the composition, the live performances sector is engaged with the commercial organisation of performances, and the recorded music industry seeks to distribute and monetise phonograms.

The relationship between composers and publishers is situated in the *music publishing* sector, as it relates to the exploitation of the *composition*. The second sector, the *live performances* industry, builds on the activities (that is, the *performances*) of performers. The *recorded music* industry, finally, requires the cooperation of both performers and record companies since it centres around the fixation of a performance (or another sound) in a *phonogram*.

While bearing in mind this fundamental three-way division, this book opts for a characterisation of the music industry on the basis of its primary categories of stakeholders. The rights and interests of these heterogenous groups are analysed in the following sections, focusing respectively on musicians, their corporate partners and users. After a brief typology, their rights and underlying interests are treated.

2.2.2 *Musicians*

2.2.2.1 Typology

While artistry is not susceptible to exhaustive categorisation, it is first useful to take a closer look at different 'types' of musicians. There are two main broad categories, namely composers/lyricists (jointly referred to as 'composers') and performers.[3]

In the category of *composers*, artists who write both music and lyrics are referred to as songwriters. Singer-songwriters are songwriters who also perform their music and are credited as such. Within the category of musical *performers*, there are two main types of musician, namely *featured artists* and *session musicians*. Featured artists' work is credited on a phonogram, while session musicians are hired on either a

[2] See Art 5(A) UK CDPA.

[3] Cf Lorenz Haidinger, *Online-Musiklizenzierung in der Europäischen Union und in den USA* (Schriften zum europäischen Urheber-, Immaterialgüter- und Informationsrecht, De Gruyter 2021) 12–16.

TABLE 2.1 *Typology of musicians*

<table>
<tr><td colspan="4">Musician</td></tr>
<tr><td colspan="2">Composer (sensu lato)</td><td colspan="2">Performer</td></tr>
<tr><td>Composer (sensu stricto)</td><td>Lyricist</td><td rowspan="2">Featured artist</td><td rowspan="3">Session musician</td></tr>
<tr><td colspan="2">Songwriter</td></tr>
<tr><td colspan="3">Singer-songwriter</td></tr>
</table>

freelance or a more lasting contractual basis to perform in recording sessions or live performances without receiving express credit.[4] Within these two types, an enormous variety exists, from singers to multi-instrumentalists.[5] Musicians that are featured on a certain phonogram may be session musicians on another, and vice versa. A final important subcategory of the broad range of session musicians includes orchestral musicians[6] and chamber music players, active in the genre of classical music. This typology may be schematically represented as shown in Table 2.1.

The process of making music varies significantly across different genres. Classical musicians most often either perform or compose music and are thus easy to categorise on that basis.[7] Contemporary classical musicians are an exception, as they often create dedicated works and perform these works themselves. This seems especially true for creations with a significant conceptual aspect. Jazz musicians combine existing music structures with their own improvisations, thus continuously crossing the line between being a performer and a composer-performer.[8] In modern music, there is a large variety of artistic processes, ranging from singer-songwriters and indie folk bands who write their own music, to pop stars who perform melodies composed entirely by a team of collaborating songwriters.

4 of the EU 2015) <https://op.europa.eu/s/zIa9> 63; Christian Castle and Claudio Feijóo, 'Study on the Artists in the Digital Music Marketplace: Economics and Legal Considerations' (WIPO, 2021) 17.

5 Ananay Aguilar, '"We Want Artists to Be Fully and Fairly Paid for Their Work": Discourses on Fairness in the Neoliberal European Copyright Reform' [2018] JIPITEC 160, 169.

6 Given the real-time influence that orchestra conductors and/or choir directors exert on the tempo and the expression of the performers, their status as a performing artist is generally accepted; see Fabienne Brison, *Het Naburig Recht van de Uitvoerende Kunstenaar* (Creatie Informatie Communicatie 7, Larcier 2001) 43; Mathilde Pavis, 'The Author–Performer Divide in Intellectual Property Law: A Comparative Analysis of the American, Australian, British and French Legal Frameworks' (University of Exeter 2016) vol I, 35.

7 Richard Arnold, 'Reflections on the Triumph of Music: Copyrights and Performers' Rights in Music' (Oxford Intellectual Property Invited Speaker Seminar, Oxford, UK, 20 October 2009) 14; Luc Gulinck, *Hier Tekenen! (en Let Niet op de Kleine Lettertjes…) Wegwijs in het Juridische en Zakelijke Labyrint van de Muziekwereld* (Academia Press 2019) 158.

8 Original improvisations are protected by copyright *sensu stricto*. See Arnold, 'Reflections on the Triumph of Music' (n 7) 5; Stefan Skopelja, 'The Boundaries of "Authorship" and "Performance" in Musical Copyright' [2015] UNSWLJ Student Series No 15-04 9.

A final group is populated by DJs, whose status as creating and/or performing musicians is disputed.[9]

2.2.2.2 Rights

In their capacity as either composers (and thus authors) or performers, musicians are granted initial ownership of rights in music: copyright *sensu stricto* in the composition and a neighbouring right in (the fixation of) a performance.

Authorship leads to initial ownership of copyright *sensu stricto*. It may only be claimed in the event of a contribution that fulfils the conditions for copyright protection.[10] Copyright protection is available to 'literary and artistic works',[11] including music.[12] It is not granted to mere abstract ideas and principles. These must be expressed in a concrete way, identifiable with sufficient precision and objectivity.[13] Copyright protection only arises if the condition of originality is fulfilled. In accordance with established case law of the European Court of Justice (ECJ),[14] this implies that the work must be an intellectual creation of the author(s) expressing free and creative choices and reflecting their personality.[15] The work must show the

[9] See eg Jan Pauly and Yannick H'Madoun, *Poppuntgids voor muzikant en dj* (Poppunt vzw no date) 62; Gulinck, *Hier Tekenen!* (n 7) 47, 411. See also the case between Dutch DJ and producer Martin Garrix and his primary corporate partners Spinnin Records and MusicAllstar Management, where the court found that Garrix qualified as both a performing artist and a phonogram producer: *Gerechtshof* (hereinafter: Court of Appeal) Arnhem-Leeuwarden 24 December 2019, docket number 200.227.882/01, ECLI:NL:GHARL:2019:11117, paras 7.77–7.86. The further appeal before the Dutch Supreme Court on matters of law failed on this particular point; see *Hoge Raad der Nederlanden* (hereinafter 'Dutch Supreme Court') 17 December 2021, docket numbers 20/01155, 20/01158, ECLI:NL:HR:2021:1923, paras 3.5.1–3.5.3.

[10] See Daniela Simone, *Copyright and Collective Authorship: Locating the Authors of Collaborative Work* (Cambridge Intellectual Property and Information Law 50, Cambridge University Press 2019) 58–69; Kathy Bowrey, *Copyright, Creativity, Big Media and Cultural Value. Incorporating the Author* (Routledge 2020) 10–28; Lionel Bently and others, *Intellectual Property Law* (6th edn, Oxford University Press 2022) 135–46.

[11] Article 2(1) Berne Convention.

[12] This refers to melody (successive sounds), harmony (simultaneous sounds) and rhythm (structure of sounds whereby the dominant sound recurs in periodical intervals), as well as the combination thereof. Arrangements of music (including variations) are also susceptible to copyright protection, see Art 2(3) Berne Convention. In the United Kingdom, 'musical works' are expressly listed as protectable subject matter, see Arts 1(1)(a) *jo* 3 UK CDPA; Bently and others, *Intellectual Property Law* (n 10) 76–77.

[13] Art 9(2) TRIPS Agreement; Art 2 WCT; Case C-310/17 *Levola Hengelo* [2018] ECLI:EU:2018:899, paras 37, 40.

[14] On the relevance of ECJ law in the United Kingdom subsequent to Brexit, see *TuneIn v Warner Music UK* [2021] *EWCA Civ* 441, [2021] *EMLR* (18) 575; Paul Torremans, 'Transposition of the DSM Copyright Directive 2019/790 in the United Kingdom' [2021] AM 374, 377; Bently and others, *Intellectual Property Law* (n 10) 24–28.

[15] See ia Case C-5/08 *Infopaq International A/S v Danske Dagblades Forening* [2009] ECLI:EU:C:2009:476; Case C-393/09 *Bezpečnostní softwarová asociace – Svaz softwarové ochrany v Ministerstvo kultury* [2010] ECLI:EU:C:2010:816; Case C-145/10 *Eva-Maria Painer v Standard*

personal stamp of the author – that is, their *authorship*. The determination of authorship in a specific case is a matter of national law.[16] The concepts of 'joint', 'collective' or 'co-' authorship differ by country and are not harmonised at the EU level.[17]

A particular dimension arises in case a work or performance is created in an employment context. Under Belgian, French and German law, the employee is awarded initial ownership.[18] In the Netherlands and the United Kingdom, the opposite rule applies to works (not performances): copyright is deemed to vest in the employer, unless contrary contractual arrangements have been made.[19]

This brief analysis of authorship and the person of the author(s) may be contrasted with the concepts of performance and performers.[20] Article 2(a) WIPO Performances and Phonograms Treaty (WPPT)[21] defines 'performers' by enumeration as 'actors, singers, musicians,[22] dancers, and other persons who act, sing, deliver, declaim, play in, interpret or otherwise perform literary or artistic works', that is, works that are susceptible to – but not necessarily subject to – copyright protection. A certain degree of artistry is required. Mere technical contributions, such as those by sound engineers, are generally deemed insufficient.[23] Ancillary performers are excluded in some jurisdictions.[24] Finally, while a performance must

VerlagsGmbH and Others [2011] ECLI:EU:C:2011:798, para 94; Case C-161/17 *Land Nordrhein-Westfalen v Dirk Renckhoff* [2018] ECLI:EU:C:2018:634, para 14; Case C-310/17 *Levola Hengelo* [2018] ECLI:EU:2018:899, para 36; Case C-469/17 *Funke Medien NRW v Bundesrepublik Deutschland* [2019] ECLI:EU:C:2019:623, para 19.

16 See ia Art 14 Term Directive.

17 See Simone, *Copyright and Collective Authorship* (n 10) 201–72.

18 Jean-Christophe Lardinois, *Les Contrats Commentés de l'Industrie de La Musique 2.0: Cadre Général et Pratique Contractuelle* (Création Information Communication Pratique 1, 2nd edn, Larcier 2009) 70; Andreas Rahmatian, 'Dealing with Rights in Copyright-Protected Works: Assignments and Licences' in Estelle Derclaye (ed), *Research Handbook on the Future of EU Copyright* (Research Handbooks in Intellectual Property, Edward Elgar 2009) 294; Brigitte Lindner, 'European Union. Part A – Copyright and Contract Law Issues' in René Viljoen (ed), *Cross-Border Copyright Licensing Law and Practice* (Elgar Intellectual Property Law and Practice, Edward Elgar 2018) 75; Jeff Keustermans and Peter Blomme, *Auteursrecht. Capita Selecta* (2nd edn, Intersentia 2021) 35–36.

19 Art 7 Dutch Copyright Act; Art 11(2) UK CDPA. A company that publicly discloses a work without mentioning a physical person as its author is designated as its author, unless this disclosure is proven to be unlawful, see Art 8 Dutch Copyright Act.

20 See Brison, *Het Naburig Recht van de Uitvoerende Kunstenaar* (n 6) 42–52, 362–74, 531–48.

21 WIPO Performances and Phonograms Treaty <www.wipo.int/wipolex/en/treaties/textdetails/12743>.

22 The concept of 'musicians' in this provision is narrower than the term used here.

23 Brison, *Het Naburig Recht van de Uitvoerende Kunstenaar* (n 6) 43–44; Bob Donnelly, 'Everything You Need to Know about Copyright Reversions' (2012) 1 St John's Entertainment, Arts and Sports Law Journal 1, 13–14; Gulinck, *Hier Tekenen!* (n 7) 55.

24 In both Belgium and France, ancillary artists are expressly excluded from neighbouring rights protection (see Art XI.205(1) Belgian CEL; Art L 212-1 French IP Code). German, Dutch and UK law do not expressly exclude ancillary artists. However, it may be argued that auxiliary artists do not fulfil the substantive requirement of artistry.

not necessarily take place during a live concert, the performer's contribution must take place at the same time as the performance.[25] Thus, performers are persons who perform.[26] A clearer definition could conceptualise performers as artists whose contribution is not deemed sufficiently original to give rise to copyright, who merely interpret the work of somebody else and operate within the boundaries of such work. This would detract from the possibility of performers also being the composers of the works they perform. In any case, the legal consequence of a musician's categorisation as a performer is the acquisition of a neighbouring right relating to (the fixation of) the performance.

Thus, the legal qualification of a musician's contribution depends on its nature and creative intensity. If a particular contribution attains the threshold of originality, the musician surpasses the bounds of performance and may in theory claim (joint) authorship of the creative musical work.[27] Many musicians fulfil a wide array of roles that may be situated somewhere on the continuum between authorship and performance, somewhere along the sliding scale of creativity.[28] Consequently, the application of legal concepts to this composer–performer spectrum may prove to be problematic. Maintaining an overly strict line in the sand between the legal regimes applicable to composing and performing musicians may be untenable in the long run. Instead, an argument may be made in favour of a largely uniform interpretation where this is possible.[29]

When sheet music leaves sufficient leeway to the performer to make free and creative choices that express their personality in the context of the performance, it could be argued that the performer may fulfil the requirement of originality and thus legitimately claim copyright protection.[30] Even outside the realm of aleatoric

[25] Gulinck, *Hier Tekenen!* (n 7) 410.

[26] See Pavis, 'The Author–Performer Divide' (n 6) vol I, 31 et seq.

[27] Luke McDonagh, 'Rearranging the Roles of the Performer and the Composer in the Music Industry: The Potential Significance of Fisher v Brooker' [2012] IPQ 64, 76.

[28] Robert Brauneis, 'Musical Work Copyright for the Era of Digital Sound Technology: Looking beyond Composition and Performance' [2014] GW Law Faculty Publications & Other Works 60, 2; Pavis, 'The Author–Performer Divide in Intellectual Property Law' (n 6) 144; Isabelle De Voldere and others, 'Mapping the Creative Value Chains. A Study on the Economy of Culture in the Digital Age. Final Report' (Publications Office of the EU 2017) <https://op.europa.eu/s/zIa8> 64; Ananay Aguilar, 'Distributed Ownership in Music: Between Authorship and Performance' (2018) 27 Social & Legal Studies 776; Nikita Malevanny, *Online Music Distribution – How Much Exclusivity Is Needed? A Study of International, European, German and US Copyright Systems and Their Objectives*, vol 12 (Munich Studies on Innovation and Competition, Springer Berlin Heidelberg 2019) 271.

[29] Cf Case C-484/18 *Spedidam* [2019] ECLI:EU:C:2019:423, Opinion of AG Hogan, para 34.

[30] Pavis, 'The Author–Performer Divide' (n 6) 125–29. Cf Arnold, 'Reflections on the Triumph of Music' (n 7) 4; McDonagh, 'Rearranging the Roles of the Performer and the Composer in the Music Industry' (n 27) 64; Flavia Marisi, 'Law and Music: Copyright and Neighboring Rights' [2013] Review of Artistic Education 25; Skopelja, 'The Boundaries of "Authorship" and "Performance" in Musical Copyright' (n 8); Mathilde Pavis, 'Is There Any-Body on Stage? A Legal (Mis)Understanding of Performances' (2016) 19 Journal of World Intellectual Property 99; Richard Arnold, *Performers' Rights* (6th edn, Sweet & Maxwell 2021) 295–309.

music, the performance of a piece of music may legitimately influence the essence of a work itself, not only inspiring future performances but also leaving a creative, lasting imprint on the score.[31] For example, over the last decades, cellists everywhere have been inspired by the specific choices made in performances of the Bach Suites by Pablo Casals, and (later) Anner Bijlsma, Pierre Fournier, Yo-Yo Ma, Pieter Wispelwey and so forth. While the desirability of requalifying such ground-breaking performances as protected works may be disputed, a consistent application of the originality criterion may yet result in such a legal requalification.[32] In that case, performance and authorship would essentially merge.[33] A valid counterargument could be that an increased (legal) valuation of musical performance and an ensuing increase in potential joint authors would lead to both an increase in disputes on copyright ownership and an undue extension of the scope of copyright protection.[34] Taking the Bach analogy one step further, it could legitimately be asked whether any sort of exclusivity may be claimed on innovative bowings, nuances, rubatoes and/or fingerings. Yet the position set out above merely pleads for a consistent application of the law *de lege lata* of the existing criterion of originality. Many performers make free and creative choices in the context of their performance(s). In a way, objections against a revaluation of musical performance may be seen as objecting to the criterion of originality as such.[35]

Independently of the above, in order to avoid unnecessary friction in the long run, it is advisable for collaborating musicians to make clear, prior written arrangements regarding the initial allocation of ownership of any rights that result from their collaboration, as well as the distribution of any ensuing revenues.[36] Whether a

[31] Cf Pavis, 'The Author–Performer Divide' (n 6) vol II, 83.

[32] See regarding this 'performative turn' recognising the value of performance in the context of the interdisciplinary field of performance studies Pavis, 'The Author–Performer Divide' (n 6) vol I, 164–67. See also ibid vol II, 58–60, 67–76, 116–43.

[33] Cf Lionel Bently, 'Authorship of Popular Music in UK Copyright Law' (2009) 12 ICS 179, 179–204; Richard Osborne, 'Is Equitable Remuneration Equitable? Performers' Rights in the UK' (2017) 40 Popular Music and Society 573, 579, 587.

[34] Cf McDonagh, 'Rearranging the Roles of the Performer and the Composer in the Music Industry' (n 27) 75; Gulinck, *Hier Tekenen!* (n 7) 53. See extensively on the relevant arguments and counterarguments in this regard Pavis, 'The Author–Performer Divide' (n 6) vol I, 36–45 and vol II, 186–97.

[35] See Pavis, 'The Author–Performer Divide' (n 6) vol II, 144–208. Among other things, Pavis pleads in favour of removing the divide between musical and audio-visual performers and offers a number of avenues open to legislators should they wish to wholly drop the author–performer divide. Possible (linked) options include introducing performers as a new sub-class of copyright holders, expressly acknowledging performances as copyrightable works and broadening the scope of the condition of originality.

[36] This is done by way of a so-called band agreement or band partnership agreement. By way of example, the songwriting partnership between John Lennon and Paul McCartney entailed a 50/50 ownership share in all of the music they wrote for the duration of the partnership, see Jostein Gripsrud, 'Creativity and the Sense of Collective Ownership in Theatre and Popular Music' in Mireille van Eechoud (ed), *The Work of Authorship* (Amsterdam University Press 2014) 229. Another option is the 'Nashville style', which entails equal ownership shares for all

theoretical claim to (joint) authorship translates into ownership of copyright largely depends on the socio-legal bargaining power of the performer.[37] Only musicians with sufficient soft power and ensuing leverage in a contractual negotiation context will be able to claim rights.[38] It appears that contributions made by performers in a collaborative music-making context, such as during a 'jam session', are traditionally undervalued in such situations precisely as a result of the imbalance in negotiating power on the part of performers.[39] In case no arrangements on ownership are spelled out in advance – and in writing, given the difficulties of proving the existence and content of oral agreements[40] – and a dispute arises after the fact, the consequences of power relations may be even more pronounced.[41] This rings all the more true where the music at issue ultimately achieves economic success.

Finally, a specific place in the popular music-making process is occupied by music producers (also known as 'studio producers').[42] They are involved in the process of recording music, but occupy a more artistic than commercial position. They oversee the recording process and seek to ensure that all parties involved contribute to the best of their abilities.[43] In other words, producers function as a kind of personified quality control.[44] Their task requires detailed knowledge of recording techniques as well as a strong affinity with music. However, unless an original contribution to the composition may be proven, music producers have no right to

those present in the room during the creative process, see Aguilar, 'Distributed Ownership in Music' (n 28) 789. Written band agreements may also lead to objectionable situations, as is evidenced by the way Lou Pearlman added himself as a sixth member of boybands Backstreet Boys and *NSYNC in the 1990s (see documentary at <https://bit.ly/3DnqXEY>). Reference may also be made to blockchain-based tools such as Bernstein <bwww.bernstein.io>: see Marie-Christine Janssens and Jozefien Vanherpe, 'Blockchain and Copyright beyond the Buzzword?' [2018] IRDI 93; Jozefien Vanherpe and Marie-Christine Janssens, 'Toepassingen van smart contracts in het auteursrecht: Tussen droom en daad' in Pieter-Jan Aerts and others (eds), *Smart contracts: een overzicht vanuit juridisch perspectief* (KU Leuven Centre for IT & IP Law, Intersentia 2020).

37 Gripsrud, 'Creativity and the Sense of Collective Ownership in Theatre and Popular Music' (n 36) 235; Aguilar, 'Distributed Ownership in Music' (n 28) 777, 780, 788, 790–91.

38 Cf Daniel McClean, 'Introduction' in Daniel McClean (ed), *Artist, Authorship & Legacy: A Reader* (Ridinghouse 2019) 14; Gulinck, *Hier Tekenen!*(n 7) 314.

39 Richard Arnold, 'Are Performers Authors?' [1999] EIPR 464, 469.

40 The fact that prior verbal arrangements may still lead to disputes is illustrated eg by the dispute between the members of rock band The Smiths, where drummer Mike Joyce successfully claimed 25 per cent ownership of The Smiths' music, despite assertions of a contrary verbal agreement by band members Morrissey and Johnny Marr (*Joyce v Morrissey* [1999] EMLR 233).

41 Pavis, 'The Author–Performer Divide' (n 6) vol I, 119-122; Gulinck, *Hier Tekenen!* (n 7) 63.

42 Well-known music producers include Brian Eno, Quincy Jones, George Martin, Nile Rodgers and Rick Rubin. See eg David Stopps, 'How to Make a Living from Music, Second Edition' (Creative Industries, WIPO 2014) 16–17, 104–05; Donald Passman, *All You Need to Know about the Music Business* (10th edn, Simon & Schuster 2019) 125–36; Chris Castle, 'Record Producer Agreements, a Practical Guide' (2023).

43 Lardinois, *Les Contrats Commentés de l'Industrie de La Musique* 2.0 (n 18) 107; De Voldere and others, 'Mapping the Creative Value Chains' (n 28) 137.

44 Gulinck, *Hier Tekenen!* (n 7) 405.

copyright protection *sensu stricto*. The Court of Appeal of Amsterdam held that music producers are not entitled to claim neighbouring rights protection as either a performing artist or a phonogram producer.[45] Producers may only claim performing artist status if the sounds they produce with their voice and/or with an instrument are incorporated into the performance and, thus, the phonogram.[46] The intervention of a music producer is not a prerequisite in the music recording process – musicians may also perform the tasks of a music producer themselves. Music producers often make their intervention in the recording process dependent on receiving credit and/or part of the exploitation rights in the composition and/or the phonogram, independent of the nature of their intervention(s).[47]

As initial rights owners, musicians obtain the exclusive, negative right to either prohibit or authorise certain acts on the part of third parties.[48] Both copyright *sensu stricto* and the neighbouring right of performing musicians have an economic and a moral dimension. On the one hand, the economic prerogatives allow musicians to extract (commercial) value from their work(s)/performance(s) by granting certain rights to other parties through exploitation contracts. This book refers to the economic prerogatives assigned under copyright law *sensu lato* as 'exploitation rights'.[49] These exploitation rights are curtailed by certain exceptions and limitations.[50] On the other hand, moral rights protect the link between authors or performers and their output.

45 Court of Appeal Amsterdam 4 May 2010, docket number 200.002.411/01, *Various Artists (Koelewijn and others) v SENA* [2010] IEF 8821; IER 2010, 516–22.

46 Gulinck, *Hier Tekenen!* (n 7) 55, 410.

47 On the role of music producers, see Virgil Moorefield, *The Producer as Composer. Shaping the Sounds of Popular Music* (MIT Press 2005). See also Lardinois, *Les Contrats Commentés de l'Industrie de La Musique* 2.0 (n 18) 108; DCMS Committee, 'Economics of Music Streaming. Second Report of Session 2021–22' (15 July 2021) 46.

48 Case C-301/15 *Soulier and Doke* [2016] ECLI:EU:C:2016:878, para 33.

49 This subsection focuses on the relevant provisions of EU law. Under national law, see ia (1) in Belgium: Frank Gotzen, 'Art XI.165' in Fabienne Brison and Hendrik Vanhees (eds), *Hommage à Jan Corbet Huldeboek* (3rd edn, Larcier 2018) 47–66; Fabienne Brison, 'Art XI.205' in Fabienne Brison and Hendrik Vanhees (eds), *Hommage à Jan Corbet Huldeboek* (3rd edn, Larcier 2018) 359–64; (2) in France: André Lucas and others, *Traité de la Propriété Littéraire et Artistique* (5th edn, LexisNexis 2017) 271–472; (3) in Germany: Gunda Dreyer and others, *Urheberrecht* (Heidelberger Kommentar, 4th edn, CF Müller 2018) 312–652, 1343–71; Philipp Möhring and Käte Nicolini, *Urheberrecht* (4th edn, CH Beck 2018) 210–382, 924–63; Malevanny, *Online Music Distribution* (n 28) 42–50; (4) in the Netherlands: JH Spoor and others, *Auteursrecht. Auteursrecht, portretrecht, naburige rechten en databankenrecht* (Recht en Praktijk, 4th edn, Wolters Kluwer 2019) 171–367, 847–53; and (5) in the United Kingdom: Arnold, *Performers' Rights* (n 30) 137–216; Bently and others, *Intellectual Property Law* (n 10) 153–97, 210–302, 374–79.

50 Malevanny, *Online Music Distribution* (n 28) 101–83; Stavroula Karapapa, *Defences to Copyright Infringement: Creativity, Innovation and Freedom on the Internet* (Oxford University Press 2020).

The first and primary exclusive exploitation right is the right to make reproductions of their protected work and/or the fixation(s) of their performance(s). This right is to be interpreted broadly and is largely harmonised at the EU level.[51] The music industry wields the term 'mechanical rights'.[52] The mechanical rights granted to composers differ from those enjoyed by performers.

Composers have the exclusive right of authorising the reproduction of their work (s) in any matter or form (by making copies), such as by recording a phonogram or by digitally storing a protected work.[53] A copy subject to the author's consent exists when it takes over original elements of the initial work.[54] While coincidental resemblance is not actionable, no bad faith is required for an infringement to arise.[55] Illicit copying may take place subconsciously.[56] The reproduction right *sensu lato* further includes the right to adaptation (making musical arrangements[57]).[58] Authors also obtain a right of translation.[59] For music, this right only bears relevance for a composition's lyrics (for example, an opera libretto).

Performing musicians first obtain a right to authorise or prevent the fixation of their performance(s).[60] Second, they are granted a right of reproduction relating to such fixations. This means that they may prevent a third party from making copies,

51 See (1) re authors: Case C-5/08 *Infopaq International* [2009] ECLI:EU:C:2009:465, para 43; Case C-145/10, *Painer v Standard* [2011] ECLI:EU:C:2011:798, para 96; Case C-301/15 *Soulier and Doke* [2016] ECLI:EU:C:2016:878, paras 30–31 and (2) re performers Case C-484/18 *Spedidam* [2019] ECLI:EU:C:2019:970, paras 36–37.

52 See eg Europe Economics and others, 'Remuneration of Authors and Performers' (n 4) 27.

53 Art 2(a) InfoSoc Directive; Art XI.165(1) paras 1–3 Belgian CEL; Arts L 122-1, L 122-2-2–L 122-4 French IP Code; Arts 15–18 German Copyright Act; Arts 13–14 Dutch Copyright Act; Arts 16–17 UK CDPA. See also Art 9 Berne Convention; Agreed Statement concerning Art 1(4) WCT <https://bit.ly/3as9Ooz>.

54 See Joined Cases C-403/08 and C-429/08, *Football Association Premier League and others (FAPL)* [2011] ECLI:EU:C:2011:631, paras 153–159.

55 Jane Ginsburg, 'Copyright' in *The Oxford Handbook of Intellectual Property Law* (Oxford Handbooks, Oxford University Press 2018) 501.

56 ibid.

57 Gulinck, *Hier Tekenen!* (n 7) 74.

58 Art 12 Berne Convention.

59 Art 8 Berne Convention.

60 Art 7(1) Rental and Lending Directive; Art XI.205(1) Belgian CEL; Art L 212-3(I) French IP Code; Art 77 German Copyright Act; Art 2(1)(a) Dutch Neighbouring Rights Act; Art 182 UK CDPA. See also Art 6(ii) WPPT. Art 2(c) WPPT defines a 'fixation' as 'the embodiment of sounds, or of the representations thereof, from which they can be perceived, reproduced or communicated through a device'. The fixation refers to 'the material object on which the sounds are fixed': see Judica Krikke, 'Directive 2006/115/EC – on Rental Right and Lending Right and on Certain Rights Related to Copyright in the Field of Intellectual Property (Rental and Lending Right Directive)' in Thomas Dreier and P Bernt Hugenholtz (eds), *Concise European Copyright Law* (2nd edn, Kluwer Law International 2016) 287. As to the rights of performers, see in detail AEPO-ARTIS, 'Performers' Rights Study 2022' (2022).

including digital storage of such copies.[61] Performing musicians do not acquire an express right of adaptation or translation.[62]

The mechanical rights granted to both composers and performing musicians further include the rental and lending right as to works embodied in phonograms and fixations of performances.[63] Finally, composers and performers acquire the exclusive right to either authorise or prohibit the distribution to the public of the original or copies of their works and/or fixations of their performances, which is limited by the principle of exhaustion.[64]

Musicians also acquire certain performing rights. First, composers obtain the exclusive right to authorise the public performance of their works by any means or process.[65] This right of public performance implies the presence of a live audience at the place of the performance.[66] In addition, composers acquire exclusive rights relating to the communication to the public of their compositions by wire or wireless means.[67] This broad concept implies a transmission to a public that is not present in the same location.[68] The scope of this right includes music played in shops, restaurants and music venues, as well as broadcasts via radio and/or TV or by satellite[69] and cable retransmission[70] (as provided for under Member State law[71]).[72]

61 Art 2(b) InfoSoc Directive; Art XI.205(1) paras 1–2 Belgian CEL; Art L 212-3(I) French IP Code; Art 77 German Copyright Act; Art 2(1)(a)–(c) Dutch Neighbouring Rights Act; Art 182A–B UK CDPA. See also Art 3(e) Rome Convention; Art 14(1) TRIPS Agreement; Art 7 WPPT; Agreed Statement concerning Arts 7, 11 and 16 WPPT <https://bit.ly/3arTY5U>.

62 Gulinck, *Hier Tekenen!* (n 7) 73.

63 Arts 2–3 Rental and Lending Directive. See also Art 7 WCT. See also Europe Economics and others, 'Remuneration of Authors and Performers' (n 4) 31; Krikke, 'Directive 2006/115/EC' (n 60) 275–95; Gulinck, *Hier Tekenen!* (n 7) 75–76; Sylvie Nérisson, 'The Rental and Lending Rights Directive' in Irini Stamatoudi and Paul Torremans (eds), *EU Copyright Law. A Commentary* (Elgar Commentaries, Edward Elgar 2021) 118–50.

64 See re composers Art 4 InfoSoc Directive; Art 6 WCT. See re performers Art 9 Rental and Lending Directive; Art 8 WPPT. See also Ansgar Ohly, 'Economic Rights' in Estelle Derclaye (ed), *Research Handbook on the Future of EU Copyright* (Research Handbooks in Intellectual Property, Edward Elgar 2009) 219–23. See re exhaustion Simon Geiregat, *Supplying and Reselling Digital Content: Digital Exhaustion in EU Copyright and Neighbouring Rights Law* (Edward Elgar 2022); Péter Mezei, *Copyright Exhaustion: Law and Policy in the United States and the European Union* (2nd edn, Cambridge University Press 2022).

65 Art XI.165(1) para 4 Belgian CEL; Arts L 122-1–L 122-2-2 French IP Code; Arts 15, 19–22 German Copyright Act; Art 12 Dutch Copyright Act.

66 Ginsburg, 'Copyright' (n 55) 504.

67 Art 3(1) InfoSoc Directive. See also Arts 11–11*bis* Berne Convention; Art 8 WCT. See Justin Koo, *The Right of Communication to the Public in EU Copyright Law* (Hart 2019); Branka Marušić, *The Autonomous Legal Concept of Communication to the Public Interpretation in EU Copyright Law* (Edward Elgar 2023).

68 Recs 23–24 InfoSoc Directive.

69 Art 4 Satellite and Cable Directive.

70 Art 8 Satellite and Cable Directive.

71 See definition in Art 1(1) Satellite and Cable Directive. See Art 2 as to the exclusive broadcasting right granted to authors regarding the communication of works to the public via satellite and Art 8 regarding the cable retransmission right.

72 Ginsburg, 'Copyright' (n 55) 504.

A final subset of this right is the right to make their works available to the public in a way that allows individualised access by the public.[73]

Performers may authorise or prevent the broadcasting by wireless means[74] (including by satellite[75] and cable retransmission[76] as provided for under Member State law) and/or the communication to the public of their performance.[77] As for composers, the right to communication to the public includes an exclusive right to making available.[78] Save this making available right, performers' right to communication to the public largely equates to an unwaivable remuneration right, subject to mandatory collective management.[79]

Following the no formalities rule, the rights granted under copyright law *sensu lato* are generated automatically, upon either the creation of the work, (the fixation of) the performance or the creation of the phonogram at issue.[80] The term of protection starts then.

Copyright *sensu stricto* in the European Union as well as in the United Kingdom lasts for seventy years after the death of the (last surviving) author, subject to a limited number of exceptions.[81] The term of protection is different for anonymous or pseudonymous works. Unless the identity of the author becomes clear within seventy years after the work has been lawfully made available to the public (starting from the first of January following that event[82]), the protection lapses after that period.[83]

The term of the rights granted to performers is somewhat more complex and has also changed over the past decades: while these rights traditionally expire fifty years after the event giving rise to the protection (for example, in case of unfixed performances),[84] a longer period of protection is granted in case of fixation on a

73 Art 3(2) InfoSoc Directive; Cheryl Foong, *The Making Available Right. Realizing the Potential of Copyright's Dissemination Function in the Digital Age* (Elgar Law, Technology and Society series, Edward Elgar 2019).

74 'Broadcasting' is defined as 'the transmission by wireless means for public reception of sounds or of images and sounds', see Art 3(f) Rome Convention.

75 Art 4 Satellite and Cable Directive.

76 Art 8 Satellite and Cable Directive.

77 Art XI.205(1) para 3 Belgian CEL; Art L 212-3(I) French IP Code; Art 78 German Copyright Act; Art 2(1)(d) Dutch Neighbouring Rights Act. Art 8 Rental and Lending Directive harmonises this right at the EU level as far as live performances are concerned. See also Art 7(1) Rome Convention; Art 14(1) TRIPS Agreement; Art 6(i) WPPT.

78 Art 3(2)(a) InfoSoc Directive. See also Art 10 WPPT.

79 Art 8(2) Rental and Lending Directive. See on the scope of the concept of 'relevant performers': Case C-265/19 *Recorded Artists Actors Performers v Phonographic Performance (Ireland)* [2020] ECLI:EU:C:2020:677. See also Art 11*bis*(2) Berne Convention; Art 15 WPPT.

80 See Art 5(2) Berne Convention re copyright *sensu stricto* and Article 20 WPPT re the neighbouring right of performing artists.

81 Art 1 Term Directive, maintained in the United Kingdom following Brexit in Art 12 UK CDPA.

82 Art 7(5) Berne Convention.

83 Art 1(3)–(7) Term Directive. See also Art 12 TRIPS Agreement.

84 As required under Art 14(5) TRIPS Agreement and Art 17 WPPT.

phonogram, namely seventy years after its publication.[85] The relatively recent[86] term extension from fifty to seventy years was prompted by the EU legislator's wish to improve the social situation of (session) musicians in view of their increased life expectancy.[87] It was controversial in view of its perceived ineffectiveness and the intrusion on the public domain that it entailed.[88]

In addition to exploitation rights, musicians acquire certain moral rights.[89] First, in some jurisdictions composers acquire a right of first disclosure, which entails the right to divulge their work(s) to the public.[90] This right does not apply to performers, which is logical, given that the performance itself constitutes a disclosure thereof. Second, the right of paternity or attribution implies that both composers and performers may (dis)claim paternity of their work and/or performance.[91] Notably,

85 Art 3 Term Directive, maintained in the United Kingdom following Brexit in Arts 13(b)–(c), 191 UK CDPA. For this extension to apply, the fixation of the performance in a phonogram must be lawfully published or communicated to the public within fifty years following the date of the performance at issue. See Lucas and others, *Traité de la Propriété Littéraire et Artistique* (n 49) 1119–26; Fabienne Brison, 'Art XI.208' in Fabienne Brison and Hendrik Vanhees (eds), *Hommage à Jan Corbet Huldeboek* (3rd edn, Larcier 2018) 371–73; Dreyer and others, *Urheberrecht* (n 49) 1361–66, 1371–73; Möhring and Nicolini, *Urheberrecht* (n 49) 932–60, 968–71; Spoor and others, *Auteursrecht* (n 49) 876–78; Arnold, *Performers' Rights* (n 30) 83–93.

86 It applies to phonograms and fixations that were still protected on 1 November 2013 (the implementation deadline of the Term Extension Directive) and later performances/phonograms, see Art 10(5) Term Directive.

87 Recs 5–7 Term Extension Directive.

88 See eg P Bernt Hugenholtz and others, 'The Recasting of Copyright & Related Rights for the Knowledge Economy' (2006) 83–137; Natali Helberger and others, 'Never Forever: Why Extending the Term of Protection for Sound Recordings Is a Bad Idea' (2008) 30 EIPR 174, 174–81; Lionel Bently and others, 'Creativity Stifled? A Joint Academic Statement on the Proposed Copyright Term Extension for Sound Recordings' (2008) 30 EIPR 341, 341–47; Reto M Hilty and others, 'Comment by the Max-Planck Institute on the Commission's Proposal for a Directive to Amend Directive 2006/116 Concerning the Term of Protection for Copyright and Related Rights' (2009) 31 EIPR 59, 59–72; Mireille van Eechoud and others, *Harmonizing European Copyright Law: The Challenges of Better Lawmaking* (Information Law Series 19, Kluwer Law International 2009) 181–234; Agnieszka Vetulani-Cęgiel, 'EU Copyright Law, Lobbying and Transparency of Policy-Making' [2015] JIPITEC 146, 151–52; Christina Angelopoulos, 'Directive 2006/116/EC – on the Term of Protection of Copyright and Certain Related Rights (Term Directive), as Amended by Directive 2011/77/EU (Term Extension Directive)' in Thomas Dreier and P Bernt Hugenholtz (eds), *Concise European Copyright Law* (2nd edn, Kluwer Law International 2016) 336–37, 356.

89 See eg Elizabeth Adeney, *The Moral Rights of Authors and Performers: A International and Comparative Analysis* (Oxford University Press 2006); Fabienne Brison and others (eds), *Moral Rights in the 21st Century. The Changing Role of the Moral Rights in an Era of Information Overload* (Larcier 2015). See re authors: Art 6bis(2) Berne Convention. See re performers: Art 5 (3) Rome Convention.

90 See Art XI.165(2) Belgian CEL; Art L121–2 French IP Code; Art 12 German Copyright Act. On Dutch law, see Spoor and others, *Auteursrecht* (n 49) 446–49. On UK law, see Bently and others, *Intellectual Property Law* (n 10) 303.

91 See re authors: Arts XI.165(2) Belgian CEL; Art L 121-1 French IP Code; Art 13 German Copyright Act; Art 25(1)(a)–(b) Dutch Copyright Act; Arts 77–79, 84 UK CDPA; Art 6*bis*(1) Berne Convention. See re performers: Art XI.204 Belgian CEL; Art L 212-2 French IP Code; Art

performers' right to paternity is limited by honest trade practices. By way of example, not all members of a symphony orchestra can claim acknowledgement on a CD cover or in the metadata of a digital music file. This privilege is reserved to the conductor, the concertmaster and possible soloists.[92] Even so, many instances of infringement of the paternity right arise, largely due to the poor quality of metadata.[93] The third moral right is referred to as the right to integrity. It implies that composers and performers may object to actions relating to their output that would bring them into disrepute.[94] In the music industry, cases regarding this moral right may, for example, relate to the combination of a pre-existing work or performance fixation with offensive lyrics.[95] Finally, German and French law provide for an express, albeit very limited, 'right to repent' for authors, as a result of which a composer may withdraw or retract their work subsequent to its initial disclosure – in other words, reverse the exercise of their moral right of disclosure.[96]

The term of moral rights varies. This term is usually linked to the duration of the exploitation rights. This is the case in Belgium, Germany, the Netherlands and the United Kingdom, the latter with a caveat as to the right to false attribution.[97] By contrast, moral rights have no limitation in time under French copyright law and thus apply in perpetuity, for composers as well as performers.[98]

If third parties want to use a musical composition, (a fixation of) a performance and/or a phonogram, consent must be acquired from the relevant right owner(s).[99] In this context, the distinction between exclusive rights and remuneration rights

74 German Copyright Act; Art 5(1)(a)–(b) Dutch Neighbouring Rights Act; Arts 205C–205E UK CDPA; Art 5(1) WPPT.

92 The right to prevent wrong acknowledgement is absolute.

93 On the difficulty to enforce moral rights online, see Gillian Davies, 'Moral Rights in the Borderless Online Environment' in Johan Axhamn (ed), *Copyright in a Borderless Online Environment* (Nordstedts Juridik 2012) 37–46.

94 See re authors: Arts XI.165(2) Belgian CEL; Art L 121-2 French IP Code; Art 14 German Copyright Act; Art 25(1)(b)–(d) Dutch Copyright Act; Arts 80–83 UK CDPA; Art 6bis(1) Berne Convention. See re performers: Art XI.204 Belgian CEL; Art L 212-2 French IP Code; Art 75 German Copyright Act; Art 5(1)(b)–(d) Dutch Neighbouring Rights Act; Arts 205F–205H UK CDPA; Art 5(1) WPPT.

95 See eg *Confetti Records & Others v Warner Music UK Ltd* [2003] *EWHC* 1274; [2003] *EMLR* 790, where it was held that no reputational prejudice had occurred as the lyrics were deemed incomprehensible.

96 Art 42 German Copyright Act; Art L 121-4 French IP Code. See below, Chapter 6, Section 6.3.

97 Frank Gotzen, 'Art XI.166' in Fabienne Brison and Hendrik Vanhees (eds), *Hommage à Jan Corbet Huldeboek* (3rd edn, Larcier 2018) 72–73; Möhring and Nicolini, *Urheberrecht*(n 49) 822; Spoor and others, *Auteursrecht* (n 49) 445–46; Bently and others, *Intellectual Property Law* (n 10) 206. See as to UK law in particular Arts 86, 205I UK CDPA.

98 Rahmatian, 'Dealing with Rights' (n 18) 296; Lucas and others, *Traité de la Propriété Littéraire et Artistique* (n 49) 545–47, 1126–28; Lindner, 'European Union. Part A' (n 18) 85.

99 Case C-301/15 *Soulier and Doke* [2016] ECLI:EU:C:2016:878, paras 33–34; Case C-161/17 *Land Nordrhein-Westfalen v Dirk Renckhoff* [2018] ECLI:EU:C:2018:634, paras 16, 29; Case C-484/18 *Spedidam* [2019] ECLI:EU:C:2019:970, para 38.

bears particular relevance.[100] This distinction applies to both copyright and neighbouring rights.

Exclusive rights may usually be transferred or licensed out. Consent is either granted on an individual basis or, optionally, through a collective management organisation (CMO). A CMO is an organisation tasked by their members-rightsholders with the management of their copyright or neighbouring rights through the grant of licences to third parties.[101] There is a large number of active CMOs.[102]

The exclusive rights of composers include almost all of the mechanical rights and the performing rights set out above. This explains why voluntary collective management is of particular importance in the music publishing industry.[103] Performers only (initially and thus subject to further transfer) acquire the exclusive right to reproduce fixations of their performances, distribute these and make them available to the public.

In the context of optional (or 'voluntary') collective management, prospective users approach the relevant CMO(s) to obtain a licence relating to the exploitation rights of protected content. The user pays the rate set by the CMO, which retains a

[100] There is also an 'in-between model' that combines the transfer of an exclusive right with a residual remuneration right. See below, Chapter 5, Section 5.5.

[101] Cf Art 3(a) CRM Directive. See ia Mihály Ficsor, *Collective Management of Copyright and Related Rights* (WIPO 2002); KEA, 'The Collective Management of Rights in Europe. The Quest for Efficiency' (2006); Maria Mercedes Frabboni, 'Collective Management of Copyright and Related Rights: Achievements and Problems of Institutional Efforts towards Harmonisation' in Estelle Derclaye (ed), *Research Handbook on the Future of EU Copyright* (Research Handbooks in Intellectual Property, Edward Elgar 2009) 373–400; Sylvie Nérisson, *La gestion collective des droits des auteurs en France et en Allemagne: quelle légitimité?* (Bibliothèque de l'Institut de recherche juridique de la Sorbonne-André Tunc 49, IRJS Editions 2013); Daniel Gervais (ed), *Collective Management of Copyright and Related Rights* (3rd edn, Kluwer Law International 2016); Malevanny, *Online Music Distribution* (n 28) 185–239.

[102] The main CMOs for composers and performers in the chosen jurisdictions are: (1) in Belgium: SABAM (Société d'Auteurs Belge – Belgische Auteurs Maatschappij) and PlayRight; (2) in France: SACEM (Société des Auteurs, Compositeurs et Éditeurs de Musique) and ADAMI for featured artists (Administration des Droits des Artistes et Musiciens Interprètes)/Spedidam for non-featured artists (Société de Perception et de Distribution des Droits des Artistes-Interprètes)/SAI for both (Société des Artistes Interprètes); (3) in Germany: GEMA (Gesellschaft für musikalische Aufführungs- und mechanische Vervielfältigungsrechte) and GVL (Gesellschaft zur Verwertung von Leistungsschutzrechten); (4) in the Netherlands: Buma/Stemra (Bureau voor Muziek-Auteursrechten/Stichting tot Exploitatie van Mechanische Reproduktierechten voor Auteurs), SENA (Stichting ter Exploitatie van Naburige Rechten)/NORMA (Naburige Rechtenorganisatie voor Musici en Acteurs); and (5) in the United Kingdom: PRS for Music and PPL (Phonographic Performance Limited).

[103] Chris Cooke, *Dissecting the Digital Dollar* (3rd edn, Music Managers Forum and CMU Insights 2020)12–13; Raquel Xalabarder, 'The Principle of Appropriate and Proportionate Remuneration for Authors and Performers in Art 18 Copyright in the Digital Single Market Directive. Statutory Residual Remuneration Rights for Its Effective National Implementation' [2020] InDret 1, 4–5.

commission-based compensation for administrative costs and transfers the remainder of the fee to the rightsholder(s).

For the exploitation of remuneration rights, no express consent from the rightsholder(s) is required. Consequently, the relevant rightsholders do not have the opportunity to prevent the exploitation at issue. Instead, in such cases, a compulsory licensing system subject to mandatory collective management applies. An equitable remuneration is collected by CMOs and subsequently transferred to the rightsholder (s) after deduction of administrative costs. Remuneration rights are unwaivable.[104] Rental and lending rights are in principle both exclusive rights, but the EU framework leaves room for a qualification of the lending right as a remuneration right under national law.[105] As to the rental right, in case a transfer of this right occurs, an equitable remuneration through a system of mandatory collective management is required.[106]

A larger proportion of performers' rights has the status of a remuneration right compared with the rights granted to authors. This explains the importance of mandatory collective management in the recorded music industry. Indeed, in addition to the above, performers' right to broadcasting and communication to the public of fixations of their performances in a phonogram are largely treated as remuneration rights (except for the making available right, which is an exclusive right).[107] This is referred to as the compulsory licence for secondary use.

The cable retransmission right has a particular status as an exclusive right that is nevertheless subject to mandatory collective management.[108] The equitable remunerations for private copying and reprography also occupy a specific position, since they function as compensation to the rightsholders for the harm inflicted through the application of private copying and reprography exceptions.[109] These two equitable remuneration regimes are also subject to mandatory collective management.

[104] Case C-277/10 *Martin Luksan v Petrus van der Let* [2012] ECLI:EU:C:2012:65; Séverine Dusollier and others, 'Contractual Arrangements Applicable to Creators: Law and Practice of Selected Member States' (Publications Office of the EU 2014) <https://op.europa.eu/s/zIba> 6, 88–89.

[105] See Art 6 Rental and Lending Directive. This is the case under Belgian law. In accordance with Arts XI.243–45 Belgian CEL, the remuneration relating to sheet music is divided 70 per cent for composers and 30 per cent for publishers, while composers, performers and producers each receive one-third of the remuneration relating to phonograms.

[106] Art 5 Rental and Lending Directive.

[107] Cf Art 8(2) Rental and Lending Directive. See also Case C-265/19 *Recorded Artists Actors Performers v Phonographic Performance (Ireland)* [2020] ECLI:EU:C:2020:677; Case C-147/19 *Atresmedia Corporación de Medios de Comunicación SA v Asociación de Gestión de Derechos Intelectuales (AGEDI), Artistas Intérpretes o Ejecutantes, Sociedad de Gestión de España (AIE)* [2020] ECLI:EU:C:2020:935.

[108] Art 9 Satellite and Cable Directive.

[109] Cf Rec 35 InfoSoc Directive.

Musicians may transfer (or 'assign'[110]) their exclusive exploitation rights to third parties, be it a natural person or a legal entity.[111] Consequently, these rights have traditionally been divested to commercial players, with the copyright in musical works being assigned from composers to music publishers and the neighbouring right of performers to record companies for the entire term of protection.[112] In return, the initial rightsholder(s) usually obtain(s) a form of compensation, either by way of a flat fee or through recurring royalty payments.[113] As a result, most copyright is owned by corporations instead of artists.[114]

As an alternative to the full transfer of rights, it is possible to grant a licence. Hereby, the counterparty obtains the right to use the object of the licence within certain limits, again usually in return for monetary compensation to the initial rights owner(s) – but not always, as is proven by open licences.[115] As opposed to a transfer of rights, which is always of an exclusive nature, a licence may be either exclusive or non-exclusive. In the latter case, the licensor(s) retain(s) the right to exploit the object of the licence and/or to grant other licences to third parties, who may then perform actions of exploitation in parallel with the initial licensee. Drawing the line between an exclusive licence and a transfer of copyright can be difficult.[116]

[110] This term is primarily used under UK law, see eg Abbe EL Brown and others, *Contemporary Intellectual Property: Law and Policy* (5th edn, Oxford University Press 2019) 220; Arnold, *Performers' Rights* (n 30) 97–99; Bently and others, *Intellectual Property Law* (n 10) 323–26.

[111] Rahmatian, 'Dealing with Rights' (n 18) 298–301; Sébastien Raimond, *La Qualification du Contrat d'Auteur* (Le Droit des Affaires. Propriété Intellectuelle 34, LexisNexis 2009) 33–56; Nathalie Blanc, *Les Contrats du Droit d'Auteur à l'Epreuve de la Distinction des Contrats Nommés et Innommés* (Nouvelle Bibliothèque de Thèses 93, Dalloz 2010) 244–61; Alain Strowel and Bernard Vanbrabant, 'Copyright Licensing: A European View' in Jacques de Werra (ed), *Research Handbook on Intellectual Property Licensing* (Research Handbooks in Intellectual Property, Edward Elgar 2013) 34–35; Bernard Vanbrabant, *La Propriété Intellectuelle. Tome 2. Régime Patrimonial* (Création Information Communication, Larcier 2018) 371–74, 401–15; Robert B Merges, 'What Kind of Rights Are Intellectual Property Rights?' in Rochelle Dreyfuss and Justine Pila (eds), *The Oxford Handbook of Intellectual Property Law* (Oxford Handbooks, Oxford University Press 2018) 62. Under German law, no full transfer of copyright *sensu stricto* is possible, see below, Chapter 4, Section 4.4.1.1.

[112] Séverine Dusollier, 'EU Contractual Protection of Creators: Blind Spots and Shortcomings' [2018] Colum J L & Arts, 436, 451.

[113] See in more detail below, Section 2.4.

[114] Orly Lobel, *Talent Wants to Be Free. Why We Should Learn to Love Leaks, Raids, and Free Riding* (Yale University Press 2013) 165.

[115] Rahmatian, 'Dealing with Rights' (n 18) 298, 301–09; Raimond, *La Qualification du Contrat d'Auteur* (n 111) 56–91; Blanc, *Les Contrats du Droit d'Auteur* (n 111) 261–82; Alexis Boisson, *La Licence de Droit d'Auteur* (Bibliothèque de Droit de l'Entreprise 86, LexisNexis 2013) 119–352; Stopps, 'How to Make a Living from Music' (n 42) 32–33; Vanbrabant, *La Propriété Intellectuelle. Tome 2* (n 111) 643–58, 690–703, 747–48; Lindner, 'European Union. Part A' (n 18) 79–81.

[116] Alain Berenboom, *Le Nouveau Droit d'Auteur et les Droits Voisins* (Création Information Communication 1, 3rd edn, Larcier 2005) 209; Rahmatian, 'Dealing with Rights' (n 18) 298–99, 301; Dusollier and others, 'Contractual Arrangements Applicable to Creators' (n 105) 30, 49; Strowel and Vanbrabant, 'Copyright Licensing' (n 111) 34–36.

In this book, contracts that establish a transfer of or a licence to the exploitation rights associated with works protected by copyright and/or fixations of performances protected by the neighbouring right of performing artists are referred to by the umbrella terms 'copyright exploitation contracts' or 'exploitation contracts'.

The exploitation of a phonogram has an impact on both the neighbouring rights associated with said phonogram and the copyright in the underlying composition embodied in the phonogram. As a result, a single exploitation activity requires permission under both copyright and neighbouring rights law.[117]

The exploitation of the exclusive rights associated with a jointly owned work and/or performance in principle requires express consent from all parties, especially if the individual contributions are not discernible. In such a case, a single rightsholder can stop others from exploiting the work and/or performance. To mitigate this, rules have been established that modulate the requirement of consent relating to live performances by large groups of performing musicians, such as orchestras or large chamber music ensembles.[118] These rules designate specific musicians as representative(s) of the group, allowing the possibility of efficient contracting in large live productions. The applicable regimes differ, from the appointment of soloists, directors and conductors (Belgium and the Netherlands) to group leaders (Belgium and Germany) or elected representatives (Germany).[119] While French and UK law do not appear to expressly regulate such situations, musicians may provide a mandate to another party for this purpose.

2.2.2.3 Interests

Several internal and external factors incentivise musicians to create and/or perform music.[120] The intrinsic wish to make music for the sake of personal development[121] and/or participation in cultural life[122] is a significant and primary driver,[123] but only constitutes part of the equation.[124] In addition, musicians are driven by a number of

[117] Cf Jeff Price, 'The Definitive Guide to Spotify Royalties' [2020] <https://shorturl.at/ADHS3> 3, 14.

[118] These specific rules should not be applied to small ensembles, such trios and quartets. In such cases, the permission of all musicians is required.

[119] See (1) in Belgium: Art XI.207 Belgian CEL; (2) in Germany: Art 80(2) *jo* 74(2) German Copyright Act; and (3) in the Netherlands: Art 13 Dutch Neighbouring Rights Act. See also Art 8 Rome Convention, which expressly allows diverging national regimes.

[120] See in detail Sarah Polcz, 'Loyalties v Royalties' (2021) 74 Hastings LJ 765.

[121] Cf Jessica Silbey, *The Eureka Myth: Creators, Innovators, and Everyday Intellectual Property* (Stanford University Press 2014) 40–41, 44, 274–75; Alan B Krueger, *Rockonomics* (John Murray 2019) 52, 57–58.

[122] See Art 27(1) UDHR and Art 15(1)(a) ICESCR.

[123] Gripsrud, 'Creativity and the Sense of Collective Ownership in Theatre and Popular Music' (n 36) 228; Silbey, *The Eureka Myth* (n 121) 1–2, 8, 13, 39; Gulinck, *Hier Tekenen!* (n 7) 9.

[124] Jonathan M Barnett, 'Copyright without Creators' (2014) 9 RLE 389, 432–33; Jane C Ginsburg, 'Exceptional Authorship: The Role of Copyright Exceptions in Promoting Creativity' in Susy

external incentives. A first important motivating factor is remuneration. This is especially true for professional musicians, whose income depends on music-related revenues.[125] However, this incentive applies across the board. Indeed, all musicians seek a certain degree of valuation of their work, of which proper remuneration constitutes an important part.[126] However, 'money isn't everything'.[127] Beyond the purely monetary self-interest, a number of non-economic external incentives play a role. Many of these incentives are covered by the broad concept of (self-)agency.[128] This includes, first and foremost, credit where credit is due.[129] Musicians want to receive acknowledgement for their work.[130] The value of music must not only translate into money, but also into attribution and ensuing personal recognition.[131] Second, musicians want their music to be heard. This implies access to audiences through exploitation of the work and the wish to build a relationship with their

Frankel and Daniel Gervais (eds), *The Evolution and Equilibrium of Copyright in the Digital Age* (Cambridge University Press 2014) 25; Bruno S Frey, *Economics of Art and Culture* (SpringerBriefs in Economics, Springer International 2019) 32; Krueger, *Rockonomics* (n 121) 3–4; Ruth Towse, *A Textbook of Cultural Economics* (2nd edn, Cambridge University Press 2019) 374–76.

125 Gripsrud, 'Creativity and the Sense of Collective Ownership in Theatre and Popular Music' (n 36) 229.

126 Martin Kretschmer and others, 'The Relationship between Copyright and Contract Law' (2010) <https://ssrn.com/abstract=2624945> 28–3267; Jane C Ginsburg, 'The Role of the Author in Copyright' in Ruth L Okediji (ed), *Copyright Law in an Age of Limitations and Exceptions* (Cambridge University Press 2017) 81; Stephanie Plamondon, 'Rational Faith: The Utility of Fairness in Copyright' (2017) 97 BU L Rev 1487, 1512–14; Aguilar, 'We Want Artists' (n 5) 169–70; Alexander Cuntz, 'Creators' Income Situation in the Digital Age' (Economic Research Working Paper, 2018) 6–7; Ole-Andreas Rognstad and Joost Poort, 'The Right to Reasonable Exploitation Concretized: An Incentive Based Approach' in P Bernt Hugenholtz (ed), *Copyright Reconstructed. Rethinking Copyright's Economic Rights in a Time of Highly Dynamic Technological and Economic Change* (Information Law Series 41, Kluwer Law International 2018) 127; Hayleigh Bosher, *Copyright in the Music Industry. A Practical Guide to Exploiting and Enforcing Rights* (Elgar Practical Guides, Edward Elgar 2021) 6–8.

127 Krueger, *Rockonomics* (n 121) 9. See also Lobel, *Talent Wants to Be Free* (n 114) 192–95; Silbey, *The Eureka Myth* (n 121) 1–2, 14; Rethink Music Initiative, 'Fair Music: Transparency and Payment Flows in the Music Industry. Recommendations to Increase Transparency, Reduce Friction, and Promote Fairness in the Music Industry' (2015) 5; Nancy K Baym, *Playing to the Crowd. Musicians, Audiences, and the Intimate Work of Connection* (New York University Press 2018) 108; Simone, *Copyright and Collective Authorship* (n 10) 210–11; Bosher, *Copyright in the Music Industry* (n 126) 8–11.

128 Tom Phillips and John Street, 'Copyright and Musicians at the Digital Margins' (2015) 37 Media, Culture & Society 342, 346; Ginsburg, 'The Role of the Author in Copyright' (n 126) 63, 79, 84; Juliet Fraser, 'Sharing the Spoils of a Shared Practice' (2019) 73 Tempo 51, 52.

129 Plamondon, 'Rational Faith' (n 126) 1511–12; Krueger, *Rockonomics* (n 121) 216.

130 Rick Carnes, 'Developing a Copyright System that Works for Songwriters' (2015) 38 Colum JL & Arts 309, 309; Baym, *Playing to the Crowd* (n 127) 198.

131 Cf Lionel Bently and Laura Biron, 'Discontinuities between Legal Conceptions of Authorship and Social Practices: What, If Anything, Is to Be Done?' in Mireille van Eechoud (ed), *The Work of Authorship* (Amsterdam University Press 2014) 267–70.

audience in order to nurture a fan base.[132] Third, agency may be associated with artistic integrity and reputation, as well as the wish to retain a certain degree of control over the exploitation of their work.[133] Both credit and reputation may be linked with moral rights protection – the right to paternity and integrity respectively.[134]

Internal motives to make music and external incentives to achieve artistic and commercial success ensure a continuous stream of hopeful music market entrants, forming a supply that significantly outstrips demand.[135] The consequences of this mismatch between supply and demand on artist income are palpable.[136] Several authoritative research projects may be mentioned, such as the study conducted by Dutch Institute for Information Law (IViR).[137] That study pointed towards an average net annual income of composers in the EU per country between approximately €15,000 and €45,000 – the higher numbers being due to a number of significant outliers.[138] The corresponding figures for performers lay between approximately €4,000 and €16,000.[139] More recently, reference may be made to the 2023 Musicians' Census in the United Kingdom, which found the average annual income from music work to be around €24,000.[140] In many cases, the income of

[132] Stopps, 'How to Make a Living from Music' (n 42) 50–51; William Deresiewicz, *The Death of the Artist. How Creators Are Struggling to Survive in the Age of Billionaires and Big Tech* (Henry Holt 2020) 122–23. See also Yannos Paramythiotis, 'Fairness in Copyright Contract Law: Remuneration for Authors and Performers under the Copyright in the Digital Single Market Directive' in Tatiana-Eleni Synodinou and others (eds), *EU Internet Law in the Digital Single Market* (Springer International 2021) 78.

[133] Séverine Dusollier, *Droit d'Auteur et Protection des Œuvres dans l'Univers Numérique. Droits et Exceptions à la Lumière des Dispositifs de Verrouillage des Oeuvres* (Création Information Communication 10, Larcier 2005) 289–90; Silbey, *The Eureka Myth* (n 121) 7, 142; Stopps, 'How to Make a Living from Music' (n 42) 52, 102; Carnes, 'Developing a Copyright System' (n 130) 309; Ginsburg, 'The Role of the Author in Copyright' (n 126) 79; Krueger, *Rockonomics* (n 121) 216. See on the importance of reputation for creators in particular Silbey, *The Eureka Myth* (n 121) 75–76, 149–83.

[134] Silbey, *The Eureka Myth* (n 121); Rebecca Tushnet, 'Intellectual Property as a Public Interest Mechanism' in Rochelle Dreyfuss and Justine Pila (eds), *The Oxford Handbook of Intellectual Property Law* (Oxford Handbooks, Oxford University Press 2018) 114.

[135] Martin Kretschmer and others, 'The Relationship between Copyright and Contract Law' (2010) 66; Mark Mulligan, *Awakening: The Music Industry in the Digital Age* (Createspace 2015) 174; Lionel Bently and others, 'Strengthening the Position of Press Publishers and Authors and Performers in the Copyright Directive' (2017) 54.

[136] Krueger, *Rockonomics* (n 121) 58; Bruno Racine, 'L'Auteur et l'Acte de Création' (January 2020) 17–27. See also Richard L Florida, *The Rise of the Creative Class* (Basic Books 2012) 53; Pierre-Michel Menger, 'The Market for Creative Labour: Talent and Inequalities' in Candace Jones and others (eds), *The Oxford Handbook of Creative Industries* (Oxford Handbooks, Oxford University Press 2015) 150; Cuntz, 'Creators' Income Situation in the Digital Age' (n 126).

[137] Europe Economics and others, 'Remuneration of Authors and Performers' (n 4). See also DCMS Committee, 'Economics of Music Streaming' (n 47) 29–30.

[138] Europe Economics and others, 'Remuneration of Authors and Performers' (n 4) 198–99.

[139] ibid 193, 203. See also DCMS Committee, 'Economics of Music Streaming' (n 47) 26–27.

[140] Help Musicians and Musicians' Union, 'Musicians' Census. Financial Insight Report' (September 2023). See also <https://bit.ly/3Pz9ORr>. On this topic, see also DCMS

musicians appears to lie below the minimum wage level, and certainly below the median wage level in the jurisdictions researched in the context of this book.[141]

As regards the position of musicians vis-à-vis other legitimate interests, three aspects are noted. First, there is an inherent, inescapable tension between the protection of the commercial interests of musicians and those of their corporate partners. Second, musicians attach great importance to the way in which they are perceived by users.[142] Third, and importantly, the heterogeneity of the group of musicians implies a large variety of perspectives and interests, which appear to overlap only partially. The fault line runs along the boundaries of the concepts of authorship and performance and the ensuing distinction between copyright *sensu stricto* and the neighbouring rights of performing artists. The interests of composers and performers are not necessarily aligned. Since both categories receive a part of the same 'pie', there is a persisting belief that increased focus on one subset of the broad category of musicians will lead to the other subset losing out.[143] Moreover, the categories of authors and performers are themselves quite fragmented, given the large amount of and variety within the cultural and creative industries (CCIs) as well as cultural differences between different (national or regional) territories.[144] Finally, for the category of performers, a significant divergence exists between the small number of well-known featured artists and the vast majority of relatively anonymous session musicians, orchestral musicians and self-releasing artists, with the former being seemingly inclined to align their views with the interests of corporate partners.[145] Musicians have therefore traditionally found it difficult to speak with a unified voice. This contributes to an underrepresentation of their interests in the music industry debate.

Committee, *Creator Remuneration. Fifth Report of Session 2023–24* (10 April 2024) <https://shorturl.at/oFNSZ>.

141 In 2022, the median net annual income amounted to €27,314 in Belgium, €23,053 in France, €25,000 in Germany, €29,537 in the Netherlands. See statistics at <https://bit.ly/3sVetEs>. For the United Kingdom, Statista reports that the median annual earnings for full-time employees amounted to approximately £33,000 in 2022, see <https://bit.ly/3ZdM5cO>.

142 Krueger, *Rockonomics* (n 121) 6.

143 Cf Pavis, 'The Author–Performer Divide' (n 6) vol I, 28–30, 106; Osborne, 'Is Equitable Remuneration Equitable?' (n 33) 582, 586–87. See also Aguilar, 'We Want Artists' (n 5) 171–72; Ananay Aguilar, 'The Collective Management of Performers' Rights in the UK: A Story of Competing Interests' (2019) 16 SCRIPTed 4, 14.

144 Peter C DiCola, 'Money from Music: Survey Evidence on Musicians' Revenue and Lessons About Copyright Incentives' (2013) 55 Ariz L Rev 301, 336–37; Bently and others, 'Strengthening the Position' (n 135) 54; Deresiewicz, *The Death of the Artist* (n 132) 310; Racine, 'L'Auteur et l'Acte de Création' (n 136) 12, 37–39. See for an overview of the CCIs in the EU: EIF, 'Market Analysis of the Cultural and Creative Sectors in Europe: A Sector to Invest In' (2021).

145 Aguilar, 'We Want Artists' (n 5) 169–70; Aguilar, 'The Collective Management of Performers' Rights in the UK' (n 143) 16–17.

The primary objective of continental copyright *sensu lato* is to protect and stimulate creativity.[146] Artists are at the centre of copyright and neighbouring rights protection.[147] Only they are granted the initial right to exploit their work.[148] Moreover, the 'high level of protection' that serves as a guiding principle for EU copyright law refers to the rights of artists, whose 'independence and dignity' must be safeguarded.[149] While the importance of internal incentives should be acknowledged, the primary objective of copyright protection is to further the external incentives for musicians to make music. This implies due attention to monetary as well as non-monetary aspects, to both agency and remuneration.

2.2.3 *Corporate Partners*

2.2.3.1 Typology

On the more commercially inclined side of the music industry, there is a wealth of individuals and (mostly) companies that perform a diverse array of intermediary services. Throughout this book, they are indicated as *corporate partners*.

A first important player is the *music publisher*, who grants licences to content providers for the use of original musical compositions in a commercial context, either directly or via a CMO.[150] This includes (part of) the copyright in the composition or a licence from the composer(s).[151] The tasks of a music publisher include pitching a piece of music to record companies, to facilitate its recording or to incentivise covers of it, contacting radio stations to ensure airplay, promoting synchronisation of the music with music supervisors, and so forth.[152] Traditionally,

[146] See eg Rochelle Cooper Dreyfuss, 'In Praise of an Incentive-Based Theory of Intellectual Property Protection' in Rochelle Cooper Dreyfuss and Elizabeth Siew-Kuan Ng (eds), *Framing Intellectual Property Law in the 21st Century* (1st edn, Cambridge University Press 2018) 1–31; Johanna Gibson, 'Basis of Protection' in JAL Sterling (ed), *Sterling on World Copyright Law* (5th edn, Sweet & Maxwell 2018) 39–111.

[147] Cf Zechariah Chafee, 'Reflections on the Law of Copyright: I' (1945) 45 Columbia Law Review 503, 506–07.

[148] Case C-301/15 *Soulier and Doke* [2016] ECLI:EU:C:2016:878, para 47; Case C-484/18 *Spedidam* [2019] ECLI:EU:C:2019:970, para 39.

[149] Recs 4, 9–11 InfoSoc Directive.

[150] Cf Cooke, *Dissecting the Digital Dollar* (n 103) 10; Europe Economics and others, 'Remuneration of Authors and Performers' (n 4) 65–68; Dusollier and others, 'Contractual Arrangements Applicable to Creators' (n 105) 21. See also Don E Tomlinson, 'Everything That Glitters Is Not Gold: Songwriter-Music Publisher Agreements and Disagreements' (1995) 18 Hastings Comm & Ent LJ 85.

[151] Europe Economics and others, 'Remuneration of Authors and Performers' (n 4) 65, 67–68; De Voldere and others, 'Mapping the Creative Value Chains' (n 28) 137, 147.

[152] Lardinois, *Les Contrats Commentés de l'Industrie de La Musique 2.0* (n 18) 116–17; Yannick H'Madoun and others, *Auteursrechten en Publishing* (Poppunt vzw 2014) 64–67; Stopps, 'How to Make a Living from Music' (n 42) 17, 107, 110; De Voldere and others, 'Mapping the Creative Value Chains (n 28) 137; Pauly and H'Madoun, *Poppuntgids voor muzikant en dj* (n 9) 189–98; Gulinck, *Hier Tekenen!* (n 7) 114, 153–55.

music publishers have also been in charge of the commercialisation of sheet music.[153]

The music publisher must acquire the exploitation rights necessary to provide licences to third parties from the composer(s), either in the form of a (partial[154] and/or temporary) transfer of the composer's copyright or in the form of a licence.[155] Exploitation agreements entered into between a composer and a publisher may take various different forms. While a 'title agreement' is limited to the rights in one or more specific pre-existing compositions, a (usually exclusive) 'songwriter agreement' or 'exclusivity agreement' relates to works that have yet to be composed during a specific time period.[156] It is also possible to limit the publisher's intervention to the administration of copyright revenue and call upon the services of a PR company for promotion and marketing purposes.[157] In the context of such an 'administration agreement' with a publishing administrator, the composer retains their copyright and the music publisher only acquires a licence.[158] Such arrangements are becoming increasingly common.[159] Composers are in no way obliged to enter into an agreement with a music publisher and may decide to perform the activities of a music publisher themselves.[160] The composers then retain their rights.

A relatively new player seeking to disrupt music publishing is Hipgnosis,[161] an investment company that purchases music publishing rights directly from (primarily established) artists and allows investment in their catalogue in a way similar to a stock or asset portfolio.[162]

153 In the analogue age, this was the main task of a music publisher. Sheet music has now become a significantly less important source of music publishing revenue.

154 This leads to a 'co-publishing' contract, where composer and publisher co-own the copyright *sensu stricto*, see DCMS Committee, 'Economics of Music Streaming' (n 47) 20.

155 P Bernt Hugenholtz and Lucie Guibault, 'Auteurscontractenrecht: Naar Een Wettelijke Regeling?' (2004) <https://bit.ly/3UvnwGx> 25; H'Madoun and others, *Auteursrechten en Publishing* (n 152) 64, 71–72; Europe Economics and others, 'Remuneration of Authors and Performers' (n 4) 65, 67–68; De Voldere and others, 'Mapping the Creative Value Chains' (n 28) 137, 147; Passman, *All You Need to Know* (n 42) 220–21; Ruth Towse, 'Dealing with Digital: The Economic Organisation of Streamed Music' (2020) 42 Media, Culture & Society 1461, 1463.

156 H'Madoun and others, *Auteursrechten en Publishing* (n 152) 70; Gulinck, *Hier Tekenen!* (n 7) 307–10, 317–42; Malevanny, *Online Music Distribution* (n 28) 78–80; Passman, *All You Need to Know* (n 42) 277–97; Towse, 'Dealing with Digital' (n 155) 1463; Haidinger, *Online-Musiklizenzierung* (n 3) 155.

157 See below, Chapter 2, Section 2.3.4.

158 Gulinck, *Hier Tekenen!* (n 7) 310; Malevanny, *Online Music Distribution* (n 28) 85–86; Passman, *All You Need to Know* (n 42) 297–303; Cooke, *Dissecting the Digital Dollar* (n 103) 34.

159 Cooke, *Dissecting the Digital Dollar* (n 103) 34.

160 H'Madoun and others, *Auteursrechten en Publishing* (n 152) 68; Pauly and H'Madoun, *Poppuntgids voor muzikant en dj* (n 9) 192.

161 <www.hipgnosissongs.com>.

162 See eg Will Schube, 'How a Wildly Ambitious Company Called Hipgnosis Is Shaking Up the Music Industry' (*Complex*, 8 October 2020) <https://bit.ly/3aMBRrC>; Matt Hendrickson, 'The Man Who's Spending $1 Billion to Own Every Pop Song' (*Medium*, 8 January 2021)

Second, the *record company* or (record) label invests in the discovery and development of musicians, as well as in the production and distribution of phonograms.[163] An important division in a record company is often called A&R (Artist & Repertoire), which focuses on the discovery and signing of artists.[164] The record company is usually responsible for the production of phonograms, the manufacture of physical copies (if applicable), physical and/or digital distribution (the latter through digital service providers (DSPs)) as well as promotion and marketing of the finished product.[165] It functions as an investor and risk aggregator.[166] In this capacity, a record company acquires a neighbouring right as a producer of the phonogram(s) at issue.[167]

Exploitation contracts with record companies take various different forms. The traditional contract model is a so-called record contract or artist deal. This exclusive deal usually entails a full transfer of rights from the musician to the record company, in return for monetary compensation.[168] In recent years, an evolving practice may be discerned, whereby musicians have more margin for negotiation and may agree on a rights transfer that is limited in time or sign an exclusive or non-exclusive licence or distribution contract.[169] For session musicians, buyouts – with a full transfer of

<https://bit.ly/3C52Fzv>; Emma Griffiths, 'Money Moves – Merck Mercuriadis on Changing Industry Paradigms and the Future of Music as an Asset Class' (*Synchtank*, 11 February 2021) <https://bit.ly/3BPwow8>; Tim Ingham, 'Merck Mercuriadis Faces the Future… and Stares down His Critics' (*Music Business Worldwide*, 16 February 2021) <https://bit.ly/3FPl9WV>; Tim Ingham, 'Blackstone Invests $1bn in Music via Hipgnosis. Are Billions More on the Way?' (*Music Business Worldwide*, 12 October 2021) <https://bit.ly/2Z3koKH>.

163 Mulligan, *Awakening* (n 135) 279; Cooke, *Dissecting the Digital Dollar* (n 103) 125–30.

164 De Voldere and others, 'Mapping the Creative Value Chains' (n 28) 137; Gulinck, *Hier Tekenen!* (n 7) 125–26.

165 Norbert J Michel, 'Digital File Sharing and Royalty Contracts in the Music Industry: A Theoretical Analysis' (2006) 3 Review of Economic Research on Copyright Issues 29, 31; Europe Economics and others, 'Remuneration of Authors and Performers' (n 4) 65–66; Rethink Music Initiative, 'Fair Music (n 127) 6; De Voldere and others, 'Mapping the Creative Value Chains (n 28) 137–38; Gulinck, *Hier Tekenen!* (n 7) 114; Cooke, *Dissecting the Digital Dollar* (n 103) 125–30.

166 Barnett, 'Copyright without Creators' (n 124) 391–92; Hyojung Sun, *Digital Revolution Tamed. The Case of the Recording Industry* (Springer International 2019) 52–53; Gulinck, *Hier Tekenen!* (n 7) 112.

167 Cf above, Section 2.2.3.2.

168 Hugenholtz and Guibault, 'Auteurscontractenrecht' (n 155) 24; Lardinois, *Les Contrats Commentés de l'Industrie de La Musique 2.0* (n 18) 83–84, 88–89; Rethink Music Initiative, 'Fair Music (n 127) 6; Pauly and H'Madoun, *Poppuntgids voor muzikant en dj* (n 9) 169–77; Gulinck, *Hier Tekenen!* (n 7) 229–31, 250–88; Malevanny, *Online Music Distribution* (n 28) 83–85; Cooke, *Dissecting the Digital Dollar* (n 103) 130–31.

169 Europe Economics and others, 'Remuneration of Authors and Performers' (n 4) 67; De Voldere and others, 'Mapping the Creative Value Chains' (n 28) 82; Pauly and H'Madoun, *Poppuntgids voor muzikant en dj* (n 9) 177–85; Gulinck, *Hier Tekenen!* (n 7) 121; Krueger, *Rockonomics* (n 121) 162; Passman, *All You Need to Know* (n 42) 205–06; Cooke, *Dissecting the Digital Dollar* (n 103) 34, 131, 137.

exclusive rights against a modest one-off fee – are still the norm.[170] Finally, as is the case for music publishing, it is not mandatory for a musician to enter into a contractual relationship with a record company.

Digitisation has given rise to a new type of corporate partners, namely DSPs, a broad category of providers of services that are provided digitally, via the internet. Examples of DSPs include online content and/or social media platforms (such as YouTube, Spotify, Facebook[171]), digital aggregators (for example, TuneCore, CD Baby[172]) and their counterparts, music publishing administrators (such as TuneCore Publishing, CD Baby Pro[173]), the latter two aiding in the online distribution of recorded music and the administration of composition royalties respectively.

A final, very broad category of relevant corporate partners includes managers, concert promoters, distributors, entertainment lawyers and booking agents.[174] Among the corporate partners in this final, broad category, the *manager* holds a privileged position, being the corporate partner whose interests are the most closely aligned with those of the musicians they represent.[175] Indeed, a music manager's income is usually made up of a percentage of the revenues amassed by 'their' musician(s). Thus, the manager sits on the fence between the artistic and commercial sides of the music industry.[176]

This book uses the umbrella term *music value chain* to refer to musicians and their managers, music publishers, record companies, CMOs, digital aggregators and music publishing administrators. Managers, publishers, record companies, CMOs, digital aggregators and music publishing administrators are referred to as *music industry corporate partners*. Other corporate partners are referred to as *external corporate partners*.

2.2.3.2 Rights

Music producers are to be distinguished from the legal concept of 'producer' under copyright law *sensu lato*. The WPPT defines a producer of phonograms as 'the person, or the legal entity, who or which takes the initiative and has the

170 Rec 9 Term Directive; Ruth Towse, 'Copyright and Economic Incentives: An Application to Performers' Rights in the Music Industry' (1999) 52 Kyklos 369 374, 380–81; McDonagh, 'Rearranging the Roles of the Performer and the Composer in the Music Industry' (n 27) 69, 75–76; Europe Economics and others, 'Remuneration of Authors and Performers' (n 4) 5, 77–78; Osborne, 'Is Equitable Remuneration Equitable?' (n 33) 581; Aguilar, 'We Want Artists' (n 5) 163, 172; Aguilar, 'Distributed Ownership in Music' (n 28) 786; Aguilar, 'The Collective Management of Performers' Rights in the UK' (n 143) 16; Gulinck, *Hier Tekenen!* (n 7) 83–84, 214–15; Cooke, *Dissecting the Digital Dollar* (n 103) 32.

171 <www.youtube.com>; <www.spotify.com>; <www.facebook.com>.

172 <www.tunecore.com>; <https://cdbaby.com/>.

173 <www.tunecore.com/music-publishing-administration>; <https://cdbaby.com/publishing>.

174 Passman, *All You Need to Know* (n 42) 32–65.

175 Jim Rogers, *The Death & Life of the Music Industry in the Digital Age* (Bloomsbury 2013) 15; Stopps, 'How to Make a Living from Music' (n 42) 73–76; Silbey, *The Eureka Myth* (n 121) 137; Passman, *All You Need to Know* (n 42) 32–53.

176 Cf Aguilar, 'We Want Artists' (n 5) 171; Cooke, *Dissecting the Digital Dollar* (n 103).

responsibility for the first fixation of the sounds of a performance or other sounds, or the representations of sounds'.[177] A 'phonogram' refers to 'the fixation of the sounds of a performance or of other sounds, or of a representation of sounds, other than in the form of a fixation incorporated in a cinematographic or other audio-visual work'.[178] The sounds at issue must not necessarily relate to a work that is protected by copyright – in other words, the phonogram's content is, as such, irrelevant.[179] In the music industry, the status of producer of a phonogram accrues to the record company, unless the musicians themselves take this position. DIY (do-it-yourself) musicians may be qualified as producers and thus acquire rights in that capacity, in addition to their status as performing artists.[180] The neighbouring right granted to producers of phonograms protects financial investments in phonograms.[181] Such investments are considered to be high in both amount and risk and necessary to secure the creation of new content.[182]

A particularity of UK law are the special provisions relating to exclusive recording contracts – contracts with a performer that exclusively entitle a person to record certain performances with a view to their commercial exploitation.[183] Record companies that qualify as such persons acquire rights under UK law similar to certain rights granted to performers.[184]

2.2.3.3 Interests

The music industry is characterised by an inherent tension between the legitimate interests of musicians and those of their corporate partners.[185] While the former have a primordial interest in the dissemination of their music, the latter are primarily interested in their ultimate return-on-investment.[186] The revenue ultimately

[177] Art 2(d) WPPT; Art 3(c) Rome Convention. The reproduction of an existing phonogram, such as by the reissue of a CD or the issue of a CD on the basis of a vinyl record, does not give rise to a new neighbouring right.

[178] Art 2(b) WPPT; Art 3(b) Rome Convention; Case C-147/19 *Atresmedia Corporación de Medios de Comunicación SA v Asociación de Gestión de Derechos Intelectuales (AGEDI), Artistas Intérpretes o Ejecutantes, Sociedad de Gestión de España (AIE)* [2020] ECLI:EU:C:2020:935, paras 37–47.

[179] Aguilar, 'Distributed Ownership in Music' (n 28) 778.

[180] Gulinck, *Hier Tekenen!* (n 7) 177.

[181] Case C-476/17 *Pelham GmbH, Moses Pelham and Martin Haas v Ralf Hütter and Florian Schneider-Esleben* [2018] ECLI:EU:C:2018:1002, Opinion of AG Szpunar, para 33.

[182] Case C-200/96 *Metronome Musik v Music Point Hokamp* [1998] ECLI:EU:C:1998:172, para 24; Case C-61/05 *Commission of the European Communities v Portuguese Republic* [2006] ECLI:EU:C:2006:467, para 27.

[183] Art 186 UK CDPA.

[184] Arts 187–88 UK CDPA; Arnold, *Performers' Rights* (n 30) 80–83; Bently and others, *Intellectual Property Law* (n 10) 373.

[185] Gulinck, *Hier Tekenen!* (n 7) 10.

[186] Richard Caves, *Creative Industries. Contracts between Art and Commerce* (Harvard University Press 2002) 4, 21; Lardinois, *Les Contrats Commentés de l'Industrie de La Musique 2.0* (n 18) 26;

accruing to corporate partners does not flow to musicians and vice versa. Put somewhat crassly by former industry executive Walter Yetnikoff: 'Most of the majors are in the fast food business and the artists are hamburgers.'[187] The interests of both sides dictate a struggle for a bigger proportion of total revenues. Corporate partners have a clear and justifiable interest in keeping the level of regulation down and maintaining the status quo for revenue distribution.[188] Their emphasis on the importance of freedom of contract is unsurprising and, moreover, legitimate.[189] Indeed, if the price demanded in the context of contract negotiations is too high, demand drops and everybody loses out – including musicians.[190]

Given their essentially commercial focus, the perspective of music industry corporate partners on musicians (and users) is largely driven by the laws of supply and demand. As a result, they more readily accept the music market's winner-takes-all tendencies.[191] Their business models leave no room for mediocrity and/or lack of success.[192] Corporate partners have an interest in acquiring a considerable share of the revenues garnered by an artist that has struck gold and in retaining that artist's 'services' for as long as possible.[193] By contrast, corporate partners are likely to seek to drop artists that have proven to be less lucky and not be required to exploit their (unsuccessful) music.[194]

The broad category of music industry corporate partners lacks homogeneity. Not only is the wealth of intermediary functions mirrored by a variety of business models, the relevant corporate partners also show an impressive range of structures and sizes,

Rethink Music Initiative, 'Fair Music' (n 127) 5; Pauly and H'Madoun, *Poppuntgids voor muzikant en dj* (n 9) 164; Aguilar, 'We Want Artists' (n 5) 172; Baym, *Playing to the Crowd* (n 127) 64–65; Rognstad and Poort, 'The Right to Reasonable Exploitation' (n 126) 127; Martin Skladany, *Big Copyright versus the People: How Major Content Providers Are Destroying Creativity and How to Stop Them* (1st edn, Cambridge University Press 2018) 9; Gulinck, *Hier Tekenen!* (n 7) 62.

187 As quoted in Stan Soocher, *They Fought the Law. Rock Music Goes to Court* (Schirmer Books 1999) 44.

188 Cf Commission, 'Report on the Responses to the Public Consultation on the Review of the EU Copyright Rules' (July 2014) 80; Aguilar, 'We Want Artists' (n 5) 172, 175–76; Morten Hviid and others, 'Digitalisation and Intermediaries in the Music Industry: The Rise of the Entrepreneur?' (2018) 15 SCRIPTed 242, 271 275.

189 See also DCMS Committee, 'Economics of Music Streaming (n 47) 33; Osborne and Sun (n 5) s 1.4.1.

190 Europe Economics and others, 'Remuneration of Authors and Performers' (n 4) 115; Stef van Gompel, '"Non, Non, Rien n'a Changé": Over Vergoedingsaanspraken voor Makers uit Hoofde van Exploitatiecontracten' [2021] Auteursrecht 3, 5.

191 Ted Shapiro, 'Remuneration Provisions in the DSM Copyright Directive and the Audiovisual Industry in the EU: The Elusive Quest for Fairness' (2020) 42 EIPR 778, 779.

192 Cf Kretschmer and others, 'The Relationship between Copyright and Contract Law' (n 135) 67.

193 Aguilar, 'We Want Artists' (n 5) 167; Baym, *Playing to the Crowd* (n 127) 64; Hviid and others, 'Digitalisation and Intermediaries' (n 188) 259; Brown and others, *Contemporary Intellectual Property* (n 110) 222.

194 Baym, *Playing to the Crowd* (n 127) 64; Brown and others, *Contemporary Intellectual Property* (n 110) 222.

from a one-man show to mammoth multinational media conglomerates. Contrary to what is the case for musicians, however, it appears that this heterogeneity has not translated into a lack of leverage in the legislative process. Instead, the major rights owners have played an important role in the push towards greater protection of copyright over recent decades.

The position of corporate partners corresponds with the objective of the neighbouring rights of producers of phonograms.[195] While copyright's primary theoretical focus lies with the creative incentives of artists, the added value of actively risk-taking commercial intermediaries should be acknowledged, and met with the opportunity to obtain an equitable return on investment and a reasonable profit margin.[196] To this end, music publishers and record companies must be able to acquire the rights necessary to effectively exploit a composition and/or a phonogram and retain a proportion of the revenues garnered through such exploitation.[197] The inherent uncertainty present in CCIs such as the music industry already makes for a tricky investment climate. The revenues obtained from successful hits serve as a subsidy for failed releases and as much as 90 per cent of all released music fails to break even.[198] Thus, disappointing financial results for musicians may be due to the 'unfavourable economics of the music industry'[199] as much as to instances of unfairness in music contracts. Due care must be shown not to overemphasise either the perspective of musicians or their corporate partners. The perverse effect of far-reaching protective mechanisms would be a sharp decrease in corporate partners' activity, which could in turn be detrimental to cultural diversity and musicians themselves.

Similar to the case of musicians, the structure and size of a corporate partner significantly affect their market position and bargaining power, vis-à-vis both musicians and external corporate partners. The heterogeneous nature of the category of corporate partners should be borne in mind. Particular reference may be made to the status of small and medium-sized enterprises (SMEs).

[195] Cf Ana Ramalho, *The Competence of the European Union in Copyright Lawmaking. A Normative Perspective of EU Powers for Copyright Harmonization* (Springer International 2016) 198–203.

[196] Chafee, 'Reflections on the Law of Copyright: I' (n 147) 509–11; William M Landes and Richard A Posner, *The Economic Structure of Intellectual Property Law* (Belknap Press of Harvard University Press 2003) 38; Barnett, 'Copyright without Creators' (n 124) 390–92. Cf Case 200/96 *Metronome Musik v Music Point Hokamp* [1998] ECLI:EU:C:1998:172, para 24.

[197] Cf Séverine Dusollier, 'An Effective and Comprehensive Contractual Protection of Creators and Performers' (Copyright in the Digital Single Market, Brussels, 30 January 2020).

[198] Caves, *Creative Industries* (n 186) 61; Landes and Posner, *The Economic Structure of Intellectual Property Law* (n 196) 233; Nicolas Suzor, 'Access, Progress, and Fairness: Rethinking Exclusivity in Copyright' (2013) 15 Vand J Ent & Tech L 297, 323; Mulligan, *Awakening* (35n 15) 86; Krueger, *Rockonomics* (n 121) 21, 36, 110; Deresiewicz, *The Death of the Artist* (n 132) 45–46.

[199] Krueger, *Rockonomics* (n 121) 21.

2.2.4 *Users*

The value of music is limited without its audience. Therefore, due account must be taken of the legitimate interests of users. This is all the more so given the rise of user-generated content (UGC) and the ensuing difficulty of drawing a line between mere consumers of analogue and/or digital music and actual creators – and thus potential copyright owners.[200] First, users have a clear interest in obtaining convenient, cheap access to protected content as well as legal certainty as to the licit nature of their activities.[201] Freedom of expression is paramount.[202] A second incentive, which mainly applies to active music fans and less so to mere passive listeners, is the wish to connect with music and the people behind it.[203]

The position of users may be linked with the secondary objective of copyright to ensure the dissemination of creative works and the ensuing access to them.[204] This objective may be linked to the socio-cultural right to participate in cultural life and 'enjoy the arts'.[205] As opposed to the debate on the appropriate balance between copyright and consumer rights such as freedom of information and expression and the right to participate in cultural life, the legitimate interests of users only play a background role in the debate surrounding the contractual dynamics within the music industry. Even so, many users attach a certain degree of importance to the remuneration of artists, in line with humankind's instinctive inclination towards the underdog.[206] A copyright framework that places due stress on the position of the artist may benefit from enhanced societal legitimacy.[207] Therefore, it is important to

200 Baym, *Playing to the Crowd* (n 127) 84; Jacqueline Seignette and Jørgen Blomqvist, 'A Future Proof Copyright System' in Jørgen Blomqvist (ed), *Copyright, to Be or Not to Be* (Ex Tuto 2019) 266–67.

201 Dusollier, *Droit d'Auteur et Protection des Œuvres dans l'Univers Numérique* (n 133) 292–93; Séverine Dusollier, 'The Relations between Copyright Law and Consumer's Rights from a European Perspective' (European Parliament 2010) 4–5, 10–11, 15–16; Mulligan, *Awakening* (n 135) xv, 13, 29, 45, 57, 59, 249–50; Baym, *Playing to the Crowd* (n 127) 103; Krueger, *Rockonomics* (n 121) 32, 203, 267.

202 Dusollier, 'The Relations between Copyright Law and Consumer's Rights from a European Perspective' (n 201) 12–13.

203 Stopps, 'How to Make a Living from Music' (n 42) 168; Baym, *Playing to the Crowd* (n 127) 10, 31–53, 81.

204 Rec 22 InfoSoc Directive; Rec 2 IPRED; Art 7 TRIPS Agreement. On the associated objective of respecting and promoting cultural diversity, see Rec 2 DSM Directive; Ramalho, *The Competence of the European Union in Copyright Lawmaking* (n 195) 190–98.

205 See Art 27(1) *jo* 22 Universal Declaration of Human Rights (UDHR) <https://bit.ly/3mTGd5H> and Art 15(1)(a)–(b) International Covenant on Economic, Social and Cultural Rights (ICESCR) <https://bit.ly/3BHXBRl>. See also Silbey, *The Eureka Myth* (n 121) 221–22.

206 See eg EUIPO, 'European Citizens and Intellectual Property: Perception, Awareness, and Behaviour' (2017) 4, 7, 25, 36–37.

207 Peter K Yu, 'Digital Copyright and Confuzzling Rhetoric' (2011) 13 Vand J Ent & Tech L 881, 914–17; Suzor, 'Access, Progress, and Fairness' (n 198) 334–35; Eddie Schwartz, 'Coda: Fair Trade Music: Letting the Light Shine In' in Susy Frankel and Daniel Gervais (eds), *The Evolution and Equilibrium of Copyright in the Digital Age* (Cambridge University Press 2014)

ensure awareness as to the division of ownership and value within the music value chain.[208] Users who feel that revenue garnered through licit exploitation of protected content largely accrues to commercial corporations might view copyright protection as illegitimate and could potentially have a larger incentive to resort to online piracy as a form of civil disobedience.[209] Moreover, increased cultural diversity stemming from a healthy music ecosystem would benefit users' access to music.[210]

2.3 THE MUSIC VALUE CHAIN IN THE STREAMING AGE

2.3.1 *Digitisation in the Music Industry*

An analysis of the music industry in the streaming age would be incomplete without a brief glance at the first stages of digitisation that preceded this (r)evolution.[211] At the turn of the millennium, the widespread use of the internet, allowing for reproductions of protected works and/or performances to be instantly transferred across the globe through peer-to-peer (P2P) file-sharing, led to uncurbed piracy of artistic

313; Martin Senftleben, 'More Money for Creators and More Support for Copyright in Society – Fair Remuneration Rights in Germany and the Netherlands' (2018) 41 Colum J L & Arts 413, 413, 421–22; Xalabarder, 'The Principle of Appropriate and Proportionate Remuneration' (n 103) 27; DCMS Committee, 'Economics of Music Streaming (n 47) 25, 35.

208 Cf the objectives of the *Fair MusE* project <https://fairmuse.eu>.

209 Cf Jane Ginsburg, 'How Copyright Got a Bad Name for Itself' (2002) 26 Colum JL & Arts 61, 61–62; Commission, 'Impact Assessment on the Modernisation of EU Copyright Rules Accompanying the Document Proposal for a Directive of the European Parliament and of the Council on Copyright in the Digital Single Market and Proposal for a Regulation of the European Parliament and of the Council Laying Down Rules on the Exercise of Copyright and Related Rights Applicable to Certain Online Transmissions of Broadcasting Organisations and Retransmissions of Television and Radio Programmes' (Staff Working Document) SWD (2016) 301 Final (14 September 2016) 186; Commission, 'Annexes to the Impact Assessment on the Modernisation of EU Copyright Rules' (Staff Working Document) SWD(2016) 301 Final (14 September 2016) 29; Gary Sinclair and Todd Green, 'Download or Stream? Steal or Buy? Developing a Typology of Today's Music Consumer' [2016] J Consumer Behav 3, 3–14.

210 See in this sense SWD(2016) 301 final (n 209) 194.

211 Many volumes have been written on the topic of digitisation and its consequences in the music industry. See eg Patrick Burkart and Tom McCourt, *Digital Music Wars: Ownership and Control of the Celestial Jukebox* (Rowman & Littlefield 2006); Peter Tschmuck, *Creativity and Innovation in the Music Industry* (2nd edn, Springer 2012); Alex Sayf Cummings, *Democracy of Sound. Music Piracy and the Remaking of American Copyright in the Twentieth Century* (Oxford University Press 2013); Rogers, *The Death & Life* (n 175); Dan Cornfield, *Beyond the Beat: Musicians Building Community in Nashville* (Princeton University Press 2015); Mulligan, *Awakening* (n 135); Stephen Witt, *How Music Got Free. The End of an Industry, the Turn of the Century, and the Patient Zero of Piracy* (Viking 2015); Steve Knopper, *Appetite for Self-Destruction: The Spectacular Crash of the Record Industry in the Digital Age* (CreateSpace 2017); Sun, *Digital Revolution Tamed* (n 166); David Arditi, *Getting Signed: Record Contracts, Musicians, and Power in Society* (Springer International 2020); David Arditi, *Streaming Culture: Subscription Platforms and the Unending Consumption of Culture* (Emerald 2021).

content. While the direct link between illegal file-sharing and the sharp decline in physical record sales[212] is disputed by some,[213] it is difficult to deny the difficulties of the recorded music industry in particular during that period.[214] The figures do not lie: in 2020, global revenues from physical music sales were five times lower than in 2001, while the global recorded music industry lost over one-third of its total revenues in the 2001–2014 period.[215] The music industry was left wondering how it could bend the forces of digitisation to its will. Continuing losses in analogue music sales were only offset by the rise in digital revenues in 2015, over a decade later.

On the music industry's side, it was repeatedly argued that the widespread use of the internet led to an 'everything is free culture', in which it became more and more difficult to monetise artistic content.[216] When the first digitisation wave hit, record companies in particular took a primarily negative view and were slow to adapt to the newfound digital reality.[217] On the other side, pitted squarely against the vested interests of the music industry, were the proponents of a free internet.[218] From their perspective, online file-sharing presents itself as an opportunity to enhance access to creative content at a lower price – and, ideally, even for free.[219] These diametrically opposed positions clash vehemently, not least regarding copyright enforcement and the legislative reform that took place as a response to digitisation and the rise of online piracy.

The instinctive reaction of the media industries to online piracy was to double down on copyright enforcement. Initial efforts focused on the repression of piracy by private users, such as through the threat of criminal sanctions.[220] Graduated

212 See eg Stan J Liebowitz, 'File Sharing: Creative Destruction or Just Plain Destruction?' (2006) 49 JL & Econ 28; Stan J Liebowitz, 'How Much of the Decline in Sound Recording Sales Is Due to File-Sharing?' (2016) 40 J Cult Econ 13; Stan J Liebowitz, 'Responding to Oberholzer-Gee and Strumpf's Attempted Defense of Their Piracy Paper' (2017) 14 Econ J Watch 23; Joost Poort and others, 'Global Online Piracy Study' (2018).

213 See eg Felix Oberholzer-Gee and Koleman Strumpf, 'The Effect of File Sharing on Record Sales: An Empirical Analysis' (2007) 115 J Political Econ 1; Felix Oberholzer-Gee and Koleman Strumpf, 'File Sharing and Copyright' (2010) 10 Innovation Policy and the Economy 19; Rogers, *The Death & Life* (n 175) 35–41; Felix Oberholzer-Gee and Koleman Strumpf, 'The Effect of File Sharing on Record Sales, Revisited' (2016) 37 Inf Econ Policy 61; Baym, *Playing to the Crowd* (n 127) 67.

214 See Rogers, *The Death & Life* (n 175) 25–70; Brett Danaher and others, 'Copyright Enforcement in the Digital Age: Empirical Economic Evidence and Conclusions' (2015); Mulligan, *Awakening* (n 135) 2–18.

215 IFPI, 'Global Music Report 2024 – State of the Industry' (2024) <https://globalmusicreport.ifpi.org> 11.

216 See eg Rogers, *The Death & Life* (n 175) 5, 61–69.

217 ibid 55–60; Mulligan, *Awakening* (n 135) 19–41; Gulinck, *Hier Tekenen!* (n 7) 111.

218 See eg Robert Levine, *Free Ride. How Digital Parasites Are Destroying the Culture Business, and How the Culture Business Can Fight Back* (Anchor 2012).

219 Glynn Lunney, *Copyright's Excess: Money and Music in the US Recording Industry* (1st edn, Cambridge University Press 2018) 194.

220 Ben Depoorter and others, 'Copyright Backlash' (2011) 84 South Calif Law Rev 1251, 1251–92; Rogers, *The Death & Life* (n 175) 72–75; Mulligan, *Awakening* (n 135) 222–23; João Pedro Quintais and Joost Poort, 'The Decline of Online Piracy: How Markets – Not Enforcement – Drive Down Copyright Infringement' (2019) 34 Am U Int'l L Rev 807, 848–54.

response strategies such as the 'three strikes and you're out' approach vis-à-vis illicit file-sharers were the subject of intense discussions in the first decade of the millennium.[221] Gradually, the industry's enforcement focus shifted to internet service providers (ISPs), obtaining injunctions against piracy websites such as The Pirate Bay and MegaUpload, and suing new DSPs.[222] Moreover, as a rule, online content platforms now provide 'notice and take down' procedures (for example, Content ID on YouTube) allowing rights owners to put a stop to particular instances of online copyright infringement. The next step is 'notice and stay down' procedures, whereby infringing content is taken down and subsequently prevented from being re-uploaded to the platform.

Over the years, several regulatory options have been explored, ranging from stronger enforcement of existing copyright rules over the introduction of new rules to the abolition of copyright altogether.[223] However, the vast amount of interests involved made – and make – for a strenuous legislative process with intensive lobbying.[224]

Major rightsholders have traditionally been able to retain the upper hand, leading to a gradual but obvious increase in protection.[225] By contrast, the interests of musicians and their audiences have traditionally remained underexposed.[226] The significant increase in the term of protection over the past few decades serves as a first example. The term extension for phonograms mainly benefited the major record companies.[227] The same appears to be true for the exclusive making available right, which is usually transferred from the initial owners to their corporate

[221] See eg Rogers, *The Death & Life* (n 175) 80.

[222] ibid 75–82; Mulligan, *Awakening* (n 135) 227–31; Quintais and Poort, 'The Decline of Online Piracy' (n 221) 854–63.

[223] See extensively Rogers, *The Death & Life* (n 175) 71–97.

[224] Cf ibid 96, 134, 179, 196–98; Vetulani-Cęgiel, 'EU Copyright Law, Lobbying and Transparency of Policy-Making' (n 88) 146–58; Ramalho, *The Competence of the European Union in Copyright Lawmaking* (195) 18; Jørgen Blomqvist, 'The Roles for Intervention and for the Market' in Silke von Lewinski (ed), *Remuneration for the Use of Works. Exclusivity vs Other Approaches* (De Gruyter 2017) 389; Stefanie Hubig, 'Keynote' in Silke von Lewinski (ed), *Remuneration for the Use of Works. Exclusivity vs Other Approaches* (De Gruyter 2017) 312; Aguilar, 'We Want Artists' (n 5) 161; Hviid and others, 'Digitalisation and Intermediaries' (n 188) 275.

[225] Rogers, *The Death & Life* (n 175) 32–33, 197; Phillips and Street, 'Copyright and Musicians at the Digital Margins' (n 128) 344; Ginsburg, 'The Role of the Author in Copyright' (n 126) 67–68; Jessica Litman, *Digital Copyright* (Michigan Publishing, University of Michigan Library 2017) ix; Osborne, 'Is Equitable Remuneration Equitable?' (n 33) 583; Lunney, *Copyright's Excess* (n 219) 196. See Benjamin Farrand, *Networks of Power in Digital Copyright Law and Policy. Political Salience, Expertise and the Legislative Process* (Routledge 2014).

[226] Gulinck, *Hier Tekenen!* (n 7) 40–41; Stef van Gompel, 'Modern Copyright Reform and the Challenges of Evidence-Based Policymaking' in Jørgen Blomqvist (ed), *Copyright, to Be or Not to Be* (Ex Tuto 2019) 139–40.

[227] Rogers, *The Death & Life* (n 175) 142; van Gompel, 'Modern Copyright Reform' (n 226) 140.

partners.[228] A third notable legislative evolution spurred by digitisation and again heavily influenced by lobbyists was the establishment of anti-circumvention laws regarding digital rights management (DRM).[229] Finally, a more recent legislative evolution in the field of copyright law is the adoption of the Digital Single Market (DSM) Directive at the EU level and its ensuing implementation into Member State law.[230]

The music industry's reactionary attitude in the first stages of the internet revolution has given way to resilience and resourcefulness. While the internet revolution was first only perceived as a threat, the focus broadened to mining the opportunities presented by the new digital reality and monetising music online. This led to the development of numerous new business models, with the establishment of new digital players and a significant impact on consumer consumption patterns.[231]

The first notable development was the establishment of the 'some rights reserved' Creative Commons[232] (CC) licences in 2001. The next was the development of digital downloads, whereby users buy a licence to a digital copy of a music file that is then permanently downloaded to the user's personal device(s).[233] Downloads have a bearing on both mechanical rights and performing rights (in particular the right to making available).[234] Further, while users may download entire albums, in reality

[228] See De Voldere and others, 'Mapping the Creative Value Chains' (n 28) 147; Rochelle Dreyfuss and Justine Pila, 'Intellectual Property Law: An Anatomical Overview' in Rochelle Dreyfuss and Justine Pila (eds), *The Oxford Handbook of Intellectual Property Law* (Oxford Handbooks, Oxford University Press 2018) 11–12.

[229] See (1) on the international level: Arts 11–12 WCT and Arts 18–19 WPPT; (2) on the EU level: Arts 6–7 InfoSoc Directive; and (3) on the national level: Arts XI.291–292 Belgian CEL, Art L 331-5 French IP Code; Arts 95a–c German Copyright Act; Arts 29a–b Dutch Copyright Act, Arts 19–19a Dutch Neighbouring Rights Act. See ia Dusollier, 'The Relations between Copyright Law and Consumer's Rights from a European Perspective' (n 201) 27–30; Marcella Favale, 'Approximation and DRM: Can Digital Locks Respect Copyright Exceptions?' (2011) 19 International Journal of Law and Information Technology 306; Séverine Dusollier, 'The Protection of Technological Measures: Much Ado about Nothing or Silent Remodeling of Copyright?' in Rochelle Cooper Dreyfuss and Jane C Ginsburg (eds), *Intellectual Property at the Edge* (Cambridge University Press 2014); Joseph P Liu, 'Paracopyright – a Peculiar Right to Control Access' in Rochelle Cooper Dreyfuss and Jane C Ginsburg (eds), *Intellectual Property at the Edge* (Cambridge University Press 2014); Reto M Hilty, 'Intellectual Property and Private Ordering' in *The Oxford Handbook of Intellectual Property Law* (Oxford Handbooks, Oxford University Press 2018) 900–06, 915–20, 928–30.

[230] See Aguilar, 'We Want Artists' (n 5) 160–78.

[231] De Voldere and others, 'Mapping the Creative Value Chains' (n 28) 133, 145.

[232] <https://creativecommons.org> <https://freesound.org>.

[233] Seth Ericsson, 'The Recorded Music Industry and the Emergence of Online Music Distribution: Innovation in the Absence of Copyright (Reform)' (2011) 79 Geo Wash L Rev 1783, 1790–91; Rethink Music Initiative, 'Fair Music' (n 127) 7; Malevanny, *Online Music Distribution* (n 28) 9–11.

[234] Revenues from digital downloads are usually divided along the following lines: 75 per cent for mechanical rights and 25 per cent for performing rights: see Cooke, *Dissecting the::igital Dollar* (n 103) 86. See also Malevanny, *Online Music Distribution* (n 28) 10; Cooke, *Dissecting the Digital Dollar* (n 103) 14–15.

there was a notable shift to unbundling of such albums and a propensity toward single-track downloading.[235]

Both MusicNet and PressPlay, the legal digital music services set up by record companies at the beginning of the 2000s, failed, leaving ample room for new business models.[236] The first to rise to the occasion of providing users with a sound legal alternative to online piracy was Apple's iTunes store, which launched in 2003 and was ultimately shut down in 2019 to the benefit of streaming service Apple Music.[237] In theory, iTunes provided a greater opportunity for musicians to reach their audience directly, bypassing traditional intermediaries. This potential for disintermediation went by largely untapped, with network effects favouring the commercial interests of major record companies.[238] Moreover, independent musicians could not directly upload their music to iTunes. This led to the emergence of online distributors such as CD Baby and The Orchard, which still exist.[239]

The gap left by iTunes allowed for the emergence of new models in subsequent years. These saw the establishment of, for example, YouTube (2005), the online platform that enables users to upload and stream video content. This in turn led to the emergence of the concept of UGC, whereby users can create and share their own content, thereby becoming artists in their own right. UGC is still on the rise: it is impossible to keep track of the growing number of blogs, podcasts, social networks and other mediums used to share photos, videos and music. As a result, the line between 'makers' and 'consumers' of musical content is growing ever thinner. However, the most viewed videos on YouTube are and have almost always been those provided by traditional media, often the major record companies.[240] Moreover, YouTube has traditionally been completely free for users. Consequently, this did not counter the global decline in music sales. Again, there was room for innovation, which led to the rise of music streaming services.

The term 'streaming' refers to a method of transmitting or receiving data, such as audio and/or video material, without actually downloading any media files.[241] The data flows through the network in a continuous way, allowing the consumer to start

[235] Rogers, *The Death & Life* (n 175) 52; Mulligan, *Awakening* (n 135) 46; Krueger, *Rockonomics* (n 121) 197; Deresiewicz, *The Death of the Artist* (n 132) 130.

[236] Rogers, *The Death & Life* (n 175) 82; Mulligan, *Awakening* (n 135) 33–35; Hviid and others, 'Digitalisation and Intermediaries' (n 188) 268–69; DCMS Committee, 'Economics of Music Streaming (n 47) 10.

[237] See in detail Mulligan, *Awakening* (n 135) 129–42.

[238] David Arditi, 'iTunes: Breaking Barriers and Building Walls' (2014) 37 Popular Music and Society 408, 416–19, 422. See also David Arditi, *iTake-Over: The Recording Industry in the Digital Era* (Rowman & Littlefield 2014).

[239] Arditi, 'iTunes' (n 238) 416–19.

[240] De Voldere and others, 'Mapping the Creative Value Chains' (n 28) 145.

[241] See on the distinction between digital downloads and streaming, and the economic differences that this entails, Ericsson, 'The Recorded Music Industry' (n 233) 1791; Mulligan, *Awakening* (n 135) 155–58; Krueger, *Rockonomics* (n 121) 189; Malevanny, *Online Music Distribution* (n 28) 9–12.

viewing and/or listening to the content while the remainder of the data is still being received. As is the case for downloads, streaming has a bearing on both mechanical rights and performing rights (in particular the making available right).[242] While the stream itself primarily constitutes a communication to the public – a form of making available – streaming also entails a technical reproduction from the source file to the DSP's server. In addition, many DSPs allow users to save – and thus copy – certain songs to their personal (offline) library.[243] Finally, the (partial) reproduction of lyrics, which occurs on some streaming services as the song is played, also constitutes a copyright-relevant act, with a bearing on the right of reproduction of the owner of the copyright in the lyrics.

The rise of streaming indicates the advent of a post-ownership mentality on the part of users, whereby access to music, by 'renting' it through a streaming platform for example, is seen as more important than actual ownership of a physical CD or a digital MP3 file. In other words, the sale of music is seeing a shift from product to services, from ownership to access. Users no longer feel the need to secure a physical and/or digital copy of artistic content, but rather opt for convenience and unlimited, real-time access.[244] This shift from ownership to access also implies another change. While the focus used to lie with securing a successful, high-sales launch for new music, the aim now is to build an audience and achieve sustained listening over time rather than immediate success, since each listen is connected with economic value.[245] This explains the rising importance of catalogues in the music streaming market, which is further underscored by the notable spike in catalogue acquisitions, including deals regarding the music of David Bowie, Bob Dylan, Bruce Springsteen and Sting.[246] Moreover, streaming entails yet a further shift away from albums and toward single tracks.

[242] Marshall Leaffer, 'Exclusive Rights. General Report: Scope and Enforcement Tools to Assure Remuneration, Part A of the Questionnaire' in Silke von Lewinski (ed), *Remuneration for the Use of Works. Exclusivity vs Other Approaches* (De Gruyter 2017) 22–24; Gulinck, *Hier Tekenen!* (n 7) 297; Malevanny, *Online Music Distribution* (n 28) 12; Cooke, *Dissecting the Digital Dollar* (n 103) 11, 14–15; DCMS Committee, 'Economics of Music Streaming' (n 47) 18. The specifics of the division of revenues from streaming between mechanical rights and performing rights differ rather significantly between the chosen jurisdictions, see Cooke, *Dissecting the Digital Dollar* (n 103) 86, 201–02. See on the difference in treatment of streaming in the recorded music and music publishing sectors: DCMS Committee, 'Economics of Music Streaming (n 47) 38–39, 103; David Hesmondhalgh and others, 'Music Creators' Earnings in the Digital Era' (2021) 60–61.

[243] Castle and Feijóo, 'Study on the Artists in the Digital Music Marketplace' (n 4) 20.

[244] De Voldere and others, 'Mapping the Creative Value Chains' (n 28) 139; Castle and Feijóo, 'Study on the Artists in the Digital Music Marketplace' (n 4) 21.

[245] On the remuneration model for streaming, see Section 2.4.

[246] See ia Ben Sisario, 'Bruce Springsteen Sells Music Catalog in Massive Deal' (*New York Times*, 15 December 2021) <https://nyti.ms/3LdR9qe>; Jem Aswad, 'David Bowie's Estate Sells His Publishing Catalog to Warner Chappell' (*Variety*, 3 January 2022) <https://bit.ly/3sqFtI3>; Murray Stassen, 'At Least $5 Billion Was Spent on Music Rights Acquisitions in 2021. Could 2022 Be Even Bigger?' (*Music Business Worldwide*, 10 January 2022) <https://bit.ly/3sv3EoH>; Ryan Faughnder, 'Music Catalogs Are Fetching Huge Deals. Are They Overvalued?' (*LA Times*, 15 January 2022) <https://lat.ms/3sqlqcQ>; Murray Stassen, 'Sony Music Acquires Bob

Streaming services now constitute the main driver for revenue growth in the music industry. While there are a number of big streaming platforms, including Spotify,[247] Apple Music, Tencent Music and Amazon Music, the diversity that is available on the music streaming market is notable.[248] While SoundCloud is known for its pioneering shift to the user-centric model,[249] Napster (formerly Rhapsody, the first 'real' music streaming service[250]) and Qobuz seek to distinguish themselves by offering both digital downloads and music streaming, Tidal focuses on sound quality, iHeartRadio offers radio, streaming and podcasts, and Resonate uses a 'stream-to-own' model.[251] Niche streaming services, such as Idagio and Primephonic for classical music, are also available.[252] Moreover, most streaming services offer a wide variety of options for users, ranging from fully ad-supported services to a variety of subscription models with multiple price tiers.[253] Prices for music are now being set by DSPs instead of by the music industry itself – a seismic shift set in motion by iTunes.[254]

The shift towards music streaming affects the music that people listen to and thus also the music that is composed, performed and recorded. First, the importance of streaming playlists that guide users through an oversupply in music is noted.[255] While some playlists are actively curated by DSPs, others are generated through

Dylan's Recorded Music Catalog' (*Music Business Worldwide*, 24 January 2022) <https://bit.ly/30zv23X>; Murray Stassen, 'Sting Sells Song Catalog to Universal for $300M+ (*Music Business Worldwide*, 10 February 2022) <https://bit.ly/3uN388A>. See also Goldmedia, 'Musik-Streaming in Deutschland: Erlössituation Im Deutschen Musik-Streaming-Markt 2022' (2023) 95–96.

[247] See extensively Maria Eriksson and others, *Spotify Teardown: Inside the Black Box of Streaming Music* (MIT Press 2019); Sven Carlsson and Jonas Leijonhufvud, *The Spotify Play. How CEO and Founder Daniek EK Beat Apple, Google and Amazon in the Race for Audio Dominance* (Diversion Books 2021).

[248] See <www.spotify.com> <www.apple.com/apple-music> <https://music.amazon.com>. In detail: DCMS Committee, 'Economics of Music Streaming (n 47) 99–102.

[249] See below, Section 2.4.3.

[250] Mulligan, *Awakening* (n 135) 144.

[251] See <https://soundcloud.com> <https://us.napster.com> <www.qobuz.com> <https://tidal.com> <www.iheart.com> <https://resonate.is>.

[252] See <www.idagio.com> <www.primephonic.com>.

[253] De Voldere and others, 'Mapping the Creative Value Chains' (n 28) 138; Krueger, *Rockonomics* (n 121) 8, 184; DCMS Committee, 'Economics of Music Streaming (n 47) 14–15.

[254] De Voldere and others, 'Mapping the Creative Value Chains' (n 28) 144.

[255] Luis Aguiar and Joel Waldfogel, 'Platforms, Promotion, and Product Discovery: Evidence from Spotify Playlists' (NBER Working Paper, 2018); Sun, *Digital Revolution Tamed* (n 166) 156–61; Deresiewicz, *The Death of the Artist* (n 132) 61; Castle and Feijóo, 'Study on the Artists in the Digital Music Marketplace' (n 4) 7, 28; DCMS Committee, 'Economics of Music Streaming (n 47) 21–22, 77; Hesmondhalgh and others, 'Music Creators' Earnings in the Digital Era' (n 242) 91–93; Will Page, *Tarzan Economics. Eight Principles for Pivoting through Disruption* (Simon & Schuster 2021) 90–91, 238–40; Rebecca Giblin and Cory Doctorow, *Chokepoint Capitalism: How Big Tech and Big Content Captured Creative Labor Markets and How We'll Win Them Back* (Beacon Press 2022) 12; Goldmedia, 'Musik-Streaming in Deutschland' (n 246) 99–100.

automated recommendation systems based on perceived user preferences.[256] Second, the fact that rightsholders only receive royalties for music that is streamed for at least thirty seconds negatively affects certain musical genres where lengthy pieces are the norm – such as classical music and certain types of electronic dance music (EDM) – and has a direct impact on the structure of new music.[257] Songs are generally shorter, with early choruses and interventions by famous featuring artists instead of lengthy buildups.[258] The objectives for rightsholders are clear: find a way into a successful playlist, grasp people's fleeting attention and maintain it for at least thirty seconds.

In addition to the rise of streaming, the past decade has also seen an increase in revenue from synchronisation rights.[259] This refers to fees paid in return for rightsholders' permission to link audio and video in order to use music in the context of advertising, film, games and TV.[260] The required permission relates to the exclusive right of reproduction of composers, performers and producers of phonograms, and thus has a bearing on the total revenues of both the recorded music and music publishing sectors.[261] Synchronisation deals are highly fact-specific and the conditions for them are usually subject to stringent confidentiality requirements.[262]

2.3.2 *The Majors' Place in the Recorded Music and Music Publishing Sectors*

Our focus now shifts to the structure of the music value chain in which contracts between musicians, record companies and publishers are embedded. Three main layers may be discerned: the levels occupied by the majors, the independent corporate partners and the independent artists.

The recorded music and music publishing sectors are characterised by a significant degree of concentration and centralisation of power. The major record companies (or 'majors'), who have traditionally enjoyed a significant degree of power in

[256] See eg <https://about-recommendations.spotify.com>.

[257] Krueger, *Rockonomics* (n 121) 5; Page, *Tarzan Economics* (n 255) 3–4. See also David Hesmondhalgh, 'Streaming's Effects on Music Culture: Old Anxieties and New Simplifications' [2021] 16 Cultural Sociology 3.

[258] Paula Mejía, 'The Success of Streaming Has Been Great for Some, but Is There a Better Way?' (*NPR*, 22 July 2019) <https://n.pr/3vxlqJd>; Krueger, *Rockonomics* (n 121) 5, 196; DCMS Committee, 'Economics of Music Streaming (n 47) 44–45; Page, *Tarzan Economics* (n 255) 56–85; Giblin and Doctorow, *Chokepoint Capitalism* (n 255) 80–81.

[259] Stephan Klingner and Julia Friedrich, 'Status Quo and Perspectives of Licensing Synchronisation Rights' (2017) 6 IJMBR 69, 69–86; Deresiewicz, *The Death of the Artist* (n 132) 135–36.

[260] Rogers, *The Death & Life* (n 175) 103, 111; Stopps, 'How to Make a Living from Music' (n 42) 112–21; De Voldere and others, 'Mapping the Creative Value Chains' (n 28) 149; Gulinck, *Hier Tekenen!* (n 7) 478–79; Passman, *All You Need to Know* (n 42) 242–50.

[261] Gulinck, *Hier Tekenen!* (n 7) 478–86.

[262] Caves, *Creative Industries* (n 186) 301. See, however, Cooke, *Dissecting the Digital Dollar* (n 103) 48–52.

the music industry, have cemented their place at the table through horizontal as well as vertical integration.[263] On the horizontal level, the three remaining majors, namely Sony, Universal Music and Warner Music, hold a combined global market share of almost 70 per cent in the recorded music market at the time of writing.[264] From a vertical perspective, all three of these major labels have a music publishing division alongside functioning as a record company.[265] This means that, in addition to serving as a risk aggregator that provides money for the development of aspiring artists, these labels play an active role in monetising creative content for licensing purposes. Together, the music publishing divisions of the majors hold a market share of almost 60 per cent.[266] Signing a contract with the record division of a major may imply an inevitable publishing deal with the same major music company. On various occasions, the majors go even further and acquire partial or even full ownership of 'new', digital intermediaries in the marketing and distribution sector.[267]

The higher the degree of consolidation and centralisation of power, the more difficult it is for musicians to run their musical careers in a purely independent manner. Buyer power is susceptible to abuse on the part of those wielding it.[268] Major corporate partners can leverage their catalogue and use their strong market

[263] Caves, *Creative Industries* (n 186) 158–59; Phillip W Hall Jr, 'Smells Like Slavery: Unconscionability in Recording Industry Contracts' [2002] Hastings Comm & Ent LJ 189202; Rogers, *The Death & Life* (n 175) 17, 181–90, 195–186; Barnett, 'Copyright without Creators' (n 124) 403; Europe Economics and others, 'Remuneration of Authors and Performers' (n 4) 66; De Voldere and others, 'Mapping the Creative Value Chains' (n 28) 135, 144; Pauly and H'Madoun, *Poppuntgids voor muzikant en dj* (n 9) 166; Matthew David, 'CD' in Claudy Op den Kamp and Dan Hunter (eds), *A History of Intellectual Property in 50 Objects* (Cambridge University Press 2019) 361–63; Passman, *All You Need to Know* (n 42) 69–72; Hyojung Sun, 'Paradox of Celestial Jukebox: Resurgence of Market Control' (2019) 12 Creative Industries Journal 105, 109; Giblin and Doctorow, *Chokepoint Capitalism* (n 255) 2, 69–70, 148–49.

[264] See below, Section 2.4.3.

[265] See eg Hall Jr, 'Smells Like Slavery' (n 263) 202; Rogers, *The Death & Life* (n 175) 17, 181–90; De Voldere and others, 'Mapping the Creative Value Chains' (n 28) 146; Sun, *Digital Revolution Tamed* (n 166) 56–57; DCMS Committee, 'Economics of Music Streaming (n 47) 56. The prevalence of vertical integration is not new. In the pre-digital age, this technique led to the integration of recording and publishing divisions with manufacturing and distribution units, resulting in significant economies of scale, see Gerben Bakker, 'Adopting the Rights-Based Model: Music Multinationals and Local Music Industries since 1945' (2012) 6 Popular Music History 307.

[266] See below, Section 2.4.3.

[267] By way of example, Universal acquired digital agency Fame House as well as distribution and marketing company INgrooves, while Warner Music purchased UPROXX, a media company focusing on cultural news, and Sony has obtained full ownership of pioneering digital distributor The Orchard. See eg <https://shorturl.at/fAEWX>; <https://bit.ly/2XYWnCJ>; <https://bit.ly/3iePHY1>; <https://bit.ly/3igTmVb>. See also Sun, 'Paradox of Celestial Jukebox' (n 263) 117, 119–20. See for an extensive case study of INgrooves: Sun, *Digital Revolution Tamed* (n 16) 227–55, 272–76.

[268] Victoria Daskalova, 'The Monopsony Paradox: Buyer Power and Enforcement of the EU Antitrust Provisions' (Tilburg University 2016) 33–76; Friso Bostoen and Jozefien Vanherpe, 'Competition Law in the Digitized Music Industry: The Winners Take It All – But Should

position to force disadvantageous and inflexible deals on musicians. The apparent omnipresence of Spotify[269] and the rise of curated streaming playlists has consolidated and even augmented the market power of the majors.[270] Industry powerhouses are simply much better placed than independent artists to get 'their' music onto such playlists. They have the marketing budget required to pay for extensive promotional campaigns and may moreover leverage the success of their catalogue.[271] Artists with the backing of a major label can therefore reach a broader audience on streaming services. In turn, this ensures the majors' future leverage, even though the protection for some of the popular back catalogue held by the majors is on its last legs.

Thus, instead of democratising the music industry, streaming appears to have led to a replication of traditional music industry dynamics. Such practices may be likened to the now illegal practice of 'payola', whereby radio DJs were paid to play certain songs on the radio.[272] Direct ties between streaming services and the majors in the form of ownership stakes give an additional reason for concern. Finally, the power of the majors is also consolidated through the technique of direct licensing between DSPs and major rights owners, which has led to the (partial) withdrawal of their catalogues from voluntary collective management. This has unfavourable consequences for independent artists and small corporate partners. They have neither the resources nor the leverage to engage in direct licensing themselves and are left with CMOs that are less potent due to the withdrawal of major right owners' repertoire.[273] Thus, music industry concentration risks negatively impacting

They?' (2021) 2 CPI Antitrust Chronicle 30, 31–34; Giblin and Doctorow, *Chokepoint Capitalism* (n 255) 10.

[269] The four biggest music streaming services (Spotify, Apple Music, Tencent Music and Amazon Music) hold a combined market share of over 70 per cent in 2023. The market share held by Spotify amounts to over 30 per cent in 2023. See data at <www.internationalmusicsummit.com/business-report>.

[270] Arditi, 'iTunes' (n 238) 408–24; Deresiewicz, *The Death of the Artist* (n 132) 130–31. See also Julie Knibbe, 'Fairness in Question: Do Music Recommendation Algorithms Value Diversity?' (*Music Tomorrow*, 21 September 2021) <https://bit.ly/3ADHAo>; Julie Knibbe, 'Is the Spotify Editorial Playlist Landscape Fair to Emerging Artists?' (*Music Tomorrow*, 27 April 2022) <https://bit.ly/3T9CEHQ>.

[271] Rogers, *The Death & Life* (n 175) 83, 147–51; Rethink Music Initiative, 'Fair Music' (n 127) 14; Ashley Cook, 'The Power of Playlisting' [2017] MBJ; Sun, 'Paradox of Celestial Jukebox' (n 263) 118–20; Cooke, *Dissecting the Digital Dollar* (n 103); Franco Mariuzzo and Peter L Ormosi, 'Independent v Major Record Labels: Do They Compete on a Level-Playing Streaming Field?' [2020] SSRN Electronic Journal; Castle and Feijóo, 'Study on the Artists in the Digital Music Marketplace' (n 4) 31; DCMS Committee, 'Economics of Music Streaming (n 47) 69, 78; Giblin and Doctorow, *Chokepoint Capitalism* (n 255) 60–61, 67, 80. See also eg <https://about-recommendations.spotify.com>, which expressly indicates that, '[i]n some cases, commercial considerations may influence [Spotify's] recommendations'.

[272] Krueger, *Rockonomics* (n 121) 10, 183; Sun, 'Paradox of Celestial Jukebox' (n 263) 108.

[273] Cf Mulligan, *Awakening* (n 135) 305; Morten Hviid and others, 'Regulating Collective Management Organisations by Competition' [2016] JIPITEC 256, 267–68; Gulinck, *Hier Tekenen!* (n 7) 539.

cultural diversity.[274] In practice, therefore, the majors still play a vital role in deciding on the scope and modalities of exploitation of a work/performance – as well as the ensuing remuneration – by entering into contracts with providers of musical content, such as online content platforms, to which musicians are not a party.[275] The market power of a rightsholder is inversely proportionate to its accountability vis-à-vis musicians, DSPs and CMOs alike. The possible preventive intervention of merger control is noted in this context, as well as the potential application of the prohibition on abuse of (individual or collective) dominance of major media conglomerates under Article 102 TFEU.[276]

2.3.3 *The Rise of Independent Music Companies*

In addition to the majors, there is a large number of independent music companies, which are generally referred to as the 'indies'.[277] The market share of such independent companies is rising.[278] Among big indie names in the recorded music sector are Beggars Group (including labels such as Rough Trade and XL Recordings) and BMG, while two of the biggest independent music publishing administration companies are Kobalt and Peermusic.[279]

Independent music companies usually operate on a more limited territorial basis than the majors and moreover do not have the benefit of vertical integration, in the sense that they do not include a distribution division.[280] In order to overcome this, many indies have entered into a distribution or partnership deal with one of the majors[281] or make use of the wide array of so-called artist and label services.[282] Such

[274] Joost Smiers and Marieke van Schijndel, *Imagine There Is No Copyright and No Cultural Conglomerates Too: An Essay* (Institute of Network Cultures 2009) 5, 7.

[275] Dusollier, 'EU Contractual Protection of Creators' (n 112) 450.

[276] See Bostoen and Vanherpe, 'Competition Law in the Digitized Music Industry' (n 268). As to the process of horizontal integration, see Jenny Kanellopoulou, *Competition Policy and the Music Industries: A Business Model Perspective* (Routledge 2022). As to Article 102 TFEU, see Daskalova, 'The Monopsony Paradox' (n 268).

[277] Passman, *All You Need to Know* (n 42) 72–73, 122–24.

[278] See eg Malevanny, *Online Music Distribution* (n 28) 325; Giblin and Doctorow, *Chokepoint Capitalism* (n 255) 77.

[279] See <www.beggars.com> <www.bmg.com> <www.kobaltmusic.com> <http://peermusic.com>. In October 2021, news broke that Kobalt had sold its catalogue; see Tim Ingham, 'Confirmed: Kobalt Sells Catalog to New KKR Venture, Chord, for $1.1 Billion' (*Music Business Worldwide*, 19 October 2021) <https://bit.ly/2XrOxBd>. AWAL, a renowned (and disruptive) independent label, was purchased from Kobalt by Sony Music in 2021. This deal was cleared by the UK Competition and Markets Authority (CMA): see <https://bit.ly/3mSEa1S>; DCMS Committee, 'Economics of Music Streaming (n 47) 54–55.

[280] Rogers, *The Death & Life* (n 175) 132; Europe Economics and others, 'Remuneration of Authors and Performers' (n 4) 66; Pauly and H'Madoun, *Poppuntgids voor muzikant en dj* (n 9) 166; Gulinck, *Hier Tekenen!* (n 7) 115; Sun, *Digital Revolution Tamed* (n 166) 57–59.

[281] Arditi, 'iTunes' (n 238) 419; De Voldere and others, 'Mapping the Creative Value Chains' (n 28) 138; Gulinck, *Hier Tekenen!* (n 7) 119.

[282] See below, Chapter 2, Section 2.3.4.

arrangements are to be distinguished from seemingly independent record companies that are in fact subsidiaries of major record companies.[283] Once an independent label becomes particularly successful, a takeover by a major may be around the corner, past examples being the acquisition of independent labels Motown, Island and Virgin.[284]

Another notable development in the independent music sector over the past few decades is a marked increase in cooperation. On the European front, reference may be made to the Independent Music Companies Association (IMPALA), a non-profit trade association that represents the interests of both independent record companies and music publishers, for example by opposing further consolidation of the majors.[285] Independent music bodies such as IMPALA are linked on a global level through the Worldwide Independent Network (WIN).[286]

In addition, the indies' answer to the rise in direct licensing on the part of the majors in the recorded music sector was the establishment of 'Merlin', a direct licensing entity for digital use that represents around 15 per cent of the total recorded music market at the time of writing.[287] It seeks to level the playing field vis-à-vis DSPs and allow independent music companies to compete with the majors in their dealings relating to digital rights by way of a collective licence, thus enhancing the value of independent music.[288] Now that Merlin has matured into an established market player, the indies' objective is to further expand the scope of cooperation within the Merlin network, such as by developing analytical tools on the basis of customer data. For music publishing, reference may be made to IMPEL (which stands for Independent Music Publishers European Licensing), which seeks to fulfil a similar role to Merlin, but for mechanical music publishing rights.[289]

2.3.4 *Independent Artists and Artist and Label Services*

It has been argued repeatedly that technological developments will bring – and to a certain extent already have brought – an end to the need for 'middlemen' in the

[283] A (non-exhaustive) list of examples in this regard includes: (1) Sony's Columbia Records, Epic Records and RCA Records; (2) Capitol Music Group, Island Records and Def Jam Recordings, which are subsidiaries of the Universal Music Group; and (3) Atlantic Records, Elektra Music Group and Parlophone, which are part of Warner Music.

[284] Rogers, *The Death & Life* (n 175) 17, 136; David, 'CD' (n 263) 363; Gulinck, *Hier Tekenen!* (n 7) 115, 117.

[285] <www.impalamusic.org>.

[286] <https://winformusic.org>.

[287] <https://merlinnetwork.org>.

[288] De Voldere and others, 'Mapping the Creative Value Chains' (n 28) 138, 142, 146; Cooke, *Dissecting the Digital Dollar* (n 103) 66; DCMS Committee, 'Economics of Music Streaming (n 47) 68–69.

[289] <www.impel-music.com>.

music industry.[290] The promise of disintermediation challenges the traditional music value chain and seeks to empower musicians on the global music market. Using the opportunities that the internet has to offer, musicians can indeed mine a new, broad and diverse audience via the so-called celestial jukebox[291] of streaming services, enter into direct contact with their listeners, get involved in the production, marketing and distribution of music, as well as build and maintain their own global audience.[292] Several established mainstream artists have already taken to distributing their music directly to fans.[293] Additionally, the (apparently faltering) interest in the opportunities offered by blockchain technology and smart contracts has led to an explosion of startups promising a disintermediated online music market where musicians automatically and quasi-instantly receive 100 per cent of royalty payments in a fully transparent way.[294]

However, the growing DIY mentality appears not to have led to large-scale disintermediation in practice.[295] The combined market share of majors and indies is significant, as is the catalogue leveraged by those commercial players vis-à-vis DSPs.[296] Mainstream commercial DIY success appears to be largely reserved to artists that have already achieved popularity under the wings of a corporate partner.[297]

[290] Gary Graham and others, 'The Transformation of the Music Industry Supply Chain. A Major Label Perspective' (2004) 24 Int J Oper Prod Man 1087, 1087–103; Smiers and Schijndel, *Imagine There is No Copyright and No Cultural Conglomerates Too* (n 274) 56. Cf Hviid and others, 'Digitalisation and Intermediaries' (n 188) 245, 260–61, 263; Rogers, *The Death & Life* (n 175) 2–3, 8–9, 129 et seq, in particular 139–41, 146; Mulligan, *Awakening* (n 135) xii.

[291] Paul Goldstein, *Copyright's Highway. From Gutenberg to the Celestial Jukebox* (2nd edn, Stanford University Press 2003). This concept refers to the possibility for users to easily access all music in a legal way – the essential premise of streaming services.

[292] See eg Rogers, *The Death & Life* (n 175) 152; Arditi, 'iTunes' (n 228) 411; Ginsburg, 'The Role of the Author in Copyright' (n 126) 72; Baym, *Playing to the Crowd* (n 127) 169.

[293] See eg Rogers, *The Death & Life* (n 175) 152; Mulligan, *Awakening* (n 135) 177; Baym, *Playing to the Crowd* (n 127) 126; Krueger, *Rockonomics* (n 121) 34; Bowrey, *Copyright, Creativity, Big Media and Cultural Value* (n 10) 189–90, 197–205; Page, *Tarzan Economics* (n 255) 116–34.

[294] The opportunities offered by blockchain technology in the music industry have been the subject of widespread discussion over the past few years. In summary, blockchain-related startups seek to optimise the ownership and/or exploitation of rights. As to the former, full transparency and certainty is sought, while, as to the latter, the objective is to ensure an automated royalty payout embedded in a transparent licensing structure. See Janssens and Vanherpe, 'Blockchain and Copyright beyond the Buzzword?' (n 36) 93; Vanherpe and Janssens, 'Toepassingen van smart contracts in het auteursrecht' (n 36); Jozefien Vanherpe, 'Non-Fungible Tokens Als Instrument Voor Intellectuele Rechten' [2023] NjW 2.

[295] See eg Hviid and others, 'Digitalisation and Intermediaries' (n 188) 252; Gulinck, *Hier Tekenen!* (n 7) 10, 107; Malevanny, *Online Music Distribution* (n 28) 76; Sun, *Digital Revolution Tamed* (n 166).

[296] Cf Rogers, *The Death & Life* (n 175) 133–34; Ginsburg, 'The Role of the Author in Copyright' (n 126) 70.

[297] Rogers, *The Death & Life* (n 175) 152; Arditi, 'iTunes' (n 238) 411; Mulligan, *Awakening* (n 135) 200–01; Deresiewicz, *The Death of the Artist* (n 132) 28.

In addition, a form of 're-intermediation' may be identified, whereby DSPs have crafted their place next to the major record companies and assumed an identity as new barriers to entry for independent artists.[298] True disintermediation is, as yet, a mirage, with new 'middlemen' having squarely positioned themselves on the online music market. Reference may be made to social media and content platforms,[299] leading music blogs[300] and digital distributors.[301] While the online environment initially presented itself as a way to foster a direct relationship with fans (direct to consumer or D2C[302]), many DSPs provide no such direct access for truly independent artists, with the exception of DIY platforms such as SoundCloud.[303] Instead, artists who seek to add their music to a DSP's catalogue for exploitation purposes call upon the services of digital distributors[304] (for phonograms) and publishing administrators[305] (for compositions) that serve as go-betweens and allow DIY artists to monetise the use of their music by DSPs, again usually in return for a commission-based remuneration.[306]

Even so, the digital context appears to be more favourable to independent artists than the analogue world. While artist independence used to be associated with an inability to get signed – and thus access an audience – it is now increasingly linked with empowerment and the possibility to enter into partnerships with a wide variety

298 Arditi, 'iTunes' (n 238) 421; Mulligan, *Awakening* (n 135) 103–04; Deresiewicz, *The Death of the Artist* (n 132) 46, 61–62; DCMS Committee, 'Economics of Music Streaming (n 47) 64. Cf Cory Doctorow, *Information Doesn't Want to Be Free: Laws for the Internet Age* (McSweeney's 2014) s 2.8.

299 Examples of this category include YouTube <www.youtube.com>, Spotify <www.spotify.com>, Facebook <www.facebook.com>, and TikTok <www.tiktok.com>.

300 See eg Pitchfork <https://pitchfork.com>. See also Beatrice Jetto, 'The Evolution of Music Blogs: From a Fan's Passion to a Promotional Outlet' (2015) 4 IJMBR 49, 49–75; George Musgrave, 'Collaborating to Compete: The Role of Cultural Intermediaries in Hypercompetition' (2017) 6 IJMBR 41, 41–68.

301 See eg Arditi, 'iTunes' (n 238); Patryk Galuszka, 'Music Aggregators and Intermediation of the Digital Music Market' [2015] Internal Journal of Communication 254; Hviid and others, 'Digitalisation and Intermediaries' (n 188) 244–46, 266–67, 272–73; Sun, *Digital Revolution Tamed* (n 189).

302 The D2C relationship is also referred to as 'direct to fan' or 'D2F'.

303 <https://soundcloud.com>.

304 See eg Amuse, CDBaby, DistroKid, Ditto Music, FreshTunes, Fuga, Horus Music, LANDR, Octiive, ONErpm, RouteNote, Songtradr, Soundrop, Stem, Symphonic and TuneCore. See <www.amuse.io> (Amuse also presents itself as a record company) <https://cdbaby.com> <https://distrokid.com> <www.dittomusic.com> <https://freshtunes.com> <https://fuga.com> <www.horusmusic.global> <www.songtradr.com> <www.landr.com> <www.octiive.com> <https://onerpm.com> <www.routenote.com> <https://soundrop.com> <https://stem.is> <https://symphonicdistribution.com> <www.tunecore.com>.

305 See eg Songtrust (part of independent music company Downtown) <www.songtrust.com>. Some big indies may also be qualified as a publishing administrator. Moreover, some digital distributors combine their activity relating to phonograms with music publishing administration for compositions, such as ONErpm, Songtradr and TuneCore.

306 Europe Economics and others, 'Remuneration of Authors and Performers' (n 4) 80–81; De Voldere and others, 'Mapping the Creative Value Chains' (n 28) 138; Gulinck, *Hier Tekenen!* (n 7) 141–43.

of service providers, under contract terms that are more tailored to the artist's needs and without excessive rights transfers.[307] These new types of intermediaries are grouped under the umbrella term 'artist and label services' (ALS). Notably, both majors and large indies acknowledge the worth of such new business models and now also offer ALS to a certain extent, either directly or through subsidiaries.[308] Thus, artists who would prefer to eschew a contractual relationship with a major music company may in practice call upon the services of ALS companies that are owned by majors.[309]

Instead of entering into a full-service contract, artists may pick and choose the services they require, depending on their goals and the specificities of their career. Services offered include marketing and promotion, financing, distribution, music publishing administration, and so forth. ALS may also be combined with a partnership contract with an independent music company. In such a case, the deal between musician and corporate partner may be characterised as a business partnership based on a services model, whereby artists retain their rights and thus control over their work, while the corporate partner only acquires a licence.[310] Independent artists who seek to become global superstars are likely to take the leap to a deal with either a big independent music company or one of the three majors at some point, in a bid to achieve global exposure.[311] An investment on the part of one of the major music companies is likely to depend on pre-existing viral and/or commercial success garnered through prior investment of the artist(s), collaborating music producer(s) and/or their manager.[312] This puts a slightly different light on the traditional function of such initial corporate partners as an investor and thus a risk-taker.[313]

At the fully DIY side of the spectrum are direct support, crowdfunding, pay-per-play and purchase sites, such as Bandcamp, Patreon, Resonate, Sonstream and SoundCloud.[314] Artists fully retain their rights and pay a modest commission-based fee to the online platform. Such platforms may function as fruitful 'hunting grounds' for the A&R departments of record companies.

[307] Mulligan, *Awakening* (n 135) 201–02; Giblin and Doctorow, *Chokepoint Capitalism* (n 255) 56.

[308] Mulligan, *Awakening* (n 135) 209, 283; Gulinck, *Hier Tekenen!* (n 7) 121.

[309] DCMS Committee, 'Economics of Music Streaming (n 47) 64.

[310] MIDEM, 'Artist & Label Services: How Technology Is Energising an Artists-First Global Business' (2020).

[311] Cf Rogers, *The Death & Life* (n 175) 138, 145, 153, 184, 191–94; Europe Economics and others, 'Remuneration of Authors and Performers' (n 4) 83; Mulligan, *Awakening* (n 135) 176, 201, 204; De Voldere and others, 'Mapping the Creative Value Chains' (n 28) 146; Baym, *Playing to the Crowd* (n 127) 66; Gulinck, *Hier Tekenen!* (n 7) 146–48; Krueger, *Rockonomics* (n 121) 40; Passman, *All You Need to Know* (n 42) 77; Sun, *Digital Revolution Tamed* (n 166) 54.

[312] Cf CMU, 'Performer Payments from Streaming' (2021) 10–11; Hesmondhalgh and others, 'Music Creators' Earnings in the Digital Era' (n 242) 86.

[313] Cf DCMS Committee, 'Economics of Music Streaming' (n 47) 34.

[314] See <https://bandcamp.com> <https://resonate.is> <https://sonstream.com> <www.patreon.com> <https://soundcloud.com>. See also Baym, *Playing to the Crowd* (n 127) 126–27; Giblin and Doctorow, *Chokepoint Capitalism* (n 255) 223, 237–38.

DIY composers, digital distributors and publishing administrators may call upon the services of ALS companies that focus on monetisation and royalty management[315] or content and data tracking.[316] ALS companies may also provide a full service akin to but conceptually separate from a record company.[317] A common thread is an increased reliance on and faith in technology such as big data and artificial intelligence (AI), whereby technological developments are seen as a choice opportunity to increase efficiency and (distribution of) revenues.

Musicians dispose of a vast range of tools to acquire and maintain their (online and offline) audience. Significant barriers to entry have disappeared. However, the wide availability of these tools implies fierce and unrelenting competition to get and maintain audiences' attention.[318] Users are faced with a veritable 'tyranny of choice', where navigating a way between the millions and millions of available songs becomes simply impossible.[319] The road to artistic and commercial success is paved with uncertainty.[320] Moreover, in the fast-paced environment of the music industry, a lack of quasi-immediate success risks equating to equally rapid failure.[321] Many variables are at play, not all of which are directly related to musical quality. Both luck and leverage have a role to play.[322] Leverage, the latter factor, may be linked to the lasting market power of the major music companies. Moreover, the limited size of the catalogue held by an independent, DIY musician in itself carries significant disadvantages in the context of contractual negotiations with DSPs. Indeed, the combination of an oversupply of music with a fragmentation of repertoire on the supply side negatively affects the leverage of smaller, independent industry players. This logic applies to both DIY musicians and small independent corporate partners. This situation is exacerbated by the rapid evolution on the music 'market': since today's hype may already be forgotten tomorrow, smaller players risk falling behind. As a result, artists are left with a dilemma: either they choose the DIY or ALS way and are likely to collect fewer total streams but a higher proportion of streaming revenue, or they seek a major label record deal that may potentially lead to much more streams in total, but a significantly lower proportionate return in terms of streaming revenue.

[315] See eg AdRev <https://adrev.net>, Audiam <www.audiam.com>, Muserk <https://muserk .com>.

[316] See eg Bitfury Surround <https://surround.com>), Pex, which combines data collection with monetisation purposes <https://pex.com> and Trqk <www.trqk.io>.

[317] See eg Vydia <https://vydia.com>.

[318] Arditi, 'iTunes' (n 238) 411; Gulinck, *Hier Tekenen!* (n 7) 10; Sun, 'Paradox of Celestial Jukebox' (n 263) 113–14; Sun, *Digital Revolution Tamed* (n 166) 197–200.

[319] Mulligan, *Awakening* (n 135) 168, 246, 298; Sun, *Digital Revolution Tamed* (n 166) 196–97.

[320] This is linked with the status of artistic content such as music as an 'experience good', the evaluation of which can only take place following its consumption and is therefore inherently unpredictable.

[321] Cf Mulligan, *Awakening* (n 135) 194; Baym, *Playing to the Crowd* (n 127) 64; Gulinck, *Hier Tekenen!* (n 7) 121; Krueger, *Rockonomics* (n 121) 16–17.

[322] Krueger, *Rockonomics* (n 121) 15.

Moreover, the music industry is inherently structured as a 'superstar', 'winner-takes-all' economy.[323] There is a small number of global superstars, whose situation starkly contrasts with the large majority of musicians who struggle to make a living, who suffer from the casualisation of creative labour in the so-called gig economy – coincidentally, musicians may be qualified as the 'original' gig workers – and whose (legal) situation is precarious.[324] This situation is enhanced by network effects and a tendency towards the mainstream.[325] The increased use of automated recommendation systems for music streaming based on prior listening data risks further exacerbating this evolution, since such playlists may function as an 'echo chamber' that makes it harder to discover new music and, moreover, entail a risk of discrimination on the basis of nationality, gender and genre.[326] There is an ensuing risk of barriers to entry for emerging artists, of decreasing diversity and of a reduction of the cultural landscape. However, recently, a trend is noted towards a consumption model that favours diversity and local artists singing in their own language rather than purely focusing on global Anglo-American superstars.[327] This evolution runs parallel with the slightly increasing market share of independent record companies and DIY artists. In view of this, it has been argued that, in order for the majors to retain their pole position, a transformation of their business model is required, including a

[323] Sherwin Rosen, 'The Economics of Superstars' (1981) 71 Am Econ Rev 845, 845–58; Scott Timberg, *Culture Crash: The Killing of the Creative Class* (Yale University Press 2015) 225–49; Frey, *Economics of Art and Culture* (n 124) 34–35; Towse, *A Textbook of Cultural Economics* (n 124) 366–68, 463–99; Deresiewicz, *The Death of the Artist* (n 132) 58–59, 61; Séverine Dusollier, 'The 2019 Directive on Copyright in the Digital Single Market: Some Progress, a Few Bad Choices, and an Overall Failed Ambition' [2020] CML Rev 979, 1021; Giblin and Doctorow, *Chokepoint Capitalism* (n 255) 3, 67.

[324] See on this topic eg George Morgan and Pariece Nelligan, *The Creativity Hoax: Precarious Work in the Gig Economy* (Anthem Press 2018); Jeremias Prassl, *Humans as a Service. The Promise and Perils of Work in the Gig Economy* (Oxford University Press 2018); Deresiewicz, *The Death of the Artist* (n 132); Jamie Woodcock and Mark Graham, *The Gig Economy – A Critical Introduction* (Polity Press 2020); Jeroen Meijerink and others (eds), *Platform Economy Puzzles: A Multidisciplinary Perspective on Gig Work* (Edward Elgar 2021). See re the music industry Towse, 'Copyright and Economic Incentives' (n 170) 385, 388; Mulligan, *Awakening* (n 135) 185–89, 209; De Voldere and others, 'Mapping the Creative Value Chains' (n 28) 135; Baym, *Playing to the Crowd* (n 127) 7, 25, 63–64; Lunney, *Copyright's Excess* (n 219) 215; Krueger, *Rockonomics* (n 121) 1, 7, 12–14, 53–55.

[325] Krueger, *Rockonomics* (n 121) 13, 86–94, 235–36.

[326] DCMS Committee, 'Economics of Music Streaming' (n 47) 24, 69, 79, 107. See also Mariuzzo and Ormosi, 'Independent v Major Record Labels' (n 271); Daniel Antal and others, 'Music Streaming: Is It a Level Playing Field?' (2021) 2 Antitrust Chronicle 14; Castle and Feijóo, 'Study on the Artists in the Digital Music Marketplace' (n 4) 9, 30–31, 50; Andres Ferraro and others, 'Break the Loop: Gender Imbalance in Music Recommenders' in (ACM 14 March 2021) Proceedings of the 2021 Conference on Human Information Interaction and Retrieval 249; Emmanuel Legrand, 'Study on the Place and Role of Authors and Composers in the European Music Streaming Market' (2022) 22–23; Centre for Data Ethics and Innovation, 'The Impact of Recommendation Algorithms on the UK's Music Industry' (9 February 2023).

[327] Cf Will Page and Chris Dalla Riva, '"Glocalisation" of Music Streaming within and across Europe' (Europe in Question, 2023).

primordial focus on all things digital and a more balanced, empowering relationship with artists. The first stages of such a shift are already visible, such as in the artist-friendly deal between US singer-songwriter Taylor Swift and (a sub-label of) Universal, according to which Swift retains ownership of the rights in phonograms of her new music.[328]

2.4 REMUNERATION IN THE STREAMING AGE

2.4.1 *Revenue Streams in the Streaming Age*

Following the outline of the music value chain in the streaming age, we move on to an analysis of the revenue streams that flow from the exploitation of rights in music for the recorded music and publishing sectors.

While unequivocal certainty regarding the actual size of these industries cannot be attained, some reliable figures are freely available online.[329] With regard to recorded music, the most-cited figures are those of the International Federation of the Phonographic Industry (IFPI). According to IFPI's *Global Music Report*, the total global revenue of the recorded music industry in 2023 amounted to over €26.6 billion, almost £23 billion (Figure 2.1).[330] This is still a long way away from the industry's peak revenue in 1999, which was around €40 billion (£34.3 billion) when adjusted for inflation.[331] This figure includes revenues from physical sales (CDs, vinyl, cassettes), digital downloads and streaming, as well as performing rights and synchronisation. In 2023, streaming accounted for over two-thirds of the recorded music industry's total revenues.[332] Physical sales still account for about one-sixth of total revenues globally, while downloads and other digital sales correspond with less than 4 per cent of revenues. The remaining percentage of global revenues is attributed to performing rights and synchronisation revenue.

Conclusive data regarding the music publishing industry is more difficult to obtain. Research by the 'Music & Copyright' blog indicates a global figure for music publishing in 2023 of around €8.4 billion (£7.1 billion).[333]

328 Jem Aswad and Chris Willman, 'Taylor Swift Signs Landmark New Deal with Universal Music Group' (*Variety*, 19 November 2018) <https://bit.ly/3aGBuih>.

329 Cf Richard E Caves, 'Contracts between Art and Commerce' (2003) 17 Journal of Economic Perspectives 73, vii. See also <https://pivotaleconomics.com/undercurrents/copyright-2021>. See as to the German market in detail Goldmedia, 'Musik-Streaming in Deutschland' (n 246). See as to the UK market in detail BPI, 'The New Music Democracy: How More Artists Are Succeeding from Streaming' (2023).

330 IFPI, 'Global Music Report 2024' (n 215) 11.

331 See inflation calculator at <https://bit.ly/3uwSyjP>.

332 The growth of streaming in the recorded music industry over the 2015–2022 period led to a multiplication in revenues of more than six times.

333 See <https://musicandcopyright.wordpress.com>. Cf CISAC, 'Annual Report 2023' (2023) 5.

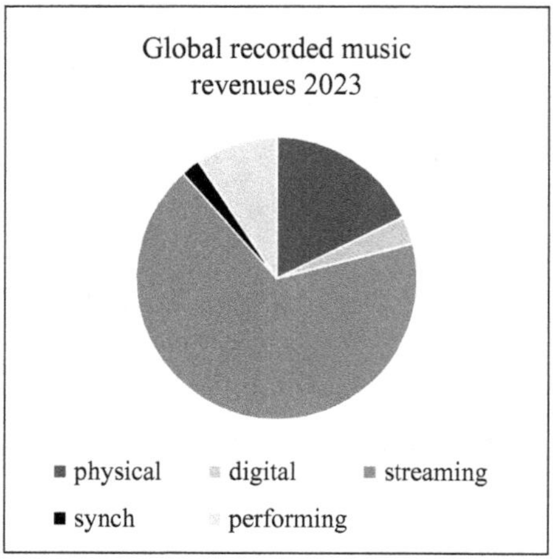

Physical	17.8%
Downloads/other digital	3.2%
Streaming (48.3% subscription, 8.7% ad-supported)	67.3%
Synchronisation	2.2%
Performing rights	9.5%

FIGURE 2.1 Global recorded music revenues 2023

There are five main revenue streams for the recorded music and music publishing sectors in the music industry. While the significance of physical sales and digital downloads is decreasing, these first two sources of revenue still make up a sizeable chunk of the music industry's total revenues.[334] Music streaming occupies an increasingly central position. The two other main sources of revenue are performing rights and synchronisation.

Since the inception of streaming services, their cost for the consumer sat steadily at €/$/£9.99.[335] In 2022, the average revenue per user (ARPU) for paid subscriptions on Spotify in particular was a mere €4.52 which, compared with the €6.84 in 2015, was quite low.[336] Among other things, this may be ascribed to a surge in multi-person and student subscription plans, which yield a lower revenue per individual user. Combined with inflation, the increase in total number of available tracks and total number of streams, and the prospective saturation of the streaming market in terms of number of subscribers, this decrease drives musicians' streaming revenue

[334] See on this ongoing decline Mulligan, *Awakening* (n 135) 54, 80.

[335] See in detail Will Page, 'Malbeconomics. Taking Stock of the Twentieth Anniversary of the 9.99 Price Point' (*Tarzan Economics*, 6 December 2021) <https://bit.ly/3rBSvTZ>.

[336] See data via <www.statista.com/statistics/813789/spotify-premium-arpu>.

further downwards.[337] The increase of subscription fees implemented by Spotify in the summer of 2023 should therefore have come as no surprise.[338]

The division of music industry revenue has four dimensions. First, revenues are shared between the music industry value chain and their external corporate partners. Second, revenues are divided between different compositions and phonograms. A third aspect relates to the division of revenues between the composition and the phonogram for a specific piece of music. Finally, there is a division between the different actors in the music value chain. For all four constitutive parts, a distinction may be made between the division of revenue for physical sales, digital downloads and streams.

2.4.2 *Division between Music Value Chain and External Corporate Partners*

The revenue distribution for physical sales varies depending on the specifics of the distribution chain. By way of an approximation, it may be argued that retailers retain around 25 per cent of the retail price (minus VAT), while the music value chain collects 75 per cent and pays all manufacturing, promotion and distribution costs, as well as artist remuneration, from its share.[339]

Agreements between rightsholders and DSPs are usually characterised as a revenue share deal based on total consumption share.[340] While every deal is different and depends on parties' relative bargaining position, such revenue share agreements with DSPs regarding digital downloads and/or music streaming usually reserve around 30 per cent of total revenues for the DSP.[341] Around 70 per cent is allocated to the members of the music value chain. However, DSP contracts have traditionally been subject to strict non-disclosure agreements (NDAs) for reasons of commercial confidentiality.[342]

337 Cf DCMS Committee, 'Economics of Music Streaming' (n 47) 20, 86; Björn Ulvaeus, 'Rebalancing the Song Economy' (TEDxSSE, April 2021); IMPALA, 'Streaming Reform Revisited – IMPALA Calls for Increased Subscription Prices, Bespoke Deals for Fans, and a Revaluation of the Share for Master Rights (for Labels and Artists), among Other Proposals for a Fairer, More Dynamic Market' (27 April 2023) <https://bit.ly/44tWlyK>.

338 See <https://bit.ly/3xKA6dB> and even more recently in France <https://bit.ly/4cHDV2o>.

339 See Gulinck, *Hier Tekenen!* (n 7) 435–39. See also Pierre-É Lalonde, 'Study Concerning Fair Compensation for Music Creators in the Digital Age' (2014) 21; Hesmondhalgh and others, 'Music Creators' Earnings in the Digital Era' (n 242) 61–62.

340 Cf Price, 'The Definitive Guide to Spotify Royalties' (n 117) 8.

341 Rethink Music Initiative, 'Fair Music' (n 127) 3, 8, 14; De Voldere and others, 'Mapping the Creative Value Chains' (n 28) 146; Jari Muikku, 'Pro Rata and User Centric Distribution Models: A Comparative Study' (30 November 2017) 5; Pauly and H'Madoun, *Poppuntgids voor muzikant en dj* (n 9) 211; Krueger, *Rockonomics* (n 4) 182; Sun, *Digital Revolution Tamed* (n 166) 162–63; Cooke, *Dissecting the Digital Dollar* (n 103) 16, 79–80; DCMS Committee (n 47) 17, 68; Hesmondhalgh and others, 'Music Creators' Earnings in the Digital Era' (n 242) 63. See Gulinck, *Hier Tekenen!* (n 7) 441–45.

342 Mulligan, *Awakening* (n 135) 82, 158; Rethink Music Initiative, 'Fair Music' (n 127) 6, 14; De Voldere and others, 'Mapping the Creative Value Chains' (n 28) 147; Krueger, *Rockonomics*

In addition to the 70/30 divide, DSP deals usually contain a number of other provisions that have a bearing on revenue allocation, both between the DSP and the music value chain and between different pieces of music. Many major rightsholders have obtained beneficial revenue share arrangements, which – in combination with the size of their catalogue – make a low payout per stream palatable. Many DSP deals contain certain minimum revenue guarantees (either as to the total amount or the per-play rate), advances and administration fees payable by the DSP.[343] The technique of 'breakage', reminiscent of the industry practice of automatic discounts for damaged physical products,[344] means that labels receive their share in revenues on the basis of the results of the preceding allocation period.[345] If the advances paid by the DSP surpass the amount that is actually due, these advances are non-refundable.[346] Further, many streaming platforms have been found willing to grant equity to the three major rightsholders.[347] Revenue allocation is also indirectly affected by marketing fees, payable by rightsholders in return for large-scale promotion of 'their' music on the streaming platform(s) at issue, including the incorporation in curated playlists.[348] Further, some DSPs – and in particular Spotify – grant rightsholders the possibility to accept a lower revenue rate in return for favourable treatment by the DSP's algorithm.[349] Finally, so-called most-favoured-nation clauses

(n 121) 181; Cooke, *Dissecting the Digital Dollar* (n 103) 8, 104–05; Hesmondhalgh and others, 'Music Creators' Earnings in the Digital Era' (n 242) 89; Osborne and Sun, 'Economics of Streaming' (n 189) s 1.4.3.

343 Mulligan, *Awakening* (n 135) 82–84, 297; Rethink Music Initiative, 'Fair Music' (n 127) 14, 16; Gulinck, *Hier Tekenen!* (n 7) 450; Cooke, *Dissecting the Digital Dollar* (n 103) 16, 65–66; Deresiewicz, *The Death of the Artist* (n 132) 130; Castle and Feijóo, 'Study on the Artists in the Digital Music Marketplace' (n 4) 34.

344 This other form of 'breakage' has a bearing on the division of revenues between musicians and their primary corporate partners, see below, Section 2.4.5.

345 Mulligan, *Awakening* (n 135) 68; Passman, *All You Need to Know* (n 42) 146–48.

346 Rethink Music Initiative, 'Fair Music' (n 127) 15; Cooke, *Dissecting the Digital Dollar* (n 103) 102; Giblin and Doctorow, *Chokepoint Capitalism* (n 255) 70–71.

347 Warner sold its stake in Spotify, see 'Warner Sells Entire Stake in Spotify, Crediting Artists with $126m of the Money' (*Music Business Worldwide*, 8 July 2018) <https://bit.ly/3FMHm7L>. A few months prior, Sony made a similar move, see 'Sony Has Sold Half of Its Spotify Shares' (*Variety*, 5 January 2018) <https://bit.ly/3ABQoko>. At the time of writing, it appears that both Sony and Universal still hold a stake in Spotify, see DCMS Committee, 'Economics of Music Streaming' (n 47) 58–60; Giblin and Doctorow, *Chokepoint Capitalism* (n 255) 72–77. See also <https://bit.ly/3rNG1f7>.

348 See above, Section 2.3.2.

349 Noah Yoo, 'Could Spotify's New Discovery Mode Be Considered Payola?' (*Pitchfork*, 9 November 2020) <https://bit.ly/3p4qnYW>; Tim Ingham, 'Indie Labels Call for End to Streaming "Payola" – as IMPALA Unveils 10-Point Plan to Reform Sector' (*Music Business Worldwide*, 23 March 2021) <https://bit.ly/30tKTb5>; Giblin and Doctorow, *Chokepoint Capitalism* (n 255) 82. See on associated issues of transparency ia DCMS Committee, 'Economics of Music Streaming' (n 47) 22, 78–79; CSPLA, 'Rapport de Mission. Les Dispositifs de Recommandation des Œuvres Audiovisuelles et Musicales sur les Services en Ligne' (2021) 47–61; Justine Haekens and Jozefien Vanherpe, 'Spotlight Op Spotify: Een Analyse van de Samenstelling van Playlists Door de Lens van Het Auteurs-

imply that, were the DSP to provide a better deal to another record company, the initial contracting record company can insist on the DSP matching that better offer.[350]

Another dimension to the division of digital revenues stems from the contracts between external corporate partners, primarily between DSPs and the app stores that offer their applications for users' mobile devices (Apple or Google), and charge a commission fee on, among other things, in-app subscriptions. As this does not have a bearing on the internal revenue division within the music value chain, it remains unexamined here.[351]

2.4.3 *Consumption Shares of Compositions and Phonograms*

For physical sales and digital downloads, the revenue distribution between different compositions and phonograms is straightforward: the revenue is attributed to the product bought by the consumer. In case of a physical sale or a digital download of an album, the revenues are proportionately allocated to all tracks on the album. In case of a physical sale or digital download of a single track, the revenue accrues to the track.

The division of streaming revenue is more complex, diverse and evolving.[352] The revenues shared by DSPs are allocated to each phonogram on the basis of its overall share in total consumption, using a model labelled as 'pro-rata' or

En Mededingingsrecht' [2023] IRDI 14; Goldmedia, 'Musik-Streaming in Deutschland' (n 246) 101, 103; Jozefien Vanherpe, 'The Regulation of AI Recommender Systems: "You Are Here"' (ALAI Congress, Paris, 22 June 2023); Parliament, 'Cultural Diversity and the Conditions for Authors in the European Music Streaming Market: A Bibliographical Review' (2024) <https://shorturl.at/cioT6>. See also Christopher Buccafusco and Kristelia García, 'Pay-to-Playlist: The Commerce of Streaming' (2021) 12 UC Irvine L Rev 1.

350 Mulligan, *Awakening* (n 135) 84; De Voldere and others, 'Mapping the Creative Value Chains' (n 28) 148.

351 See Friso Bostoen and Daniel Mândrescu, 'Assessing Abuse of Dominance in the Platform Economy: A Case Study of App Stores' (2020) 16 European Competition Journal 431, 431–91. In March 2024, The European Commission fined Apple over €1.8 billion for abusing its dominant position in the market for the distribution of music streaming apps to iPhone and iPad users through its App Store: see *Apple – App Store Practices (Music Streaming)* (Case AT.40437) Commission Decision C(2024) 1307 final) <https://shorturl.at/FHMNT>.

352 See in more detail 'The Ten Things People Get Wrong about Streaming – Part One' directed by Andy Malt and Chris Cooke (Podcast, Setlist, 5 November 2020) <https://bit.ly/3papHkF>. For a detailed case study, albeit focusing on Swedish artists, see also Daniel Johansson, 'Revenue Distribution from Music Streaming – A Quantitative Analysis of Swedish Artists on Spotify' (2023). Since 1 April 2024, Spotify has changed its revenue distribution model. As this change took place following the finalisation of the manuscript for this book, it is not discussed in detail here. More information is available at, for example <https://shorturl.at/cmpWZ>. See also in detail Frederik Juul Jensen, 'Rethinking Royalties: Alternative Payment Systems on Music Streaming Platforms' [2024] J Cult Econ <https://rdcu.be/dHsmY>.

'market-centric'.[353] If no users have streamed a phonogram during the relevant period, no revenue is allocated to it. The overall consumption share is calculated by dividing the amount of streams for a certain phonogram on the platform by the total amount of streams on that platform in the relevant period.[354] The calculation of this percentage takes place per country and per subscription type. Streams from emerging markets, where a lower subscription fee is charged to users, have a lower yield. The same is true for streams by users that do not pay a subscription fee (for example, ad-supported platforms) or only pay a discounted subscription fee (for example, students, users with a family plan or a streaming subscription that is included in a mobile plan).[355] Streams that cannot be attributed to the correct rightsholder(s), due to incomplete metadata information, are labelled as 'non-allocable income' and are usually divided between other rightsholders on the basis of market share.[356]

Based on this percentage, the DSP sets aside a given amount for each member of the music value chain from whom they have acquired a licence. The allocation to phonograms takes place primarily on the basis of the International Standard Recording Code (ISRC) that uniquely identifies phonograms as to title, record company, country of recording, date of recording and/or publication and, ideally, full and correct data regarding performer contributions.[357] In reality, the information is all too often incomplete and/or incorrect.[358] The allocation to compositions is even less straightforward since, contrary to the case for phonograms, DSPs have no full knowledge of the compositions recorded on a given phonogram. In practice, the relevant streaming information is transferred to publishers and CMOs, which then have the task of matching the ISRC codes in their own databases with the relevant International Standard Work Code (ISWC)[359] of the compositions they represent and invoice the DSP on this basis, again separately per country and per product type.[360]

Once the allocated revenue is shared with the music value chain, it is possible to calculate a per-play rate – the amount paid out per stream by a certain DSP. For many DSPs, this average rate falls significantly below €0.01.[361] However, such average figures

[353] See eg Rasmus Rex Pedersen, 'A Meta Study of User-Centric Distribution for Music Streaming' (2020) 4–5; Castle and Feijóo, 'Study on the Artists in the Digital Music Marketplace' (n 4) 8; Alberto Arenal and others, 'Giants with Feet of Clay: The Sustainability of the Business Models in Music Streaming Services' (2022) 31 El Profesional de la información.

[354] Cooke, *Dissecting the Digital Dollar* (n 103) 67; Castle and Feijóo, 'Study on the Artists in the Digital Music Marketplace' (n 4) 33–34.

[355] Rethink Music Initiative, 'Fair Music' (n 127) 20.

[356] ibid 16, 27; Gulinck, *Hier Tekenen!* (n 7) 172; DCMS Committee, 'Economics of Music Streaming' (n 47) 51.

[357] See <https://isrc.ifpi.org>; <https://winformusic.org/mp-files/factsheet-isrc-en.pdf>; Serona Elton, 'Standardized Identifiers and Electronic Data Interchange Rules for Music' in Sean M O'Connor (ed), *The Oxford Handbook of Music Law and Policy* (Oxford University Press 2020).

[358] See below, Section 2.5.

[359] See <www.iswc.org>.

[360] Rethink Music Initiative, 'Fair Music' (n 127) 23; Cooke, *Dissecting the Digital Dollar* (n 103) 17, 76, 194–95.

[361] See eg figures available at <https://bit.ly/3Fgxkvx>; <https://bit.ly/2WKBRFe>.

paint a blended picture that takes no due account of the different variables at play in the calculation.[362] By way of example, the generalised per-play rate for Amazon Music is higher than it is for Spotify, since the former does not offer a free tier. Therefore, such figures should be approached with caution. A final note on per-play rates is that, due to the fixed nature of streaming subscriptions, the total revenue from streaming does not depend on the total amount of streams. As a result, contrary to conventional supply-and-demand logic, if the amount of streams doubles, the per-play rate halves.

There is a significant degree of concentration of market share among the majors, with almost 70 and 60 per cent of revenues accruing to them for recorded music and music publishing respectively (Figures 2.2 and 2.3).[363]

Arguably, this model plays out in favour of aggregated copyright ownership, to the disadvantage of emerging artists, regional markets and niche genres such as classical music and jazz.[364] This is detrimental to cultural diversity. Moreover, the pro-rata model delinks users' streaming subscriptions from the music they listen to and thus intervenes in the relationship between musicians and their fans. A significant amount of revenue garnered from users' subscription fees eventually accrues to rightsholders of music these users never listen to, but who hold a bigger market share.[365] Pro-rata distribution also leaves a streaming platform vulnerable to artificial inflation of streaming numbers in a bid to maximise profits.[366] Additional concern is engendered by the rising proportion of AI-generated content on music streaming platforms.

An alternative solution is presented by the user-centric payment system (UCPS). Instead of using the proportion of total streams as a calculation base, this model matches the subscription fees of listeners to the music they actually listen to.[367] Some DSPs have already made the change to UCPS, such as Idagio and Primephonic for classical music, which have implemented a pay-per-second model that pays out more the longer a certain piece is played. One of the most vocal

362 Krueger, *Rockonomics* (n 121) 188; Price, 'The Definitive Guide to Spotify Royalties' (n 117) 10, 47. Cf David Hesmondhalgh, 'Is Music Streaming Bad for Musicians? Problems of Evidence and Argument' [2020] New Media & Society 1, 5–10.

363 2023 data acquired via Statista <https://statista.com>.

364 Deresiewicz, *The Death of the Artist* (n 132) 132–33; DCMS Committee, 'Economics of Music Streaming' (n 47) 45–46.

365 Castle and Feijóo, 'Study on the Artists in the Digital Music Marketplace' (n 4) 8, 31–33.

366 Centre Nationale de la Musique, 'Manipulation des écoutes en ligne' (2023); Goldmedia, 'Musik-Streaming in Deutschland' (n 246) 106. Cf the (at the time of writing) ongoing investigation in Norway of Jay-Z's streaming service Tidal, which is alleged to have artificially inflated listening statistics for Beyoncé's 'Lemonade' and Ye's 'The Life of Pablo', see Elsa Keslassy, 'Norwegian Court Approves Data-Fraud Investigation of Tidal' (*Variety*, 11 June 2020) <https://bit.ly/2YPgJPf>. See also Joseph Dimont, 'Royalty Inequity: Why Music Streaming Services Should Switch to a Per-Subscriber Model' (2018) 69 Hastings LJ 675, 688–90; Page, *Tarzan Economics* (n 255) 171–72.

367 DCMS Committee, 'Economics of Music Streaming' (n 47) 91; Hesmondhalgh, 'Is Music Streaming Bad for Musicians?' (n 362); Ulvaeus, 'Rebalancing the Song Economy' (n 337); Daniel Johansson, 'Streams & Dreams: A Fair Music Economy for All, Part 1' (2022) 30–38; Pro Musik, 'Payment Option Transparency: On the Impact of Alternative Payment Models in Music Streaming' (9 June 2023).

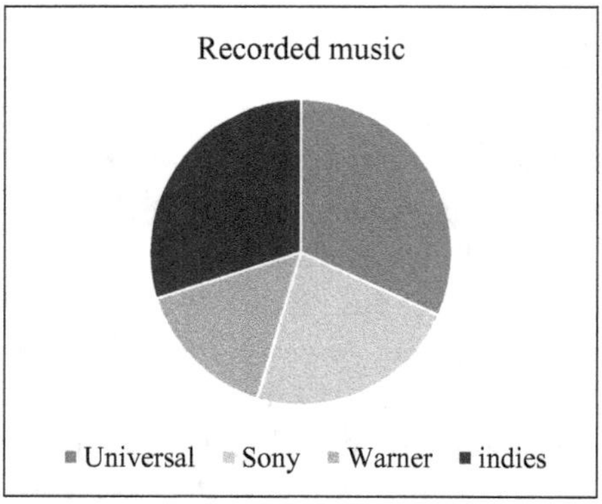

Universal Music Group (UMG)	31.7%
Sony Music Entertainment (SME)	22.9%
Warner Music Group (WMG)	15.5%
Independent labels/performers	29.9%

FIGURE 2.2 2023 market share in the recorded music sector

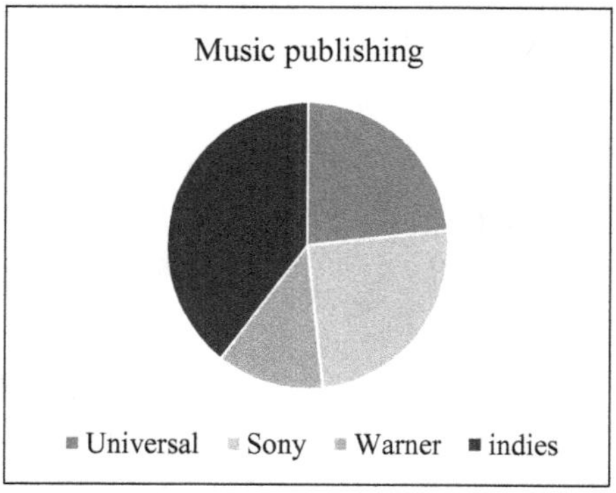

Universal (UMPG)	23.3%
Sony Music Publishing, EMI Music Publishing (EMI MP), and Sony Music Publishing Japan	24.9%
Warner Chappell Music (WCM)	12.4%
Independent publishers/composers	39.4%

FIGURE 2.3 2023 market share in the music publishing sector

proponents of UCPS is French DSP Deezer.[368] From April 2021 onwards, DIY-centred DSP SoundCloud has made the shift to UCPS, labelling its new revenue distribution model 'fan-powered royalties' and paving the way for a similar move by Tidal in November 2021.[369]

There are two sides in the debate on the desirability of the switch to UCPS. Proponents argue that it is intrinsically fairer, given its transparency and the re-establishment of a connection between a musician and their audience. A switch from pro-rata revenue distribution to UCPS could make a potential increase in subscription fees more palatable for users.[370] UCPS is also said to prevent fraud, since it limits the effects of distortions by paid bots that 'listen' to a song for 30 seconds[371] 24/7 to the money initially invested in the fraudulent subscription at issue.[372] Moreover, such bots may be distinguished from actual listeners and removed from the royalty calculation process, thus avoiding the artificial inflation of streaming counts.[373]

The main substantive counterargument to UCPS is that its promise of a transformation of music streaming through enhanced fairness in terms of revenue distribution remains, at present, unfulfilled.[374] Given the efficiency[375] and ease of administration of the pro-rata distribution system, where every stream is accorded the same value, (primarily corporate) stakeholders hesitate to take the leap to UCPS. The consequences of a shift to UCPS are not yet entirely clear and, while several studies are already available,[376] further research is desirable. The data required for

[368] See eg <www.deezer.com/en/ucps>; Giblin and Doctorow, *Chokepoint Capitalism* (n 255) 69.

[369] See eg 'SoundCloud Introduces Fan-Powered Royalties' (*SoundCloud Newsroom*, 2 March 2021) <https://bit.ly/3vsbrF1>; Stuart Dredge, 'Tidal Reveals Its User-Centric Payout Plans and Adds a Free Tier' (*Music Ally*, 17 November 2021) <https://bit.ly/3BspQEk>. See more recently on the intermediate results of this switch Mark Hogan, 'SoundCloud Says Portishead Song Earned 500% More under New Royalty Plan' (*Pitchfork*, 15 September 2021) <https://bit.ly/3jazflE>.

[370] 'The Ten Things People Get Wrong about Streaming – Part Two' directed by Andy Malt and Chris Cooke (Podcast, 18 May 2020) <https://bit.ly/3ZVkoYl>.

[371] Ie the minimum period to generate revenues on most DSPs, see Castle and Feijóo, 'Study on the Artists in the Digital Music Marketplace' (n 4) 34; Goldmedia, 'Musik-Streaming in Deutschland' (n 246) 90.

[372] Pedersen, 'A Meta Study of User-Centric Distribution for Music Streaming' (n 353) 3, 16–17; Centre National de la Musique and Deloitte, 'Étude Relative à l'Impact du Passage à l'UCPS par les Services de Musique en Ligne. Rapport Détaillé' (2021) 28; Tim Ingham, 'The Boomy/Spotify Streaming Fraud Debacle Proves "Pro-Rata" Must Go – Urgently' (*Music Business Worldwide*, 4 May 2023) <https://bit.ly/42poaYO>.

[373] 'The Ten Things People Get Wrong about Streaming – Part Two' (n 370); DCMS Committee, 'Economics of Music Streaming' (n 47) 91.

[374] 'The Ten Things People Get Wrong about Streaming – Part Two' (n 370).

[375] See on the tradeoff between efficiency and fairness in terms of revenue distribution, Will Page and David Safir, 'Money In, Money Out: Lessons From CMOs in Allocating and Distributing Licensing Revenue' [2018] Music & Copyright Newsletter 23, 23–31.

[376] See eg Muikku, 'Pro Rata and User Centric Distribution Models' (n 341); Pedersen, 'A Meta Study of User-Centric Distribution for Music Streaming' (n 353); Centre National de la

such research is, at present, siloed, which precludes firm assertions on this topic for now.[377] Tentative economic research indicates that the main prospective 'losers' of UCPS – who thus appear to be disproportionately privileged by the current pro-rata distribution model – would-be internationally renowned major label artists (including English-speaking music in non-English-speaking territories) and urban artists.[378] It would make sense for these findings to constitute an additional incentive for major corporate partners to advocate in favour of maintaining the current model. Prospective winners would appear to be niche genres, mid-level artists and local artists performing in their native language.[379] Consequently, some argue that UCPS would contribute to a more diverse music market and provide some welcome pushback against the forces of the superstar economy.[380] Sceptics counter that, while some mid-level artists would do better under UCPS, others would receive lower revenues – merely resulting in a form of 'musical chairs' in the mid-level.[381] Also under UCPS, session musicians risk drawing the short straw, with no presently proposed UCPS models offering any remuneration to non-featured artists that have transferred their rights against a flat fee.[382] In other words, the distribution of revenues could remain rather similar overall.[383]

Regardless of the economic effect in terms of revenue distribution, UCPS holds significant value. With UCPS, users' subscription fee benefits the musicians they choose to support by listening to their music. Users' money is connected with what they – personally – assign value to, establishing a more direct connection between musicians and their audience.[384] Moreover, UCPS may have a levelling effect on the current distortion of the payment system in favour of intensive users (also known

Musique and Deloitte, 'Étude Relative à l'Impact du Passage à l'UCPS' (n 372); Castle and Feijóo, 'Study on the Artists in the Digital Music Marketplace' (n 4); Janek Meyn and others, 'Consequences of Platforms' Remuneration Models for Digital Content: Initial Evidence and a Research Agenda for Streaming Services' (2023) 51 Journal of the Academy of Marketing Science 114.

377 Cf Giblin and Doctorow, *Chokepoint Capitalism* (n 255) 163.

378 Cooke, *Dissecting the Digital Dollar* (n 103) 69; Castle and Feijóo, 'Study on the Artists in the Digital Music Marketplace' (n 4) 41; Centre National de la Musique and Deloitte, 'Étude Relative à l'Impact du Passage à l'UCPS' (n 372) 21–26; DCMS Committee, 'Economics of Music Streaming' (n 47) 91. See also Xiaochang Lei, 'Pro-Rata vs User-Centric in the Music Streaming Industry' (2023) 226 Economics Letters 111111.

379 Dimont, 'Royalty Inequity' (n 366) 694–95; Cooke, *Dissecting the Digital Dollar* (n 103) 69; Pedersen, 'A Meta Study of User-Centric Distribution for Music Streaming' (n 353) 7–11; Centre National de la Musique and Deloitte, 'Étude Relative à l'Impact du Passage à l'UCPS' (n 372) 27.

380 See eg Centre National de la Musique and Deloitte, 'Étude Relative à l'Impact du Passage à l'UCPS' (n 372) 27.

381 Castle and Feijóo, 'Study on the Artists in the Digital Music Marketplace' (n 4) 9, 40–43, 49.

382 ibid 42–43.

383 Cf Pedersen, 'A Meta Study of User-Centric Distribution for Music Streaming' (n 353) 14; Castle and Feijóo, 'Study on the Artists in the Digital Music Marketplace' (n 4) 5, 40–43.

384 This direct link is reminiscent of the approach taken by Patreon, whereby users have the opportunity to pay specific artists directly in return for certain products and/or services; cf

as 'heavy streamers').[385] While logic would seem to dictate the existence of a link between users' listening habits and ultimate distribution of revenues – and while many users assume the existence thereof – such a link is currently partial at best. The mere fact that many users assume that UCPS is already prevalent constitutes a reason to actually make the switch.[386] Users who are aware of where their money is going may be more inclined to move to a DSP that uses UCPS – making the switch to UCPS on the part of DSPs a good PR move, at the very least. However, such a move would be subject to the authorisation of all licensors, including the major rightsholders.[387] Given the uncertain effects of UCPS on majors' revenue streams, their consent will likely be withheld.[388] The transaction costs associated with a move to UCPS on the part of DSPs may be prohibitively high.[389] Therefore, while UCPS appears to have certain advantages, its large-scale materialisation appears improbable.

An argument may also be made in favour of moving away from a pro-rata distribution of unallocated streaming revenue.[390] Such a practice results in the most frequently streamed music effectively bringing in more revenues than is objectively merited. A potentially valuable alternative would be to ensure that unallocated income is put back into the music community, supporting emerging artists, knowledge creation and dissemination.[391] However, as is the case for the potential switch to UCPS, the stakeholders with the highest amount of soft power have the least incentives to make such a change.[392]

The most recent addition to the music streaming vernacular is the so-called artist-centric model, which came to the fore following an agreement entered into between Universal Music Group and streaming service Deezer in the summer of 2023.[393] This model is set to boost royalty payments to artists that achieve a minimum threshold in terms of streams and unique listeners, as well as tracks actively searched for by users to the disadvantage of listens acquired through algorithmic playlists. The

DCMS Committee, 'Economics of Music Streaming' (n 47) 91; Page, *Tarzan Economics* (n 255) 135–43.

385 See eg Centre National de la Musique and Deloitte, 'Étude Relative à l'Impact du Passage à l'UCPS' (n 372) 27.

386 'The Ten Things People Get Wrong about Streaming – Part Two' (n 370).

387 Pedersen, 'A Meta Study of User-Centric Distribution for Music Streaming' (n 353) 3.

388 Castle and Feijóo, 'Study on the Artists in the Digital Music Marketplace' (n 4) 40, 49.

389 ibid 42, 49; DCMS Committee, 'Economics of Music Streaming' (n 47) 92.

390 Giblin and Doctorow, *Chokepoint Capitalism* (n 255) 71, 226.

391 Cf Cooke, *Dissecting the Digital Dollar* (n 103) 186, 210–11; DCMS Committee, 'Economics of Music Streaming' (n 47) 51–52.

392 Cf Cooke, *Dissecting the Digital Dollar* (n 103) 186.

393 See eg Stuart Dredge, 'UMG and Deezer Reveal Plans for "Artist-Centric" Streaming Payouts' (*Music Ally*, 6 September 2023) <https://bit.ly/48EFhcr>; Mark Mulligan, 'How to Make Artist Centric Artist Centric' (*LinkedIn*, 6 September 2023) <https://bit.ly/3Q2xqhC>; Murray Stassen, 'Popular Artists to Get "royalty Boost" on Deezer as Platform Readies "Artist-Centric" Model with Universal Music Group' (*Music Business Worldwide*, 6 September 2023) <https://bit.ly/3RLcCMV>.

intention is to reduce the effect of recommender algorithms and tackle streaming fraud.

2.4.4 *Division between Composition and Phonogram*

The revenues garnered through the exploitation of a phonogram that contains the recording of a specific composition are also divided between the composition and the phonogram.

For physical sales, record companies acquire a licence from the relevant publisher(s), usually via collective management.[394] Record companies retain the lion's share of revenues, with publishers in most cases having to make do with under 10 per cent of total revenues.[395] This significant difference was deemed justified on the basis of the financial risk taken by record companies in bringing new music to the market.[396] For physical sales, the record company's activities include artist development, manufacturing and distribution of physical products as well as marketing and promotion and destruction of unsold stock.[397] It was argued that record companies required a larger share of the revenues in order to recoup the costs associated with all of these activities and obtain a return on their investment. The publisher's contribution, on the other hand, was deemed much more limited, resulting in an equally limited share of the revenues.

When digital downloads emerged, new arrangements had to be made. An important shift compared with physical sales is that for downloads, as is the case for streaming, record companies and music publishers (and/or their CMOs) enter into separate licensing relationships with DSPs.[398] As for the division of revenues, representatives of the phonogram industry leaned towards a continuation of the division model used for physical sales, whereby iTunes was characterised as a digital version of a CD store.[399] This position was met with protest on the part of music publishers, composers and their CMOs, who argued that digital music sales entailed significantly fewer activities and associated costs for record companies and that therefore the disproportionate division of revenues was not justified for digital downloads. The costs of digital reproduction are very close to zero. While some costs remain (such as artist development, marketing and promotion), digital sales

[394] Cooke, *Dissecting the Digital Dollar* (n 103) 14, 44–45.

[395] ibid 44. In the publishing sector, voluntary collective management of such revenues is common.

[396] ibid 44, 82; Ulvaeus, 'Rebalancing the Song Economy' (n 337).

[397] See eg Hugenholtz and others, 'The Recasting of Copyright & Related Rights for the Knowledge Economy' (n 88) 99–100, 111–15; DCMS Committee, 'Economics of Music Streaming' (n 47) 39.

[398] Cooke, *Dissecting the Digital Dollar* (n 103) 14, 57–61. The record company is usually the first to licence. Given the big part of revenues claimed by record companies, much less is left for music publishers to negotiate about, see Cooke, *Dissecting the Digital Dollar* (n 103) 83.

[399] Mulligan, *Awakening* (n 135) 213.

undeniably entail significant cost savings for record companies. Ultimately, the phonogram industry partially heeded the call for change. The proportion of digital sales revenue granted to the composition increased vis-à-vis physical sales, but only by a few percentage points.

The increased popularity of streaming again gave rise to discussions regarding the appropriate distribution of revenue.[400] As is the case for digital downloads, streaming costs the recorded music industry proportionately rather little. Again, the publishing industry sought to increase its revenue share. Its efforts have achieved only moderate success, resulting in an allocated share of total streaming revenue that is about double the share accorded to the composition for physical sales. As a result, while specific proportions may vary per contract, of the 70 per cent of total revenues that the DSP shares with the music value chain, between 10 and 20 per cent is accorded to the composition (publishers and CMOs), while the phonogram's share usually varies between 50 and 60 per cent of the total revenues.[401]

The current division of digital and streaming revenue between composition and phonogram, whereby the phonogram receives approximately four times what the composition does, is fiercely criticised by composers, non-major publishers and their CMOs.[402] These representatives of the composition feel that their contribution is undervalued.[403]

As is the case for digital downloads, the activity of streaming has an impact on both the exclusive reproduction right and the right of making available. Some aspects of music streaming appear substantively more akin to radio, which is fully subject to the right of communication to the public, and which, at least for performers, has the status of a remuneration right.[404] Intuitively, a distinction may be made between on-demand streaming and the use of playlists. For streaming playlists and discovery modes on DSPs, users are not, as such, actively involved in the choice of music – effectively opting for a 'lean-back' form of music consumption and ceding this task to the DSP's algorithm in a way not dissimilar to (personalised) radio.[405] Music streaming may be perceived as a digital, more interactive version of radio, where equal revenue shares for composition and phonogram are common.[406] On-demand streaming bears a greater likeness to downloads, especially if the user

[400] See in more detail 'The Ten Things People Get Wrong about Streaming – Part One' (n 352); 'The Ten Things People Get Wrong about Streaming – Part Two' (n 370).

[401] Mulligan, *Awakening* (n 135) 213; Rethink Music Initiative, 'Fair Music' (n 127) 10; Cooke, *Dissecting the Digital Dollar* (n 103) 15–16, 76, 81–82, 193; DCMS Committee, 'Economics of Music Streaming' (n 47) 43–44.

[402] DCMS Committee, 'Economics of Music Streaming' (n 47) 43–49, 70–72; Goldmedia, 'Musik-Streaming in Deutschland' (n 246) 63–64.

[403] See eg Hesmondhalgh and others, 'Music Creators' Earnings in the Digital Era' (n 242) 84–87.

[404] See 'The Ten Things People Get Wrong about Streaming – Part One' (n 352); Cooke, *Dissecting the Digital Dollar* (n 103) 92.

[405] Hesmondhalgh and others, 'Music Creators' Earnings in the Digital Era' (n 242) 93–95.

[406] See AEPO-ARTIS, 'Performers' Rights in International and European Legislation: Situation and Elements for Improvement' (2018) 26–29. Cf Cooke, *Dissecting the Digital Dollar* (n 103)

decides to save the song(s) to their offline music library. Even so, it is noted that DSPs active in the music streaming market are increasingly also vying for a share of linear radio listeners.[407] This position finds empirical support in the waning popularity of radio over the past decade in favour of music consumption through streaming platforms.[408] In view of the perceived potential substitutability of radio for music streaming, can a strict distinction between both ways of listening to music really be maintained? Understandably, composers, non-major publishers and their CMOs submit that this question merits a negative answer.[409] The argument in favour of according a higher proportion to the composition holds water. Taking the equal division of radio revenues as a benchmark, a proportion of one-third or even a half may be envisaged.[410]

Yet there are several complicating factors. First, major music companies that house both a publishing division and a label division have a clear economic interest in maintaining the status quo.[411] As explained further on in this section, music publishing deals are significantly more artist-friendly than the standard deal with a major record company.[412] The current division between composition and phonogram allows the major record companies to retain a larger revenue share than would be the case if a larger proportion of revenues were to be accorded to the composition. The majors' reluctance to make a change in this regard is unsurprising.[413]

Second, the licensing process for streaming appears not to be conducive to change. In analogue times, the rights in the composition were first licensed to the record company which then, in turn, took care of the further steps of the commercial exploitation process, paying a portion of revenues to the owners of the rights in the composition (often through collective management).[414] In the streaming age, negotiations with the DSP take place separately, with publishers and CMOs negotiating on the side of the composition, and record companies and/or distributors closing the deal on the part of the phonogram.[415] Since not all parties are present at

42, 92; DCMS Committee, 'Economics of Music Streaming' (n 47) 18; Hesmondhalgh and others, 'Music Creators' Earnings in the Digital Era' (n 242) 69.

[407] See eg Cherie Hu, 'Spotify and Apple Music Disagree on the Future of Radio. Who's Right?' (*Water & Music*, 24 August 2020) <www.patreon.com/posts/40800408>; Castle and Feijóo, 'Study on the Artists in the Digital Music Marketplace' (n 4) 6.

[408] DCMS Committee, 'Economics of Music Streaming' (n 47) 21, 32, 37–38.

[409] 'The Ten Things People Get Wrong About Streaming – Part One' (n 352).

[410] Cf Cooke, *Dissecting the Digital Dollar* (n 103) 90; DCMS Committee, 'Economics of Music Streaming' (n 47) 49, 104. See for more detailed proposals ECSA, 'Songwriters' Fee & Master Point Guidelines' (2021) <https://bit.ly/3Ba85JD>.

[411] See above, Section 2.3.2. See also Cooke, *Dissecting the Digital Dollar* (n 103) 84; Giblin and Doctorow, *Chokepoint Capitalism* (n 255) 70.

[412] See below, Section 2.4.5.

[413] Cf Cooke, *Dissecting the Digital Dollar* (n 103) 84; DCMS Committee, 'Economics of Music Streaming' (n 47) 70–72, 106.

[414] Cooke, *Dissecting the Digital Dollar* (n 103) 14–15, 44–45.

[415] ibid 14–15, 57–58, 82–84.

the negotiation table at the same time, this process is unlikely to result in significant changes to the division between composition and phonogram.

2.4.5 *Division between Musicians and Music Industry Corporate Partners*

Finally, the revenues are shared between musicians and their primary music industry partners.[416] As to the distribution of recorded music revenue, session musicians and featured artists occupy a different position. Session musicians generally transfer their exclusive neighbouring rights to record companies in return for a flat fee and receive no further share in the phonogram's revenues.[417] Featured artists more often receive a proportionate share of the phonogram's revenues in the form of royalty payments.[418] Compared with physical sales and digital downloads, a somewhat larger portion of revenues is accorded to performers for streaming. This may be linked with the decreased costs and activities associated with streaming for record companies. However, taken as a whole, a 2015 study showed that record companies retain almost three-quarters of DSP royalties, not much less than for physical sales and/or digital downloads.[419]

For the greater part of the twentieth century, the royalty percentages granted to featured artists were very limited – almost exclusively below 10 per cent.[420] Often, a differentiated rate was set depending on the territorial source of revenues.[421] In parallel with the rise of digital music distribution, this percentage started to rise, with average royalties around the 15 per cent mark.[422] For streaming, the royalty rate

416 See for empirical research on net musician revenue over the past decades ia Kretschmer and others, 'The Relationship between Copyright and Contract Law' (n 135) 48–64; Europe Economics and others, 'Remuneration of Authors and Performers' (n 4) 192–207; Malevanny, *Online Music Distribution* (n 28) 265–70; Castle and Feijóo, 'Study on the Artists in the Digital Music Marketplace' (n 4).

417 Towse, 'Copyright and Economic Incentives' (n 170) 369,374; Europe Economics and others, 'Remuneration of Authors and Performers' (n 4) 77–78; DCMS Committee, 'Economics of Music Streaming' (n 47) 31–32; CMU, 'Performer Payments from Streaming' (n 312) 16; Hesmondhalgh and others, 'Music Creators' Earnings in the Digital Era' (n 242) 67. Session musicians do not incur any commercial risk regarding the phonogram, cf Kretschmer and others, 'The Relationship between Copyright and Contract Law' (n 135) 24.

418 Hesmondhalgh and others, 'Music Creators' Earnings in the Digital Era' (n 242) 66. This implies a form of risk-sharing between the artist and the corporate partner, cf Kretschmer and others, 'The Relationship between Copyright and Contract Law' (n 135) 24.

419 Rethink Music Initiative, 'Fair Music' (n 127) 14. See also Goldmedia, 'Musik-Streaming in Deutschland' (n 246) 77.

420 By way of example the 1992 deal between George Michael and Sony, which provided for 8 per cent royalties for the United Kingdom and 6 per cent for the rest of the world; see Soocher, *They Fought the Law* (n 187) 46. The Beatles' initial deal with Capitol Records provided for an even lower rate, see Soocher, *They Fought the Law* (n 187) 87.

421 Cf Hall Jr, 'Smells Like Slavery' (n 263) 206–08.

422 See eg Towse, 'Copyright and Economic Incentives' (n 170) 373; Hugenholtz and others, 'The Recasting of Copyright & Related Rights for the Knowledge Economy' (n 88) 121; Michel, 'Digital File Sharing and Royalty Contracts in the Music Industry' (n 165) 37; Aisling Quinn,

again increased. At the time of writing, a royalty percentage of around 15–20 per cent appears to be generally accepted.[423] In licensing deals, musicians receive a higher rate.[424] In new deals, a featured artist with high bargaining power may receive up to 30 or 50 per cent of streaming revenue, perhaps even more.[425] Indies usually grant a higher royalty percentage than the majors do, with figures up to 50 per cent and above circulating in the sector.[426] It is also possible to foresee a 'sliding scale' of remuneration or 'escalations', whereby the royalty percentage increases as the phonogram(s) at issue become(s) more successful.[427] While certain trends may be discerned, there is no such thing as an 'average' contract in the music industry.[428] Caution is therefore advised against unwarranted oversimplifications.

In addition to the royalty percentage, the impact of the calculation base on the distribution of revenues should not be underestimated. Traditionally, royalties are calculated as a percentage of the published price to dealer (PPD).[429] Before the calculation takes place, a number of discounts are applied. For physical sales, it used to be common to apply a 25 per cent packaging charge, a 10 per cent deduction for damaged goods (so-called breakages), as well as technology charges, discounts for products provided to retailers for free, returned products and so on.[430] Musician revenue is driven further downwards by remuneration arrangements accorded to music producers and/or guest artists.[431] In addition, the distinction between an 'at source' or a 'receipts' royalty basis is relevant: while royalties calculated 'at source' are linked with the amount paid by the third party using the work, 'receipts' refer to

'Are Online Music Platforms Undermining the Principles of Copyright Law?' (2018) 13 JIPLP 49, 51; CMU, 'Performer Payments from Streaming' (n 312) 16.

423 See eg Gulinck, *Hier Tekenen!* (n 7) 289; Krueger, *Rockonomics* (n 121) 36, 162; Malevanny, *Online Music Distribution* (n 28) 84–85; Passman, *All You Need to Know* (n 42) 92; Cooke, *Dissecting the Digital Dollar* (n 103) 16–17, 69, 79; DCMS Committee, 'Economics of Music Streaming' (n 47) 28; CMU, 'Performer Payments from Streaming' (n 312) 11, 15; Goldmedia, 'Musik-Streaming in Deutschland' (n 246) 75.

424 Gulinck, *Hier Tekenen!* (n 7) 289.

425 CMU, 'Performer Payments from Streaming' (n 312) 13; Giblin and Doctorow, *Chokepoint Capitalism* (n 255) 58; Goldmedia, 'Musik-Streaming in Deutschland' (n 246) 75.

426 Mulligan, *Awakening* (n 135) 87, 159.

427 Lardinois, *Les Contrats Commentés de l'Industrie de La Musique* 2.0 (n 18) 89; Pauly and H'Madoun, *Poppuntgids voor muzikant en dj* (n 9) 174; Passman, *All You Need to Know* (n 42) 95–96; Gulinck, *Hier Tekenen!* (n 7) 290–91; Stef van Gompel and others, 'Evaluatie Wet Auteurscontractenrecht: Eindrapport' (2020) <https://bit.ly/3UBZrh4> 102.

428 Cf Cooke, *Dissecting the Digital Dollar* (n 103) 133; Hesmondhalgh and others, 'Music Creators' Earnings in the Digital Era' (n 242) 131.

429 Sometimes, the calculation base is the recommended retail price (RRP), which is sometimes also indicated as the suggested retail list price (SRLP), see Stopps, 'How to Make a Living from Music' (n 42) 99; Passman, *All You Need to Know* (n 42) 82.

430 Soocher, *They Fought the Law* (n 187) 54; Caves, 'Contracts between Art and Commerce' (n 329) 62–63; Hugenholtz and Guibault, 'Auteurscontractenrecht' (n 155) 24; Lardinois, *Les Contrats Commentés de l'Industrie de La Musique* 2.0 (n 18) 90–95; Gulinck, *Hier Tekenen!* (n 7) 138–39; Passman, *All You Need to Know* (n 42) 82–84; Cooke, *Dissecting the Digital Dollar* (n 103) 88–89, 134; CMU, 'Performer Payments from Streaming' (n 312) 11.

431 CMU, 'Performer Payments from Streaming' (n 312) 12, 15–16.

the amount received by the publisher after deduction of costs, such as commissions charged by sub-publishers.[432] Some of these discounts and deductions are still applied, even for digital downloads and streaming, where reference is made to 'overhead' costs.[433] Finally, many deals with DSPs grant minimum guarantees and/or equity to major rights owners. While this revenue has recently been (partially) shared with artists, this does not appear to be common practice and the modalities of such revenue sharing are often unclear.[434]

Several other factors affect the calculation and the payment of royalties. A first relevant industry practice, albeit less frequent than before,[435] is that of non-returnable but recoupable advances, by which musicians receive a lump sum advance that allows them to focus on their music career for a certain period of time. This advance payment is recouped out of future royalty payments, together with operational costs for the recording, production and promotion of the music, including the costs for music videos.[436] Under a recoupment deal, the label's return on investment is computed only on the basis of the share of revenues allotted to the artist, while under a 'profit-sharing' agreement, the total revenue is taken into account.[437] Thus, under a recoupment deal, the record company may have already

[432] Stopps, 'How to Make a Living from Music' (n 42) 108; Passman, *All You Need to Know* (n 42) 93–94, 256–58; CMU, 'Performer Payments from Streaming' (n 312) 11–12.

[433] Stopps, 'How to Make a Living from Music' (n 42) 99–100; Mulligan, *Awakening* (n 135) 68; Rethink Music Initiative, 'Fair Music' (n 127) 3, 14; De Voldere and others, 'Mapping the Creative Value Chains' (n 28) 147; Pauly and H'Madoun, *Poppuntgids voor muzikant en dj* (n 9) 174; David, 'CD' (n 263) 362; Gulinck, *Hier Tekenen!* (n 7) 293–94.

[434] Mulligan, *Awakening* (n 135) 82; Rethink Music Initiative, 'Fair Music' (n 127) 4; De Voldere and others, 'Mapping the Creative Value Chains' (n 28) 147–48; Gulinck, *Hier Tekenen!* (n 7) 450; Cooke, *Dissecting the Digital Dollar* (n 103) 99–102.

[435] It has been argued that the music industry has recently been characterised by a lower willingness to invest and a trend towards conservativeness concerning new music, resulting from an increased risk aversity. This manifests itself in a decrease in the amount of advances offered to emerging artists: see eg Stopps, 'How to Make a Living from Music' (n 42) 10; Mulligan, *Awakening* (n 135) 192; Baym, *Playing to the Crowd* (n 127) 55; Gulinck, *Hier Tekenen!* (n 7) 110, 113, 120, 266; DCMS Committee, 'Economics of Music Streaming' (n 47) 31; Hesmondhalgh and others, 'Music Creators' Earnings in the Digital Era' (n 242) 86.

[436] Towse, 'Copyright and Economic Incentives' (n 170) 373; Hall Jr, 'Smells Like Slavery' (n 263) 213; Caves, 'Contracts between Art and Commerce' (n 329) 64–66; Michel, 'Digital File Sharing and Royalty Contracts in the Music Industry' (n 165) 37; Lardinois, *Les Contrats Commentés de l'Industrie de La Musique* 2.0 (n 18) 96–97; Kretschmer and others, 'The Relationship between Copyright and Contract Law' (n 135) 46; Europe Economics and others, 'Remuneration of Authors and Performers' (n 4) 68; Rethink Music Initiative, 'Fair Music' (n 127) 6, 14; De Voldere and others, 'Mapping the Creative Value Chains' (n 28) 137; Osborne, 'Is Equitable Remuneration Equitable?' (n 33) 580; Passman, *All You Need to Know* (n 42) 85–87, 96–101; Kristelia García, 'Contracts and Copyright: Contemporary Musician Income Streams' in Sean M O'Connor (ed), *The Oxford Handbook of Music Law and Policy* (Oxford Handbooks, Oxford University Press 2020) s 1.1; Towse, 'Dealing with Digital' (n 155) 1463; Castle and Feijóo, 'Study on the Artists in the Digital Music Marketplace' (n 4) 18; Giblin and Doctorow, *Chokepoint Capitalism* (n 255) 53–54.

[437] Quinn, 'Are Online Music Platforms Undermining the Principles of Copyright Law?' (n 422) 51; Cooke, *Dissecting the Digital Dollar* (n 103) 32–33, 134, 137–38; CMU, 'Performer Payments

recouped their investment for several years before starting to pay out royalties to the artist.[438] Between the day that the corporate partner breaks even and that the artist has recouped, the corporate partner's profit margin is significant.

The degree of recoupment is enhanced even further, such as with the technique of cross-collateralisation, whereby several contracts are linked together, including recording, publishing and merchandising contracts.[439] The technique of including several revenue streams in a single contract is referred to as a 'multiple rights deal'.[440] When the idea of cross-collateralisation is taken to its extreme, we arrive at so-called 360-degree deals, whereby the record company obtains part of the revenue stemming from peripheral revenue streams that are unrelated to phonograms, including live performances, music publishing and/or merchandising.[441] Such arrangements lead to a significant centralisation of power.[442] Famous examples of 360-degree deals primarily date from the 2000s and include the ground-breaking arrangement between Robbie Williams and the (now defunct[443]) EMI, as well as the deals between promoter Live Nation and Madonna and Jay-Z.[444] As a result of 360-degree arrangements, for example, artists who generate significant profits through music publishing, but make losses on recorded music, ultimately lose out on royalties.[445]

from Streaming' (n 312) 13; DCMS Committee, 'Economics of Music Streaming' (n 47) 19, 28; Hesmondhalgh and others, 'Music Creators' Earnings in the Digital Era' (n 242) 87–89, 123.

438 DCMS Committee, 'Economics of Music Streaming' (n 47) 28–29; Giblin and Doctorow, *Chokepoint Capitalism* (n 255) 53–54, 63, 181.

439 Kretschmer and others, 'The Relationship between Copyright and Contract Law' (n 135) 46; Rogers, *The Death & Life* (n 175) 126–27, 184–85; Pauly and H'Madoun, *Poppuntgids voor muzikant en dj* (n 9) 175; Gulinck, *Hier Tekenen!* (n 7) 292; Passman, *All You Need to Know* (n 42) 88–89.

440 Gulinck, *Hier Tekenen!* (n 7) 245–46.

441 The rise of 360-degree deals is linked with the decline of physical revenues and record companies' contention that ancillary revenue streams arise from record companies' investment, marketing and promotion efforts. See eg Ian Brereton, 'The Beginning of a New Age: The Unconscionability of the 360-Degree Deal' (2009) 27 Cardozo Arts & Ent LJ 168, 168–97; Sara Karubian, '360° Deals: An Industry Reaction to the Devaluation of Recorded Music' (2009) 18 S Cal Interdisc LJ 395, 395–462; Douglas Okorocha, 'A Full 360: How the 360 Deal Challenges the Historical Resistance to Establishing a Fiduciary Duty between Artist and Label' (2010) 18 UCLA Ent L Rev 1, 1–32; Daniel Gervais and others, 'The Rise of 360 Deals in the Music Industry' (2011) 3 Landslide 40, 40–45; Lee Marshall, 'The 360 Deal and the "New" Music Industry' (2013) 16 EJCS 77, 77–99; Rogers, *The Death & Life* (n 175) 124–27, 183; Stopps, 'How to Make a Living from Music' (n 42) 10, 103; Passman, *All You Need to Know* (n 42) 102–07.

442 Rogers, *The Death & Life* (n 175) 127.

443 See Eamonn Forde, *The Final Days of EMI. Selling the Pig* (Omnibus Press 2019).

444 Marshall, 'The 360 Deal and the "New" Music Industry' (n 441) 77–96; De Voldere and others, 'Mapping the Creative Value Chains' (n 28) 139; Cooke, *Dissecting the Digital Dollar* (n 103) 32.

445 Rogers, *The Death & Life* (n 175) 126; Mulligan, *Awakening* (n 135) 193; David, 'CD' (n 263) 362.

The revenue division between musicians and music industry corporate partners is more beneficial to composers than it is to performers.[446] While the secret and deal-specific nature of revenue share arrangements is again emphasised, it may be stated with a significant degree of confidence that composers receive at least half of all publishing revenue.[447] Notably, statutes of publisher CMOs set a threshold in this regard: for example, in Belgium and France, the maximum limit for publishers is half of revenues.[448] In any case, it has been stated that recent composer–publisher deals grant as much as 80 per cent of revenue (or even more) to the composer. In some cases, recoupable advances and/or a 'sliding scale' of remuneration are foreseen.[449] It is also possible to include so-called kickbacks, where a music publisher agrees to transmit part of the revenue received by them in a first stage to the composer, thus providing a better deal than the initial 50/50 division.[450] Another type of potential 'kickbacks' is less beneficial to the composer, since it forces them to pay the publisher part of the CMO revenues they receive on the basis of their remuneration rights.[451] Finally, reference may be made to the (fading) practice of controlled composition clauses. Such clauses limit the percentage of royalties paid to musicians for certain musical content that they have written themselves and are therefore deemed to be within their sphere of 'control'.[452]

Net musician revenue may be calculated after deducting the commission-based fees granted to a number of corporate partners. In particular, an external distributor may ask between 15 and 30 per cent commission.[453] For online revenues,

446 Cooke, *Dissecting the Digital Dollar* (n 103) 24, 33, 85–87; DCMS Committee, 'Economics of Music Streaming' (n 47) 19–20.

447 See eg Lardinois, *Les Contrats Commentés de l'Industrie de La Musique* 2.0 (n 18) 33; H'Madoun and others, *Auteursrechten en Publishing* (n 152) 67; Mulligan, *Awakening* (n 135) 184; Krueger, *Rockonomics* (n 121) 32; Malevanny, *Online Music Distribution* (n 28) 79; Cooke, *Dissecting the Digital Dollar* (n 103) 79; Towse, 'Dealing with Digital' (n 155) 1464.

448 H'Madoun and others, *Auteursrechten en Publishing* (n 152) 84–85; Gulinck, *Hier Tekenen!* (n 7) 201, 305, 333–34. See the regulations of Belgian CMO SABAM, available online at <https://bit.ly/3mZeqAO>. See the regulations of French CMO SACEM, in particular Art 76, available online at <https://bit.ly/3AHAaX2>.

449 See in more detail H'Madoun and others, *Auteursrechten en Publishing* (n 152) 75; Pauly and H'Madoun, *Poppuntgids voor muzikant en dj* (n 9) 196–97.

450 Pauly and H'Madoun, *Poppuntgids voor muzikant en dj* (n 9) 196; Gulinck, *Hier Tekenen!* (n 7) 305.

451 Hugenholtz and Guibault, 'Auteurscontractenrecht (n 155) 25; Lionel Bently, 'Between a Rock and a Hard Place: The Problems Facing Freelance Creators in the UK Media Market-Place. A Briefing Document on Behalf of the Creators' Rights Alliance. Third and Final Draft' (2009) 9–11; van Gompel and others, 'Evaluatie Wet Auteurscontractenrecht: Eindrapport' (n 427) 55.

452 Stopps, 'How to Make a Living from Music' (n 42) 59–60; Passman, *All You Need to Know* (n 42) 264–65.

453 Pauly and H'Madoun, *Poppuntgids voor muzikant en dj* (n 9) 184, 211; Gulinck, *Hier Tekenen!* (n 7) 289; Cooke, *Dissecting the Digital Dollar* (n 103) 135–37; Towse, 'Dealing with Digital' (n 155) 1470; CMU, 'Performer Payments from Streaming' (n 312) 10.

independent musicians and small independent corporate partners may call upon the services of a digital distributor and/or a publishing administrator for the exploitation of 'their' phonograms and/or compositions. These corporate partners receive a commission-based fee that amounts to up to 10–15 per cent of revenues.[454] Musician revenue is subject to a commission fee for the manager(s) of around 15–20 per cent as well as, ultimately, taxes.[455]

Throughout recent decades, attempts have been made to transplant analogue music business practices to the present-day digital reality, to the benefit of major rights owners.[456] As a result, despite the artist-centred nature of continental EU copyright and copyright's stated purpose for music to incentivise musicians through reward, the reality is often that the record companies and music publishers reap the lion's share of the rewards.[457] First, the fairness of buyouts of session musicians against a flat fee is questioned, especially for music that becomes commercially successful. The main issue is simple: while it may be argued that a flat fee is always unfair in case of success, another perspective might only take issue with the level of such payments. The picture regarding royalty payments is more complex.[458] Contractual clauses regarding payment to musicians are often quite detailed and technical.[459] Moreover, new modes of exploitation are constantly emerging. It is therefore hard to assess the fairness of the clause itself or its performance in practice.[460] Regardless, a number of issues are impossible to deny, as to both the

[454] See Pauly and H'Madoun, *Poppuntgids voor muzikant en dj* (n 9) 138–39. Some digital distributors charge a fixed price per phonogram/album, such as TuneCore and DistroKid. The commission charged by the digital distributor may vary depending on the size of the contracting partner.

[455] Caves, 'Contracts between Art and Commerce' (n 329) 61; Lardinois, *Les Contrats Commentés de l'Industrie de La Musique 2.0* (n 18) 54–57; Stopps, 'How to Make a Living from Music' (n 42) 78; Gulinck, *Hier Tekenen!* (n 7) 367–77; Krueger, *Rockonomics* (n 121) 129; Towse, *A Textbook of Cultural Economics* (n 124) 481; CMU, 'Performer Payments from Streaming' (n 312) 12. See on management contracts Lardinois, *Les Contrats Commentés de l'Industrie de La Musique 2.0* (n 18) 44–61; Stopps, 'How to Make a Living from Music' (n 42) 73–84, 223–36; Gulinck, *Hier Tekenen!* (n 7) 367–404; Passman, *All You Need to Know* (n 42) 32–53.

[456] See also Eric E Johnson, 'Intellectual Property and the Incentive Fallacy' (2012) 39 Fla St U L Rev 623.

Cf Rogers, *The Death & Life* (n 175) 178–99; Mulligan, *Awakening* (n 135) 242; Baym, *Playing to the Crowd* (n 127) 63; Irina Eidsvold-Tøien, 'Remunerating Authors and Performers: Are Statutory Compensation Provisions Sufficient?' in Jens Schovsbo (ed), *The Exploitation of Intellectual Property Rights: In Search of the Right Balance* (ATRIP Intellectual Property, Edward Elgar 2023) 197.

[457] Cf Baym, *Playing to the Crowd* (n 127) 25.

[458] See for simulations of artist remuneration for streaming: (1) for recorded music <https://dealsim.createos.app> and (2) for music publishing: <https://pubsim.createos.app>.

[459] There is an argument in favour of simplifying royalty clauses, such as by instituting a flat-rate royalty percentage without any deductions, see eg Stopps, 'How to Make a Living from Music' (n 42) 100.

[460] Dusollier, 'EU Contractual Protection of Creators' (n 112) 448.

royalty percentage and the calculation base.[461] Finally, it is possible to write a royalty cap into the contract or simply refuse to pay.[462]

In summary, the division of digital revenues is largely based on last-century payment principles that apply to the advantage of major rights owners.[463] Two decades ago, Ruth Towse argued that 'despite high aggregate earnings from copyright in the music industry, the vast majority of musicians earn relatively little from specific copyright and performers' rights'.[464] This statement holds true, especially for legacy artists, whose contracts date back to the purely analogue age, when room for manoeuvre was very limited and usually led to a full transfer of rights and an exceedingly low royalty rate – if not a low flat fee.[465] While the speculative nature of art in general and music in particular is undeniable and justifies proper remuneration of risk-takers and investors, the benefits of success should be fairly allocated. Arguably, this is not the case in the streaming age.[466]

2.5 TRANSPARENCY IN THE STREAMING AGE

The previous section discussed the different dimensions of revenue division in the streaming age. All four dimensions are pervaded by a conspicuous, persisting lack of transparency. There is still much to be desired in terms of transparent reporting by corporate partners to musicians.[467] Musicians are often unable to obtain credible data on digital use and streaming of their music.[468] By way of example, it is unclear to what extent and how exactly equity shares and breakage received from DSPs are shared with musicians.[469]

The confidential nature of direct licensing deals between major rights owners and DSPs, including the trend of UGC deals, makes it impossible to assess whether

[461] See in more detail below, Chapter 5, Section 5.3.2.2.

[462] For an example of the latter and the ensuing legal proceedings between legacy artists The Shirelles, BJ Thomas and music publishing company GML Inc in the US, see Soocher, *They Fought the Law* (n 187) 65–84. See also Yu, 'Digital Copyright and Confuzzling Rhetoric' (n 207) 915; Deresiewicz, *The Death of the Artist* (n 132) 151. See also more recently Nancy Dillon, 'Black Sheep Files Class Action Claiming Universal 'Unlawfully Retained' $750 Million in Royalties' (*Rolling Stone*, 4 January 2023) <https://bit.ly/3FCRL7v>.

[463] Cf Rethink Music Initiative, 'Fair Music' (n 127) 28.

[464] Towse, 'Copyright and Economic Incentives' (n 170) 388.

[465] Cf Baym, *Playing to the Crowd* (n 127) 65–66; Lunney, *Copyright's Excess* (n 219) 198–99; DCMS Committee, 'Economics of Music Streaming' (n 47) 28; Giblin and Doctorow, *Chokepoint Capitalism* (n 255) 57, 221; Osborne and Sun, 'Economics of Streaming' (n 189) s 1.4.3.

[466] Rethink Music Initiative, 'Fair Music' (n 127) 10; Ginsburg, 'Copyright' (n 55) 497.

[467] De Voldere and others, 'Mapping the Creative Value Chains' (n 28) 137.

[468] See eg Rethink Music Initiative, 'Fair Music' (n 127); Price, 'The Definitive Guide to Spotify Royalties' (n 117) 48.

[469] Giblin and Doctorow, *Chokepoint Capitalism* (n 255) 72. See however in relation to Warner Music in particular Tim Ingham, 'Warner Pays Artists Share of Spotify Advances. . . and Has for 6 Years' (*Music Business Worldwide*, 29 May 2015) <https://bit.ly/3HCQwUY>.

these contracts are actually fair to all stakeholders.[470] A notable exception to this shroud of secrecy is the revenue share agreement between Sony Music and Spotify, which was leaked in 2015, uncovering a significant revenue stream of advances and pays-per-stream from Spotify to Sony Music.[471] There has been a recent move towards more transparency, primarily on the part of independent labels, but also by the major record companies.[472] Even so, as long as there is an information asymmetry, it is almost impossible to evaluate whether the calculation and ensuing distribution of revenues takes place correctly and fairly.[473]

Furthermore, as streaming revenue is distributed within the music value chain, a significant amount of money either ends up with the wrong recipient or is lost entirely and cannot be accounted for.[474] At each stage, the margin for human error gives rise to a risk of significant loss in revenues. This opacity is labelled the 'royalty chain issue' or the 'black box'.[475] There are no definitive figures on the exact amount of streaming revenue that is not accurately distributed as a result, but the total size of this black box has been estimated at over 20 per cent of the total revenues from streaming.[476] This 'royalty chain issue' is in urgent need of a comprehensive solution, especially in the context of music publishing, where the royalty chains are particularly long, leading to significant delays in payment.[477] This issue may be linked with the difficult process of streaming royalty payouts,[478] which, in turn, is closely linked to the highly fragmented nature of rights in music and the persisting conundrum of music metadata.[479] Both issues are discussed below.

470 Cf Europe Economics and others, 'Remuneration of Authors and Performers' (n 4) 136; Carnes, 'Developing a Copyright System' (n 130) 313–14; Hviid and others, 'Digitalisation and Intermediaries' (n 188) 271; Gulinck, *Hier Tekenen!* (n 7) 539; Cooke, *Dissecting the Digital Dollar* (n 103) 104.

471 See Micah Singleton, 'This Was Sony Music's Contract with Spotify. The Details the Major Labels Don't Want You to See' (*The Verge*, 19 May 2015) <https://bit.ly/3vcuhjr>; Quinn, 'Are Online Music Platforms Undermining the Principles of Copyright Law?' (n 422) 57.

472 Mulligan, *Awakening* (n 135) 86; Rethink Music Initiative, 'Fair Music' (n 127) 10, 14–15; Quinn, 'Are Online Music Platforms Undermining the Principles of Copyright Law?' (n 422) 58.

473 Cf Hall Jr, 'Smells Like Slavery' (n 263) 210.

474 Rethink Music Initiative, 'Fair Music' (n 127) 3.

475 Stopps, 'How to Make a Living from Music' (n 42) 49; Rethink Music Initiative, 'Fair Music' (n 127) 4–5, 15–16; Passman, *All You Need to Know* (n 42) 259; Ulvaeus, 'Rebalancing the Song Economy' (n 337).

476 Mulligan, *Awakening* (n 135) 215; Rethink Music Initiative, 'Fair Music' (n 127) 26; DCMS Committee, 'Economics of Music Streaming' (n 47) 53; Andre Paine, 'Black Box Disorder: Ivors Academy Research Reveals £500m Streaming Data Gap' (16 August 2021) <https://bit.ly/3vkEZV2>; Giblin and Doctorow, *Chokepoint Capitalism* (n 255) 224.

477 Cooke, *Dissecting the Digital Dollar* (n 103) 182–86, 196–204; 'The Ten Things People Get Wrong About Streaming – Part Two' (n 370).

478 See above, Section 2.4.

479 Europe Economics and others, 'Remuneration of Authors and Performers' (n 4) 24; Mulligan, *Awakening* (n 135) 243; Baym, *Playing to the Crowd* (n 127) 66.

Several factors contribute to rights fragmentation. First, the move towards direct licensing leads to fragmentation between the catalogues of major rights owners and those represented by CMOs. In addition, the high number of collaborators in musical projects leads to joint and thus fragmented initial ownership of both copyright *sensu stricto* and neighbouring rights. Third, the principle of territoriality implies a separate copyright title for each country. Finally, subsequent (partial) transfers may lead to shared or full ownership on the part of third parties. The effects of this fragmentation are exacerbated in the online environment.

A user who wishes to enter into a licence agreement for either commercial or private use is confronted with a multitude of potential licensors, who all hold a small piece of the global fragmented music repertoire. Difficulties in locating rightsholders and obtaining proper licences for the exploitation of protected music, combined with an absence of full blanket licences (one-stop shops) lead to enormous transaction costs.[480] Separate negotiations lead to a variety in licensing structures, especially when it comes to complex remuneration regimes.

The effects of rights fragmentation are significant and a streamlining on all fronts would be desirable. Competition law solutions may be envisaged, such as recourse to the prohibition on abuse of dominance through excessive pricing or the qualification of repertoire as an essential facility.[481] In addition, the EU regime on orphan works may offer solace, albeit only to a limited extent.[482] Initiatives for industry-led change, including the establishment of user-friendly, multi-territorial one-stop shops, are ongoing.[483]

Another contributor to the black box of streaming is the lack of a complete database that contains all music metadata information. This gives rise to a pervasive challenge in the music industry that is colloquially referred to as the 'metadata issue'.[484] Ideally, such a database would not only be complete in the sense that it would contain all relevant authorship, performance and ownership data, but it

[480] Hviid and others, 'Digitalisation and Intermediaries' (n 188) 270; Lucius Klobučník, 'Ameliorating the Impact of Rights' Fragmentation on New Online Music Services by Legislative Action' (Fostering Innovation in Europe: Intellectual Property Policies and Law, 25 June 2020).

[481] See eg Lucius Klobučník, 'Navigating the Fragmented Online Music Licensing Landscape in Europe: A Legislative Compass in Sight?' (2020) 11 JIPITEC 340; Giblin and Doctorow, *Chokepoint Capitalism* (n 255) 150. See also extensively CMA, 'Music and Streaming: Final Report' (29 November 2022).

[482] See Arts 1–12 Orphan Works Directive.

[483] Ginsburg, 'The Role of the Author in Copyright' (n 126) 78.

[484] On this topic, see eg Frank Lyons and others, 'Music 2025 – The Music Data Dilemma: Issues Facing the Music Industry in Improving Data Management' (2019); Norbert Gronau and Martin Schaefer, 'Why Metadata Matters for the Future of Copyright' (2021) 43 EIPR 488; DCMS Committee, 'Economics of Music Streaming' (n 47) 49–52; Martin Senftleben and others, 'Ensuring the Visibility and Accessibility of European Creative Content on the World Market: The Need for Copyright Data Improvement in the Light of New Technologies' [2021] SSRN 20, ss 2, 4.2. This may be linked with the absence of a registration requirement under copyright law.

would also be secure, consistent (standardised), correct, accessible and interoperable.[485] Existing structures such as the CIS[486]-Net network of CMO databases[487] and the AllMusic, Discogs, Gracenote, MusicBrainz and Songdex databases[488] are vast and undoubtedly helpful to those with access, but are not infallible and are siloed.[489] By way of a cursory example, between the many options for the spelling of Russian composers such as Shostakovich and Tchaikovsky, some are fated to fall between the cracks. Room for error also exists, for instance, in case of modulated transfer of rights in the context of a mergers and acquisitions (M&A) deal. Errors may lead to incorrect remuneration of rightsholders. This issue has become even more pressing in view of the significant increase in the amount of (self-)released music. The release of a physical product also requires due attention to relevant data, but not nearly to the same extent as digital music. Indeed, such music may be put online, copied infinitely and transmitted across the globe without any (of the correct) metadata. This has a clear potential negative impact on online monetisation opportunities for rightsholders.[490]

A global, comprehensive database of all music rights information, with full guarantees as to public availability and accessibility, as well as accuracy and standardisation of data input, would be ideal. The ultimate objective is for all stakeholders to have transparent and real-time access to full and accurate music rights information. However, as the failure of past initiatives such as the Global Repertoire Database (GRD) project has shown, to date, such an ideal world is only to be hoped for.[491] A more realistic alternative would be to optimise the ISRC and ISWC systems that are already in place[492] and secure the interoperability of existing databases through the establishment of an industry-wide qualitative metadata standard, applicable to CMOs as well as individual rights owners and DSPs.[493] This

[485] Cf Recs 41–42, Arts 25–26 CRM Directive; Cooke, *Dissecting the Digital Dollar* (n 103) 76; Racine, 'L'Auteur et l'Acte de Création' (n 136) 64–65.

[486] Abbreviation of Common Information System.

[487] <www.cisac.org/services/information-services/cis-net>.

[488] See <www.allmusic.com> <www.discogs.com> <www.gracenote.com> <https://musicbrainz.org> <www.songdex.com>.

[489] Mulligan, *Awakening* (n 135) 214; Giblin and Doctorow, *Chokepoint Capitalism* (n 255) 224.

[490] Some more recently established corporate partners seek to remedy this situation, see reference to content and data tracking companies Bitfury Surround and Pex above, Section 2.3.4.

[491] Rethink Music Initiative, 'Fair Music' (n 127) 26; Giblin and Doctorow, *Chokepoint Capitalism* (n 255) 225–26.

[492] See also 'New Improved Music Identifier Will Help Creators in the All-Important Digital Market' (*CISAC*, 24 September 2020) <https://bit.ly/3jaKiBG>; Legrand, 'Study on the Place and Role of Authors and Composers in the European Music Streaming Market' (n 326) 34–37.

[493] William F Patry, *How to Fix Copyright* (Oxford University Press 2011) 183; Rethink Music Initiative, 'Fair Music' (n 127) 3, 14, 25; Cooke, *Dissecting the Digital Dollar* (n 103) 154, 211–12; DCMS Committee, 'Economics of Music Streaming' (n 47) 51. See eg <www.rdx-portal.org>; <https://metad.media>; <www.creditsdue.org>; <https://jaxsta.com>; <www.rightsholder.io>.

avenue has the advantage of being able to lean fully on existing databases, while also furthering the objective of enhancing transparency in a meaningful way.

2.6 BRIDGE

This chapter outlined the primary structure of the music industry and showed the main relevant dynamics and revenue flows. Streaming is the music industry's focal point for the foreseeable future. Simultaneously, the importance of synchronisation revenue is rising and the music industry is tapping into UGC platforms as a new source of revenue. An interesting evolution is the music industry's attitude towards technology: wariness towards new business models has given way to a much more open frame of mind towards opportunities for further growth of the industry.

The recorded music and publishing industries are characterised by a wealth of possible contracting partners both internal and external to the music value chain and a corresponding abundance of varying exploitation agreements, ranging from simple transfers against flat fees to complex online (sub-)licensing arrangements on a multi-territorial level. The digitisation wave has provided many options for D2C contact to independent artists. However, in practice, a fully DIY music career is almost impossible, given the amount of intermediaries on the music market.

It is clear that certain forces of change are at work within the music industry in the streaming age. However, there are many spinning plates, the issue of information asymmetry is likely to persist and, while a more artist-friendly environment is growing, vested interests argue in favour of maintaining the status quo.[494] It therefore appears unlikely that bottom-up change will lead to an outcome that duly considers the justified interests of all stakeholders. If the music industry itself does not succeed in achieving a fair ecosystem, the legal framework should step in. This is the topic of the next chapters.

[494] Cf Parliament, 'Resolution of 21 November 2023 with Recommendations to the Commission on an EU Framework for the Social and Professional Situation of Artists and Workers in the Cultural and Creative Sectors' 2023/2051(INL); Parliament, 'Resolution of 17 January 2024 on Cultural Diversity and the Conditions for Authors in the European Music Streaming Market' 2023/2054(INI); Parliament, Committee on Culture and Education, 'Report of 4 December 2023 on Cultural Diversity and the Conditions for Authors in the European Music Streaming Market' A9-0388/2023 <https://shorturl.at/covxK>.

3

Law and Policy in the Streaming Age

So what better alternative is there
than an agreement between citizens themselves
reached under conditions that are fair for all?

—John Rawls[1]

3.1 INTRO

This chapter crosses the bridge from music industry practice to the analysis of the legal regimes deemed most relevant in securing a fair(er) balance in music contracts in the streaming age. Particular focus lies with the effect of the law on contracts entered into between musicians and record companies and/or music publishers as to individually managed exclusive rights.

First, this chapter analyses the role of the legal framework in achieving this book's policy objective of moving towards a fair(er) balance in the streaming age, fleshing out both the substantive and procedural dimension of what may be perceived as 'fair' in this particular context (Section 3.2). It then goes on to provide a typology of the relevant substantive legal regimes, categorising these limitations to parties' freedom of contract in terms of substantive, geographical and temporal scope and analysing the interplay between them (Section 3.3). Finally, the chapter sets out to establish the appropriate level(s) and method(s) of further potential policy initiatives aimed at contributing to the elusive fair balance that this book advocates (Section 3.4).

[1] John Rawls, *Justice as Fairness: A Restatement* (Harvard University Press 2001) para 6.1.

3.2 TOWARDS A FAIR BALANCE IN THE STREAMING AGE

3.2.1 *Balancing Copyright and Other Fundamental Rights*

Copyright falls within the scope of the fundamental right to ownership.[2] Both the material and moral dimensions of copyright are also protected as a sociocultural right.[3] A risk of conflict arises with other fundamental rights, including freedom of expression and information.[4] In this regard, achieving a fair balance is key.[5] Three different dimensions may be discerned.

First, an appropriate balance is required between the protection of copyright as exclusive property and the provision of legal certainty and third parties' freedom to create. This encompasses questions pertaining to (joint) authorship and the creative reuse of existing works.[6] The latter questions the appropriate line between copyright infringement and use that falls within the scope of applicable exceptions and limitations.

The second dimension refers to the balance between copyright owners and users as well as exploiters of content protected by copyright. This brings, inter alia, freedom of commerce, expression and information as well as the right to privacy and data protection into the picture. In the debate concerning the digitised

[2] Art 17 UDHR; Art 1 Prot 1 European Convention on Human Rights (ECHR) <https://bit.ly/3v2xGRL>; Guide on Article 1 of Protocol No. 1 to the European Convention on Human Rights (2020) <https://bit.ly/3v4anqz> 8, 13 and cited case law; Art 17(2) Charter of Fundamental Rights of the European Union [2012] OJ C326/391 (hereinafter: EU Charter).

[3] Art 27(2) UDHR; Art 15(1)(c) ICESCR. See Christophe Geiger, 'Copyright's Fundamental Rights Dimension at EU Level' in Estelle Derclaye (ed), *Research Handbook on the Future of EU Copyright* (Research Handbooks in Intellectual Property, Edward Elgar 2009) 31.

[4] Art 10 ECHR; Art 11 EU Charter; Art 19 UDHR. See Jonathan Griffiths and Uma Suthersanen, *Copyright and Free Speech. Comparative and International Analyses* (Oxford University Press 2005); Reto M Hilty and Sylvie Nérisson (eds), *Balancing Copyright: A Survey of National Approaches* (MPI studies on Intellectual Property and Competition Law 18, Springer 2012); Susy Frankel and Daniel Gervais (eds), *The Evolution and Equilibrium of Copyright in the Digital Age* (Cambridge Intellectual Property and Information Law, Cambridge University Press 2014); Christophe Geiger (ed), *Research Handbook on Human Rights and Intellectual Property* (Research Handbooks in Intellectual Property, Edward Elgar 2016); Oreste Pollicino and others (eds), *Copyright and Fundamental Rights in the Digital Age: A Comparative Analysis in Search of a Common Constitutional Ground* (Edward Elgar 2020); Paul Torremans (ed), *Intellectual Property Law and Human Rights* (Information Law Series 34, 4th edn, Kluwer Law International 2020) pt II; Tatiana-Eleni Synodinou, 'The Desirability of Unification of European Copyright Law' in Eleonora Rosati (ed), *The Routledge Handbook of EU Copyright Law* (Routledge Handbooks, 1st edn, Routledge 2021) 18–38.

[5] Rec 31 InfoSoc Directive; Rec 2 IPRED; Rec 6 DSM Directive; Case C-275/06 *Productores de Música de España (Promusicae) v Telefónica de España SAU* [2008] ECLI:EU:C:2008:54, paras 62–68; Joined Cases C-403/08 and C-429/08 *Football Association Premier League and others* [2011] ECLI:EU:C:2011:631, para 164.

[6] See also Giorgos D Vrakas, 'Does Copyright Support Musical Creativity in a Remix Era?' in Tatiana-Eleni Synodinou and others (eds), *EU Internet Law in the Digital Single Market* (Springer International 2021).

entertainment industry, this dimension is linked with the colloquial 'size of the pie' that is, the total revenue stream accruing to the content value chain.

The balance between the artistic and commercial players within this value chain provides the third dimension, which concerns the division of artistic and commercial value between the relevant players – in other words, how the abovementioned 'pie' is 'sliced'.[7] This dimension of the copyright balance is the primary focal point of this book.

3.2.2 *Conceptualising a 'Fair(er) Balance' in the Streaming Age*

The objective is to contribute to a legal framework that is conducive to a fair(er) balance between the interests of the primary music industry stakeholders in the streaming age.[8] A distinction may be made between substantive and procedural aspects. Substantively speaking, the appropriate allocation of resources within a society comes to the fore. This is associated with the objective of ensuring that stakeholders receive a 'fair share'. Fairness also implies the procedural dimension of 'fair play'. In order to ensure that the allocated share is and remains fair, relevant processes should attain certain procedural benchmarks. Keywords in this context include transparency and legal certainty.

As to the question of 'fair share', the framework provided by varying theories of distributive justice forms a welcome starting point.[9] Theories of distributive justice accord varying weight to considerations such as efficiency, equality, liberty and entitlement in justifying 'their' account of what should be considered as a just allocation of resources. Broadly speaking, a distinction may be made between egalitarian and libertarian schools of thought, whereby the primary focus either lies with securing equality and equal treatment, or autonomy and freedom.

A prevailing (liberalist) egalitarian theory is John Rawls' perspective on justice as fairness.[10] Rawls theorises about a hypothetical scenario in which a group of people

[7] Cf David Felipe Alvarez-Amezquita and Florelia Vallejo-Trujillo, 'Limiting Freedom of Contract' in Jens Schovsbo (ed), *The Exploitation of Intellectual Property Rights: In Search of the Right Balance* (ATRIP Intellectual Property, Edward Elgar 2023) 216–18.

[8] Cf Stefan Scheuerer, 'The Fairness Principle in Competition-Related Economic Law' [2023] GRUR International 1; Giuseppe Mazziotti and Heritiana Ranaivoson, 'Can Online Music Platforms Be Fair? An Interdisciplinary Research Manifesto' [2024] 55 IIC 249–279.

[9] See Serena Olsaretti (ed), *The Oxford Handbook on Distributive Justice* (Oxford University Press 2018).

[10] Rawls, *Justice as Fairness: A Restatement* (n 1); John Rawls, *A Theory of Justice* (original ed, Belknap Press 2005). On other egalitarian theories, see ia Ronald Dworkin, 'What Is Equality? Part 2: Equality of Resources' (1981) 10 Philosophy and Public Affairs 283; Richard J Arneson, 'Equality and Equal Opportunity for Welfare' (1989) 56 Philosophical Studies 77; Gerald A Cohen, 'On the Currency of Egalitarian Justice' (1989) 99 Ethics 906; GA Cohen, *Rescuing Justice and Equality* (Harvard University Press 2008); Lars Lindblom, 'The Structure of a Rawlsian Theory of Just Work' (2011) 101 Journal of Business Ethics 577; Eliane Saadé, *The Concept of Justice and Equality: On the Dispute between John Rawls and*

must decide on the modalities of their society – what counts as fair terms of cooperation – without knowing what place they will occupy in it.[11] The chosen principles are to be binding to all and, moreover, irrevocable once the veil of ignorance is lifted. Rawls posits that, starting from this 'original position' and conscious of the irrevocable nature of the choices made in this context, a political and economic basic structure will be unveiled that operates under conditions that are fair for all.[12] In Rawls' view, the principles of justice that participants in his thought experiment would agree upon are twofold. First, each citizen would be guaranteed a set of certain equal basic, fundamental liberties, including freedom of thought and speech and the right to bodily integrity.[13] Second, social and economic inequalities would be attached to positions and offices that are open to all and would moreover work to the advantage of those worst off.[14] The former principle is referred to as 'fair equality of opportunity', while the latter is referred to as the 'difference principle'. This view on society requires a certain degree of direct involvement of the state, whose primary goal is to improve the lot of those least fortunate.[15] Rawls' theory is not free from criticism, including for its individualistic conception of what is good and thus worth pursuing, the ideal setting of the 'original position' thought experiment and the difficulties in operationalising the difference principle.[16]

Gerald Cohen (Practical Philosophy 20, De Gruyter 2015); Richard J Arneson, 'Dworkin and Luck Egalitarianism' in Serena Olsaretti (ed), *The Oxford Handbook of Distributive Justice* (Oxford University Press 2018).

11 Rawls, *Justice as Fairness: A Restatement* (n 1) paras 6.2–6.4.

12 See Jean Hampton, 'Contracts and Choices: Does Rawls Have a Social Contract Theory?' (1980) 77 Journal of Philosophy 315.

13 Rawls does not consider the freedom of contract to be a basic liberty in the sense of this first principle of justice, see Rawls, *A Theory of Justice* (n 10) 62; Josse Klijnsma, 'Contract Law as Fairness' (2015) 28 Ratio Juris 68, 84.

14 See eg John Rawls, *Political Liberalism* (The John Dewey Essays in Philosophy 4, Columbia University Press 1993) 289–371; Maciej Barczewski and Dorota Pyć, 'Intellectual Property and Sustainable Development: A Distributive Justice Perspective' in Graeme B Dinwoodie (ed), *Methods and Perspectives in Intellectual Property* (ATRIP Intellectual Property, Edward Elgar 2013) 208; Michael Freeman, *Lloyd's Introduction to Jurisprudence* (9th edn, Sweet & Maxwell 2014) 481–92.

15 Anupam Chander and Madhavi Sunder, 'Is Nozick Kicking Rawls's Ass? Intellectual Property and Social Justice' (2007) 40 UC Davis Law Review 563, 567; Anthony K Kronman, 'Contract Law and Distributive Justice' in Joel Feinberg and Jules Coleman (eds), *Philosophy of Law* (8th edn, Thomson Wadsworth 2008) 820.

16 See eg Donald Schroeder, 'John Rawls and Contract Theory' (1973) 56 Soundings: An Interdisciplinary Journal 338; Robert Paul Wolff, *Understanding Rawls – A Reconstruction and Critique of a Theory of Justice* (Princeton University Press 1977); Roberto Alejandro, *The Limits of Rawlsian Justice* (Johns Hopkins University Press 1998); Henry S Richardson and Paul J Weithman (eds), *The Philosophy of Rawls – A Collection of Essays – 3. Opponents and Implications of* A Theory of Justice (A Garland Series. Readings in Philosophy, Garland 1999); Chandran Kukathas (ed), *John Rawls. Critical Assessments of Leading Political Philosophers – Volumes I through IV* (Routledge 2002); Freeman, *Lloyd's Introduction to Jurisprudence* (n 14) 486–87.

Libertarianism puts much greater emphasis on personal autonomy, responsibility and respect for individual rights. A minimal state is advanced as the most 'just' way to regulate society. One of the main proponents of libertarianism is the entitlement theory advanced by Robert Nozick.[17] Simply put, a transaction pertaining to certain resources is deemed fair from a libertarian point of view if it is voluntary. Thus, the free-market economy is placed squarely in the centre and state intervention that is labelled as paternalistic and overly intrusive is rejected.

The perspective of egalitarians and libertarians also diverges as to the perceived role of (copyright) contract law. The question thus is whether or not contract law should make a conscious effort to influence the allocation of resources within a society through the regulation of transactions.[18] From a libertarian perspective, the answer is negative. A compulsory transfer of resources is considered theft. A Nozickian libertarian's focus on personal responsibility and the protection of both private property and freedom of contract would bring them to consider the idea of countering the results of voluntary transactions on the basis of considerations of equality as implemented through the provisions of contract law as 'unfair'.[19] Conversely, Rawls' theory of 'justice as fairness' may point towards a different conclusion on the basis of egalitarian considerations of equality and inclusivity. The fundamental perceived need to allocate resources in an inclusive way that duly acknowledges the contributions of relevant actors and secures equal opportunities for all stakeholders steers this book in such a direction.[20] The mere fact that both parties have consented to a certain transaction does not in itself imply that the transaction is actually 'voluntary'.[21] The bargaining power of the parties plays a key role. The 'voluntary' nature of copyright-related transactions in the streaming age – the actual 'freedom of contract' in the real sense of the word – is often merely a mirage.[22]

The Rawlsian principles of distributive justice are meant to shape the institutions that contain the 'basic structure'[23] of society from a macro perspective; they provide for fair background conditions, while allowing members of this society to be as free as possible to pursue their own conception of what is good through micro, voluntary

[17] See eg Robert Nozick, *Anarchy, State, and Utopia* (Basic Books 1974); Freeman, *Lloyd's Introduction to Jurisprudence* (n 14) 492–98. See also Martín Hevia, *Reasonableness and Responsibility: A Theory of Contract Law*, vol 101 (Law and Philosophy Library, Springer Netherlands 2013) 33–44. See on other libertarian perspectives eg Peter Vallentyne and Hillel Steiner, *The Origins of Left-Libertarianism* (Palgrave Macmillan UK 2000).

[18] See Hans-Wolfgang Micklitz, 'Social Justice and Access Justice in Private Law' (EUI Working Papers, 2011); Hevia, *Reasonableness and Responsibility* (n 17) vol 101, p. See also Kronman, 'Contract Law and Distributive Justice' (n 15) 809–10.

[19] Cf Kronman, 'Contract Law and Distributive Justice' (n 15) 811, 820.

[20] See for a more elaborate, convincing argument in the same direction eg Kronman, 'Contract Law and Distributive Justice' (n 15) 809–29.

[21] ibid 812.

[22] See Chapter 2, Sections 2.3–2.4.

[23] See on this concept Rawls, *Political Liberalism* (n 14) 257–88.

transactions.[24] It has been argued that Rawls considered this basic structure not to include private contractual relations and that such transactions should remain free from government interference in view of the contracting parties' personal autonomy and responsible agency.[25] The contrary position has also been defended.[26] Independently of the exact appropriate scope of Rawls' 'basic structure', the shaping of contract law should not take place independently of distributive considerations. The mere fact that 'fair' background conditions are available in a given society does not in itself imply that parties will be able to assume personal responsibility and protect themselves against unfair advantage-taking in the context of foreground contractual transactions.[27] There is a risk that less advantaged parties enter into contractual transactions that 'purport to deprive them of resources beyond a Rawlsian sufficiency baseline'.[28] In such cases, the law should intervene, at least to a certain extent. The distributive effects of the relevant contract law framework should not be ignored.[29] If contract law steers away from distributive considerations, it risks losing its moral acceptability.[30]

It would be a bridge too far to assess every individual transaction in terms of its (re) distributive qualities.[31] The original position thought experiment does not require us to presuppose individual parties' intentions and wishes from behind a veil of ignorance. Instead, the presumed veil of ignorance may be said to apply on a more macro level. Rawls' perspective on justice as fairness does not give a definitive answer to the question how a specific rule should be shaped and/or how it should be applied to a particular situation.[32] Instead, it provides a general, overarching thought framework that encourages and guides lawmakers.[33] Micro-level inequalities in bargaining power are deemed relevant for fairness-assessment purposes if they mirror structural inequalities at a more macro level, such as in the case of

[24] Kronman, 'Contract Law and Distributive Justice' (n 15) 821; Lindblom, 'The Structure of a Rawlsian Theory of Just Work' (n 10) 578; Zhong Xing Tan, 'Where the Action Is: Macro and Micro Justice in Contract Law' (2020) 83 Mod Law Rev 725.

[25] See eg Arthur Ripstein, 'Private Order and Public Justice: Kant and Rawls' (2006) 92 Va L Rev 1391, 1393, 1397–98; Kronman, 'Contract Law and Distributive Justice' (n 15) 821.

[26] See eg Kevin A Kordana and David H Tabachnick, 'Rawls and Contract Law' (2005) 73 Geo Wash L Rev 598; Klijnsma, 'Contract Law as Fairness' (n 13); Samuel Scheffler, 'Distributive Justice, the Basic Structure and the Place of Private Law' (2015) 35 Oxford J Legal Stud 213.

[27] Tan, 'Where the Action Is' (n 24) 756.

[28] ibid 757.

[29] Kronman, 'Contract Law and Distributive Justice' (n 15) 822, 826.

[30] Cf ibid 810; Scheffler, 'Distributive Justice' (n 26) 217.

[31] Kronman, 'Contract Law and Distributive Justice' (n 15) 822, 826; Klijnsma, 'Contract Law as Fairness' (n 13) 77. Cf in the context of employment contracts Lindblom, 'The Structure of a Rawlsian Theory of Just Work' (n 10) 586.

[32] Cf Kordana and Tabachnick, 'Rawls and Contract Law' (n 26) 600, 614–15; Ripstein, 'Private Order and Public Justice' (n 25) 1409.

[33] 'Only the complete scheme of all legal and political institutions is directly answerable to the difference principle', see Kordana and Tabachnick, 'Rawls and Contract Law' (n 26) 621.

employment or consumer contracts.[34] A party's status as either an employee or a consumer serves as a proxy for their presumed bargaining power. In classifying a group of people in such a way, the costs of excessive fine-tuning are to be balanced against the objective of being sensitive to inequalities in bargaining power.[35] There are structural inequalities in the streaming age that point towards the appropriateness of classifying musicians – in particular legacy artists – as the category of stakeholders that should be considered 'worst off' and which therefore merits specific and sustained attention when shaping the relevant legal framework from the perspective of fairness.

The goal should be to craft a legal regime that allows stakeholders to arrive at an allocation of resources through contractual transactions that acquires its perceived fairness on the basis of the legal regime.[36] Thus, the fairness assessment takes place independently of the intention of the contracting parties.[37] A balance is required between the objective of securing stakeholders' individual autonomy and the need to set certain limits to the freedom of contract from the perspective of securing equality of opportunity and the operationalisation of the difference principle.[38] If contract law is fair, the fairness of contracts entered into within the framework of this law is presumed.

The development of Rawlsian fairness invites us to further flesh out to which resources the distributive perspective of this book applies. In other words, what relevant resources are there to be (fairly) allocated? Again, various theories may offer fruitful ground for further concretisation.

Pierre Bourdieu's 1986 essay on the forms of capital provides a first useful building block.[39] Bourdieu defines capital as an accumulation of labour and uses it as a way to explain how power is divided in a society.[40] He distinguishes three separate but interconnected types of capital, namely economic, cultural and social capital. First, economic capital focuses on direct remuneration and property (how much money one has). The latter two types of capital are more abstract and symbolic, and only have an indirect monetary link.[41] Cultural capital refers to familiarity with culture and is impacted by personal development, interaction with cultural goods (such as

34 Cf Tan, 'Where the Action Is' (n 24) 738–54.

35 ibid 742.

36 Cf Kordana and Tabachnick, 'Rawls and Contract Law' (n 26) 599–600, 620–23; Klijnsma, 'Contract Law as Fairness' (n 13) 69, 77.

37 Cf Kordana and Tabachnick, 'Rawls and Contract Law' (n 26) 599–600, 620–23; Klijnsma, 'Contract Law as Fairness' (n 13) 69, 77.

38 Kordana and Tabachnick, 'Rawls and Contract Law' (n 26) 626; Klijnsma, 'Contract Law as Fairness' (n 13) 70.

39 Pierre Bourdieu, 'The Forms of Capital' in JG Richardson (ed), *Handbook of Theory and Research for the Sociology of Education* (Greenwood Press 1986). The inclusion of Bourdieu's essay on this topic in the analysis was inspired by Juliet Fraser, 'Sharing the Spoils of a Shared Practice' (2019) 73 Tempo 51.

40 Bourdieu, 'The Forms of Capital' (n 39) 241.

41 ibid 243.

music) and formal education.[42] In the music industry, some degree of cultural capital appears to be a precondition for entry.[43] Social capital is associated with the credentials of belonging to a certain group and the strength of members of a connected network.[44] Capital begets more capital, in the sense that it enhances the owners' capacity for success. The accumulation of capital over time implies the entrenchment of power relations. In the streaming age, issues arise regarding the division of economic and social capital. Reference may be made to (respectively) the distribution of revenues and the negotiating and/or lobbying position of the various stakeholder groups. The perceived added value of Bourdieu's theory in the context of this book lies in its express acknowledgement that allocable resources can have both a direct and an indirect monetary link and that both aspects have an impact on the position of stakeholders in a society. Thus, the road towards a fair(er) balance in the music industry must take due account of both commercial and other incentives.

The body of literature devoted to the 'capability approach' to social justice adds another dimension.[45] It seeks to empower people to live a full and dignified life, by asking (1) what people are actually able to do and be (what their 'internal capabilities' are), (2) what real opportunities are available to them and, ultimately, (3) how public authorities can aid people in realising their capabilities.[46] The capability approach focuses on people's agency and freedom to choose among various options to achieve certain 'doings and beings' they perceive (with reason) to be valuable.[47]

A final aspect that may be added to the baseline of Rawlsian justice in the contractual sphere is the idea of 'reciprocity', of 'reasonableness'.[48] This relational perspective advances the position that 'others are owed a fair return to what they have given you, just as you are owed a fair return for what you have given others'.[49] It presupposes that contracting parties wish to cooperate on fair terms and goes

42 ibid 243–48.

43 This depends on the musical genre, with formal education taking a much prominent place in the field of eg classical music than is the case for popular music.

44 Bourdieu, 'The Forms of Capital' (n 39) 248–52.

45 See ia Martha Nussbaum, *Creating Capabilities. The Human Development Approach* (Belknap Press of Harvard University Press 2011); Amartya Sen, *The Idea of Justice* (Penguin Books 2010); Amartya Sen, *Rationality and Freedom* (Belknap Press of Harvard University Press 2004); Amartya Sen, *Commodities and Capabilities* (Oxford University Press India 1999).

46 See ia Nussbaum, *Creating Capabilities* (n 45) xi, x, 12–14, 18–21, 30–31, 65, 106, 167–69 and 176; Sen, *The Idea of Justice* (n 45) xi, 18, 231 and 233; Justin Hughes and Robert Merges, 'Copyright and Distributive Justice' (2016) 92 Notre Dame L Rev 513, 521–22.

47 Sen, *Rationality and Freedom* (n 45) 585; Ingrid Robeyns, 'The Capability Approach: A Theoretical Survey' (2005) 6 Journal of Human Development 93; Jonathan Wolff and Avner de-Shalit, *Disadvantage* (Oxford University Press 2007) 21–84, 180; Sen, *The Idea of Justice* (n 45) 19, 227–28, 231, 253; Nussbaum, *Creating Capabilities* (n 45) 10–26, 43.

48 See in particular Lindblom, 'The Structure of a Rawlsian Theory of Just Work' (n 10); Hevia, *Reasonableness and Responsibility* (n 17) vol 101, p; Tan, 'Where the Action Is' (n 24) 745–49. Cf also Scheffler, 'Distributive Justice' (n 26) 233–35.

49 Andrea Sangiovanni, 'Global Justice, Reciprocity, and the State' (2007) 35 Philosophy & Public Affairs 3, 26.

beyond the aim of advancing the position of those worst off posited by the difference principle.[50]

In sum, contract law should have a capacity-building role and empower stakeholders who find themselves in a context that postdates the original position to both accomplish their goals through (truly) voluntary transactions and have genuine, sufficiently viable options in this regard.[51] Simultaneously, due account must be taken of stakeholders' legitimate, reciprocal claims for a fair return. Only then can an inclusive, equal division of economic, cultural and social capital be attained.

The translation of these ideas to the music industry in the streaming age requires us first to circle back to the interests of the categories of stakeholders analysed in Chapter 2, namely musicians, corporate partners and users. The relevant findings may be summarised as shown in Table 3.1.

On the part of musicians, a clear focus on agency and remuneration may be discerned. As a result, fairness from the perspective of musicians may be seen to require a certain degree of exploitation of their work(s)/performance(s), with due acknowledgement of their contribution and proper remuneration. Corporate partners' commercial focus on the recoupment of their investment, on the other hand, implies that a fair balance may only be attained if there is no disproportionate limitation of the principle of freedom of contract. Swinging the pendulum too much towards either side may lead to detrimental effects in practice. On the one hand, if the legal framework overreaches and provides a framework that is altogether too protective of musicians in a contractual context, the perverse effect may be that their corporate

TABLE 3.1 *Overview of main legitimate interests*

	Musicians	*Corporate partners*	*Users*
Who?	See typology[52]	Publishers/labels	Private users as group/ individuals
What?	Create/perform disseminate; obtain remuneration	Obtain return on investment; (disseminate)	Access; create (UGC)
Why?	Artistic incentives; economic incentives	Primarily economic incentives	Convenience; legal certainty
Fairness	Agency (exploit / acknowledge); remuneration	Focus on investment (commercial); no undue limitation of freedom of contract	Limited interest; enhance knowledge; account of access

[50] Cf Lindblom, 'The Structure of a Rawlsian Theory of Just Work' (n 10) 577, 583–84.

[51] Cf Nicolas Suzor, 'Access, Progress, and Fairness: Rethinking Exclusivity in Copyright' (2013) 15 Vand J Ent & Tech L 297, 328–29; Bhamati Viswanathan, *Cultivating Copyright: How Creators and Creative Industries Can Harness Intellectual Property to Survive the Digital Age* (Routledge 2019) 231.

[52] See Chapter 2, Section 2.2.2.1.

partners cut back on, or even cease, their investments in the music industry ecosystem. This could in turn leave all parties involved in a worse position than before, begging the question whether a 'bad' contract is better than no contract at all. On the other hand, overtly and fully championing the principle of freedom of contract, allowing the free market to fully run its course, could lead to equally (if not more) perverse effects. Given the rightful central position that the artist holds under the basic tenets of copyright law, such an outcome is undesirable. Finding a fruitful, reciprocal middle ground that does not unduly violate stakeholders' basic liberties in the Rawlsian sense and contributes to the improvement of the situation of the category of stakeholders least well off must therefore be the objective. Third, while users only have a limited interest in the division of resources within the content value chain, this does not mean that their perspective should be cast aside. Instead, a fair(er) balance in the streaming age requires consumer education, while taking account of users' interest in gaining convenient access to protected content. Concomitantly, reference may be made to the presumptive resulting increase in the dissemination of creative works and the enhancement of cultural heritage, which is beneficial to users.

In essence, the objective is to achieve a more balanced contractual playing field in relation to all three stages of the contracts under review.[53] In the contract formation stage, detailed in Chapter 4 below, the keyword in this regard will be a 'fair scope' of rights granted. The transfer of rights to a corporate partner is not considered to be inherently problematic. The question is rather whether the musician receives sufficient return. Thus, in relation to the performance phase of the contract, the focal point of Chapter 5, the question will be whether the contract leads to both 'fair exploitation' and 'fair remuneration'. If either is deemed not to occur, a fair balance requires the musician to be able to either retain or reclaim the relevant rights.[54] Chapter 6 therefore seeks to increase fairness as to the termination of the contracts under review.

The procedural aspect of fairness may be linked with the concept of 'fair play'. It implies due attention to legal certainty and transparency.[55] Here, again, the legal

53 Cf Ananay Aguilar, '"We Want Artists to Be Fully and Fairly Paid for Their Work": Discourses on Fairness in the Neoliberal European Copyright Reform' [2018] JIPITEC 160, 162; Nikita Malevanny, *Online Music Distribution – How Much Exclusivity Is Needed? A Study of International, European, German and US Copyright Systems and Their Objectives*, vol 12 (Munich Studies on Innovation and Competition, Springer Berlin Heidelberg 2019) 317–39.

54 Cf Jane C Ginsburg, 'The Role of the Author in Copyright' in Ruth L Okediji (ed), *Copyright Law in an Age of Limitations and Exceptions* (Cambridge University Press 2017) 70.

55 Cf P Bernt Hugenholtz and Lucie Guibault, 'Auteurscontractenrecht: Naar Een Wettelijke Regeling?' (2004) <https://bit.ly/3UvnwGx> 25, 77; Commission, 'Impact Assessment on the Modernisation of EU Copyright Rules Accompanying the Document Proposal for a Directive of the European Parliament and of the Council on Copyright in the Digital Single Market and Proposal for a Regulation of the European Parliament and of the Council Laying Down Rules on the Exercise of Copyright and Related Rights Applicable to Certain Online Transmissions of Broadcasting Organisations and Retransmissions of Television and Radio Programmes' (Staff Working Document) SWD (2016) 301 Final (14 September 2016) 134.

framework and technological developments must work in tandem. Relevant provisions must be well-structured and clear. Vague concepts that are difficult to apply in practice should be avoided. For musicians, such vagueness, combined with a weaker relative bargaining power, increases the risk of disadvantageous clauses in practice. For corporate partners, legal uncertainty leads to increased transaction costs and a more difficult investment climate.[56]

Moreover, rules must be set at the appropriate level. First, regulatory measures must be suitably divided between the international, EU and national level. Second, focus must not only lie with options for legislative amendments that lead to hard law, but also with the possible value of soft law alternatives. These aspects contribute to a streamlined, transparent regulatory framework that provides legal certainty for all interested parties. This is necessary for its impact on the freedom of contract to be as limited as possible while simultaneously securing protection for musicians as the weaker contracting party.

Further, in order to ensure both substantive and procedural fairness, the application of the legal framework in practice must be secured. In this context, this book supplements Rawlsian idealism with ambitious pragmatism. Unfair situations in the music industry are exacerbated by its characteristics as a high-risk, high-reward concentrated marketplace with a pronounced inclination towards superstars. Precisely those characteristics lead to obstacles between the legislator's objectives and their translation into practice – in other words: between the 'law in the books' and the 'law in action'. This explains the express focus on the application of the legal framework in practice in Chapter 7 below.

3.3 TYPOLOGY OF THE SELECTED SUBSTANTIVE LEGAL REGIMES

3.3.1 *General Limitations to Freedom of Contract*

The freedom of contract is a central tenet of contract law.[57] It implies parties' freedom to (not) enter into a contractual relationship with one another, as well as

[56] Cf Aguilar, 'We Want Artists' (n 53) 167.

[57] See eg (1) in Belgium: Art 1134 Belgian CC; Sophie Stijns, *Verbintenissenrecht. Boek 1* (die Keure 2005) 37–54; Ignace Claeys and Thijs Tanghe, *Algemeen Contractenrecht. Handboek voor Nu en Straks* (Intersentia 2021) 43–53; (2) in France: Art 1102 French CC; Yvaine Buffelan-Lanore and Virginie Larribau-Terneyre, *Droit Civil. Les obligations* (16th edn, Sirey 2018) 294–96, 331–34; François Terré and others, *Droit Civil. Les Obligations* (Précis. Droit privé, 12th edn, Dalloz 2019) 34–38, 159–61; (3) in Germany: Art 2(1) *Grundgesetz für die Bundesrepublik Deutschland* (in English: 'German Basic Law') <www.gesetze-im-internet.de/gg/BJNR000010949.html>; Basil S Markesinis and others, *The German Law of Contract. A Comparative Treatise* (2nd edn, Hart 2006) 43–46; Dieter Medicus and Stephan Lorenz, *Schuldrecht I. Allgemeiner Teil* (Juristische Kurz-Lehrbücher, 21st edn, CH Beck 2015) 26–32; Wolfgang Fikentscher and Andreas Heinemann, *Schuldrecht: Allgemeiner und Besonderer Teil* (De Gruyter Studium, 11th edn, De Gruyter 2017) 70–90; (4) in the Netherlands: Art 6:248 Dutch CC; Hugenholtz and Guibault, 'Auteurscontractenrecht' (n 55) 77; Carel Asser,

their freedom to determine a contract's content. Parties' freedom of contract is limited on several fronts. The general limitations under contract law in the continental European jurisdictions under review in this book are included in the main civil codes.[58] A first general limitation is provided by the principle of good faith that applies in contractual situations.[59] This principle implies that contract parties' behaviour is subjected to an obligation of loyalty and limited to what befits a reasonable participant of society.[60] The principle of good faith may provide a legal basis to set aside contractual provisions that are excessive, unreasonable, unacceptable and thus deemed contrary to good faith.[61] In a way, this leads to an objectification of parties' expected behaviour. No articulated general contractual duty to perform in good faith applies under UK law.[62]

Associated limitations stem from the rules concerning vitiated consent and the general prohibition of abuse of law. Parties may not exploit the vulnerability or the inferior position of their counterparty in a way that leads to a manifest disproportion between the obligations of the contracting parties.[63] Parties' freedom of contract is also limited by the requirements of public policy and good morals.[64] For the United

Verbintenissenrecht. Algemeen Overeenkomstenrecht (Asser Serie 6.III*, 13th edn, Kluwer 2008) 33–50; Jac Hijma and others, *Rechtshandeling en Overeenkomst* (Studiereeks burgerlijk recht 3, 9th edn, Kluwer 2019) 14; and (5) in the United Kingdom: Joseph Chitty and Hugh Beale, *Chitty on Contracts* (32nd edn, Sweet & Maxwell 2015) 22–24; Neil Andrews, *Contract Rules: Decoding English Law* (Intersentia 2016) 3–6; Edwin Peel, *Treitel on the Law of Contract* (15th edn, Sweet & Maxwell 2020) 3–4; Mindy Chen-Wishart, *Contract Law* (7th edn, Oxford University Press 2022) 14–15. See also Giuseppina D'Agostino, 'Contract Lex Rex: Towards Copyright Contract's Lex Specialis' in Graeme Dinwoodie (ed), *Intellectual Property and General Legal Principles* (Edward Elgar 2015) 6–10.

58 See (1) in Belgium: *'Burgerlijk Wetboek'/'Code Civil'* (commonly abbreviated as 'BW'/'CC', with ongoing codification of the existing *'oud Burgerlijk Wetboek'/'ancien Code Civil'*, hereinafter: Belgian CC), full text at <www.ejustice.just.fgov.be>; (2) in France: *'Code Civil'* (commonly abbreviated as CC, hereinafter: French CC), full text at <https://bit.ly/3ArdSIM>; (3) in Germany: *'Bürgerliches Gesetzbuch'* (commonly abbreviated as BGB, hereinafter: German CC), full text at <www.gesetze-im-internet.de/bgb>; and (4) in the Netherlands: *'Burgerlijk Wetboek'* (commonly abbreviated as BW or NBW, hereinafter: Dutch CC), full text at <https://wetten.overheid.nl>.

59 See (1) in Belgium: Art 1134 para 3 old Belgian CC; Art 5.73 new Belgian Civil Code; (2) in France: Art 1104 French CC; (3) in Germany: Art 242 German CC; and (4) in the Netherlands: Arts 6:2, 6:248 Dutch Civil Code.

60 Lucie Guibault, *Copyright Limitations and Contracts: An Analysis of the Contractual Overridability of Limitations on Copyright* (Information Law Series 9, Kluwer Law International 2002) 146; Lucie Guibault and P Bernt Hugenholtz, 'Study on the Conditions Applicable to Contracts Relating to Intellectual Property in the European Union' (2002) <https://bit.ly/4bzdGud> 13.

61 Guibault, *Copyright Limitations and Contracts* (n 60) 146.

62 Chitty and Beale, *Chitty on Contracts* (n 57) 35–38; Andrews, *Contract Rules* (n 57) 15–16; Peel, *Treitel on the Law of Contract* (n 57) 2–3; Chen-Wishart, *Contract Law* (n 57) 619–21.

63 See eg (1) in Belgium: Art 1134(3) Belgian CC; (2) in France: Art 1104 French CC; (3) in Germany: Art 226 *jo* 242 German CC; and (4) in the Netherlands: Art 3:13 *jo* 6:248 Dutch CC.

64 See eg (1) in Belgium: Arts 2, 1133 Belgian Civil Code; (2) in France: Arts 6, 1162 French Civil Code; (3) in Germany: Art 138 German Civil Code; (4) in the Netherlands: Art 3:40(1) Dutch

Kingdom in particular, the doctrines of undue influence and restraint of trade are noted.[65]

Theoretical restrictions on parties' behaviour set by general principles of contract law are only applied in exceptional situations, with judges traditionally favouring the freedom of contract.[66] Moreover, the open-ended nature of many of these restrictions makes it hard to predict their application in practice, which in turn leads to legal uncertainty.[67] In view of this, the intervention of more specific substantive legal regimes may be desirable. In order to fill this perceived gap, parties' contractual freedom is additionally curtailed by specific legal regimes, the scope of which is analysed in the next section.

3.3.2 *Scope of Selected Substantive Legal Regimes*

3.3.2.1 Structure

The following chapters of this book analyse the relevant substantive provisions of copyright contract law and the law of unfair B2B contract terms and trade practices, as well as their interplay with the main relevant provisions of general contract law.

Before delving into the substantive analysis of these provisions in Chapters 4–6, it is important to have a clear view on the scope of and interplay between these seemingly diverse fields of law. Following an overview of the relevant legislative sources of copyright contract law and the law of unfair B2B contract terms and trade practices, the substantive scope of the selected legal regimes in the chosen jurisdictions is analysed. This analysis not only focuses on the scope of *ratione materiae* and *ratione personae* – that is, based on the object of and the parties to the contract respectively – but also on the interplay between these fields of law. Then, this section analyses the geographical scope of the selected legal regimes. Finally, the temporal scope of the applicable legal regimes is reviewed.

3.3.2.2 Overview of Legislative Sources

The relevant provisions of copyright contract law are included in the acts that provide the national copyright framework in the chosen jurisdictions: the Belgian

Civil Code; and (5) in the UK: Chitty and Beale, *Chitty on Contracts* (n 57) 1235–40; Andrews, *Contract Rules* (n 57) 64–97; Chen-Wishart, *Contract Law* (n 57) 488–90.

65 Chitty and Beale, *Chitty on Contracts* (n 57) ch 8, 16; Andrews, *Contract Rules* (n 57) 81–84, 130–33; Peel, *Treitel on the Law of Contract* (n 57) 512–29, 605–32; Lionel Bently and others, *Intellectual Property Law* (6th edn, Oxford University Press 2022) 347–52.

66 Hugenholtz and Guibault, 'Auteurscontractenrecht' (n 55) 30, 76; Alexandre Cruquenaire, *L'Interprétation des Contrats en Droit d'Auteur* (Création Information Communication 11, Larcier 2007) 411; Barbara Baarsma and Nicole Rosenboom, 'Oneerlijke Handelspraktijken. Voldoet Bestaande (Zelf)regulering?' (2013) 21; Séverine Dusollier and others, 'Contractual Arrangements Applicable to Creators: Law and Practice of Selected Member States' (Publications Office of the EU 2014) <https://op.europa.eu/s/zIba> 6 51.

67 Cf Baarsma and Rosenboom, 'Oneerlijke Handelspraktijken' (n 66) 20–21, 24.

CEL, the French IP Code, the German Copyright Act, and the Dutch Copyright Act and Act on Neighbouring Rights. Under German law, a separate act provides a specific, albeit largely contractually waivable regime for publishing contracts that applies to works of literature and music, namely the *Verlagsgesetz* (in English: Publishing Act).[68] It is referred to below as the German Publishing Act.

The United Kingdom is the 'odd one out' here, as no specific copyright contract law applies to exploitation contracts.[69] Instead, the law of contracts applies.[70] However, change may be on the horizon, even though the UK legislator decided not to proceed with the implementation of the DSM Directive subsequent to Brexit.[71] At the close of 2021, a bill was introduced in the UK Parliament that sought to establish a number of limitations on parties' freedom in relation to copyright exploitation contracts, partially mirroring certain requirements set by the DSM Directive.[72] This bill, referenced below as the 'Brennan Bill', did not materialise into hard law.[73] However, the UK Intellectual Property Office (UKIPO) provided extensive additional support for potential legislative action in the form of a report published in February 2023.[74] This issue therefore appears still to be on the agenda of the UK legislator.

The contractual relationships under review may also be affected by legal regimes concerning unfair B2B contract terms and trade practices. Specific legal provisions in the chosen jurisdictions prohibit the inclusion of unfair terms in contract, as well as certain trade practices labelled as unfair.[75] As opposed to what is the case in B2C situations,[76] the law of unfair B2B contract terms and trade practices largely lacks

68 *Gesetz über das Verlagsrecht*, full text at <www.gesetze-im-internet.de/verlg>. See Wirt Soetenhorst, *De bescherming van de uitgeefprestatie* (WEJ Tjeenk Willink 1993); Ludwig Delp, *Der Verlagsvertrag. Handbuch für die Praxis* (8th edn, CH Beck 2008).

69 Although some specific legislative measures have been maintained subsequent to Brexit, specifically those accompanying the increased duration of protection for phonograms, see Chapter 5, Sections 5.2.2.3.1 and 5.3.2.2.1.

70 Richard Arnold, *Performers' Rights* (6th edn, Sweet & Maxwell 2021) 275, 280; Lionel Bently and others, *Intellectual Property Law* (6th edn, Oxford University Press 2022) 347.

71 *Copyright: EU Action: Written Question – 4371 of 2020* UK Parliament, UK Parliament (2020); Paul Torremans, 'Transposition of the DSM Copyright Directive 2019/790 in the United Kingdom' [2021] AM 374 374–75; Paul Torremans and Alina Trapova, 'The Copyright Contracts of Tomorrow: A British Point of View' in Simon Geiregat and Hendrik Vanhees (eds), *Copyright Contracts Tomorrow* (LeA 2023) 85–90.

72 Copyright (Rights and Remuneration of Musicians, Etc.) HC Bill (2021–22) 19; Chris Cooke, 'Kevin Brennan MP's Controversial Music Copyright Proposals Discussed in Parliament' (*CMU*, 3 December 2021) <https://bit.ly/3Lo5YGY>; Stuard Dredge, 'Brennan Bill Second Reading: What Happened… And What Happens Next' (*Music Ally*, 3 December 2021) <https://bit.ly/34Pw4Co>.

73 Bently and others, *Intellectual Property Law* (n 70) 353–54.

74 Richard Osborne and Hyojung Sun, 'Economics of Streaming: Contract Adjustment and Rights Reversion' (6 February 2023).

75 The concept of unfair trade practices also includes unfair behaviour linked to an individual contractual relationship.

76 See Andrews, *Contract Rules* (n 57) 239–42.

harmonisation at the EU level. The relevant provisions of Belgian law as to both B2B unfair contract terms and trade practices are included in Book VI of the Belgian CEL. In Belgium, relevant legislative changes were made by a 2019 act, which added a number of particularly stringent provisions concerning B2B relationships that have a significant impact on the freedom of contract.[77] The French legal framework on law of unfair B2B contract terms and trade practices is somewhat fragmented: both the French Commercial Code[78] (as amended in 2019[79]) and the French Civil Code[80] bear relevance.[81] In Germany, there is no general restriction on unfair B2B contract terms that were negotiated individually. As to unfair trade practices, the uniform regime applicable to both B2B and business-to-consumer (B2C) situations set by the *Gesetz gegen den unlauteren Wettbewerb*[82] is noted. Finally, in the Netherlands, no separate general restrictions exist as to either unfair B2B contract terms or trade practices. Instead, the B2B sphere is regulated through principles of general contract law and extra-contractual liability.[83]

A related doctrine, associated with the law of unfair contract terms and trade practices in some jurisdictions, but with competition law in others, is that of abuse of economic dependence.[84] In the chosen jurisdictions, at the time of writing, this doctrine exists in Belgium, France and Germany.[85]

77 *Wet van 4 april 2019 houdende Wijziging van het Wetboek van Economisch Recht met Betrekking tot Misbruiken van Economische Afhankelijkheid, Onrechtmatige Bedingen en Oneerlijke Marktpraktijken tussen Ondernemingen, Belgisch Staatsblad* (Belgian Official Gazette, hereinafter: BS) 24 May 2019, 50066 (hereinafter: Belgian B2B Act).

78 See Arts L 442-1–L 442-8 French Commercial Code.

79 See *Ordonnance no 2019-359 du 24 avril 2019 portant refonte du titre IV du livre IV du code de commerce relatif à la transparence, aux pratiques restrictives de concurrence et aux autres pratiques prohibées, Journal Officiel de la République Française* (French Official Gazette, hereinafter: JORF) No 0097, 25 April 2019.

80 See Art 1171 French Civil Code.

81 See also as to the potential relevance of the *Code de la Consommation* in a B2B context Sofie De Pourcq, *Oneerlijke Handelspraktijken en Bedingen in Contracten Tussen Ondernemingen* (Intersentia 2018) 161–62, 352.

82 In English: Act on Unfair Competition, commonly abbreviated as UWG.

83 See eg Baarsma and Rosenboom, 'Oneerlijke Handelspraktijken (n 66) 7–17; Léon Korsten and Jolein Movig, 'Belgische wetswijziging introduceert B2B-bescherming; een voorbeeld voor Nederland?' (2020) 23 M&M 68, 74–76.

84 The doctrine of abuse of economic dependence is deemed to be part of competition law if the relevant provisions require the behaviour at issue to have an anticompetitive effect, as is the case in Belgium (see Art IV.2/1 Belgian CEL), as to *pratiques anticoncurrentielles* in France (see Art L 420-2(2) French Commercial Code) and in Germany (see Art 20 *Gesetz gegen Wettbewerbsbeschränkungen*, in English: Act against Restraints of Competition, commonly abbreviated as GWB). This is not the case if no anticompetitive effect is required, such as is the case with *pratiques restrictives de concurrence* in France (Arts L 442-1–L 442-8 French Commercial Code).

85 The Dutch legal system does not foresee a dedicated regime prohibiting abuse of economic dependence. Instead, recourse may be had to the prohibition of abuse of a dominant position under competition law, general contract law mechanisms or instances of self-regulation, see Baarsma and Rosenboom, 'Oneerlijke Handelspraktijken' (n 66) 7–37.

3.3.2.3 Substantive Scope

3.3.2.3.1 OBJECT OF THE CONTRACT The substantive scope of the selected substantive legal regimes may first be qualified on the basis of the object of the contract. This refers to the legal consequences of a contract and, thus, the resulting obligations for the parties. Provisions of general contract law are not limited to a certain type of contract and thus apply regardless of the contract's object.

Copyright contract law applies to contracts that have as their object to establish a transfer of or a licence to works protected by copyright and/or fixations of performances protected by the neighbouring right of performing artists ('copyright exploitation contracts').

A first, general category of provisions of copyright contract law applies to all copyright exploitation contracts, both when the contract at issue results in a transfer of exploitation rights and in case a licence is granted. The rules applicable to exclusive and non-exclusive licences are not identical.[86] Further, given the particular status of moral rights, the law applicable to such rights differs from the rules that apply to the grant of exploitation rights.

The relevant provisions of French law only refer to the concept of *cession*.[87] However, it is commonly accepted that this concept (which may be equated to the English 'assignment') includes both transfer (*aliénation*) and licence (*licence*) contracts.[88] The relevant provisions of Belgian copyright contract law expressly refer to both transfers and licences.[89] German law does not allow authors to transfer exclusive rights.[90] For performers, Article 79(2a) German Copyright Act expressly specifies that the protective rules of copyright contract law apply to both transfers and licences. Dutch law, finally, defines the scope of application of the relevant provisions relating to copyright *sensu stricto* by referring to the grant of a right to

[86] See eg Chapter 5, Section 5.2.2.3 concerning indirect duties to exploit.

[87] This book does not treat the specific regimes applicable under French law to so-called *contrats à compte d'auteur* and *contrats de compte à demi*, for want of any *cession* that takes place in such a case (Art L 132-2–3 French IP Code). See Hendrik Vanhees, *Een Juridische Analyse van de Grondslagen, Inhoud en Draagwijdte van Auteursrechtelijke Exploitatiecontracten* (Maklu 1993) 17–19; André Lucas and others, *Traité de la Propriété Littéraire et Artistique* (5th edn, LexisNexis 2017) 682–84; Pierre-Yves Gautier, *Propriété Littéraire et Artistique* (11th edn, Presses Universitaires de France 2019) 618–19; Christophe Caron, *Droit d'Auteur et Droits Voisins* (6th edn, LexisNexis 2020) 482–84.

[88] See eg Sébastien Raimond, *La Qualification du Contrat d'Auteur* (Le Droit des Affaires. Propriété Intellectuelle 34, LexisNexis 2009) 455–56; Brigitte Lindner, 'European Union. Part A – Copyright and Contract Law Issues' in René Viljoen (ed), *Cross-Border Copyright Licensing Law and Practice* (Elgar Intellectual Property Law and Practice, Edward Elgar 2018) 81; Lucas and others, *Traité de la Propriété Littéraire et Artistique* (n 87) 608–10, 1129–30.

[89] Arts XI.167, XI.205 Belgian CEL.

[90] See Chapter 4, Section 4.4.1.1.

exploit.[91] Thus, in these jurisdictions, the qualification of a copyright exploitation contract as a licence does not allow contracting parties to evade the relevant provisions.

Copyright contract law also provides different sets of rules for certain contract types. These specific regimes differ as to their effect on parties' freedom of contract. The first contract type subject to specific regulation in Belgium, France and Germany is the publishing contract.[92] Such a contract may be defined as a contract through which the author of a work protected by copyright *sensu stricto* (or, in certain cases, their successor(s) in title), grants their corporate partner (the 'publisher') the right to reproduce or have reproduced, make available and distribute this work for the purpose of publication and dissemination.[93] These rules apply to contracts between composers and music publishers, but not to contracts between performers and record companies.[94] The researched provisions particular to publishing contracts were clearly drafted with a literary context in mind. Regardless, the concept of 'publishing contracts' is interpreted broadly as including both literary publishing and music publishing.[95]

A specific set of rules is sometimes foreseen in employment situations and for certain categories of commissioned music – either compositions or performances.[96] In such cases, the contractual playing field is considered to be more level and thus the objective of protecting artists as presumed weaker parties to a contract is deemed to apply to a lesser extent.[97] On the one hand, musicians may be active under an employment contract or deemed to be employees in accordance with the applicable social statute. Although factually and legally distinct from the US concept of works

91 Art 25b(1) Dutch Copyright Act; Dirk Visser and others, *ACR: Auteurscontractenrecht* (DeLex 2016) 49–82; Dirk Visser, 'Dutch Copyright Contract Law' in Simon Geiregat and Hendrik Vanhees (eds), *Copyright Contracts Tomorrow* (LeA 2023) 25–27.

92 See (1) in Belgium: Arts XI.195–XI.200 Belgian CEL; (2) in France: Arts L 132-1–L 132-17-8 French IP Code; and (3) in Germany: German Publishing Act.

93 Cf (1) under Belgian law: Fernand De Visscher and Benoît Michaux, *Précis du Droit d'Auteur et des Droits Voisins* (Bruylant 2000) 343–45; Hendrik Vanhees, 'Art XI.195' in Fabienne Brison and Hendrik Vanhees (eds), *Hommage à Jan Corbet Huldeboek* (3rd edn, Larcier 2018) 309–10; Hendrik Vanhees, 'Auteurscontract' [2019] OBO 1, 37–39; (2) under French law: Art L 132-1 *jo* L 132-2, 132-3 French IP Code; Lucas and others, *Traité de la Propriété Littéraire et Artistique* (n 87) 680–84; and (3) under German law: Art 1 German Publishing Act; Delp, *Der Verlagsvertrag* (n 68) 4–9; Friedrich Karl Fromm and Wilhelm Nordemann, *Urheberrecht. Kommentar zum Urheberrechtsgesetz, zum Verlagsgesetz und zum Urheberrechtswahrnehmungsgesetz* (Rechtswissenschaften und Verwaltung, 10th edn, Kohlhammer 2008) 2030–37.

94 Fabienne Brison, *Het Naburig Recht van de Uitvoerende Kunstenaar* (Creatie Informatie Communicatie 7, Larcier 2001) 448; Alain Berenboom, *Le Nouveau Droit d'Auteur et les Droits Voisins* (Création Information Communication 1, 3rd edn, Larcier 2005) 228; Dusollier and others, 'Contractual Arrangements Applicable to Creators' (n 66) 123.

95 See Vanhees, 'Art XI.195' (n 93) 310.

96 See (1) in Belgium: Arts XI.167(3), XI.205(4) Belgian CEL; (2) in France: Art L132–31 French IP Code; and (3) in the Netherlands: Art 25b(3) Dutch Copyright Act; Art 3 Dutch Neighbouring Rights Act.

97 Cf Rec 72 DSM Directive.

'made for hire',[98] this refers to music that the musicians at issue were, in essence, 'hired' to make. For specific rules to apply, the relevant music must arise in the course *and* in the context of the performance of the employment relationship.[99] Notably, under Dutch law, the employer is deemed to be the author of works created by the employee. As a result, the relevant protective provisions of copyright contract law do not apply to employees that create works susceptible to protection under copyright *sensu stricto*.[100] This rule does not apply as such to performers. Instead, under Dutch law, employers of performers are granted the right to exploit the exclusive rights granted to performers to the extent that this is foreseen in the contract, or follows from either the nature of the contract, common practices or reasonableness.[101] Further, not all of the chosen jurisdictions provide specific rules applicable to employment situations: German law expressly provides that the protective rules of copyright contract law also apply to employment relationships, unless the terms or the nature of this relationship dictate otherwise.[102] French law contains no such specification, but does not foresee any specific rules pertaining to the rights of employed musicians either. Finally, Belgian law provides a number of specifications as to the regime applicable to employment contracts, as well as 'commissioned' content.[103]

On the other hand, specific rules are also foreseen for 'commissioned' music, which result from a specific 'commission' for a particular context or purpose. The protective provisions of Dutch copyright contract law do not apply to commissioned content that is primarily intended for 'use by the commissioning party'.[104] Also under Belgian and French law, more permissive regimes apply.[105]

Thus, the law foresees differing rules for music made in an employment context and/or on commission, in terms of both ownership and exploitation. There are

98 See eg Hannibal Travis, *Copyright Class Struggle: Creative Economies in a Social Media Age* (1st edn, Cambridge University Press 2018) 21–55; Donald Passman, *All You Need to Know about the Music Business* (10th edn, Simon & Schuster 2019) 307–10.

99 Brison, *Het Naburig Recht van de Uitvoerende Kunstenaar* (n 94) 451–52.

100 Art 7 Dutch Copyright Act.

101 Art 3 Neighbouring Rights Act.

102 Art 43 German Copyright Act.

103 De Visscher and Michaux, *Précis du Droit d'Auteur* (n 93) 335–41; Marina Markellou, *Le Contrat d'Exploitation d'Auteur. Vers un Droit d'Auteur Contractuel Européen. Analyse Comparative des Systèmes Juridiques Allemand, Belge, Français et Hellénique* (Création Information Communication, Larcier 2012) 127–29. See eg Chapter 4, Section 4.4.3.

104 This may lead to issues for tunes or jingles, see P Bernt Hugenholtz, 'Towards Author's Paradise: The New Dutch Act on Authors' Contracts' in Gunnar Karnell and others (eds), *Liber Amicorum Jan Rosén* (eddy.se ab 2016) 401–02; Stef van Gompel and others, 'Evaluatie Wet Auteurscontractenrecht: Eindrapport' (2020) <https://bit.ly/3UBZrh4> 23–25.

105 See (1) in Belgium: Hendrik Vanhees, *De wettelijke regeling inzake auteurscontracten* (Recht en Praktijk 69, Kluwer 2012) 75–83; Vanhees, 'Auteurscontract' (n 93) 75–85 and (2) in France: Art L 132-31 French IP Code; Conseil Supérieur de la Propriété Littéraire et Artistique (CSPLA), 'Rapport de Mission. Le Contrat de Commande', 2020, available (with annexes) at <https://bit.ly/4b8aQfT>.

several arguments in favour of increased simplicity.[106] This rings especially true in the music industry, where recourse to employee status through short-term employment contracts for specific creative output is a recurring strategy to ensure social security protection and mitigate precarious social situations.[107] A linked observation is that the day-to-day practice of employed and freelance musicians is often quite similar – with large ensembles frequently calling upon the services of musicians of both categories and many freelance musicians consistently being asked to work for a select set of corporate partners or even a single corporate partner.[108] The distinct treatment of employees and non-employees may therefore be problematic.[109] A solution could be to presume the existence of an employment relationship in cases where a situation of economic dependence exists for the artist.[110] This concept may be defined by analogy to the regimes concerning abuse of economic dependence in B2B situations, namely as a situation where the market power of an undertaking vis-à-vis their contracting party allows them to force certain contract conditions on this contracting party that would not have been accepted in the absence of such market power.[111] Alternatively, freelancers in a situation comparable to that of employees, in the sense that they cannot determine their own conduct on the music market, may be qualified as 'false self-employed'. This, in turn, supports the argument in favour of an analogue legal status.[112]

Finally, copyright contract law may provide specific rules for performance contracts[113] and audio-visual production contracts.[114] Save the presumption of transfer of exploitation rights in an audio-visual context,[115] these regimes are not discussed in detail in this volume.

[106] Alain Strowel and Bernard Vanbrabant, 'Copyright Licensing: A European View' in Jacques de Werra (ed), *Research Handbook on Intellectual Property Licensing* (Research Handbooks in Intellectual Property, Edward Elgar 2013) 46–47.

[107] European Copyright Society, 'Comment of the European Copyright Society Addressing Selected Aspects of the Implementation of Articles 18 to 22 of the Directive (EU) 2019/790 on Copyright in the Digital Single Market' [2020] JIPITEC 132, 136.

[108] Lionel Bently and others, 'Strengthening the Position of Press Publishers and Authors and Performers in the Copyright Directive' (2017)52.

[109] European Copyright Society, 'Comment' (n 107) 136, 146.

[110] Cf Art L 7121-3 *jo* Art L 7121-4 French Labour Code; Europe Economics and others, 'Remuneration of Authors and Performers for the Use of Their Works and the Fixations of Their Performances. Final Report' (Publications Office of the EU 2015) <https://op.europa.eu/s/zIa9> 58, 140–41, 150–51; Lucas and others, *Traité de la Propriété Littéraire et Artistique* (n 87) 1138; Caron, *Droit d'Auteur et Droits Voisins* (n 87) 638–39.

[111] See eg in Belgium: Art I.6(12*bis*) Belgian CEL.

[112] Cf Case C-413/13 *FNV Kunsten Informatie en Media (KIEM) v Staat der Nederlanden* [2014] ECLI:EU:C:2014:2411, para 31.

[113] See (1) in Belgium: Arts XI.201–202 Belgian CEL and (2) in France: Arts L 132-18–L 132-22 French IP Code.

[114] See (1) in Belgium: Arts XI.179–XI.185 and XI.206 Belgian CEL and (2) in France: Arts L 132-23–L 132-30 and L 212-4–L 212-9 French IP Code.

[115] See Chapter 4, Section 4.3.1.

3.3.2.3.2 PARTIES TO THE CONTRACT This subsection treats the personal scope of the selected substantive legal regimes. Principles of general contract law apply regardless of the identity of the parties to the contract. Conversely, both the relevant provisions of copyright contract law and the law of unfair B2B contract terms and trade practices seek to level the contractual playing field in situations where one of the parties has a weaker bargaining position than the other. The personal scope of these regimes is tailored to cases where such a protective attitude is merited.

The personal scope of application of the protective regimes of both copyright contract law and the law of unfair B2B contract terms and trade practices as to corporate partners is quite broad.

First, the identity of the corporate partner does little to affect the scope of application of the relevant provisions of copyright contract law, provided that the object of the contract is for the corporate partner to carry out exploitation activities in accordance with the contract.[116] Illustrative reference may be made to Recital 72 DSM Directive, which provides that its provisions on copyright exploitation contracts do not apply when the corporate partners merely act as end users and do not exploit the music themselves.[117]

Second, the personal scope of the law of unfair contract terms and trade practices differs slightly between the chosen jurisdictions.[118] In any case, one would be hard-pushed to find a corporate partner engaged in the music industry contracts under review that does not fall within the scope of all of them.

The personal scope of copyright contract law vis-à-vis musicians is simultaneously broader and narrower in scope than is the case for the law of unfair B2B contract terms and trade practices. Subject to specific regimes that apply to music made in an employment context or on commission, the protective provisions of copyright contract law apply to persons that qualify as authors and/or performers under the law of copyright.[119] Natural persons who are active as musicians thus fall within the scope of the protective regimes.[120] As confirmed by Recital 72 DSM Directive, the

[116] Cf Hendrik Vanhees, 'Auteurscontracten en de Problematiek inzake Werken Gemaakt in Opdracht of in Uitvoering van een Arbeidsovereenkomst of Statuut' in Frank Gotzen (ed), *Belgisch Auteursrecht van Oud naar Nieuw Le Renouveau du Droit d'Auteur en Belgique* (CIR 11, Bruylant 1996) 295; Raimond, *La Qualification du Contrat d'Auteur* (n 88) 227–28; Nathalie Blanc, *Les Contrats du Droit d'Auteur à l'Epreuve de la Distinction des Contrats Nommés et Innommés* (Nouvelle Bibliothèque de Thèses 93, Dalloz 2010) 47–49. As to the status of investment companies such as Hipgnosis under copyright contract law, see Dirk Visser and Syb Terpstra, 'De stelling van Pythagoras. De lumpsumoverdracht van muziekrechten aan investeringsmaatschappijen en het auteurscontractenrecht' [2023] Auteursrecht 4.

[117] Rec 72 DSM Directive.

[118] See in detail De Pourcq, *Oneerlijke Handelspraktijken* (n 81) 157–71, 398–401.

[119] See, however, Art 48 German Publishing Act, which provides that the provisions of this Act also apply if the person concluding the contract with the publisher is not the author.

[120] Vanhees, 'Auteurscontracten en de Problematiek inzake Werken Gemaakt in Opdracht of in Uitvoering van een Arbeidsovereenkomst of Statuut' (n 116) 292; Dirk Visser, 'Pippi Langkous en het nieuwe auteurscontractenrecht' [2015] NJB 1289, 1291; Hugenholtz, 'Towards Author's

same should be true for musicians who conduct their activities through the vessel of a legal entity, such as a one-person company.[121] This is especially true since the mere fact of having recourse to a legal entity to enter into contracts does not appear to affect one's bargaining power. However, if a musician's company may be considered exceedingly powerful in the music marketplace, a convincing argument may be made against the applicability of the protective regimes.[122] In such a case, the musician is no longer a weaker party to the contract and the regime's objective no longer applies.[123] A similar line of argument applies to hereditary rightsholders: while the scope of application of the relevant provisions of copyright contract law is in principle extended to heirs, this extension should not extend to powerful heirs that assume a similar status to corporate partners.[124] Determining when a musician acting through a legal entity or the heir(s)/estate of a musician should lose their status as a perceived weaker party is difficult and requires an analysis of all relevant circumstances. A cautious approach is merited.

The protective rules of copyright contract law also do not apply within secondary relationships between corporate partners and third parties, since neither the objective of protecting a weaker party nor the aim of furthering the position of artists are deemed to apply in such a case.[125] However, as will become clear, artists may in some cases stake a claim vis-à-vis such third parties in order to protect their own interests.[126]

As to provisions on unfair B2B contract terms and trade practices, again the scope in the chosen jurisdictions varies. Depending on the national framework at issue, the relevant question is whether the musician engages in an economic activity or acts for purposes related to their craft. In the past, the European Commission (EC) has held that performing musicians are deemed to engage in economic activities insofar as they commercially exploit their artistic performances.[127] In view of this, it

Paradise' (n 104) 402; Vanhees, 'Auteurscontract' (n 93) 12–15; Raquel Xalabarder, 'The Remuneration of Authors and Performers' [2020] RIDA 129, 133–34.

[121] Cf Vanhees, *De wettelijke regeling inzake auteurscontracten* (n 105) 9; Visser, 'Pippi Langkous en het nieuwe auteurscontractenrecht' (n 120) 1292; European Copyright Society, 'Comment' (n 107) 135; Raquel Xalabarder, 'The Principle of Appropriate and Proportionate Remuneration for Authors and Performers in Art 18 Copyright in the Digital Single Market Directive. Statutory Residual Remuneration Rights for Its Effective National Implementation' [2020] InDret 1, 17.

[122] Rec 72 DSM Directive. Cf Vanhees, 'Auteurscontracten en de Problematiek inzake Werken Gemaakt in Opdracht of in Uitvoering van een Arbeidsovereenkomst of Statuut' (n 116) 293.

[123] ibid; Hugenholtz and Guibault, 'Auteurscontractenrecht' (n 55) 77.

[124] See eg Art 25b(4) Dutch Copyright Act, which limits the application of Dutch copyright contract law to heirs that are natural persons.

[125] Cf Art 25b(3) Dutch Copyright Act, which excludes the applicability of the protective provisions of copyright contract law to the benefit of employers.

[126] See Chapter 4, Section 4.5 and Chapter 5, Section 5.4.

[127] *RAI/UNITEL* (Case IV/29.559) Commission Decision 78/516/EEC [1978] OJ L 157/39; Phillip W Hall Jr, 'Smells Like Slavery: Unconscionability in Recording Industry Contracts' [2002] Hastings Comm & Ent LJ 189, 200; Valérie-Laure Bénabou, 'European Competition Law and

may be argued that provisions on unfair B2B contract terms and trade practices do not apply to amateur musicians, with the exception of those who are (sufficiently) commercially active in the music industry. Drawing a line in the sand in this regard, however, is rather difficult. Moreover, once amateur musicians enter into a copyright *exploitation* contract with a corporate partner in the music industry, it may be argued that the commercial *exploitation* of their music is on the horizon and thus that those musicians lose their amateur status. Excluding such musicians from the scope of application of the protective framework would leave them exceedingly vulnerable from a legal perspective. The bargaining power of an amateur musician entering into a copyright exploitation contract without any 'professional' aspirations at the moment of contract formation may even be lower than that of a musician who purposefully seeks to 'enter' the music industry. As the risk of unfairness may be considered as inversely proportionate to the bargaining power of the weaker party, the amateur status of a musician should not have any impact on the scope of the relevant provisions on unfair B2B contract terms and trade practices with regard to the music industry contracts under review. Further, the applicability of these provisions is not affected by the fact that a musician conducts their activities through a legal entity, or that the contract is entered into by the musician's successors in title – hereditary or otherwise. Finally, no separate rules apply to the use of either exploitation rights or moral rights, and the legal framework applies indiscriminately to composers and performers.

While the provisions on copyright exploitation contracts in the DSM Directive do not distinguish between contracts with authors and performers, it will be shown that the applicable legal framework in the chosen jurisdictions nevertheless differs markedly.[128] Independently of the legal (re)qualification thereof, the contribution of musical performers risks being accorded less artistic and/or commercial value than that made by a composer.[129] In other words, performers' share of music's social,

Copyright: Where Do We Stand? Where Do We Go?' in Estelle Derclaye (ed), *Research Handbook on the Future of EU Copyright* (Research Handbooks in Intellectual Property, Edward Elgar 2009) 546; Jules Stuyck and Bert Keirsbilck, *Handels- en Economisch Recht. Deel 2. Mededingingsrecht. A. Handelspraktijken en Contracten met Consumenten* (Beginselen van Belgisch Privaatrecht XIII, 5th edn, Wolters Kluwer 2019) 89.

128 See also Jan Corbet, *Auteursrecht* (Algemene Praktische Rechtsverzameling, Story-Scientia 1997) 96; Brison, *Het Naburig Recht van de Uitvoerende Kunstenaar* (n 94) 443, 448; Brison, 'Art XI.205' (n 93) 363.

129 Richard Arnold, 'Are Performers Authors?' [1999] EIPR 464, 468–69; Luke McDonagh, 'Rearranging the Roles of the Performer and the Composer in the Music Industry: The Potential Significance of Fisher v Brooker' [2012] IPQ 64, 64; Stefan Skopelja, 'The Boundaries of "Authorship" and "Performance" in Musical Copyright' [2015] UNSWLJ Student Series No 15-04, 9; Mathilde Pavis, 'The Author–Performer Divide in Intellectual Property Law: A Comparative Analysis of the American, Australian, British and French Legal Frameworks' (University of Exeter 2016) vol I, 27, 75–76, 117 and vol II, 4, 84, 102–07; Ananay Aguilar, 'Distributed Ownership in Music: Between Authorship and Performance' (2018) 27 Social & Legal Studies 776 777, 793; Fraser, 'Sharing the Spoils of a Shared Practice' (n 39) 52–53; Bently and others, *Intellectual Property Law* (n 70) 370.

cultural and economic capital is more limited than that of composers.[130] While the creative genius of a composer is often quite readily accepted, many performing musicians – especially session musicians – are considered to be mere craftsmen, as providers of a certain service.[131] On a contractual level, this perceived status is usually accompanied by standard contracts, with a full assignment of rights in return for a flat fee.[132]

This apparent underprivileged nature of performance may be unmerited.[133] 'Music' in itself does not exist in a palpable way, only the score does. A composition consisting of melody, harmony and rhythm requires a performance to bring it to life.[134] Illustrative reference may be made to variations in timbre, rhythmic articulation and other sound elements that often cannot be exhaustively recorded through musical notation.[135] The artistic value of the creative, interpretative work done by performing musicians should receive due recognition, thus increasing performer agency.[136] Because of the overarching importance attached to notation in music, to the musical score, such aspects risk remaining underexposed.[137] In a way, the emphasis put on a musical score in a certain genre is inversely proportionate to the valuation of musical performance in practice.[138] In the

[130] Cf above regarding Pierre Bourdieu's *Forms of Capital*. See also Brison, *Het Naburig Recht van de Uitvoerende Kunstenaar* (n 94) 15; Fraser, 'Sharing the Spoils of a Shared Practice' (n 39) 53–55.

[131] Daniel Leech-Wilkinson, 'Classical Music as Enforced Utopia' (2016) 15 Arts and Humanities in Higher Education 325, 326; Pavis, 'The Author–Performer Divide' (n 129) vol I, 76; Aguilar, 'Distributed Ownership in Music' (n 129) 785; Ananay Aguilar, 'The Collective Management of Performers' Rights in the UK: A Story of Competing Interests' (2019) 16 SCRIPTed 4, 31; Fraser, 'Sharing the Spoils of a Shared Practice' (n 39) 52.

[132] See Chapter 2, Section 2.4.5.

[133] See Pavis, 'The Author–Performer Divide' (n 129). See also Kanchana Kariyawasam and Rangika Palliyaarachchi, 'The Song Would Be Nothing Without Someone to Sing It: Copyright and Performers' Rights in Music' [2020] Int Rev Law Comput Technol 1; Mathilde Pavis, 'Sixty Years of International Performers' Rights: Time for a Performers' Copyright?' in Hayleigh Bosher and Eleonora Rosati (eds), *Developments and Directions in Intellectual Property Law* (Oxford University Press 2023).

[134] Leech-Wilkinson, 'Classical Music as Enforced Utopia' (n 131) 330.

[135] The influence of such variations is readily noticeable in pieces of (classical) music that have been around for centuries, with significant evolutions in performance styles over the years. As noted by Leech-Wilkinson: 'the same notes can make (and have made) substantially different music'. See Skopelja, 'The Boundaries of "Authorship" and "Performance"' (n 129); Leech-Wilkinson, 'Classical Music as Enforced Utopia' (n 131) 327–28, 332.

[136] Cf Rec 4 Term Directive. See also Leech-Wilkinson, 'Classical Music as Enforced Utopia' (n 131) 326, 334–35; Richard Osborne, 'Is Equitable Remuneration Equitable? Performers' Rights in the UK' (2017) 40 Popular Music and Society 573, 578–79, 587–88; Aguilar, 'Distributed Ownership in Music' (n 129) 777.

[137] Robert Brauneis, 'Musical Work Copyright for the Era of Digital Sound Technology: Looking beyond Composition and Performance' [2014] GW Law Faculty Publications & Other Works 8–10, 15–17. See, however, on the waning role of the score in popular music and the consequences thereof, albeit from the perspective of US law, ibid 18 et seq.

[138] Cf Skopelja, 'The Boundaries of "Authorship" and "Performance"' (n 129).

field of classical music in particular, the score determines and separates the roles of musicians: the composer writes and owns the score, while performers merely interpret it and work in its service.[139] In such a context, possibly (mis)guided by a lack of knowledge regarding the legal status of their activities, performers see themselves as 'mere' performers. In other musical genres, where emphasis on the score is more limited (for example, pop music, R&B or EDM), performing musicians may value the nature of their contribution more highly.[140] Attention to the appropriate artistic and commercial valuation of performances is therefore necessary.

Legally speaking, this translates into the desirability of a legal framework that does not force performers to always 'play second fiddle'. Composers and performers are entitled to an analogue level of protection, unless the specifics of their situation dictate otherwise in particular situations.[141] Significantly, the minimum thresholds for copyright exploitation contracts set by the DSM Directive apply equally to the broad category of 'authors and performers', which includes all types of musician. In terms of application of the existing rules, this implies a desirability of uniform interpretation of analogue provisions.

3.3.2.4 Interplay between Relevant Legal Regimes

Analysis of the scope of the selected substantive legal regimes reveals a significant overlap. The interplay between the different applicable sets of rules is therefore relevant. This relationship may be qualified on the basis of the legal distinction between general and specific rules (*leges generales* and *leges speciales*). General contract law serves as a *lex generalis* and applies in a complementary way to copyright exploitation contracts, to the extent that no specific rules to the contrary exist.[142] In practice, the broad scope of application of general contract law and the lack of tailoring to the specificities of contractual dynamics of the CCIs (including

[139] This clear distinction is moreover seemingly perpetuated through formal education channels such as music conservatoires. See Leech-Wilkinson, 'Classical Music as Enforced Utopia' (n 131) 325–36; Aguilar, 'Distributed Ownership in Music' (n 129) 783–85, 787–88, 794; Daniel Leech-Wilkinson, *Challenging Performance: Classical Music Performance Norms and How to Escape Them* (ebook, 2020). Full text at <https://challengingperformance.com/the-book>. See in particular chapter 18.1. Even so, it is noted that scores of early music leave much leeway for the performer, see Richard Caves, *Creative Industries. Contracts Between Art and Commerce* (Harvard University Press 2002) 273.

[140] Aguilar, 'Distributed Ownership in Music' (n 129) 794.

[141] Cf Hugenholtz and Guibault, 'Auteurscontractenrecht' (n 55) 78; European Copyright Society, 'Comment' (n 107) 132, 134.

[142] Guibault and Hugenholtz, 'Study' (n 60) 11; Blanc, *Les Contrats du Droit d'Auteur* (n 116) 443; Strowel and Vanbrabant, 'Copyright Licensing: A European View' (n 106) 29; Gautier, *Propriété Littéraire et Artistique* (n 87) 493; Caron, *Droit d'Auteur et Droits Voisins* (n 87) 412–13; van Gompel and others, 'Evaluatie Wet Auteurscontractenrecht: Eindrapport' (n 104) 14.

the music industry) limit its application in practice, to the benefit of the relevant specific legal regimes.[143]

Copyright contract law and contract-related provisions on unfair B2B contract terms and trade practices may be qualified as a *lex specialis* vis-à-vis general contract law, with an overlapping but distinct substantive scope. While the scope of copyright contract law is more limited than that of provisions on unfair B2B contracts in terms of object, it may apply to a broader category of parties (that is, also to musicians that do not qualify as undertakings). This renders the absolute categorisation of either regime as 'general' or 'specific' tricky. A simultaneous application of both legal regimes may be sought. While copyright contract law is more tailored to the contracts under review, the rules on unfair B2B contract terms fulfil a complementary, fallback role.

Finally, the regimes applicable to certain specific copyright exploitation contracts may be qualified as a *lex specialis* vis-à-vis the more general provisions of copyright contract law. Again, the more general rules apply in a subsidiary way to the extent that no deviating specific provision is applicable.[144] For this book, this distinction is chiefly relevant for publishing contracts and music made in an employment context or on commission.

3.3.2.5 Geographical Scope

Contract law has traditionally been largely embedded in national traditions. Further, as dictated by the principle of territoriality, the geographical scope of the relevant rules of copyright (contract) law is limited to the national territory. Over recent decades, the importance of the EU level to the regulation of copyright law has increased. Until recently, there was no substantive regulatory EU intervention in the field of copyright contract law, with the EU legislator traditionally favouring the principle of freedom of contract over the protection of parties with weaker bargaining power in B2B situations. While several EU directives refer to the need to secure appropriate remuneration for artists[145], substantive rules were, until recently, limited to the contract measures included in the Term Extension Directive and the criteria for appropriate remuneration of rightsholders set forth in Article 16(2) CRM Directive – which were implemented into UK law prior to Brexit and subsequently retained.[146]

[143] Séverine Dusollier, 'EU Contractual Protection of Creators: Blind Spots and Shortcomings' [2018] Colum J L & Arts, 436, 443.

[144] Vanhees, 'Auteurscontract' (n 93) 36–37; Raad voor de Intellectuele Eigendom, 'Advies betreffende de omzetting in Belgisch recht van richtlijn 2019/790/EU van 17 april 2019 inzake auteursrechten en naburige rechten in de digitale eengemaakte markt en tot wijziging van Richtlijnen 96/9/EG en 2001/29/EG' (19 June 2020) 67.

[145] See eg Recs 10–11, 35 InfoSoc Directive, Rec 3 Resale Right Directive, Rec 5 Rental and Lending Directive.

[146] See Chapter 5, Sections 5.2.2.3.1 and 5.3.2.2.1.

The first step to fill this gap was taken with the DSM Directive, which was meant to lead to EU-wide express provisions on the negotiation of artists' contracts.[147] As will become clear throughout the analysis of the substantive provisions in the following chapters, the harmonising effect of the DSM Directive is only partial. The relevant provisions are of a minimum harmonising nature and the Member States retain a significant margin of implementation.

Finally, the international regulatory level deals with copyright exploitation contracts only in an indirect way.[148] In particular, reference may be made to the recognition that artists have a right to see their interests protected, as is acknowledged in Article 27(2) UDHR and Article 15(1)(c) ICESCR.

3.3.2.6 Temporal Scope

3.3.2.6.1 PRINCIPLES OF INTERTEMPORAL LAW The third aspect that determines the relationship between the different relevant legal regimes is their application in time. This issue is governed by the principles of transition law, also referred to as 'intertemporal' law. Two distinct but interlinked questions arise.[149] First, it must be determined when exactly a new legal regime enters into force, when an act becomes binding. Second, there must be a delineation of the concrete situations to which the new legal regime at issue applies. Three main types of hypothetical circumstances may be discerned. First, both the legal fact and its consequences – here, the music industry contract and its performance through exploitation and remuneration – may take place before the entry into force of the new act. In such a case, unless the new regime is expressly imbued with retroactive effect, the old regime remains applicable. In the second category of situations, both legal fact and consequences arise after the entry into force of the new act. Again, settling the issue of temporal application is quite simple: the new regime applies to such cases. The third set of circumstances provides more food for discussion. Indeed, when the legal fact occurs before the new act's entry into force, but its legal consequences (partially) take place only after this moment, resolving the issue of temporal application is contentious. By way of example, such a situation arises in case a music industry contract is concluded before the entry into force of the new regime and is still ongoing when the new legal regime enters into force.

In determining the applicable legal regime, a balance must be sought between considerations of substantive and procedural fairness.[150] On the one hand, a new legal regime may be considered to bring progress in terms of equality and justice.

[147] On the implementation of the DSM Directive in the Member States, see <https://bit.ly/2X26syc>; <https://bit.ly/3uWybNo>.

[148] Xalabarder, 'The Principle of Appropriate and Proportionate Remuneration' (n 121) 5.

[149] Thijs Vancoppernolle, *Intertemporeel Recht* (Intersentia 2019) 20–26.

[150] Case C-168/09 *Flos v Semeraro* [2011] ECLI:EU:C:2011:29, paras 56–57.

A broad application in time of a new legal regime may be considered to further fairness in substantive terms. This translates into an immediate application of the new legal regime to the legal consequences of ongoing contracts that postdate its entry into force.

On the other hand, grounds of 'fair play' rather argue in favour of applying the old regime to existing contractual relationships. Contracting parties may legitimately expect their relationship to be governed by the law applicable at the moment of contract formation. This leads to a parallel application of two differing legal regimes: contracts concluded following the new regime's entry into force are subject to this new regime, while ongoing contracts are still governed by the old regime. As such contracts fade out over time, so does the old legal regime. This engenders both transparency and legal certainty for contracting parties, who are likely to have negotiated their contractual relationships solely in view of the legal framework applicable at that time.[151] It may be argued that the contractual balance thus reached between the parties should not be disturbed ex post.

However, a principled choice for immediate application of new legal regimes could be the most beneficial. Such a solution would both provide clarity and avoid the unequal treatment (and thus risk of discrimination) that a choice for continued application of the old regime to ongoing contracts would entail.[152] Other arguments in favour of such a choice include furthering of progress through the enhanced justice that the new legal regime is assumed to bring.

A new legal regime may include an express provision regarding its entry into force and/or its applicability in time, such as by including a transition period.[153] If it does not, a set of default rules applies. In the chosen EU jurisdictions, the default rules regarding entry into force of an act range from (in principle) a day (France[154]), ten days (Belgium[155]) or fourteen days (Germany[156]) to one or two months (Netherlands[157]) following its publication.[158]

[151] Vancoppernolle, *Intertemporeel Recht* (n 149) 59–61.

[152] Cf ibid 53–54.

[153] ibid 28–30. On UK law, see <www.legislation.gov.uk/understanding-legislation>.

[154] See Art 1 French Civil Code.

[155] See Art 4(2) *Wet 31 mei 1961 betreffende het gebruik der talen in wetgevingszaken, het opmaken, bekendmaken en inwerkingtreden van wetten en verordeningen*, BS 21 June 1961, 5171.

[156] See Art 82(2) German Basic Law.

[157] See Art 10(1) *Wet van 4 februari 1988, houdende regeling van de uitgifte van het Staatsblad en de Staatscourant en van de bekendmaking en de inwerkingtreding van wetten, algemene maatregelen van bestuur en vanwege het Rijk anders dan bij wet of algemene maatregel van bestuur vastgestelde algemeen verbindende voorschriften* <https://bit.ly/3viaQpm>.

[158] See in more detail Vancoppernolle, *Intertemporeel Recht* (n 149) 21. In the United Kingdom, the application of new laws is specified in the 'Commencement' section of an Act. If this is not the case, the application in time is set by the Secretary of State for the relevant government department. In the absence a statute pertaining to the regulation of copyright exploitation contracts under UK law, considerations as to the application of UK legislation in time are not included here.

The default rules regarding an act's application in time usually adhere to four main principles. The first is the fundamental principle of non-retroactivity, which dictates that new acts generally do not apply to past situations, and is motivated by the wish to protect legal certainty and the legitimate expectations of legal subjects.[159] Second, new acts generally apply immediately and exclusively to current and future situations.[160] Third, the legal consequences of ongoing contracts are usually governed by the old regime.[161] The fourth rule provides for exceptions to the third, leading to immediate application of certain acts, even to ongoing contracts.[162] The precise details of this fourth rule differ. In Belgium, both mandatory acts and acts that relate to public order apply immediately, save if the act at issue provides otherwise.[163] A more restrictive view is taken in France and Germany, where the immediate application to ongoing contracts is limited to those new acts where particularly imperative public policy considerations apply – a rather vague concept in itself.[164] An – interesting, yet somewhat unpredictable – alternative approach that has to some extent been accepted in Germany and the Netherlands seeks to solve intertemporal conflicts on a case-by-case basis, referring to a set of criteria that includes the new law's objective, the perceived injustice caused by the old law and the legitimate expectations of the relevant parties.[165]

A convincing argument may be made to remodel intertemporal law based on conflict-of-law rules, focusing on the legitimate expectations of parties whose situation is adversely affected by the new legal regime.[166] If this party (or these parties) may legitimately expect the old regime to apply, this would be the outcome of the case, unless the result would not be in conformity with applicable higher norms, such as the constitution.[167]

[159] Concerning the lack of retroactivity of acts under the laws of the chosen EU jurisdictions, the consequences of this principle and the exceptions thereto, see Vancoppernolle, *Intertemporeel Recht* (n 149) 34–48. See also the extensive source materials cited there. In essence, because of this principle, rights that have arisen (such as a right to damages), cannot be removed through the application of the new law, and rights that have been removed (such as through the statute of limitations) cannot arise again.

[160] This is indicated in Dutch as *onmiddellijke werking*, in French as *effet immédiat* and in German as *Sofortwirkung* or *sofortige Anwendung*. See Vancoppernolle, *Intertemporeel Recht* (n 149) 49–58, 87. For a clear nuance regarding the German legal system, see ibid 52. For various corrective mechanisms, see ibid 52–58.

[161] This is indicated in Dutch as *eerbiedigende werking*, in French as *effet différé*, *survie de la loi ancienne* or *effet post-actif* and in German as *Nachwirkung des alten Gesetzes*. See Vancoppernolle, *Intertemporeel Recht* (n 149) 58–62, 87.

[162] ibid 62–75.

[163] Art 1.2 new Belgian CC; Vancoppernolle, *Intertemporeel Recht* (n 149) 62–66.

[164] ibid 66–67.

[165] ibid 75–79.

[166] ibid 151–202, 609–11, 855–58.

[167] ibid 205–602, 611–16, 876–81.

3.3.2.6.2 APPLICATION TO LEGAL FRAMEWORK A full discussion of the temporal application of general contract law falls outside the scope of this research.[168] However, particular attention is devoted to the relevant provisions of copyright contract law in the continental EU jurisdictions under review, which have evolved significantly over recent decades.

In Belgium, the existing provisions of the 1994 Belgian Copyright Act were included in Book XI, Title 5 Belgian CEL by way of the Belgian Act of 19 April 2014.[169] These codified provisions apply to all works and performances that are protected when this act entered into force on 1 January 2015.[170]

The French legal framework saw an important substantive amendment with a 2014 decree that changed provisions concerning publishing contracts in particular.[171] The French legislator expressly applied these new, restrictive rules to pre-existing contracts in the literary sector.[172] Further, a 2016 act brought significant changes to the rules that apply to contracts between performing musicians and their record companies, in addition to setting up an alternative dispute resolution (ADR) mechanism specific to the music sector.[173] While most of the relevant provisions concerning copyright exploitation contracts do not apply to contracts ongoing at the entry into force of these provisions, an exception was made for a particular transparency obligation specific to record companies.[174]

Over recent decades, the German legislator amended and supplemented the provisions of copyright contract law under review in this book by way of acts dating

[168] See (1) in Belgium: Claeys and Tanghe, *Algemeen Contractenrecht* (n 57) 25–38; (2) in France: Buffelan-Lanore and Larribau-Terneyre, *Droit Civil. Les obligations* (n 57) 5–42; Terré and others, *Droit Civil. Les Obligations* (n 57) 31–86; (3) in Germany: Markesinis and others, *The German Law of Contract* (n 57) 6–16; Fikentscher and Heinemann, *Schuldrecht* (n 57) 1022–28; and (4) in the Netherlands: Asser, *Verbintenissenrecht* (n 57) x–xi, 5–8.

[169] *Wet van 19 april 2014 houdende Invoeging van Boek XI, 'Intellectuele Eigendom' in het Wetboek van Economisch Recht, en houdende Invoeging van Bepalingen eigen aan Boek XI in de Boeken I, XV en XVII van Hetzelfde Wetboek*, BS 12 June 2014, 44352 (hereinafter: Belgian Act 19 April 2014).

[170] Art 40(1) para 1 Belgian Act 19 April 2014. The provisions of that act concerning the resale right relating to artworks (see Chapter 5, Section 5.4.3.1) entered into force on 1 July 2015.

[171] *Ordonnance no 2014-1348 du 12 novembre 2014 modifiant les dispositions du code de la propriété intellectuelle relatives au contrat d'édition*, JORF No 0262, 13 November 2014 (hereinafter: French Decree of 12 November 2014).

[172] See Arts 9–12 French Decree of 12 November 2014; Caron, *Droit d'Auteur et Droits Voisins* (n 87) 444–45.

[173] *Loi no 2016-925 du 7 juillet 2016 relative à la liberté de la création, à l'architecture et au patrimoine*, JORF No 0158, 8 July 2016 (hereinafter: French Act of 7 July 2016). On ADR under French law, see Chapter 7, Section 7.5.

[174] Art 110 French Act of 7 July 2016. The provision subject to immediate application is Art 212-15 French IP Code. on transparency obligations under French law, see Chapter 5, Sections 5.3.3 and 5.4.3.2.

from 2002,[175] 2007[176] and 2016.[177] The German legislator has combined the traditional route of having the legal consequences of ongoing contracts be governed by the old regime with the immediate application of some protective provisions to ongoing contracts.[178] First, while most of the provisions of the German Act of 28 March 2002 only apply to contracts that were concluded, and/or facts that occurred, from 1 July 2002 (the day the 2002 act entered into force), limited immediate application was accorded to the right of fair remuneration as to contracts concluded between 1 June 2001 and 30 June 2002 if the content at issue was/is exploited after 30 June 2002.[179] In addition, the contract adjustment mechanism applies to all facts that have occurred since 28 March 2002 – also those stemming from contracts predating the German Act of 28 March 2002.[180] The main change effected by the German Act of 28 October 2007 was the introduction of the possibility for authors to grant rights relating to future methods of exploitation under certain conditions.[181] The relevant transitional provision foresees that contracts dating between 1 January 1966 and 2008 that exclusively grant all essential exploitation rights to the corporate partner, without limitation in either place or time, also include methods of exploitation that were not yet known at the time of contract

[175] *Gesetz zur Stärkung der vertraglichen Stellung von Urhebern und ausübenden Künstlern Vom 28. März 2002*, *Bundesgesetzblatt* (German Official Gazette, hereinafter: BGBl) 2002 Part I No 21, 1155 (hereinafter: German Act of 28 March 2002). See also Adolf Dietz, 'Amendment of German Copyright Law in Order to Strengthen the Contractual Position of Authors and Performers' [2002] IIC 828; Adolf Dietz, 'News from Germany. Significant Legislative and Case Law Developments in Copyright Contract Law in Germany' [2003] RIDA 146; Adolf Dietz, 'Copyright Contract Law According to the New German Legislation and Practice' [2005] AMI 20; Eva Inés Obergfell (ed), *Zehn Jahre reformiertes Urhebervertragsrecht: 1. Josef Kohler-Symposion* (Josef Kohler-Symposion, Berlin/Boston, Walter De Gruyter 2013).

[176] *Zweites Gesetz zur Regelung des Urheberrechts in der Informationsgesellschaft Vom 28. Oktober 2007*, BGBl 2007 Part I No 54, 2513 (hereinafter: German Act of 28 October 2007). See also Agnès Lucas-Schloetter, 'Qu'y a-t-Il Dans La "Deuxième Corbeille"? La Loi Allemande Du 26 Octobre 2007 Relative Au Droit d'Auteur Dans La Société de l'Information' [2008] PI 368; Silke von Lewinski, 'News from Germany. Developments in Germany from Mid-2005 until the End of 2010. Part I' [2011] RIDA 164, 167, 181–91.

[177] *Gesetz zur verbesserten Durchsetzung des Anspruchs der Urheber und ausübenden Künstler auf angemessene Vergütung und zur Regelung von Fragen der Verlegerbeteiligung Vom 20. Dezember 2016*, BGBl 2016 Part I No 63, 3037 (hereinafter: German Act of 20 December 2016). See also Agnès Lucas-Schloetter, 'Das neue Urhebervertragsrecht' [2017] GRUR 235.

[178] Art 132 German Copyright Act; Gerhard Schricker, *Urheberrecht. Kommentar* (3rd edn, CH Beck 2006) 2196–204; Fromm and Nordemann, *Urheberrecht* (n 93) 1963–71; Gunda Dreyer and others, *Urheberrecht* (Heidelberger Kommentar, 4th edn, CF Müller 2018) 1699–704; Philipp Möhring and Käte Nicolini, *Urheberrecht* (4th edn, CH Beck 2018) 1453–61.

[179] Art 132(3)–(4) German Copyright Act. On the right of fair remuneration under German law see below, Section 3.3.2.2.

[180] Art 132(3)–(4) German Copyright Act. On the contract adjustment mechanism under German law see below, Section 3.3.2.3.1.

[181] More specifically, this led to the repeal of Art 31(4) German Copyright Act and the introduction of Art 31a German Copyright Act: see Chapter 4, Section 4.4.1.2.

formation, unless the author objects in a timely manner.[182] As for the 2016 amendment of the German Copyright Act, the new provisions concerning copyright exploitation contracts only apply to contracts concluded from 1 March 2018 onwards, with the exception of the right of revocation, which applies to all facts that occur after 1 March 2018, independent of their contractual origins.[183]

The 2015 Dutch act on copyright exploitation contracts contains a wide range of protective rules. Before the entry into force of this act, copyright exploitation contracts were largely governed by the general provisions of the Dutch Civil Code.[184] In principle, the provisions of the 2015 act only apply to contracts that postdate its entry into force, with some exceptions.[185] The most relevant exceptions to this principle are the limitation as to future works, the general requirement of reasonableness and the right of revocation.[186] Those protective rules also apply to pre-existing contracts. Several amendments of the legal framework are on the table in the Netherlands at the time of writing.[187]

In addition, in the past decade, the implementation of two relevant EU directives into national law led to several amendments of copyright contract law in the chosen jurisdictions that bear relevance to the legal framework applicable to the music industry contracts under review, namely the Term Extension Directive and the DSM Directive.

The extended term of protection for phonograms applies to all content that qualified for neighbouring rights protection on 1 November 2013, as well as all posterior content.[188] The rights in phonograms granted to corporate partners on

[182] Art 137l(1) German Copyright Act.

[183] Art 132(3a)–(4) German Copyright Act. On the right of revocation under German law see below, Section 3.2.2.

[184] Hugenholtz, 'Towards Author's Paradise' (n 104) 399.

[185] *Wet van 30 juni 2015 tot wijziging van de Auteurswet en de Wet op de naburige rechten in verband met de versterking van de positie van de auteur en de uitvoerende kunstenaar bij overeenkomsten betreffende het auteursrecht en het naburig recht, Staatsblad* (Dutch Official Gazette, hereinafter: Stb) 2015, 257 (hereinafter: Dutch Act of 30 June 2015). See Visser and others, *ACR: Auteurscontractenrecht* (n 91) 307–13; JH Spoor and others, *Auteursrecht. Auteursrecht, portretrecht, naburige rechten en databankenrecht* (Recht en Praktijk, 4th edn, Wolters Kluwer 2019) 558–59; Stef van Gompel, 'Omzetting van de DSM Auteursrecht Richtlijn 2019/790 in Nederland' [2021] AM 338, 335.

[186] Art III Dutch Act of 30 June 2015.

[187] See <https://bit.ly/3Uze3Ov>. See also Commissie Auteursrecht, 'Advies over concept wetsvoorstel auteurscontractenrecht II' (5 September 2022) <https://bit.ly/3S767nQ>.

[188] See (1) in Belgium: Art 40(4) para 1 Belgian Act 19 April 2014; (2) in France: Art 8(I) *Loi no 2015-195 du 20 février 2015 portant diverses dispositions d'adaptation au droit de l'Union européenne dans les domaines de la propriété littéraire et artistique et du patrimoine culturel,* JORF No 0045, 22 February 2015 (hereinafter: French Act of 20 February 2015); (3) in Germany: Art 137m(1) German Copyright Act; (4) in the Netherlands: Art III(2) *Wet van 9 oktober 2013 tot wijziging van de Wet op de naburige rechten in verband met de omzetting van Richtlijn 2011/77/EU van het Europees Parlement en de Europese Raad van 27 september 2011 tot wijziging van de Richtlijn 2006/116/EG betreffende de beschermingstermijn van het auteursrecht en bepaalde naburige rechten,* Stb 2013, 383 (hereinafter: Dutch Act of 9 October 2013); and (5) in the United Kingdom: Arts 1, 21 Copyright and Duration of Rights in Performances Regulations 2013, SI 2013/1782.

1 November 2013 continue to produce effects for the extended period of protection of twenty years, unless the contract itself clearly indicates otherwise.[189] It is difficult to envisage a such a deviating contractual provision, given the inherent difficulties associated with predicting future legislative developments. It may therefore be said with relative certainty that prior grants remain applicable for the full period of seventy years. This arrangement is ostensibly prompted by concerns of legal certainty,[190] but appears to be a policy decision in favour of corporate partners. This term extension was coupled with several measures that sought to ensure that musicians reaped part of the additional revenues associated with the term extension.[191] These measures apply to contracts that predate the entry into force of the Term Extension Directive, effective from the fifty-first year of protection. While this immediate effect favours musicians, this is countervailed by the continuing effect of prior grants during the extended period of protection.

The other legislative instrument of note at the EU level is the DSM Directive, which dates from 2019.[192] The implementation of this Directive into Member State law was due by 7 June 2021. The provisions of the DSM Directive apply in respect of 'all works and other subject matter that are protected by national law in the field of copyright' on or after this date.[193] This implies that the DSM Directive may apply to pre-existing music.[194] However, the application in time of the DSM Directive is expressly limited by the proviso that it does not affect 'any acts concluded and rights acquired before 7 June 2021'.[195] Alternative interpretations are possible, especially as to its application to pre-existing licence agreements. The provision apparently perceives the contractual relationships at issue as a static environment, whereby a singular relevant point in time may be pinpointed. While this may be true for contracts resulting in a transfer of rights, such a single moment in time is much more difficult to determine in a licensing context.[196]

On the one hand, it could be argued that the concepts of 'acts concluded' and 'rights acquired' refer to all copyright exploitation agreements entered into before 7 June 2021, be it through a transfer or a licence. This would mean that the minimum benchmarks set by the DSM Directive only apply to contracts postdating the DSM implementation deadline. This interpretation clearly favours the interests of corporate partners. It risks undermining the objective of the DSM Directive to secure enhanced protection for artists.[197]

189 Art 10a(1) Term Directive; Recital 15 Term Extension Directive.
190 Rec 15 Term Extension Directive.
191 See Chapter 5, Sections 5.2.2.3.2 and 5.3.2.2.
192 See <https://bit.ly/2YSDGRz>.
193 Art 26(1) DSM Directive.
194 Cf Ted Shapiro, 'Remuneration Provisions in the DSM Copyright Directive and the Audiovisual Industry in the EU: The Elusive Quest for Fairness' (2020) 42 EIPR 778, 787.
195 Art 26(2) DSM Directive.
196 Shapiro, 'Remuneration Provisions in the DSM Copyright Directive' (n 194) 787.
197 European Copyright Society, 'Comment' (n 107) 132, 139.

The alternative interpretation is that the concept of 'acts concluded' refers to acts of exploitation, not agreements.[198] This position is supported by the Dutch DSM Implementation Act, which provides that it does not apply to exploitation activities (in Dutch: *exploitatiehandelingen*) and rights granted (in Dutch: *verworven rechten*) predating its entry into force.[199] This interpretation would bring acts of exploitation conducted on the basis of earlier contracts into the temporal scope of application of the DSM Directive. This interpretation would be favourable to the interests of musicians.[200]

In interpreting this provision, recourse may be had to ECJ case law interpreting the transitional provision of the InfoSoc Directive, which provides that its provisions apply 'without prejudice to any acts concluded and rights acquired before 22 December 2002'.[201] In the context of the *VG Wort* case concerning private copying, the phrase 'acts concluded' was interpreted as referring to 'acts of exploitation' by the ECJ.[202] However, this argument is specific to the context of private copying and has no place in a contractual situation.[203] The indiscriminate copying of the concept 'acts concluded' from the InfoSoc Directive is regrettable. A clearer formulation, as was included, for example, in the Unfair Contract Terms Directive,[204] the Consumer Rights Directive,[205] the Sale of Goods Directive[206] and the Digital Content Directive,[207] would have been preferable.

Independently of the above, the question arises how certain triggers that occur after the formation of the contract may affect the legal framework to which the

[198] This has apparently been the position of the EC, see Shapiro, 'Remuneration Provisions in the DSM Copyright Directive' (n 194) 787. See also Case C-168/09 *Flos v Semeraro* [2011] ECLI: EU:C:2011:29, para 51; Yannos Paramythiotis, 'Fairness in Copyright Contract Law: Remuneration for Authors and Performers Under the Copyright in the Digital Single Market Directive' in Tatiana-Eleni Synodinou and others (eds), *EU Internet Law in the Digital Single Market* (Springer International 2021) 94.

[199] Art VI Dutch DSM Implementation Act. Cf the reference to the concept of *exploitatiehandelingen* in Art 40(4) para 2 Belgian Act 19 April 2014, which implemented the Term Extension Directive into national law.

[200] See European Copyright Society, 'Comment' (n 107) 139.

[201] Art 10(2) InfoSoc Directive. On the legislative history of this provision, see the Opinion of AG Sharpston in Joined Cases C-457/11 to C-460/11 *Verwertungsgesellschaft Wort (VG Wort) and Others* [2013] ECLI:EU:C:2013:34, paras 132–33.

[202] Joined Cases C-457/11–C-460/11 *Verwertungsgesellschaft Wort (VG Wort) and Others* [2013] ECLI:EU:C:2013:34, para 28. See also AG Sharpston, referring to 'acts of reproduction': Joined Cases C-457/11–C-460/11 *Verwertungsgesellschaft Wort (VG Wort) and Others* [2013] ECLI:EU: C:2013:34, para 135.

[203] Shapiro, 'Remuneration Provisions in the DSM Copyright Directive' (n 194) 787–88.

[204] See Art 10(1) para 2 Unfair Contract Terms Directive, which declares its provisions applicable to all contracts concluded after 31 December 1994.

[205] Art 28(2) Consumer Rights Directive, which declares its provisions applicable to contracts concluded after 13 June 2014.

[206] Art 24(2) Sale of Goods Directive, which declares its provisions inapplicable to contracts concluded before 1 January 2022.

[207] Art 24(2) Digital Content Directive, which declares its provisions applicable to the supply of digital content or digital services which occurs from 1 January 2022, except for Arts 19, 20, which only apply to contracts concluded from that date.

contract must adhere. Reference may be made to clauses that foresee a renegotiation or termination of the contract in case certain circumstances arise.[208] Does the concept of 'acts concluded' include such 'new' agreements based on a contractual relationship that predates the DSM Directive? The text of the DSM Directive suggests that the minimum benchmarks do not apply to exploitation activities that took place before 7 June 2021.[209] The 'lack of clarity supports application of the general rule against retroactivity'.[210]

Finally, the requirement of transparency[211] applies from 7 June 2022 onwards.[212] This grace period seeks to enable corporate partners to adapt their existing reporting practices to the minimum benchmarks set by the DSM Directive.[213] However, the DSM Directive has failed to specify expressly whether, following the expiry of this grace period, the requirement of transparency will apply to contracts concluded before 7 June 2022 (or even 7 June 2021).[214]

The absence of clear legislative guidance on the temporal application of the DSM Directive is regrettable, since it leaves the door open for legal uncertainty and regulatory divergences at the national level. A preliminary reference filed with the ECJ by the Belgian Council of State will hopefully provide such guidance. This case is pending under the docket number C-575/23 at the time of writing and concerns the neighbouring rights of the performing musicians of the National Orchestra of Belgium.

The Netherlands was the first of the chosen jurisdictions to implement the DSM Directive into national law, on 16 December 2020.[215] Subject to the specifications on 'acts concluded' reviewed above, the provisions on artist contracts of the Dutch DSM Implementation Act entered into force on 7 June 2021.[216] The reporting

[208] Shapiro, 'Remuneration Provisions in the DSM Copyright Directive (n 194) 787.

[209] ibid.

[210] ibid.

[211] See Art 19 DSM Directive and Chapter 5, Sections 5.3.3 and 5.4.3.2.

[212] Art 27 DSM Directive.

[213] Rec 77 DSM Directive.

[214] See, however, Christophe Geiger and Franciska Schönherr, 'The Information Society Directive' in Irini Stamatoudi and Paul Torremans (eds), *EU Copyright Law. A Commentary* (Elgar Commentaries, Edward Elgar 2021) 760.

[215] *Wet van 16 december 2020 tot wijziging van de Auteurswet, de Wet op de naburige rechten, de Databankenwet en de Wet toezicht en geschillenbeslechting collectieve beheersorganisaties auteurs- en naburige rechten in verband met de implementatie van Richtlijn (EU) 2019/790 van het Europees parlement en de Raad van 17 april 2019 inzake auteursrechten en naburige rechten in de digitale eengemaakte markt en tot wijziging van de Richtlijnen 96/9/EG en 2001/29/EG (Implementatiewet richtlijn auteursrecht in de digitale eengemaakte markt)*, Stb 2020, 558 <https://bit.ly/30F3rPC> (hereinafter: Dutch DSM Implementation Act).

[216] *Besluit van 18 december 2020 tot vaststelling van het tijdstip van inwerkingtreding van de Implementatiewet richtlijn auteursrecht in de digitale eengemaakte markt*, Stb 2020, 559 <https://bit.ly/3uQg0Jo> (hereinafter: Dutch Decree of 18 December 2020). See also clarifications added in the course of the ongoing review process of the Dutch regulatory framework at <https://bit.ly/3Uze3Ov>.

obligations entered into force on 7 June 2022.[217] The Dutch DSM Implementation Act does not expressly treat the issue of application of the reporting obligations to ongoing contracts.[218]

Second, on 12 May 2021 the French government issued a decree[219] partially implementing the DSM Directive, including the provisions on artist contracts.[220] The French decree only specifies its temporal application as to the provisions that implement Article 17 (7 June 2021) and Article 19 DSM Directive (7 June 2022).[221] The French DSM Implementation Decree expressly specifies that the reporting obligations will apply to ongoing contracts.[222] No specification was added as to the provisions implementing Articles 18 and 20 through 23 DSM Directive.

The third of the chosen jurisdictions to implement the DSM Directive was Germany, on 19 May 2021.[223] The amendments of the German Copyright Act pertaining to copyright exploitation contracts entered into force on 7 June 2021, while the separate act implementing Article 17 DSM Directive entered into force on 1 August 2021.[224] Detailed provisions have been foreseen on the temporal application of the amendments to ongoing contracts. Contracts with either composers or performers that were concluded and/or facts that occurred from 1 July 2002 until 28 February 2017 in principle remain subject to the legal framework as applicable on 28 February 2017.[225] In principle, the law as applicable on 1 March 2017 remains applicable to contracts with either composers or performers that were concluded and/or facts that occurred from 1 March 2017 until 6 June 2021.[226] Since 7 June 2021, the legislative amendments pertaining to the use-it-or-lose-it clause[227] and the contract adjustment mechanism[228] also apply to ongoing contracts.[229] From

[217] See under Dutch law the Dutch Decree of 18 December 2020 and under French law Art 13(II) *jo* Arts 5, 12 French DSM Implementation Decree.

[218] See Visser, 'Dutch Copyright Contract Law' (n 91) 37.

[219] In French: *Ordonnance*.

[220] *Ordonnance no 2021-580 du 12 mai 2021 portant transposition du 6 de l'article 2 et des articles 17 à 23 de la directive 2019/790 du Parlement européen et du Conseil du 17 avril 2019 sur le droit d'auteur et les droits voisins dans le marché unique numérique et modifiant les directives 96/9/CE et 2001/29/CE*, JORF No 0111, 13 May 2021 (hereinafter: French DSM Implementation Decree).

[221] Art 13 French DSM Implementation Decree.

[222] Article 13(II) French DSM Implementation Decree.

[223] *Gesetz zur Anpassung des Urheberrechts an die Erfordernisse des digitalen Binnenmarktes, Drucksache* 19/29894 <https://bit.ly/3FthVYG> (hereinafter: German DSM Implementation Act). Art 17 DSM Directive was implemented by way of a separate act, namely the *Gesetz über die urheberrechtliche Verantwortlichkeit von Diensteanbietern für das Teilen von Online-Inhalten* ('*Urheberrechts-Diensteanbieter-Gesetz*' or 'UrhDaG', hereinafter: German OCSSP Act).

[224] Art 5 German DSM Implementation Act.

[225] Arts 132(3a), 132(4) German Copyright Act.

[226] Arts 133(1), 133(4) German Copyright Act.

[227] Art 41 German Copyright Act. See Chapter 5, Section 5.2.2.3.2.

[228] Art 32a German Copyright Act. See Chapter 5, Section 5.3.2.3.1.

[229] Arts 133(2), 133(4) German Copyright Act.

7 June 2022, the amended provisions setting forth active reporting obligations[230] also apply to ongoing contracts.[231]

Finally, in Belgium, a remarkable evolution has taken place. The 2021 Belgian implementing act specified that its entry into force did not prejudice rights granted by law or through prior acts of exploitation.[232] This formulation indicated an intended restrictive application in time and a lack of application of the new rules to ongoing contracts.[233] However, consequent to a legislative amendment dating from the spring of 2024, the mandatory provisions of this act now expressly apply to ongoing contracts.[234]

Both the law of unfair B2B contract terms and trade practices[235] and general contract law have undergone changes over recent decades. The 2019 Belgian rules concerning unfair contract terms apply to contracts that have been concluded, renewed and/or modified after 1 December 2020,[236] while the amended regime concerning unfair trade practices applies to undertakings' behaviour on or after 1 September 2019.[237] Recent relevant amendments to the French regime on unfair B2B contract terms and trade practices, intended to significantly simplify the applicable regime and render it more intelligible, entered into force on 26 April 2019, without an express qualification as to the temporal effects of the amended provisions under review in this book.[238] Further, the provision specific to contracts of adhesion under French law initially stems from contract law reform dating from 2016, whereby pre-existing contracts were excluded from the scope of application, and was subsequently amended in 2018, as to contracts entered into from 1 October 2018 onwards.[239]

Before substantively analysing the applicable legal framework, it is difficult to comprehensively assess the choices of national and EU legislators concerning the

230 Arts 32d, 32e German Copyright Act. See Chapter 5, Sections 5.3.3 and 5.4.3.2.

231 Arts 133(3)–(4) German Copyright Act.

232 Art 99 Belgian DSM Implementation Act.

233 Cf Emmanuel Cornu and Romain Meys, 'La transposition en droit belge de la directive sur le droit d'auteur et les droits voisins dans le marché unique numérique: Une modification significative du cadre contractuel d'exploitation des droits' [2022] JT 773, 787–88.

234 Art 196 *Wet van 9 februari 2024 houdende diverse bepalingen inzake economie*, Belgian Official Gazette 21 March 2024, 34577.

235 See in detail De Pourcq, *Oneerlijke Handelspraktijken* (n 81).

236 Art 39 para 4 Belgian B2B Act.

237 Art 39 para 1 Belgian B2B Act.

238 *Ordonnance no 2019-359 du 24 avril 2019 portant refonte du titre IV du livre IV du code de commerce relatif à la transparence, aux pratiques restrictives de concurrence et aux autres pratiques prohibées*, JORF No 0097, 25 April 2019. A specification as to temporal application was included only for the legislative amendments pertaining to payment terms, see Art 5.

239 See Art 1171 French Civil Code *jo* Art 9 *Ordonnance no 2016-131 du 10 février 2016 portant réforme du droit des contrats, du régime général et de la preuve des obligations*, JORF No 0035, 11 February 2016 and Art 16(I) *Loi n° 2018-287 du 20 avril 2018 ratifiant l'ordonnance no 2016-131 du 10 février 2016 portant réforme du droit des contrats, du régime général et de la preuve des obligations*, JORF No 0093, 21 April 2018.

temporal scope of the relevant legal framework. Only after the relevant rules have been reviewed and evaluated, the application of the legal framework in time may be put to the 'fairness test'.

3.4 ESTABLISHING THE APPROPRIATE LEVEL(S) AND METHOD(S) OF REGULATION

Before delving into the substance of the law, the appropriate level(s) and method(s) of regulation merit closer attention. At present, the relevant legal framework spans protective regimes across several fields of law and provides several rules that vary depending on the type of contract – with different rules applying to music publishing contracts and contracts with record companies, as well as to employment situations or commissioned music.[240] The different substantive scope of the relevant protective regimes allows for an approach that is tailored to the wide spectrum of musicians: both composing and performing musicians, either with or without an employment status, active in big or small groups or as a soloist, and so on. Doing justice to the diversity that exists in practice is a legitimate objective.

However, given the continuous emergence of new business models and methods of exploiting protected content, an equally legitimate question is whether attaining this objective is at all feasible. In addition, more simplicity and uniformity in terms of the applicable rules may be beneficial. Therefore, an argument may be made in favour of a more streamlined, harmonised legal framework. Such a framework may be less tailored to specific situations, but would provide a coherent, transparent set of rules that engenders legal certainty. While stopping short of a full uniformisation of the applicable rules, this consideration is to be borne in mind throughout this book. It is valid at both the national and EU levels, the latter from an internal market perspective. Notably, the DSM Directive does not distinguish between different types of contracts. It not only applies to the broad spectrum of creations (both works and performances), but also to a multiplicity of economic and cultural sectors – not only the music industry.[241]

The field of law considered to be the most suitable for the purposes of this book is copyright contract law, given its proximity to the CCIs and the music industry in particular. Provisions of general contract law and those curtailing unfair B2B contract terms and trade practices may act as a fallback rebalancing measure in certain exceptionally unfair situations. However, the general nature of these rules makes it hard to effectively invoke them in the context of the contracts under review.[242] Conversely, given their focus on relationships characterised by a

[240] See above, Section 3.3.2.

[241] Cf Séverine Dusollier, 'An Effective and Comprehensive Contractual Protection of Creators and Performers' (Copyright in the Digital Single Market, Brussels, 30 January 2020).

[242] Dusollier and others, 'Contractual Arrangements Applicable to Creators' (n 66) 60–61.

difference in (bargaining) power, the provisions pertaining to unfair B2B contract terms and trade practices may serve as a source of inspiration. The benefits of the threefold structure of (1) a list of per se prohibitions, (2) a grey list subject to an impact test and (3) a general norm based on fairness considerations are hard to deny. As argued by Ohly, this approach 'combines certainty in clear cases with flexibility to deal with unforeseen situations'.[243] However, this would require compiling a list of appropriate per se prohibitions that is both clear and complete – and does justice to the diversity of CCIs as well as within the music industry itself.[244] Potential express prohibitions spring to mind of tying practices between music publishers and record companies, of undue limitations of royalty calculation bases, of excessive discounts and deductions, of the grant of rights to future methods of exploitation without separate remuneration, of unbridled option clauses and indefinite terms, and so forth.[245] This list may very well be partly subjective, and it is almost certain that some stakeholders would not agree with its formulation. Moreover, research of the same kind in other CCIs would undoubtedly lead to a similar but different list of terms and practices to be considered per se unfair. Therefore, formulating a comprehensive regime of unfair B2B contract terms and trade practices in the CCIs would be rather challenging. A generalised harmonisation of the law of unfair B2B contract terms and trade practices at the EU level – also extending beyond the CCIs – is therefore unlikely.[246] In any case, from the perspective of good lawmaking, hard law regulatory intervention as to the music industry alone appears to be inefficient and overly sectorial. In view of this, the area of unfair B2B contract terms and trade practices does not appear to provide fruitful ground for further harmonisation for the purposes of this book.

Finally, the potential contribution of competition law to a fair(er) balance in the music industry is noted, as well as the need to approach copyright (and IP in general) contracts and competition from a holistic perspective.[247]

[243] Ansgar Ohly, 'A Fairness-Based Approach to Economic Rights' in P Bernt Hugenholtz (ed), *Copyright Reconstructed. Rethinking Copyright's Economic Rights in a Time of Highly Dynamic Technological and Economic Change* (Information Law Series 41, Wolters Kluwer 2018) 91.

[244] Cf more in general ibid.

[245] Cf Dusollier and others, 'Contractual Arrangements Applicable to Creators' (n 66) 103; Dusollier, 'EU Contractual Protection of Creators' (n 143) 456.

[246] Cf De Pourcq, *Oneerlijke Handelspraktijken* (n 81) 693–700. The EU legislator has undertaken specific initiatives in this regard, such as (1) Directive (EU) 2019/633 of the European Parliament and of the Council of 17 April 2019 on unfair trading practices in business-to-business relationships in the agricultural and food supply chain [2019] OJ L111/59 and (2) Regulation (EU) 2019/1150 of the European Parliament and of the Council of 20 June 2019 on promoting fairness and transparency for business users of online intermediation services [2019] OJ L186/57.

[247] Cf Friso Bostoen and Jozefien Vanherpe, 'Competition Law in the Digitized Music Industry: The Winners Take It All – But Should They?' (2021) 2 CPI Antitrust Chronicle 30, 30–38. See also extensively CMA, 'Music and Streaming: Final Report' (29 November 2022).

The next step is to determine the regulatory level that appears the most appropriate for enhancing fairness in the music industry. The global reach of online music and, consequently, the cross-border nature of the contracts under review beg the question whether further harmonisation of the copyright contract law should take place at the international regulatory level. However, regardless of possible substantive arguments in favour of global harmonisation, the realisation of hard-law rules on copyright contracts at the global level appears, at the time of writing, to be wholly unrealistic. Consequent to the principle of territoriality, the applicable national copyright laws differ by country, with a significant divide still persisting between civil law and common law countries. Therefore, for the foreseeable future, an international consensus on the appropriate copyright contract law framework seems illusory. Regardless, the consequences of the further globalisation and increasing homogeneity of the music market may yet surprise us all.[248]

Awaiting such potential surprises, the main question as to the appropriate regulatory level is whether and to what extent further European harmonisation of copyright contract law is merited – even though the United Kingdom would not be covered by such regulatory evolution. Subsequent to the principle of conferral, the EU has only the competences conferred on it by the Treaty on European Union (TEU) and the Treaty on the Functioning of the European Union (TFEU), in order to achieve the objectives contained in these treaties.[249] EU competences are either exclusive[250] (including the establishment of competition rules necessary for the functioning of the internal market), shared[251] (including internal market) or supporting[252] (including culture). The exercise of the EU's competences is further subject to the principles of subsidiarity and proportionality. The former implies that the EU may only act under its shared and/or supporting competences if the objectives of the proposed action can be better achieved at the EU regulatory level.[253] If this is not the case, national regulation is considered a better fit. Second, subsequent to the principle of proportionality, the EU may not act in a way that exceeds what is necessary to achieve the objectives of the TEU and/or the TFEU.[254]

[248] Alan B Krueger, *Rockonomics* (John Murray 2019) 232.
[249] Art 5(2) TEU; Ana Ramalho, *The Competence of the European Union in Copyright Lawmaking. A Normative Perspective of EU Powers for Copyright Harmonization* (Springer International 2016) 106–09.
[250] Art 3 TFEU.
[251] Art 4 TFEU.
[252] Art 6 TFEU.
[253] Art 5(3) TEU.
[254] Art 5(4) TEU.

The EU legislator does not have a generalised competence for copyright contract law.[255] However, Article 114 TFEU grants the EU legislator power to adopt measures for the establishment and functioning of the internal market. Further, Article 118 TFEU specifies that the EU is competent to establish measures for the creation of EU-wide IP rights.[256] So far, harmonising EU measures relating to copyright have primarily been based on the objective of furthering the internal market.[257] Not only is EU harmonisation deemed to contribute to the proper functioning of this internal market, it is also said to simultaneously stimulate innovation, creativity, investment and production of new content.[258] For EU action to be legitimately based on the internal market competence, the measures at issue must genuinely have as their aim and content to improve the conditions for the establishment and functioning of the internal market.[259] In this context, the ECJ deems a 'mere finding of disparities between national rules and of the abstract risk of obstacles to the exercise of fundamental freedoms or of distortions of competition liable to result therefrom' to be insufficient.[260] As contract law is traditionally a national field of law, there was a certain hesitation regarding harmonisation of the law applicable to copyright exploitation contracts.[261] This reticence was further fuelled by the wish to acknowledge territorial differences between CCIs.[262] A final hurdle for harmonisation

[255] Silke von Lewinski, 'Copyright Contracts' in Tatiana-Eleni Synodinou (ed), *Codification of European Copyright Law Challenges and Perspectives* (Information Law Series 29, Kluwer Law International 2012) 242; Reto M Hilty and Valentina Moscon, 'Part D – Copyright Contract Law (Article 10 and Articles 14–16 COM(2016) 593 Final)' in Reto M Hilty and Valentina Moscon (eds), *Modernisation of the EU Copyright Rules Position Statement of the Max Planck Institute for Innovation and Competition* (Max Planck Institute for Innovation and Competition Research Paper Series 17–12, Max Planck Institute for Innovation and Competition 2017) 73. See in detail on the EU's competence concerning copyright law Ramalho, *The Competence of the European Union in Copyright Lawmaking* (n 249). See on EU external action in particular Yole Tanghe, 'EU Trade Policy and Copyright Law: On Competence Boundaries and Balancing Copyright Protection with Other Fundamental Rights' (KU Leuven 2019).

[256] See eg Synodinou, 'The Desirability of Unification of European Copyright Law' (n 4) 6.

[257] See eg Recs 1–7 InfoSoc Directive; Recs 9–15 Resale Right Directive; Recs 1–10 IPRED; Recs 1, 5 CRM Directive; Rec 1 Satellite and Cable Directive II; Recs 1–2 DSM Directive. See in detail Ramalho, *The Competence of the European Union in Copyright Lawmaking* (n 249) 10–13, 28–36, 92–95; Synodinou, 'The Desirability of Unification of European Copyright Law' (n 4) 4–6, 15.

[258] Rec 2 DSM Directive.

[259] Case C-376/98, *Germany v Parliament and Council* [2000] ECLI:EU:C:2000:544, paras 83–84.

[260] Hilty and Moscon, 'Part D – Copyright Contract Law (Article 10 and Articles 14–16 COM(2016) 593 Final)' (n 255) 73.

[261] Andreas Rahmatian, 'Dealing with Rights in Copyright-Protected Works: Assignments and Licences' in Estelle Derclaye (ed), *Research Handbook on the Future of EU Copyright* (Research Handbooks in Intellectual Property, Edward Elgar 2009) 313–14.

[262] Cf Commission, 'Report on the Responses to the Public Consultation on the Review of the EU Copyright Rules' (July 2014) <https://bit.ly/3yjVQN8> 80.

efforts in the field of copyright contract law was the limited harmonisation of initial ownership[263] and moral rights.[264]

A shift towards harmonisation in the field of copyright exploitation contracts was first indicated by the rules on contractual relationships with CMOs in the CRM Directive.[265] The need for further harmonisation was subsequently identified in the runup to the DSM Directive.[266] The undeniability of the cross-border dimension is confirmed by the harmonising measures that are already in place at the EU level.[267] The measures included in the DSM Directive in particular seek to allow rightsholders to better exercise their rights in the online environment, thus improving the functioning of the Digital Single Market.[268] The legislative approach in the jurisdictions under review varies rather widely. This sits uneasily with the online and thus potentially global nature of the music contracts under review. Fragmentation, a lack of transparency and ensuing shortcomings in terms of legal certainty arise, as well as a risk of forum shopping.[269] The effect is a validation and continuation of existing power relationships. The potential for further harmonising efforts is clear.[270]

The next step is to determine the appropriate method of regulation. A first important distinction in this regard is that between hard and soft law. The former refers to binding legal instruments and has the benefits of transparency and legal certainty. However, a further increase in such top-down regulation risks entailing a disproportionate encroachment on the freedom of contract and may moreover lead

[263] Michel M Walter and Silke von Lewinski, 'Status of Harmonization and Outlook' in Silke von Lewinski and Michel M Walter (eds), *European Copyright Law A Commentary* (Oxford University Press 2010) 1465–71; Antoon Quaedvlieg, 'Authorship and Ownership: Authors, Entrepreneurs and Rights' in Tatiana-Eleni Synodinou (ed), *Codification of European Copyright Law Challenges and Perspectives* (Information Law Series 29, Kluwer Law International 2012) 197–232. See eg on the initial ownership of rights in audio-visual works, Art 2(2) Rental and Lending Directive.

[264] Guibault and Hugenholtz, 'Study' (n 60) 153; Hugenholtz and Guibault, 'Auteurscontractenrecht' (n 55) 2; Lucie Guibault, 'Relationship between Copyright and Contract Law' in Estelle Derclaye (ed), *Research Handbook on the Future of EU Copyright* (Research Handbooks in Intellectual Property, Edward Elgar 2009) 525.

[265] Arts 11–32 CRM Directive.

[266] Report on the Public Consultation (n 262) 78–79, 82; Commission, 'A Digital Single Market Strategy for Europe' (Communication) COM(2015) 192 Final' (5 June 2015) 7; SWD (2016) 301 final (n 55) 175–91.

[267] SWD(2016) 301 final (n 55) 194.

[268] ibid 132.

[269] Dusollier and others, 'Contractual Arrangements Applicable to Creators' (n 66) 49, 101–02; Hilty and Moscon, 'Part D – Copyright Contract Law (Article 10 and Articles 14–16 COM(2016) 593 Final)' (n 255) 72.

[270] See eg regulatory efforts in the European Parliament concerning the EU framework for the social and professional situation of artists and workers in the CCIs (2023/2051(INL)) <https://bit.ly/3FkTUEm> and 'Cultural Diversity and the Conditions for Authors in the European Music Streaming Market' (2023/2054(INI)). See also OMC Working Group of Member States' Experts, 'The Status and Working Conditions of Artists and Cultural and Creative Professionals' (European Union Publications Office June 2023).

to inefficiencies due to an increase in administration and transaction costs.[271] More malleable, flexible soft law may be said to contribute to a dynamic framework that is more likely to be able to keep up with market changes than somewhat static and all too often unwieldy top-down regulation.[272] In addition, the often sector-specific nature of soft law may aid in acknowledging the specificity of the various CCIs, allowing for a list of per se prohibitions without having to compile one list that 'works' for all CCIs. Finally, soft law that stands the test of time may, over time, be cemented into hard law.[273] This also applies to collectively bargained solutions that may be made generally binding.

The CCIs are extremely diverse, especially across different national territories. Even within the music industry itself, there are relevant genre-specific practices, such as the distinction between employed and freelance orchestral musicians.[274] Drawing the line between an overly specific sectorial framework and a one-size-fits-all regulatory approach that does not take due account of this diversity may be problematic.[275] A potential solution to this conundrum may be to reserve the applicable hard law framework for general rules and essential principles, which are then fleshed out in complementary sector-specific soft law and best practices fuelled by recurring, inclusive stakeholder dialogues. The French implementation process of the DSM Directive may serve as an example, as it leaves much of the specifics of the protective legal framework to collective bargaining.[276] Cross-border – and preferably sector-specific – initiatives in this regard would be most welcome. There may even be room for soft law regarding copyright exploitation contracts at the international level.[277] A particular role in this regard may be envisaged for the World Intellectual Property Organization (WIPO), and in particular the open public–private partnership 'WIPO for Creators'[278] that was launched by WIPO and the Music Rights Awareness Foundation in 2020.[279] While this initiative was primarily set up for awareness-raising purposes, a potential enhancement of its role

[271] Martin Kretschmer and others, 'The Relationship between Copyright and Contract Law' (2010) <https://ssrn.com/abstract=2624945> 5.

[272] Cf Guibault and Hugenholtz, 'Study' (n 60) 157; eg P Bernt Hugenholtz and others, 'The Recasting of Copyright & Related Rights for the Knowledge Economy' (2006) 83–137 214–15; De Pourcq, *Oneerlijke Handelspraktijken* (n 81) 624–25, 701–04.

[273] Hugenholtz and others, 'The Recasting of Copyright & Related Rights for the Knowledge Economy' (n 272) 214–15.

[274] See Chapter 2, Section 2.2.2.1.

[275] Bently and others, 'Strengthening the Position' (n 108) 54.

[276] See Chapter 5, Sections 5.2–3. See also the stakeholder dialogues that took place in 2019 and 2020 concerning the application of Art 17 DSM Directive, which led to Commission, 'Guidance on Article 17 of Directive 2019/790 on Copyright in the Digital Single Market' (Communication) COM(2021) 288 final.

[277] Strowel and Vanbrabant, 'Copyright Licensing: A European View' (n 106) 48.

[278] <www.wipo.int/wipoforcreators/en>.

[279] In this context, Universal Music's decision to become the first corporate sponsor of WIPO for Creators in October 2021 constitutes a step in the right direction, see <https://bit.ly/360UTeJ>.

in terms of standard-setting could be contemplated.[280] However, the potential of sector dialogue should not serve as an excuse for the legislator to avoid making hard (law) decisions.

Empirical research associated with evidence-based lawmaking is difficult and its results are often unpredictable. Nevertheless, additional qualitative and quantitative evidence obtained through independent research that uses a solid methodology should be welcomed.[281] Further evidence may be obtained on the impact of the law on the overall income of musicians, on the investment climate for corporate partners and on the position of users, as well as on the functioning of reporting, contract adjustment and ADR mechanisms in practice. Further interdisciplinary research that brings together the law, economics and sociology is to be supported.[282] A promising initiative in this regard is the 'Copyright Evidence' project, which was developed by the CREATe Centre at the University of Glasgow in partnership with the AHRC[283] Creative Industries Policy & Evidence Centre (PEC).[284] This project houses an open platform that collects empirical studies relating to copyright. It has already catalogued over 900 studies at the time of writing. At the EU level, reference may be made to the Music Moves Europe (MME) strategic initiative, which may lead to the creation of a European Music Observatory.[285] The impact assessments drafted in support of regulatory action at the EU level may also play a contributing role.[286] Finally, the inclusion of the objective of achieving a 'competitive, fair and sustainable European music ecosystem' in the context of the EU

[280] For WIPO standards that apply in the context of industrial property rights, see <https://bit.ly/3mCgjDF>.

[281] Reference may be made to the market study of the UK CMA, 'Music and Streaming: Final Report' (n 247). This report is available online at <https://bit.ly/3YHoQoc>. See also Work Package 3 of the 'ReCreating Europe' project, funded under the Horizon 2020 programme, which includes a survey of authors and performers regarding digitisation, copyright and the digital single market: eg Joost Poort and others, 'Mapping Document on Income Development of Authors and Performers and Copyright Reversal in EU' (2021); Joost Poort and Abeer Pervaiz, 'Survey Data Perspectives Authors and Performers' (2022). See also <www.recreating.eu>.

[282] Stef van Gompel, 'Modern Copyright Reform and the Challenges of Evidence-Based Policymaking' in Jørgen Blomqvist (ed), *Copyright, to Be or not to Be* (Ex Tuto 2019) 129, 132. See also Emily Hudson, *Drafting Copyright Exceptions: From the Law in Books to the Law in Action* (Cambridge Intellectual Property and Information Law, Cambridge University Press 2020); Giulia Priora, 'Distributive Justice in EU Copyright Law: A Function-Based Assessment for a Sustainable Harmonization' (Sant'Anna School of Advanced Studies 2020).

[283] Abbreviation of 'Arts and Humanities Research Council', a British research council that supports research and postgraduate study in the arts and humanities.

[284] <www.copyrightevidence.org>.

[285] <https://bit.ly/3lojIq2>. On the potential for a European Music Observatory, see Panteia and KEA, *Feasibility Study for the Establishment of a European Music Observatory: Final Report* (Publications Office of the European Union 2020).

[286] See eg Commission, 'Impact Assessment on the Legal and Economic Situation of Performers and Record Producers in the European Union' (Staff Working Document) SEC(2008) 2287' (27 July 2008); Commission, 'Impact Assessment Reforming Cross-Border Collective Management of Copyright and Related Rights for Legitimate Online Music Services' (Staff Working Document) SEC(2005) 1254 (11 October 2005); SWD(2016) 301 final (n 55).

research and innovation framework programme Horizon Europe is noted with assent.[287]

3.5 OUTRO

This chapter has analysed the normative criterion of achieving a 'fair(er) balance' between the legitimate interests of the relevant music industry players on both a procedural and substantive level, with a focus on exclusive, individually managed rights in the recorded music and music publishing sector. It then went on to analyse the scope of the relevant substantive legal regimes in substance, place and time. Following an overview of the relevant legislative sources at the national, EU and international levels, the substantive scope of the different protective regimes was assessed. In addition to a categorisation based on the object of the contract, it was found that the identity of the parties to the contract may also affect the applicable legal rules. Given the overlap between the different legislative regimes, their interplay was subsequently reviewed, revealing a multitude of *leges generales et speciales*. Geographically speaking, the continued importance of the national regulatory level in the field of contract law was highlighted, both as to general contract law, copyright contract law and provisions on unfair B2B contract terms and trade practices. This chapter then delved into the crucial issue of intertemporal law, highlighting the essential principles and the conservative application in terms of time of the progressively more protective legal regimes in the chosen jurisdictions. Finally, the appropriate level(s) and method(s) of regulation were treated, arguing in favour of evidence-based lawmaking that combines a hard law approach to general rules and essential principles, to be specified through soft law and sector-specific best practices.

This brings us to the substance of the relevant regulatory framework. Three types of measures may be distinguished. First, there may be certain formal requirements, such as the need for a written document for purposes of proof or validity. Second, the legal framework may result in the prohibition of certain clauses deemed unfair or excessive, either under the framework of (copyright) contract law or the law of unfair B2B contract terms and trade practices. By way of example, the scope of rights transferred may be limited to a certain extent, such as by the principle of strict interpretation, the need for a proper specification of the scope and terms of the transferred/licenced right(s) and restrictions to the transfer of/licence to certain rights – for example, to future works and/or unknown modes of exploitation. Other rules may limit contract transfers, sub-licensing and/or excessive contract duration, or prohibit other contract terms and/or trade practices deemed unfair. Third, the legal framework may impose certain substantive obligations on one (or

[287] See HORIZON-CL2-2022-HERITAGE-01-05 in Commission, 'Horizon Europe Work Programme 2021–2022. 5. Culture, Creativity and Inclusive Society' (2021) 60–61.

more) of the contracting parties in favour of the weaker contract party (or parties). Such measures seek to level the contractual playing field and include certain exploitation obligations and requirements regarding appropriate remuneration for the transferee/licensee. While formal contract requirements are largely confined to the formation stage of the contract and apply in an ex ante way, the latter two categories transcend the abovementioned triad based on the stages of the contract and combine legislative intervention relating to the conditions at the outset of the contract with ex post mechanisms that seek to rectify situations labelled as unfair.

Many of the legislative provisions under review in this book also apply outside the music industry context, to other CCIs. However, given this book's focus on the music industry, the analysis of the relevant legal regimes focuses on their application to the music industry contracts under review. Where deemed relevant, prior analogous research relating to other CCIs is referenced in the footnotes.

The analysis of each category of regulatory measures in the following chapters is two-pronged. First, the substantive scope of application of the measure is analysed, confirming whether it applies to both transfers and licences, and to both composers and performers. Specifications as to scope are not only made on an individual level, but also based on the collective dimension of copyright exploitation. In particular, the influence of the idea of collectiveness (concretised through both collective bargaining and the intervention of CMOs) on the scope of application of the measure at issue is highlighted. Subsequently, the content of the measure is reviewed, focusing on the applicable conditions of application, the appropriate interpretation of the resulting obligations for the contract partners and the question whether the measures at issue may be subject to contractual deviation.

4

Negotiation and Formation of the Contract

Interviewer: 'What came first, the lyrics or the music?'
George Gershwin: 'What came first was the contract.'[1]

4.1 INTRO

Artists who wish to sign over their rights, and who have a full understanding of the consequences of such a decision, must be free to do so. The relevant criterion is the musician's objective: if their primary objective is to obtain financial gain and they are willing to relinquish control over the exploitation of their music to achieve this goal, the legal framework should not unduly hinder them. Even so, differences in bargaining power may lead to excessive transfers and unfair situations in practice, when the scope of the transfer is either unwittingly or purposely unclear and/or goes beyond what is necessary for exploitation purposes and/or leads to an undue transfer of economic value stemming from exploitation of protected content.[2] This rings especially true for early-career musicians, who often do not fully comprehend the scope of a full rights transfer and/or the consequences for their future career.

1 Quoted by Lewis Minkin, *Exits and Entrances: Political Research as a Creative Art* (Sheffield Hallam University Press 1997), 90.

2 Lucie Guibault, 'Relationship between Copyright and Contract Law' in Estelle Derclaye (ed), *Research Handbook on the Future of EU Copyright* (Research Handbooks in Intellectual Property, Edward Elgar 2009) 519; Séverine Dusollier and others, 'Contractual Arrangements Applicable to Creators: Law and Practice of Selected Member States' (Publications Office of the EU 2014) <https://op.europa.eu/s/zIba> 81; Commission, 'Report on the Responses to the Public Consultation on the Review of the EU Copyright Rules' (July 2014) <https://bit.ly/3yjVQN8> 79; Commission, 'Annexes to the Impact Assessment on the Modernisation of EU Copyright Rules' (Staff Working Document) SWD(2016) 301 Final (14 September 2016) 29; Brigitte Lindner, 'European Union. Part A – Copyright and Contract Law Issues' in René Viljoen (ed), *Cross-Border Copyright Licensing Law and Practice* (Elgar Intellectual Property Law and Practice, Edward Elgar 2018) 62.

By way of illustration, while it has been argued that such practices occur less and less,[3] reference may be made to tying practices where musicians are offered contracts that require them to sign with both the record company and music publishing divisions of a major music company.[4] In addition, the much-used technique of recoupable advances[5] may raise an eyebrow, as corporate partners (in the event of a transfer) still retain ownership after the advances have been recouped entirely. While mere licences have become much more prevalent, full buyouts still occur often, especially for session musicians.[6] Such practices may be questioned, especially for music that turns out to be a huge commercial success.

The rise of digital and streaming revenue has led to an additional concern as to contracts with so-called legacy artists. This term, used interchangeably with the term 'heritage artists', comes from the United States and refers to artists whose catalogue largely predates the introduction of copyright protection for phonograms in the United States in 1972. Many of these artists signed unfavourable record deals, leading to persisting unfair situations.[7] As to the grant of rights in particular, 'digital sales' and 'streaming' as forms of exploitation of music did not exist in the analogue age. Deals that predate the internet revolution do not mention these methods of exploitation – or the right to making available, since this had not yet been established then.[8] Some music companies argued that general transfers of copyright pertaining to the right of communication to the public that took place before the turning of the millennium also include these new forms of exploitation, thus allegedly releasing labels from the obligation to provide musicians with additional remuneration for digital exploitation.[9] Others have been known to hold out on offering music on streaming services until the artists conceded to low royalty rates.[10]

This chapter analyses limitations to parties' freedom of contract in the negotiation and formation stage of the contracts under review that are aimed at remedying situations such as those outlined above. These limitations seek to ensure that such contracts have a 'fair scope'. As yet, awaiting potential EU harmonisation of authorship and initial ownership, there are no relevant harmonising rules at the EU level.

3 Stef van Gompel and others, 'Evaluatie Wet Auteurscontractenrecht: Eindrapport' (2020) <https://bit.ly/3UBZrh4>106.

4 P Bernt Hugenholtz and Lucie Guibault, 'Auteurscontractenrecht: Naar Een Wettelijke Regeling?' (2004) 25; Luc Gulinck, *Hier Tekenen! (en Let Niet op de Kleine Lettertjes…) Wegwijs in het Juridische en Zakelijke Labyrint van de Muziekwereld* (Academia Press 2019) 153.

5 See Chapter 2, Section 2.4.5.

6 ibid.

7 See eg re artists The Shirelles and BJ, Thomas: Soocher (n 210) 65–84.

8 Cf Jim Rogers, *The Death & Life of the Music Industry in the Digital Age* (Bloomsbury 2013) 88–89; Mark Mulligan, *Awakening: The Music Industry In The Digital Age* (Createspace 2015) 19–20; Gulinck, *Hier Tekenen!* (n 4) 65.

9 Dusollier and others, 'Contractual Arrangements Applicable to Creators' (n 2) 11, 66–76; Chris Cooke, *Dissecting the Digital Dollar* (3rd edn, Music Managers Forum and CMU Insights 2020) 97.

10 Mulligan, *Awakening* (n 8) 19–20.

Instead, focus lies with relevant restrictions under national law. First, objectionable precontractual behaviour may be sanctioned by precontractual liability, giving rise to damages (Section 4.2). Subsequently, the requirement of consent is subject to certain requirements (Section 4.3). Third, the law limits parties' freedom as to the scope of rights that may be transferred or licenced and provides tools to determine this scope in practice (Section 4.4). Finally, this chapter turns to the negotiation and formation stage of secondary contractual relationships that may arise once the initial contract has been entered into (Section 4.5), and concludes with an overview of the main findings (Section 4.6).

4.2 NEGOTIATION OF THE CONTRACT: PRECONTRACTUAL LIABILITY

Parties' freedom of contract implies a liberty to enter into and conduct contractual negotiations at will. While restrictions to parties' behaviour in a precontractual context are limited, they must abide by a duty of care, lest liability arise.[11] The scope of this duty of care is subject to national law. On the one hand, such liability may arise when parties unduly leave the negotiation table, resulting in a right to claim damages for the scorned party under certain circumstances.[12] On the other hand, parties may have an obligation to actively provide their (prospective) counterparty with certain information.[13]

[11] In some cases, providing faulty or even deceptive information may lead to vitiated consent on the part of the counterparty, with potential consequences as to the validity of the contract.

[12] See eg (1) in Belgium: Art 5.17 new Belgian CC; (2) in France: Art 1112 French CC; Jacques Ghestin and Hugo Barbier, *Traité de Droit Civil. Introduction Générale. Tome 2* (5th edn, LGDJ – lextenso éditions 2020) 508–13; (3) in Germany: Art 311(2) German Civil Code; Basil S Markesinis and others, *The German Law of Contract. A Comparative Treatise* (2nd edn, Hart 2006) 91–102; Dieter Medicus and Stephan Lorenz, *Schuldrecht I. Allgemeiner Teil* (Juristische Kurz-Lehrbücher, 21st edn, CH Beck 2015) 242–53; Wolfgang Fikentscher and Andreas Heinemann, *Schuldrecht: Allgemeiner und Besonderer Teil* (De Gruyter Studium, 11th edn, De Gruyter 2017) 70; and (4) in the Netherlands: on the basis of the general provision on good faith, Art 6:2(1) Dutch CC; Jan M van Dunné, *Verbintenissenrecht. Deel 1. Contractenrecht* (5th edn, Kluwer 2004) 238–85; Carel Asser, *Verbintenissenrecht. Algemeen Overeenkomstenrecht* (Asser Serie 6.III*, 13th edn, Kluwer 2008)156–70; RPJL Tjittes, 'De Aansprakelijkheid Voor Afgebroken Onderhandelingen – Een Kritisch Overzicht' [2016] Rechtsgeleerd Magazijn THEMIS 237; Jac Hijma and others, *Rechtshandeling en Overeenkomst* (Studiereeks burgerlijk recht 3, 9th edn, Kluwer 2019) 65–72.

[13] See eg (1) in Belgium: Ignace Claeys and Thijs Tanghe, *Algemeen Contractenrecht. Handboek voor Nu en Straks* (Intersentia 2021) 69–83; W Van Gerven and A Van Oevelen, *Verbintenissenrecht* (Studie Juri, 6th edn, Acco 2021) 154–55; (2) in France: Arts 1112-1, 1116 French CC; Julie Groffe, *La Bonne Foi en Droit d'Auteur* (Institut Universitaire Varenne Collection des Thèses 106, LGDJ – lextenso éditions 2015) 266–68, 308–10; Yvaine Buffelan-Lanore and Virginie Larribau-Terneyre, *Droit Civil. Les obligations* (16th edn, Sirey 2018) 353–58; François Terré and others, *Droit Civil. Les Obligations* (Précis. Droit privé, 12th edn, Dalloz 2019) 273–76; (3) in Germany: on the basis of the provisions on mistake and/or fraud, leading to vitiated consent, Arts 119, 123 German CC; see also Art 276 German CC; Markesinis and others, *The German Law of Contract* (n 12) 103; and (4) in the Netherlands: on

Negotiating parties are not obliged to tell each other everything and may use previously acquired knowledge to their advantage. A contrary solution would run counter to commercial practice and would significantly deter investment. However, providing incorrect or incomplete information may give rise to liability, either based on a general duty of care or because of a duty of information imposed by law in a specific context.[14] The scope of a negotiating party's general duty to provide information is affected by, among other things, the applicable law – as, for example, UK law does not articulate a general pre-contractual duty to conduct negotiations in good faith and instead relies on a number of flexible contractual doctrines to regulate the negotiation context[15] – as well as the reasonable expectations and information needs of the counterparty. These are, in turn, shaped by several factors, such as the relevance of the information in view of the contract and the experience of the counterparty. Translated to the streaming age, a corporate partner's duty to inform will be more extensive if they are faced with a musician at the start of their career.[16] Conversely, parties may have a duty of research or control, in the sense that it is expected for them to have a certain degree of knowledge about the subject of the contract. Legally speaking, therefore, musicians should not simply accept all information and should conduct a certain amount of prior research.

In addition to these grounds for pre-contractual liability, non-harmonised national regimes concerning unfair trade practices in B2B situations may fulfil a complementary role.[17] Under these rules, aggressive or misleading behaviour that exploits the vulnerable position of the counterparty may be sanctioned.[18] Unfair trade practices are usually sanctioned by an injunction that puts an end to the behaviour.[19] In addition, damages may be

the basis of the provisions on mistake and/or fraud, leading to vitiated consent, ia Art 3:44(1)–(3), Art 6:228 Dutch CC; Asser, *Verbintenissenrecht* (n 12) 156–57.

14 Annick De Boeck, *Informatierechten en -Plichten bij de Totstandkoming en Uitvoering van Overeenkomsten* (Intersentia 2002). See also Alexandre Cruquenaire, *L'Interprétation des Contrats en Droit d'Auteur* (Création Information Communication 11, Larcier 2007) 328–29, 398–99; Dusollier and others, 'Contractual Arrangements Applicable to Creators' (n 2) 52.

15 Neil Andrews, *Contract Rules: Decoding English Law* (Intersentia 2016) 21, 97–127.

16 Cf Cruquenaire, *L'Interprétation des Contrats en Droit d'Auteur* (n 14) 420.

17 Cf Art 10*bis* Paris Convention of 20 March 1883 for the Protection of Industrial Property (as amended), available online at <https://wipolex.wipo.int/en/text/287556>.

18 See (1) in Belgium: Arts VI.104/1, VI.105, VI.105/1, VI.109/1, VI.109/3 Belgian CEL; (2) in France: Art L 442-1 French Commercial Code; and (3) in Germany: Arts 4, 4a, 5, 5a UWG. The concept of unfair trade practices also includes unfair behaviour linked to an individual contractual relationship. See in a B2C context as to a misleading trade practice Case C-388/13 *Nemzeti Fogyasztóvédelmi Hatóság v UPC Magyarország* [2015] ECLI:EU:C:2015:225. See in more detail, Sofie De Pourcq, *Oneerlijke Handelspraktijken en Bedingen in Contracten Tussen Ondernemingen* (Intersentia 2018) 401–06. Provisions on unfair B2B trade practices are not limited to the pre-contractual phase.

19 De Pourcq, *Oneerlijke Handelspraktijken* (n 18) 480–93; Jules Stuyck and Bert Keirsbilck, *Handels- en Economisch Recht. Deel 2. Mededingingsrecht. A. Handelspraktijken en Contracten met Consumenten* (Beginselen van Belgisch Privaatrecht XIII, 5th edn, Wolters Kluwer 2019) 157–79.

claimed.[20] On a more conceptual level, a prohibition on misleading conduct may imply a specification of the duty to inform the other contracting party before contract conclusion.

Applicable duties of care and information are exceedingly fact- and country-specific and, thus, difficult to generalise. Considerations of distributive justice argue in favour of a duty for both contracting parties to provide certain information. Such a duty may help to counter the information asymmetry surrounding the contracts under review and may prevent parties from exploiting the advantage that flows from such an asymmetry to the detriment of their counterparty.[21] Indeed, the law should not 'burden citizens with requirements of knowledge and foresight that they cannot normally meet'.[22] However, these restrictions on party behaviour are rather vague. This leads to questions of interpretation, the need for a case-by-case analysis and the importance of case law as a source of interpretation. Moreover, the breadth of the relevant concepts makes them susceptible to overreach. A careful and restrictive application is merited, in view of the freedom of contract and the duty of research that applies in B2B situations such as those in the contractual relationships under review.[23]

It may also be questioned to what extent imposing liability on one of the contract partners really contributes to achieving a fair balance between stakeholders' interests, given the limited impact of such liability on the actual substance of the contractual relationship.[24] Legal provisions that *do* have such an impact are discussed below.

4.3 FORMATION OF THE CONTRACT: REQUIREMENT OF CONSENT

This section focuses on substantive and formal aspects of the requirement of consent that have a particular bearing on the contracts under review, either for reasons of public policy or with a view to protecting one or more of the parties in a contractual context. The subsection on substantive requirements posits the principle of express consent as the rule. Exceptions to this rule that are relevant to this research mainly apply in the audio-visual sector and to music made in an employment context or on commission. Formally speaking, focus lies with applicable requirements of a written contract.

20 De Pourcq, *Oneerlijke Handelspraktijken* (n 18) 480–93.

21 Anthony K Kronman, 'Contract Law and Distributive Justice' in Joel Feinberg and Jules Coleman (eds), *Philosophy of Law* (8th edn, Thomson Wadsworth 2008) 812–13. See for an extensive analysis of this issue and advocating in favour of an objective standard for parties' behaviour, albeit from the perspective of corrective justice, Martín Hevia, *Reasonableness and Responsibility: A Theory of Contract Law*, vol 101 (Law and Philosophy Library, Springer Netherlands 2013) 157–69.

22 John Rawls, *Political Liberalism* (The John Dewey Essays in Philosophy 4, Columbia University Press 1993) 268.

23 Cf Cruquenaire, *L'Interprétation des Contrats en Droit d'Auteur* (n 14) 327.

24 Cf ibid 329–38, 356–57.

4.3.1 *Material Requirements*

The requirement of a consensus between parties for a contract to be concluded is one of the main building blocks – if not the foundation – of contract law. Without consent, there can be no contract. The principles regarding vitiated consent have a similar consequence: if a party's consent is tainted with a defect, the entire contract could be declared non-binding.[25] For a detailed analysis of the substantive requirements of consent, the reader is referred to detailed legal doctrine on this topic.[26]

Generally, parties' consent to enter into a copyright exploitation contract must be express.[27] Express consent may be defined as an authorisation that is explicitly communicated by the consenting party before the exploitation, and is contrasted with presumptive consent, which refers to implicit authorisation deduced from certain strictly defined external factors.[28] In view of the principle of express consent, presumptive consent to transfer or grant a licence to certain rights to a corporate partner will not often be accepted.[29] Subsequent to the ECJ judgment in the *Soulier*

[25] ibid 373–76; Dusollier and others, 'Contractual Arrangements Applicable to Creators' (n 2) 55; Bernard Vanbrabant, *La Propriété Intellectuelle. Tome 2. Régime Patrimonial* (Création Information Communication, Larcier 2018) 781–85. See for two examples where recourse to the principles concerning vitiated consent was not accepted: Court of Appeal Arnhem-Leeuwarden 24 December 2019, docket number 200.227.882/01, ECLI:NL:GHARL:2019:11117; District Court Amsterdam 17 January 2024, docket number C/13/714130 HA ZA 22-167, ECLI:NL:RBAMS:2024:345.

[26] See (1) in Belgium: Arts 1108–1122 Belgian Civil Code; Sophie Stijns, *Verbintenissenrecht. Boek 1* (die Keure 2005) 80–93; Claeys and Tanghe, *Algemeen Contractenrecht* (n 13) 150–66; Van Gerven and Van Oevelen, *Verbintenissenrecht* (n 13) 114–26; (2) in France: Arts 1128–1144 French Civil Code; Buffelan-Lanore and Larribau-Terneyre, *Droit Civil. Les obligations* (n 13) 371–407, 469–508; Pierre-Yves Gautier, *Propriété Littéraire et Artistique* (11th edn, Presses Universitaires de France 2019) 507–13; Terré and others, *Droit Civil. Les Obligations* (n 13) 182–365, 611–68; (3) in Germany: Arts 116–124 German Civil Code; Markesinis and others, *The German Law of Contract* (n 12) 55–81, 276–318; Fikentscher and Heinemann, *Schuldrecht* (n 12) 109–12; (4) in the Netherlands: Arts 3:44, 6:228, Dutch Civil Code; van Dunné, *Verbintenissenrecht* (n 12) 515–606; Asser, *Verbintenissenrecht* (n 12) 133–223; Barbara Baarsma and Nicole Rosenboom, 'Oneerlijke Handelspraktijken. Voldoet Bestaande (Zelf)regulering?' (2013) 21 10–11; Hijma and others, *Rechtshandeling en Overeenkomst* (n 12) 23–77, 156–91; and (5) in the United Kingdom: Joseph Chitty and Hugh Beale, *Chitty on Contracts* (32nd edn, Sweet & Maxwell 2015) chs 2–8; Andrews, *Contract Rules* (n 15) 97–136; Edwin Peel, *Treitel on the Law of Contract* (15th edn, Sweet & Maxwell 2020) chs 2–4; Mindy Chen-Wishart, *Contract Law* (7th edn, Oxford University Press 2022) 43–395. See also Study Group on a European Civil Code and the Research Group on EC Private Law (Acquis Group), *Principles, Definitions and Model Rules of European Private Law. Draft Common Frame of Reference (DCFR)* (2008) <https://bit.ly/2XvvoxZ>.

[27] See eg Sébastien Raimond, *La Qualification du Contrat d'Auteur* (Le Droit des Affaires. Propriété Intellectuelle 34, LexisNexis 2009) 76–77.

[28] Cf Case C-301/15 *Soulier and Doke* [2016] ECLI:EU:C:2016:878. See also Cruquenaire, *L'Interprétation des Contrats en Droit d'Auteur* (n 14) 97–103.

[29] However under UK law see eg *Godfrey v Lees* [1995] *EMLR* 307 and the potential implied obligation to transfer copyright to the commissioner under UK law, Lionel Bently and others, *Intellectual Property Law* (5th edn, Oxford University Press 2018) 151–52, 327. See also Michael

case (concerning authors of literary works), presumptive consent is only accepted if (1) the author is actually informed of the intended use of their work and (2) they have been put in a position to prohibit the use if they so desire.[30] If no actual and individual information is proven, a mere lack of opposition on the part of the author does not equal the requisite consent.[31] Because of copyright's no-formalities rule, authors must be able to stop unauthorised exploitation by a third party without having to go through cumbersome formalities.[32] This conclusion applies to composers. The same must be true for performers, in view of the identical formulation of the relevant provisions[33] and the principled equal nature of the rights granted to composers and performers.[34]

The requirement of express consent plays a key role in ensuring informed consent to the contracts under review and ensuing agency of all parties. Therefore, a generalised requirement of express consent in the music industry is merited, also in the streaming age. As to the concrete interpretation of the requirement of express material consent, inspiration may be drawn from the realm of consumer law. A separate, prior, clear and comprehensible expression of parties' wills may be envisaged.[35] Musicians must be aware of both the legal and economic consequences of signing a contract with a corporate partner and have ample opportunities to discuss and set fair arrangements in terms of contract performance.[36] The grant of exploitation rights should not be hidden in the general terms and conditions that apply in a given contractual relationship.[37]

Even so, presumptive consent often exists in an employment context. Regarding music created in (legally presumed or actual) employment situations, the scope of the substantive requirement of consent for the grant of rights differs.[38] Under

Beurskens and others, 'Implied Consent – a Silent Revolution in Digital Copyright Law. US, German and French Perspectives' [2013] RIDA 2; Georgia Jenkins, 'An Extended Doctrine of Implied Consent – A Digital Mediator?' (2021) 52 IIC 706; Bently and others, *Intellectual Property Law* (n 29) 331–32. The concept of presumptive licences is to be distinguished from remuneration rights.

30 Case C-301/15 *Soulier and Doke* [2016] ECLI:EU:C:2016:878, paras 35–36. See also Caterina Sganga, 'From Soulier to the EU Copyright Law Reform: What Future for Non-Voluntary Collective Management Schemes?' (2018) 19 ERA Forum 137. See also Case C-392/19 *VG Bild-Kunst v Stiftung Preußischer Kulturbesitz* [2021] ECLI:EU:C:2021:181, para 38.

31 ibid paras 37–43.

32 Case C-301/15 *Soulier and Doke* [2016] ECLI:EU:C:2016:878, paras 51–52.

33 See at the EU level Art 2(a)–(b) InfoSoc Directive regarding the reproduction right and Art 3 (1)–(2) InfoSoc Directive regarding composers' right to communication to the public and performers' making available right.

34 Case C-484/18 *Spedidam* [2019] ECLI:EU:C:2019:423, Opinion of AG Hogan, para 35.

35 Cf Arts 5–8 Consumer Rights Directive.

36 Dusollier and others, 'Contractual Arrangements Applicable to Creators' (n 2) 32, 69; ; Séverine Dusollier, 'EU Contractual Protection of Creators: Blind Spots and Shortcomings' [2018] Colum J L & Arts, 436, 439.

37 Van Gompel and others, 'Evaluatie Wet Auteurscontractenrecht' (n 3) 22.

38 Cf Chapter 3, Section 3.3.2.3.

Belgian,[39] French[40] and German[41] law, in principle, the employee retains their rights unless contractually provided otherwise.[42] Regardless, case law has accepted that the existence of presumptive consent in case content is created in an employment context under certain circumstances. This is particularly true if the creation process falls within the scope of the performance of the employee's duties as an employee and thus the object of the contract.[43]

Under French law, presumptive consent may also apply to music commissioned for advertising purposes.[44] More specifically, the grant of exploitation rights to a corporate partner is (rebuttably) presumed if a certain duty to specify is fulfilled: if the contract specifies a distinct remuneration for each method of exploitation, geographical and temporal scope, the size of the *tirage*[45] and the nature of the medium/carrier.[46] Finally, Dutch law grants initial ownership in a work that has

[39] No rules regarding presumptive consent apply to the particular category of commissioned works and/or performances under Belgian law. The initial author and/or performer receives initial ownership. The corporate partner must obtain express consent to secure the transfer and/or licence of those relevant rights.

[40] See Art L 111-3 French IP Code.

[41] Art 43 German Copyright Act. This rule is subject to the prohibition under German law to transfer copyright *sensu stricto*, see below, Section 4.4.1.1. See Gerhard Schricker, *Urheberrecht. Kommentar* (3rd edn, CH Beck 2006) 879–933; Friedrich Karl Fromm and Wilhelm Nordemann, *Urheberrecht. Kommentar zum Urheberrechtsgesetz, zum Verlagsgesetz und zum Urheberrechtswahrnehmungsgesetz* (Rechtswissenschaften und Verwaltung, 10th edn, Kohlhammer 2008) 910–32; Gunda Dreyer and others, *Urheberrecht* (Heidelberger Kommentar, 4th edn, CF Müller 2018) 857–67; Philipp Möhring and Käte Nicolini, *Urheberrecht* (4th edn, CH Beck 2018) 626–31; Patrick Zurth, 'Implementation of the DSM Directive's Contract Provisions into German Law' in Simon Geiregat and Hendrik Vanhees (eds), *Copyright Contracts Tomorrow* (LeA 2023) 49.

[42] As indicated in Chapter 3, Section 3.3.2.3, the opposite rule applies as to copyright *sensu stricto* in the Netherlands and the United Kingdom: a presumption of ownership applies to the benefit of the employer, unless contrary contractual arrangements have been made.

[43] See case law referenced in Lucie Guibault and P Bernt Hugenholtz, 'Study on the Conditions Applicable to Contracts Relating to Intellectual Property in the European Union' (2002) <https://bit.ly/4bzdGud> 63–64; Schricker, *Urheberrecht. Kommentar* (n 41) 1522–23; Cruquenaire (n 14) 112–14; Raimond, *La Qualification du Contrat d'Auteur* (n 27) 76–79; Marina Markellou, *Le Contrat d'Exploitation d'Auteur. Vers un Droit d'Auteur Contractuel Européen. Analyse Comparative des Systèmes Juridiques Allemand, Belge, Français et Hellénique* (Création Information Communication, Larcier 2012) 102–04, 128–34; Alexis Boisson, *La Licence de Droit d'Auteur* (Bibliothèque de Droit de l'Entreprise 86, LexisNexis 2013) 558–62; Dusollier and others, 'Contractual Arrangements Applicable to Creators' (n 2) 44, 132. See also Eugen Ulmer, *La propriété intellectuelle et le droit international privé* (Commission des communautés européennes. Collection études. Série secteur culturel 3, Office for Official Publications of the European Communities 1980) 47.

[44] The regime that applies to music on commission under Belgian law requires the grant of rights to be express.

[45] In English: edition.

[46] Art L 132-31 French IP Code; Guibault and Hugenholtz, 'Study on the Conditions Applicable to Contracts Relating to Intellectual Property in the European Union' (n 43) 64; Markellou, *Le Contrat d'Exploitation d'Auteur* (n 43) 98–100; André Lucas and others, *Traité de la Propriété Littéraire et Artistique* (5th edn, LexisNexis 2017) 773–82; Christophe Caron, *Droit d'Auteur et*

been created according to the design of another person and under the latter's supervision to the commissioner that fulfils these criteria – a rule that has been held to have a limited scope of application in the past.[47]

A final example of presumptive consent in the relationship between musicians and their corporate partners relates to contributions to audio-visual works. All three regulatory layers under review provide for such presumptive consent under certain circumstances, for both authors and performers.[48] The rebuttable presumption usually (except in Germany for copyright *sensu stricto*[49]) gives rise to a statutory assignment of rights to the producer of the audio-visual work at issue and an unwaivable right to equitable remuneration on the part of the artist. Compositions specifically created for and used in a film are excluded from the scope of such presumptions of transfer.[50]

Over the past decade, presumptive consent has led to several preliminary references to the ECJ. First, the *Luksan* case[51] concerned a presumptive, rebuttable transfer under Austrian law of authors' exploitation rights regarding audio-visual works to the film producer. The principal director of a documentary film sought to challenge this presumption. However, his efforts eventually proved to be fruitless. In its judgment, the ECJ primarily refers to the need to protect the significant and high-risk investments made by producers in the production of both films and

Droits Voisins (6th edn, LexisNexis 2020) 484–86. See for a potential alternative solution for commissioned works under French law Bruno Racine, 'L'Auteur et l'Acte de Création' (January 2020) 96–103.

47 Art 6 Copyright Act; Guibault and Hugenholtz, 'Study on the Conditions Applicable to Contracts Relating to Intellectual Property in the European Union' (n 43) 47.

48 See (1) at the international level: Art 14*bis* Berne Convention (for authors; see regarding the applicability of this provision in the EU: Case C-277/10 *Martin Luksan v Petrus van der Let* [2012] ECLI:EU:C:2012:65, paras 54–64) and Art 19 Rome Convention and Art 12 Beijing Treaty (for performers); (2) at the EU level: Art 3(5) (for authors) and 3(1–4) and 3(6) Rental Directive (for performers); and (3) at the national level: Arts XI.182 (for authors) and XI.206 (for performers) Belgian CEL, Arts L 132-24 (for authors) and L 212-4 (for performers) French IP Code, Arts 89 (for authors) and 92 (for performers) German Copyright Act; Art 45d Dutch Copyright Act (for authors) and Art 4 Dutch Neighbouring Rights Act (for performers); Arts 93A, 191F UK CDPA; Fabienne Brison, *Het Naburig Recht van de Uitvoerende Kunstenaar* (Creatie Informatie Communicatie 7, Larcier 2001) 454–60, 619–21, 632–38, 647–49; Markellou, *Le Contrat d'Exploitation d'Auteur* (n 43) 95–98; Europe Economics and others, 'Remuneration of Authors and Performers for the Use of Their Works and the Fixations of Their Performances. Final Report' (Publications Office of the EU 2015) <https://op.europa.eu/s/zIa9> 33–35; Dirk Visser and others, *ACR: Auteurscontractenrecht* (DeLex 2016) 237–85, 291; Hendrik Vanhees, 'Auteurscontract' [2019] OBO 1, 59–63; Richard Arnold, *Performers' Rights* (6th edn, Sweet & Maxwell 2021) 99–100.

49 Under German law, no full transfer of copyright *sensu stricto* is possible, see below, Section 4.4.1.1.

50 See (1) in Belgium: Art XI.182 Belgian CEL; (2) in France: Art L 132-24 (1) French IP Code; (3) in Germany: Art 89(3) German Copyright Act; (4) in the Netherlands: Art 45d(1) Dutch Copyright Act; and (5) in the United Kingdom: Art 93A(3) UK CDPA.

51 Case C-277/10 *Martin Luksan v Petrus van der Let* [2012] ECLI:EU:C:2012:65.

phonograms.[52] According to the ECJ, adequate protection of film producers' interests is required to secure their income and to allow them to recoup their investment.[53] Film producers must be able to exploit the films they produce.[54] They cannot be expected to acquire every contributor's express agreement.[55] The presumption of transfer at issue is therefore accepted, not only for the rental right (where it is expressly provided for under EU law[56]), but also for the reproduction right and the right of communication to the public (where this is not the case).[57] Importantly, the presumption must be rebuttable.[58] Moreover, the author's unwaivable right to equitable remuneration for private copying, the only remuneration right expressly at issue in this case, must be ensured.[59]

A similar line of reasoning was applied in the *Spedidam* judgment, which concerned the rights of performers. This case concerned a rebuttable presumption of consent under French law[60] and the consequences for the exclusive economic rights of a jazz drummer who was a performer in a series of audio-visual works spanning over almost two decades. The performer was considered to have authorised the fixation and exploitation of their performances for the mere fact of having been involved in the recording. The ECJ again held that this was allowable, provided that the presumption is rebuttable and appropriate remuneration is ensured.[61] The ECJ confirmed that consent may be presumed based on certain actions.[62]

In other words, if the performer has the possibility of entering into contrary contractual arrangements and receives some form of payment for the exploitation, presumptive consent passes the ECJ's test. This focus on remuneration may be welcomed, given the irrefutable importance of paying artists for their work, but only cautiously so. First, on a conceptual level, the apparent spillover between exclusive

52 ibid para 77.

53 ibid paras 77–79. See also Dusollier and others, 'Contractual Arrangements Applicable to Creators' (n 2) 47–48.

54 Cf Brison, *Het Naburig Recht van de Uitvoerende Kunstenaar* (n 48) 454.

55 Cf Case C-277/10 *Martin Luksan v Petrus van der Let* [2012] ECLI:EU:C:2011:545, Opinion of AG Trstenjak, paras 105–06.

56 See Art 3(4) and (5) Rental Directive.

57 Case C-277/10 *Martin Luksan v Petrus van der Let* [2012] ECLI:EU:C:2012:65, paras 82–86. See also Lindner, 'European Union. Part A' (n 2) 73–74.

58 Case C-277/10 *Martin Luksan v Petrus van der Let* [2012] ECLI:EU:C:2012:65, paras 80–81 and 87.

59 ibid paras 88–109.

60 Art L 212-4 French IP Code *jo*. Article 49 of Freedom of Communication Act No. 86-1067 of 30 September 1986, which gives the French *Institut national de l'audiovisuel* (INA) the right to exploit the audio-visual archives of national broadcasting companies.

61 Case C-484/18 *Spedidam* [2019] ECLI:EU:C:2019:970, paras 40–46. The French Supreme Court later also accepted the presumptive consent in this case, see French Supreme Court, Civil Chamber, 22 January 2020, docket number 17-18.177, ECLI:FR:CCASS:2020:C100047. See also Amélie Blocman, 'INA's Exploitation of Performances Approved by CJEU and Court of Cassation' [2020] IRIS 3:1/25.

62 Case C-484/18 *Spedidam* [2019] ECLI:EU:C:2019:970, para 42.

and remuneration rights on the part of the ECJ should not be downplayed. The *Spedidam* case relates to a performer's exclusive rights of reproduction and making available, which depend on the rights owner's consent, while the ECJ's focus lies with remuneration. The mere fact that a performer receives remuneration in case of exploitation does not change the fact that such an exploitation connected with an exclusive right constitutes an infringement without the required consent.[63] The remuneration does not in itself justify a legal presumption of consent, especially if it is unfairly low in practice. A similar uneasiness may exist regarding the second safeguard – the rebuttable nature of the presumption – since the possibility of reaching contrary contractual arrangements risks remaining largely theoretical. The ECJ's current, rather lax treatment of presumptive transfers in the audio-visual sector therefore deserves closer scrutiny.

The ECJ attaches importance to the specific nature of audio-visual works, the production of which requires considerable financial investment.[64] The presumptive transfer of rights is thus primarily a policy choice, the result of the balancing exercise that enables film producers to recoup their investment while safeguarding artists' right to remuneration. The scope of this presumption should remain limited to what is necessary to achieve this policy objective. Otherwise, the presumption may constitute a disproportionate interference with exclusive artists' rights.[65] It should therefore only apply to film producers, not to the benefit of third parties that seek to exploit audio-visual works without having (at least partially) funded their production.[66] The indiscriminate application of any legal presumption of consent, as seemingly accepted by the ECJ, given that the middleman in the *Spedidam* case was a public body and not a film producer, is difficult to justify.

Exceptions to the requirement of express consent such as those outlined above should be confined to a workable minimum, such as for certain audio-visual productions and music made in an employment context or for hire – albeit with a marked preference for express consent as regards the latter category. Various legislative solutions exist in this context, as exemplified by the Belgian, French and German legal frameworks. Instances of presumptive consent should moreover be limited to what is strictly necessary to allow the corporate partner to recoup their investment, and/or to an implied licence instead of a transfer in other cases where presumptive consent presents itself as desirable, such as for archiving or other

63 Cf by analogy Case C-301/15 *Soulier and Doke* [2016] ECLI:EU:C:2016:536, Opinion of AG Wathelet, para 41.

64 Rec 10 InfoSoc Directive; Rec 5 Rental Directive; Case C-61/05 *Commission of the European Communities v Portuguese Republic* [2006] ECLI:EU:C:2006:467, para 27; Case C-277/10 *Martin Luksan v Petrus van der Let* [2012] ECLI:EU:C:2012:65, paras 77 and 83.

65 Case C-484/18 *Spedidam* [2019] ECLI:EU:C:2019:423, Opinion of AG Hogan, paras 40 and 43–44.

66 ibid paras 40–42.

cultural purposes.[67] Only by limiting presumptive consent to situations where the need arises may agency on the part of all contracting parties be secured.

4.3.2 *Formal Requirements*

Contracts generally arise solely when certain substantive conditions are fulfilled, without there being any need to fulfil specific formalities.[68] This is true for copyright exploitation contracts in Belgium, France and Germany. As a result, a written instrument is in principle not a requirement of validity and parties' consent in principle suffices for a transfer and/or licence to exclusive exploitation rights in music to be valid in those countries.

The contrary is true in the Netherlands and the United Kingdom, save for non-exclusive licences. In those countries, the law requires (either full or partial) transfers and exclusive licences by either authors or performers to be by way of a signed document.[69] In the Netherlands, in the absence of such a document, the grant may be declared non-binding.[70] In the United Kingdom, while an oral assignment is ineffective at law, equitable ownership is likely to arise, provided that the necessary consideration is present.[71]

[67] Cf Case C-484/18 *Spedidam* [2019] ECLI:EU:C:2019:423, Opinion of AG Hogan, para 45.

[68] See eg (1) in Belgium: Stijns, *Verbintenissenrecht. Boek 1* (n 26) 42; Claeys and Tanghe, *Algemeen Contractenrecht* (n 13) 55–69; Van Gerven and Van Oevelen, *Verbintenissenrecht* (n 13) 158; (2) in France: Arts 1172 *jo* 1109, 1113 French Civil Code; Nathalie Blanc, *Les Contrats du Droit d'Auteur à l'Epreuve de la Distinction des Contrats Nommés et Innommés* (Nouvelle Bibliothèque de Thèses 93, Dalloz 2010) 45; Buffelan-Lanore and Larribau-Terneyre, *Droit Civil. Les obligations* (n 13) 296; Terré and others, *Droit Civil. Les Obligations* (n 13) 226–30; (3) in Germany: impliedly ia Arts 125, 145 German Civil Code; Markesinis and others, *The German Law of Contract* (n 12) 55–56; Medicus and Lorenz, *Schuldrecht I. Allgemeiner Teil* (n 12) 28; Fikentscher and Heinemann, *Schuldrecht* (n 12) 46; (4) in the Netherlands: Art 3:37 Dutch Civil Code; Hugenholtz and Guibault, 'Auteurscontractenrecht' (n 4) 6; van Dunné, *Verbintenissenrecht* (n 12) 7–14; Asser, *Verbintenissenrecht* (n 12) 225–26; Hijma and others, *Rechtshandeling en Overeenkomst* (n 12) 14–15, 149–50; and (5) in the United Kingdom: Chitty and Beale, *Chitty on Contracts* (n 26) 94; Andrews, *Contract Rules* (n 15) 49–51; Chen-Wishart, *Contract Law* (n 26) 160–64; Peel, *Treitel on the Law of Contract* (n 24) 204.

[69] See as to (1) the Netherlands: Art 2(3) Dutch Copyright Act; Art 9(2) Dutch Neighbouring Rights Act; the legislative process available at <https://bit.ly/3Uze3Ov>; Visser and others, *ACR: Auteurscontractenrecht* (n 48) 21–47, 293–94; JH Spoor and others, *Auteursrecht. Auteursrecht, portretrecht, naburige rechten en databankenrecht* (Recht en Praktijk, 4th edn, Wolters Kluwer 2019) 516–20, 543, 872–73; van Gompel and others, 'Evaluatie Wet Auteurscontractenrecht' (n 3) 19–20 and (2) the United Kingdom: Arts 90(3), 92(1), 191B(3), 191D(1) UK CDPA; Arnold, *Performers' Rights* (n 48) 97, 104–05; Bently and others, *Intellectual Property Law* (n 29) 325, 327. As proposed by the Wittem Group for transfers in particular, see Art 2.3(4) European Copyright Code.

[70] Art 3:40 Dutch Civil Code; Explanatory Memorandum Dutch Act of 2015, *Kamerstukken* II 2012/13, 33008-6, 14; Dirk Visser, 'Pippi Langkous en het nieuwe auteurscontractenrecht' [2015] NJB 1289, 1291; Visser and others, *ACR: Auteurscontractenrecht* (n 48) 22; van Gompel and others, 'Evaluatie Wet Auteurscontractenrecht (n 3) 20–21.

[71] Bently and others, *Intellectual Property Law* (n 29) 325.

Aside from the general rules of evidence, specific requirements apply pursuant to relevant provisions of copyright contract law. In France, the requirement of written evidence has been made explicit for contracts with both authors[72] and performers.[73] Belgian law expressly requires written evidence vis-à-vis the artist in the context of all copyright exploitation contracts.[74] The artist, on the other hand, may prove both the existence and content of the agreement by any other means.[75] In addition, the duty to specify that exists under Belgian and French law indirectly results in a requirement of written form for all copyright exploitation contracts to which such a duty to specify applies.[76]

In Germany, an express requirement of written form only exists if the exploitation contract pertaining to copyright *sensu stricto* relates to unspecified rights in future music[77] and/or future methods of exploitation.[78] For other copyright exploitation

[72] Art L 132-7 French IP Code *jo* Art 1173 French Civil Code for publishing contracts. See also Art L 131-2 French IP Code for transfer contracts. See also Art L 131-3 para 3 French IP Code for audio-visual adaptation contracts. See in more detail Boisson, *La Licence de Droit d'Auteur* (n 43) 515–25; Lucas and others, *Traité de la Propriété Littéraire et Artistique* (n 46) 615–17, 629–31, 684–85; Gautier, *Propriété Littéraire et Artistique* (n 26) 495–504; Caron, *Droit d'Auteur et Droits Voisins* (n 46) 420–21.

[73] Art L 212-3(I) French IP Code, as amended by Art 11 French DSM Implementation Decree, *jo* Art 1173 French Civil Code. See also Brison, *Het Naburig Recht van de Uitvoerende Kunstenaar* (n 48) 629; Guibault and Hugenholtz, 'Study on the Conditions Applicable to Contracts Relating to Intellectual Property in the European Union' (n 43) 66–67; Lucas and others, *Traité de la Propriété Littéraire et Artistique* (n 46) 1134.

[74] Arts XI.167(1) para 2, XI.205(3) para 1 Belgian CEL; Belgian Supreme Court 18 June 2020, docket number C.19.0017.N <https://juportal.be>. See for a recent application pertaining to musicians of the Belgian National Orchestra: Court of Appeal Brussels 7 May 2021, docket number 2020/AR/1222, not published. The appeal before the Belgian Supreme Court was rejected, see Belgian Supreme Court 29 April 2022, docket number C.21.0358.F <https://juportal.be>. See also Markellou, *Le Contrat d'Exploitation d'Auteur* (n 43) 182–90; Lindner, 'European Union. Part A' (n 2) 60; Vanbrabant, *La Propriété Intellectuelle* (n 25) 440–44, 792–95; Hendrik Vanhees, 'Art XI.167' in Fabienne Brison and Hendrik Vanhees (eds), *Hommage à Jan Corbet Huldeboek* (3rd edn, Larcier 2018) 79; Vanhees, 'Auteurscontract' (n 48) 16–20. Written clauses must moreover be drafted in a clear and comprehensible way, see Art VI.91/2(1) Belgian CEL.

[75] See eg Brison, *Het Naburig Recht van de Uitvoerende Kunstenaar* (n 48) 443, 629; Alain Strowel and Bernard Vanbrabant, 'Copyright Licensing: A European View' in Jacques de Werra (ed), *Research Handbook on Intellectual Property Licensing* (Research Handbooks in Intellectual Property, Edward Elgar 2013) 37.

[76] See below, Section 4.4.2.

[77] Art 40(1) *jo* 79(2a) German Copyright Act. See Bart Jan Lenselink, *De Verlening van Exploitatiebevoegdheden in het Auteursrecht. Een Rechtsvergelijkend Onderzoek naar Overdracht en Licentieverlening in Auteursrechtelijke Exploitatieverhoudingen naar Nederlands, Duits en Amerikaans Recht* (Sdu Uitgevers 2005) 263; Schricker, *Urheberrecht. Kommentar* (n 41) 842–50; Europe Economics and others, 'Remuneration of Authors and Performers' (n 48) 36; Lindner, 'European Union. Part A' (n 2) 59.

[78] Art 31a(1) German Copyright Act. This rule is subject to an exception relating to open licences. The right to a written contract is not waivable in advance, see Art 31a(4) German Copyright Act.

contracts, no such requirement applies, and proof of consent may arise from circumstantial evidence.[79]

A requirement of written proof of copyright exploitation contracts vis-à-vis artists helps enhance their position, without imposing excessive obligations on corporate partners. Conversely, the qualification of a written instrument as a validity requirement appears to be disproportionate.

Procedurally speaking, a written contract leads to increased transparency and legal certainty as to the scope and modalities of the contractual relationship.[80] This benefits all parties: it is not only the musician(s) that has an interest in securing clear, written contract terms; the corporate partner(s) may also invoke such written contract as a means of proof. This would not imply a move away from the reliance on consensus as a founding principle, since the contractual relationship itself still arises from a consensus between the parties. On a substantive level, the requirement of written proof seeks to ensure that the parties exchange all relevant information, thus contributing to parties' informed consent.[81] A requirement of written form indirectly obliges the parties to sit down and negotiate the terms of the contract before its conclusion.[82] This may help counter the persisting information asymmetry between musicians and their corporate partners and may enhance musicians' understanding of the contracts they enter into.[83] It may even have a positive substantive impact on contracts' substance, as the requirement to put pen to paper directs a spotlight on potentially unfair aspects of the contractual relationship that may otherwise have been left unseen.[84] Written contract terms may also assist either party in a post-contractual setting, such as in building a case concerning the enforcement of the contract.[85]

Finally, the mere requirement of (briefly) writing down the essence of a contractual relationship would not lead to excessive compliance costs. For contracts with large groups of musicians, the designation of certain representatives of such groups

[79] Markellou, *Le Contrat d'Exploitation d'Auteur* (n 43) 165–68; Dusollier and others, 'Contractual Arrangements Applicable to Creators' (n 2) 31, 127.

[80] Strowel and Vanbrabant, 'Copyright Licensing: A European View' (n 75) 38; Europe Economics and others, 'Remuneration of Authors and Performers' (n 48) 117.

[81] Hendrik Vanhees, *Een Juridische Analyse van de Grondslagen, Inhoud en Draagwijdte van Auteursrechtelijke Exploitatiecontracten* (Maklu 1993) 521; Guibault and Hugenholtz, 'Study on the Conditions Applicable to Contracts Relating to Intellectual Property in the European Union' (n 43) 31–32; Jean-Christophe Lardinois, *Les Contrats Commentés de l'Industrie de La Musique 2.0: Cadre Général et Pratique Contractuelle* (Création Information Communication Pratique 1, 2nd edn, Larcier 2009) 8; Strowel and Vanbrabant, 'Copyright Licensing: A European View' (n 75) 37.

[82] Dusollier and others, 'Contractual Arrangements Applicable to Creators' (n 2) 30; Dusollier, 'EU Contractual Protection of Creators' (n 36) 438.

[83] Strowel and Vanbrabant, 'Copyright Licensing: A European View' (n 75) 38; Dusollier, 'EU Contractual Protection of Creators' (n 36) 438–41.

[84] Cf Europe Economics and others, 'Remuneration of Authors and Performers' (n 48) 132.

[85] Dusollier, 'EU Contractual Protection of Creators' (n 36) 438.

as having the power to grant express consent on behalf of their fellow musicians may act as a mitigating factor in terms of administrative costs. Moreover, the digitised, globalised context clearly points towards allowing purely digital communication and accepting emails and digital signatures, provided that express consent is safeguarded.[86]

The perceived value of the requirement of a written (possibly digital) instrument for purposes of proof vis-à-vis musicians is only the first part of a large puzzle. The fairness of a contract largely depends on its actual content in terms of scope, performance and termination. While the substance and form of consent matter, the main focus is on the legal and factual consequences of such consent, both in theory and in practice. The next step is therefore to analyse the consequences of consent at the moment of contract formation. This brings us to the scope of the rights transferred or licensed as constrained by the legal framework.

4.4 FORMATION OF THE CONTRACT: SUBSTANCE OF RIGHTS GRANTED

4.4.1 *Limitations in Theory*

4.4.1.1 Prohibition of Transfer

In addition to the requirement of consent, the law sets forth several limitations to the scope of rights granted through copyright exploitation contracts. The four chosen EU jurisdictions include detailed restrictions on the scope of rights granted – and thus what is to be considered as 'fair scope'. Following the analysis of the general prohibition on transfer of copyright *sensu stricto* under German law in this subsection, the next subsections focus on limitations as to specific categories of rights, namely as to future music and future methods of exploitation, and complementary limitations based on a reasonableness assessment.

At first sight, the most drastic restriction is the general prohibition on the transfer of copyright *sensu stricto* under German law, which does not apply to performers[87] and does not exist in the other jurisdictions under review.[88] This prohibition flows from the long tradition of German copyright law as a 'monist' system that considers

[86] Cf van Gompel and others, 'Evaluatie Wet Auteurscontractenrecht (n 3) 21–22.

[87] Art 79(1) German Copyright Act; Schricker, *Urheberrecht. Kommentar* (n 41) 1510–11; Nikita Malevanny, *Online Music Distribution – How Much Exclusivity Is Needed? A Study of International, European, German and US Copyright Systems and Their Objectives*, vol 12 (Munich Studies on Innovation and Competition, Springer Berlin Heidelberg 2019) 74.

[88] Art 29 German Copyright Act; Schricker, *Urheberrecht. Kommentar* (n 41) 627–34; Fromm and Nordemann, *Urheberrecht* (n 41) 461–69; Dreyer and others, *Urheberrecht* (n 41) 655–58; Möhring and Nicolini, *Urheberrecht* (n 41) 385–90.

exploitation rights and moral rights to be inextricably intertwined.[89] According to this theory, copyright protection is seen as a personality right and therefore unalienable.[90] This principle is foundational to German copyright law. Under German law, therefore, rights in compositions may only be subject to a licence,[91] on either an exclusive or non-exclusive basis.[92] Given that the economic effect attained through an exclusive licence is substantively similar to that of a transfer, this prohibition does not appear to substantively affect the position of the artist.[93] In view of this and in combination with the encroachment on freedom of contract that this would entail, there is no pressing need to extend the prohibition on the transfer of copyright *sensu stricto* to copyright systems with a 'dualist' theory, such as the other jurisdictions under review.[94]

On a more general level, the transfer of rights is, in and of itself, largely unproblematic. The question is rather what the musician gets in return – whether agency is secured. Even if the grant of rights is limited to a licence, contract terms may disproportionately favour the corporate partner(s) in terms of scope, exploitation, remuneration and/or termination.[95] Provided that both (1) freedom of choice and informed consent at the outset and (2) fairness throughout the contract's performance are secured, it makes commercial and legal sense to allow exploiters to obtain control over all relevant rights. Absent sufficient rights on the part of the corporate partner, exploitation may lead to infringement, which would be undesirable and thoroughly inefficient.[96] Transfers and licences are not contradictory, but rather complementary routes to exploit protected content, with distinctive characteristics in terms of, for example, risk allocation, and a specific role to play depending on the objectives of either party.[97]

89 See ia Vanhees, *Een Juridische Analyse van de Grondslagen* (n 81) 444, 448, 501–03; Jan Corbet, *Auteursrecht* (Algemene Praktische Rechtsverzameling, Story-Scientia 1997) 11–13; Lenselink, *De Verlening van Exploitatiebevoegdheden in het Auteursrecht* (n 77) 65–66; Malevanny, *Online Music Distribution* (n 87) 73. This 'monist' tradition may be contrasted with the 'dualist' perspective on copyright as a hybrid right, which consists of part property right (exploitation rights) and part personality right (moral rights);

90 Corbet, *Auteursrecht* (n 89) 11–13.

91 This implies the grant of so-called *Nutzungsrechte*, which translates into 'rights of use'.

92 Art 29(2) *jo* 31 German Copyright Act.

93 Cf Guibault and Hugenholtz, 'Study on the Conditions Applicable to Contracts Relating to Intellectual Property in the European Union' (n 43) 29–30; Lenselink, *De Verlening van Exploitatiebevoegdheden in het Auteursrecht* (n 77) 109–212.

94 Cf Andreas Rahmatian, 'Dealing with Rights in Copyright-Protected Works: Assignments and Licences' in Estelle Derclaye (ed), *Research Handbook on the Future of EU Copyright* (Research Handbooks in Intellectual Property, Edward Elgar 2009) 296; Malevanny, *Online Music Distribution* (n 87) 73.

95 See Chapters 5 and 6.

96 Guibault, 'Relationship between Copyright and Contract Law'(n 2) 521.

97 Martin Kretschmer and others, 'The Relationship between Copyright and Contract Law' (2010) <https://ssrn.com/abstract=2624945> 65.

4.4.1.2 Limitations Regarding Future Music and/or Methods of Exploitation

The inclusion of future music in the scope of the rights granted is beneficial to the corporate partner and provides them with a clear incentive to invest in musicians.[98] This consideration applies to both compositions that have not yet been written and (fixations of) performances that have yet to take place. Granting rights in future music may provide musicians with some degree of career certainty. However, a musician whose output proves to be commercially successful may want to improve the conditions of their contractual relationship with a corporate partner, or even seek new horizons. Extending the scope of a contract to future music may, in such a case, lead to undue musician lock-in. In order to protect early-career musicians against such unfavourable contracts, some national legislators have established restrictions on the inclusion of future music in the scope of copyright exploitation contracts. These restrictions do not apply to the relationship between musicians and CMOs.[99]

The possibility to transfer copyright in future music is not expressly limited under UK law.[100] However, specific provisions apply as to the prospective ownership of such music.[101]

Conversely, under French law, the global grant of rights in future compositions is null and void.[102] Once the works have come into existence, the grant may be confirmed.[103] Apparently, this is done in practice, leading to periodic updates of the contract as time goes by.[104] No corresponding prohibition exists for performances.[105]

The other chosen EU jurisdictions require the grant of certain rights in future music to be either in writing or sufficiently detailed – not only by way of the general

[98] Dusollier and others, 'Contractual Arrangements Applicable to Creators' (n 2) 33–34; Europe Economics and others, 'Remuneration of Authors and Performers' (n 48) 149.

[99] Europe Economics and others, 'Remuneration of Authors and Performers' (n 48) 140.

[100] Bently and others, *Intellectual Property Law* (n 29) 325.

[101] Arts 91, 191C UK CDPA; Arnold, *Performers' Rights* (n 48) 98.

[102] Art L 131-1 French IP Code. An exception applies to performance contracts, see Art L 132-18 French IP Code. See Vanhees, *Een Juridische Analyse van de Grondslagen* (n 81) 289–92; Lucie Guibault, *Copyright Limitations and Contracts: An Analysis of the Contractual Overridability of Limitations on Copyright* (Information Law Series 9, Kluwer Law International 2002) 146; Guibault and Hugenholtz, 'Study on the Conditions Applicable to Contracts Relating to Intellectual Property in the European Union' (n 43) 68–69; Rahmatian, 'Dealing with Rights in Copyright-Protected Works' (n 94) 300, 308; Markellou, *Le Contrat d'Exploitation d'Auteur* (n 43) 111–17; Lucas and others, *Traité de la Propriété Littéraire et Artistique* (4n 46) 636–41; Gautier, *Propriété Littéraire et Artistique* (n 26) 552–56; Caron, *Droit d'Auteur et Droits Voisins* (n 46) 425–27.

[103] Markellou, *Le Contrat d'Exploitation d'Auteur* (n 43) 114–17; Dusollier and others, 'Contractual Arrangements Applicable to Creators' (n 2) 118.

[104] Hugenholtz and Guibault, 'Auteurscontractenrecht' (n 4) 42; Dusollier and others, 'Contractual Arrangements Applicable to Creators' (n 2) 34.

[105] See, however, as to the duty to specify under French law below, Section 4.4.2.

contract law requirement of precision of the contract's object[106] but also through specific requirements. In addition, substantive limitations apply regarding the duration of the grant of rights in future music.

Under Belgian law, the period of exclusivity resulting from any grant of exploitation rights regarding future music must be limited, either in time or referring to a specific number of works and/or performances.[107] The actual resulting effective period of exclusivity is not subject to an express maximum. The assessment of the reasonableness thereof may depend per sector – for example allowing a longer duration for genres with a longer 'shelf life', such as classical music.[108] In any case, clauses referring to an exclusivity 'for life' are deemed unacceptable.[109] In addition to the limitation in time, the contract must specify the types and genres of works and/or performances to which the grant pertains in a sufficiently precise manner.[110] Non-respect of these conditions is sanctioned with relative nullity of the grant, meaning that the musician may invoke this.

In Germany, unspecified exploitation rights regarding future music must be granted in writing.[111] No additional duty to specify applies. Instead, German law grants either party the right to terminate a contract that grants the corporate partner rights relating to future music after a period of five years following its conclusion.[112] This right may not be waived in advance.[113] Music that is yet to be supplied upon termination of the contract falls outside the scope of the contractual relationship.[114] In this way, the German legislator sought to allow artists to mine future business opportunities.

Article 40a German Copyright Act also furthers this objective regarding authors in particular. This provision grants authors who have entered into an exclusive licence contract under a lump sum arrangement the right to grant another licence to

[106] See (1) in Belgium: Arts 1129–1130 old Belgian CC; (2) in France: Art 1163 French Civil Code; (3) in Germany: Art 154 German Civil Code; and (4) in the Netherlands: Arts 3:97, 6:227 Dutch Civil Code.

[107] Arts XI.167(2), XI.205(3) para 6 Belgian CEL; Fernand De Visscher and Benoît Michaux, *Précis du Droit d'Auteur et des Droits Voisins* (Bruylant 2000) 328–31; Brison, *Het Naburig Recht van de Uitvoerende Kunstenaar* (n 48) 446; Vanhees, 'Auteurscontract' (n 48) 33–36.

[108] Brison, *Het Naburig Recht van de Uitvoerende Kunstenaar* (n 48) 447. An express limitation in time, to five years for example, was not retained.

[109] ibid.

[110] Arts XI.167(2), XI.205(3) para 6 Belgian CEL; Alain Berenboom, *Le Nouveau Droit d'Auteur et les Droits Voisins* (Création Information Communication 1, 3rd edn, Larcier 2005) 218–19, 383.

[111] See above, Section 4.3.2.

[112] Art 40(1) *jo* Art 79(2a) German Copyright Act. A notice period of six months applies, unless the contracts provides for a shorter period. See Vanhees, *Een Juridische Analyse van de Grondslagen* (n 81) 298–303; Schricker, *Urheberrecht. Kommentar* (n 41) 842–50; Fromm and Nordemann, *Urheberrecht* (n 41) 863–74; Markellou, *Le Contrat d'Exploitation d'Auteur* (n 43) 109–10; Dreyer and others, *Urheberrecht* (n 41) 829–34; Möhring and Nicolini, *Urheberrecht* (n 41) 593–98.

[113] Art 40(2) *jo* Art 79(2a) German Copyright Act.

[114] ibid.

another corporate partner after ten years following either the grant of the right or the delivery of the work at issue if this occurs later.[115] If the author invokes this right and grants an additional licence, the licence of the first corporate partner becomes non-exclusive for the remainder of its duration.[116] The author may waive this right to grant another licence (1) five years after having granted the right[117] or (2) when their contribution is merely secondary.[118] Other contractual deviations to the detriment of the author are only allowed where these arise from collective bargaining. This right to grant another licence does not apply to performers.

Yet another approach is taken in the Netherlands, where the unwaivable[119] limiting rules only apply to transfers and exclusive licences – not to non-exclusive licences.[120] No requirement applies as to the specification of the type of future music involved. However, Dutch law limits the duration of any clause that grants exclusive exploitation rights concerning future music to what is reasonable.[121] Such a clause must moreover specify the intended duration of the grant of rights in a sufficiently specified manner.[122] In the absence of due specification, the clause at issue is sanctioned by relative nullity.[123]

These protective provisions do not always apply to music made in an employment context or on commission. The relevant provisions of Belgian law expressly allow the grant of rights relating to future music in the context of employment situations and/or commissioned content.[124] The Dutch provisions of copyright contract law do not apply to employment situations relating to copyright *sensu stricto*.[125] As to performers, employers obtain rights in future music if this follows from the terms or nature of the employment contract, custom or considerations of reasonableness.[126] This reference to the terms or nature of the contractual relationship also returns under German law.[127] In France, finally, a pragmatic approach is adopted.[128] While the

[115] Art 40a(1) German Copyright Act; Dreyer and others, *Urheberrecht* (n 41) 834–37; Möhring and Nicolini, *Urheberrecht* (n 41) 598–609; Malevanny, *Online Music Distribution* (n 87) 97–98.

[116] Agnès Lucas-Schloetter, 'The Remuneration of Authors and Performers in Copyright Contract Law' in Paul Torremans (ed), *Research Handbook on Copyright Law* (Research Handbooks in Intellectual Property, 2nd edn, Edward Elgar 2017) 268.

[117] Art 40a(2) German Copyright Act.

[118] Art 40a(3) German Copyright Act.

[119] Art 25h(1) Dutch Copyright Act *jo* Art 2b Dutch Neighbouring Rights Act.

[120] Arts 25b(2) *jo* 25f(1) Dutch Copyright Act.

[121] Art 25f(1) Dutch Copyright Act; Art 2b Dutch Neighbouring Rights Act; Visser and others, *ACR: Auteurscontractenrecht* (n 48) 189–98.

[122] ibid.

[123] ibid.

[124] Arts XI.167(3) para 3, XI.205(4) para 3 Belgian CEL; Strowel and Vanbrabant, 'Copyright Licensing: A European View' (n 75) 32; Dusollier and others, 'Contractual Arrangements Applicable to Creators' (n 2) 115; Vanhees, 'Auteurscontract' (n 48) 70–71.

[125] See Chapter 3, Section 3.3.2.3.

[126] Art 3 Dutch Neighbouring Rights Act.

[127] Art 43 German Copyright Act.

[128] See in detail Markellou, *Le Contrat d'Exploitation d'Auteur* (n 43) 122–34.

principled prohibition of the global grant of rights in future works has been held to apply to employment contracts, the automatic grant of rights to the employer upon the creation of original works as provided for by the contract has been held to be in line with French copyright contract law.[129]

The scope of music contracts is usually limited to a certain amount of content (such as a number of albums/songs, or the content provided during a specific period in time), combined with a right of first refusal on the part of the corporate partner as to further content.[130] The use of options has a substantively similar economic effect to a grant of rights concerning future music, resulting in a risk of musician lock-in.[131] The substantive considerations that support restrictions to the grant of rights in future music thus also apply to option clauses.[132] In France, Germany and the Netherlands, option clauses have been found to fall within the scope of the above-mentioned restrictions. First, the French regime applicable to publishing contracts expressly allows authors to include a right of first refusal as to future works in their contracts with publishers, provided that the genre(s) is(are) sufficiently specified, and limited to either five new works or a period of five years.[133] The express inclusion of this authorisation in the French IP Code implies that it is seen as an exception to the general prohibition on the global grant of rights in future works that applies under French law and that, therefore, the scope of this prohibition in principle extends to option contracts.[134] Further, authoritative legal doctrine from the Netherlands refers to the practice of granting option clauses as an apparent synonym of the grant of rights in future works.[135] It may therefore be argued that, under Dutch law, the grant of options is restricted.[136] The same conclusion is reached in legal doctrine pertaining to Article 40 German Copyright Act, the relevant provision under German law.[137] Conversely, legal scholars analysing the

[129] Guibault and Hugenholtz, 'Study on the Conditions Applicable to Contracts Relating to Intellectual Property in the European Union' (n 43) 68–69; Hugenholtz and Guibault, 'Auteurscontractenrecht' (n 4) 42.

[130] Europe Economics and others, 'Remuneration of Authors and Performers' (n 48) 149.

[131] Cf Raimond, *La Qualification du Contrat d'Auteur* (n 27) 79.

[132] Cf Vanhees, *Een Juridische Analyse van de Grondslagen* (n 81) 570–71.

[133] Art L 132-4 French IP Code; Hugenholtz and Guibault, 'Auteurscontractenrecht' (n 4) 42–43; Rahmatian, 'Dealing with Rights in Copyright-Protected Works' (n 94) 308; Raimond, *La Qualification du Contrat d'Auteur* (n 27) 96–97, 402–07; Lucas and others, *Traité de la Propriété Littéraire et Artistique* (n 46) 688–94; Gautier, *Propriété Littéraire et Artistique* (n 26) 556–67; Caron, *Droit d'Auteur et Droits Voisins* (n 46) 454–56.

[134] Art L 131-1 French IP Code. See also Code des Usages et des Bonnes Pratiques de l'Edition des Œuvres Musicales (4 October 2017) s 2.

[135] P Bernt Hugenholtz, 'Towards Author's Paradise: The New Dutch Act on Authors' Contracts' in Gunnar Karnell and others (eds), *Liber Amicorum Jan Rosén* (eddy.se ab 2016) 404.

[136] See also as to the relevance of the restriction on unreasonable clauses under Art 25f Dutch Copyright Act below, Section 4.4.1.3.

[137] Vanhees, *Een Juridische Analyse van de Grondslagen* (n 81) 301–03; Hugenholtz and Guibault, 'Auteurscontractenrecht' (n 4) 32; Lenselink, *De Verlening van Exploitatiebevoegdheden in het Auteursrecht* (n 77) 439; Schricker, *Urheberrecht. Kommentar* (n 41) 844–45; Fromm and

Belgian provisions have found that they do *not* have a bearing on option mechanisms.[138]

In addition to limitations regarding future music, copyright contract law may also significantly restrict the scope of contracts insofar as they pertain to 'future methods of exploitation'. These restrictions tie in with emerging opportunities for exploitation that arise as a result of technological progress and the accompanying switch from analogue to digital exploitation.[139] An extension of the scope of music industry contracts to methods of exploitation unknown or unknowable at the moment of contract formation (such as digital downloads and streaming in legacy contracts) would be favourable to corporate partners, whose exploitation rights would then increase over time.[140] However, this would lead to an undue transfer of economic value stemming from exploitation of protected content to corporate partners. Therefore, the legislators in the chosen jurisdictions seek to limit or even prevent contracts concerning exploitation activities that are still shrouded in uncertainty at the moment of contract formation.[141] Again, these restrictions do not apply to the relationship between musicians and CMOs.[142]

The scope of these limitations hinges on the interpretation of the concept 'method of exploitation' as well as of the word 'future'.

A 'method of exploitation' may be defined as a form of use of protected content that is concrete, specific and autonomous, as well as technically and – in principle – economically distinct.[143] The term 'use' refers to an application that falls within the scope of the exclusive rights of the rightsholder(s) and thus, in principle, requires their permission. As for the criteria of distinctiveness, it has been argued that, given that the economic consequences of a certain method of exploitation are impossible to predict, primary focus should lie with the technical aspect.[144]

Applied to music, analogue and digital exploitation constitute separate methods of exploitation of exclusive rights in music. Also within those categories, there are several distinctions. As for the physical production of music, exploitation on

Nordemann, *Urheberrecht* (n 41) 866–67; Dreyer and others, *Urheberrecht* (n 41) 831; Möhring and Nicolini, *Urheberrecht* (n 41) 398, 595.

[138] Vanhees, *Een Juridische Analyse van de Grondslagen* (n 81) 280–85; De Visscher and Michaux, *Précis du Droit d'Auteur et des Droits Voisins* (n 107) 329; Brison, *Het Naburig Recht van de Uitvoerende Kunstenaar* (n 48) 447; Lardinois, *Les Contrats Commentés de l'Industrie de La Musique 2.0* (n 81) 139.

[139] Dusollier and others, 'Contractual Arrangements Applicable to Creators' (n 2) 35.

[140] ibid.

[141] See as to the interplay with general contract law, Hugenholtz and Guibault, 'Auteurscontractenrecht' (n 4) 9.

[142] Europe Economics and others, 'Remuneration of Authors and Performers' (n 48) 140.

[143] Cf Raimond, *La Qualification du Contrat d'Auteur* (n 27) 42–43; Markellou, *Le Contrat d'Exploitation d'Auteur* (n 43) 89–94; Dreyer and others, *Urheberrecht* (n 41) 700; Vanhees, 'Art XI.167' (n 74) 79; Malevanny, *Online Music Distribution* (n 87) 74.

[144] Cf Raimond, *La Qualification du Contrat d'Auteur* (n 27) 43; Europe Economics and others, 'Remuneration of Authors and Performers' (n 48) 148.

cassettes, vinyl and CDs may definitely be distinguished. In the digital realm, a clear distinction may be made between digital downloads, streams and sync.[145] An additional distinction within music streaming may be made between ad-supported and subscription-based streams, given the different revenue source. In addition, in view of the different way in which listeners engage with interactive (on-demand) and non-interactive (through playlists) streaming, an argument is to be made in favour of distinguishing these two types of streaming as separate methods of exploitation.[146] A more recent addition to the streaming landscape is 'lossless' streaming, where the use of an uncompressed sound file leads to a higher sound quality.[147] This does not appear to be a new method of exploitation: while a technical distinction with 'traditional' music streaming may be made, it uses a technique that has already existed for analogue music for several decades. A mere technical improvement of an existing technique should not qualify as a distinct method of exploitation.[148] Moreover, more and more streaming services offer lossless streaming to their subscribers at no additional cost, thus excluding the possibility of an economic distinction.[149]

Further, no real technical distinction may be made between the same method of exploitation in a different geographical setting. The grant of rights for a single method of exploitation may therefore encompass global rights for the corporate partner. The initial contract may grant global rights, even if only a limited geographical release is planned at the outset, to be (potentially) followed by global exploitation in case commercial success arises.

The next concept is 'future'. Substantive considerations support a broad interpretation in order to safeguard the interests of the parties in the event unforeseen and unforeseeable circumstances arise.[150] Consequently, restrictions on the grant of rights relating to future methods of exploitation include techniques that do not yet exist at the time of contract formation as well as techniques that already exist, but are

[145] Cf Hugenholtz, 'Towards Author's Paradise' (n 135) 403.

[146] Cf Seth Ericsson, 'The Recorded Music Industry and the Emergence of Online Music Distribution: Innovation in the Absence of Copyright (Reform)' (2011) 79 Geo Wash L Rev 1783, 1788–89.

[147] See eg Matthew Kronsberg, 'Why Apple, Amazon and Spotify Are Embracing Hi-Def Music: A Guide to "Lossless" Streaming' (*Wall Street Journal*, 26 June 2021) <https://on.wsj.com/2XihjnE>.

[148] See German case law referred to in Hugenholtz and Guibault, 'Auteurscontractenrecht' (n 4) 38.

[149] See eg Brandt Ranj, 'How to Stream High-Resolution Music' (*Rolling Stone*, 17 May 2021) <https://bit.ly/3vkfvqN>; 'Spotify vs Apple Music vs Tidal: 12 Best Music Streaming Services in 2021' (*MusicTech*, 18 May 2021) <https://bit.ly/3pamTDZ>; Kronsberg, 'Why Apple, Amazon and Spotify Are Embracing Hi-Def Music' (n 147).

[150] See eg Arts L 131-6, 212-11 para 2 French IP Code. This position is in line with the principle of restrictive interpretation that applies under Belgian and French law (see below, Section 4.4.2). If the scope of the methods of exploitation covered is to be interpreted strictly, emerging uses of protected content are likely to not be included.

not yet commonly known or applied.[151] The required novelty of a future method of exploitation does not require this method to lead to a 'new audience'.[152]

Protective regimes as to future methods of exploitation range from a full ban on their inclusion in contracts to a set of conditions attached thereto. A full ban applies in Belgium for both composers and performers, sanctioned by relative nullity of the grant concerning the future method(s) of exploitation at issue.[153]

In the other chosen continental EU jurisdictions, focus lies with ensuring due specification, a right to revocation and/or appropriate remuneration through specific conditions. In France, the grant of rights relating to future methods of exploitation must be express and subject to proportionate remuneration.[154] Under Dutch law, save in an employment situation,[155] the artist has an unwaivable[156] right to additional remuneration for revenues garnered through the exploitation of new methods of exploitation.[157] A combination of all three focal points exists under German law, albeit in a regime limited to copyright *sensu stricto*. In addition to a requirement of written form,[158] Article 31a German Copyright Act links the inclusion of future methods of exploitation in an exploitation contract with a right of revocation on the part of the author.[159] A corporate partner who wishes to start exploiting a work using a new method must inform the author without delay.[160] The author then has three months to revoke the grant for this new method of exploitation.[161] Alternatively, the author may invoke a right to additional remuneration for the new method, as provided by Article 32c German Copyright Act.[162] If the parties have agreed on such

[151] Brison, *Het Naburig Recht van de Uitvoerende Kunstenaar* (n 48) 446; Raimond, *La Qualification du Contrat d'Auteur* (n 27) 47–48; Europe Economics and others, 'Remuneration of Authors and Performers' (n 48) 37.

[152] Cf Brison, *Het Naburig Recht van de Uitvoerende Kunstenaar* (n 48) 446.

[153] Arts XI.167(1) para 6, XI.205(3) para 5 Belgian CEL. The nullity only affects the clause at issue.

[154] Arts L 131-6, L 212-11 para 2 French IP Code; Rahmatian, 'Dealing with Rights in Copyright-Protected Works' (n 94) 300–01; Raimond, *La Qualification du Contrat d'Auteur* (n 27) 46–48; Markellou, *Le Contrat d'Exploitation d'Auteur* (n 43) 83–85; Dusollier and others, 'Contractual Arrangements Applicable to Creators' (n 2) 35; Lucas and others, *Traité de la Propriété Littéraire et Artistique* (n 46) 625–27, 1151–52.

[155] Art 25b(3) Dutch Copyright Act.

[156] Art 25h(1) Dutch Copyright Act *jo* Art 2b Dutch Neighbouring Rights Act.

[157] Art 25c(6) Dutch Copyright Act; Art 2b Dutch Neighbouring Rights Act; Visser and others, *ACR: Auteurscontractenrecht* (n 48) 275–85.

[158] See above, Section 4.3.2.

[159] Art 31a(1) German Copyright Act; Lenselink, *De Verlening van Exploitatiebevoegdheden in het Auteursrecht* (n 77) 424–37; Fromm and Nordemann, *Urheberrecht* (n 41) 665–96; Markellou, *Le Contrat d'Exploitation d'Auteur* (n 43) 85–87; Dreyer and others, *Urheberrecht* (n 41) 714–25; Möhring and Nicolini, *Urheberrecht* (n 41) 416–24.

[160] Art 32c(1) German Copyright Act.

[161] Art 31a(1) German Copyright Act. This right of revocation expires upon the author's death, see Art 31a(2) German Copyright Act. The exercise of the right of revocation is limited by the doctrine of good faith in case of consolidated and/or collaborative works, see Art 31a(3) German Copyright Act.

[162] Art 32c(1) German Copyright Act. See also Chapter 5, Section 5.3.2.2.

a separate remuneration or if a joint remuneration agreement[163] applies, recourse to the revocation right mentioned above is no longer possible.[164] Authors' right to claim either revocation or additional remuneration for future methods of exploitation may not be waived in advance.[165] In addition, again, reference may be made to the right granted to certain authors under German copyright law to grant a licence to another corporate partner after ten years.[166] Performers have no equivalent right of revocation, nor can they invoke the right to other exploitation after ten years in case of flat-rate remuneration. However, they may claim additional remuneration in case the corporate partner starts using a method of exploitation that was not known at the time of contract formation.[167] This distinct regime for authors and performers is based on practical considerations connected with multi-performer projects, but has been the subject of criticism.[168]

Theoretical limitations on the scope of rights granted seek to prevent artists in general and musicians in particular from signing away rights the economic value of which is not (yet) clear.[169] This objective circles back to the general aim of securing well-informed consent. On the one hand, this enhances musician agency. Instead of relinquishing control, musicians may choose other exploitation routes for emerging (digital) possibilities. If they choose the same partner, an opportunity may arise to secure better conditions.[170] However, a musician whose work has little commercial success may have a considerably weaker bargaining position at the renegotiation table.[171] Musicians favouring long-term security over favourable contract terms may conceivably wish to grant future rights to their corporate partners. Therefore, as is the case for the choice between a transfer and a licence, fully excluding the transfer of future rights and/or methods of exploitation appears excessive.

Interestingly, theoretical limitations on the grant of rights in future methods of exploitation appear to have had limited effects in practice when it comes to the internet revolution. Understandably, legacy contracts did not expressly include the grant of exploitation rights regarding digital use. Parties that wished to include such

[163] See Chapter 5, Section 5.3.2.2.
[164] Art 31a(2) German Copyright Act.
[165] Arts 31a(4), 32c(3) German Copyright Act. These rules are subject to an exception for open licences, see Arts 31a(1), 32c(3) German Copyright Act.
[166] Art 40a German Copyright Act.
[167] Art 79b German Copyright Act.
[168] See Hugenholtz and Guibault, 'Auteurscontractenrecht' (n 4) 38–39. See also *Bundesgerichtshof* (BGH, hereinafter: German Federal Court of Justice) 10 October 2002, docket number I ZR 180/00 <https://bit.ly/3tVCMP1>.
[169] Europe Economics and others, 'Remuneration of Authors and Performers' (n 48) 156; Lionel Bently and others, 'Strengthening the Position of Press Publishers and Authors and Performers in the Copyright Directive' (2017) 51; Dusollier, 'EU Contractual Protection of Creators' (n 36) 441.
[170] Cf Europe Economics and others, 'Remuneration of Authors and Performers' (n 48) 139, 148.
[171] ibid 148.

rights in their contractual relationship had to renegotiate.[172] However, many musicians, faced with the choice to either not 'go digital' and face musical obscurity, or to accept contract terms similar to those relating to physical sales and be able to offer their music on digital platforms, chose the latter.[173] Thus, the renegotiation process often did not have a favourable outcome for musicians.

For methods of exploitation emerging subsequent to the digital transition and the accompanying rise of digital downloads and streaming, the application of the protective framework is even more difficult. Indeed, the first round of contract renegotiations, at the turn of the millennium, led to the inclusion of 'digital' methods of exploitation – a broad concept the confines of which are not clear-cut. Corporate partners may argue that the word 'digital' encompasses all digital 'methods of exploitation', even though the mere inclusion of 'digital' does not do justice to the available and emerging digital methods of exploitation.[174] Musicians risk not pushing back on such a broad interpretation.[175] Furthermore, if we argue that each new method of digital exploitation requires a renegotiation to bring it within a contract's scope, every music industry contract risks becoming obsolete in the (possibly very) short term, given the fast pace of evolution in the digital music market.[176] The inevitable increase in transaction costs that this would entail leads to questions of efficiency and cost allocation.[177] In addition, legal uncertainty arises, as does the risk of unreasonable contractual outcomes. This leads to a chasm between theory and practice. While the restrictions on future methods of exploitation therefore serve a commendable purpose, it may be questioned whether they are actually futureproof.[178]

Additionally, limitations relating to future methods of exploitation – and maybe even relating to future music – lose some (if not all) of their appeal if fair exploitation and remuneration, sanctioned by rights reversion, are secured in the performance stage of the contract.[179] As noted above, German law allows authors to grant another licence to their work after a decade if a lump sum remuneration arrangement applies. This measure enhances musician agency. Then again, economics scholars have argued that this may actually harm authors in the long run, as the risk of increased future competition may negatively affect publishers' willingness to invest, or induce them to internalise this risk by offering lower remuneration in

[172] Cf Dusollier, 'EU Contractual Protection of Creators' (n 36) 448.

[173] Christian Castle and Claudio Feijóo, 'Study on the Artists in the Digital Music Marketplace: Economics and Legal Considerations' (WIPO, 2021) 19.

[174] Dusollier, 'EU Contractual Protection of Creators' (n 36) 448.

[175] Cf Stef van Gompel, '"Non, Non, Rien n'a Changé": Over Vergoedingsaanspraken voor Makers uit Hoofde van Exploitatiecontracten' [2021] Auteursrecht 3, 4.

[176] Dusollier and others, 'Contractual Arrangements Applicable to Creators' (n 2) 13.

[177] Cf Europe Economics and others, 'Remuneration of Authors and Performers' (n 48) 117–18, 144, 148–49.

[178] Van Gompel, 'Non, Non, Rien n'a Changé' (n 175) 4.

[179] See Chapter 5.

the initial contract.[180] Moreover, the grant of a right to additional remuneration in relation to future methods of exploitation may render the restrictions discussed here obsolete.[181]

4.4.1.3 Complementary Limitations

Provisions of the law of unfair B2B contract terms and trade practices may further restrict the scope of rights granted. The law varies widely across the chosen jurisdictions. The spectrum of potential sanctions ranges from a right to claim an injunction and/or damages, over the moderation of contract terms labelled as problematic to what is deemed reasonable, to an impact on the validity of the term(s) at issue or even the entire contract – the latter in case the unfair term(s) cannot be severed from the contract or in case of a contravention of norms of public order and/or good morals.[182]

Both Belgian and French law contain general restrictions on the inclusion of contract clauses that create a manifest imbalance between the rights and obligations of the parties that apply to all B2B contracts.[183] Belgian law first sets a list of per se prohibited clauses.[184] Second, it includes a list of clauses that are presumed to be illicit unless the contrary is proven.[185] Third, it labels as unlawful contract clauses that create a manifest imbalance between the rights and obligations of the parties, either by themselves or in conjunction with one or more other terms.[186] Core, characterising clauses of the contracts at issue that are drafted clearly and comprehensibly fall outside the scope of this prohibition.[187] This exclusion also applies to the issue of equivalence between the remuneration and the 'products' to be

180 Roland Kirstein and Michael Karas, 'More Rights, Less Income? An Economic Analysis of the New Copyright Law in Germany' (Working Paper Series, 2017).

181 See Chapter 5, Section 5.3.2.2. Cf Hugenholtz and Guibault, 'Auteurscontractenrecht' (n 4) v.

182 See (1) in Belgium: Arts VI.91/6, XV.83(13°) XVII.4 Belgian CEL; Art 5.52 new Belgian Civil Code; (2) in France: Arts L 442-1–8 French Commercial Code and Art 1171 French Civil Code; (3) in Germany as to standard terms: Arts 307–309 German Civil Code; and (4) in the Netherlands as to standard terms: Arts 6:233–234 Dutch Civil Code. See Guibault, *Copyright Limitations and Contracts* (n 102) 122; De Pourcq, *Oneerlijke Handelspraktijken* (n 18) 315–26, 487–93.

183 German law does not provide a general restriction of unfair B2B contract terms that were negotiated individually. Instead, its rules on unfair B2B contract terms are confined to standard terms, see Arts 307–310 German Civil Code.

184 Art VI.91/4 Belgian CEL.

185 Art VI.91/5 Belgian CEL.

186 Art VI.91/3(1) Belgian CEL. The 'imbalance' refers to the clause itself, independent of its performance in practice and of the existence of an imbalance between the parties at the moment of contract formation. The existence of a 'manifest imbalance' is assessed at the moment of contract formation, on the basis of the circumstances applicable at that time, the general economy of the contract, sector practices and all other relevant contractual clauses, see Art VI.91/3(2) Belgian CEL. See also Art 5.52 new Belgian CC.

187 Arts VI.91/3(2) *jo* VI.91/2(1) Belgian CEL.

delivered, subject to the requirement of clarity and intelligibility.[188] Thus, transparency plays a key role in the legal assessment of the (un)fair character of B2B contract terms under Belgian law.

The equivalent provision of the French Commercial Code prohibits contract parties from obtaining, or attempting to obtain, a benefit that corresponds to no consideration or that is manifestly disproportionate to the consideration provided.[189] There is no exclusion relating to core clauses. A more generic prohibition applies to situations where a significant imbalance between the rights and obligations of the parties is created.[190] Finally, a specific reasonableness test applies to contracts of adhesion. This concept refers to contracts singularly drafted by one of the potential contracting parties, where the other party does not have any margin for negotiation concerning the terms of the contract.[191] Such a non-negotiable clause is unenforceable under French law if it creates a significant imbalance between the rights and obligations of the parties, save when that clause relates to the principal subject matter of the contract or when the adequacy of the remuneration is concerned.[192]

In the Netherlands, finally, a supplementary limitation specific to copyright exploitation contracts results from Article 25f(2) Dutch Copyright Act.[193] This provision subjects the grant of exclusive exploitation rights to an unwaivable[194] reasonableness test. It provides that all clauses included in a transfer contract or an exclusive licence contract that are unreasonably burdensome to the artist are to be sanctioned by relative nullity.[195] Relevant considerations include the nature and content of the agreement, how it came into existence and the (knowable) interests of the contracting parties.[196] General restrictions may provide fruitful ground for musicians to resist the inclusion of excessive option clauses.[197] An analogue argument may be envisaged for other terms that may be considered unreasonable, such as obligations to sign a contract with both the recorded music and publishing divisions of an integrated music company.[198] Circumstances that arise subsequent

[188] Arts VI.91/3(2) *jo* VI.91/2(1) Belgian CEL.

[189] Art L 442-1(I) 1° French Commercial Code.

[190] Art L 442-1(I) 2° French Commercial Code.

[191] Cf Art 1110 French Civil Code; Stijns, *Verbintenissenrecht. Boek 1* (n 26) 31–32; Claeys and Tanghe, *Algemeen Contractenrecht* (n 13) 136.

[192] Art 1171 French Civil Code; Caron, *Droit d'Auteur et Droits Voisins* (n 46) 414; Racine, 'L'Auteur et l'Acte de Création' (n 46) 99.

[193] *Jo* Art 2b Dutch Neighbouring Rights Act for performers; Visser and others, *ACR: Auteurscontractenrecht* (n 48) 189–98. See also Iris Houben and Dirk Visser, 'De Beëindiging van Muziekexploitatieovereenkomsten' [2022] ATR 135, 138–39.

[194] Art 25h(1) Dutch Copyright Act *jo* Art 2b Dutch Neighbouring Rights Act.

[195] This rule does not apply to non-exclusive licences, see Art 25b(2) *jo* 25f(2) Dutch Copyright Act.

[196] Lindner, 'European Union. Part A' (n 2) 61.

[197] Spoor and others, *Auteursrecht* (n 69) 579–80.

[198] Visser and others, *ACR: Auteurscontractenrecht* (n 48) 190–93; Spoor and others, *Auteursrecht* (n 69) 581. A complaint filed with the Dutch Competition Authority on, among other things, such tying practices was rejected, based on the consideration that a restriction of competition was not apparent, see *Nederlandse Mededinging.sautoriteit* (Dutch Competition Authority)

to contract formation may not be taken into account, as the Dutch Supreme Court found in its judgment in the dispute between Martin Garrix and corporate partner Spinnin Records.[199] The Court of Appeal Arnhem-Leeuwarden had ruled that the option for the latter to extend a contract for two years on the same terms was unreasonable in view of the commercial success of Garrix's music and the disproportionality in terms of revenue distribution that this entailed.[200] The appeal by Spinnin Records on this aspect was successful. The Dutch Supreme Court considered that the alleged unreasonableness of a clause should be judged at the time of contract formation and not on the basis of circumstances that may or may not arise at a later stage, including the performance of the agreement and the commercial success of the music.[201] This decision restricts the potential effect of Article 25f(2).

The Belgian and French 'manifest imbalance' test appears to be more restrictive than the Dutch 'unreasonably burdensome' test. Consequently, the added value of these complementary regimes is difficult to assess. Moreover, in interpreting the appropriate scope of the complementary limitations reviewed in this section, the overarching influence of the freedom of contract should be borne in mind. Caution is therefore advised against an expansive interpretation of the relevant concepts, particularly for contracts subject to individual negotiations.

In terms of appropriate sanctions, corporate partners may argue that the moderation of a clause deemed unlawful to what is considered reasonable is preferable to declaring the clause (and sometimes even the entire contract) non-binding. However, such a solution is suboptimal. As argued by Lobel in the context of non-compete clauses, 'if businesses know that an unreasonable control provision will be modified to its reasonable limit by the court, then there would be practically no cost of overreaching – they would always attempt to define restrictions on human capital as broadly as possible'.[202] Thus, an impact on the validity of the contract appears merited in order to sufficiently deter unreasonable clauses stemming from overreach by corporate partners.[203]

Finally, the principles of general contract law apply as the ultimate *lex generalis*, bringing the doctrines of good faith, abuse of law, public policy, good morals and

27 April 2012, docket number 7213/27 (*Platform Makers v NPO and Others*). The appeal against this decision was denied, see District Court Rotterdam 5 December 2013, docket number AWB-13_02790, ECLI:NL:RBROT:2013:9461.

[199] Dutch Supreme Court 17 December 2021, docket numbers 20/01155, 20/01158, ECLI:NL:HR:2021:1923, paras 3.1.1–3.1.4, 3.4.1–3.4.2.

[200] Court of Appeal Arnhem-Leeuwarden 24 December 2019, docket number 200.227.882/01, ECLI:NL:GHARL:2019:11117; van Gompel and others, 'Evaluatie Wet Auteurscontractenrecht (n 3) 53–54. A similar argument could have been made under the Dutch provision concerning the grant of rights in future music, see above, Section 4.4.1.2.

[201] Dutch Supreme Court 17 December 2021, docket numbers 20/01155, 20/01158, ECLI:NL:HR:2021:1923, paras 3.1.1–3.1.4, 3.4.1–3.4.2.

[202] Orly Lobel, *Talent Wants to Be Free. Why We Should Learn to Love Leaks, Raids, and Free Riding* (Yale University Press 2013) 208.

[203] Cf De Pourcq, *Oneerlijke Handelspraktijken* (n 18) 324–33, 726–27.

undue influence into the equation.[204] On the basis of these provisions, exceptionally unreasonable situations may be remedied and truly disadvantageous contractual bargains set aside. The potential application of general contract law also came to the fore in the Garrix case. In particular, the Court of Appeal had neglected to analyse the contested clauses on the basis of the general principles of reasonableness, which Garrix had invoked in a subsidiary manner. The Dutch Supreme Court considered that the Court of Appeal was wrong to not have expressly analysed whether the clauses at issue fulfilled the general standard of reasonableness, which is to be assessed taking account of all relevant circumstances (including from an ex post perspective).[205] Regardless, if a certain situation is deemed acceptable under the applicable *leges speciales*, it seems unlikely that the application of general contract law principles would bring a judge to a different conclusion in practice.

In sum, a complementary reasonableness test and the relevant principles of general contract law provide fallback mechanisms to curb instances of unfairness that do not fall within the scope of the restrictions pertaining to either future music or methods of exploitation.[206] However, their scope in practice appears to be limited.

4.4.2 *Determination in Practice*

The above overview focused on theoretical limitations to rights granted. The next step is to establish how the substantive scope of such rights is actually determined. A certain degree of specification in the contract is required. Musicians must know what they are signing up for and be conscious of the contract's scope.[207] Not only does such transparency further procedural fairness; it also substantively mitigates the consequences of the structural information asymmetry between musicians and their corporate partners, and aids them in proving their claims in either a judicial or extra-judicial setting.[208] The scope of rights granted should not go beyond what is necessary for the exploitation.[209] This not only has the benefit of efficiency, but

[204] See Chapter 3, Section 3.3.1 and sources referenced there.

[205] Dutch Supreme Court 17 December 2021, docket numbers 20/01155, 20/01158, ECLI:NL:HR:2021:1923, paras 3.2.1–3.2.2. At the time of writing, the case on the merits is pending before the Court of Appeal of Den Bosch.

[206] See above, Section 4.4.1.2.

[207] Europe Economics and others, 'Remuneration of Authors and Performers' (n 48) 156; Bently and others, 'Strengthening the Position' (n 169) 51; Dusollier, 'EU Contractual Protection of Creators' (n 36) 441.

[208] Europe Economics and others, 'Remuneration of Authors and Performers' (n 48) 118, 143.

[209] Cf European Copyright Society, 'Comment of the European Copyright Society Addressing Selected Aspects of the Implementation of Articles 18 to 22 of the Directive (EU) 2019/790 on Copyright in the Digital Single Market' [2020] JIPITEC 132 147; Raquel Xalabarder, 'The Principle of Appropriate and Proportionate Remuneration for Authors and Performers in Art 18 Copyright in the Digital Single Market Directive. Statutory Residual Remuneration Rights for Its Effective National Implementation' [2020] InDret 1, 15.

also ensures that musicians can exploit the remaining rights themselves or choose another corporate partner that might be a better fit.[210]

There are several regulatory approaches to this issue. Belgian and French law require copyright exploitation contracts to specify their scope in detail. Under German and Dutch law, the principle of purpose-limitation applies, limiting ambiguous rights granted to what is necessary to fulfil the contract's purpose. UK law does not provide specific rules on the appropriate interpretation of copyright exploitation contracts. Instead, the general rules on contract interpretation apply.[211] Such principles of (B2B) contract interpretation may also influence the balance in the music contracts under review at the formation stage in other jurisdictions, as *leges generales*.[212] While the primary objective of finding the parties' common intention applies in all five chosen jurisdictions, the intricacies of the applicable legal regimes pertaining to contract interpretation differ, with a more pronounced focus on either the subjective will of the parties or a more objective perspective infused with considerations of reasonableness.[213] The objective of all regimes pertaining to contract interpretation is to achieve a balance between party autonomy and legal certainty – between the subjective intention of the parties as reflected in the contract and the more objective perspective of a (hypothetical) reasonable person wishing to avoid instances of unfairness.[214]

The formalistic duty to specify under Belgian and French law implies that copyright exploitation contracts must specify the rights granted to the corporate partner, including the type of exclusive right(s) and the methods of exploitation

[210] Cf Europe Economics and others, 'Remuneration of Authors and Performers' (n 48) 136.

[211] Arnold, *Performers' Rights* (n 48) 279–87; Bently and others, *Intellectual Property Law* (n 29) 328.

[212] On the regimes in ia Belgium, France and the Netherlands, see Johanna Waelkens, *Interpretatie van Overeenkomsten en Eenzijdige Rechtshandelingen. Deel I* (Intersentia 2016). On the applicable regimes in ia France, Germany and the Netherlands, see CJW Baaij and others (eds), *Interpretation of Commercial Contracts in European Private Law* (The Common Core of European Private Law 1, Intersentia 2020). On the applicable regime in the United Kingdom, see Gerard McMeel, *The Construction of Contracts: Interpretation, Implication and Rectification* (Oxford University Press 2007).

[213] See (1) in Belgium: Arts 1156–1164 Belgian CC; Cruquenaire, *L'Interprétation des Contrats en Droit d'Auteur* (n 14) 137–84; (2) in France: Arts 1188–1192 French CC; (3) in Germany: Arts 133, 157 German CC; Guibault and Hugenholtz, 'Study on the Conditions Applicable to Contracts Relating to Intellectual Property in the European Union' (n 43) 14; Markesinis and others, *The German Law of Contract* (n 12) 133–43; Fikentscher and Heinemann, *Schuldrecht* (n 12) 109–12; (4) in the Netherlands primarily Dutch Supreme Court 13 March 1981, docket number 11.647, ECLI:NL:HR:1981:AG4158 *jo* Art 6:248 Dutch Civil Code; Dutch Supreme Court 25 August 2023, docket number 22/04170, ECLI:NL:HR:2023:1131; Hugenholtz and Guibault, 'Auteurscontractenrecht' (n 4) 8, 10, 75; Hijma and others, *Rechtshandeling en Overeenkomst* (n 12) 290–300; Spoor and others, *Auteursrecht* (n 69) 550–53; and (5) in the United Kingdom: Chitty and Beale, *Chitty on Contracts* (n 26) ch 13; Andrews, *Contract Rules* (n 15) 199–230; Peel, *Treitel on the Law of Contract* (n 24) ch 6; Chen-Wishart, *Contract Law* (n 26) 413–32.

[214] Waelkens, *Interpretatie van Overeenkomsten en Eenzijdige Rechtshandelingen* (n 212); Baaij and others, *Interpretation of Commercial Contracts in European Private Law* (n 212).

covered.[215] The relevant provisions of French law also refer to the need to specify the intended public.[216] The duty to specify applies to both composing and performing musicians.[217] Under Belgian law, the duty to specify does not apply to either commissioned music or music made by employees, in which case the express grant of rights is deemed to suffice.[218] In both Belgium and France, the requirement of specification extends to the geographical scope and duration of the grant. Moreover, if the corporate partner wishes to obtain an option, this must be specified in the contract.[219] As to the substance of the rights granted, it is insufficient for the contract to merely refer to the grant of rights relating to the right of reproduction or the right of communication to the public.[220] Exactly how specific the enumeration of relevant methods of exploitation must be is fuel for debate.[221] Pragmatism argues against an unduly strict interpretation. In any case, it is difficult to fulfil the duty to specify without a written contract.[222] Thus, even though this is not a validity requirement under either Belgian or French law, a written instrument is likely to arise.[223] In case the duty to specify applies and no adequate specification is included in the contract, the sanction is relative nullity of the unspecified grant, to be invoked by the musician.[224]

As non-specified methods of exploitation remain in the hands of the artist(s), the associated objective of this requirement is to allow artist(s) to retain control over the exploitation of 'their' content.[225] However, the duty to specify appears to miss its mark in practice. The result of this duty is often a long, very detailed list of potentially relevant methods of exploitation and a resulting risk that the rights granted exceed what is necessary for exploitation of the content.[226] Musicians'

[215] See Art XI.167(1) para 4 Belgian CEL; Art L 131-3 French IP Code.

[216] Arts L 131-3, L 212-11 French IP Code; Raimond, *La Qualification du Contrat d'Auteur* (n 27) 44–45.

[217] See as to performers Art XI.205(3) para 3 Belgian CEL; Art L 212-11 French IP Code.

[218] Arts XI.167(3) paras 1–4, XI.205(4) paras 1–4 Belgian CEL. The substance of the grant may be determined by collective agreement.

[219] Raimond, *La Qualification du Contrat d'Auteur* (n 27) 89–90.

[220] See Art L 121-17-1 French IP Code as to literary publishing.

[221] See on the scope of the concept 'method of exploitation' above, Section 4.4.1.2. Uses of protected content that are concrete and autonomous on a technical level should be specified separately.

[222] The duty to specify under Belgian law is complemented by the requirement for written B2B contract terms to be clear and comprehensible, see Art VI.91/2 Belgian CEL.

[223] Cf Blanc, *Les Contrats du Droit d'Auteur* (n 68) 46; Dusollier and others, 'Contractual Arrangements Applicable to Creators' (n 2) 118.

[224] Berenboom, *Le Nouveau Droit d'Auteur et les Droits Voisins* (n 10) 220–21; Hendrik Vanhees, *De wettelijke regeling inzake auteurscontracten* (Recht en Praktijk 69, Kluwer 2012) 18; Dusollier and others, 'Contractual Arrangements Applicable to Creators' (n 2) 32–33; Vanhees, 'Auteurscontract' (n 48) 22–23.

[225] Berenboom, *Le Nouveau Droit d'Auteur et les Droits Voisins* (n 110) 215.

[226] Dusollier and others, 'Contractual Arrangements Applicable to Creators' (n 2) 102.

weaker bargaining power may force them to accept such long lists.[227] The law does not offer much protection in such a case: provided that the substantive, geographical and temporal scope of the rights granted is sufficiently detailed in the contract, these rights may pertain to all exclusive rights for the entire term of protection, on a global level – subject to the limitations analysed in Section 4.4.1 above.[228] In addition to this risk of overreach, an overly detailed list of methods of exploitation leads to increased complexity and administrative costs associated with contract formation.[229] This risks negatively affecting musicians. First, if the corporate partner(s) cannot transfer increased transaction costs to users, these costs are likely to be passed on to musicians with weak(er) bargaining power.[230] Second, unwarranted complexity endangers the achievement of the main objective of the duty to specify, namely ensuring informed consent.[231] Finally, undue complexity has spillover effects on contract performance: the more specific the list of methods of exploitation, the more opaque the operationalisation of remuneration arrangements risks becoming.[232] A sustained focus on the requirement of clarity, as it applies to B2B contracts under Belgian law, may have a positive impact.

In case the scope of rights granted is unclear, the principle of restrictive interpretation comes into play.[233] An exclusive right or method of exploitation that is not clearly specified in the contract is presumed to fall outside the scope of the contract.[234] For example, an exploitation contract pertaining to certain music does not imply the right to release a compilation album of a selection of songs if the contract does not expressly grant permission to do so.[235]

[227] Strowel and Vanbrabant, 'Copyright Licensing: A European View' (n 75) 38; Europe Economics and others, 'Remuneration of Authors and Performers' (n 48) 145; Dusollier, 'EU Contractual Protection of Creators' (n 36) 447.

[228] Berenboom, *Le Nouveau Droit d'Auteur et les Droits Voisins* (n 110) 214–15; Dusollier and others, 'Contractual Arrangements Applicable to Creators' (n 2) 33.

[229] Dusollier and others, 'Contractual Arrangements Applicable to Creators' (n 2) 83; Europe Economics and others, 'Remuneration of Authors and Performers' (n 48) 143–44.

[230] Europe Economics and others, 'Remuneration of Authors and Performers' (n 48) 144.

[231] ibid 145.

[232] Dusollier, 'EU Contractual Protection of Creators' (n 36) 440–41.

[233] See (1) in Belgium: Arts XI.167(1) para 3, XI.205(3) para 2 Belgian CEL; De Visscher and Michaux, *Précis du Droit d'Auteur et des Droits Voisins* (n 107) 316–18; Cruquenaire, *L'Interprétation des Contrats en Droit d'Auteur* (n 14) 27–122; Markellou, *Le Contrat d'Exploitation d'Auteur* (n 43) 72–73; Vanhees, *De wettelijke regeling inzake auteurscontracten* (n 224) 19–21; Vanhees, 'Auteurscontract' (n 48) 24–26 and (2) in France: Art 122-7 French IP Code; Cruquenaire, *L'Interprétation des Contrats en Droit d'Auteur* (n 14) 126–30; Lucas and others, *Traité de la Propriété Littéraire et Artistique* (n 46) 641–49; Gautier, *Propriété Littéraire et Artistique* (n 26) 588–91; Caron, *Droit d'Auteur et Droits Voisins* (n 46) 416.

[234] See eg French Supreme Court 30 September 2010, docket number 09-15091 <https://bit.ly/3kp4798>; Dusollier and others, 'Contractual Arrangements Applicable to Creators' (n 2) 41.

[235] See for Belgian case law in this sense, Court of Appeal Brussels 29 November 2000, IRDI 2001, 145 (*Helmut Lotti v BMG*); see also Civil Court Brussels 24 September 2001, AM 2002, 357 (*Gielen and Maes v Antler*); Lardinois, *Les Contrats Commentés de l'Industrie de La Musique*

This rule appears to be favourable to the interests of musicians. However, its scope is not that broad. If the contract contains general, vague terms that are open to interpretation, it may offer a fruitful avenue. However, there is no restrictive interpretation if the rights transfer is clear.[236] This rule arguably does not amount to a generalised principle of interpretation in favour of the artist. Instead, its application is limited to the determination of the scope of rights granted.[237]

An alternative to the duty to specify combined with the principle of restrictive interpretation is to limit the scope of rights granted to what is reasonably necessary to fulfil the contract's objective. This approach has been adopted in Germany and the Netherlands, for both authors and performers.

Under German law, the parties may specify the methods of exploitation to which the grant at issue pertains. Such specification is usually done in practice.[238] The relevant methods of exploitation must be sufficiently clearly definable within the contract, as well as technically and economically independent.[239] In the absence of due specification, the scope of the rights granted is determined on the basis of the contract's purpose.[240] This restriction has a bearing on both the exclusive or non-exclusive nature of the licence granted and the methods of exploitation that fall within the contract's scope.[241] Methods of exploitation that the parties did not envisage at the time of contract formation fall outside the contract's scope.[242] Similar rules of interpretation apply in other cases, such as where there is doubt as

2.0 (n 81) 71. On French case law taking a moral rights perspective, see Groffe, *La Bonne Foi en Droit d'Auteur* (n 13) 259–60.

[236] Brigitte Dauwe, 'Overeenkomsten in het Oude en in het Nieuwe Auteursrecht' in Frank Gotzen (ed), *Belgisch Auteursrecht van Oud naar Nieuw Le Renouveau du Droit d'Auteur en Belgique* (CIR 11, Bruylant 1996) 260, 262; Dusollier and others, 'Contractual Arrangements Applicable to Creators' (n 2) 53.

[237] Cruquenaire, *L'Interprétation des Contrats en Droit d'Auteur* (n 14) 27–122.

[238] Europe Economics and others, 'Remuneration of Authors and Performers' (n 48) 37.

[239] Hugenholtz and Guibault, 'Auteurscontractenrecht' (n 4) 35; Lenselink, *De Verlening van Exploitatiebevoegdheden in het Auteursrecht* (n 77) 409–10; Dreyer and others, *Urheberrecht* (n 41) 705–07; Malevanny, *Online Music Distribution* (n 87) 74.

[240] Arts 31(5), 79(2a) German Copyright Act; Schricker, *Urheberrecht. Kommentar* (n 41) 661–76, 1516–17. See also Art 37 German Copyright Act; Vanhees, *Een Juridische Analyse van de Grondslagen* (n 81) 178–94; Brison, *Het Naburig Recht van de Uitvoerende Kunstenaar* (n 48) 615; Guibault, *Copyright Limitations and Contracts* (n 102) 146; Hugenholtz and Guibault, 'Auteurscontractenrecht' (n 4) 44–46; Lenselink, *De Verlening van Exploitatiebevoegdheden in het Auteursrecht* (n 77) 405–15; Cruquenaire, *L'Interprétation des Contrats en Droit d'Auteur* (n 14) 130–34, 450; Fromm and Nordemann, *Urheberrecht* (n 41) 638–59; Rahmatian, 'Dealing with Rights in Copyright-Protected Works' (n 94) 306; Markellou, *Le Contrat d'Exploitation d'Auteur* (n 43) 78–81; Dusollier and others, 'Contractual Arrangements Applicable to Creators' (n 2) 12, 32, 42, 131; Dreyer and others, *Urheberrecht* (n 41) 707–14, 1362; Dusollier, 'EU Contractual Protection of Creators' (n 36) 440, 446–47; Möhring and Nicolini, *Urheberrecht* (n 41) 413–15.

[241] Art 31(5) German Copyright Act.

[242] Dusollier, 'EU Contractual Protection of Creators' (n 36) 440.

to whether the scope of rights granted includes the right to consent to adaptations.[243] In view of these rules, it makes commercial sense for corporate partners to insist upon a detailed formulation of the scope of rights granted in the contract, as is often done.[244]

In the Netherlands, for transfer contracts as well as exclusive licences, the scope of rights granted is limited to what is expressly mentioned in the written contract or what necessarily follows from the nature and scope of the grant.[245] For non-exclusive licences, a similar result may follow from the application of general contract law rules on the interpretation of contracts.[246]

Thus, as is the case for the duty to specify, the purpose-limitation rule does not protect musicians against clear, extensive lists of methods of exploitation. It only comes into play in case the scope of rights granted is ambiguous. Consequently, the substantive impact of both types of regimes on the position of the weaker party to the contract appears to be limited. Procedurally speaking, while something is definitely to be said for the elegance of the purpose-limitation principle, the duty to specify appears to provide the more transparent solution.[247] Moreover, as the substantive and geographical scope of rights granted, as well as the duration and the applicable remuneration arrangements, are determined in advance, legal certainty may be said to benefit from a duty to specify.[248] Coupled with a requirement of clarity and intelligibility, purpose-limitation as a sanction and acknowledging the limited effect of this rule on the actual scope of rights granted in practice, it may yet provide us with the 'best of both worlds' in terms of determination of the scope of rights granted in the context of primary music industry relationships.[249]

[243] Art 37 German Copyright Act; Schricker, *Urheberrecht. Kommentar* (n 41) 814–19; Fromm and Nordemann, *Urheberrecht* (n 41) 835–43; Dreyer and others, *Urheberrecht* (n 41) 816–18; Möhring and Nicolini, *Urheberrecht* (n 41) 566–68. See also Art 44(1) German Copyright Act, which confirms that – in case of doubt – the sale of an original of a work does not in itself imply the grant of a licence. On this topic see ia Schricker, *Urheberrecht. Kommentar* (n 41) 934–41; Fromm and Nordemann, *Urheberrecht* (n 41) 933–34; Dreyer and others, *Urheberrecht* (n 41) 868–69; Möhring and Nicolini, *Urheberrecht* (n 41) 633.

[244] Hugenholtz and Guibault, 'Auteurscontractenrecht' (n 4) 44–45; Markellou, *Le Contrat d'Exploitation d'Auteur* (n 43) 80; Dusollier and others, 'Contractual Arrangements Applicable to Creators' (n 2) 42. See, however, German Federal Court of Justice 27 September 1995, docket number I ZR 215/93 <https://bit.ly/39lvz1j>.

[245] Art 2(3) Dutch Copyright Act; Art 9(3) Dutch Neighbouring Rights Act. See Hugenholtz and Guibault, 'Auteurscontractenrecht' (n 4) 524–28; Europe Economics and others, 'Remuneration of Authors and Performers' (n 48) 37; Hugenholtz, 'Towards Author's Paradise' (n 135) 405; Visser and others, *ACR: Auteurscontractenrecht* (n 48) 41–42.

[246] Visser and others, *ACR: Auteurscontractenrecht* (n 48) 41.

[247] Cf Hugenholtz and Guibault, 'Auteurscontractenrecht' (n 4) 79; Dusollier and others, 'Contractual Arrangements Applicable to Creators' (n 2) 41. See also Hevia, *Reasonableness and Responsibility* (n 21) 91–102.

[248] Hugenholtz and Guibault, 'Auteurscontractenrecht' (n 4) 79.

[249] Cf Art 2.4 European Copyright Code.

A final observation as to the determination of the substance of rights granted in practice brings us back to the impact of digitisation. Consequent to the applicable rules on the temporal application of the substantive legal framework, these theoretical limitations do not apply to certain legacy contracts. As to contracts that postdate the internet revolution, digital rights may be granted in fairly broad terms, such as 'downloading' and/or 'streaming', without any further specification.[250] This engenders questions as to the scope of the duty to specify and the purpose-limitation principle. First, it may be argued that methods of exploitation that were unknown or unknowable at the time of contract formation cannot have been duly specified at that moment in time, thus excluding those methods from the scope of the grant – provided that a duty to specify applied in the jurisdiction at issue at that time. Conversely, the potential applicability of the principle of purpose-limitation in such a case will depend on (the temporal application of this rule and) the nature and scope of the contract. If the purpose is defined broadly as maximising revenues through exploitation, emerging uses may yet be covered by the grant, while a strict view that limits exploitation to the methods available at the time of contract formation on the basis of considerations of reasonableness[251] could lead to an outcome that is more favourable to the musician. This ambiguity is not conducive to legal certainty. Moreover, imbalances in relative bargaining power have 'resolved' this ambiguity by either express extensions of the rights granted to digital exploitation or by the simple commencement of digital exploitation by corporate partners, trusting musicians not to take legal action.[252] Also on a substantive level, questions may be raised regarding the effects of legal provisions determining the 'fair scope' of a contract, despite the incremental establishment of restrictions on the scope of rights granted.

4.5 FORMATION OF THE CONTRACT: SECONDARY RELATIONSHIPS

Subsequent to the initial grant of rights, further transfers of or sub-licences to exclusive rights occur frequently – either as a standalone transaction or in the context of a larger deal, such as through mergers and acquisitions, or in case of insolvency of a corporate partner.[253] Such further transactions have a significant impact on the exploitation of protected music and the ensuing remuneration.[254]

250 Dusollier and others, 'Contractual Arrangements Applicable to Creators' (n 2) 67, 70.

251 For Dutch case law in this sense, see Hugenholtz and Guibault, 'Auteurscontractenrecht' (n 4) 9.

252 Dusollier and others, 'Contractual Arrangements Applicable to Creators' (n 2) 66; van Gompel and others, 'Evaluatie Wet Auteurscontractenrecht (n 3) 30.

253 Cf Phillip W Hall Jr, 'Smells Like Slavery: Unconscionability in Recording Industry Contracts' [2002] Hastings Comm & Ent LJ 189, 220; CMA, 'Music and Streaming: Final Report' (29 November 2022) 66–72.

254 Cf Dusollier, 'EU Contractual Protection of Creators' (n 36) 450; Séverine Dusollier, 'An Effective and Comprehensive Contractual Protection of Creators and Performers' (Copyright in the Digital Single Market, Brussels, 30 January 2020).

This implies a further relinquishing of control that may lead to unfair situations in practice, especially when the third parties are deemed ill-suited for the exploitation of the music.[255] A salient example is the 2019 takeover by US entrepreneur Scott 'Scooter' Braun's Ithaca Holdings of Big Machine Label Group.[256] This transaction included the transfer of the rights to a number of albums by Taylor Swift. The latter, citing a long-running feud with Mr Braun and her own wish to own the rights in these albums, sought to resist the transfer.[257] In autumn 2020, the rights were transferred further to Shamrock Capital, yet another company, leaving Ms Swift to ponder the merits of rerecording the compositions on the albums at issue, a feat that she has since successfully accomplished.[258] Regardless of this success, this saga leads to the following observation: if even global superstars do not succeed in exerting control over further transfers of their music, all musicians could find themselves in a similar position.

The conclusion of secondary contracts by primary corporate partners is subject to certain limitations, to avoid a disproportionate loss of control and agency on the part of musicians. Not only must musicians be aware of who holds what rights to their music, they should also have the opportunity to object in good faith prior to the conclusion of the contract, at least when the circumstances so allow.

The first, overarching limitation to the further transfer of rights stems from the foundational principle of contract law that prevents parties from transferring more rights than they have obtained. Consequently, the further transfer of rights is limited to those that have been transferred to the corporate partner in the primary contract, to the exclusion of those to which the corporate partner merely received a licence. Moreover, this implies that the limitations set as to the substance of exclusive exploitation rights granted, such as for future music and/or methods of exploitation,[259] also restrict the scope of possible secondary relationships.[260] Finally, this scope is also affected by remuneration rights of musicians, as well as their moral rights, which cannot be fully waived and may merely be modulated as to their enforcement in practice. These restrictions apply to both composers and performers.

[255] This may be illustrated by the difficulty for artists in getting their corporate partners to agree to a so-called key player provision, whereby the contract's continued existence is made dependent on the presence of a certain person (or group of persons) within the corporate partner, see eg Hall Jr, 'Smells Like Slavery' (n 253) 216–19; Gulinck, *Hier Tekenen!* (n 4) 284.

[256] Ann Herman, 'You Belong with Me: Recording Artists' Fight for Ownership of Their Masters' (2021) 18 Nw J Tech & Intell Prop 239.

[257] See eg Taylor Swift, 'Untitled' (*Tumblr*, 30 June 2019) <https://bit.ly/3lGCh9e>.

[258] See Taylor Swift, 'Tweet' (*Twitter*, 16 November 2020) <https://bit.ly/3AVeOpj>. See also Geoff Mayfield, 'Taylor Swift's Masters: What Shamrock Gets for $300 Million, Why It Matters, and What's Next' (*Variety*, 19 November 2020) <https://bit.ly/3BWAGS8>; Lucas Shaw, 'The End of Taylor Swift's $300 Million Fight With Scooter Braun' (*Bloomberg*, 22 November 2020) <https://bloom.bg/3lH8xsD>; Herman, 'You Belong with Me' (n 256).

[259] See above, Section 4.4.1.2.

[260] The duty to specify under Belgian and French law does not extend to secondary relationships, see Strowel and Vanbrabant, 'Copyright Licensing: A European View' (n 75) 38.

Other restrictions to the formation of secondary contractual relationships arise from the applicable provisions of (copyright) contract law, both as to further transfers thereof and/or sub-licences thereto. When entering into a primary contractual relationship, both musicians and their corporate partners do so with the specific characteristics of their contracting party in mind. It therefore makes sense to subject changes in the (economic) identity of one of the parties to the express consent of the other party.[261] Regulatory responses range from a requirement of consent – mandatory in some cases and subject to contractual deviation in others – to the attachment of the grant of further rights to certain modalities, such as a requirement to notify the parties involved and/or the emergence of joint and several liability on the part of the corporate partner and the third party.

Belgium and France have set particular conditions for the formation of secondary relationships in a publishing context in particular. Under Belgian law, the requirement of author consent in such a case is mandatory.[262] In the absence of consent, the author may invoke the relative nullity of the grant to the third party.[263] This requirement of consent does not apply if the grant to the third party is accompanied by a partial or complete transfer of the publisher's business.[264] The relevant provision of French law concerning publishing contracts also expressly requires the consent of the author in case of a secondary grant of rights to a third party, unless a transfer of the publisher's business occurs.[265] However, this rule is accompanied by a safeguard for the author: if this secondary grant severely undermines the author's interests, the author may terminate the contract.[266] The French provision concerning audiovisual production contracts requires any transfer of such a contract to be preceded by a prior notification by the transferor to their co-author(s), at least one month prior

[261] Vanhees, *Een Juridische Analyse van de Grondslagen* (n 81) 317–18, 326, 332–33.

[262] Hugenholtz and Guibault, 'Auteurscontractenrecht' (n 4) 67; Yves Van Couter and Bernard Vanbrabant, *Handboek Licentieovereenkomsten* (Bibliotheek Handelsrecht Larcier. Mededinging, Handelspraktijken en Intellectuele Rechten 7, Larcier 2008) 16, 87–88; Vanhees, *De wettelijke regeling inzake auteurscontracten* (n 224) 43–44; Vanhees, 'Art XI.195' (n 74) 312, 317–18; Vanhees, 'Auteurscontract' (n 48) 45–47.

[263] De Visscher and Michaux, *Précis du Droit d'Auteur et des Droits Voisins* (n 107) 347; Vanhees, 'Art XI.195' (n 74) 318.

[264] Art XI.196(3) Belgian CEL; Berenboom, *Le Nouveau Droit d'Auteur et les Droits Voisins* (n 110) 233.

[265] Art L 132-16 para 1 French IP Code; Vanhees, *Een Juridische Analyse van de Grondslagen* (n 81) 328–20; Guibault and Hugenholtz, 'Study on the Conditions Applicable to Contracts Relating to Intellectual Property in the European Union' (n 43) 72–73; Hugenholtz and Guibault, 'Auteurscontractenrecht' (n 4) 66; Dusollier and others, 'Contractual Arrangements Applicable to Creators' (n 2) 124; Lucas and others, *Traité de la Propriété Littéraire et Artistique* (n 46) 716–19; Gautier, *Propriété Littéraire et Artistique* (n 26) 638–40, 725–31; Caron, *Droit d'Auteur et Droits Voisins* (n 46) 447–48.

[266] Art L 132-16 para 1 French IP Code; Dusollier and others, 'Contractual Arrangements Applicable to Creators' (n 2) 124.

to the effective date of the transfer.[267] This requirement of consent furthers stakeholder agency.[268]

German copyright contract law foresees a detailed, balanced regime that distinguishes the further transfer of rights from the grant of sub-licences.[269] It applies to both composing and performing musicians. On the one hand, German law in principle requires artist consent to further transfer(s).[270] In the absence of the required consent, no transfer can take place.[271] Consent may only be refused in good faith.[272] No consent is required if the transfer is accompanied by a full or partial sale of the corporate partner's business. In such a case, the artist may revoke the initial grant if exploitation of the protected content by the transferee cannot be reasonably demanded of the musician.[273] Moreover, the transferor and the transferee become jointly and severally liable for the obligations towards the musician(s) under the initial contract.[274] Neither the right of revocation nor the right to invoke the transferee's liability may be waived in advance.[275] On the other hand, the grant of a sub-licence is subject to less stringent rules. While German law posits the need for consent, such consent may only be refused in good faith, and no consent is required if the sub-licence is granted solely to serve the interests of the musician (s).[276] Regrettably, the relevant provisions do not expressly qualify the rights of musicians as to the grant of sub-licences as unwaivable.[277] For the remainder, however, the German regime may be considered as a balanced solution that takes due account of the interests of all stakeholders.[278]

Finally, neither Dutch nor UK law contain any specific restrictions on the further grant of rights to third parties in a copyright contract context. However, many copyright exploitation contracts may be said to have a strictly personal nature.[279]

[267] Art L 132-28 para 3 French IP Code.

[268] Dusollier and others, 'Contractual Arrangements Applicable to Creators' (n 2) 55–56.

[269] See ia Vanhees, *Een Juridische Analyse van de Grondslagen* (n 81) 319–25; Fromm and Nordemann, *Urheberrecht* (n 41) 789–810; Dreyer and others, *Urheberrecht* (n 41) 782–96; Möhring and Nicolini, *Urheberrecht* (n 41) 492–503.

[270] Art 34(1) *jo* 79(2a) German Copyright Act; Vanhees, *Een Juridische Analyse van de Grondslagen* (n 81) 319–22; Hugenholtz and Guibault, 'Auteurscontractenrecht' (n 4) 65–66; Rahmatian, 'Dealing with Rights in Copyright-Protected Works' (n 94) 303; Dusollier and others, 'Contractual Arrangements Applicable to Creators' (n 2) 43, 131.

[271] Lenselink, *De Verlening van Exploitatiebevoegdheden in het Auteursrecht* (n 77) 113.

[272] Art 34(1) *jo* 79(2a) German Copyright Act.

[273] Art 34(3) *jo* 79(2a) German Copyright Act. The right of revocation also applies in case of a substantial change to the corporate partner's shareholders.

[274] Art 34(4) *jo* 79(2a) German Copyright Act; Rahmatian, 'Dealing with Rights in Copyright-Protected Works' (n 94) 303.

[275] Art 34(5) *jo* 79(2a) German Copyright Act.

[276] Art 35(1)–(2) *jo* 34(1) *jo* 79(2a) German Copyright Act; Schricker, *Urheberrecht. Kommentar* (n 41) 751–55.

[277] See Arts 35(2) *jo* 34(5) *jo* 79(2a) German Copyright Act.

[278] Vanhees, *Een Juridische Analyse van de Grondslagen* (n 81) 332–33.

[279] See eg Van Couter and Vanbrabant, *Handboek Licentieovereenkomsten* (n 262) 16, 87–88; Lucas and others, *Traité de la Propriété Littéraire et Artistique* (n 46) 715–16; Gautier, *Propriété*

This may prevent the further transfer of exclusive exploitation rights and/or the grant of sub-licences thereto by the corporate partner without the artist's clear and undisputable – although potentially oral – consent.[280]

In determining the appropriate form of regulation, heed must be paid to both the interests of musicians in maintaining a degree of control regarding the identity of the third party/parties involved, and those of corporate partners in securing efficient, revenue-maximising exploitation of the protected content. The regime foreseen in Articles 34 and 35 German Copyright Act appears to be the most fairly balanced of the analysed provisions.[281] These provisions are quite comprehensive and very detailed.[282] Moreover, they make a distinction between further transfers and sub-licences.[283] Consequently, transparency and legal certainty benefit. Moreover, these regimes take due account of the interests of all stakeholders and do not appear to lead to a disproportionate encroachment upon parties' freedom of contract. Informed consent – and thus agency – appears to be safeguarded. In view of this, a move towards the German rules on further transfers and sub-licences is to be supported and, moreover, qualified as mandatory law.[284]

The provision pertaining to the further transfer of rights may moreover be of particular help in the context of insolvency of the corporate partner(s). Indeed, both composing and performing musicians who have transferred their rights or have granted an exclusive licence thereto should in such a situation be able to terminate the grant under certain circumstances, allowing them to reclaim their rights and seek other avenues for the exploitation of their music.[285] A less intrusive, but arguably also effective and fair alternative would be to grant musicians the right to revoke the exclusivity of licences granted when the corporate partner becomes insolvent.

4.6 OUTRO

This chapter has analysed the legal framework as applicable to the formation stage of the contracts under review, seeking to ascertain what exactly qualifies as 'fair scope' and what the impact of the legal framework is. First, a brief precontractual perspective was taken, focusing on the applicable duties of care and information, as well as potentially relevant provisions on unfair B2B trade practices.

Littéraire et Artistique (n 26) 725–26; Caron, *Droit d'Auteur et Droits Voisins* (n 46) 445–46; Arnold, *Performers' Rights* (n 48) 287–88.

280 Van Couter and Vanbrabant, *Handboek Licentieovereenkomsten* (n 262) 16, 87–88; Arnold, *Performers' Rights* (n 48) 287–88.

281 See regarding performers, Art 79(2a) German Copyright Act.

282 Cf Vanhees, *Een Juridische Analyse van de Grondslagen* (n 81) 333, 575.

283 ibid.

284 Cf Vanhees, *Een Juridische Analyse van de Grondslagen* (n 81) 575.

285 Hugenholtz and Guibault, 'Auteurscontractenrecht' (n 4) vi, xii, 82.

A significantly more extensive section was devoted to the substantive and formal aspects of the requirement of consent. In this regard, the principled need for express consent was highlighted, with certain exceptional instances of presumptive consent. On a formal level, the requirement of a written document that applies in some of the chosen jurisdictions was explored further.

Subsequently, the substance of rights granted through the contracts under review was analysed. Focus first lay on theoretical limitations to the scope of such rights and then shifted to practical considerations that determine the scope of rights granted. As to the former, following a brief highlight of the prohibition of transfer of copyright *sensu stricto* under German law, limitations set as to future music and future methods of exploitation were analysed, in addition to a number of complementary limitations based on requirements of reasonableness. These limitations are sanctioned by relative nullity, to be invoked by the musician. As to the determination of the scope of rights granted, the duty to specify under Belgian and French law was contrasted with the principle of purpose-limitation under Dutch and German law. The effect of both rules in practice is the interpretation of the scope of rights granted in favour of the musician(s) if the contract is ambiguous.

Finally, a section was devoted to the rules that govern the further transfer or sub-licence of exclusive exploitation rights to secondary contract partners. While the applicable legal regimes posit the need for consent on the part of musicians as a general principle, contractual deviations remain possible in many cases.

Regulatory choices differ significantly. To date, legislators' freedom in this context is not curtailed through harmonisation at either the EU or the international level.[286] Given the lack of harmonisation on the issue of initial ownership, EU harmonisation is, as yet, unlikely. Regulatory convergence at a global level appears to be an even more distant dream. Regardless, this chapter made several regulatory recommendations. An important common thread is the aim of securing informed consent and ensuing agency on the part of all contracting parties, through measures that seek to alleviate existing structural information asymmetries. The measures reviewed in this chapter are primarily of a negative nature, providing restrictions on the scope of rights granted. These measures are important, as they define the boundaries of the contractual relationship at the time of contract formation. However, in view of the temporal application of the incremental amendments of the legal framework, these measures do not appear to have had a profound impact on the scope of legacy contracts. This illustrates the difficulties of righting past wrongs in the music

[286] Reto M Hilty and Valentina Moscon, 'Part D – Copyright Contract Law (Article 10 and Articles 14-16 COM(2016) 593 Final)' in Reto M Hilty and Valentina Moscon (eds), *Modernisation of the EU Copyright Rules Position Statement of the Max Planck Institute for Innovation and Competition* (Max Planck Institute for Innovation and Competition Research Paper Series 17-12, Max Planck Institute for Innovation and Competition 2017) 74; Séverine Dusollier, 'The 2019 Directive on Copyright in the Digital Single Market: Some Progress, a Few Bad Choices, and an Overall Failed Ambition' [2020] CML Rev 979, 1022.

industry. Further, as to 'modern' music industry contracts, information asymmetries persist, as do detailed lists of methods of exploitation included in clauses pertaining to the grant of rights. Therefore, the risks of unfairness associated with the excessive transfer of rights remain. Moreover, these measures do not provide any positive obligations regarding the effective exploitation of music and/or the ensuing remuneration. We must therefore look beyond the scope of the rights granted and adopt a dynamic perspective that takes account of the performance of the contract over time.[287] This is done in the next chapter, which focuses on the performance stage of music contracts in the streaming age.

[287] Cf Dusollier and others, 'Contractual Arrangements Applicable to Creators' (n 2) 23; Dusollier, 'EU Contractual Protection of Creators' (n 36) 447.

5

Performance of the Contract

The big print giveth
and the small print taketh away.

—Tom Waits[1]

5.1 INTRO

The difference in the relative bargaining power of musicians and their corporate partners not only has consequences for the negotiation and formation phase of the contract, but also for its performance, consisting of the exploitation of protected content and the ensuing remuneration. Unfair situations may arise as to both aspects.[2]

This chapter analyses to what extent the legal framework intervenes – and should intervene. First, it reviews exploitation obligations, in terms of both the existence and scope of a duty to exploit and possible limitations to the content of exploitation activities (Section 5.2). Subsequently, the requirement of 'fair' remuneration, the available tools for ex post contract adjustment, and legislative measures seeking to enhance transparency in the music value chain are scrutinised (Section 5.3). The chapter moves on to the performance stage of contracts in secondary relationships (Section 5.4), before making a case for a harmonised residual remuneration right for digital exploitation (Section 5.5), and then concluding (Section 5.6).

[1] Excerpt from the song 'Step Right up' (album Small Change, 1976); cf Luc Gulinck, *Hier Tekenen! (en Let Niet op de Kleine Lettertjes...) Wegwijs in het Juridische en Zakelijke Labyrint van de Muziekwereld* (Academia Press 2019) 14.

[2] See eg Steve Albini, 'The Problem with Music' [1993] The Baffler <https://bit.ly/3uUPXAi>; Courtney Love, 'Courtney Love Does the Math' [2000] Salon <https://bit.ly/3AuPo2O>; Mark Hogan, 'The Record Industry Expects a Windfall. Where Will the Money Go?' [2019] Pitchfork <https://bit.ly/3DuMls1>.

5.2 EXPLOITATION

5.2.1 *Structure*

The concept of 'exploitation' encompasses all activities undertaken by corporate partners in order to build an audience for the music to which they have obtained certain rights of use. Corporate partners to which musicians have transferred or exclusively licensed their rights control the modalities of exploitation of a work/performance in practice, including the remuneration therefor. This may be problematic for a musician who seeks to retain artistic oversight regarding the use of their work/performance.[3] Without a generalised obligation to exploit the music, the musician has no real guarantee that it will be effectively exploited and, if so, how this exploitation will take place. Further, it is difficult for a musician to have a full, transparent insight into what exploitation activities are actually undertaken.[4] This risk of 'under-exploitation' increases with the decreased competition resulting from vertical and horizontal concentration in the music industry.[5] All of this sits uneasily with the exclusive nature of many recording contracts.[6]

The issue of exploitation also has a bearing on the moral rights of musicians. A lack of enforcement of both the right to paternity and the right to integrity may lead to instances of unfairness in practice. A particular example is provided by the plight of composers whose music is uploaded to online platforms. While the name of the featured artist is usually listed in the track's title, more often than not, the songwriter(s) is(are) not identified.[7] Not only may this lead to a lack of remuneration for the exploitation of a piece of music, it also unduly severs the connection between a composer and their work, resulting in a loss of agency.[8]

3 Cf Phillip W Hall Jr, 'Smells Like Slavery: Unconscionability in Recording Industry Contracts' [2002] Hastings Comm & Ent LJ 189, 214.

4 Commission, 'Impact Assessment on the Modernisation of EU Copyright Rules Accompanying the Document Proposal for a Directive of the European Parliament and of the Council on Copyright in the Digital Single Market and Proposal for a Regulation of the European Parliament and of the Council Laying Down Rules on the Exercise of Copyright and Related Rights Applicable to Certain Online Transmissions of Broadcasting Organisations and Retransmissions of Television and Radio Programmes' (Staff Working Document) SWD (2016) 301 Final (14 September 2016) 174.

5 Cf Jim Rogers, *The Death & Life of the Music Industry in the Digital Age* (Bloomsbury 2013) 186–87.

6 Orly Lobel, *Talent Wants to Be Free. Why We Should Learn to Love Leaks, Raids, and Free Riding* (Yale University Press 2013) 51; Séverine Dusollier, 'EU Contractual Protection of Creators: Blind Spots and Shortcomings' [2018] Colum J L & Arts 436, 446.

7 Mark Mulligan, *Awakening: The Music Industry In The Digital Age* (Createspace 2015) 210.

8 Rethink Music Initiative, 'Fair Music: Transparency and Payment Flows in the Music Industry. Recommendations to Increase Transparency, Reduce Friction, and Promote Fairness in the Music Industry' (2015) 4, 25. This problem is linked with the metadata issue, see Chapter 2, Section 2.5.

This section focuses on the legal release commitments for corporate partners in terms of the exploitation of compositions and (fixated) performances in the streaming age. First, it reviews and evaluates existing positive obligations concerning the extent of exploitation required, as well as the consequences if no or insufficient exploitation takes place. Second, this section analyses and evaluates whether and how musicians may exert control over the content of corporate partners' exploitation activities.

5.2.2 *Duty to Exploit*

5.2.2.1 Overview

Musicians want their music to be exploited in order for it to be heard and, in most cases, result in remuneration.[9] The exploitation activities of the corporate partner play a key role in achieving this goal. Corporate partners have a parallel commercial interest in exploiting music. In the absence of exploitation of the music at issue, neither party will obtain remuneration. However, corporate partners' appetite for exploitation (understandably) lessens significantly if their commercial expectations are not met. The law seeks to balance these overlapping but simultaneously conflicting interests by way of two types of legal provisions.

A first category gives rise to a direct duty on the corporate partners to exploit. Second, so-called use-it-or-lose-it provisions grant musicians the right to reclaim their exclusive exploitation rights if the corporate partner does not perform any acts of exploitation or when such activities are deemed insufficient, without expressly formulating a direct duty to exploit. Thus, an indirect duty to exploit arises: if the corporate partner wishes to maintain the rights granted, they must exploit the music at issue. On the basis of these duties, a requirement of 'fair exploitation' may be conceptualised.

5.2.2.2 Direct Duty to Exploit

Some jurisdictions expressly impose a direct duty to exploit on the corporate partner, either in a general way or specific to a certain contract type.[10] The Belgian legislator has opted for an express general duty to exploit subject to honest trade practices. This duty applies to all copyright exploitation contracts with both composers and performers, except as to music in employment situations and commissioned music.[11]

[9] Cf Rec 80 DSM Directive.

[10] On the substantive scope of this duty to exploit, conceptualised as the requirement of 'fair exploitation', see below, Section 5.2.2.4.

[11] On composers, see Art XI.167(1) para 5 Belgian CEL and on performers, Art XI.205(3) para 4 Belgian CEL; Fernand De Visscher and Benoît Michaux, *Précis du Droit d'Auteur et des Droits Voisins* (Bruylant 2000) 331–33; Hendrik Vanhees, 'Auteurscontract' [2019] OBO 1, 42.

No such general duty applies under German, Dutch or UK law. As to the French legal framework, it has been argued that the unwaivable principle of proportionate remuneration[12] implies a duty to exploit on the part of the corporate partner.[13]

Independently of the existence of a general duty to exploit, provisions of copyright contract law in Belgium, France and Germany (not in the Netherlands) establish a specific, direct duty to exploit for publishing contracts, such as between composers and music publishers.

Under Belgian law, upon sanction of relative nullity of the publishing contract, it must set a minimum number of 'copies' for the first edition, unless the author is guaranteed an advance.[14] The concept of 'copies' refers to reproductions in fixed material form – that is, physical products.[15] This particular direct duty to exploit therefore has no real consequences in the digital sphere. This concretisation of the general duty to exploit under Belgian law only applies to the first (physical) edition of the publication.[16] The French IP Code obliges music publishers to mine potential avenues for exploitation in a permanent way, including through the promotion of the work(s) at issue.[17] A similar rule regarding a minimum number of copies applies, as is the case under Belgian law, provided that the contract does not set the payment of a minimum royalty.[18] The German Publishing Act also includes an

[12] See below, Section 5.3.2.2.

[13] See Sébastien Raimond, *La Qualification du Contrat d'Auteur* (Le Droit des Affaires. Propriété Intellectuelle 34, LexisNexis 2009) 126–31; Alexis Boisson, *La Licence de Droit d'Auteur* (Bibliothèque de Droit de l'Entreprise 86, LexisNexis 2013) 595–625. See however Jean-Michel Bruguière, 'The Irresistible Rise of the Exploitation Obligation in Literary and Artistic Property Agreements' [2022] RIDA 3, 11–12.

[14] Art XI.195 Belgian CEL.

[15] This position is supported by the text of Art XI.199(1) Belgian CEL and Art L 132-17(1) French IP Code, which grant the author the opportunity to rescind the publishing contract in case the publisher 'destroys' all the copies of the work at issue. This provision is difficult to apply in a digital environment.

[16] Alain Berenboom, *Le Nouveau Droit d'Auteur et les Droits Voisins* (Création Information Communication 1, 3rd edn, Larcier 2005) 232.

[17] Art L 132-12 French IP Code. See also Art L 131-3 para 4 French IP Code. See ia Marina Markellou, *Le Contrat d'Exploitation d'Auteur. Vers un Droit d'Auteur Contractuel Européen. Analyse Comparative des Systèmes Juridiques Allemand, Belge, Français et Hellénique* (Création Information Communication, Larcier 2012) 308–17; Séverine Dusollier and others, 'Contractual Arrangements Applicable to Creators' (Publications Office of the EU 2014) <https://op.europa.eu/s/zIba> 6, 46; André Lucas and others, *Traité de la Propriété Littéraire et Artistique* (5th edn, LexisNexis 2017) 698–706; Pierre-Yves Gautier, *Propriété Littéraire et Artistique* (11th edn, Presses Universitaires de France 2019) 627–41; Christophe Caron, *Droit d'Auteur et Droits Voisins* (6th edn, LexisNexis 2020) 427–28, 458–65; Bruguière, 'The Irresistible Rise' (n 13) 8–15. Regarding literary publishing, cf Arts L 132-17-2(I), L 132-17-5 French IP Code.

[18] Arts L 132-10, L 132-11 French IP Code. See also Jean-Christophe Lardinois, *Les Contrats Commentés de l'Industrie de La Musique 2.0: Cadre Général et Pratique Contractuelle* (Création Information Communication Pratique 1, 2nd edn, Larcier 2009) 121; Raimond, *La Qualification du Contrat d'Auteur* (n 13) 133–36; Dusollier and others, 'Contractual Arrangements Applicable to Creators' (n 17) 46.

express, albeit waivable, obligation for the publisher to reproduce and distribute the work, as appropriate and customary in the sector.[19]

Taken as a whole, duties to exploit applicable to publishers in particular cater to the literary sector.[20] Their operationalisation appears ill-suited to the music industry in the streaming age. While the manufacture and distribution of (copies of) sheet music used to be an important part of music publishers' commercial activities, this aspect has become much less prevalent. As a result, the activities of music publishers centre to a much lesser extent around 'copies'.

Finally, French law establishes a specific provision concerning the non-use of exploitation rights by record companies. Article L 212-12 French IP Code provides that civil courts may order all appropriate measures in the event of clearly abusive non-exploitation by a record company of the exploitation rights that it has acquired.[21] No equivalent provisions were found.

More general provisions may further affect a corporate partner's duty to exploit. The objective of exploitation that is inherent to copyright exploitation contracts implies the performance of at least some exploitation activities by the corporate partner.[22] This rings especially true in case of transfers and exclusive licences, since the exploitation of the music in such a case depends on the activities of the corporate partner(s).[23] The duty of good-faith contract performance implies a duty to exploit on the part of the corporate partner, at least to a certain extent.[24] A lack of exploitation may exceptionally be qualified as an abuse of right or even lead to the voidability of a contract on the basis of vitiated consent if exploitation is considered

[19] Arts 1, 14, 16 German Publishing Act; Bart Jan Lenselink, *De Verlening van Exploitatiebevoegdheden in het Auteursrecht. Een Rechtsvergelijkend Onderzoek naar Overdracht en Licentieverlening in Auteursrechtelijke Exploitatieverhoudingen naar Nederlands, Duits en Amerikaans Recht* (Sdu Uitgevers 2005) 261; Ludwig Delp, *Der Verlagsvertrag. Handbuch für die Praxis* (8th edn, CH Beck 2008) 10–12; Markellou, *Le Contrat d'Exploitation d'Auteur* (n 17) 304–06.

[20] Lardinois, *Les Contrats Commentés de l'Industrie de La Musique 2.0* (n 18) 120; Raimond, *La Qualification du Contrat d'Auteur* (n 13) 133–34.

[21] Lucas and others, *Traité de la Propriété Littéraire et Artistique* (n 17) 1152–53.

[22] Cf Hendrik Vanhees, *Een Juridische Analyse van de Grondslagen, Inhoud en Draagwijdte van Auteursrechtelijke Exploitatiecontracten* (Maklu 1993) 210–18; De Visscher and Michaux, *Précis du Droit d'Auteur et des Droits Voisins* (n 11) 332; Dusollier and others, 'Contractual Arrangements Applicable to Creators' (n 17) 22; Julie Groffe, *La Bonne Foi en Droit d'Auteur* (Institut Universitaire Varenne Collection des Thèses 106, LGDJ – lextenso éditions 2015) 292–93.

[23] cf Brigitte Dauwe, 'Overeenkomsten in het Oude en in het Nieuwe Auteursrecht' in Frank Gotzen (ed), *Belgisch Auteursrecht van Oud naar Nieuw Le Renouveau du Droit d'Auteur en Belgique* (CIR 11, Bruylant 1996) 282.

[24] See (1) in Belgium: Art 1134 para 3 Belgian CC; (2) in France: Art 1134 para 3 French CC; (3) in Germany: Art 242 German CC; Ludwig Delp, *Der Verlagsvertrag. Handbuch für die Praxis* (8th edn, CH Beck 2008) 10; and (4) in the Netherlands: Arts 6:2, 6:248 Dutch Civil Code; Vanhees, *Een Juridische Analyse van de Grondslagen* (n 22) 230–34.

to be an essential element thereof.[25] However, given the restrictive application of limitations to freedom of contract on the basis of general contract law rules, and the fact that these rules are not tailored to the creative sector, it seems unlikely that a substantive general duty to exploit would be inferred from them in practice.

Breach of contract regarding the direct duties to exploit is usually sanctioned by specific performance and/or a right to damages, in accordance with general contract law.[26] In serious cases, the contract may be rescinded, either on the basis of general contract law, specific provisions of copyright contract law, or a specific clause in the contract.[27] French copyright contract law expressly establishes the sanction of contract termination if a publisher falls short in fulfilling their duty to exploit after having been given due notice thereof, as did Belgian law prior to the implementation of the DSM Directive.[28] As the result is a reversal of rights, this adds an *in*direct duty to exploit to the equation.

The provisions that establish a duty to exploit on the part of corporate partners give rise to the question whether there is a parallel duty for musicians. One may think of delivery obligations, instances of mandatory cooperation with promotion and marketing, as well as the negative duty not to engage in activities that risk hindering the exploitation of the music.[29] Such obligations will usually arise from express provisions in the contract.[30] In the absence of such provisions, the requirement of good-faith contract performance implies the existence of a general duty in this sense, as does the requirement for transferors and/or licensors to provide indemnification to their counterparty for their own actions and, to a certain extent, the actions of third parties (for example, in case of copyright infringement

25 Cf Dauwe, 'Overeenkomsten in het Oude en in het Nieuwe Auteursrecht' (n 23) 283; Dusollier and others, 'Contractual Arrangements Applicable to Creators' (n 17) 55–56.

26 Lardinois, *Les Contrats Commentés de l'Industrie de La Musique* 2.0 (n 18) 29–30, 121; Agnès Lucas-Schloetter, 'European Copyright Contract Law: A Plea for Harmonisation' (2017) 48 IIC 897, 899; Agnès Lucas-Schloetter, 'The Remuneration of Authors and Performers in Copyright Contract Law' in Paul Torremans (ed), *Research Handbook on Copyright Law* (Research Handbooks in Intellectual Property, 2nd edn, Edward Elgar 2017) 266; Ula Furgał, 'Interpreting EU Reversion Rights: Why "Use-It-or-Lose-It" Should Be the Guiding Principle' (2021) 43 EIPR 283, 287.

27 For an application in Belgium, expressly noting the mandatory nature of the direct duty to exploit under the Belgian regime concerning publishing contracts, see Court of Appeal Brussels 4 March 2008, docket number 2005/AR/1986, not published; Joris Deene, 'Intellectuele Rechten Kroniek 2008' [2009] NJW 523.

28 See (1) in Belgium: Art XI.196(1) para 3 Belgian CEL and (2) in France: Art L 132-17 French IP Code. On digital exploitation in literary publishing, see Art L 132-17-5 French IP Code.

29 On publishing contracts see (1) in France: Arts L 132-8, L 132-9 French IP Code; Markellou, *Le Contrat d'Exploitation d'Auteur* (n 17) 329–63; Groffe, *La Bonne Foi en Droit d'Auteur* (n 22) 283–90; Lucas and others, *Traité de la Propriété Littéraire et Artistique* (n 17) 694–98; Gautier, *Propriété Littéraire et Artistique* (n 17) 620–22; Caron, *Droit d'Auteur et Droits Voisins* (n 17) 450–53 and (2) in Germany: Arts 2(1), 30, 31, 33(2), 39(2) German Publishing Act.

30 Delp, *Der Verlagsvertrag* (n 24) 13; Lardinois, *Les Contrats Commentés de l'Industrie de La Musique* 2.0 (n 18) 76–77, 96–97.

allegations).[31] In extreme cases, such as active deception, musicians' behaviour may even be qualified as an unfair trade practice. It deserves to be emphasised, however, that a musician cannot be held responsible if their music lacks commercial success.[32]

Due account for both the artistic and commercial interests involved cautions against a direct duty to exploit on the part of corporate partners in the streaming age.[33] While not expressly and directly requiring exploitation may appear anathema to the essence of copyright exploitation contracts, the potential indirect effects of such a direct duty to exploit are undesirable. A corporate partner forced to actively invest in exploitation activities for a piece of music, at the penalty of breaching their contract and being liable for damages, is likely to hold off on investment in that music. Given that commercial success in the CCIs is never guaranteed, this would negatively affect the investment climate – and thus corporate partners' agency – in a significant way.[34] Ultimately, this would again leave musicians at the losing end of the equation.

5.2.2.3 Indirect Duty to Exploit

The second category of relevant legal provisions consists of so-called use-it-or-lose-it provisions, whereby the lack of (sufficient) exploitation by the corporate partner results in a right of revocation for the musician(s) under certain circumstances.[35] Such revocations not only operate to the benefit of musicians, but also have an associated public interest objective. By allowing artists to reclaim their rights, the

[31] See ia (1) in Belgium: Vanhees, *Een Juridische Analyse van de Grondslagen* (n 22) 98–103, 111, 123–28; Dauwe, 'Overeenkomsten in het Oude en in het Nieuwe Auteursrecht' (n 23) 267–68; De Visscher and Michaux, *Précis du Droit d'Auteur et des Droits Voisins* (n 11) 353; Yves Van Couter and Bernard Vanbrabant, *Handboek Licentieovereenkomsten* (Bibliotheek Handelsrecht Larcier. Mededinging, Handelspraktijken en Intellectuele Rechten 7, Larcier 2008) 10, 60–62, 70; Bernard Vanbrabant, *La Propriété Intellectuelle. Tome 2. Régime Patrimonial* (Création Information Communication, Larcier 2018) 867–74; (2) in France: Raimond, *La Qualification du Contrat d'Auteur* (n 13) 95–96, 424–42; Markellou, *Le Contrat d'Exploitation d'Auteur* (n 17) 340–49; Boisson, *La Licence de Droit d'Auteur* (n 13) 632–72; Gautier, *Propriété Littéraire et Artistique* (n 17) 622–27; Caron, *Droit d'Auteur et Droits Voisins* (n 17) 450–52; and (3) in Germany: Delp, *Der Verlagsvertrag* (n 24) 12; Markellou, *Le Contrat d'Exploitation d'Auteur* (n 17) 337–40.

[32] Cf Van Couter and Vanbrabant, *Handboek Licentieovereenkomsten* (n 31) 68–69.

[33] Vanhees, *Een Juridische Analyse van de Grondslagen* (n 22) 532–34; Hendrik Vanhees, 'Auteurscontracten en de Problematiek inzake Werken Gemaakt in Opdracht of in Uitvoering van een Arbeidsovereenkomst of Statuut' in Frank Gotzen (ed), *Belgisch Auteursrecht van Oud naar Nieuw Le Renouveau du Droit d'Auteur en Belgique* (CIR 11, Bruylant 1996) 305.

[34] Dauwe, 'Overeenkomsten in het Oude en in het Nieuwe Auteursrecht' (n 23) 284.

[35] For an overview of relevant revocation mechanisms in Member States, see <https://bit.ly/3lxpEgN>. See Ula Furgał, 'Reversion Rights in the European Union Member States' (CREATe Working Paper, 19 November 2020). No parallel type of provisions applies to musicians' exploitation activities.

aim is to avoid 'warehousing' of dormant, unused catalogues by inactive players, instead enabling exclusive rights to be held by those who will exploit them in the most productive way and ultimately enhancing access to protected content for users.[36] Artists who are at liberty to reclaim their rights in case their music remains unexploited may do so, and by seeking other 'exploitation horizons' enhance competition between corporate partners.[37]

The relevant national provisions have been partially harmonised at the EU level. First, the Term Extension Directive sets forth a rights reversion regime specific to performing musicians who have granted exclusive rights to their corporate partner (s). Second, Article 22 DSM Directive applies to copyright exploitation contracts with both composers and performers. The harmonising effect of these provisions is quite limited, in view of their scope and the broad margin for implementation left to Member States.[38] The divergences between the applicable national regimes are not conducive to legal certainty.[39] Further, the differences in scope and application of harmonising regimes at the EU level lead to additional complexity. Both types of measures are discussed in turn below.

5.2.2.3.1 INDIRECT DUTY TO EXPLOIT SPECIFIC TO THE RECORDED MUSIC SECTOR The first revocation mechanism harmonised at the EU level only applies to performers whose performance has been fixed in a phonogram and who have transferred (not licensed) their exclusive rights to a corporate partner. This mechanism grants such performing musicians the unwaivable right to reclaim their exclusive rights if the record company does not 'sufficiently' exploit the phonogram (s) at issue during the extended term of protection of the phonogram – that is, from the fifty-first to the seventieth year of protection.[40] This regime was implemented in

36 This ties in with the difference between the limited exploitation period of artistic content in practice and the long term of copyright protection. See Tim Brooks, *Survey of Reissues of US Recordings* (Optimizing Collections and Services for Scholarly Use, Council on Library and Information Resources, and Library of Congress 2005); P Bernt Hugenholtz, 'Towards Author's Paradise: The New Dutch Act on Authors' Contracts' in Gunnar Karnell and others (eds), *Liber Amicorum Jan Rosén* (eddy.se ab 2016) 404; Rebecca Giblin and Kimberlee Weatherall, 'A Collection of Impossible Ideas' in Rebecca Giblin and Kimberlee Weatherall (eds), *What If We Could Reimagine Copyright?* (ANU Press 2017) 326–27; Martin Kretschmer and Rebecca Giblin, 'Getting Creators Paid: One More Chance for Copyright Law' (2021) 43 EIPR 279, 279–80. See also Marcella Favale, 'Bouncing Back from Oblivion: Can Reversionary Copyright Help Unlock Orphan Works?' (2019) 41 EIPR 339.

37 Hugenholtz, 'Towards Author's Paradise' (n 36) 404.

38 Ted Shapiro, 'Remuneration Provisions in the DSM Copyright Directive and the Audiovisual Industry in the EU: The Elusive Quest for Fairness' (2020) 42 EIPR 778, 784.

39 ibid 778, 784; Furgał, 'Interpreting EU Reversion Rights' (n 27) 286, 291.

40 Art 3(2a) Term Directive; Recs 8, 10 Term Extension Directive. If the phonogram has been published, the term is linked with the date of publication. In case no publication has taken place, the term is linked with the lawful communication of the phonogram to the public.

all chosen jurisdictions.[41] It gives rise to an indirect duty to exploit on the part of the corporate partner. There is no specific corresponding indirect obligation for the first fifty years of the contract. Cynics might therefore argue that this implies that the 'fair' term to start exploiting a phonogram was/is half a century.[42]

Under the harmonised regime, the record company must offer sufficient 'copies'[43] for sale or make the phonogram available to the public by wire or wireless means. If they do not fulfil this obligation, the musician can notify the record company of their intention to terminate the contract. Following such notice, the record company has one year to exploit the phonogram by offering sufficient copies for sale and making it available to the public.[44] This implies an obligation to exploit on both the analogue and digital markets – an obligation that may run counter to current (and especially future) music industry practices.[45] Without such 'sufficient' exploitation, the musician may reclaim their rights and seek DIY exploitation of the phonogram, or call upon the services of another corporate partner. Arguably, the termination automatically arises following the expiry of the grace period.[46]

The final aspect of the analysis is how the use-it-or-lose-it clause is applied in practice in the case of collaborations between multiple performing musicians. The harmonised regime does not impose any rules in this regard. In principle, each musician may assert their rights in accordance with national law, leading to a corresponding loss of rights on the part of the record company.[47] This may allow one musician to block the further exploitation of a phonogram. French law seeks to pre-empt this issue by establishing that the exercise of the right of revocation for a phonogram that contains contributions by multiple performers must take place by common consent, in the absence of which a judge is to rule on the matter.[48]

[41] See (1) in Belgium: Art XI.210(1) Belgian CEL; (3) in France: Arts L 212-3-5, L 212-3-6 French IP Code; (iii) in Germany: Art 79(3) German Copyright Act; (4) in the Netherlands: Art 12(4) Dutch Neighbouring Rights Act; and (5) in the United Kingdom: Art 191HA UK CDPA.

[42] Dusollier and others, 'Contractual Arrangements Applicable to Creators' (n 17) 79.

[43] On the scope of the word 'copies', see ia below, Section 5.2.2.4.

[44] The grace period of one year applies in all chosen jurisdictions. In Belgium, France and Germany, this period is included in the relevant provision. In the Netherlands, the applicability of the one-year grace period follows from an intricate web of interlinked provisions (see Arts 2b, 9a, 12(4) Dutch Neighbouring Rights Act *jo* Art 25e Dutch Copyright Act, see Dirk Visser and others, *ACR: Auteurscontractenrecht* (DeLex 2016) 295–306). On the scope of the requirement of 'sufficient' or 'fair' exploitation, see below, Section 5.2.2.4.

[45] Ana Ramalho and Aurelio Lopez-Tarruella, 'Implementation of the Directive 2011/77/EU: Copyright Term of Protection' (2018) 33–34, 49.

[46] Cf Fabienne Brison, 'Art XI.210' in Fabienne Brison and Hendrik Vanhees (eds), *Hommage à Jan Corbet Huldeboek* (3rd edn, Larcier 2018) 386.

[47] Cf Rec 8 Term Extension Directive. In Belgium, the record label only loses its own relevant exclusive exploitation rights as a producer if each musician terminates the contract regarding a certain phonogram, see Art XI.210(1) para 4 Belgian CEL. It has been argued that this implementation is contrary to the Term Extension Directive, see Brison, 'Art XI.210' (n 46) 387.

[48] Art L 212-3-6 French IP Code; Ramalho and Lopez-Tarruella, 'Implementation of the Directive 2011/77/EU' (n 45) 23–24.

In Germany, the revocation mechanism is to be set in motion by an elected representative or by the leader of a group of musicians.[49] In effect, this implies the requirement of a majority decision on the matter of rights revocation.[50] This may provide a more efficient solution.

5.2.2.3.2 INDIRECT DUTY TO EXPLOIT IN THE MUSIC PUBLISHING AND RECORDED MUSIC SECTORS The DSM Directive offers a second chance for a high-performing harmonised use-it-or-lose-it clause. Article 22 DSM Directive sets certain minimum requirements for regimes that apply to copyright exploitation contracts with authors and/or performers where there is no exploitation. The harmonised regime does not apply to non-exclusive licences. Moreover, as is the case for the other relevant provisions of the DSM Directive, the substantive scope of Article 22 DSM Directive is limited to exploitation rights that have been harmonised under EU law – that is, the rights of reproduction *sensu stricto*, communication to the public and distribution, to the exclusion of the right of adaptation.[51] Regardless, in order to maintain the internal coherence of the national legal frameworks, Member States may also be expected to implement the harmonised regime for non-harmonised rights.[52]

Subsequent to Article 22 DSM Directive, musicians (either composers or performers) who have transferred their rights or granted an exclusive licence thereto must be able to reclaim these rights, either in whole or in part, if the corporate partner does not perform any exploitation activities.[53] The regime harmonised by Article 22 DSM Directive does not apply to non-exclusive licences. However, given the minimum harmonising nature of this provision, Member States may establish a use-it-or-lose-it provision for non-exclusive licences as well.

Article 22 DSM Directive leaves significant leeway for Member States as to its implementation into national law, allowing several differences between the applicable national legal regimes.[54] First, Member States are free to further specify the revocation mechanism under national law, taking account of the specific nature of certain CCIs and types of artistic content.[55] In addition, the EU legislator allows for

49 Cf Art 74(2) German Copyright Act; Ramalho and Lopez-Tarruella, 'Implementation of the Directive 2011/77/EU' (n 45) 24.

50 ibid 7, 23–24, 33–34, 49.

51 Cf Rec 72 DSM Directive.

52 Raquel Xalabarder, 'The Remuneration of Authors and Performers' [2020] RIDA 129, 135–36.

53 Art 22(1) DSM Directive. Cf Lucas-Schloetter, 'European Copyright Contract Law' (n 26) 899.

54 Fair Internet Coalition, 'Joint Guidelines for the Implementation of the 2019 Copyright Directive' (2019) 25; Séverine Dusollier, 'The 2019 Directive on Copyright in the Digital Single Market: Some Progress, a Few Bad Choices, and an Overall Failed Ambition' [2020] CML Rev 979,1025; European Copyright Society, 'Comment of the European Copyright Society Addressing Selected Aspects of the Implementation of Articles 18 to 22 of the Directive (EU) 2019/790 on Copyright in the Digital Single Market' [2020] JIPITEC 132, 145; Furgał, 'Interpreting EU Reversion Rights'(n 27) 284.

55 Art 22(2)(a) DSM Directive. See also Rec 80 DSM Directive.

specifications of national law for co-creations or co-performances based on the relative importance of artists' contributions and the legitimate interests of the artists involved.[56] The broad language of Article 22 DSM Directive further indicates that Member States' discretion extends beyond the possibility of sector-specific rules and provisions particular to collaborative content.[57]

The use-it-or-lose-it provision included in the German Copyright Act applies to both composing and performing musicians and is limited to exclusive rights (exclusive licences of rights of composers and either transfers or exclusive licences of rights of performers).[58] In addition, for publishing contracts, the German Publishing Act grants the author a waivable right to revocation in case the publisher does not exercise their right to publish a new edition of a work.[59]

The Dutch regime applies to both authors and performers and, contrary to what is the case under German law, does not limit its applicability to exclusive contracts.[60] It applies to transfer contracts and both exclusive and non-exclusive licences.

Third, pre-DSM, both Belgian and French law only contained a reversion regime specific to publishing contracts – that is, applicable to music publishing, but not to recorded music – as a sanction in case of breach of the direct duty to exploit

[56] Art 22(2)(b) DSM Directive.

[57] Shapiro, 'Remuneration Provisions in the DSM Copyright Directive and the Audiovisual Industry in the EU' (n 38) 784.

[58] Art 41(1) *jo* 79(2a) German Copyright Act. See in detail P Bernt Hugenholtz and Lucie Guibault, 'Auteurscontractenrecht: Naar Een Wettelijke Regeling?' (2004) <https://bit.ly/3UvnwGx> 25, 68–70; Lenselink, *De Verlening van Exploitatiebevoegdheden in het Auteursrecht* (n 19) 266–68; Gerhard Schricker, *Urheberrecht. Kommentar* (3rd edn, CH Beck 2006) 850–59; Friedrich Karl Fromm and Wilhelm Nordemann, *Urheberrecht. Kommentar zum Urheberrechtsgesetz, zum Verlagsgesetz und zum Urheberrechtswahrnehmungsgesetz* (Rechtswissenschaften und Verwaltung, 10th edn, Kohlhammer 2008) 874–93; Ulrich Loewenheim, 'Rückruf des Nutzungsrechts nach § 41 UrhG und Fortbestehen der Enkelrechte' in Kirsten-Inger Wöhrn and others (eds), *Festschrift für Artur-Axel Wandtke zum 70 Geburtstag am 26 März 2013* (Walter De Gruyter 2013) 199–207; Gunda Dreyer and others, *Urheberrecht* (Heidelberger Kommentar, 4th edn, CF Müller 2018) 837–44; Philipp Möhring and Käte Nicolini, *Urheberrecht* (4th edn, CH Beck 2018) 609–17; Gernot Schulze, 'Das Urhebervertragsrecht nach Erlass der EU-Richtlinie über das Urheberrecht im digitalen Binnenmarkt' [2019] GRUR 682, 685.

[59] Art 17 German Publishing Act. This right is not expressly limited to copyright exploitation contracts that grant an exclusive right. Art 8 German Publishing Act provides that publishing contracts that fall within the scope of this act are, in principle, exclusive, unless the contract specifies otherwise.

[60] Art 25e Dutch Copyright Act for authors *jo* Art 2b Dutch Neighbouring Rights Act for performers; Visser and others, *ACR: Auteurscontractenrecht* (n 44) 163–87; JH Spoor and others, *Auteursrecht. Auteursrecht, portretrecht, naburige rechten en databankenrecht* (Recht en Praktijk, 4th edn, Wolters Kluwer 2019) 569–79. For a rare (albeit indirect) application of this provision in the music industry the case between the Dutch rock band Golden Earring and their music publisher, see District Court Amsterdam 9 May 2012, docket number C/13/496699 HA ZA 11-2296, ECLI:NL:RBAMS:2013:5971; Court of Appeal Amsterdam 31 March 2015, docket number 200.148.383, ECLI:NL:GHAMS:2015:1201; Dutch Supreme Court 7 July 2017, docket number 15/03787, ECLI:NL:HR:2017:1270.

discussed above.[61] In addition to the rule specific to publishing contracts, the French legal framework now provides a revocation mechanism to the benefit of both authors and performers, albeit limited to transfers and exclusive licences.[62] Conversely, the Belgian legislator has amended the pre-existing mechanism specific to publishing contracts, to the benefit of a new mechanism that applies to both authors and performers.[63] The scope of the Belgian revocation mechanism excludes both non-exclusive licences and music made either in an employment context or on commission.[64] The same is true for insignificant contributions, to the extent that the exercise of the revocation right by one artist would unduly prejudice the interests of the other artists involved.[65]

The conditions for application of the relevant national regimes differ. The first main substantive difference is whether the reversion regimes require 'sufficient' use on the part of the corporate partner[66] or whether any use suffices to exclude its application. Further, some regimes include an express proportionality test that limits the substantive scope of application of the reversion regime, while others do not.

The scope of the revocation mechanism included in Article 22 DSM Directive is limited to situations of non-exploitation.[67] It could therefore be argued that one stream of a phonogram on a single DSP constitutes an exploitation activity that is sufficient to render the harmonised revocation mechanism wholly inoperative.[68] At present, such an interpretation is not expressly excluded, given the lack of legal qualification of music streaming beyond the fact that it is covered by both the reproduction right and the making-available right.

However, some jurisdictions are more artist-friendly and require more than any form of exploitation to evade application of the revocation mechanism. General revocation mechanisms relating to insufficient exploitation are, as yet, not harmonised at the EU level.[69]

61 See respectively Art XI.196(1) Belgian CEL and former Art L 132-17(2) French IP Code; Hugenholtz and Guibault, 'Auteurscontractenrecht' (n 58) 70–71.

62 See respectively Arts L 131-5-2, L 212-3-3 French IP Code.

63 Arts XI.167/4, XI.205/4 Belgian CEL.

64 Raad voor de Intellectuele Eigendom, 'Advies betreffende de omzetting in Belgisch recht van richtlijn 2019/790/EU van 17 april 2019 inzake auteursrechten en naburige rechten in de digitale eengemaakte markt en tot wijziging van Richtlijnen 96/9/EG en 2001/29/EG' (19 June 2020) 103; Explanatory Memorandum Belgian Draft DSM Implementation Act (2020) 60–62, 107.

65 Raad voor de Intellectuele Eigendom (n 64) 103; Explanatory Memorandum Belgian Draft DSM Implementation Act (n 64).

66 On the scope of the requirement of 'sufficient' or 'fair' exploitation, see below, Section 5.2.2.4.

67 Furgał, 'Interpreting EU Reversion Rights'(n 27) 285–86.

68 Ananay Aguilar, 'The New Copyright Directive: Fair Remuneration in Exploitation Contracts of Authors and Performers – Part II, Articles 20–23' (*Kluwer Copyright Blog*, 1 August 2019) <https://bit.ly/3Qh8WBl>.

69 As to the specific revocation mechanism foreseen in the Term Extension Directive, see above, Section 5.2.2.3.1.

The Dutch regime requires 'sufficient' exploitation for the corporate partner to be able to avoid termination of the contract by the artist.[70] The same is true under German law.[71] The corporate partner must be granted two years to start exploiting the content at issue.[72] While the Belgian provisions do not expressly require 'sufficient' exploitation by the corporate partner, this may be deduced from the general duty to exploit in accordance with sector practices.[73]

Under French law, both the post-DSM generalised revocation mechanism and the pre-existing regime for publishing contracts only come into play if no exploitation activities take place.[74]

Article 22 DSM Directive does not expressly require a proportionality test. However, the harmonised reversion right does *not* apply if the lack of exploitation is predominantly due to circumstances that the musician 'can reasonably be expected to remedy' – in other words, where the non-exploitation is attributable to the artist.[75] This proviso expressly applies under Belgian, German and Dutch law. At the time of writing, no equivalent requirement exists under French law. The national regimes under review also include other considerations of proportionality. For example, the Belgian regime expressly establishes its disapplication if the corporate partner had a legitimate reason not to exploit the content at issue, interpreted as a reason that is foreign to them, such as a fire in the warehouses leading to a destruction of stock.[76] Another example is that German law expressly requires artists to indemnify the corporate partner if this is deemed fair and equitable.[77] A strict interpretation of the proportionality requirement is desirable. The same is true for the abovementioned provisions of national law that implement proportionality considerations. Otherwise, there is a risk of undue circumvention of the protection that the revocation mechanism offers to musicians.[78] This rings especially true for music streaming, where it may be argued that legitimate reasons

70 Art 25e Dutch Copyright Act *jo* Art 2b Dutch Neighbouring Rights Act.

71 Amended Arts 41(1) *jo* 79(2a) German Copyright Act.

72 Arts 41(2) *jo* 79(2a) German Copyright Act.

73 See, however, arguing in favour of the inclusion of an express requirement of 'sufficient' exploitation, Raad voor de Intellectuele Eigendom, 'Advies' (n 64) 100.

74 Arts L 131-5-2(I), L 212-3-3(I), L 132-17(2) French IP Code; Jean Lapousterle, 'La Révocation Des Contrats d'auteurs et d'artistes-Interprètes' [2021] PI 36.

75 Art 22(4) DSM Directive. See (1) in Belgium: Arts XI.167/4(4)(1°), XI.205/4(4)(1°) Belgian CEL; (2) in Germany: Art 41(1) *jo* 79(2a) German Copyright Act; and (3) in the Netherlands: Art 25e Dutch Copyright Act *jo* Art 2b Dutch Neighbouring Rights Act.

76 Art XI.167/4(3), XI.205/4(3) Belgian CEL

77 Arts 41(6) *jo* 79(2a) German Copyright Act. See, questioning the compatibility of this requirement with Art 22 DSM Directive, Patrick Zurth, 'Implementation of the DSM Directive's Contract Provisions into German Law' in Simon Geiregat and Hendrik Vanhees (eds), *Copyright Contracts Tomorrow* (LeA 2023) 61.

78 As argued in European Copyright Society, 'Comment' (n 54) 132, 134.

not to exploit content would routinely arise, thus easily allowing the harmonised revocation mechanism to be bypassed.[79]

Further, the application of the harmonised use-it-or-lose-it clause in time merits closer attention. The appropriate temporal application of a certain protective measure depends on a balance between procedural considerations of legal certainty and substantive considerations of enhanced protection.[80] In view of the limited scope of the harmonising mechanism (which only applies in case of non-use) and the procedural safeguards included to the benefit of corporate partners (such as the requirement of a notice of default), its consequences in practice – and thus its impact on the freedom of contract – are limited. The immediate application of this mechanism to acts of exploitation stemming from ongoing contracts from 7 June 2021 is therefore merited.[81]

Legal mechanisms securing an indirect duty to exploit should simultaneously be of a mandatory nature and a measure of last resort.[82]

As to the former, the harmonised revocation mechanism is not expressly qualified as mandatory law in Article 23 DSM Directive and may therefore in principle be subject to contractual derogations.[83] Legislative approaches differ. While the Dutch regime has been labelled as unwaivable,[84] the French legislator has not done this – although this may yet occur following a collective negotiation process.[85] In Germany and Belgium, an alternative route was chosen: derogations to the detriment of artists are only possible if they stem from collective negotiations.[86] This route is expressly mentioned in Article 22 DSM Directive.[87] In practice, such provisions lead to a qualification of the revocation mechanism as mandatory law, albeit only indirectly.[88]

The latter aspect is linked with the objective of maintaining the position of corporate partners. Musicians should not be able to reclaim their rights on a whim. Substantive conditions, such as a requirement of proportionality, as well as procedural steps, such as a notice of default and an additional grace period, play an

79 Aguilar, 'The New Copyright Directive: Part II, Articles 20–23' (n 68).

80 See Chapter 3, Section 3.3.2.6.

81 Cf European Copyright Society, 'Comment' (n 54) 139–40; Eleonora Rosati, *Copyright in the Digital Single Market. Article-by-Article Commentary to the Provisions of Directive 2019/790* (Oxford University Press 2021) 406–07.

82 European Copyright Society, 'Comment' (n 54) 145.

83 See Art 23(1) DSM Directive, which does not include Art 22 DSM Directive.

84 Art 25h(1) Dutch Copyright Act *jo* Art 2b Dutch Neighbouring Rights Act.

85 See respectively Arts L 131-5-2, L 212-3-3 French IP Code.

86 Art 41(4) *jo* 79(2a) German Copyright Act; Arts XI.167/5 *jo* XI.167/6, XI.205/5 *jo* XI.205/6 Belgian CEL.

87 Art 22(5) DSM Directive. See also Aguilar, 'The New Copyright Directive: Part II, Articles 20–23' (n 68).

88 Cf Shapiro, 'Remuneration Provisions in the DSM Copyright Directive and the Audiovisual Industry in the EU' (n 38) 784.

important role.[89] The application of the revocation mechanism is indeed subject to procedural conditions. Care must be taken to ensure that these steps are not too arduous for artists, in order to avoid an enforcement gap in practice.[90]

First, a logical substantive prerequisite is that corporate partners must have a reasonable amount of time to start exploiting the music following the grant of rights, such as the period of two years that applies under German law.[91] Under the generalised French revocation mechanism, this period is to be set through collective bargaining.[92]

The musician(s) must notify the corporate partner and set a reasonable deadline for the desired exploitation activities.[93] Only after the expiry of that deadline do the applicable sanctions apply.[94] For publishing contracts in particular, French law provides for automatic expiry of the contract if two requests for delivery of copies remain unanswered within three months.[95] Under German law, no grace period must be granted to the corporate partner if it is impossible for them to conduct exploitation activities, if they refuse to take action, or if such a grace period would unduly prejudice the artist's interests.[96]

In order for musicians to be able to assess whether fair exploitation is actually taking place, an argument may be made in favour of transparency obligations comparable to those in place for fair remuneration.[97]

As to the scope of the rights reclaim, it is an interesting option to seek to merely revoke exclusivity instead of opting for a full rights revocation,[98] or to seek revocation

89 Séverine Dusollier, 'An Effective and Comprehensive Contractual Protection of Creators and Performers' (Copyright in the Digital Single Market, Brussels, 30 January 2020).

90 See Chapter 7. See also Rita Matulionyte, 'Empowering Authors via Fairer Copyright Contract Law' (2019) 42 UNSWLJ 681, 708.

91 Art 22(3) DSM Directive. See also Rec 80 DSM Directive.

92 Arts L 131-5-2(II), L 212-3-3(II) French IP Code.

93 See (1) in Belgium: Arts XI.167/4, XI.205/4 Belgian CEL; (2) in France: no express provision, awaiting determination by collective agreement (see, however, Art L 132-17-2(II)–(III) French IP Code, which sets a deadline of six months following a notice of default for literary publishing); (3) in Germany: Art 41(3) *jo* 79(2a) German Copyright Act; and (4) in the Netherlands: Art 25e(3) Dutch Copyright Act *jo* Art 2b Dutch Neighbouring Rights Act.

94 Art 22(3) *jo* (2) DSM Directive. As to the effect of this sanction, see ongoing legislative developments in the Netherlands, where the references to the retroactive termination of the contract in the relevant Art 25e Dutch Copyright Act will be modified to references to non-retroactive termination, see <https://bit.ly/3Uze3Ov>. See also Iris Houben and Dirk Visser, 'De Beëindiging van Muziekexploitatieovereenkomsten' [2022] Auteursrecht 3, 135–49.

95 Art L 132-17(2) French IP Code.

96 Art 41(3) *jo* 79(2a) German Copyright Act; Art 17 German Publishing Act.

97 Cf below, Section 5.3.3. See also under Dutch law the former Art 25e(4) Dutch Copyright Act *jo* Art 2b Dutch Neighbouring Rights Act.

98 Pre-DSM, German law did not foresee the possibility for artists to revoke the exclusivity of the licence, providing only the option of revocation. Artists may now choose between full revocation or mere revocation of exclusivity, see amended Art 41(5) *jo* 79(2a) German Copyright Act. Dutch law does not expressly provide the possibility for the artist to revoke the exclusivity of a licence. However, it does foresee a right to compensation if the corporate partner does not act

only for certain specific methods of exploitation. As to the latter, inspiration may be drawn from the French model for literary publishing, which allows authors to invoke the applicable use-it-or-lose-it mechanism separately for analogue and digital exploitation.[99]

A final aspect of the analysis is how the revocation mechanism is applied where multiple musicians are involved. A blanket exclusion of the music sector from the harmonised revocation mechanism, as appears to be allowed under Article 22 DSM Directive, would be excessive.[100] This option was not chosen by any of the selected jurisdictions. Neither German nor Belgian law provide any express rule for collaborative music. Conversely, the French regime mandates a joint exercise of the right of revocation in such a case; in the absence of consensus, the matter is to be brought before a judge.[101] Similarly, under Dutch law, rights pertaining to collaborative content that cannot be separated can only be revoked if all artists involved provide their consent.[102] If the undue refusal of one of the artists disproportionately prejudices the interests of the others (that is, constitutes an actionable form of abuse of law), the contract may only be rescinded through court proceedings.[103] Coupling the principled requirement for joint consent with a prohibition of the abusive refusal thereof indeed appears to be the most balanced solution. However, given the difficulties associated with legal proceedings in music industry,[104] the mandated intervention of a judge risks being slightly unproductive.

5.2.2.4 Requirement of Fair Exploitation

A duty of fair exploitation may have an indirect (but tangible) consequence for the scope of the grant at the contract's formation stage. A duty to exploit for each pertinent method of exploitation is likely to induce corporate partners to limit the grant to what is relevant.[105] This would be a positive evolution. The duty should be indirect: if a corporate partner does not fulfil the minimum requirements in terms of exploitation, musicians should be able to exercise their agency as an independent

quickly enough following the exercise of the right to revocation, see Art 25e(7) Dutch Copyright Act *jo* Art 2b Dutch Neighbouring Rights Act.

[99] Art L 132-17-2 French IP Code.

[100] Cf Aguilar, 'The New Copyright Directive: Part II, Articles 20–23' (n 68).

[101] Art L 131-5-2(IV) French IP Code.

[102] Art 25e(2) Dutch Copyright Act *jo* Art 2b Dutch Neighbouring Rights Act; Visser and others, ACR: *Auteurscontractenrecht* (n 44) 164–65; Stef van Gompel and others, 'Evaluatie Wet Auteurscontractenrecht: Eindrapport' (2020) <https://bit.ly/3UBZrh4> 49–50.

[103] Art 25e(2) Dutch Copyright Act *jo* Art 2b Dutch Neighbouring Rights Act; Visser and others, ACR: *Auteurscontractenrecht* (n 44) 164–65.

[104] See Chapter 7, Section 7.4.

[105] Cf Dusollier and others, 'Contractual Arrangements Applicable to Creators' (n 17) 72, 102–03; Elena Cooper, 'Reverting to Reversion Rights? Reflections on the Copyright Act 1911' (2021) 43 EIPR 292, 292.

actor by having recourse to a high-performing rights reversal mechanism.[106] This offers a fairly unintrusive way to achieve stakeholder agency and a fair balance between the interests at play. The amount of exploitation activities required to avoid revocation may be shaped through soft law along the lines of the concept of 'fair exploitation' conceptualised here.

The criteria set forth below are based on an interpretation of the current legal framework and do not require any substantive amendments – an approach that is deemed preferable to far-reaching amendments and/or additions to the existing rules.

The international and EU regulatory levels offer some initial, tentative tools for concretisation. First, the definition of 'published works' and 'publication' under the Berne and Rome Conventions respectively may bear relevance. The Berne Convention defines 'published works' as 'works published with the consent of their authors, whatever may be the means of manufacture of the copies, provided that the availability of such copies has been such as to satisfy the reasonable requirements of the public, having regard to the nature of the work'.[107] The Rome Convention defines 'publication' as the 'offering of copies of a phonogram to the public in reasonable quantity'.[108] While these provisions are not expressly linked with any type of duty to exploit, the expressly mentioned lack of relevance of the 'means of manufacture' gives support to the argument that both analogue and digital exploitation activities may fulfil a corporate partner's duty to sufficiently exploit.

At the EU level, the requirement of 'sufficient' exploitation under the use-it-or-lose-it mechanism set by the Term Extension Directive refers to the need to both offer 'copies' of the phonogram(s) at issue and make them available on demand, thus requiring exploitation of not only the reproduction right, but also the making-available right.

While the international and EU frameworks remain very high-level on the issue of 'sufficient' exploitation, it may be concluded that fair exploitation requires attention to both analogue and digital methods of exploitation. This translates into a requirement of exploitation activities as to both the reproduction and making available right. Of further note is the consistent requirement for corporate partners to offer certain 'copies' on the market.

However, the streaming age is fuelled by a new method of consuming music that does not require physical copies, or (in many cases) full digital copies. The

[106] Cf Dusollier and others, 'Contractual Arrangements Applicable to Creators' (n 17) 14; Joshua Yuvaraj, 'Back to the Start: Re-Envisioning the Role of Copyright Reversion in Australia and Other Common Law Countries' (Monash University 2021).

[107] Art 3(3) Berne Convention; cf Brison, 'Art XI.210' (n 46) 386.

[108] Art 3(d) Rome Convention. Interestingly, Rec 8 Term Extension Directive expressly refers to the Rome Convention with regard to the scope of 'sufficient' exploitation under the Term Extension Directive, without further specifying which provision of the Rome Convention bears relevance in this regard. The referenced Art 3(d) Rome Convention appears to be the only possibly relevant provision.

usefulness of the term 'copies' is therefore rapidly decreasing. An alternative basis for the concrete implementation of the requirement of fair exploitation is merited. Below, a set of guiding criteria is developed. In turn, the concept of fair exploitation is shaped on a substantive, personal, geographical and temporal level. The substantive analysis takes account the use of both the musician's contribution in the music at issue and the music as such, also considering the overarching impact of digitisation. Due account is taken of relevant sector practices and the potential contribution of collective arrangements.

On a substantive level, the concept of exploitation in music may be analysed from two separate angles – the use of a certain contribution in music and the subsequent use of that music in the offline and/or online environment.

The former aspect relates to the intrinsic value and significance of a musician's contribution and the intensity and frequency of its use in a given piece of music (such as the inclusion of a short excerpt on repeat throughout the piece[109]).

A musician who has significantly contributed to a piece of music has a stronger claim as to fair exploitation than a musician whose contribution is limited. As indicated above,[110] the EU legislator allows for specifications of the harmonised revocation mechanism under national law for co-creations or co-performances, based on the relative importance of artists' contributions and the legitimate interests of the artists involved.[111] Member States may even exclude content from the scope of application of the revocation mechanism where such content usually contains contributions of a plurality of artists.[112] Given the steep increase of collaborations in the creation and performance of music[113] and the practical issues that may arise

[109] Cf Commission, SWD(2016) 301 final (n 4) 174; Nikita Malevanny, *Online Music Distribution – How Much Exclusivity Is Needed? A Study of International, European, German and US Copyright Systems and Their Objectives*, vol 12 (Munich Studies on Innovation and Competition, Springer Berlin Heidelberg 2019) 92.

[110] See above, Section 5.2.2.3.

[111] Art 22(2)(b) DSM Directive.

[112] Art 22(2) DSM Directive.

[113] For example, in popular music a trend may be discerned where a rising number of songwriters on the composition side is complemented by, on the performing artists' side, a successful megastar featuring a range of artists attempting to 'ride their coattails' to (inter)national stardom. This increased dispersion of creativity may ultimately result in nobody being able to raise a fair claim to authorship; cf Jane C Ginsburg, 'The Role of the Author in Copyright' in Ruth L Okediji (ed), *Copyright Law in an Age of Limitations and Exceptions* (Cambridge University Press 2017) 66. See also Richard Arnold, 'Reflections on the Triumph of Music: Copyrights and Performers' Rights in Music' (Oxford Intellectual Property Invited Speaker Seminar, Oxford, UK, 20 October 2009) 13; Jostein Gripsrud, 'Creativity and the Sense of Collective Ownership in Theatre and Popular Music' in Mireille van Eechoud (ed), *The Work of Authorship* (Amsterdam University Press 2014) 227; Isabelle De Voldere and others, 'Mapping the Creative Value Chains. A Study on the Economy of Culture in the Digital Age. Final Report' (Publications Office of the EU 2017) <https://op.europa.eu/s/zIa8> 64; Nancy K Baym, *Playing to the Crowd. Musicians, Audiences, and the Intimate Work of Connection* (New York University Press 2018) 73; Alan B Krueger, *Rockonomics* (John Murray 2019) 32–33, 64–66; Kai Riemer and others (eds), *Collaboration in the Digital Age. How Technology Enables*

from the application of the revocation mechanism in multi-musician situations in practice, such specifications may prove to be useful.

Musicians' individual contributions are often not discernible after the fact. This may be ascribed to the nature of the collaborative musical process, which is unpredictable and often takes place in an integrative way. A collaboration starts with a number of (unprotected) abstract ideas that are concretised and transformed throughout the group process. When several authors make a concrete, original contribution to the creation of a work protected by copyright, joint authorship may arise.[114] However, unless every intervention is recorded in detail, untangling this creative process and determining who contributed what is arduous. Subsequent to the principle of distributive creativity, it may even be argued that the distinction of individual contributions to a musical work is impossible.[115] Even if the individual contributions are separable, the question arises when exactly the weight of a musician's contribution should be assessed – at the moment of the contribution or at a later stage. It may be argued that a musician's contribution can only be properly assessed with hindsight. A short, insignificant sequence of notes contributed by a session musician may ultimately prove to be the main reference point for its target audience, leaving a significant imprint on the piece of music over time.

A contribution's intrinsic worth refers to its artistic value,[116] which is inherently subjective and subject to a qualitative, not quantitative assessment. The significance of a certain contribution in the context of a larger whole is somewhat easier to quantify, but still difficult to gauge in advance. Both the intrinsic value and the significance of a musician's contribution are particularly hard to grasp in an objective way. This may be illustrated by relevant case law from the United Kingdom in several high-stakes disputes concerning authorship in the music industry.

A first notable case, *Hadley v Kemp*, concerns the dispute between the members of new-wave band Spandau Ballet that was brought before the UK High Court of Justice in the late 1990s. Following the commercial success of Spandau Ballet's first five albums, vocalist Tony Hadley, drummer John Keeple and multi-instrumentalist Steve Norman claimed joint ownership in a number of songs – including and

Individuals, Teams and Businesses (Progress in IS, Springer International 2019); Daniela Simone, *Copyright and Collective Authorship: Locating the Authors of Collaborative Work* (Cambridge Intellectual Property and Information Law 50, Cambridge University Press 2019) 1. For an illustration, see also eg Andrew Unterberger, 'Only 13 No. 1 Hot 100 Hits This Century Were Penned without Co-Writers' (*Billboard*, 25 January 2022) <https://bit.ly/3rC6fhz> and the searchable music rights database Songdex at <https://bit.ly/39BEZWN>.

[114] See (1) in Belgium: Arts XI.168–169 Belgian CEL; (2) in France: Arts L 113-2–L 113-5 French IP Code; (3) in Germany: Art 8 German Copyright Act; (4) in the Netherlands: Arts 5(1), 26 Dutch Copyright Act; and (5) in the United Kingdom: Arts 10–10A UK CDPA.

[115] See Laura Bishop, 'Collaborative Musical Creativity: How Ensembles Coordinate Spontaneity' (2018) 9 Front Psychol 1.

[116] Fabienne Brison, *Het Naburig Recht van de Uitvoerende Kunstenaar* (Creatie Informatie Communicatie 7, Larcier 2001) 440–41.

importantly the hit 'True', which contained Norman's signature saxophone solo – and sued Gary Kemp, guitarist and acknowledged composer of the band. The creative process of the band usually consisted of Kemp first providing the general structure, melody and chords of a certain piece of music and the band then completing the finalised, recorded product together. The High Court rejected the band members' claims entirely.[117] This judgment was met with significant criticism.[118] Influencing considerations included a focus on melody and chord progression as a core of the music and the fact that Kemp maintained artistic control throughout the creative process. In two further cases, the English courts showed greater deference to the artistic contribution of performers. In the case leading to the UK Court of Appeal decision in *Beckingham v Hodgens*, violinist Robert James Beckingham claimed joint authorship in the adaptation of The Bluebells' version of the song 'Young at Heart'. Beckingham had contributed a violin solo that features several times throughout the song, in return for a modest flat session fee. The Court of Appeal deemed the session musician's contribution significant and original enough to warrant joint authorship in the song.[119] A similar outcome was reached in *Fisher v Brooker*, a case regarding authorship of Procol Harum's 1967 hit song 'A Whiter Shade of Pale' that went all the way up to the UK Supreme Court (then still the House of Lords). This case revolved around an introductory organ solo created by Matthew Fisher, clearly inspired by a Bach chorale prelude, combined with an organ accompaniment to the song's vocal parts. In return for his services, Fisher received a modest fee. However, the brief solo turned out to be an important part of the song, eventually allowing Fisher to successfully claim joint authorship. The High Court decision[120] awarded Fisher joint authorship of the musical work itself, while the Court of Appeal,[121] confirmed in this position by the House of Lords,[122] only granted Fisher joint authorship of the arrangement as recorded, in view the existence of an earlier demo to which he had not contributed.

Musicology experts play an important role in such court cases.[123] These expert witnesses draft extensive reports containing detailed analyses of the music at issue as well as historical and conceptual arguments. Thus, they seek to objectify the creative process. The assessment appears to be both quantitative and qualitative. As to the

[117] *Hadley v Kemp* [1999] EMLR 589.
[118] See eg Richard Arnold, 'Are Performers Authors?' [1999] EIPR 464, 468–69.
[119] *Hodgens v Beckingham* [2003] EWCA Civ 143, [2003] EMLR 18 (first instance decision: *Beckingham v Hodgens* [2002] EWCA Civ 1901); Dominic Free, 'Beckingham v. Hodgens: The Session Musician's Claim to Music Copyright' (2003) 13 Entertainment Law Review 93.
[120] *Fisher v Brooker* [2006] EWHC 3239 (Ch), [2007] EMLR 256, [2007] FSR 12.
[121] *Brooker v Fisher* [2008] EWCA Civ 287.
[122] *Fisher v Brooker* [2009] UKHL 41.
[123] Arnold, 'Reflections on the Triumph of Music: Copyrights and Performers' Rights in Music' (n 113) 8–9; Lionel Bently, 'Authorship of Popular Music in UK Copyright Law' (2009) 12 ICS 179; Stefan Skopelja, 'The Boundaries of "Authorship" and "Performance" in Musical Copyright' [2015] UNSWLJ Student Series No 15-04.

latter, a high degree of importance is seemingly placed on melody and chord progressions, leaving less room for focus on rhythm. Regardless, any court decision assessing a given contribution's 'significance' is inherently fact-specific and bears a significant subjective aspect.[124] Ultimately, it all comes down to the question of how the court (more often than not composed of musical laymen) assesses the value of a certain contribution.

In view of the difficulty in assessing artists' relative contributions to a certain piece of music, shaping national law in this regard as allowed under Article 22 may prove to be problematic.[125] Care must therefore be taken not to overemphasise the importance of this criterion in the conceptualisation of fair exploitation. Internal distribution mechanisms used by CMOs that quantify performers' contributions by using a proportionate division drawing from a points-based system may fulfil a clarifying role in this regard. By way of example, in the context of the division of remuneration rights, the Belgian performer CMO PlayRight accords fifteen points to both featured artists and conductors of groups that exceed twelve musicians, while session musicians are granted five points per instrument group[126] to which their performance relates, with a maximum of three instrument groups.[127] After the points have been added, a proportionate division takes place, with a minimum guarantee of 30 per cent to the benefit of featured artists and conductors.[128] German performer CMO GVL accords four points to featured artists, conductors and full band members and one point to session musicians.[129] Similarly, Dutch performer CMO SENA accords five points to featured artists and full band members, three points to conductors and one point to session musicians per instrument played (including vocals) with a maximum of three points per musician and a total maximum of 50 per cent of revenues for all session musicians combined.[130] In France, the division has been rather contentious over the years, leading to an evolving CMO landscape with the establishment of the Société des Artistes Interprètes (SAI) by performer CMOs ADAMI (for featured artists) and Spedidam (for non-featured artists).[131] SAI is an example of a CMO that does not use a points-based system. Instead, it opts for an

[124] Arnold, 'Reflections on The Triumph of Music: Copyrights and Performers' Rights in Music' (n 113) 2; Lionel Bently and Laura Biron, 'Discontinuities between Legal Conceptions of Authorship and Social Practices: What, If Anything, Is to Be Done?' in Mireille van Eechoud (ed), *The Work of Authorship* (Amsterdam University Press 2014) 262; Skopelja, 'The Boundaries of "Authorship" and "Performance" in Musical Copyright' (n 123).

[125] Cf Fair Internet Coalition, 'Joint Guidelines' (n 54) 25.

[126] The seven instrument groups referred to are keyboard, string and wind instruments, percussion, melodic percussion, mechanical instruments and vocals.

[127] Art 26 *Algemeen Reglement PlayRight* (2020) <https://bit.ly/3lM9iQ2>.

[128] ibid.

[129] *Anlage 1 zum Verteilungsplan Nr 2 ab 2017 ab dem Verteilungsjahr 2019 Punktwerte (Gewichtung) der Mitwirkendenkategorien* (2020) <https://bit.ly/3tZNTqw>.

[130] Arts 7–8 *Repartitiereglement SENA* (2024) <https://shorturl.at/mqrD8>.

[131] <https://la-sai.fr/>.

equal distribution among all identified eligible performing artists.[132] The distribution rules of UK CMO Phonographic Performance Limited (PPL), finally, provide a detailed procedure to aptly allocate featured and non-featured performers' revenue shares.[133]

The other side of the exploitation 'coin' is the (partial or full) use of a composition and/or fixation of a performance by a third party in a way that falls within the scope of the exclusive rights of the rightsholder(s) and thus, in principle, requires their permission. Applied to the music industry, corporate partners should exert a certain degree of effort to build and maintain an audience for (and thus ultimately maximise the revenue garnered by) music to which they have been granted certain rights, through marketing and promotion activities.[134]

As for physical music sales, fair exploitation also implies responsibility in terms of the manufacturing and distribution of copies – the steps required to bring the physical music product to the end user. In the context of a direct duty to exploit, this requirement has been quantified in terms of a minimum number of 'copies'.[135] In the online environment, corporate partners' appropriate exploitation activities are much more difficult to objectify.[136]

One of the questions is whether the mere fact that users have downloaded or streamed the music at issue in itself provides proof of exploitation on the part of the relevant corporate partners, even if they have not undertaken any active exploitation activities themselves in terms of marketing, promotion or other means to improve the 'findability' of a given piece of music – that is, its prominence on relevant online platforms.[137] If streams and digital downloads qualify as 'copies' in the sense of the duty to exploit under copyright contract law, the answer is clear: a copy is an act of exploitation. However, digital downloads and streams are not equivalent to physical copies – on a technological or economic level. Theoretically speaking, both digital downloads and streams may occur without the active intervention of a corporate partner, as opposed to physical copies. Moreover, the economics of streaming are vastly different from those associated with either digital downloads or physical copies.[138]

[132] See <https://shorturl.at/zAHI6>.

[133] Schedule 5, Performer Allocation Rules (2015) <https://bit.ly/46d4noh>.

[134] Regarding the perceived obligation (under French law) for a music publisher to contact a record company for securing the use of a certain composition, see eg Dusollier and others, 'Contractual Arrangements Applicable to Creators' (n 17) 123. See also Groffe, *La Bonne Foi en Droit d'Auteur* (n 22) 295–96; Spoor and others, *Auteursrecht* (n 60) 573–74. As to the exploitation by third parties, see below, Section 5.4.2.

[135] See above, Section 5.2.2.2.

[136] European Copyright Society, 'Comment' (n 54) 133.

[137] Kretschmer and Giblin, 'Getting Creators Paid' (n 36) 280; Dirk Visser, 'Dutch Copyright Contract Law' in Simon Geiregat and Hendrik Vanhees (eds), *Copyright Contracts Tomorrow* (LeA 2023) 34–35.

[138] This has required a modification to the way in which music chart metrics function and, more in general, how the popularity of music is assessed. This has led to recourse to the 'album-equivalent unit', a measurement unit that refers to the consumption of music that is deemed equal to the purchase of one album copy. The precise number of digital downloads and/or

The legal framework offers little concrete guidance. For example, since many of the relevant legal provisions predate the internet revolution, it is not beyond dispute whether the term 'copies' used in such provisions only covers physical copies, or whether this also extends to digital downloads of phonograms. As indicated above, the link with 'copies' is even more tenuous for streaming, and may even become non-existent for the next potentially disruptive technology. Instead of holding on to the pre-digital concept of 'copies', alignment should be sought with the legal concepts of the right of reproduction *sensu stricto* and the right of communication to the public (including the right of making available).[139] Logic dictates that fair exploitation should relate to both prongs of exclusive rights. This implies the need for both (physical as well as digital) reproduction and (digital) making available of the music at issue. This corresponds with the approach of the EU legislator in the context of the Term Extension Directive for phonograms subject to transfer contracts, where loss of rights can ultimately only be avoided if the corporate partner's exploitation activities relate to both the reproduction right and the making-available right. By analogy, the requirement for literary publishers under French law to commit to exploitation activities concerning the literary work(s) at issue both on paper and as an e-book may be referenced.[140]

However, the specification of fair exploitation as the need for both physical and digital exploitation activities is still very vague. More concrete support for the operationalisation of 'fair exploitation' may be found in the concept of 'methods of exploitation' of protected content, which groups certain types of use in separate categories. Above, it was argued that there are several separate methods of exploitation in the music industry, in particular requiring a distinction between digital downloads and streaming. This begs the question whether the concept of fair exploitation requires the corporate partner to mine all existing and emerging methods of exploitation for the purpose of building an audience for the music to which they have been granted rights, or whether their activities may be limited to more traditional methods of exploitation, such as digital downloads, the existing models for music streaming, sync and merchandising.

A link may be made with the legal restrictions on the scope of rights granted, both as to requirements pertaining to the specification thereof (mainly in Belgium and France) and possible limitations as to the grant of rights regarding future methods of

streams deemed relevant in this regard differs per jurisdiction. By way of example, the Recording Industry Association of America (RIAA) equates 10 permanent downloads and 1,500 streams to 1 album sale, see eg <https://bit.ly/3lo8qlN>. On the partially confidential chart metric methodology wielded by IFPI, see <https://bit.ly/3mBRw2o>. See also Luis Aguiar and Joel Waldfogel, 'Streaming Reaches Flood Stage: Does Spotify Stimulate or Depress Music Sales?' (JRC Technical Reports, 2015).

139 See Chapter 2, Section 2.2.2.2. Cf Dusollier, 'EU Contractual Protection of Creators' (n 6) 456.

140 Arts L 132-17-1–8 French IP Code as amended on the basis of the French Decree of 12 November 2014, which was ratified by Art 107 French Act of 7 July 2016.

exploitation (in all four chosen EU jurisdictions).[141] These restrictions aim to counter excessive rights transfers and ensure informed consent on the part of the musician(s) at the moment of contract formation. Attaching a duty to exploit to each existing and emerging method of exploitation in the performance stage of the contract would strengthen the effect of these restrictions. This would mean that corporate partners would have to weigh the benefits of obtaining rights regarding a certain method of exploitation up against the burden of having to conduct exploitation activities – the latter at the pain of having to give up the rights at issue in case the musician(s) reclaim(s) them. Not accepting the right of the musician to (partially) reclaim their rights in such a case would amount to consolidating musician lock-in, at least where the contract at issue results in a transfer or an exclusive licence.

A less burdensome alternative for the corporate partner, with a more limited direct impact on the freedom of contract, would be to only attach a duty to exploit to methods of exploitation deemed 'significant' – again a vague concept relating to which further concretisation would be welcome.[142]

These theoretical considerations offer us little to no practical guidance in determining what exactly constitutes 'sufficient' exploitation in the digital sphere.[143] A first avenue to make 'sufficient' exploitation more concrete could be to set a minimum revenue benchmark, either in total or as to ensuing remuneration granted to the musician.[144] However, it seems disproportionate to attach the continued grant of rights to the corporate partner to the content's commercial success, given its inherent unpredictability. A more fruitful alternative form of objectification may be provided by the concept of 'findability' of a given piece of music.[145] Fair exploitation implies active steps towards improving such 'findability', bringing it to the attention of users through marketing and promotion activities. In other words, fair exploitation means that the corporate partner must seek to increase the 'actual or potential number of persons who enjoy or wish to enjoy'[146] the music they represent. The mere online availability of a piece of music on a digital download and/or streaming platform is insufficient, regardless of the size (and thus the potential audience) of the platform.[147] Otherwise, given the ubiquitous availability of content online, this

[141] See Chapter 4, Section 4.4.1.2.

[142] Cf Dusollier and others, 'Contractual Arrangements Applicable to Creators' (n 17) 102–03; Lucas-Schloetter, 'The Remuneration of Authors and Performers in Copyright Contract Law' (n 26) 267; Dusollier, 'EU Contractual Protection of Creators' (n 6) 455.

[143] Cf Furgał, 'Interpreting EU Reversion Rights' (n 27) 289.

[144] The latter solution is foreseen by the standard contract for original Dutch literary works in the Netherlands, see Art 15(1)(c) at <https://shorturl.at/lozQ4>.

[145] Furgał, 'Interpreting EU Reversion Rights'(n 27) 290, 291; Kretschmer and Giblin, 'Getting Creators Paid' (n 36) 280.

[146] Cf Joined Cases C-403/08 and C-429/08 *Football Association Premier League (FAPL) and Others* [2011] ECLI:EU:C:2011:631, para 109.

[147] Cf Fair Internet Coalition, 'Joint Guidelines' (n 54) 26; van Gompel and others, 'Evaluatie Wet Auteurscontractenrecht: Eindrapport' (n 102) 48; Furgał, 'Interpreting EU Reversion Rights' (n

requirement of exploitation risks remaining an empty shell. At the close of this subsection, an attempt is made to concretise these considerations into practical criteria.

The identity of the parties may also have an impact on the level of exploitation activities required. On the commercial side, account should be taken of the level of professionalism, and the size and financial capacity of the corporate partner, implying a lighter obligation for SMEs.[148] On the artistic side, a sliding scale of fame may serve as a way to frame musicians' legitimate expectations concerning the level of exploitation activities required from their corporate partner(s).[149]

In the online world, the potential geographical market for a certain piece of music extends across the globe. Even in a purely physical setting, it may be argued that fair exploitation requires activities across national borders, especially if the music at issue has already proven to be commercially successful in the home country.[150] However, requiring global exploitation activities by the corporate partner would be excessive. Fair exploitation requires commercial opportunities to be mined in all territories where sufficient market potential may be discerned.[151] Parties' legitimate expectations as expressed throughout the contract negotiation process should provide more specific indications in this regard.

Temporal considerations also play a role. The requisite exploitation activities must take place within a reasonable period following the formation of the contract.[152] This may be linked with the reasonable time granted to corporate partners in the context of the indirect duty to exploit, such as two years under German law.[153]

An important question is whether fair exploitation only implies an obligation for the corporate partner at the outset of contract performance, or whether it should lead to an obligation of sustained, continuous exploitation over time. An example of the former is provided by the Belgian regime, which appears to be limited to situations where there is a lack of initial exploitation.[154] An example of the latter may be found under Dutch law, which expressly renders the right to revocation applicable both if no sufficient exploitation takes place at the outset of the contract and if, following sufficient exploitation at first, this ceases to be the case after a

27) 290. See, however, Ramalho and Lopez-Tarruella, 'Implementation of the Directive 2011/77/EU' (n 45) 49.

148 Cf Brison, *Het Naburig Recht van de Uitvoerende Kunstenaar* (n 116) 445.

149 Cf ibid.

150 For French case law on music publishing contracts, see Lardinois, *Les Contrats Commentés de l'Industrie de La Musique* 2.0 (n 18) 122.

151 Van Gompel and others, 'Evaluatie Wet Auteurscontractenrecht: Eindrapport' (n 102) 51.

152 Brison, *Het Naburig Recht van de Uitvoerende Kunstenaar* (n 116) 444.

153 Art 22(3) DSM Directive; Arts 41(2) *jo* 79(2a) German Copyright Act. See also Rec 80 DSM Directive. See above, Section 5.2.2.3.2.

154 Arts XI.167/4, XI.205/4 Belgian CEL; Raad voor de Intellectuele Eigendom, 'Advies' (n 64) 99, 125–26; Furgał, 'Interpreting EU Reversion Rights' (n 27) 288.

certain period.[155] If commercial success is not forthcoming despite corporate partners' best efforts, their obligations in this context should not be unduly maintained. However, given the varying potential shelf life of different musical genres (with pop music, for example, having a faster 'expiry date' than classical music), care must be taken not to adopt an excessively restrictive stance. Moreover, if an indirect rather than a direct duty to exploit applies, the result of its application in practice is merely a rights reversal, mostly without an associated right to damages for the artist. In view of this, as well as the fact that rights reversal furthers the public interest objective of combating undue 'warehousing' of artistic content, sustained exploitation over time to avoid rights reversal appears to be wholly defensible.[156]

Further, in order to maintain a fair balance, a temporal restriction on musicians' behaviour is merited: once it is established that the corporate partner at issue will not comply with the requirement of fair exploitation, the musician should not remain unduly inactive. Failure to oppose a lack of (sufficient) exploitation by the corporate partner(s) indicates that the exploitation of their music is not the primary focus and points away from the existence of a substantive duty to exploit on the part of the corporate partner.

The exact timing of appropriate behaviour is rather fluid and fact-specific.[157] In a bid to remedy this, under pre-DSM Belgian law, all publishing contracts must set a specific time limit for the required exploitation activities, in the absence of which reference is made to sector practices.[158] This approach was maintained in the new generalised use-it-or-lose-it clause.[159] An express contract provision regarding timing could indeed be beneficial in terms of clarity, but would again be subject to the relative bargaining power of the parties. Thus, while a set term for requisite action would benefit procedural fairness, it risks hindering substantive fairness. In order to maintain flexibility, recourse to sector practices is preferable.

This reference to sector practices as a tool for operationalisation is common to all of the criteria discussed above, either implicitly or explicitly.[160] Rules that are specific to the music sector and that take account of the particularities of the exploitation of music are desirable. Sector-specific arrangements remain possible after the partial harmonisation of the revocation mechanism under EU law. Indeed,

155 Art 25e(1) Dutch Copyright Act; Furgał, 'Reversion Rights in the European Union Member States' (n 35) 288.

156 Hugenholtz, 'Towards Author's Paradise' (n 36) 404; van Gompel and others, 'Evaluatie Wet Auteurscontractenrecht: Eindrapport' (n 102) 46; Furgał, 'Interpreting EU Reversion Rights' (n 27) 283.

157 Cf Vanhees, 'Auteurscontracten en de Problematiek inzake Werken Gemaakt in Opdracht of in Uitvoering van een Arbeidsovereenkomst of Statuut' (n 33) 306.

158 Art XI.196(1) paras 1–2 Belgian CEL; Dusollier and others, 'Contractual Arrangements Applicable to Creators' (n 17) 46; Hendrik Vanhees, 'Art XI.195' in Fabienne Brison and Hendrik Vanhees (eds), *Hommage à Jan Corbet Huldeboek* (3rd edn, Larcier 2018) 314.

159 Arts XI.167/4, XI.205/4 Belgian CEL.

160 For express references to sector practices, see eg Arts L 132-11, L 132-12, L 132-13 French IP Code; Art 14 German Publishing Act.

Member States are free to specify this mechanism under national law, taking account of the specific nature of certain CCIs and types of artistic content.[161]

Specific reference may be made to the possibility for Member States to restrict the application of the revocation mechanism to a certain time frame.[162] Such a limitation makes sense for music that has a relatively long shelf life, where the exploitation of such music is intended to take place over a longer period of time. In such cases, the corporate partner recoups their investment over a longer time and a limitation of the right to revocation appears to be justified.[163]

Another example is the evolution of the activities of music publishers over time. Contrary to what is the case for classical music, the production and distribution of sheet music appears to be much less important for contemporary music, where the music publisher's task instead focuses on offering the composition(s) for reproduction using new production techniques.[164]

It may be asked whether the reference to trade practices may result in the duty to exploit becoming moot. If corporate partners in a certain CCI make a habit of not exploiting creative content or ceasing exploitation if commercial success is not immediately forthcoming, this risks elevating non-exploitation to the status of a commercial practice.[165] However, given the objective of exploitation that is – or at least should be – central to copyright exploitation contracts at the moment of their formation, this risk is unlikely to materialise in practice.

Finally, the principle of fair exploitation may be shaped further by having recourse to collective bargaining.[166] In the context of the DSM implementation process, both Belgium[167] and France[168] have embraced this possibility. In France, the modalities of the new revocation mechanism are largely left up to sector-specific collective bargaining, the outcome of which may be declared legally binding for all stakeholders.[169] If the collective negotiation process is not successful, the French Conseil d'État is to set the specifics of the revocation mechanism.[170] Also in Belgium, express reference is made to the benefits of collective bargaining in further fleshing out the general revocation mechanism.[171]

Recourse to collectivity is not a new tool for the French music industry. This is shown by the French code of practice signed by six representative organisations of

[161] Art 22(2)(a) DSM Directive. See also Rec 80 DSM Directive. See above, Section 5.2.2.3.2.
[162] Art 22(2) DSM Directive. See also Rec 80 DSM Directive.
[163] Aguilar, 'The New Copyright Directive: Part II, Articles 20–23' (n 68).
[164] Jan Corbet, *Auteursrecht* (Algemene Praktische Rechtsverzameling, Story-Scientia 1997) 85.
[165] Cf Vanhees, *Een Juridische Analyse van de Grondslagen* (n 22) 536–38.
[166] Cf European Copyright Society, 'Comment' (n 54) 133, 138, 145–46.
[167] Arts XI.167/5, 205/5 Belgian CEL. For a prior example in the Belgian literary sector, see Association des éditeurs belges (ADEB), *Code des usages des éditeurs de langue française de belgique* (2012).
[168] Art L 132-25-1 French IP Code.
[169] Arts L 131-5-2(II)–(III), 212-3-3(II)–(III) French IP Code.
[170] Arts L 131-5-1(III), L 212-3-1(III) French IP Code.
[171] Arts XI.167/5, XI.205/5 Belgian CEL.

composers and music publishers in 2017.[172] This code applies mandatorily to all contracts entered into after 1 July 2018 by any member of the signatory organisations. As to exploitation, throughout the contract reference may be made to the signatories' stated commitment to sustained exploitation activities that seek to ensure the best possible exploitation for a given piece of music,[173] as well as the need to make explicit the applicable duties to exploit in the contract.[174] In order to be able to fulfil these duties, the publisher must, throughout the contract, retain a copy of the music, in the form of its full score, and, if applicable, a phonographic recording.[175] This code of practice also contains a detailed list of relevant exploitation activities that distinguishes between classical and contemporary music and sets a minimum benchmark for 'sufficient' exploitation by music publishers.[176]

Despite a sustained effort at concretisation, the above analysis remained at times rather theoretical. A further translation into practical criteria is therefore merited.

A first *conditio sine qua non* for fair exploitation in the music industry is that a graphic version or phonographic recording of the composition is made available offline and online. In the physical world, this should lead to commercialisation of mechanical copies, such as on vinyl and CD, and possibly also on DVD – as long as that format is still in use. If orders are being placed, fair exploitation implies securing delivery of such orders without undue delay. In the digital sphere, availability of the phonograms at issue on digital download and music-streaming platforms should be a prerequisite of fair exploitation. In addition, sheet music should be available in printed version and online if this is common practice as to the genre of the music. Beyond the mere availability of compositions and/or (fixated) performances, corporate partners should take steps to push further reproduction and making available of the music at issue – in essence, to increase its audience in both the home territory and abroad. For compositions, this may imply the addition to analogue and digital catalogues and other relevant databases, as well as other efforts towards enhancing opportunities for compositions to be adapted or arranged. For both compositions and phonograms, possible opportunities leading to the diffusion of the music via radio and/or TV, synchronisation with video material (such as for the purpose of advertising), the inclusion as a sample and/or as part of a compilation album should be mined. As regards streaming platforms in particular, certain steps should be taken to promote inclusion on streaming playlists. Proof of fair exploitation may also be supported by the conclusion of sub-publishing contracts and/or investments in merchandising or video footage pertaining to the musician(s) and their music, such as music videos, live concert videos and/or documentaries. Finally, fair exploitation

[172] Code des Usages et des Bonnes Pratiques de l'Edition des Œuvres Musicales (4 October 2017).

[173] ibid ss 3, 3.4.

[174] ibid s 3.3. The publisher has a year to start exploiting the composition. This period is extended to two years for classical music.

[175] ibid s 3.4.

[176] ibid.

may also result from efforts seeking to secure the public performance of a certain composition or by a (group of) performing musician(s), such as by securing and maintaining contacts with, for example, booking agents and festival organisers.

In essence, exploitation may only be deemed fair if it relates to all significant methods of exploitation, both analogue and digital. Given that the concept of 'copies' is largely inoperative in the digital sphere, focus should lie with minimum requirements to improve the 'findability' of a piece of music, implying a minimum benchmark for promotion and marketing activities. On a temporal level, initial exploitation at the outset of the contract arguably does not suffice. In order to tackle the issue of content 'warehousing', there is a need for sustained exploitation over time.[177]

5.2.3 *Control of Exploitation Activities*

Following the analysis of the requisite extent of exploitation activities to be undertaken by the corporate partner, our attention shifts to the possibilities for the musician(s) to assert control. In addition, several courses of action are possible on the basis of moral rights protection. Moral rights play an important role in ensuring due acknowledgement for artists as well as in enhancing agency. The former task mainly rests on the shoulders of the right to paternity (for authors, and for performers to a lesser extent), while the latter falls upon the right of disclosure[178] (for authors, not performers) and the right to integrity[179] (for both authors and performers).[180] By way of example, musicians may invoke the latter right to prevent the synchronisation of their music with a certain video,[181] or the inclusion of their music on a compilation album.[182] Moral rights are, as such, unwaivable, but their application in practice may be subject to specification in the contract. The possibility for musicians to invoke their moral rights in a specific situation may therefore be limited.[183]

In addition to the right to integrity, another moral right may prove to be relevant in certain, albeit exceptional cases. French law provides for a express, unwaivable

[177] Furgał, 'Interpreting EU Reversion Rights' (n 27) 288.

[178] For an example, see Lardinois, *Les Contrats Commentés de l'Industrie de La Musique 2.0* (n 18) 124–25.

[179] See eg Jeff Keustermans and Peter Blomme, *Auteursrecht. Capita Selecta* (2nd edn, Intersentia 2021) 196–205.

[180] Cf Art 39 German Copyright Act. See also Schricker, *Urheberrecht. Kommentar* (n 58) 829–42; Fromm and Nordemann, *Urheberrecht* (n 58) 851–63; Dreyer and others, *Urheberrecht* (n 58) 823–29; Möhring and Nicolini, *Urheberrecht* (n 58) 586–93.

[181] See eg Court of Appeal Paris 27 September 1996 (*Farmer v Sony Music Entertainment*), see Lardinois, *Les Contrats Commentés de l'Industrie de La Musique 2.0* (n 18) 123.

[182] See eg French Supreme Court 12 July 2001 (*Dutronc*), French Supreme Court 10 July 2002 (*Jean Ferrat v Universal Music*), *Tribunal de Grande Instance* ('TGI') Paris 10 January 1990 (*Rostropovich*); TGI Paris 10 May 1996, all discussed in ibid 75–76, 123.

[183] As to all copyright exploitation contracts, see Vanhees, *Een Juridische Analyse van de Grondslagen* (n 22) 360–412, 578–91.

'right to repent' for authors (not performers), as a result of which a composer may withdraw or retract their work subsequent to its initial disclosure.[184] The exercise of this *droit de retrait et de repentir* requires a change of conviction on the part of the author, as well as the indemnification of the initial corporate partner.[185] Purely economic reasons, such as the wish to call upon the services of another publisher that, for example, spends more on marketing or offers a better royalty rate, do not suffice.[186] In any case, if the artist wishes to resume exploitation at a later stage, they must offer a right of use to their initial corporate partner under the same conditions as initially agreed.[187]

Similarly, in Germany, the artist has a right of revocation in case of a change of conviction concerning the work that makes the exploitation in the way originally agreed impossible to accept.[188] This right may not be waived in advance.[189] The (artistic and other) reasons for this change of conviction must be substantiated. Moreover, as is the case under French law, the corporate partner has a right to reasonable compensation for costs incurred,[190] as well as a right of first refusal in case of further exploitation – albeit not necessarily under the same conditions as initially agreed, but under 'reasonable' conditions.[191] The conditions attached to the exercise of this right, combined with the possibly limited financial resources of the

184 Art L 121-4 French IP Code. See ia Edouard Fortunet, 'The Author's Moral Right to Withdraw a Work (Droit de Repentir): A French Perspective' (2011) 6 JIPLP 535, 535–41; Dusollier and others, 'Contractual Arrangements Applicable to Creators' (n 17) 78; Lucas and others, *Traité de la Propriété Littéraire et Artistique* (n 17) 503–08, 1078–79.

185 Hugenholtz and Guibault, 'Auteurscontractenrecht' (n 58) 71; Andreas Rahmatian, 'Dealing with Rights in Copyright-Protected Works: Assignments and Licences' in Estelle Derclaye (ed), *Research Handbook on the Future of EU Copyright* (Research Handbooks in Intellectual Property, Edward Elgar 2009) 309–10; Daniel Chozick, 'Help! Fixing the Problem of Copyright Termination Inconsistencies through Public and Private International Law' (2018) 49 Georget J Int Law 1461, 1466–68; Caron, *Droit d'Auteur et Droits Voisins* (n 17) 250–51.

186 See French Supreme Court 14 May 1991, docket number 89-21.701 <https://bit.ly/3uOCBYg>.

187 Art L 121-4 French IP Code.

188 Art 42(1) German Copyright Act (*Rückrufsrecht wegen gewandelter Überzeugung*). See also Art 35(1) German Publishing Act. See in detail Hugenholtz and Guibault, 'Auteurscontractenrecht' (n 58) 72; Lenselink, *De Verlening van Exploitatiebevoegdheden in het Auteursrecht* (n 19) 266–69; Schricker, *Urheberrecht. Kommentar* (n 58) 859–72; Delp, *Der Verlagsvertrag* (n 24) 16–18; Fromm and Nordemann, *Urheberrecht* (n 58) 893–903; Rahmatian, 'Dealing with Rights in Copyright-Protected Works' (n 185) 309; Dusollier and others, 'Contractual Arrangements Applicable to Creators' (n 17) 77–78; Europe Economics and others, 'Remuneration of Authors and Performers for the Use of Their Works and the Fixations of Their Performances. Final Report' (Publications Office of the EU 2015) <https://op.europa.eu/s/zIa9> 43–44; Lucas-Schloetter, 'The Remuneration of Authors and Performers in Copyright Contract Law' (n 26) 267; Dreyer and others, *Urheberrecht* (n 58) 844–49; Möhring and Nicolini, *Urheberrecht* (n 58) 617–23.

189 Art 42(2) *jo* 79(2a) German Copyright Act.

190 Art 42(3) *jo* 79(2a) German Copyright Act; Art 35(2) German Publishing Act.

191 Art 42(4) German Copyright Act.

author(s) at issue, clearly limit the application of this right of withdrawal in practice.[192]

In Belgium, the Netherlands and the United Kingdom, no such express right exists, bar the Dutch provision that allows authors to modify the work in a reasonable way and the general prohibition on the abuse of rights.[193] Finally, it is possible to establish a provision in the contract that expressly allows a right of withdrawal. However, such a clause is unlikely to materialise, given the difference in bargaining power to the benefit of the corporate partner and the significant effect on the binding force of the contract that such a provision would entail.

The limited right of withdrawal described above constitutes a severe restriction on the principled binding force of a contract.[194] Its application should be limited to extreme cases and subject to the requirement of good faith on the part of the musician, which may manifest itself by requiring timely protest on their behalf.[195] Moreover, recourse to a right of withdrawal should only be allowed in circumstances where the continued performance of the initial contract would constitute an abuse of rights on the part of the corporate partner.[196]

Other, more general provisions of the selected substantive legal regimes may further affect musicians' right to exert control in the context of a corporate partner's exploitation activities, such as good-faith performance of a contract and abuse of rights on the part of the counterparty.[197] Save requirements that stem from the protection of public order and good morals, possible lines of action on the basis of general contract law are, in principle, waivable by the musician(s). Given the restrictive application of the relevant provisions in practice, their incidence in the music contracts under review is limited.

Independently of the possible ground(s) for action, the operationalisation of musician agency regarding the extent as well as the content of exploitation activities of their corporate partners depends on the transparency in terms of exploitation that exists in the context of the contractual relationship and the actual application of the legal framework.[198]

Moreover, even if appropriate control and agency may be achieved for all parties through obligations relating to exploitation, the crux of the matter of contractual

[192] Rahmatian, 'Dealing with Rights in Copyright-Protected Works' (n 185) 309.

[193] Art 25(4) Dutch Copyright Act.

[194] Cf Vanhees, *Een Juridische Analyse van de Grondslagen* (n 22) 461.

[195] Lardinois, *Les Contrats Commentés de l'Industrie de La Musique* 2.0 (n 18) 125.

[196] Cf Nicolas Debruyne, *Commerciële Exploitatie van de Menselijke Afbeelding, Naam en Stem* (Recht en Onderneming 54, die Keure 2021) 309.

[197] See (1) in Belgium: Art 1134 para 3 Belgian CC; (2) in France: Art 1134 para 3 French CC; (3) in Germany: Art 242 German CC; and (4) in the Netherlands: Arts 6:2, 6:248 Dutch Civil Code. See also eg Brison, *Het Naburig Recht van de Uitvoerende Kunstenaar* (n 116) 376; Spoor and others, *Auteursrecht* (n 60) 449–51. See also Chapter 3, Section 3.3.1 and sources referenced there.

[198] See in more detail below, Section 5.3.3 and Chapter 6.

balance is whether such exploitation leads to fair remuneration for all parties. This is the topic of the next section.

5.3 REMUNERATION

5.3.1 *Structure*

The exploitation of music does not in itself guarantee any remuneration, given that the consumption of artistic content depends on market demand, and since music may in certain cases be consumed for free.[199] In view of the importance of remuneration as an incentive, achieving fairness in terms of remuneration will go a long way to attaining a fairer balance in the music contracts under review. This section examines how the law affects the division of revenues in the streaming age. First, while acknowledging the justified interest of corporate partners in acquiring part of the economic value garnered through the exploitation of protected music, it discusses and evaluates the scope of the legal requirement to fairly remunerate artists. Second, given the importance of transparency to the operationalisation of fairness and the significant margin for improvement that exists in this regard in the music industry,[200] a separate subsection specifically focuses on the operationalisation of transparency in the music industry.

5.3.2 *Fair Remuneration*

5.3.2.1 Overview

This subsection approaches the concept of fair remuneration in the context of primary contractual relationships in both an ex ante and ex post fashion.[201] First, the principle of fair remuneration is made more concrete by way of a number of guiding criteria that take account of the dynamic market environment of the music industry. Subsequently, mechanisms that may allow the ex post modification of remuneration arrangements are discussed.

5.3.2.2 Requirement of Fair Remuneration

5.3.2.2.1 LEGAL REQUIREMENTS OF FAIR REMUNERATION Article 18 DSM Directive requires all Member States to ensure that artists who enter into copyright exploitation contracts 'are entitled to receive appropriate and proportionate

[199] See eg Lionel Bently and others, 'Strengthening the Position of Press Publishers and Authors and Performers in the Copyright Directive' (2017) 53.

[200] See Chapter 2, Section 2.5.

[201] As to secondary relationships, see below, Section 5.4.3.

remuneration'.[202] This minimum ex ante benchmark, which is referred to in this book as the principle of 'fair' remuneration, seeks to contribute to a sustainable marketplace for content creation, exploitation and consumption.[203] The principle of fair remuneration was not included in the initial Commission Proposal.[204] It was added by the European Parliament[205] under the influence of the 'Fair Internet for Performers' campaign.[206] The recognition of this principle of fair remuneration in EU legislation was primarily welcomed by stakeholders on the artistic side of the copyright aisle.[207] A countervailing force is provided by the second paragraph of Article 18, which requires Member States to take due account of the freedom of contract in its implementation into national law, and thus achieve a fair balance between the rights and interests of all involved.[208]

Article 18 DSM Directive complements two prior, narrower harmonising measures taken in the context of the Term Extension Directive, namely the right to supplementary compensation and the 'clean slate' provision. These fairly detailed measures are meant to ensure that the term extension for neighbouring rights associated with phonograms actually benefits performing musicians that have transferred their exclusive neighbouring rights.[209] The first measure relates to exploitation contracts where a transfer of rights – not a licence – is effected in return for a lump sum. Thus, it primarily applies to session musicians. It purports to grant such musicians an unwaivable right to annual supplementary remuneration during the extended term of protection of the phonogram.[210] This remuneration is payable by the record company and distributed through collective management.[211] In order to secure payment, the record label must set aside and reserve one-fifth of revenues

[202] Art 18(1) DSM Directive. Cf Art 15(5) DSM Directive, which provides that authors of works incorporated in press publications are to receive an 'appropriate share of the revenues' that press publishers obtain from licensing the new neighbouring right of press publishers concerning online uses.

[203] See eg Case C-62/79 *Coditel and Others* [1980] ECLI:EU:C:1980:84, para 13; Case C-92/92 *Phil Collins and Others* [1993] ECLI:EU:C:1993:847, paras 12, 21; Joined Cases C-403/08 and C-429/08 *Football Association Premier League and Others* [2011] ECLI:EU:C:2011:631, paras 107-8; Case C-351/12 *OSA v Léčebné lázně Mariánské Lázně* [2014] ECLI:EU:C:2014:110, para 23. Cf Raquel Xalabarder, 'The Principle of Appropriate and Proportionate Remuneration for Authors and Performers in Art 18 Copyright in the Digital Single Market Directive. Statutory Residual Remuneration Rights for Its Effective National Implementation' [2020] InDret 1, 13.

[204] Commission, 'Proposal for a Directive of the European Parliament and of the Council on Copyright in the Digital Single Market' (14 September 2016) COM(2016) 593 final.

[205] Parliament, 'Report on the Proposal for a Directive of the European Parliament and of the Council on Copyright in the Digital Single Market (COM(2016)0593 – C8–0383/2016 – 2016/0280(COD)) (29 June 2018) A8–0245/2018, 67.

[206] See also below, Section 5.5.

[207] The reference to artists' right to appropriate reward is not new, see Recs 10–11 InfoSoc Directive, Rec 5 Rental and Lending Right Directive, Rec 3 Resale Right Directive.

[208] Art 18(2) DSM Directive.

[209] Rec 5 Term Extension Directive.

[210] Art 3(2b) Term Directive.

[211] Art 3(2d) Term Directive *jo* Rec 12 Term Extension Directive.

derived from the exploitation of exclusive rights associated with the phonogram(s) at issue during that time, before deducting costs.[212] An extension of the annual supplementary remuneration for performing musicians on the basis of the Term Extension Directive to musicians having granted an exclusive licence to their rights should be considered, given that the economic effects of an exclusive licence are so similar to those of a full rights transfer that maintaining this difference could amount to a form of discrimination.

The second course of action, the 'clean slate' provision, is aimed at royalty-based contracts that include a transfer of rights – again not a licence.[213] It sets forth that record labels may not deduct unrecouped advances or contractually defined deductions from royalties associated with exploitation activities during the extended term of protection.[214] Both of these measures may assist in shaping the requirement of fair remuneration.

The principle of 'appropriate and proportionate' remuneration is in tune with this book's objective of securing a fair return in terms of economic capital for all contracting parties and therefore constitutes a significant step forward in terms of relational Rawlsian substantive fairness as to music contracts in the streaming age.[215] Indeed, a fair return infuses the idea of true reciprocity in the contracts under review. This principle may be seen as safeguarding parties' basic liberties as well as ensuring fair equality of opportunity and furthering the difference principle. First, fair remuneration contributes to the voluntary nature of the transactions under review.[216] The parties are free to determine the essence of the contractual bargain, thus safeguarding their individual autonomy. Second, it also allows musicians to work towards improving their position in the marketplace in terms of both economic and social capital.[217] Finally, the implicit objective of the principle of fair remuneration to secure a minimum level of remuneration can be linked with a Rawlsian baseline of resources that are to be allocated to members of society.[218]

The principle of fair remuneration as included in Article 18 DSM Directive is remarkably vague and allows a continuation of divergences between national laws.[219] The scope of appreciation for Member State legislators is significant, as is

[212] Art 3(2c) Term Directive *jo* Recs 11–12 Term Extension Directive.

[213] See Recs 10, 14 Term Extension Directive.

[214] Art 3(2e) Term Directive.

[215] Cf Oren Bracha and Talha Syed, 'Beyond Efficiency: Consequence-Sensitive Theories of Copyright' (no date) 29, 89, 295; Stephanie Plamondon, 'Rational Faith: The Utility of Fairness in Copyright' (2017) 97 BU L Rev 1487 1521.

[216] Cf in relation to consumer contracts Zhong Xing Tan, 'Where the Action Is: Macro and Micro Justice in Contract Law' (2020) 83 Mod Law Rev 725, 751–52.

[217] Cf in relation to consumer and/or employment contracts Lars Lindblom, 'The Structure of a Rawlsian Theory of Just Work' (2011) 101 Journal of Business Ethics 577, 580; Tan, 'Where the Action Is' (n 216) 751.

[218] Cf in relation to employment contracts Tan, 'Where the Action Is' (n 216) 753.

[219] Cf Dusollier, 'The 2019 Directive on Copyright in the Digital Single Market' (n 54) 1023; Giulia Priora, 'Catching Sight of a Glimmer of Light: Fair Remuneration and the Emerging

shown by the use of broad concepts such as 'appropriate', 'disproportionate' and 'real' or 'potential' economic value, as well as the lack of concrete benchmarks for appreciation, especially in a digital context. This is bound to affect legal certainty in a negative way.[220] The inevitable further contractual definition of these concepts is associated with increased transaction costs and may perpetuate and reinforce imbalances in bargaining power. Below, the relevant legal framework at all three regulatory levels is reviewed, in a bid to further concretise the principle of fair remuneration in the streaming age.

First, a brief overview of the essence of the legal requirements as to remuneration in the chosen jurisdictions is provided, since 'fair remuneration' is intrinsically connected with the legal provisions that seek to attain this. Even before the implementation of the DSM Directive, both the German and Dutch legal frameworks already provided a general principle of fair remuneration to the benefit of both composers and performers, upon which Article 18 DSM Directive was modelled. Under German law, in the absence of contractual determination of the amount of remuneration, the contract is presumed to establish fair remuneration.[221] If the contractually agreed amount is unfair, the musician may require the corporate partner to consent to a modification of the agreement that remedies this and balances out the interests of both parties.[222] Conversely, a corporate partner may not invoke a clause that deviates from the legal regime to the detriment of the musician(s).[223] In practice, therefore, the right to fair remuneration under German law is unwaivable. Under Dutch law, both composers and performers have an unwaivable right to fair remuneration in return for the grant of exploitation rights to a third party, unless in an employment context or for commissioned content.[224]

Distributive Rationale in the Reform of EU Copyright Law' [2020] JIPITEC 330, 343; Xalabarder, 'The Principle of Appropriate and Proportionate Remuneration' (n 203) 10; Yannos Paramythiotis, 'Fairness in Copyright Contract Law: Remuneration for Authors and Performers under the Copyright in the Digital Single Market Directive' in Tatiana-Eleni Synodinou and others (eds), *EU Internet Law in the Digital Single Market* (Springer International 2021) 83.

220 Cf Dusollier and others, 'Contractual Arrangements Applicable to Creators' (n 17) 38.

221 Art 32(1) *jo* 79(2a) German Copyright Act; Art 22(2) German Publishing Act; Schricker, *Urheberrecht. Kommentar* (n 58) 677–701, 1518; Fromm and Nordemann, *Urheberrecht* (n 58) 696–752; Dreyer and others, *Urheberrecht* (n 58) 725–48; Möhring and Nicolini, *Urheberrecht* (n 58) 424–50.

222 Art 32(1) *jo* 79(2a) German Copyright Act; *Bundesverfassungsgericht* ('BVerfG', General Federal Constitutional Court), Order of the First Senate of 23 October 2013, 1 BvR 1842/11, paras 1–115, '*Destructive Emotions*' <https://bit.ly/3FzgUyi>.

223 Art 32(3) *jo* 79(2a) German Copyright Act. This rule is subject to an exception for open licences.

224 Arts 8 jo 25c(1) jo 25h(1) Dutch Copyright Act jo Art 2b Dutch Neighbouring Rights Act. See, however, Art 3 Dutch Neighbouring Rights Act, which grants employed performers a right to fair remuneration for each method of exploitation, unless the terms or nature of the contract provide otherwise, or if this follows from common practice or considerations of reasonableness. See Visser and others, *ACR: Auteurscontractenrecht* (n 44) 83–137; Spoor and others, *Auteursrecht* (n 60) 563–65; van Gompel and others, 'Evaluatie Wet Auteurscontractenrecht:

France has traditionally taken a different approach. Instead of expressly requiring remuneration arrangements in the context of copyright exploitation contracts pertaining to copyright *sensu stricto* to be 'fair', French law requires such contracts to set proportionate remuneration, a rule that is qualified as pertaining to public order and is, therefore, unwaivable.[225] Prior to the implementation of the DSM Directive, this rule applied to authors only.[226] Subsequent to the implementation of the DSM Directive, performers have a right to appropriate and proportionate remuneration.[227] This principle of appropriate and proportionate remuneration is deemed to be of a public order nature.[228] The French legislator's choice not to add the requirement that the remuneration arrangement be 'appropriate' for authors was held to be incompatible with Article 18 DSM Directive.[229] While it has been argued that the principle of proportionality in itself implies a requirement of (fair) remuneration in copyright exploitation contracts, French law also expressly establishes the possibility for such contracts to be entered into without any remuneration.[230] For performing musicians whose performance has been fixed in a phonogram, French law has provided for a few years that the contract should set a minimum guaranteed remuneration per method of exploitation (with a separate provision for analogue

Eindrapport' (n 102) 27–29; ; Stef van Gompel, '"Non, Non, Rien n'a Changé": Over Vergoedingsaanspraken voor Makers uit Hoofde van Exploitatiecontracten' [2021] Auteursrecht 3, 5, 9.

225 Art L 131-4 jo 131-5-3 French IP Code. See Art L 132-5 jo L 131-4, L 132-6 French IP Code for publishing contracts. In addition, Art L 132-17-6 French IP Code requires that authors obtain fair remuneration from all revenues that derive from the commercialisation and dissemination of digital editions of their literary works. See Lucie Guibault, *Copyright Limitations and Contracts: An Analysis of the Contractual Overridability of Limitations on Copyright* (Information Law Series 9, Kluwer Law International 2002) 146; Hugenholtz and Guibault, 'Auteurscontractenrecht' (n 58) 51–54; Markellou, *Le Contrat d'Exploitation d'Auteur* (n 17) 209–26; Dusollier and others, 'Contractual Arrangements Applicable to Creators' (n 17) 119–20; Europe Economics and others, 'Remuneration of Authors and Performers' (n 188) 39–40; Lucas and others, *Traité de la Propriété Littéraire et Artistique* (n 17) 651–71, 707–10, 728–33; Pierre Sirinelli, 'La Rémuneration de l'Auteur Dans La Réforme Française Du Contrat d'Edition Du 12 Novembre 2014' in Silke von Lewinski (ed), *Remuneration for the Use of Works. Exclusivity vs Other Approaches* (De Gruyter 2017) 244–54; Gautier, *Propriété Littéraire et Artistique* (n 17) 641–48; Caron, *Droit d'Auteur et Droits Voisins* (n 17) 428–38, 456–58.

226 Europe Economics and others, 'Remuneration of Authors and Performers' (n 188) 40; Christophe Caron, 'La Fixation de La Rémunération de l'auteur' [2021] PI 16.

227 Art L 212-3(II) French IP Code; Anne-Emmanuelle Kahn, 'La Fixation de La Rémunération de l'artiste-Interprète' [2021] PI 22.

228 Art L 212-3-4 French IP Code.

229 *Conseil d'État* 15 November 2022, docket number 454477 <https://bit.ly/3QVgI4P>; Séverine Dusollier and Léo Pascault, 'Contractual Protection of Authors and Performers in France after the CDSM Directive' in Simon Geiregat and Hendrik Vanhees (eds), *Copyright Contracts Tomorrow* (LeA 2023) 67–72.

230 Art L 122-7 French IP Code; Raimond, *La Qualification du Contrat d'Auteur* (n 13) 106–09; Theodoros Chiou, 'On Royalties and Transfers without (Monetary) Consideration – Looking for the "Magic Formula" for Assessing the Validity of Remuneration Clauses of Copyright Transfers under French Copyright Law' (2013) 44 IIC 585; Lucas and others, *Traité de la Propriété Littéraire et Artistique* (n 17) 649–50. See also Art L 122-7-1 French IP Code.

and digital use).[231] In addition, since 2016, the French IP Code mandates that performing musicians should receive a minimum remuneration for streaming, proportionate to the economic value of their rights.[232]

In Belgium, the principle of appropriate and proportionate remuneration to the benefit of both authors and performers was established in Articles XI.167/1 and XI.205/1 Belgian CEL, which is qualified as mandatory law.[233]

As to performers having entered into transfer contracts in particular, all five chosen jurisdictions have implemented the unwaivable, collectively managed right to annual supplementary remuneration and the 'clean slate' provision as harmonised under the Term Extension Directive.[234] The success of these measures has rightfully been called into question on various occasions.[235] While a royalty of 20 per cent of gross revenue is at the high end of what most performing musicians achieve through contract negotiations and while discounts and advances have a very real impact on musician revenue,[236] the concrete impact of these well-intended steps has remained limited. This may be linked to the fact that the temporal application of the measures is limited to twenty years. Moreover, empirical research has discerned a trend on the part of record labels to remaster and/or remix existing recordings and focus on the exploitation of newly released phonograms instead of the sustained exploitation of older phonograms that benefit from the term extension.[237] In the absence of further active marketing of the original phonograms, ensuing musician revenue appears to have stagnated. As to the right to annual supplementary remuneration, an EU study on the application of the Term Extension Directive has indicated that the revenues collected and distributed have been rather limited, as a result of difficulties in identifying performers that are entitled to such supplementary remuneration on

[231] Art L 212-13 French IP Code; Bently and others, 'Strengthening the Position' (n 199) 59.

[232] Art L 212-14 French IP Code. In French: *diffusions en flux*. See Lucas and others, *Traité de la Propriété Littéraire et Artistique* (n 17) 1155–56.

[233] Arts XI.167/6, XI.205/6 Belgian CEL; Raad voor de Intellectuele Eigendom, 'Advies' (n 64) 76.

[234] See (1) in Belgium: Art XI.210 Belgian CEL; (2) in France: Arts L 212-3-7, L 212-3-8 French IP Code (these provisions refer back to Art L 212-3 French IP Code, which pertains to both transfer and licence contracts); (3) in Germany: Art 79a German Copyright Act (this provision expressly refers to both transfer and licence contracts); (4) in the Netherlands: Art 9b Dutch Neighbouring Rights Act; and (5) in the United Kingdom: Art 191HB UK CDPA. The French regime provides for a limitation of the annual supplementary remuneration for record companies whose total yearly revenues do not exceed €2 million, on the basis of proportionality considerations.

[235] Dusollier and others, 'Contractual Arrangements Applicable to Creators' (n 17) 86; Richard Osborne, 'Is Equitable Remuneration Equitable? Performers' Rights in the UK' (2017) 40 Popular Music and Society 573, 581; Ramalho and Lopez-Tarruella, 'Implementation of the Directive 2011/77/EU' (n 45) 8–9, 26–28, 47; Xalabarder, 'The Principle of Appropriate and Proportionate Remuneration' (n 203) 6.

[236] See Chapter 2, Section 2.4.5.

[237] Ramalho and Lopez-Tarruella, 'Implementation of the Directive 2011/77/EU' (n 45) 8, 16, 20; Ananay Aguilar, 'The Collective Management of Performers' Rights in the UK: A Story of Competing Interests' (2019) 16 SCRIPTed 4, 40.

the basis of record companies' databases.[238] Thus, despite the efforts of the EU legislator on this front, the intended effects seem to not have materialised in practice.

Other legal regimes may also have an impact on a musician's right to fair remuneration. Under general contract law, in addition to the overarching principle of good-faith contract performance that curtails excessively unfair behaviour,[239] particular reference may be made to Article 138(2) German Civil Code, which qualifies the acquisition of disproportionate pecuniary advantages through the exploitation of another party's weaker position as contrary to public policy, resulting in the nullity of the legal transaction at issue.[240] Reference may also be made to the regimes applicable to unfair B2B contract terms, namely the 'manifest imbalance' test under Belgian and French law, and the 'reasonableness' test under Dutch law.[241]

5.3.2.2.2 OPERATIONALISATION OF LEGAL REQUIREMENTS The inherent unpredictability of commercial success in the streaming age, combined with the wide spectrum of contractual relationships and technological advancements that open up new avenues for digital exploitation, render it particularly difficult to pinpoint ex ante what exactly constitutes 'fair' remuneration.

The international and EU regulatory levels offer some tentative tools for concretisation. On the international level, the Rome Convention and the WPPT refer to the need for rightsholders to receive 'equitable remuneration' in the context of the compulsory licence for secondary use, but without adding any further clarification of what should be considered 'equitable'.[242] The EU level holds significantly more potential for the concretisation of equitability in terms of remuneration. Indeed, 'appropriate' or 'equitable' remuneration is a recurring concept within the EU copyright acquis.[243] The objective of securing an appropriate economic reward for

[238] Ramalho and Lopez-Tarruella, 'Implementation of the Directive 2011/77/EU' (n 45) 26–27, 47. See also AEPO-ARTIS, 'Performers' Rights in International and European Legislation: Situation and Elements for Improvement' (2018) 138.

[239] See (1) in Belgium: Art 1134 para 3 Belgian CC; (2) in France: Art 1134 para 3 French CC; (3) in Germany: Art 242 German CC; and (4) in the Netherlands: Arts 6:2, 6:248 Dutch Civil Code. By way of illustration, see District Court Amsterdam 9 March 2021, docket number C/13/696035 / KG ZA 21-32, ECLI:NL:RBAMS:2021:1041, paras 5.12, 5.14. See also Chapter 3, Section 3.3.1 and sources referenced there. Cf Bryan Lesser, 'Record Labels Shot the Artists, but They Did Not Share the Equity' (2018) 16 Geo JL & Pub Pol'y 289.

[240] See Basil S Markesinis and others, *The German Law of Contract. A Comparative Treatise* (2nd edn, Hart 2006) 253–60; Dieter Medicus and Stephan Lorenz, *Schuldrecht I. Allgemeiner Teil* (Juristische Kurz-Lehrbücher, 21st edn, CH Beck 2015) 58, 90–91, 268–69; Wolfgang Fikentscher and Andreas Heinemann, *Schuldrecht: Allgemeiner und Besonderer Teil* (De Gruyter Studium, 11th edn, De Gruyter 2017) 85–86.

[241] See Chapter 4, Section 4.4.1.3. See Visser and others, *ACR: Auteurscontractenrecht* (n 44) 190–93.

[242] Art 12 Rome Convention; Art 15 WPPT. See also Art 12 Beijing Treaty.

[243] Valid criticism has been voiced over the lack of a clear delineation of these concepts, see eg Reto M Hilty and Valentina Moscon, 'Part D – Copyright Contract Law (Article 10 and Articles

artists is a common theme throughout the recitals of various EU directives that pertain to copyright.[244] The concepts of 'equitable remuneration'[245] and 'fair compensation'[246] also return in the context of remuneration rights subject to collective management. On various occasions, the ECJ has had the opportunity to interpret the scope of these concepts and dubbed them autonomous concepts of EU law.[247] From this case law, a number of takeaways may be deduced. First, the broad margin for Member States to shape the form, detailed arrangements and level of compensation in the context of mechanisms for exceptions and limitations to copyright may be highlighted.[248] As indicated above, such leeway also exists for the benchmark of fair remuneration set by Article 18 DSM Directive. However, this freedom is not unlimited: in view of internal market considerations, Member States should avoid unnecessary inconsistencies between national regimes.[249] A harmonised interpretation would therefore be beneficial. Second – and unsurprisingly – the ECJ refers to the need to take account of, and find a balance between, the interests of all stakeholders.[250] On a more concrete level, fair compensation for rightsholders in the context of exceptions and limitations serves as a recompense for the harm suffered by the rightsholders, and a link is required between these negative effects and the remuneration granted.[251] The economic value of the content at issue serves

14–16 COM(2016) 593 Final)' in Reto M Hilty and Valentina Moscon (eds), *Modernisation of the EU Copyright Rules Position Statement of the Max Planck Institute for Innovation and Competition* (Max Planck Institute for Innovation and Competition Research Paper Series 17–12, Max Planck Institute for Innovation and Competition 2017) 75–76; Reto M Hilty and Valentina Moscon, 'Part F – Claims to Fair Compensation (Article 12 COM(2016) 593 Final)' in Reto M Hilty and Valentina Moscon (eds), *Modernisation of the EU Copyright Rules Position Statement of the Max Planck Institute for Innovation and Competition* (Max Planck Institute for Innovation and Competition Research Paper Series 17–12, Max Planck Institute for Innovation and Competition 2017) 89–93.

[244] See eg Recs 10–11, 35 InfoSoc Directive, Rec 3 Resale Right Directive, Rec 5 Rental and Lending Directive.

[245] See Arts 3(6), 5 Rental and Lending Directive.

[246] See Art 5(2)(a)–(b) InfoSoc Directive.

[247] See eg Case C-245/00 *SENA v NOS* [2003] ECLI:EU:C:2003:68, paras 23–24 regarding 'equitable remuneration' under the Rental and Lending Directive; Case C-467/08 *Padawan v SGAE* [2010] ECLI:EU:C:2010:620, para 33 regarding 'fair compensation' under the InfoSoc Directive.

[248] See eg Case C-245/00 *SENA v NOS* [2003] ECLI:EU:C:2003:68, paras 34, 40; Case C-521/11 *Amazon.com and Others v Austro-Mechana* [2013] ECLI:EU:C:2013:515, paras 20–21; Case C-463/12 *Copydan Båndkopi v Nokia Danmark* [2015] ECLI:EU:C:2015:144, para 20.

[249] Case C-467/08 *Padawan v SGAE* [2010] ECLI:EU:C:2010:620, paras 35–36; Case C-435/12 *ACI Adam and Others v Stichting de Thuiskopie and Others* [2014] ECLI:EU:C:2014:254, para 49.

[250] See eg Case C-245/00 *SENA v NOS* [2003] ECLI:EU:C:2003:68, para 36; C-462/09 *Stichting de Thuiskopie v Opus Supplies and Others* [2011] ECLI:EU:C:2011:397, para 25; Case C-435/12 *ACI Adam and Others v Stichting de Thuiskopie and Others* [2014] ECLI:EU:C:2014:254, para 53.

[251] See eg Case C-467/08 *Padawan v SGAE* [2010] ECLI:EU:C:2010:620, paras 39–40, 42; C-462/09 *Stichting de Thuiskopie v Opus Supplies and Others* [2011] ECLI:EU:C:2011:397, paras 24, 34; Joined Cases C-457/11 to C-460/11 *VG Wort v Kyocera and Others* [2013] ECLI:EU:

as a particularly relevant criterion.[252] Moreover, the determination of what is fair should be based on objective criteria – be it variable or fixed.[253] Finally, the possible added value of collective bargaining is acknowledged.[254]

Similarly, there is a reference to 'appropriate remuneration' in Article 16 CRM Directive, which sets out the criteria for licensing terms set by CMOs.[255] Rightsholders are said to have a right to be remunerated appropriately, taking account of (again) the economic value of the rights at issue and the nature as well as scope of the use.[256]

Additional inspiration may be sourced from the competition law concept of excessive pricing under Article 102 TFEU, which labels a price as abusive – and thus unfair – if a contractual party has acquired an undue commercial advantage.[257] This is said to be the case in the absence of a reasonable proportion of the price at issue to the relevant economic value; if there is no objective economic justification for it.[258]

Applying the above by analogy to the concept of 'fair remuneration', it may be argued that the remuneration granted to parties to the music contracts under review can only be deemed 'fair' if there is an objective, sufficiently strong connection between the economic value of music (in a way the 'positive effects' thereof) and the division of revenues between those playing a primary role in securing this value.

Recital 73 DSM Directive seeks to clarify the principle of fair remuneration by specifying that artists' remuneration should be 'appropriate and proportionate to the

C:2013:426, para 31; Case C-521/11 *Amazon.com and Others v Austro-Mechana* [2013] ECLI:EU:C:2013:515, para 47; Case C-435/12 *ACI Adam and Others v Stichting de Thuiskopie and Others* [2014] ECLI:EU:C:2014:254, para 50; Case C-463/12 *Copydan Båndkopi v Nokia Danmark* [2015] ECLI:EU:C:2015:144, para 21.

[252] See eg Case C-245/00 *SENA v NOS* [2003] ECLI:EU:C:2003:68, para 37. cf Joined Cases C-403/08 and C-429/08 *FAPL and Others* [2011] ECLI:EU:C:2011:631, paras 108–109, confirming the need for remuneration for the use of IP-protected content to be reasonable, taking account of the economic value of said content.

[253] See eg Case C-245/00 *SENA v NOS* [2003] ECLI:EU:C:2003:68.

[254] See eg ibid para 45.

[255] See also Rec 61 DSM Directive.

[256] Art 16(2) *jo* Rec 31 CRM Directive; Tristan Azzi, 'Exclusive Rights. General Report: Mechanisms to Ensure Adequate Remuneration for Creators and Performers' in Silke von Lewinski (ed), *Remuneration for the Use of Works. Exclusivity vs Other Approaches* (De Gruyter 2017) 86; Matanovac Vučković, 'The Role of Collective Management Organisations in New Business Models – Challenges for the Legislature and Courts' in Silke von Lewinski (ed), *Remuneration for the Use of Works. Exclusivity vs Other Approaches* (De Gruyter 2017) 416; Xalabarder, 'The Principle of Appropriate and Proportionate Remuneration' (n 203) 14; Paramythiotis, 'Fairness in Copyright Contract Law' (n 219) 82.

[257] Case C-27/76, *United Brands v Commission* [1978] ECLI:EU:C:1978:22, para 249.

[258] Case C-26/75, *General Motors Continental v Commission* [1975] ECLI:EU:C:1975:150, para 12; Case C-27/76, *United Brands v Commission* [1978] ECLI:EU:C:1978:22, para 250; Case C-226/84, *British Leyland v Commission* [1986] ECLI:EU:C:1986:421, para 27; Case C-52/07, *Kanal 5, TV 4 v Föreningen Svenska Tonsättares Internationella Musikbyrå (STIM)* [2008] ECLI:EU:C:2008:703, paras 28; Case C-372/19 *Belgische Vereniging van Auteurs, Componisten en Uitgevers (SABAM) v Weareone.World, Wecandance* [2020] ECLI:EU:C:2020:598, para 28.

actual or potential economic value of the licensed or transferred rights'.[259] The inherent demand uncertainty in CCIs such as the music industry and the qualification of music as a so-called experience good render the task of quantifying the economic value of music particularly hard.[260] In the CCIs, '[r]ather than asymmetrical information, there is symmetrical ignorance'.[261] Since neither party can calculate the exact economic value of music in advance, ex ante assessing the fairness of remuneration arrangements may be problematic.[262] Instead of relying on the 'actual or potential' economic value of music, it may be more fruitful to look at the value that may be ex ante 'reasonably expected' on the basis of a number of guiding criteria. As was done for the scope of fair exploitation in Section 5.2.2.4 above, the following analysis again leans on relevant tools provided by legislation, case law and legal doctrine in the chosen jurisdictions.

First, the conceptual question arises whether the terminology of 'appropriate and proportionate' remuneration has certain implications for the nature of such remuneration as either a royalty or a lump sum payment. In other words, can a lump sum be 'proportionate', or does this provision require a royalty payment for all copyright exploitation contracts – either in combination with a flat fee or not? Recital 73 DSM Directive confirms that a lump sum may be proportionate and thus satisfy the 'fairness' threshold set by Article 18 DSM Directive, while it should not be the rule.[263] At the European level, therefore, no absolute requirement of proportionate remuneration appears to exist. This may be contrasted with the sustained, fierce criticism on the part of artist organisations of 'buy-out contracts', whereby a full transfer of rights is agreed for a flat fee.[264]

[259] The reference to the economic value of the rights corresponds to what was stated above regarding rightsholders' right to compensation in the context of exceptions and limitations, as well as in the context of the CRM Directive.

[260] Martin Kretschmer and others, 'The Relationship between Copyright and Contract Law' (2010) <https://ssrn.com/abstract=2624945> 19–21; Dusollier and others, 'Contractual Arrangements Applicable to Creators' (n 17) 22; Europe Economics and others, 'Remuneration of Authors and Performers' (n 188) 105.

[261] Richard Caves, *Creative Industries. Contracts Between Art and Commerce* (Harvard University Press 2002) 14.

[262] Dusollier, 'EU Contractual Protection of Creators' (n 6) 446.

[263] Cf Answer given by Mr Breton on behalf of the European Commission, E-006228/2020 (29 January 2021); Answer given by Mr Breton on behalf of the European Commission, E-001244/2022 (30 June 2022).

[264] See eg Dusollier and others, 'Contractual Arrangements Applicable to Creators' (n 17) 84; Fair Internet Coalition, 'Joint Guidelines' (n 54) 5–6; European Copyright Society, 'Comment' (n 54) 141–42; Xalabarder, 'The Remuneration of Authors and Performers' (n 52) 137; Raquel Xalabarder, 'Role of Collective Administration in Such Business Models? Introduction' in Silke von Lewinski (ed), *Remuneration for the Use of Works. Exclusivity vs Other Approaches* (De Gruyter 2017) 15; ECSA, 'ECSA's Vision on How Europe Can Prevent Buyout Contracts. An Insight into Buyouts Affecting Audiovisual Composers and Actual Solutions to Prevent Them' (2021).

In the chosen EU jurisdictions, a requirement of proportionality only applies under certain circumstances. As the law stands, France is the only country of these jurisdictions where the legal framework sets out a general rule of proportionate compensation for contracts with both authors and performers.[265] This general rule of proportionate remuneration is subject to a range of exceptions.[266] Relevant exceptions include situations where there is no practical calculation basis and/or no adequate means of supervision, where a proportionate payment would lead to disproportionate costs or where this would be impossible in view of the artist's insignificant contribution to the work, or when the artist requests the royalty to be converted to a lump sum payment.[267] In the specific context of publishing contracts, a lump sum is also allowed if one of the parties is established abroad.[268] Conversely, the German legislator has shied away from setting a generally applicable requirement of proportionality. Regardless, relevant case law has repeatedly held that a lump sum payment is often not appropriate and therefore unfair, especially when exploitation rights are granted without limitation in time or scope and a reasonable interest in the overall exploitation revenues is not secured.[269] Moreover, German law now provides that a lump sum is only allowed if it guarantees an appropriate share for the artist in the expected total income from exploitation and is justified by the specifics of the industry.[270] Finally, Belgian law does not establish a general obligation of proportionality for copyright exploitation contracts. The requirement of proportionate remuneration for publishing contracts is waivable.[271]

A final aspect is the calculation basis of a proportionate remuneration arrangement. In France, the basis deemed appropriate is the retail price, which is the actual price paid by users and therefore includes the margin for the distributor.[272] Since the

[265] Arts L 131-4, L 212-3(II) French IP Code.

[266] Dusollier and others, 'Contractual Arrangements Applicable to Creators' (n 17) 38, 120; Bently and others, 'Strengthening the Position' (n 199) 58; Lucas and others, *Traité de la Propriété Littéraire et Artistique* (n 17) 660–64.

[267] Arts L 131-4, L 212-3 French IP Code; Markellou, *Le Contrat d'Exploitation d'Auteur* (n 17) 246–56.

[268] Art L 132-6 para 2 French IP Code.

[269] See eg German Federal Court of Justice 7 October 2009, docket number I ZR 38/07 <https://openjur.de/u/71662.html>; German Federal Court of Justice 31 May 2012, docket number I ZR 73/10 <https://openjur.de/u/434129.html>. See also Dusollier and others, 'Contractual Arrangements Applicable to Creators' (n 17) 57, 128–30; Bently and others, 'Strengthening the Position' (n 199) 66; Lucas-Schloetter, 'European Copyright Contract Law' (n 26) 898; Lucas-Schloetter, 'The Remuneration of Authors and Performers in Copyright Contract Law' (n 26) 259.

[270] Art 32(2) *jo* 79(2a) German Copyright Act. On the temporal application of this new rule to ongoing contracts, see Chapter 3, Section 3.3.2.6.

[271] Berenboom, *Le Nouveau Droit d'Auteur et les Droits Voisins* (n 16) 230; Dusollier and others, 'Contractual Arrangements Applicable to Creators' (n 17) 38.

[272] Dusollier and others, 'Contractual Arrangements Applicable to Creators' (n 17) 37–38, 46. Regarding literary publishing, see also in particular Art L 132-17-6 French IP Code, which refers to the sales price without taxes.

retail price is often not known to the primary corporate partner, the lack of a clear reference point renders the operationalisation of proportionate remuneration difficult.[273] An alternative position may be found under Belgian law for publishing contracts, whereby the gross revenue accumulated by the publisher is used as the basis for calculation, unless there is a contractual provision to the contrary.[274]

Instinct and logic draw us firmly towards a proportionate allocation of revenues amassed by the exploitation of artistic content over time.[275] In practice, the choice between a lump sum and proportionate remuneration ultimately depends on administrative considerations, risk-sharing arrangements and incentives for the parties.[276] In the absence of risk – and/or if large groups of musicians with minor individual contributions are involved – a lump sum is the logical choice.[277] However, success is highly unpredictable, resulting in the need for risk allocation. In case the contract sets a non-recoupable lump sum advance, the risk falls upon the corporate partner – a risk that is mitigated if the advance is recoupable. Under a royalty arrangement without any advances, the parties share the risk.[278] All of these risk allocation choices may be considered fair under certain circumstances.[279] By way of example, artists may deem a lump sum 'appropriate' if they are risk averse and prefer short-term financial certainty to uncertain incremental payments over an extended period of time, regardless of the net present value of such a royalty.[280]

[273] Lucas-Schloetter, 'The Remuneration of Authors and Performers in Copyright Contract Law' (n 26) 256–57.

[274] Dusollier and others, 'Contractual Arrangements Applicable to Creators' (n 17) 46.

[275] Cf Lucas-Schloetter, 'The Remuneration of Authors and Performers in Copyright Contract Law' (n 26) 259; European Copyright Society, 'Comment' (n 54) 133.

[276] For a detailed economic analysis in this regard, see Europe Economics and others, 'Remuneration of Authors and Performers' (n 188) 104–11.

[277] Lucie Guibault and P Bernt Hugenholtz, 'Study on the Conditions Applicable to Contracts Relating to Intellectual Property in the European Union' (2002) <https://bit.ly/4bzdGud> 33; Hugenholtz and Guibault, 'Auteurscontractenrecht' (n 58) 50; Kretschmer and others, 'The Relationship between Copyright and Contract Law' (n 260) 25–26; Kate Darling, 'Occupy Copyright: A Law & Economic Analysis of US Author Termination Rights' (2015) 63 Buffalo Law Review 147, 165; Dirk Visser, 'Pippi Langkous en het nieuwe auteurscontractenrecht' [2015] NJB 1289, 1294. cf Xalabarder, 'The Principle of Appropriate and Proportionate Remuneration' (n 203) 15.

[278] Kretschmer and others, 'The Relationship between Copyright and Contract Law' (n 260) 24.

[279] In exceptional circumstances, the allocation of risk to one of the contracting parties may be considered contrary to the provisions on unfair B2B contract terms. See eg Art VI.91/5 3° Belgian CEL.

[280] Dusollier and others, 'Contractual Arrangements Applicable to Creators' (n 17) 120; Darling, 'Occupy Copyright' (n 277) 181–84, 202; Europe Economics and others, 'Remuneration of Authors and Performers' (n 188) 106–07; Azzi, 'Exclusive Rights' (n 256) 90; Lucas-Schloetter, 'The Remuneration of Authors and Performers in Copyright Contract Law' (n 26) 256; Michael Karas and Roland Kirstein, 'Efficient Contracting under the US Copyright Termination Law' (2018) 54 Int Rev Law Econ 39, 45; Dusollier, 'The 2019 Directive on Copyright in the Digital Single Market' (n 54) 1023; van Gompel and others, 'Evaluatie Wet Auteurscontractenrecht: Eindrapport' (n 102) 56; Xalabarder, 'The Principle of Appropriate and Proportionate Remuneration' (n 203) 16; DCMS Committee, 'Economics of Music Streaming. Second

Especially in the streaming age, which is characterised by a shift in focus from a phonogram's release to the objective of achieving sustained listening over time, a choice for instant gratification is defensible. However, it would be unfair for such an immediate payment to be wildly non-commensurate with the long-term value of the musical content. While royalty arrangements are usually considered to be more musician-friendly, corporate partners may wish to provide proportionate remuneration to ensure the cooperation of musicians in promoting the music at issue.[281] Indeed, musicians who receive royalties have a commercial incentive in this sense.[282] However, the lower proportion of revenues accorded to corporate partners under a royalty arrangement may decrease their incentive to exploit and thus indirectly result in lower musician revenue in absolute terms.[283]

Depending on the circumstances, therefore, both lump sum and royalty arrangements may be deemed 'appropriate and proportionate'. In view of this, it appears unwise to simplistically remove parties' freedom in this regard.[284] Instead, we must look beyond the distinction between lump sums and royalties and shape the requirement of fair remuneration in an alternative way.

Below, a set of guiding criteria is developed, based on an analysis of relevant legislation, case law and legal doctrine. A clear parallel may be discerned with the criteria applied to the concept of fair exploitation. Again, focus first lies with substantive aspects and the impact of digitisation, before bringing personal, geographical and temporal dimensions into the equation. Sector practices and collectively bargained solutions serve as an additional guideline. The application of these criteria may lead to a broad spectrum of results in practice – indeed, it could be argued that, under some circumstances, a fair remuneration may equal zero.

Substantively speaking, the significance of individual musicians' contributions[285] and their perceived intrinsic value is pertinent, as is the concrete frequency and extent of exploitation of the protected content as a unit.[286] The former two aspects

Report of Session 2021–22' (15 July 2021) 33. Cf regarding the audio-visual sector Shapiro, 'Remuneration Provisions in the DSM Copyright Directive and the Audiovisual Industry in the EU' (n 38) 781.

[281] Kretschmer and others, 'The Relationship between Copyright and Contract Law' (n 260) 24, 66; Alain Strowel and Bernard Vanbrabant, 'Copyright Licensing: A European View' in Jacques de Werra (ed), *Research Handbook on Intellectual Property Licensing* (Research Handbooks in Intellectual Property, Edward Elgar 2013) 41; Europe Economics and others, 'Remuneration of Authors and Performers' (n 188) 110.

[282] Musicians who are remunerated by way of a lump sum also have such an incentive, but only to the extent that this would help them to secure future contracts.

[283] Europe Economics and others, 'Remuneration of Authors and Performers' (n 188) 111.

[284] The EU legislator allows Member States 'to define specific cases for the application of lump sums, taking into account the specificities of each sector', see Rec 73 DSM Directive.

[285] Rec 73 DSM Directive; Art L 212-3(II) French IP Code for performers; Case C-265/19 *Recorded Artists Actors Performers v Phonographic Performance (Ireland) and Others* [2020] ECLI:EU:C:2020:677, para 56; Brison, *Het Naburig Recht van de Uitvoerende Kunstenaar* (n 116) 440–41.

[286] Cf Arts XI.167/1, XI.205/1 Belgian CEL; Art L 212-3(II) French IP Code for performers; Art 32(2) *jo* 79(2a) German Copyright Act.

relate to the use of the contribution in the music and are difficult to quantify and assess in advance. Above, an attempt was made to render these concepts more concrete.[287] However, the fact-specific nature of such concretisation makes it difficult to accord a high degree of relevance to this first criterion in the conceptualisation of 'fair remuneration'. Regardless, as an overarching observation, it is submitted that a higher degree of use of a musician's contribution should correspond to a higher remuneration for such musician.

Since remuneration is garnered through exploitation activities, the following relevant criterion is the concrete scope of such activities, with the concept of fair exploitation both on- and offline[288] as a pertinent benchmark.[289] However, while fair exploitation should focus on methods of exploitation deemed significant, the calculation base for fair remuneration should include *all* methods of exploitation.

An interlinked question is whether the remuneration should be contractually specified for each separate method of exploitation and in how much detail the calculation method should be described in the contract.[290] Reference may be made to the duty to specify that applies under both Belgian and French law.[291] While such a specification is in principle beneficial for both transparency and legal certainty through the reduction of information asymmetries, the substantive added value is questionable.[292] It is likely to merely lead to the inclusion of long, complex lists in the contract, thus resulting in a negative follow-on effect in terms of transparency.[293]

The legal framework regarding fair remuneration must respond to the challenges set by digitisation.[294] Traditional, analogue revenue sources grafted onto the sale of 'copies' have been joined – and, to a significant extent, even replaced – by new, digital models where income is derived from consumer subscriptions and/or advertising. Futureproof fairness in terms of remuneration may only be achieved if all parties receive a fair share of all relevant revenues connected with the exploitation of music, whatever the source.[295] Digital methods of exploitation should be accompanied by appropriately tailored remuneration arrangements.[296] Restrictions

[287] See above, Section 5.2.2.4.

[288] See Section 5.2.2.4. See also Rec 73 DSM Directive.

[289] Cf Art L 212-3(II) French IP Code for performers; Art 32(2) *jo* 79(2a) German Copyright Act.

[290] Dusollier and others, 'Contractual Arrangements Applicable to Creators' (n 17) 15; Europe Economics and others, 'Remuneration of Authors and Performers' (n 188) 156; Bently and others, 'Strengthening the Position' (n 199) 51–52; Dusollier, 'EU Contractual Protection of Creators' (n 6) 439, 449, 456; Xalabarder, 'The Remuneration of Authors and Performers' (n 52) 136. The difficulties for musicians in obtaining transparency and achieving control over their corporate partners' activities are treated in more detail in Chapter 7.

[291] See Chapter 4, Section 4.4.2.

[292] Cf Dusollier and others, 'Contractual Arrangements Applicable to Creators' (n 17) 103–04; Europe Economics and others, 'Remuneration of Authors and Performers' (n 188) 143.

[293] Europe Economics and others, 'Remuneration of Authors and Performers' (n 188) 143, 145.

[294] European Copyright Society, 'Comment' (n 54) 133.

[295] Dusollier, 'An Effective and Comprehensive Contractual Protection of Creators and Performers' (n 89).

[296] European Copyright Society, 'Comment' (n 54) 138.

regarding the scope of rights granted may provide a (partial) solution.[297] Another positive mitigating strategy, which has been followed in both Germany and the Netherlands, is to link emerging methods of exploitation with an unwaivable right to additional remuneration on the part of both composing and performing musicians.[298] This combines efficiency considerations as to exploitation with the objective of securing fair remuneration. The criteria that may shape fair remuneration should apply in order to ensure that this additional remuneration for new methods of exploitation does not remain purely symbolic. In case no guarantee may be provided, the grant of rights for new methods of exploitation should be reversible.[299]

Many of the discounts applied in the analogue age are unfit for a digitised context.[300] Yet while many music industry deals have become more artist-friendly, discounts still apply to a certain extent and the lion's share of digital revenue still accrues to the major rights owners.[301] Fairness in royalty arrangements requires discounts, deductions and other costs indicated as 'overheads' to be limited to what is reasonable. These should correspond to justifiable costs incurred by corporate partners throughout the exploitation process. Structural discounts and deductions that cannot be justified by specific actions by the corporate partner should be avoided.[302] Full transparency on applied discounts and deductions is required.[303]

[297] See Chapter 4, Section 4.4.1.

[298] See (1) in Germany: Arts 32c, 79b German Copyright Act (see also Art 137l(5) German Copyright Act); Fromm and Nordemann, *Urheberrecht* (n 58) 781–86; Dreyer and others, *Urheberrecht* (n 58) 771–75; Möhring and Nicolini, *Urheberrecht* (n 58) 467–77 and (2) in the Netherlands: Arts 25c(6) *jo* 25h(1) Dutch Copyright Act *jo* Art 2b Dutch Neighbouring Rights Act; Visser and others, *ACR: Auteurscontractenrecht* (n 44) 132–37; Spoor and others, *Auteursrecht* (n 60) 565–67. See also European Copyright Society, 'Comment' (n 54) 138. Regarding audio-visual works, see in particular Art 45d Dutch Copyright Act, Art 3 Dutch Neighbouring Rights Act; Visser and others, *ACR: Auteurscontractenrecht* (n 44) 275–85. On the application of this right to additional remuneration in the context of secondary relationships, see below, Section 5.4.3.1.

[299] On the termination phase of the contract, see Chapter 6.

[300] Gulinck, *Hier Tekenen!* (n 1) 452.

[301] Donald Passman, *All You Need to Know about the Music Business* (10th edn, Simon & Schuster 2019) 94; Chris Cooke, *Dissecting the Digital Dollar* (3rd edn, Music Managers Forum and CMU Insights 2020) 86–91; van Gompel and others, 'Evaluatie Wet Auteurscontractenrecht: Eindrapport' (n 102) 106; DCMS Committee, 'Economics of Music Streaming' (n 280) 39, 61, 63.

[302] Gulinck, *Hier Tekenen!* (n 1) 452; van Gompel and others, 'Evaluatie Wet Auteurscontractenrecht: Eindrapport' (n 102) 54. See Visser and others, *ACR: Auteurscontractenrecht* (n 44) 190–93; Spoor and others, *Auteursrecht* (n 60) 581. As this potential ground of unreasonableness refers to the corporate partner's contract performance, it may be argued that Art 25f(2) Dutch Copyright Act cannot apply subsequent to the Dutch Supreme Court judgment in the Garrix case (see Chapter 4, Section 4.4.1.3 and Dutch Supreme Court 17 December 2021, docket numbers 20/01155, 20/01158, ECLI:NL:HR:2021:1923, paras 3.1.1–3.1.4, 3.4.1–3.4.2). Such an interpretation of the judgment at issue is unmerited, especially if the structural disproportion at issue was already present at the moment of contract formation. Cf Art 12 *jo* Recs 28, 30 CRM Directive.

[303] Cf CMU, 'Performer Payments from Streaming' (2021) 13. On transparency, see below, Section 5.3.3.

As to the calculation of royalties, the royalty percentage applied to digital downloads and streaming revenue should be significantly higher than what is the case for physical sales.[304] Indeed, the overhead costs associated with shipping, packing, manufacturing and distributing physical products have all but disappeared, as has the risk of damaged goods.[305] However, in order to maintain the flexibility needed to ensure a futureproof legal framework, this book does not argue in favour of a regulatory minimum royalty percentage. Regardless, a royalty rate of 30 per cent for streaming should be a standard, rather than an outlier. In many cases, a convincing argument may even be made in favour of a 50/50 division of streaming revenue, such as for artists who signed only recently, after having nurtured their own fan base until a corporate partner took note of them.[306] Moreover, the use of a sliding royalty scale is to be supported, as is the use of profit-sharing deals over recoupment deals – including the potential cancellation of unrecouped advances after a given period.[307] Conversely, excessive kickback arrangements that force a musician to forgo a part of CMO revenue obtained through remuneration rights to their corporate partners should be (more than) frowned upon, as should instances of excess cross-collateralisation and controlled composition clauses.[308]

The primary takeaways as to the distribution of streaming revenue are that musician revenue (1) should be calculated on the basis of all quantifiable revenues stemming from exploitation, (2) using a fair royalty rate and (3) without excessive

[304] Rogers, *The Death & Life of the Music Industry in the Digital Age* (n 5) 11; Mulligan, *Awakening* (n 7) 160; Baym, *Playing to the Crowd* (n 113) 68; Gulinck, *Hier Tekenen!* (n 1) 294–96, 443, 446, 465; CMU, 'Performer Payments from Streaming' (n 303) 14–15; DCMS Committee, 'Economics of Music Streaming' (n 280) 39, 67–68.

[305] Rogers, *The Death & Life of the Music Industry in the Digital Age* (n 5) 11; Baym, *Playing to the Crowd* (n 113) 68; Gulinck, *Hier Tekenen!* (n 1) 443, 446; DCMS Committee, 'Economics of Music Streaming' (n 280) 39, 67–68; Rebecca Giblin and Cory Doctorow, *Chokepoint Capitalism: How Big Tech and Big Content Captured Creative Labor Markets and How We'll Win Them Back* (Beacon Press 2022) 60.

[306] Cf Pierre-É Lalonde, 'Study Concerning Fair Compensation for Music Creators in the Digital Age' (2014) 2–4, 24, 27; Hannibal Travis, *Copyright Class Struggle: Creative Economies in a Social Media Age* (1st edn, Cambridge University Press 2018) 161–62; 'The Ten Things People Get Wrong about Streaming – Part Two' directed by Andy Malt and Chris Cooke (Podcast, 18 May 2020) <https://bit.ly/3ZVkoYl>; Raad voor de Intellectuele Eigendom, 'Advies' (n 64) 80; Giblin and Doctorow, *Chokepoint Capitalism* (n 305) 222.

[307] Mulligan, *Awakening* (n 7) 160; Gulinck, *Hier Tekenen!* (n 1) 294–96, 465; van Gompel and others, 'Evaluatie Wet Auteurscontractenrecht: Eindrapport' (n 102) 37; Christian Castle and Claudio Feijóo, 'Study on the Artists in the Digital Music Marketplace: Economics and Legal Considerations' (WIPO 2021) 19; DCMS Committee, 'Economics of Music Streaming' (n 280) 28–29, 103.

[308] See Chapter 2, Section 2.4.5. See also Ginsburg, 'The Role of the Author in Copyright' (n 113) 78; Passman, *All You Need to Know About the Music Business* (n 301) 89; van Gompel, 'Non, Non, Rien n'a Changé' (n 224) 55. Cf Code of Conduct Muziekuitgevers (15 June 2020) s a). On the possible applicability of Art 25f(2) Dutch Copyright Act, quoting the relevant sections of the Explanatory Memorandum of the 2015 Dutch Copyright Contract Act, see Visser and others, *ACR: Auteurscontractenrecht* (n 44) 190–93; Spoor and others, *Auteursrecht* (n 60) 581.

analogue discounts and/or deductions. In general, a move away from recoupment deals and toward profit-sharing deals is to be stimulated.

Things are moving in the right direction. A first example relates to the long-standing practice of recoupment deals. The specific nature of such deals implies that corporate partners are often already making a profit on the music while incoming revenues are still subject to recoupment.[309] The majors' initiatives not to apply existing unrecouped balances to certain revenues obtained on the basis of legacy contracts hold promise.[310] Other notable examples include the policy of the Beggars group to write off a quarter of the unrecouped balance after fifteen years.[311]

Article 18 DSM Directive does not expressly refer to forms of revenue flowing to corporate partners that are not directly linked with particular exploitation activities, such as breakage, equity and profits from sale, non-allocable income assigned to corporate partners and, finally, the economic value of the ability to leverage back catalogue to secure coveted positions on streaming playlists.[312] Many of these revenues cannot be attributed to a given piece of music, let alone to a specific musician. In view of the significant commercial value of indirect remuneration arrangements, the requirement of fair remuneration should also cover indirect revenue flows – provided that these are quantifiable.[313] Reference may be made to revenues flowing from breakage, equity and non-allocable income. An analogue rule has already been included in French law for literary publishing.[314] As is the case in Germany, the corporate partner's profits may serve as an additional criterion, if applicable profit margins are excessive.

The identity of the parties may also play a role in determining what remuneration arrangements qualify as fair. A uniform approach to composing and performing musicians is merited. For the musician, an increase in fame should go hand in hand with an increase in remuneration, at least to a certain extent. The application of

309 See Chapter 2, Section 2.4.5.

310 Andre Paine, 'UMG Wipes Out Unrecouped Balances for Legacy Artists' Royalties' (*Music Week*, 1 April 2022) <https://bit.ly/46WMYcB>; Murray Stassen, 'Sony Music to Expand Unrecouped Balance Program to More Artist and Songwriters' (*Music Business Worldwide*, 26 May 2022) <https://bit.ly/3tBNyyo>; Murray Stassen, 'Warner's Dismissal of Legacy Unrecouped Advances Has already Increased Earnings of 4.500 Artists and Producers Globally' (*Music Business Worldwide*, 26 January 2023) <https://bit.ly/46zBbRw>. See also Richard Osborne and Hyojung Sun, 'Economics of Streaming: Contract Adjustment and Rights Reversion' (6 February 2023) s 4.2–4.3.

311 Castle and Feijóo, 'Study on the Artists in the Digital Music Marketplace' (n 307) 19, 48; DCMS Committee, 'Economics of Music Streaming' (n 280) 29; David Hesmondhalgh and others, 'Music Creators' Earnings in the Digital Era' (2021) 99; Giblin and Doctorow (n 305) 59.

312 Dusollier, 'An Effective and Comprehensive Contractual Protection of Creators and Performers' (n 89).

313 Cf Dusollier and others, 'Contractual Arrangements Applicable to Creators' (n 17) 104.

314 See Art L 132-17-6 French IP Code, which expressly requires indirect revenues stemming from digital exploitation to be included in the calculation base. For music publishing, see Code des Usages et des Bonnes Pratiques de l'Edition des Œuvres Musicales (n 172) s 3.6.

sliding-scale remuneration arrangements, whereby the royalty rate increases in a way commensurate to the music's commercial success, may be helpful. If a group of musicians is involved, reference may be made to conventional relations of hierarchy, such as those between different roles in an orchestra and/or in a band, while shying away from undue generalisation.[315] On the corporate partner's side, account should be taken of the market conditions at the time of investment, as well as the costs incurred and the amount of risk.[316] In addition, the structure, size and profit margin of corporate partners may be considered relevant – suggesting a somewhat more lenient application of the law vis-à-vis SMEs.

The next question is whether remuneration is provided for the entire time of exploitation, as well as when it is paid out.[317] Payment should take place within a reasonable period following the exploitation to which the remuneration relates. A certain diligence on the part of corporate partners may be expected, by way of a specification of the general duty of good-faith contract performance, which implies the need for a mechanism that efficiently collects revenues from external corporate partners and pays musicians what they are due without unnecessary delay.[318] Inspiration may be drawn from the regime applicable to literary publishing under French law, according to which the publisher must pay authors what is due to them within six months after closing the accounts for a given period, unless a collective agreement specifies otherwise.[319]

In terms of geographical scope, fair remuneration requires sharing revenues with musicians for exploitation in all relevant territories where exploitation takes place. A clear preference goes out to an 'at source' calculation of royalties that does not deduct potentially excessive commissions charged by additional intermediaries, such as sub-publishers.[320]

The shaping of the concept of fair remuneration should also take due account of sector practices, referring to the compensation that is common in the sector for the

[315] European Copyright Society, 'Comment' (n 54) 141.

[316] Malevanny, *Online Music Distribution* (n 109) 92; van Gompel and others, 'Evaluatie Wet Auteurscontractenrecht: Eindrapport' (n 102) 28.

[317] Cf Art 32(2) *jo* 79(2a) German Copyright Act.

[318] See (1) in Belgium: Art 1134 para 3 Belgian CC; (2) in France: Art 1134 para 3 French CC; (3) in Germany: Art 242 German CC; and (4) in the Netherlands: Arts 6:2, 6:248 Dutch Civil Code.

[319] Art L 132-17-3-1 French IP Code. If the literary publisher fails to deliver, the author may send a notice of default within a year, which grants the publisher an additional three months. If no payment is made, the publishing contract is automatically rescinded. This rule mandating timely payment was rendered generally binding by the French Act of 7 July 2016 and also applies to contracts that were already ongoing at that time (see Art 107(IV) French Act of 7 July 2016). See also Code des Usages et des Bonnes Pratiques de l'Edition des Œuvres Musicales (n 172) s 3.5.

[320] Cf Art 15 *jo* Rec 30 CRM Directive as to limitations that apply to deductions in the context of the international collective management of copyright through reciprocity agreements.

exploitation activity at issue.[321] The parameters used by CMOs in the context of revenue distribution may provide a source of inspiration.[322]

Further, when nearly all market participants receive a similar amount for a similar grant of rights, this consideration may contribute to a finding of fairness concerning a given remuneration arrangement.[323] However, existing practices should not be followed blindly. Indeed, the mere fact that a certain type of remuneration arrangement is customary does not in itself imply that it is fair.[324]

Together with relevant rules stemming from provisions on unfair B2B contract terms and provisions of general contract law, this may lead to many of the unfair remuneration practices in the music industry becoming a thing of the past. The express prohibition of contractual deviations from this right in the chosen jurisdictions is a promising step.[325] As to the temporal application of Article 18 DSM Directive, a balance must be found between legal certainty and enhanced fairness. In view of the internal balancing measures, such as the principled allowance of a lump sum, the temporal application to ongoing contracts from 7 June 2021 onwards is defensible, provided that any retroactive application to past exploitation activities is excluded.[326]

5.3.2.2.3 COLLECTIVE BARGAINING Collectiveness may enhance fairness within the music value chain. Collective entities such as trade unions may support and even represent musicians in the context of specific negotiations with certain corporate partners, as well as contribute to industry-wide good practices. Several forms of self-regulation may be envisaged, such as guidelines, best practices, codes of

[321] Rec 73 DSM Directive; Art L 212-3(II) French IP Code for Performers; Art 32(2) *jo* 79(2a) German Copyright Act; Lucas-Schloetter, 'The Remuneration of Authors and Performers in Copyright Contract Law' (n 26) 259; Dusollier, 'EU Contractual Protection of Creators' (n 6) 439–40.

[322] See above, Section 5.2.2.4. Cf Tobias Holzmüller, 'Remuneration Rights. General Report: Mechanisms to Ensure Adequate Remuneration for Authors and Performers' in Silke von Lewinski (ed), *Remuneration for the Use of Works. Exclusivity vs Other Approaches* (De Gruyter 2017) 198, 201.

[323] Malevanny, *Online Music Distribution* (n 109) 92.

[324] German Federal Court of Justice 7 October 2009, docket number I ZR 38/7 <https://openjur.de/u/71662.html>; Hugenholtz and Guibault, 'Auteurscontractenrecht' (n 58) 50; Visser, 'Pippi Langkous en het nieuwe auteurscontractenrecht' (n 277) 1292; Hugenholtz, 'Towards Author's Paradise' (n 36) 402; Visser and others, *ACR: Auteurscontractenrecht* (n 44) 86; Bently and others, 'Strengthening the Position' (n 199) 65; Lucas-Schloetter, 'The Remuneration of Authors and Performers in Copyright Contract Law' (n 26) 259; Martin Senftleben, 'More Money for Creators and More Support for Copyright in Society – Fair Remuneration Rights in Germany and the Netherlands' (2018) 41 Colum J L & Arts 413, 424–25; Caron, *Droit d'Auteur et Droits Voisins* (n 17) 417; Raad voor de Intellectuele Eigendom, 'Advies' (n 64) 80; Paramythiotis, 'Fairness in Copyright Contract Law' (n 219) 85.

[325] Cf Dusollier and others, 'Contractual Arrangements Applicable to Creators' (n 17) 15.

[326] Cf European Copyright Society, 'Comment' (n 54) 140.

conduct, memoranda of understanding and/or model agreements.[327] By way of example, such arrangements may determine non-mandatory remuneration rates for digital exploitation.[328] The active promotion of such best practices by public authorities is likely to be beneficial.[329] In this context, too, much is to be said for an industry-wide dialogue that brings together all significant stakeholder representatives, as was included in the initial Commission Proposal for the DSM Directive regarding the operationalisation of the chapter on copyright exploitation contracts.[330] Some of the existing good practices relevant to the music industry were already discussed.[331] On the international level, illustrative reference may, among other things, be made to the 2014 'Fair Digital Deals Declaration' championed by WIN, which commits independent record companies (not the majors) to transparency in DSP contracts and revenue sharing with artists.[332]

Taking the idea of self-regulation one step further is the potential recourse to collective bargaining. Positive aspects thereof include an undeniable reduction in transaction costs, as well as the advantage of transcending the problems of enforcement associated with the application of the protective legal framework to individual contractual relationships.[333] In the music industry, initiatives like Merlin are gaining significant traction in the – traditionally very fragmented – independent music community.[334] The leverage of digital aggregators in negotiations with DSPs may fulfil a similar role for independent musicians. The opportunities offered by collective bargaining with primary corporate partners bear particular relevance to session musicians (including orchestra musicians), whose relative bargaining power in individual negotiations is especially limited.[335] It is therefore unsurprising that the legal framework repeatedly refers to the role of collective bargaining in further

[327] Lardinois, *Les Contrats Commentés de l'Industrie de La Musique 2.0* (n 18) 78–105; Dusollier and others, 'Contractual Arrangements Applicable to Creators' (n 17) 15, 105; European Copyright Society, 'Comment' (n 54) 138; van Gompel and others, 'Evaluatie Wet Auteurscontractenrecht: Eindrapport' (n 102) 11, 45, 86; van Gompel, 'Non, Non, Rien n'a Changé' (n 224) 8; Amy Thomas and others, 'Authors' Earnings in the UK' (17 August 2023) 10.

[328] Cf Dusollier and others, 'Contractual Arrangements Applicable to Creators' (n 17) 76.

[329] Bruno Racine, 'L'Auteur et l'Acte de Création' (January 2020) 62–64.

[330] Commission, SWD(2016) 301 final (n 4) 41. Cf Rec 77 DSM Directive on the consultation of all stakeholders as to the operationalisation of the transparency obligations under Art 19 DSM Directive.

[331] See *Protocole d'Accord pour un Développement Equitable de la Musique En Ligne* – Memorandum of Understanding for the Equitable Development of Music Online (2 October 2015); Code des Usages et des Bonnes Pratiques de l'Edition des Œuvres Musicales (n 172); Code of Conduct Muziekuitgevers (n 308).

[332] See <https://winformusic.org/fair-digital-deals>.

[333] Silke von Lewinski, 'Collectivism and Its Role in the Frame of Individual Contracts' in Jan Rosén (ed), *Individualism and Collectiveness in Intellectual Property Law* (ATRIP Intellectual Property, Edward Elgar 2012) 118; Dusollier, 'An Effective and Comprehensive Contractual Protection of Creators and Performers' (n 89); European Copyright Society, 'Comment' (n 54) 142.

[334] See Chapter 2, Section 2.3.3.

[335] Cf Europe Economics and others, 'Remuneration of Authors and Performers' (n 188) 45.

shaping the applicable legal framework – especially for the performance phase of the contract.[336]

Collective bargaining appears to be on the rise in all jurisdictions under review here – at least in theory. Germany, for one, has been a strong proponent of self-regulation in the CCIs for some years, and this has shone through in the legal framework.[337] Most notably, joint remuneration arrangements that set general guidelines for appropriate fees[338] – to be distinguished from traditional collective bargaining between trade unions – are irrefutably presumed to be fair in the sense of German copyright contract law.[339] This process is meant to enable representatives of both artists and corporate partners to enter into negotiations on joint remuneration agreements.[340] Joint remuneration agreements may be established either through informal negotiations, or with the intervention of an arbitration board.[341] The representative associations must be independent and have the requisite competence to enter into such agreements.[342] If they represent a significant proportion of artists in a certain CCI, their competence is presumed until proof to the contrary.[343] Where a joint remuneration agreement applies (including when the corporate partner is not a party to it but is a member of an association that entered into the joint remuneration agreement), no deviations are allowed to the detriment of the

336 As to publishing contracts under French law, see Art L 132-17-8 French IP Code. See also Jeremy de Beer, 'Making Copyright Markets Work for Creators, Consumers and the Public Interest' in Rebecca Giblin and Kimberlee Weatherall (eds), *What If We Could Reimagine Copyright?* (ANU Press 2017) 167; European Copyright Society, 'Comment' (n 54) 133.

337 Dusollier and others, 'Contractual Arrangements Applicable to Creators' (n 17) 62; Malevanny, *Online Music Distribution* (n 109) 91.

338 In German: *Gemeinsame Vergütungsregeln*.

339 Arts 32(2), (4) *jo* 79(2a) German Copyright Act; Nikolaus Reber, 'The "Further Fair Participation" Provision in Art 32 a (2) German Copyright Act – Claims against a Third-Party Exploiter of a Work' (2016) 11 Journal of Intellectual Property Law & Practice 382, 382; Senftleben, 'More Money for Creators and More Support for Copyright in Society' (n 234) 428; Malevanny, *Online Music Distribution* (n 109) 91. Collectively bargained remuneration arrangements may also be used as a basis to determine what constitutes fair remuneration in music contracts that were concluded at an earlier stage, see Art 32(2a) *jo* 79(2a) German Copyright Act. A similar rule is on the table in the Netherlands at the time of writing. More specifically, an addition in this sense to Art 25c Dutch Copyright Act is envisaged, see <https://bit.ly/3Uze3Ov>.

340 Von Lewinski, 'Collectivism and Its Role in the Frame of Individual Contracts' (n 333) 119–20. For detail on the German regime regarding joint remuneration agreements, see ia Schricker, *Urheberrecht. Kommentar* (n 58) 755–814; Fromm and Nordemann, *Urheberrecht* (n 58) 811–29; Dreyer and others, *Urheberrecht* (n 58) 797–807; Möhring and Nicolini, *Urheberrecht* (n 58) 503–37.

341 In German: *Schlichtungsstelle*. Arts 36(3)–(4) *jo* 36a *jo* 79(2a) German Copyright Act; Fromm and Nordemann, *Urheberrecht* (n 58) 829–35; Dreyer and others, *Urheberrecht* (n 58) 807–14; Möhring and Nicolini, *Urheberrecht* (n 58) 537–52.

342 Arts 36(2) *jo* 79(2a) German Copyright Act.

343 ibid.

artist.[344] Courts may extend the application of a joint remuneration agreement to the entire sector, and may moreover use an existing agreement in a similar sector to guide them in the determination of what is fair in situations that, strictly speaking, fall outside its scope.[345] Despite these extensive rules, it appears that the system of joint remuneration agreements has had little success so far, due to an unwillingness on the part of corporate partners to participate.[346]

The French legislator has also expressly enabled collective bargaining for remuneration arrangements under national law.[347] Moreover, collective agreements relating to remuneration between representative organisations may be certified by the minister for culture and thus made mandatory for a particular sector.[348] Reference may be made to the collective labour agreement on phonographic publishing, dating back to 2008.[349] The effect of this agreement was legally extended to the entire music sector in 2009 and, since then, negotiations as to its amendment have been taking place on an annual basis.[350] This collective agreement has not been without criticism, as it is said to lead to standardised contracts whereby the transfer of exclusive rights is the norm and where the room left for negotiation on the part of individual musicians is too limited.[351] Under the impetus of French performers' CMO Spedidam, lengthy judicial proceedings were conducted against its application.[352] Outside the sphere of employment, in 2015 French stakeholders signed a Memorandum of Understanding in which they expressed their committal

344 Violations of this prohibition are sanctioned with a right to injunctive relief on the part of the author, see Art 36b German Copyright Act. Subsequent to Art 36c German Copyright Act, artists may demand the agreement at issue be amended so as to remove the deviation at issue.

345 See eg German Federal Court of Justice 7 October 2009, docket number I ZR 38/7 <https://openjur.de/u/71662.html>; German Federal Court of Justice 21 May 2015, docket number I ZR 62/14 <https://openjur.de/u/862676.html>; Senftleben, 'More Money for Creators and More Support for Copyright in Society' (n 234) 425.

346 See eg Thomas Hoeren, 'Was bleibt von §§ 32, 32a, 36 UrhG? Überlegungen zur Zukunft des Urhebervertragsrechts' in Kirsten-Inger Wöhrn and others (eds), *Festschrift für Artur-Axel Wandtke zum 70 Geburtstag am 26 März 2013* (Walter De Gruyter 2013) 174–79, 186; Visser and others, *ACR: Auteurscontractenrecht* (n 44) 103–05; Lucas-Schloetter, 'European Copyright Contract Law' (n 26) 898.

347 See extensively Séverine Dusollier, 'L'expérience française des négociations sectorielles et collectives' (Studiedag Belgische Vereniging voor Auteursrecht, Brussels, 21 April 2023). See also *Conseil d'État* 28 December 2021 and 15 November 2022, docket number 454477 <https://bit.ly/3QVgI4P>.

348 Lucas-Schloetter, 'The Remuneration of Authors and Performers in Copyright Contract Law' (n 26) 261.

349 *Convention Collective Nationale de l'Édition Phonographique* of 30 June 2008 <https://bit.ly/3Dr2EGk>.

350 This was done through a decree of 20 March 2009; Europe Economics and others, 'Remuneration of Authors and Performers' (n 188) 46.

351 ibid.

352 See most recently Court of Appeal Versailles 27 January 2022, docket number 21/01141 <https://bit.ly/44AJQBj>; French Supreme Court 13 January 2021, docket number 19-13.977, ECLI:FR:CCASS:2021:SO00072.

to securing fair remuneration of musicians in the digital sphere.[353] They affirmed many of the points made in this chapter, such as the need to include indirect revenues in the calculation base for musician remuneration[354] and to limit contractual deductions to what is reasonable,[355] as well as to ensure a minimum remuneration for performers as to online exploitation.[356] Furthermore, the abovementioned minimum remuneration for streaming for performing musicians under French law[357] led to a stakeholder agreement, the application of which was extended by Ministerial Decree on 1 July 2022.[358]

In 2015, the Dutch legislator established a regime of government approval of remuneration schemes that result from collective bargaining. Upon the joint request of relevant independent associations representing both artists and their corporate partners, the competent minister may certify the amount of such fair remuneration in a sector-specific way.[359] An attempt to have recourse to this system by representatives of composers and music publishers was rejected in 2019.[360] The successful completion of this procedure has yet to occur at the time of writing. The same is true for the possibility to set up a so-called *standaardregeling*[361] under Dutch civil law, which allows a commission that consists of the majority of representatives of collective organisations to establish a regime that is subsequently meant to apply in a general way.[362] Alternatively, cooperation in the context of collective negotiations may be sought from the *Autoriteit Consument & Markt* (ACM, the Dutch competition authority).[363] As to performers, there are multiple recommended models for copyright exploitation contracts dating from 2018 and 2019, provided jointly by Dutch representative organisations for record companies and

353 Memorandum of Understanding 2 October 2015 (n 331). While this Memorandum was due to be renewed in 2018, that did not happen: see Denis Berthomier, 'Médiateur de la musique. Rapport annuel 2019–2020' (2020) 5. Nevertheless, its contents are still relevant today.

354 Memorandum of Understanding 2 October 2015 (n 331) s 5.2. The issue of equity shares in DSPs is also expressly acknowledged, see ibid s 5.3. As to music publishing, see also Code des Usages et des Bonnes Pratiques de l'Edition des Œuvres Musicales (n 1727) s 3.5.

355 Memorandum of Understanding 2 October 2015 (n 331) s 5.4.

356 ibid s 5.5.

357 Art L 212-14 French IP Code.

358 *Arrêté du 29 juin 2022 pris en application de l'article L 212-14 du code de la propriété intellectuelle et rendant obligatoire l'accord du 12 mai 2022 relatif à la garantie de rémunération minimale*, JORF No 0151, 1 July 2022. See also <https://bit.ly/3Pgrov1>; Dusollier and Pascault, 'Contractual Protection of Authors and Performers in France after the CDSM Directive' (n 229) 72.

359 Art 25c(2)-(5) Dutch Copyright Act *jo* Art 2b Dutch Neighbouring Rights Act; Visser and others, *ACR: Auteurscontractenrecht* (n 44) 98–131.

360 See van Gompel and others, 'Evaluatie Wet Auteurscontractenrecht: Eindrapport' (n 102) 33.

361 In English: 'standard arrangement' or 'standard regulation'.

362 Art 6:214 Dutch Civil Code and *Wet Commissies Standaardregelingen* <https://bit.ly/3BLEEo1>; van Gompel and others, 'Evaluatie Wet Auteurscontractenrecht: Eindrapport' (n 102) 89.

363 ibid 34; van Gompel, 'Non, Non, Rien n'a Changé' (n 224) 9.

musicians.[364] In addition, on 15 June 2020, representative organisations from the music publishing sector entered into a sector agreement that, among other things, guarantees musicians two-thirds of revenue from collectively managed remuneration rights.[365] More generally, for all CCIs, the launch of a 'Fair Practice Code' is noted, which expressly refers to the need to fairly remunerate artists.[366] Finally, the Dutch government recently proposed to (1) establish a legal presumption that a collectively negotiated remuneration is fair, mirroring the abovementioned German rule and (2) allow for specification of the Dutch provisions of copyright contract law through collective bargaining.[367]

Subsequent to the implementation of the DSM Directive, Belgian law establishes a collective mechanism meant to intervene in the determination of fair remuneration.[368] Some industry-led collective initiatives may already be highlighted, such as the *Juist is Juist* soft law principles for collaborations in the CCIs, that focus on transparency and shared responsibility.[369]

The most notable example in the UK music industry, finally, are the agreed rates, terms and conditions between the Musicians' Union and the BPI (British Recorded Music Industry) for session musicians for commercial audio release.[370]

Despite legislative efforts to bolster collective bargaining, available data suggests a limited impact on the level of remuneration in the music sector – albeit with some exceptions.[371] This has been attributed to the procedural steps involved, as well as the limited number of representative artist associations, combined with an apparent unwillingness of corporate partners to participate, leading to delay strategies in the negotiation process.[372] While laudable initiatives are ongoing, the opportunities of enhanced collectiveness are yet to be fully mined.

364 See (1) *Aanbevelingen Artiestenovereenkomsten* <https://bit.ly/30RGAAF>; (2) *Aanbevelingen Licentiecontracten* <https://bit.ly/2YBC260>; and (3) *Sessie-overeenkomst* <https://bit.ly/3FxX8U8>.

365 Code of Conduct Muziekuitgevers (n 308).

366 <https://fairpracticecode.nl>.

367 See draft amendments to Arts 25c, 25h Dutch Copyright Code <https://bit.ly/4407vot>.

368 Arts XI.167/5, 205/5 Belgian CEL; Explanatory Memorandum Belgian Draft DSM Implementation Act (n 64) 40–41, 63–65 jo 107; Raad voor de Intellectuele Eigendom, 'Advies' (n 64) 79–80.

369 <www.juistisjuist.be>.

370 <https://bit.ly/3KOzVRJ>; Richard Arnold, *Performers' Rights* (6th edn, Sweet & Maxwell 2021) 283–87.

371 Von Lewinski, 'Collectivism and Its Role in the Frame of Individual Contracts' (n 333) 120; Europe Economics and others, 'Remuneration of Authors and Performers' (n 188) 44–45, 131; Bently and others, 'Strengthening the Position' (n 199) 65; Lucas-Schloetter, 'The Remuneration of Authors and Performers in Copyright Contract Law' (n 26) 260–61; Dusollier, 'EU Contractual Protection of Creators' (n 6) 443; Senftleben, 'More Money for Creators and More Support for Copyright in Society' (n 234) 433; Malevanny, *Online Music Distribution* (n 109) 94–95; van Gompel and others, 'Evaluatie Wet Auteurscontractenrecht: Eindrapport' (n 102) 34–35; van Gompel, 'Non, Non, Rien n'a Changé' (n 224) 8.

372 Von Lewinski, 'Collectivism and Its Role in the Frame of Individual Contracts' (n 333) 120; Lucas-Schloetter, 'The Remuneration of Authors and Performers in Copyright Contract Law'

There are limits as to what collective action through interest groups can achieve. Certain legal constraints apply. In particular, guild-style collective bargaining in the contract negotiation process leading to standard agreements may run counter to the applicable principles of competition law, in particular Article 101 TFEU[373] and its equivalent under UK law, Section 2 Competition Act 1998,[374] which prohibit anticompetitive agreements, decisions and concerted practices.[375]

Collective labour agreements contravene competition law when they are concluded between undertakings. By contrast, employees – including employed musicians – do not constitute separate undertakings. Given that they perform work for and under the direction of undertakings, they form a single economic unit with that undertaking.[376] As a result, they can freely enter into agreements among themselves without falling foul of the cartel provision.[377]

The possibility of artists to enter into collective bargaining agreements thus turns on their status as undertaking or employee. Freelance musicians are generally considered as undertakings, while orchestra musicians may be employed by 'their' orchestra. Undertakings may try to prevent musicians from bargaining collectively by explicitly qualifying them as non-workers. In the *FNV Kiem* judgment, however, the ECJ held that such strategies were ineffective.[378]

This case concerned a number of substitute orchestra musicians who had entered into a collective labour agreement setting minimum fees. These freelance musicians carried out the same work as the musicians employed by the orchestra, but did so on a self-employed basis. A Dutch court wondered whether such collective agreements

(n 26) 260; Xalabarder, 'The Remuneration of Authors and Performers' (n 52) 140; van Gompel, 'Non, Non, Rien n'a Changé' (n 224) 8.

373 Treaty on the Functioning of the European Union [2012] OJ C326/47.

374 See <www.legislation.gov.uk/ukpga/1998/41/section/2>.

375 Kretschmer and others, 'The Relationship between Copyright and Contract Law' (n 260) 11; Commission, 'Report on the Responses to the Public Consultation on the Review of the EU Copyright Rules' (July 2014) 80; Visser and others, *ACR: Auteurscontractenrecht* (n 44) 99–101; Lucas-Schloetter, 'The Remuneration of Authors and Performers in Copyright Contract Law' (n 26) 261; Senftleben, 'More Money for Creators and More Support for Copyright in Society' (n 234) 433; Dirk Visser, 'Copyright Contract Law in the DSM Directive' (Copyright in the Digital Single Market, Brussels, 30 January 2020); Friso Bostoen and Jozefien Vanherpe, 'Competition Law in the Digitized Music Industry: The Winners Take It All – But Should They?' (2021) 2 CPI Antitrust Chronicle 30; Bernd Waas and Christina Hießl (eds), *Collective Bargaining for Self-Employed Workers in Europe* (Bulletin of Comparative Labour Relations, Kluwer Law International 2021).

376 Case C-22/98 *Criminal Proceedings against Jean Claude Becu and Others* [1999] ECLI:EU:C:1999:419, para 26.

377 Case C-67/96 *Albany International v Stichting Bedrijfspensioenfonds Textielindustrie* [1999] ECLI:EU:C:1999:430, paras 52–69 (see also the opinion of Advocate General Jacobs, in particular paras 191–93).

378 See also Victoria Daskalova, 'Regulating the New Self-Employed in the Uber Economy: What Role for EU Competition Law?' (2018) 19 Ger Law J 461; Friso Bostoen, 'Competition Law in the Peer-to-Peer Economy' in Bram Devolder (ed), *The Platform Economy* (Intersentia 2019) 154–55.

fell under the cartel prohibition. However, the ECJ clarified that this situation falls outside of the provision's scope if the service providers 'are in fact "false self-employed", that is to say, service providers in a situation comparable to that of employees'.[379] The most pertinent criterion is whether the musicians independently determine their conduct on the market. This is affected by their ability to choose the time, place and content of their activities and whether they bear any commercial risk.[380] If the musicians can determine their own market conduct, they are marked as 'undertakings' from a competition law standpoint and, as a result, subject to the cartel prohibition. *FNV Kiem* prevents misclassified workers from being subject to competition law.[381] This judgment does not allow actual freelance musicians to bargain collectively in the EU. However, a significant margin is offered by the 2022 EC 'Guidelines on the application of EU competition law to collective agreements regarding the working conditions of solo self-employed persons'.[382] These Guidelines apply to persons who are not employed and who rely primarily on their personal labour for the provision of certain services.[383] Solo self-employed persons who are in a comparable situation in terms of subordination and similarity of tasks as employees of the same counterparty should be able to bargain collectively without falling foul of competition law.[384] This proviso is likely to apply to freelance orchestra musicians whose colleagues operate under an employment contract.[385] Such situations fall outside the scope of the cartel prohibition. In addition, the Guidelines specify that the EC will not intervene against certain categories of

379 Case C-413/13 *FNV Kunsten Informatie en Media (KIEM) v Staat der Nederlanden* [2014] ECLI:EU:C:2014:2411, para 31.

380 Europe Economics and others, 'Remuneration of Authors and Performers' (n 188) 56, 140.

381 The exact consequences of the *FNV Kiem* judgment of the ECJ on the dichotomy between 'worker' and 'undertaking' that determines the scope of this prohibition are yet to be definitively delineated, see in detail Daskalova, 'Regulating the New Self-Employed in the Uber Economy' (n 378).

382 Commission, 'Guidelines on the application of Union competition law to collective agreements regarding the working conditions of solo self-employed persons' (Communication) 2022/C 374/02. See also Commission, 'Collective Bargaining Agreements for Self-Employed – Scope of Application of EU Competition Rules' (Inception Impact Assessment) Ares(2021) 102652; Commission, 'Impact Assessment Report accompanying the document Communication from the Commission, Guidelines on the application of EU competition law to collective agreements regarding the working conditions of solo self-employed persons (Commission Staff Working Document) SWD(2022)321 final; Parliament, 'Recommendations to the Commission on an EU Framework for the Social and Professional Situation of Artists and Workers in the Cultural and Creative Sectors' (Draft Report) 2023/2051(INL), paras 15–17; Ecorys et al, *Study to Support the Impact Assessment of a Possible EU Initiative to the Application of Competition Rules to Collective Bargaining by Self-Employed (COMP/2020/008): Final Report* (Publications Office 2022).

383 Commission, 'Guidelines on the application of Union competition law to collective agreements regarding the working conditions of solo self-employed persons' (Communication) 2022/C 374/02, para 2(a).

384 ibid, paras 26–27.

385 ibid, Example 4.

collective agreements entered into by solo self-employed persons who are not in a similar situation to employees.[386] Prior to the Guidelines, the Dutch legislator had already expressly labelled its scheme providing for government approval of collectively bargained remuneration arrangements[387] as being compliant with competition law standards.[388] Reference may also be made to the German Collective Bargaining Act, which expressly allows collective labour agreements for specific categories of authors and performers – albeit mainly in the press and audio-visual sectors.[389] Finally, neither the EC nor any of the national competition authorities have taken any action against collective bargaining in the CCIs in the past.

This indicates that collective bargaining in the music industry has little to fear in terms of competition law enforcement.[390] Indeed, it seems logical that the original gig economy workers – musicians, and possibly also artists in other CCIs, who often depend on corporate partners in a way analogous to employees despite their potential formal status as self-employed freelancers – would be able to benefit from a potential derogation or exemption.[391]

A hard law amendment that simplifies existing procedures concerning government approval of collectively bargained remuneration schemes could further bolster collective bargaining. By way of example, the removal of the need under Dutch law for a joint request to the competent minister if a good-faith attempt at negotiation was unsuccessful[392] may help in bringing corporate partners to the collective negotiation table. A final question is whether it should be possible to extend the mandatory nature of collectively bargained solutions to sector stakeholders that did not take part in the collective negotiation process. This possibility has been established under Belgian, French, German and Dutch law subsequent to the implementation of the DSM Directive.[393] This could lead to a disproportionate encroachment upon either the freedom of contract or the freedom to provide

386 ibid, para 32.

387 Art 25c Dutch Copyright Act *jo* Art 2b Dutch Neighbouring Rights Act.

388 Visser, 'Pippi Langkous en het nieuwe auteurscontractenrecht' (n 277) 1293; Hugenholtz, 'Towards Author's Paradise' (n 36) 402; van Gompel and others, 'Evaluatie Wet Auteurscontractenrecht: Eindrapport' (n 102) 85; van Gompel, 'Non, Non, Rien n'a Changé' (n 224) 9. On the position of the Dutch competition authority, see ACM, 'Leidraad Tariefafspraken Zzp'ers' [2020] 26. See also P Bernt Hugenholtz, 'Artikel 18-23 DSM-richtlijn: Exploitatiecontracten' [2020] AMI 187, 188.

389 Art 12a Collective Bargaining Act; Hugenholtz and Guibault, 'Auteurscontractenrecht' (n 58) 29, 60–62; Europe Economics and others, 'Remuneration of Authors and Performers' (n 188) 56–58, 140–41, 150–51.

390 Senftleben, 'More Money for Creators and More Support for Copyright in Society' (n 234) 428.

391 Hugenholtz and Guibault, 'Auteurscontractenrecht' (n 58) vii, xiii, 84–85; Senftleben, 'More Money for Creators and More Support for Copyright in Society' (n 234) 428. cf Commission, 'Report on the Responses to the Public Consultation on the Review of the EU Copyright Rules' (n 375) 80; European Copyright Society, 'Comment' (n 54) 142.

392 Van Gompel and others, 'Evaluatie Wet Auteurscontractenrecht: Eindrapport' (n 102) 34, 36–37; van Gompel, 'Non, Non, Rien n'a Changé' (n 224) 8.

393 European Copyright Society, 'Comment' (n 54) 138, 142.

services, or both.[394] However, such a hard law regulatory choice goes a long way in promoting not only collectively negotiated remuneration arrangements, but also the resulting substantive fairness in practice.[395] Moreover, for want of extension of the binding effect thereof, the application of such collectively bargained arrangements in practice may prove to be problematic.

The law is not the only obstacle to collective bargaining. In addition, a number of practical obstacles have led to a slow uptake of collective bargaining processes. In the multi-layered music industry, practical issues arise in bringing all stakeholders to the negotiation table. Corporate partners may need a greater incentive to participate, such as the potential qualification of cooperation to collective bargaining processes as a prerequisite to government subsidisation for certain specific projects.[396] The stakeholders ultimately occupying a place at the negotiation table must be representative and accountable, while the bargaining process itself must be transparent.[397] Building a tradition of collective bargaining that satisfies these conditions is difficult and takes time.[398] Another limitation of collective bargaining in practice is that it risks having little to no impact on fairness in situations where usually a full transfer of exclusive rights takes place at the outset of the contract, such as is the case for session musicians.[399] In such a case, the leverage of artists' representatives is limited, even when acting collectively.

5.3.2.2.4 SANCTIONS The final aspect of the analysis is how unfair behaviour should be sanctioned. Securing fair remuneration largely qualifies as an obligation of means, whereby a party's (in)action is tested against the benchmark of what is reasonable. If this minimum threshold is not reached, sanctions applicable under general national contract law apply.[400] Serious breach of contract may be

[394] Visser and others, *ACR: Auteurscontractenrecht* (n 44) 101–02; Senftleben, 'More Money for Creators and More Support for Copyright in Society' (n 234) 427–28; OECD, 'The Future of Work. Expert Meeting on Collective Bargaining for Own-Account Workers (Summary Report)' (2020) 5.

[395] Lucas-Schloetter, 'European Copyright Contract Law' (n 26) 898–99; Xalabarder, 'The Principle of Appropriate and Proportionate Remuneration' (n 203) 21.

[396] Van Gompel and others, 'Evaluatie Wet Auteurscontractenrecht: Eindrapport' (n 102) 37, 87–89; van Gompel, 'Non, Non, Rien n'a Changé' (n 224) 8.

[397] European Copyright Society, 'Comment' (n 54) 138, 142.

[398] Xalabarder, 'The Principle of Appropriate and Proportionate Remuneration' (n 203) 21, 46.

[399] Cf ibid 21.

[400] See ia (1) in Belgium: Arts 1134–1155, 1184 Belgian Civil Code; Ignace Claeys and Thijs Tanghe, *Algemeen Contractenrecht. Handboek voor Nu en Straks* (Intersentia 2021) 429–55, 573–742; W Van Gerven and A Van Oevelen, *Verbintenissenrecht* (Studie Juri, 6th edn, Acco 2021) 184–216; (2) in Germany: Arts 241–292, 320–326 German Civil Code; Markesinis and others, *The German Law of Contract* (n 240) 379–540; Medicus and Lorenz, *Schuldrecht I. Allgemeiner Teil* (n 240) 47–103, 137–78, 238–70; Fikentscher and Heinemann, *Schuldrecht* (n 240) 278–97; (3) in France: Arts 1217–1231-7 French CC; Yvaine Buffelan-Lanore and Virginie Larribau-Terneyre, *Droit Civil. Les obligations* (16th edn, Sirey 2018) 593–644; François Terré and others, *Droit Civil. Les Obligations* (Précis. Droit privé, 12th edn, Dalloz

sanctioned with contract rescission and ensuing rights reversion, possibly accompanied with a right to claim damages. However, the primary sanction of specific performance should lead to the potential adjustment of the remuneration set in the contract to what is deemed fair and, thus, a renegotiation of the contractual conditions.[401] Such ex post mechanisms to modify remuneration arrangements in the contracts under review are analysed in the next subsection.

5.3.2.3 Modification of Remuneration Arrangements

5.3.2.3.1 COPYRIGHT CONTRACT LAW: CONTRACT ADJUSTMENT MECHANISMS Above, the focus was on the principle of fair remuneration. This ex ante form of contract regulation risks leading to a static analysis that does not take appropriate account of the dynamic, evolving nature of a contractual relationship. Therefore, an ex post approach in the form of a contract adjustment mechanism that remedies disproportionate remuneration arrangements is merited, again from the perspective of reciprocity that is associated with the application of Rawlsian principles of distributive justice to a contractual setting.[402] While the costs and inevitable legal uncertainty associated with contract renegotiations are acknowledged, it is believed that the enhanced substantive fairness that a balanced contract adjustment mechanism entails counterbalances such legitimate considerations of procedural fairness.[403] A well-functioning contract adjustment mechanism may nudge corporate partners towards the ex ante inclusion of fair remuneration arrangements in primary music industry contracts.[404] In addition, a certain ex post effect may be envisaged. However, given the significant interference of the application of a contract adjustment mechanism with freedom of contract, shaping such a mechanism requires due attention to the interests of both musicians and their corporate partners.[405]

The contract adjustment mechanism included in Article 20 DSM Directive effectuates a partial harmonisation of the contract adjustment mechanisms in the

2019) 807–968; (4) in the Netherlands: primarily Arts 6:74–94 Dutch Civil Code; Jan M van Dunné, *Verbintenissenrecht. Deel 1. Contractenrecht* (5th edn, Kluwer 2004) 607–63; Carel Asser, *Verbintenissenrecht. De Verbintenis in het Algemeen, Eerste Gedeelte* (Asser Serie 6.I*, 14th edn, Kluwer 2012) 221–346, 567–600; and (5) in the United Kingdom: Neil Andrews, *Contract Rules: Decoding English Law* (Intersentia 2016) 266–364.

401 See eg van Gompel and others, 'Evaluatie Wet Auteurscontractenrecht: Eindrapport' (n 102) 28.

402 Cf Tan, 'Where the Action Is' (n 216) 746–47.

403 Cf Visser, 'Pippi Langkous en het nieuwe auteurscontractenrecht' (n 277) 1290; Commission, SWD(2016) 301 final (n 4) 187–88.

404 Justin Hughes and Robert Merges, 'Copyright and Distributive Justice' (2016) 92 Notre Dame L Rev 513, 575.

405 Hugenholtz and Guibault, 'Auteurscontractenrecht' (n 58) 55; Dusollier and others, 'Contractual Arrangements Applicable to Creators' (n 17) 40; Lucas-Schloetter, 'The Remuneration of Authors and Performers in Copyright Contract Law' (n 26) 258.

chosen EU jurisdictions. It applies to all musicians, regulates both transfers and licences, and the rights it grants are mandatory.[406] Analogue provisions were proposed in the United Kingdom in 2021, albeit limited to transfers and exclusive licences.[407]

In terms of material scope, no alternative regime is (or should be) expressly established for SMEs. While the position of SMEs in the CCIs may be tenuous at times, other measures aimed at furthering the position of SMEs on the market, such as incubators and government support, are a better fit to take account of the specific needs of SMEs.[408] Moreover, the conceptualisation of fair remuneration leaves room for personal considerations, such as the size and structure of the corporate partner. Regardless, musicians should not be penalised for choosing to cooperate with a corporate partner having SME status.

Further, while the EU mechanism is primarily intended for contracts of long duration, its scope is not limited to contracts of a certain length, or to artists' contributions that meet a certain quantitative or qualitative threshold.[409] No limitation based on the amount of remuneration agreed in the contract is anticipated either. As a result, in theory, its scope extends to contracts where the initially set remuneration equals zero – unless it is accepted that the harmonising provisions of the DSM Directive *only* apply to contracts where a form of remuneration is set. In any case, the inclusion of such contracts would be undesirable in some cases, such as where the musician has granted an open licence (for example, a CC licence) to their work – a concept that is anathema to a request for additional remuneration.[410] Extending the scope of application of contract adjustment mechanisms to open licences risks leading to a chilling effect for users, who may not be willing to risk having to pay a licence fee at a later stage. While Recital 82 DSM Directive expressly refers to the possibility for rightsholders to grant open licences, an express exclusion of open licences from the scope of the harmonised contract adjustment mechanism would have been beneficial. The corresponding provision of German law could have served as a source of inspiration, as it expressly acknowledges artists' right to grant an 'unremunerated non-exclusive exploitation right for every person'.[411]

[406] Art 23(1) *jo* Rec 81 DSM Directive.

[407] Arts 2–3 Copyright (Rights and Remuneration of Musicians, Etc.) HC Bill (2021–22) 19, proposing Arts 93E, 191O UK CDPA.

[408] Cf Shapiro, 'Remuneration Provisions in the DSM Copyright Directive and the Audiovisual Industry in the EU' (n 38) 778.

[409] Rec 78 DSM Directive.

[410] Cf Thomas Dysart, 'Author-Protective Rules and Alternative Licences: A Review of the Dutch Copyright Contract Act' (2015) 37 EIPR 601, 605–07; Bently and others, 'Strengthening the Position' (n 199) 52–53.

[411] Art 32a(3) German Copyright Act. cf Bently and others, 'Strengthening the Position' (n 199) 64, 84. See also Arts 31a(1), 32c(3) German Copyright Act.

Article 20 DSM Directive only applies to exploitation rights that have been harmonised under EU law.[412] In principle, therefore, it has no bearing on the right of adaptation.[413] Given the minimum harmonising nature of Article 20 DSM Directive, an extension of the contract adjustment mechanism to non-harmonised rights under national law is in any case allowed – and merited.

All four chosen EU jurisdictions already provided for some form of contract adjustment mechanism prior to the implementation of the DSM Directive, either for all copyright exploitation contracts (Germany[414] and the Netherlands[415]) or in the context of publishing relationships only (Belgium[416] and France[417]).[418] While the implementation of the DSM Directive leads to only minor changes in both the German and Dutch systems, it has a more significant impact on the Belgian and French regimes.[419]

The waivability of the contract adjustment mechanism is severely restricted. Under German law, no advance waiver is possible.[420] Also in Belgium, the rights granted to artists are expressly qualified as mandatory law.[421] Third, the rights under the Dutch regime are categorised as unwaivable.[422] The draft regime under UK law also expressly qualified contrary contractual arrangements as ineffective.[423] Finally, the most restrictive rule applies under the new French regime, which qualifies the relevant provisions as pertaining to public order.[424]

The harmonised contract adjustment mechanism is affected by the collective dimension to copyright management in several ways. First, it does not apply to

412 Recs 72, 78 DSM Directive.

413 See *contra* Explanatory Memorandum Belgian Draft DSM Implementation Act (n 64) 57.

414 Arts 32a *jo* 79(2a) German Copyright Act. For detail on the contract adjustment mechanism under German law, see Schricker, *Urheberrecht. Kommentar* (n 58) 701–18; Fromm and Nordemann, *Urheberrecht* (n 58) 752–72; Markellou, *Le Contrat d'Exploitation d'Auteur* (n 17) 277–80; Dreyer and others, *Urheberrecht* (n 58) 748–67; Möhring and Nicolini, *Urheberrecht* (n 58) 450–65.

415 Art 25d Dutch Copyright Act *jo* Art 2b Dutch Neighbouring Rights Act; Visser and others, *ACR: Auteurscontractenrecht* (n 44) 139–61; Spoor and others, *Auteursrecht* (n 60) 567–69.

416 Art XI.196(2) Belgian CEL; Markellou, *Le Contrat d'Exploitation d'Auteur* (n 17) 257–62.

417 Former Art L 131-5 French IP Code; Markellou, *Le Contrat d'Exploitation d'Auteur* (n 17) 257–62; Lucas and others, *Traité de la Propriété Littéraire et Artistique* (n 17) 665–71.

418 All pre-DSM contract adjustment mechanisms in the chosen jurisdictions applied to both transfers and licences.

419 See (1) in Belgium: Arts XI.167/3, XI.205/3 Belgian CEL and (2) in France: Arts L 131-5(I)-(II), 212-3-2 French IP Code; Jean-Michel Bruguière, 'La Révision de La Rémunération de l'auteur et de l'artiste-Interprète' [2021] PI 28.

420 Art 32a(3) *jo* 79(2a) German Copyright Act; Rahmatian, 'Dealing with Rights in Copyright-Protected Works' (n 185) 307; Bently and others, 'Strengthening the Position' (n 199) 64. This rule is subject to an exception for open licences.

421 Arts XI.167/6, XI.205/6 Belgian CEL.

422 Art 25h(1) Dutch Copyright Act *jo* Art 2b Dutch Neighbouring Rights Act; Visser and others, *ACR: Auteurscontractenrecht* (n 44) 142.

423 Draft Arts 93E, 191O UK CDPA.

424 Arts L 131-5-3 *jo* L 131-5, L 212-3-4 *jo* L 212-3-2 French IP Code.

CMOs.[425] Second, Member States may substitute this mechanism by a comparable regime based on collective bargaining.[426] A cautious approach is merited: the collective nature of a remuneration arrangement does not entirely exclude the possibility for a disproportion to arise in terms of remuneration.[427] This possibility was prompted by German law. The relevant provision of the German Copyright Act excludes its application where the remuneration arrangement at issue has been collectively determined, but expressly safeguards artists' right to claim additional remuneration under the substantive conditions set by the contract adjustment mechanism.[428] Subsequent to the implementation of the DSM Directive, the Belgian and French contract adjustment mechanisms contain a similar reference to collective bargaining: where a sector agreement provides a comparable regime, the contract adjustment mechanism is substituted by the collectively bargained alternative.[429] Dutch law does not expressly mention the influence of a collectively bargained solution on the application of the contract adjustment mechanism. Regardless, even if the collectively bargained nature of a remuneration arrangement does not exclude it from the scope of the contract adjustment mechanism, it may be relevant for the interpretation of the criterion of disproportionality analysed below.[430]

The additional compensation that is available to musicians under the harmonised contract adjustment mechanism may be claimed not only by the musicians themselves, but also by their duly mandated representatives – a concept that deserves a broad interpretation, to include CMOs, artist guilds, trade unions and other representative organisations.[431]

Article 20 DSM Directive grants Member States significant leeway as to its implementation. Consequently, its impact in practice risks remaining limited.[432] The Member States have a margin of appreciation as to the substantive conditions, the procedure to be followed, and the consequences of the application of the contract adjustment mechanism in practice.

The contract adjustment mechanism under Article 20 DSM Directive applies if the remuneration that was initially set 'turns out to be disproportionately low compared to all the subsequent relevant revenues derived from the exploitation of the works or performances'.[433] This benchmark of disproportionality is, in itself,

[425] Art 20(2) *jo* Rec 78 DSM Directive; draft Art 93E(4) UK CDPA.

[426] This reference to collective bargaining did not figure in the initial Commission Proposal for the DSM Directive. It did figure in draft Art 93E(4)(b) UK CDPA.

[427] Cf Fair Internet Coalition, 'Joint Guidelines' (n 54) 18.

[428] Art 32a(4) German Copyright Act.

[429] Arts XI.167/3, XI.205/3 Belgian CEL *jo* Arts XI.167/5, XI.205/5 Belgian CEL; Arts L 131-5(III), L 212-3-2 French IP Code.

[430] Rec 78 DSM Directive. cf Art 32a(4) *jo* 32(2a) German Copyright Act.

[431] Art 20(1) DSM Directive; Fair Internet Coalition, 'Joint Guidelines' (n 54) 19.

[432] Cf Bently and others, 'Strengthening the Position' (n 199) 51, 84.

[433] Art 20(1) DSM Directive. See also drafts Arts 93E(1), 191O(1) UK CDPA.

rather vague and engenders questions concerning both the amount and requisite timing and nature of the success.

The first aspect is the reference point to determine whether or not a given remuneration is disproportionately low. The appropriate calculation base consists of all relevant revenues derived from the exploitation of the content at issue.[434] Since there is no express categorisation, revenues from both existing and emerging methods of exploitation qualify as 'revenues'. As was argued regarding the principle of fair remuneration,[435] 'revenues' should be held to include both direct and indirect revenues.[436] This is supported by Recital 78 DSM Directive, which notes that the relevant base includes merchandising revenue – a source of revenue that is not directly linked to the exploitation of a certain piece of music. Finally, in order to avoid excessive cost deduction, a calculation taking account of gross revenues appears appropriate.[437]

Due consideration of the interests of corporate partners requires the calculation to take account of the entire contractual relationship.[438] In other words: the calculation for a musician who has released a chart-topping fourth album while the first three albums flopped should bring all four albums into the equation – at least to a certain extent.[439] The nature of the initial deal between musician and corporate partner, namely a recoupment versus a profit-sharing arrangement, bears relevance.[440] As a recoupment deal is significantly more beneficial to the corporate partner, the application of the contract adjustment mechanism in such a case may demand a correspondingly greater focus on the legitimate interests of musicians. In addition, the practice of cross-financing is noted, whereby (part of) the revenues garnered through the exploitation of commercially successful content are used as a way to compensate for content exploited at a loss. Corporate partners that are not able to cross-finance within their portfolio may be inclined to offer fewer opportunities to emerging artists, or musicians active in niche genres.

434 Art 20 DSM Directive. See: (1) in Belgium: Arts XI.167/3, XI.205/3 Belgian CEL; (2) in France: Art L 131-5(I)-(II) French IP Code; (3) in Germany: Art 32a(1) *jo* 79(2a) German Copyright Act; and (4) in the Netherlands: Art 25d Dutch Copyright Act *jo* Art 2b Dutch Neighbouring Rights Act. In the *Soof* 2 case, the Dutch ADR commission considered that the relevant calculation base consisted of the total (net) revenues of the entire value chain. In the absence of full transparency in this regard, the calculation in this case took place solely on the basis of the revenues garnered by the primary corporate partners, see *Geschillencommissie Auteurscontractenrecht* (hereinafter: Geschillencie ACR) 18 April 2018, docket numbers 113417 (director) and 113462 (screenwriter), <www.degeschillencommissie.nl>. See also Joost Poort and Dirk Visser in IER 2018/43 and by P Bernt Hugenholtz in AMI 2018/15. See also van Gompel and others, 'Evaluatie Wet Auteurscontractenrecht: Eindrapport' (n 102) 39–40.

435 See above, Section 5.3.2.2.

436 Cf European Copyright Society, 'Comment' (n 54) 133.

437 Van Gompel and others, 'Evaluatie Wet Auteurscontractenrecht: Eindrapport' (n 102) 41.

438 Cf ibid 37.

439 Cf Vanhees, *Een Juridische Analyse van de Grondslagen* (n 22) 264; Visser, 'Pippi Langkous en het nieuwe auteurscontractenrecht' (n 277) 1295.

440 On the difference between recoupment and profit-sharing deals, see Chapter 2, Section 2.4.5.

An associated question is whether focus should only lie with the amount of revenue collected, or whether the size of a corporate partner's profits may be relevant too. Neither French nor Dutch law expressly refer to the relevance of a corporate partner's profits. The German regime mentions the corporate partner's revenues as well as their profits.[441] Finally, while the pre-DSM Belgian regime relating to publishing contracts posited the publisher's profits as the relevant calculation base, the new mechanism refers to the revenues garnered through exploitation.[442]

The condition of disproportionality also offers grounds for debate.[443] While Recital 78 requires the disproportion to be 'clear', corresponding provisions of national law refer to this as needing to be 'manifest' (Belgium[444]), 'exaggerated' or 'excessive' (France for royalty arrangements applicable to authors[445] and for performers[446]). The relevant provision of Dutch law used to require the disproportionality to be 'serious',[447] while the German equivalent referred to the need for the disproportion to be 'conspicuous'.[448] The latter two qualifications were removed on the implementation of the DSM Directive.[449]

Recital 78 offers a number of relevant circumstances, including the artist's contribution, sector practices and whether the contract is based on a collective agreement – criteria that were also discussed above as contributing to the conceptualisation of fair remuneration.[450] The assessment should include revenues accrued through both existing and emerging methods of exploitation as well as both direct and indirect revenues, and that it should take account of the entire contractual relationship. Both lump sums and royalty arrangements may lead to disproportionality under certain circumstances. This still gives us no real wieldable tool to determine what should be considered disproportionate 'enough' to warrant modification of contractual remuneration arrangements. German case law predating the abolition of the requirement of 'conspicuous' disproportionality has deemed such a

[441] Art 32a(1) German Copyright Act. On secondary relationships, see Art 32a(2) German Copyright Act.

[442] Art XI.196(2) para 2 Belgian CEL; Arts XI.167/3, XI.205/3 Belgian CEL.

[443] Osborne and Sun, 'Economics of Streaming' (n 310) s 3.2.1.

[444] Vanhees, 'Art XI.195' (n 158) 315.

[445] Art L 131-5(II) French IP Code (in French: *exagérément*).

[446] Art L 212-3-2 French IP Code (in French: *exagérément*).

[447] Former Art 25d Dutch Copyright Act (in Dutch: *ernstig*); van Gompel, 'Non, Non, Rien n'a Changé' (n 224) 7–8.

[448] Former Art 32a(1) German Copyright Act (in German: *auffällig*). See eg Senftleben, 'More Money for Creators and More Support for Copyright in Society' (n 234) 430.

[449] See (1) in the Netherlands: Art 25d Dutch Copyright Act and (2) in Germany: Art 32a(1) German Copyright Act; Zurth, 'Implementation of the DSM Directive's Contract Provisions into German Law' (n 77) 56–57. See also drafts Arts 93E(1), 191O(1) UK CDPA.

[450] See eg the reference to the artist's contribution in Art L 131-5(II) French IP Code.

disproportionality to be definitely present if the fee paid is less than half – and a fortiori one-third – of what would have been reasonable.[451]

Further, the disproportion must arise after the formation of the contract – that is, in the course of contract performance. Indeed, the objective of the harmonised contract adjustment mechanism is to remedy unfairness in terms of remuneration that arises over time, not remuneration arrangements that may be qualified as unfair at the outset of the contract.[452] The latter are meant to be covered by the principle of fair remuneration.[453]

Questions also arise on the nature of the disproportion – namely whether the reasons and/or the source(s) thereof are relevant, as well as whether the disproportion must be unforeseen. Unnecessary sub-conditions should be avoided. As to the former, therefore, the reason of the disproportion is – or should be – irrelevant.[454] The same is true for the source: it should not matter whether the disproportion stems from existing or new methods of exploitation. The relevant legal provisions do not provide any indication to the contrary. As to the latter, Article 20 DSM Directive does not really provide a plain answer. The relevant provision of German law expressly qualifies the foreseen or foreseeable nature of the disproportionality as irrelevant.[455] This qualification appears to be largely unnecessary when it comes to disproportionality resulting from commercial success, given its inherently unpredictable nature in CCIs such as the music industry. In view of this, the nature of disproportion does not – and should not – substantively affect the application of the contract adjustment mechanism.[456]

The next step is to analyse the procedural aspects. Also on this point, Article 20 DSM Directive remains characteristically vague. Member States are free to determine the appropriate procedural steps, as long as they ensure that artists are 'entitled to claim' what is due to them.[457] This implies that the modification of the contract must be expressly requested, either by the artist (Belgium,[458] Germany,[459]

[451] German Federal Court of Justice 10 May 2012, docket number I ZR 145/11 <https://openjur.de/u/557201.html>; Bently and others, 'Strengthening the Position' (n 199) 53, 63; Senftleben, 'More Money for Creators and More Support for Copyright in Society' (n 234) 430. Cf Malevanny, *Online Music Distribution* (n 109) 97. See also Hugenholtz and Guibault, 'Auteurscontractenrecht' (n 58) 57; Fromm and Nordemann, *Urheberrecht* (n 58) 758–59; Visser and others, *ACR: Auteurscontractenrecht* (n 44) 143; Shapiro, 'Remuneration Provisions in the DSM Copyright Directive and the Audiovisual Industry in the EU' (n 38) 782.

[452] Bently and others, 'Strengthening the Position' (n 199) 48–49.

[453] See above, Section 5.3.2.2.

[454] Cf Vanhees, 'Art XI.195' (n 158) 315; van Gompel and others, 'Evaluatie Wet Auteurscontractenrecht: Eindrapport' (n 102) 38.

[455] Art 32a(1) German Copyright Act.

[456] Cf European Copyright Society, 'Comment' (n 54) 144.

[457] Art 20(1) DSM Directive.

[458] Arts XI.167/3, XI.205/3 Belgian CEL.

[459] Art 32a(1) German Copyright Act.

France,[460] the Netherlands[461] and the draft UK mechanism[462]) or their representative (expressly in this sense, France[463] and the draft UK mechanism[464]). The regulatory framework should accord more express attention to the invocation of the contract adjustment mechanism in case of large productions with many collaborators. The potential for collective invocation of rights should not be negated, including for the follow-on effect that this would engender.[465] Considerations of good faith may set a certain benchmark of reasonable behaviour.[466] This not only points towards the need for an accommodating stance on the part of the corporate partner, but also restricts the musician's behaviour, who should, for example, take action within a reasonable period after having discovered the disproportionality at issue. If no outcome is reached that is satisfactory to both parties, judicial or extra-judicial proceedings may be commenced.[467] In such a case, a reversion of rights may provide an alternative solution.[468]

The final stage of the analysis is to establish the consequences of successful recourse to the contract adjustment mechanism – namely the review of the contractual remuneration arrangements and the ensuing payment of 'additional, appropriate and fair remuneration'.[469] The adjustment is meant to remove the perceived disproportionality and bring the remuneration in line with the economic value of the music at issue.[470] The link with the requirement of fair remuneration is clear: the remuneration arrangements must be amended to reflect what is deemed fair based on the criteria analysed above.[471] While relevant case law is limited, it may be tentatively found that external (either judicial or extra-judicial) review of remuneration arrangements on the basis of contract adjustment mechanisms may lead to an increase in remuneration by about half of the remuneration (flat fee or royalty) that was initially set.[472] However, if the result of the application of a contract adjustment

[460] Arts L 141-5(III) para 2, L 212-3-2 para 2 French IP Code.
[461] Art 25d(1) Dutch Copyright Act *jo* Art 2b Dutch Neighbouring Rights Act.
[462] Draft Arts 93E(1), 191O(1) UK CDPA.
[463] Arts L 141-5(III) para 2, L 212-3-2 para 2 French IP Code.
[464] Draft Arts 93E(1), 191O(1) UK CDPA.
[465] See Chapter 7.
[466] Cf (1) in Belgium: Art 1134 para 3 Belgian CC; (2) in France: Art 1134 para 3 French CC; (3) in Germany: Art 242 German CC; and (4) in the Netherlands: Arts 6:2, 6:248 Dutch Civil Code.
[467] See Rec 78 DSM Directive.
[468] Cf Dusollier and others, 'Contractual Arrangements Applicable to Creators' (n 17) 15.
[469] Art 20(1) DSM Directive.
[470] Cf Art 32a(1) German Copyright Act.
[471] See above, Section 5.3.2.2.
[472] See eg District Court Amsterdam 1 November 2019, docket number 7329753 CV EXPL 18-24837, ECLI:NL:RBAMS:2019:8099 and District Court Amsterdam 1 November 2019, docket number 7329738 CV EXPL 18-24835, ECLI:NL:RBAMS:2019:8119, where the original remuneration arrangement was increased by 50 per cent. This case has in the meantime been settled, as noted in Dirk Visser, 'EU Copyright Contract Law from a Dutch Perspective' (Copyright Contracts Tomorrow, Ghent, 23 September 2022). See also eg Geschillencie ACR 18 April 2018, docket numbers 113417 (director) and 113462 (screenwriter), <www

mechanism is the award of a remuneration that significantly surpasses the market price for a given piece of artistic content, corporate partners are likely to shy away from further investments.[473] Consequently, an initial bias in favour of the interests of musicians, resulting in an overly broad application of contract adjustment mechanisms, risks negatively affecting the music industry ecosystem, especially given the exceptionally limited commercial success rate of music.[474] In such a situation, both corporate partners and musicians risk losing out.[475] Therefore, contract adjustment mechanisms should be limited to exceptional circumstances, through an effective application of the requirement of disproportionality.[476]

Further, the application of the contract adjustment mechanism should have retroactive effect, in the sense that the resulting adjustment of the remuneration arrangement should retroactively ensure fairness over the entire course of the contract term – not only starting from the moment of successful renegotiation. A hard law confirmation of this position would remove any existing uncertainties. Moreover, this would contribute to remuneration arrangements that are in tune with both the actual and potential value of the music to which the contract relates, as required by the principle of appropriate and proportionate remuneration and the underlying objective of ensuring Rawlsian reciprocity, translated into a fair return for all contracting parties.

More generally, from the point of view of musicians, a big question arises as to the application of contract adjustment mechanisms in practice, given the very limited nature of available case law.[477] This may point towards a lack of recourse to the contract adjustment mechanism and/or to the potential use of this mechanism as leverage in the context of contract negotiations.[478] Recent research on the Dutch music industry indicates that contract adjustment mechanisms are seldom invoked, in view of the (laudable and abovementioned) practice of sliding scale royalties.[479] Moreover, in case of overwhelming success, despite the principled binding force of contracts, contract renegotiations appear to take place frequently.[480] In such a context, successful musicians may leverage their enhanced bargaining power to claim higher royalties.[481] This allows corporate partners to extend the contractual

.degeschillencommissie.nl>, where the original remuneration was increased by 50 per cent for the screenwriter and from 7 to 12 per cent for the director.

473 Visser, 'Pippi Langkous en het nieuwe auteurscontractenrecht' (n 277) 1293; Visser, 'Copyright Contract Law in the DSM Directive' (n 375).

474 See Chapter 3, Sections 3.3–3.4.

475 Cf Shapiro, 'Remuneration Provisions in the DSM Copyright Directive and the Audiovisual Industry in the EU' (n 38) 778; Visser, 'Copyright Contract Law in the DSM Directive' (n 375).

476 Visser, 'Copyright Contract Law in the DSM Directive' (n 375).

477 See in more detail, Chapter 7, Section 7.4.

478 Commission, SWD(2016) 301 final (n 4) 187.

479 Van Gompel and others, 'Evaluatie Wet Auteurscontractenrecht: Eindrapport' (n 102) 41.

480 ibid 30, 41, 45, 106.

481 ibid.

relationship.[482] To the extent fairness in scope, exploitation and remuneration is maintained, such industry evolutions should not be hindered. In case contractual renegotiation fails, however, an argument may be made in favour of termination of the contractual relationship under certain circumstances.[483]

Finally, to the extent that a balance between the interests of all parties is attained, there is no convincing argument against the immediate application of the harmonised contract adjustment mechanism to ongoing contracts, provided that exploitation activities predating 7 June 2021 remain unaffected.[484] At the most, consideration may be given to the proviso that the grace period set for reporting obligations until 7 June 2022[485] may be (partially) extended to the contract adjustment mechanism, given that the objective of the reporting obligations established by the DSM Directive is to secure the operationalisation of the contract adjustment mechanism.[486]

5.3.2.3.2 GENERAL CONTRACT LAW: CHANGED CIRCUMSTANCES In addition to the above, the question arises whether it is possible and desirable to revise contract terms if the circumstances of the contract (including the economic conditions thereof) change significantly.[487] Such a measure would have as its objective to ensure the continued fairness of the remuneration arrangements in a given contract and, in some cases, operate as an alternative to rights reversion through contract rescission or application of the use-it-or-lose-it clause.[488] It could also have a beneficial effect in the context of negotiations pertaining to emerging methods of exploitation, in countries where no express right to additional remuneration for such emerging use applies.[489] Some provisions of (copyright) contract law already entertain the possibility of periodically reviewing the conditions of (copyright exploitation) contracts.

At the EU level, reference may be made to the express – albeit rather vague – reference in the Term Extension Directive to the possibility for Member States to provide that certain terms in royalty-based copyright exploitation contracts may be renegotiated in favour of performers.[490] This broadly worded provision applies to

482 ibid 41.
483 See Chapter 6.
484 Cf Rosati, *Copyright in the Digital Single Market* (n 81) 391–92.
485 See Chapter 3, Section 3.3.2.6 and below Section 5.3.3.2.
486 Cf European Copyright Society, 'Comment' (n 54) 139.
487 Dusollier and others, 'Contractual Arrangements Applicable to Creators' (n 17) 15; Lucas-Schloetter, 'The Remuneration of Authors and Performers in Copyright Contract Law' (n 26) 264; Dusollier, 'EU Contractual Protection of Creators' (n 6) 449; Dusollier, 'An Effective and Comprehensive Contractual Protection of Creators and Performers' (n 89); European Copyright Society, 'Comment' (n 54) 147.
488 European Copyright Society, 'Comment' (n 54) 147.
489 Cf ibid.
490 Art 10a *jo* Rec 16 Term Extension Directive; Ramalho and Lopez-Tarruella, 'Implementation of the Directive 2011/77/EU' (n 45) 21, 30.

both transfers and licences, but its personal scope is limited to performers and thus excludes composers. If Member States decide to allow such a possibility of renegotiation, the relevant recital of the Term Extension Directive adds that they should also have 'procedures in place to cover the eventuality that the renegotiation fails'.[491] This appears to do nothing else than confirm parties' freedom to amend contracts with mutual consent as well as the need for a functioning dispute resolution system. It does not delineate any conditions, such as a substantive benchmark that establishes when renegotiations should take place, the procedure that should be followed in such a context, or the desired result. The language is wholly non-committal and offers no protection in the context of contractual negotiations. Its added value is therefore limited. Regardless, the Belgian and French legislator acted upon this possibility and provided, without any further specification, that royalty contracts entered into before 1 November 2013 may be amended during the extended term of protection.[492] As for the required 'procedures', the general rules on judicial and extra-judicial dispute resolution were ostensibly deemed to be sufficient.[493]

Other national legal arrangements applicable to changed contract circumstances also already exist as a *lex generalis*.[494] By way of example, that publishing contracts that relate to e-books must, under French law, include a clause establishing a periodic review of remuneration arrangements over time.[495] While this provision does not apply to the music industry, it may serve as an indication that recurring contract revision in the context of exploitation contracts is not taboo at present, especially in a digital context.

Under general contract law, there may also be a possibility to revise the terms to a contract if unforeseen changes occur that significantly affect the contractual balance between the parties. UK law does not contain separate rules allowing for contract revision and instead relies on associated doctrines such the doctrine of frustration, which only applies in exceptional cases.[496] Among the other researched jurisdictions, conditions for recourse to such potential contract revision vary. First, the new

[491] Rec 16 Term Extension Directive.

[492] Art 40(4) para 5 Belgian Act 19 April 2014; Art 8(II) French Act of 20 February 2015. This provision was not expressly implemented in either Germany or the Netherlands, in view of the existing contract adjustment regimes, see Ramalho and Lopez-Tarruella, 'Implementation of the Directive 2011/77/EU' (n 45) 30–31.

[493] See eg Explanatory Memorandum Belgian Act 19 April 2014, 79.

[494] Rec 78 DSM Directive. The language used in this recital ('without prejudice to the law applicable to contracts in Member States') is rather imprecise and may serve as a tool for the ECJ to expand its jurisdiction in the field of contract law, cf Bently and others, 'Strengthening the Position' (n 199) 49.

[495] Art L 132-17-7 French IP Code; Lucas-Schloetter, 'The Remuneration of Authors and Performers in Copyright Contract Law' (n 26) 264.

[496] Andrews, *Contract Rules* (n 400) 246–63; Thomas Kadner Graziano, *Comparative Contract Law: Cases, Materials and Exercises* (2nd edn, Edward Elgar 2019) 426–32.

Article 5.74 Belgian Civil Code allows contract revision under the strict conditions that the changes are both significant and unforeseeable, that they are not imputable to or flowing from a risk assumed by the party invoking the circumstances and that the other party does not have legitimate expectations as to the further performance of the unrevised contract.[497] Second, Article 1195 French Civil Code provides that a party that did not assume the risk regarding a set of unforeseeable changed circumstances can request the contract to be revised if those circumstances render the contract excessively onerous for that party.[498] The German Civil Code also attaches the possibility of contract revision to several conditions. The changes at issue must be both significant and unforeseen.[499] Moreover, it is required that prior knowledge of these changes would have induced the parties not to enter into the contract, or under different conditions. Finally, the changes must lead to one of the parties not being able to reasonably expect the contract to be upheld without alteration. Under Dutch law, parties to a contract can ask a judge to modify the contract in view of unforeseen circumstances that lead to the other party not being able to legitimately expect the contract to remain as it is.[500] Given the inherently unpredictable nature of success in CCIs such as the music industry, the condition of lack of foreseeability may be fulfilled in the case of remuneration arrangements in music contracts that become unfair over time. However, the restrictive application of the other conditions limits the potential use of the doctrine of changed circumstances to extreme situations, to safeguard legal certainty.[501]

Finally, it may be argued that the continued insistence on the enforcement of remuneration arrangements that lead to unfair situations in practice, without offering the possibility of renegotiation, may be qualified as an abuse of law.[502] In turn, this may lead to judicial moderation of the remuneration arrangement(s) at issue – albeit again only in exceptional circumstances.

[497] Art 5.74 new Belgian Civil Code.

[498] See Buffelan-Lanore and Larribau-Terneyre, *Droit Civil. Les obligations* (n 400) 529–42; Kadner Graziano, *Comparative Contract Law* (n 496) 416–25; Terré and others, *Droit Civil. Les Obligations* (n 400) 704–22.

[499] Art 313(1) German Civil Code; Medicus and Lorenz, *Schuldrecht I. Allgemeiner Teil* (n 240) 260–65; Fikentscher and Heinemann, *Schuldrecht* (n 240) 148–56.

[500] Art 6:258 Dutch Civil Code; Hugenholtz and Guibault, 'Auteurscontractenrecht' (n 58) 12; van Dunné, *Verbintenissenrecht* (n 400) 751–96; Carel Asser, *Verbintenissenrecht. Algemeen Overeenkomstenrecht* (Asser Serie 6.III*, 13th edn, Kluwer 2008) 369–86; Barbara Baarsma and Nicole Rosenboom, 'Oneerlijke Handelspraktijken. Voldoet Bestaande (Zelf)regulering?' (2013) 10; Jac Hijma and others, *Rechtshandeling en Overeenkomst* (Studiereeks burgerlijk recht 3, 9th edn, Kluwer 2019) 318–29; Iris Houben and Dirk Visser, 'De Beëindiging van Muziekexploitatieovereenkomsten' [2022] ATR 135, 143.

[501] Dusollier and others, 'Contractual Arrangements Applicable to Creators' (n 17) 60.

[502] Nathalie Blanc, *Les Contrats du Droit d'Auteur à l'Epreuve de la Distinction des Contrats Nommés et Innommés* (Nouvelle Bibliothèque de Thèses 93, Dalloz 2010) 422; Dusollier and others, 'Contractual Arrangements Applicable to Creators' (n 17) 60.

5.3.3 *Transparency*

5.3.3.1 Passive Reporting Obligations

Following the analysis of the amount of remuneration required for it to be considered 'fair', the next step is to make fair remuneration work in practice. The music value chain is notoriously complex and opaque. This pervading lack of transparency gives rise to a significant information asymmetry and leads to unfairness in practice.[503] There is a commercial incentive towards secrecy.[504] However, parties to music contracts must be able to effectively assess the economic value of music and, ultimately, ascertain whether the remuneration they receive is 'fair'.[505] Without a transparent royalty chain, fair remuneration cannot be guaranteed. Musicians cannot decide whether or not to invoke a contract adjustment mechanism if they do not have access to the information required to assess the economic value of their contributions and establish whether the payments they receive correspond to this value.[506] A transparent value chain empowers musicians to claim what they are due and enhances musician agency. Moreover, detailed knowledge of this economic value is likely to assist musicians in future contract negotiations.[507] Royalty portals operated by both DSPs and corporate partners should therefore offer a high level of transparency in terms of both exploitation and remuneration.

Several legislative measures seek to enhance transparency by way of reporting obligations. Passive obligations imply a duty for the corporate partner to comply with requests for information.[508] The express inclusion of a contractual clause in this sense is an important step. It has also been proposed to mandate a right to audit under national law.[509] A relevant precedent in this context is the 'right of access' granted to authors (not performers) under some national laws.[510] Such a right is meant to allow the artist to make copies or adaptations of their work, and can hardly be said to imply a full-fledged right to audit.[511] Moreover, it only applies in case of

503 See extensively, Chapter 2, Section 2.5.

504 Giblin and Doctorow, *Chokepoint Capitalism* (n 305) 160–61.

505 Recs 74–75 DSM Directive. Reference may be made to the Das Boot case, whereby the director of photography (Jost Vacano) invoked the German contract adjustment mechanism (see Section 5.3.2.3.1) after having requested information on the basis of the German transparency provision.

506 Cf Giblin and Doctorow, *Chokepoint Capitalism* (n 305) 161.

507 Commission, SWD(2016) 301 final (n 4) 183; Giblin and Doctorow, *Chokepoint Capitalism* (n 305) 161–62.

508 The next subsection focuses on active reporting obligations.

509 See eg European Copyright Society, 'Comment' (n 54) 143. See also Art 4 UK Voluntary Code of Good Practice on Transparency in Music Streaming (31 January 2024) <https://bit.ly/4bbBx32>.

510 See (1) in Belgium: Art XI.167(1) para 3 Belgian CEL; (2) in France: Art L 111-3 French IP Code; and (3) in Germany: Art 25(1) German Copyright Act.

511 Hendrik Vanhees, 'Art XI.167' in Fabienne Brison and Hendrik Vanhees (eds), *Hommage à Jan Corbet Huldeboek* (3rd edn, Larcier 2018) 85–86; Keustermans and Blomme, *Auteursrecht* (n 179) 208–09.

need, such as when the artist does not own a sufficiently qualitative copy.[512] Its effect is therefore limited. However, there is merit to an effective audit of corporate partners' activities, for both ongoing and future contracts.[513] A right to request access to relevant information should extend to all relevant information on both exploitation and remuneration, allowing artists to determine whether they have either a right to revocation and/or additional remuneration.[514] Reference may be made to the code of practice for French music publishers, which establishes a right for composers to request an audit of the music publisher's exploitation activities every five years.[515] There is a similar right to audit for the music publisher's revenues.[516] However, even if a generalised right to audit were to be mandated by law, obstacles to its implementation remain.[517]

At the EU level, Article 3(2c) Term Extension Directive requires Member States to ensure that, upon request, record companies provide performers (or their CMOs[518]) who are entitled to annual supplementary remuneration[519] with any information required to secure payment thereof. This provision, which only applies to transfer contracts with performers where the remuneration takes the form of a lump sum, was implemented in all five chosen jurisdictions.[520] In addition, a right to audit may be implied in the formulation of Article 19 DSM Directive, which is discussed in the next subsection.[521]

5.3.3.2 Active Reporting Obligations

While rules allowing artists to request information from their corporate counterparties undoubtedly contribute to transparency, requiring the active cooperation of corporate partners has a much larger impact. While the (ex post) associated consequences for the freedom of contract are undeniable, it is difficult to see on what

[512] Vanhees, 'Art XI.167' (n 511) 86.

[513] Cf Hall Jr, 'Smells Like Slavery' (n 3) 227–28; Cooke, *Dissecting the Digital Dollar* (n 301) 153, 176; Giblin and Doctorow, *Chokepoint Capitalism* (n 305) 54–55. That such a right to audit is not a panacea is illustrated by a recent judgment in the *Garrix v Spinnin Records* case, see District Court Amsterdam 4 August 2023, docket number C/13/735802 / KG ZA 23-550 VVV/MB, ECLI:NL:RBAMS:2023:4976.

[514] See above, Sections 5.2.2.3 and 5.3.2.3.

[515] Code des Usages et des Bonnes Pratiques de l'Edition des Œuvres Musicales (n 172) s 3.4.

[516] ibid 3.6.

[517] Osborne and Sun, 'Economics of Streaming' (n 310) s 1.4.3.

[518] Cf Ramalho and Lopez-Tarruella, 'Implementation of the Directive 2011/77/EU' (n 45) 35, 49.

[519] See above, Section 5.3.2.3.

[520] See (1) in Belgium: Art XI.210(3) para 2 Belgian CEL (the right to request information under Belgian law is exercised in a purely collective manner, the compatibility of which with the Term Extension Directive is questionable, see Brison, 'Art XI.210' (n 46) 388; (2) in France: Art L 212-3-7(III) French IP Code; (3) in Germany: Art 79a(4) German Copyright Act; (4) in the Netherlands: Art 15g(2)–(3) *jo* 9b Dutch Neighbouring Rights Act; and (5) in the United Kingdom: Art 181HB(5)–(6) UK CDPA.

[521] Cf Bently and others, 'Strengthening the Position' (n 199) 45–46.

basis corporate partners may object to enhanced transparency – if not to perpetuate the current lack of transparency to their (commercial) advantage.[522]

This subsection focuses on the reporting obligations applicable to primary music contracts.[523] In the EU jurisdictions, these national provisions were partially harmonised by Article 19 DSM Directive. Analogue provisions were proposed in the United Kingdom in 2021.[524]

5.3.3.2.1 SCOPE OF ACTIVE REPORTING OBLIGATIONS Article 19(1) DSM Directive sets forth the first general, unwaivable[525] minimum benchmark for transparency as imposed by Member State laws on corporate partners who enter into a copyright exploitation contract with one or multiple musicians. It imposes on corporate partners an active duty to inform during the course of contract performance. The mechanism proposed in the United Kingdom in 2021 also expressly excluded contractual deviations, but was limited to transfers and exclusive licences and excluded employed artists from its scope.[526]

In Belgium and France, unwaivable active reporting obligations for contracts with both authors and performers were established in 2022.[527] The French legislator has opted to leave some aspects of the implementation of Article 19 DSM Directive open to sector-specific collective bargaining.[528] In the absence of a collective agreement, the modalities of the reporting obligations are to be set by the copyright exploitation contract. If the collective negotiation process is successful, the government may declare its results binding to all stakeholders – if not, the French Conseil d'État is set to intervene.[529] The pre-existing obligation under French law for record companies to actively report to performing musicians if the contract sets a royalty that is payable directly to the musician by the record company continues to apply.[530] This is also true for the waivable regime for publishing contracts under which the publisher has to provide the author with a detailed set of data upon request.[531]

522 Cf Commission, SWD(2016) 301 final (n 4) 183, 187.

523 As to secondary relationships, see below Section 5.4.3.2.

524 Arts 2–3 Copyright (Rights and Remuneration of Musicians, Etc.) HC Bill (2021–22) 19, proposing Arts 93D, 191N UK CDPA.

525 Art 23(1) *jo* Rec 81 DSM Directive.

526 Draft Arts 93D(1), (5), (6)(b), 191N(1), (5), (6) UK CDPA.

527 See (1) in Belgium: Arts XI.167/2 *jo* XI.167/6, XI.205/2 *jo* XI.205/6 Belgian CEL – the pre-existing Art XI.198 Belgian CEL was abolished and (2) in France: Arts L 131-5-3 *jo* L 131-5-1, L 212-3-4 *jo* 212-3-1 French IP Code; Vincent Varet, 'L'obligation de Transparence' [2021] PI 45.

528 Such as the frequency of reporting and the applicability exemption for insignificant contributions, see Arts L 131-5-1, 212-3-1 French IP Code.

529 Arts L 131-5-1(III), L 212-3-1(III) French IP Code.

530 Art L 212-15 French IP Code; Lucas and others, *Traité de la Propriété Littéraire et Artistique* (n 17) 1156. This rule was rendered generally binding by the French Act of 7 July 2016 and also applies to contracts that were already ongoing at that time (see Art 110 French Act of 7 July 2016).

531 Art L 132-13 French IP Code; Lucas and others, *Traité de la Propriété Littéraire et Artistique* (n 17) 710–12. Cf Art L 131-7 French IP Code. See also in the context of literary publishing, Arts

The German Copyright Act did not provide for general active reporting prior to the implementation of the DSM Directive – only a right to request information, which applied to both transfers (for performers) and licences (for composers and performers).[532] In 2022, the German legislator transformed this obligation into a generalised active reporting obligation.[533] The German Publishing Act also still establishes a (waivable) reporting obligation for publishing contracts.[534]

Dutch law, finally, used to only provide a right to audit aimed at operationalising artists' right to termination of the contract in case of non-exploitation.[535] Article 25ca Dutch Copyright Act establishes an unwaivable[536] general reporting obligation under Dutch law.[537]

Specific reporting obligations may apply to other types of copyright exploitation contracts, such as performance contracts[538] and audio-visual production contracts.[539] Moreover, EU copyright law sets other analogous reporting obligations, such as the transparency obligations imposed on CMOs through the CRM Directive,[540] the right to information established in the context of the value gap provision[541] and the resale right.[542]

The first step of the analysis of Article 19 DSM Directive is to determine its scope. Article 19 covers contracts resulting in either a transfer or a licence to exclusive exploitation rights and covers both composing and performing musicians.[543] As is the case for Articles 20 and 22 DSM Directive, Article 19 DSM Directive covers the exploitation rights that have been harmonised under EU law – so not the right to

L 132-17-3, L 132-17-4 French IP Code; Lucas and others, *Traité de la Propriété Littéraire et Artistique* (n 17) 735–37.

532 Former Art 32d *jo* 79(2a) German Copyright Act. See Schulze, 'Das Urhebervertragsrecht' (n 58) 684.

533 Amended Art 32d *jo* 79(2a) German Copyright Act; Jan Bernd Nordemann and others, 'Transposition of the DSM Copyright Directive 2019/790 in Germany' [2021] AM 325, 327.

534 Art 24 German Publishing Act; Fromm and Nordemann, *Urheberrecht* (n 58) 2105–07.

535 Art 25e(4) Dutch Copyright Act *jo* Art 2b Dutch Neighbouring Rights Act; Visser and others, *ACR: Auteurscontractenrecht* (n 44) 166. On the use-it-or-lose-it provision under Dutch law, see above Section 5.2.2.3.2.

536 New Art 25h(1) Dutch Copyright Act *jo* Art 2b Dutch Neighbouring Rights Act.

537 As to performers, see Art 2b Dutch Neighbouring Rights Act.

538 See (1) in Belgium: Art XI.202 Belgian CEL and (2) in France: Art L 132-21 French IP Code. No specific rules applicable to performance contracts were found under German, Dutch or UK law.

539 See (1) in Belgium: former Arts XI.183(2), XI.206(4) Belgian CEL (both abolished in 2022) and (2) in France: Art L 132-28 French IP Code. Except for the presumption of transfer of exploitation rights, no specific rules applicable to audio-visual production contracts were found under German, Dutch or UK law.

540 Arts 18–23 CRM Directive.

541 Art 17(8) DSM Directive. See (1) in Belgium: Arts XI.228/5(2), XI.228/6 Belgian CEL; (2) in France: Arts L 137-3, L 219-3 French IP Code; (3) in Germany: Art 19 German OCSSP Act; and (4) in the Netherlands: Art 29c(4) Dutch Copyright Act.

542 Art 9 Resale Right Directive. See (1) in Belgium: Art XI.178(4) Belgian CEL; (2) in France: Art L 122-8 para 4 French IP Code; (3) in Germany: Art 26(4)–(5) German Copyright Act; and (4) in the Netherlands: Art 43d Dutch Copyright Act.

543 Art 19(1) *jo* Rec 77 DSM Directive. On secondary relationships, see below, Section 5.4.3.2.

adaptation.[544] Recital 75 DSM Directive refers somewhat vaguely to rights that are 'relevant' to the exploitation, including merchandising revenues.[545] The type and amount of remuneration set in the contract are irrelevant. Thus the reporting obligation affects contracts with either royalty arrangements or lump sum fees – in order for the artist to be able to secure relevant information for the application of contract adjustment mechanisms under national law.[546] Finally, as opposed to the relevant provision under German law,[547] Article 19 does not expressly exclude contracts where the agreed remuneration equals zero, such as open licences. While Recital 74 indicates that the need for reporting obligations does not arise in such a case, an express exclusion of open licences would have been beneficial.[548]

The harmonised active reporting obligation does not apply to contributions deemed 'not significant' and cases where this would be 'disproportionate'.[549] The open language of these exemptions engenders legal uncertainty[550] and leaves significant margin for abuse. A broad interpretation of those 'escape routes' would result in reporting obligations that ultimately only benefit a small minority.[551] An additional reason for a restrictive interpretation of these exemptions is that the harmonised contract adjustment mechanism is not subject to a limitation based on the insignificance of artists' contributions, or a proportionality clause. As reporting obligations seek to operationalise contract adjustment mechanisms, coherency considerations advocate in favour of a broad scope of the reporting obligation.

First, Member States may render the reporting obligations inapplicable if the artist's contribution is 'not significant having regard to the overall work or performance', unless the artist needs to obtain access to the information in order to be able to have recourse to the contract adjustment mechanism.[552] Germany, the Netherlands and Belgium have opted to include such an exemption in their national legal framework.[553] German law refers to 'secondary' contributions.

[544] Rec 74 DSM Directive.

[545] Despite the absence of EU harmonisation regarding merchandising (save as to trademark law), merchandising revenues are also expressly included in the amount to be taken into account for the application of the harmonised contract adjustment mechanism, see above, Section 5.3.2.3.1.

[546] See above, Section 5.3.2.3.

[547] Art 32d(1) German Copyright Act.

[548] Cf Bently and others, 'Strengthening the Position' (n 199) 84; European Copyright Society, 'Comment' (n 54) 137.

[549] Ananay Aguilar, 'The New Copyright Directive: Fair Remuneration in Exploitation Contracts of Authors and Performers – Part 1, Articles 18 and 19' (*Kluwer Copyright Blog*, 15 July 2019) <https://bit.ly/3PTLw3L>.

[550] Shapiro, 'Remuneration Provisions in the DSM Copyright Directive and the Audiovisual Industry in the EU' (n 38) 778, 782.

[551] Ananay Aguilar, '"We Want Artists to Be Fully and Fairly Paid for Their Work". Discourses on Fairness in the Neoliberal European Copyright Reform' [2018] JIPITEC 160, 167; European Copyright Society, 'Comment' (n 54) 132, 134.

[552] Art 19(4) DSM Directive. See also Rec 77 DSM Directive.

[553] See (1) in Germany: Art 32d(2)(1) German Copyright Act; (2) in the Netherlands: Art 25ca(3) Dutch Copyright Act *jo* Art 2b Dutch Neighbouring Rights Act; and (3) in Belgium: Art XI.167/2(3), XI.205/2(3) Belgian CEL.

A contribution is deemed secondary and thus insignificant if it has little influence on the overall impression created by the content at issue, for example because it is not the typical content.[554] France leaves the issue open for determination through sector-specific collective bargaining.[555]

This reference to the 'significance' of a certain contribution may be linked to the substantive criterion of the use of a certain contribution in a given piece of music as a way to determine what is 'fair'.[556] Actually determining the 'significance' of a given (musical) contribution in the context of a larger whole amounts to guesswork in many cases, and moreover runs counter to the collaborative process of music-making.[557] While the use of a flexible sliding scale may be helpful in establishing what is 'fair' exploitation and/or remuneration, drawing a line in the sand between an 'insignificant' and a 'significant' contribution is an altogether different story. Contractual modulation and a broad interpretation of this concept are to be expected – presumably to the disadvantage of musicians.[558] The initial removal of this cut-off criterion by the European Parliament is therefore understandable.[559] This limitation was reinserted at a later stage of the legislative process at the EU level, but with a proviso meant to safeguard the interests of artists, namely that the application of the contract adjustment mechanism should be assured. The scope of this specification is unclear. Indeed, all musicians' requests for information may be associated with the application of the contract adjustment mechanism. Why would musicians want transparency in terms of remuneration if not to determine whether they are paid what is due to them and whether they have a right to claim additional remuneration? This would render the exemption of insignificant contributions very difficult to operationalise. This, in turn, begs the question what the remaining scope of this exemption is.[560] The application of the general prohibition on abuse of law may have been a (significantly) more elegant solution. The next best alternative may be to interpret the exclusion of insignificant contributions restrictively.[561] Inspiration may be sought from the draft UK mechanism, which excluded 'incidental' embodiments of a work from its scope.[562]

In addition, Member States may limit the reporting obligation to what may reasonably be expected in view of the (modest) amount of revenues garnered by

[554] Art 32d(2)(1) German Copyright Act; Bently and others, 'Strengthening the Position' (n 199) 61; Dreyer and others, *Urheberrecht* (n 58) 777; Möhring and Nicolini, *Urheberrecht* (n 58) 482.

[555] Arts L 131-5-1(I) para 2, L 212-3-1(I) para 2 French IP Code.

[556] See above, Sections 5.2.2.4 and 5.3.2.2.

[557] See above, Section 5.2.2.4.

[558] Cf Bently and others, 'Strengthening the Position' (n 199) 47.

[559] Parliament, 'Report on the Proposal for a Directive of the European Parliament, A8–0245/2018 (n 205) 69.

[560] The answer to this question likely lies in the lobbying process leading up to the DSM Directive, see Fair Internet Coalition, 'Joint Guidelines' (n 54) 16.

[561] Cf Hilty and Moscon, 'Part D – Copyright Contract Law (Article 10 and Articles 14–16 COM (2016) 593 Final)' (n 243) 74; Fair Internet Coalition, 'Joint Guidelines' (n 54) 15, 16.

[562] Draft Art 93D(6)(a) UK CDPA.

the content.[563] This is done under Belgian, German and Dutch law.[564] Conversely, the French regime does not include an express limitation based on proportionality considerations. However, such a limitation may yet arise from sector-specific collective bargaining. This limitation is meant to avoid disproportionate administrative burdens for corporate partners (such as SMEs) and leads to less stringent information obligations in terms of the types and level of information to be provided.[565]

For corporate partners, the compliance cost associated with the increased reporting obligations is undeniable.[566] The amount depends, first, on the size and roster of artists of the corporate partner: major corporate partners may divide these costs over a large number of artists, while smaller players do not have that luxury. As a result, reporting obligations affect SMEs in a particularly unfavourable way.[567] However, the objective of securing transparency is too essential to truly allow for a reporting obligation 'light' for SMEs.[568] Musicians should not be the 'victim' of the size of their corporate partner.[569]

Other criteria that affect the amount of compliance costs include the relevant methods of exploitation, the frequency of required reporting, the quality of data received from secondary exploiters such as DSPs, and already existing reporting practices.[570] In the music industry, the practice of active reporting is well-established.[571] While administrative costs may be quite high at present, technological progress leads to a significant and increasing degree of automation. Reference may be made to the automatic content recognition technology and rights management systems offered by companies like Audible Magic.[572] In the near future, this may lead to a further steep decrease in costs associated with the collection, processing and management of relevant data.[573] Moreover, if blockchain technology ever fulfils

563 Art 19(3) DSM Directive.

564 See (1) under Belgian law: Art XI.167/2(2); XI.205/2(2) Belgian CEL; (2) under German law: Art 32d(2)(2) German Copyright Act; and (3) under Dutch law: Art 25ca Dutch Copyright Act *jo* Art 2b Dutch Neighbouring Rights Act.

565 Art 19(3) DSM Directive.

566 Cf Europe Economics and others, 'Remuneration of Authors and Performers' (n 188) 146; Shapiro, 'Remuneration Provisions in the DSM Copyright Directive and the Audiovisual Industry in the EU' (n 38) 782.

567 Cf Shapiro, 'Remuneration Provisions in the DSM Copyright Directive and the Audiovisual Industry in the EU' (n 38) 778.

568 Cf Commission, SWD(2016) 301 final (n 4) 186.

569 On other ways in which SMEs could be supported, see Racine, 'L'Auteur et l'Acte de Création' (n 329) 65.

570 Cf Commission, SWD(2016) 301 final (n 4) 183–85.

571 Cf ibid.

572 <www.audiblemagic.com>.

573 Cf Europe Economics and others, 'Remuneration of Authors and Performers' (n 188) 146; Commission, SWD(2016) 301 final (n 4) 185; Aguilar, 'The New Copyright Directive: Part 1, Articles 18 and 19' (n 549).

its promise of an accurate, decentralised global copyright database, administrative costs may decrease even further.[574]

However, this optimistic view is unlikely to fully materialise in practice if no satisfactory solution is found to the metadata issue in the music industry.[575] Regardless, the vagueness of the disproportionality exemption may render it excessive. Moreover, its added value vis-à-vis the general contract law framework may be questioned. Indeed, if the application of a reporting obligation were actually disproportionate, such a claim could be deflected by the general prohibition on abuse of law. Therefore, a restrictive interpretation is merited.[576]

The scope of the harmonised reporting obligation is further affected by the collective dimension of copyright. First, Article 19 DSM Directive does not apply to contracts concluded between rightsholders and CMOs.[577] Further, as is the case for exploitation and remuneration,[578] collective bargaining may play a beneficial role in terms of enhancing transparency.[579] The EU legislator has sought to bolster this opportunity in the DSM Directive, by allowing Member States to favour collective bargaining agreements between stakeholders on transparency. In order to benefit from this, the transparency resulting from such collective agreements must be of the same or a higher level than the minimum requirements established by Article 19 DSM Directive.[580]

The French legislator has taken the opportunity to call upon the collective negotiation process in order to shape the new reporting obligations in the different CCIs.[581] The abovementioned 2017 code of practice of French music publishers contains express commitments in this sense.[582] Another example of more stringent transparency requirements based on collective action is provided by the Memorandum of Understanding signed by French music industry stakeholders in 2015.[583] The corresponding provision of German law also allows derogations from the right to information resulting from collective bargaining, assuming that such collective solutions guarantee a level of transparency comparable to the statutory

574 Hilty and Moscon, 'Part D – Copyright Contract Law (Article 10 and Articles 14–16 COM(2016) 593 Final)' (n 243) 74.

575 See Chapter 2, Section 2.5.

576 Cf Hilty and Moscon, 'Part D – Copyright Contract Law (Article 10 and Articles 14–16 COM (2016) 593 Final)' (n 243) 74; Fair Internet Coalition, 'Joint Guidelines' (n 54) 15, 16.

577 Art 19(6) *jo* Rec 77 DSM Directive; European Copyright Society, 'Comment' (n 54) 137.

578 See above, Sections 5.2.2.4 and 5.3.2.2.

579 Cf Aguilar, 'The New Copyright Directive: Part 1, Articles 18 and 19' (n 549); Fair Internet Coalition, 'Joint Guidelines' (n 54) 16; European Copyright Society, 'Comment' (n 54) 133, 138, 143; Xalabarder, 'The Remuneration of Authors and Performers' (n 52) 145–46.

580 Art 19(5) *jo* Rec 77 DSM Directive.

581 Arts L 131-5-1, L 212-3-1 French IP Code.

582 Code des Usages et des Bonnes Pratiques de l'Edition des Œuvres Musicales (n 172) s 3.5, 3.6.

583 Memorandum of Understanding 2 October 2015 (n 331).

benchmark.[584] A similar solution has been implemented under Belgian law.[585] The corresponding provision of Dutch law does not expressly refer to the added value of collective bargaining in further shaping active reporting obligations.[586]

Finally, a note on the temporal scope of reporting obligations is merited. The argument against their application to ongoing contracts is not convincing, given the seminal importance of transparency throughout the music value chain. As the DSM Directive already dates from 2019, corporate partners had sufficient time by June 2022 to enhance their reporting practices in a way that adheres to the minimum benchmarks.[587] Conversely, any retroactive application of reporting obligations to past exploitation activities is to be excluded.

5.3.3.2.2 CONTENT OF ACTIVE REPORTING OBLIGATIONS The next step is to review the content of the active reporting obligations and interpret the resulting commitments for corporate partners. The objective is to ensure a high level of transparency.[588]

The first issue to be tackled is which information is covered by the reporting obligations.[589] Article 19 DSM Directive requires information to be transmitted as regards both exploitation and remuneration. Recital 75 DSM Directive adds that the information must be up-to-date, relevant and comprehensive. The first requirement refers to the need for artists to have access to recent data. The second requirement indicates that the information must relate to exploitation[590] of the music for which the musician(s) is(are) supposed to obtain remuneration. If there is no exploitation, logic dictates that the reporting obligation should cease to apply.[591] However, a musician also has the right to know that no exploitation takes place, to allow effective recourse to the use-it-or-lose-it clause.[592] In any case, if the music is (again) subject to exploitation, information relating to it must be adequate and accurate for

[584] Art 32d(3) German Copyright Act; Dreyer and others, *Urheberrecht* (n 58) 778; Möhring and Nicolini, *Urheberrecht* (n 58) 789.

[585] Art XI.167/5(4°), XI.205/5(4°) Belgian CEL.

[586] See, however, the reference to transparency in the Dutch Fair Practice Code at <https://bit.ly/3joPsQv>.

[587] Cf European Copyright Society, 'Comment' (n 54) 139; Rosati, *Copyright in the Digital Single Market* (n 81) 380.

[588] Art 19(3) DSM Directive. The initial Commission proposal referred to the need to secure an 'appropriate' level of transparency. This was changed to a 'high' level by the European Parliament, see Parliament, 'Report on the Proposal for a Directive of the European Parliament, A8–0245/2018 (n 205) 68–69.

[589] An associated issue is the interplay of reporting obligations with trade secrets and data protection rules. Both regimes may lead to obstacles to the implementation of reporting obligations in practice, see Chapter 7, Section 7.3.

[590] See above, Section 5.2.

[591] See Recs 72, 74 DSM Directive; Rosati, *Copyright in the Digital Single Market* (n 81) 376–77. See expressly in Belgium: Arts XI.167/2, XI.205/2 Belgian CEL, subject to a requirement to notify the artist(s) that exploitation has ceased.

[592] See above, Section 5.2.2.3.

the requirement of relevance to be fulfilled. Third, the information must cover all relevant sources of revenue.[593]

In addition to the three general requirements set forth above, sector-specific regulation established through scoping stakeholder consultations may further concretise the information that is to be provided.[594] Important work has already been done. In particular, reference may be made to the Transparency Guide compiled by Chris Cooke with the aid of the Music Manager's Forum (MMF, based in the United Kingdom),[595] the 2015 memorandum of understanding signed by French music industry stakeholders[596] and the 2023 UK Industry Agreement on Music Streaming Metadata.[597]

Information should first and foremost be available on the content itself, such as the ISRC and ISWC codes and information on all contributors and/or rightsholders.[598] Further information to be provided consists of three pillars, namely the relevant exploitation activities, the revenues garnered by the corporate partner(s) and the remuneration provided to the artist on this basis.[599]

The first aspect of the relevant information pertains to the way in which the content is exploited. We can rely on the conceptualisation of 'methods of exploitation'.[600] The main distinction is that between physical sales, digital sales and streaming.

For physical and digital sales, the relevant information may be usefully linked with the concept of 'copies'. For physical sales, the information includes the number of copies manufactured in the course of the year, the number in stock, the number sold, the number used for marketing purposes or otherwise provided for free, as well as the number of copies that have been returned or destroyed, or otherwise deemed unusable.[601] The information regarding digital sales may also refer to copies, but without specifications particular to analogue copies, such as the number manufactured, in stock, returned or destroyed. Thus, relevant information regarding digital copies includes the number of sales, the number provided for free and the number deemed unusable for technical reasons.

[593] As indicated above, Art 19 DSM Directive includes merchandising revenues in the potentially relevant sources of revenue.

[594] Rec 77 DSM Directive. Cf Commission, SWD(2016) 301 final (n 4) 178.

[595] Cooke, *Dissecting the Digital Dollar* (n 301) 142–55. See also Chris Cooke, 'CMU + TGE: Music + Data' (The Great Escape Conference, Brighton and Hove, 2022).

[596] Memorandum of Understanding 2 October 2015 (n 331).

[597] UK IPO, Guidance: United Kingdom Industry Agreement on Music Streaming Metadata (31 July 2023) <https://bit.ly/3EqYsZI>.

[598] Cooke, *Dissecting the Digital Dollar* (n 301) 113.

[599] Cf European Copyright Society, 'Comment' (n 54) 143.

[600] See Chapter 4, Section 4.4.1.2.

[601] This list was largely based Art L 132-13 French IP Code (and, by analogy, Art L 132-17-3 French IP Code).

When it comes to streaming, the concept of 'copies' is moot.[602] In the streaming age, the relevant unit is a stream. This is why the total number of streams or 'track plays' should be reported, as well as the source of such plays – a direct user request, the user's feed or personal library, or a playlist.[603] Additional relevant information includes whether the user skipped (part of) a track and whether it was added to a playlist and/or personal library.[604] Finally, it is important for musicians to know their total listener count and/or follower numbers, including their demographics (such as gender or age) and location, the latter in order to inform the organisation of concert tours.[605]

For physical sales, digital downloads and streaming, the information should be provided separately per method of exploitation.[606] As to digital downloads and streaming, the report should provide separate information per DSP as to number of units. Finally, the report should clearly state what territories are covered.[607]

On the revenue side, for both physical and digital sales, the relevant information includes the unit price (the income received by the corporate partner from the sales per unit[608]), information regarding value-added tax (VAT), as applicable, and an overview of the total revenues.[609] For streaming, information should be provided as to the ex post calculated per-stream rate, applicable VAT and the total revenues – with distinct information per DSP.[610] For all methods of exploitation, the revenues should be distinguished per relevant territory, given that separate remuneration arrangements may apply.

Transparency is also required as to quantifiable indirect revenue sources, in particular breakage, equity and non-allocable income assigned to corporate partners.[611] Article 19 does not expressly include such indirect revenue flows. The requirement of relevance seems to indicate the need for a causal link between the revenues to which the reporting obligation applies and the exploitation of the content. The same conclusion follows from an analysis of the relevant provisions of national law.[612] The requisite strength of such causal link, however, is up for debate. Full transparency is merited for all quantifiable revenue flows, including

602 See also above, Sections 5.2.2 and 5.3.2.2.

603 Commission, SWD(2016) 301 final (n 4) 212; Cooke, *Dissecting the Digital Dollar* (n 301) 146, 167.

604 Cooke, *Dissecting the Digital Dollar* (n 301) 146–47.

605 ibid 147.

606 Memorandum of Understanding 2 October 2015 (n 331) s 5.6.

607 ibid; Commission, SWD(2016) 301 final (n 4) 212.

608 Cf what is foreseen for literary publishing in Art L 132-17-3(I)(2) French IP Code.

609 Memorandum of Understanding 2 October 2015 (n 331) s 5.6; Commission, SWD(2016) 301 final (n 4) 212.

610 Commission, SWD(2016) 301 final (n 4) 212; Cooke, *Dissecting the Digital Dollar* (n 301) 148.

611 Cf European Copyright Society, 'Comment' (n 54) 143.

612 See (1) in Belgium: Arts XI.167/2, XI.205/2 Belgian CEL; (2) in France: Arts L 131-5-1(I), L 212-3-1 (I) French IP Code (which refer to the *revenus générés par l'exploitation*, ie the revenues generated by the exploitation); (3) in Germany: Art 32d(1) German Copyright Act (which refers to the *Umfang der Werknutzung und die hieraus gezogenen Erträge und Vorteile*, ie the extent of the exploitation of the work and the revenues and profits *derived therefrom*); (4) in the Netherlands: Art 25ca(1) Dutch Copyright Act (which refers to the methods of exploitation and

indirect sources of revenues. Article 19 DSM Directive does not stand in the way of such an interpretation.[613] This position is supported by the express inclusion of merchandising revenue in the scope of the harmonised reporting obligation, as confirmed by Recital 75 DSM Directive. Moreover, even if Article 19 DSM Directive were not to include indirect revenues, Member States may include them in the national regimes, in view of the minimum harmonising nature of Article 19 DSM Directive. Artists should be able to gain access to the total revenues generated, as well as the total remuneration due.

The question further arises whether the artist should also obtain access to information regarding their corporate partners' profits. This is linked with the appropriate scope of the contract adjustment mechanism. If the application of the contract adjustment mechanism depends on the corporate partner's revenues, the provision of information on revenues may be sufficient. If the contract adjustment mechanism is linked with profits, the operationalisation of the contract adjustment mechanism requires the artist to also have access to this information. The relevant provisions in Belgium, France and the Netherlands do not expressly mandate transparency as to the corporate partner's profits. Nor does the draft UK mechanism. Conversely, the German reporting obligation refers to both revenues and profits.[614] Independent of that, it may be argued that the good-faith performance of contracts requires corporate partners to inform artists of their profits, while the overarching principle of freedom of contract cautions against overreach in this regard.

The final pillar of the reporting obligation consists of comprehensive information concerning the remuneration due. Reports should not only provide the total amount due and the payment date(s), but also give a clear overview of the applicable royalty rates for each separate category of units (if a sliding scale of remuneration is used), indicating clearly which deductions and/or discounts are applied (including those by intermediary parties) – as well as the contractual basis.[615] In addition, clear information should be provided as to the calculation method of an artist's share relating to a given exploitation activity in case of collaborations.[616] In order to allow artists to fully grasp and assess their overall remuneration, the average royalty rate per unit should be provided as well. The total amounts due and paid should also be included.[617] If the remuneration arrangement makes use of an advance, the total

de daarmee gegenereerde inkomsten, ie the revenues *generated therewith*); and (5) in the United Kingdom: draft Arts 93D(1), 191N(1) UK CDPA.

613 Cf European Copyright Society, 'Comment' (n 54) 133.

614 Art 32d(1) German Copyright Act.

615 Memorandum of Understanding 2 October 2015 (n 331) s 5.6; Cooke, *Dissecting the Digital Dollar* (n 301) 148–49, 200, 207–08. Cf Arts 1(h), 2(b)(v)–(vi) *jo* 3 of the Annex to the CRM Directive.

616 Cf European Copyright Society, 'Comment' (n 54) 143.

617 Art L 132-13 French IP Code.

amount should be clearly indicated, as should the unrecouped part of this advance, if it is recoupable.[618]

The provision of all of the data listed above is necessary to give musicians insight into the fairness of their remuneration. However, it also risks leading to an information overload, with stakeholders drowning in data.[619] Digitisation has caused a dramatic increase in potentially available information on music exploitation and remuneration as well as general information pertaining to listeners in terms of listening and spending behaviour – 'audience data'.[620] An effective implementation of reporting obligations gives rise to an enormous and ever-expanding flow of data.[621] Much of the effectiveness of these reporting obligations will depend on how the relevant information is provided to corporate partners and, ultimately, musicians.[622]

The next step is to determine *how* corporate partners should provide information to musicians. Subsequent to Article 19 DSM Directive, corporate partners have an active duty to provide this information on a recurring basis throughout the course of contract performance.[623] At a minimum, artists should receive a report once every year.[624] The draft UK mechanism even speaks of quarterly reports, while the 2024 UK Voluntary Code of Good Practice on Transparency in Music Streaming refers to a report 'no less than twice a year'.[625] Further, under the EU mechanism, information relevant to a certain exploitation activity should be transmitted within a reasonable period following the exploitation.[626] The obligation to provide this report may be qualified as an obligation of result, while its quality (as well as that of the information included in it) rather implies an obligation of means. The report should be comprehensible and user-friendly, and should moreover allow artists to effectively assess the economic value of the rights – and thus whether the remuneration they

[618] Commission, SWD(2016) 301 final (n 4) 212.

[619] See eg Emmanuel Legrand, 'Synchtank Panel Addresses the Issue of Too Much Data' (*Legrand Network*, 18 May 2021) <https://bit.ly/3pb79k9>.

[620] Cf Baym, *Playing to the Crowd* (n 113) 115–19; Cooke, *Dissecting the Digital Dollar* (n 301) 112, 114, 135, 143.

[621] Rethink Music Initiative, 'Fair Music: Transparency and Payment Flows in the Music Industry' (n 8) 19; Cooke, *Dissecting the Digital Dollar* (n 301) 112, 143–44.

[622] See below, Section 5.4.3.2.

[623] Rec 75 DSM Directive.

[624] Art 19(1), Rec 75 DSM Directive. See (1) in Belgium: Arts 167(1), 205(3) Belgian CEL, requiring at least yearly reporting; (2) in France: Art L 132-13 French IP Code granting an at least annual right to request information in the context publishing contracts; Art L 212-15 French IP Code requiring bi-annual reporting in the context of royalty contracts with performing musicians; new Arts L 131-5-1, L 212-3-1 French IP Code, requiring at least yearly reporting; (3) in Germany: amended Art 32d(1) *jo* 79(2a) German Copyright Act, requiring at least yearly reporting; and (4) in the Netherlands: new Art 25ca Dutch Copyright Act *jo* Art 2b Dutch Neighbouring Rights Act, requiring at least yearly reporting.

[625] Draft Arts 93D(1), 191N(1) UK CDPA; Art 1.6 UK Voluntary Code of Good Practice on Transparency in Music Streaming (31 January 2024) <https://bit.ly/4bbBx32>.

[626] Cf Explanatory Memorandum Belgian Draft DSM Implementation Act (n 64) 48.

have received is appropriate and proportionate.[627] The link with the requirement of fair remuneration[628] is thus rendered explicit. Further, for efficiency reasons and to promote full transparency, the provision of information should be standardised.[629] More specific good practices refer to the use of an electronic format and the appointment of a representative acting as a one-stop-shop for reporting obligations within large(r) corporate partners.[630]

At the time of writing, it is too soon to gauge the substantive effects of Article 19 DSM Directive and assess whether additional regulatory intervention is desirable. This being said, the minimum benchmarks set by the DSM Directive are less stringent than the detailed accounting and reporting requirements that apply to CMOs, vis-à-vis both their members and users of protected content.[631] This is remarkable, especially since the interests of CMOs may be more aligned with those of artists than is the case for corporate partners.[632] The express link between the active reporting obligation and the transparency requirements for CMOs under UK law in the draft UK mechanism may therefore be welcomed.[633] Further concretisation and ensuing upward harmonisation of active reporting obligations of corporate partners may be merited, perhaps by way of a soft law instrument. The detailed operationalisation of reporting obligations in the music industry set out above may serve as a source of inspiration. Moreover, the establishment of a detailed industry standard as to the form and content of reports by corporate partners would be beneficial. An argument may also be made in favour of obliging transparency regarding the legal and governance structure of the corporate partner, relevant sister and parent companies, the revenues collected from DSPs that have not (yet) been allocated to a specific (group of) musician(s), and so forth.[634] As to the latter, requiring corporate partners to share certain information on the remuneration arrangements set up in secondary contracts with DSPs may be possible.[635] However, care must be taken to tailor the applicable rules in a sector-specific way.

[627] Rec 75 DSM Directive; Commission, SWD(2016) 301 final (n 4) 201.
[628] See above, Section 5.3.2.2.
[629] Cf Bently and others, 'Strengthening the Position' (n 199) 73.
[630] Memorandum of Understanding 2 October 2015 (n 331) s 5.6.
[631] See in particular Arts 18–22 *jo* Recs 34, 36, 55 CRM Directive.
[632] Cf Sylvie Nérisson, 'L'Article 5.7 de La Directive 2014/26/UE, Une Introduction Diabolique Du Droit Des Contrats Dans Le Droit d'Auteur de l'Union Européenne' in Silke von Lewinski (ed), *Remuneration for the Use of Works. Exclusivity vs Other Approaches* (De Gruyter 2017) 262–63; Pál Tomori, 'Need and Options for Regulatory Intervention' in Silke von Lewinski (ed), *Remuneration for the Use of Works. Exclusivity vs Other Approaches* (De Gruyter 2017) 403; AEPO-ARTIS, 'Performers' Rights in International and European Legislation: Situation and Elements for Improvement' (n 238) 141.
[633] Draft Arts 93D(2), 191N(2) UK CDPA.
[634] Cf the content of the annual transparency report mandated by Art 22(2) CRM Directive, as set forth in of the Annex to the CRM Directive.
[635] Cf Cooke, *Dissecting the Digital Dollar* (n 301) 150–52.

The final issue is what happens if corporate partners fail to fulfil their obligations. In order for transparency requirements to be effective, a clear sanction mechanism must be available. This issue is not addressed at the EU level. National legislators are free to determine the applicable sanction(s).[636] Given the importance of transparency to the functioning of the music ecosystem, the corporate partner's sustained inaction should be sanctionable with termination of the contract and rights reversion – independent of the amount of information that is to be provided.[637] The proposed amendments of the European Parliament to the Commission Proposal for the DSM Directive covered the extension of the scope of the harmonised right of revocation – including the right to revoke exclusivity – to function as a sanction for sustained non-compliance with the active reporting obligation.[638] The proposed revocation mechanism was to apply to transfers and exclusive licences by authors or performers in case of a 'continuous lack of regular reporting' in accordance with the active reporting obligation.[639] Moreover, it allowed Member States to establish sector-specific national rules and set certain procedural requirements, including the need to grant corporate partners a reasonable time to comply following a written notification of their shortcomings.[640] This proposal eventually did not make the cut. While a similar outcome could be reached through the application of general contract rules regulating breach of contract, an express provision in this sense, allowing for contract termination in case of serious breach of applicable reporting obligations, would have been beneficial.[641] Moreover, this would increase coherency with the revocation mechanism harmonised through Article 22 DSM Directive.[642] It would also increase incentives for corporate partners to comply with active reporting obligations. The French regime as to literary publishing may serve as an additional source of inspiration.[643] In the context of music publishing, the French 2017 code of conduct establishes a sanction of termination both if the music publisher does not provide a report within three months after having been put on notice, as well as if the deadline for active reporting is missed too often over the course of three years.[644]

636 Cf Rosati, *Copyright in the Digital Single Market* (n 81) 378.

637 Raad voor de Intellectuele Eigendom, 'Advies' (n 64) 101; European Copyright Society, 'Comment' (n 54) 143.

638 See Parliament, 'Report on the Proposal for a Directive of the European Parliament, A8–0245/2018 (n 205) 70–71.

639 Draft Art 16a(1) DSM Directive, as proposed by the European Parliament.

640 Draft Art 16a(1)–(2) DSM Directive, as proposed by the European Parliament.

641 Cf the outcome in *Crosstown Music Co 1 LLC v Rive Droite Music Ltd* [2010] EWCA Civ 1222; [2012] Ch 68.

642 See above, Section 5.2.2.3.

643 See relevant case law referred to in Lardinois, *Les Contrats Commentés de l'Industrie de La Musique 2.0* (n 18) 122. French law provides for additional specifications for the book sector, see Art L 132-17-3(II)-(III), 132-17-4 French IP Code.

644 Code des Usages et des Bonnes Pratiques de l'Edition des Œuvres Musicales (n 172) s 3.6. Cf Hugenholtz and Guibault, 'Auteurscontractenrecht' (n 58) 74; Racine, 'L'Auteur et l'Acte de Création' (n 329) 111.

If the corporate partner produces a report, but no corroborating evidence, the sanction under French law is to force the corporate partner to provide the evidence that is needed to establish the accuracy of information provided.[645] Reference may also be made to the new injunction right under German law, which comes into play if an exploiter systematically violates active reporting obligations.[646] These sanctions are quite far-reaching, but appear justified given the large potential contribution of transparency to the music ecosystem. If the information is deficient, musicians should be able to obtain supplementary information that fulfils the substantive requirements set out above. If the corporate partner refuses to provide such information, the route of rights reversion should be available.[647]

5.4 REGULATION OF SECONDARY RELATIONSHIPS

5.4.1 *Structure*

This section reviews the scattered regulatory framework applicable to the performance phase of secondary relationships between musicians' initial corporate partners and third parties. These relationships play a seminal role in the music ecosystem and affect contracts with musicians in a significant way. This is especially true for streaming services, whose exploitation (and ensuing remuneration) activities are governed by contracts to which musicians are not a party. This section analyses how musicians can leverage the legal framework to exert influence on questions of exploitation and/or remuneration of protected music vis-à-vis parties who have been granted rights through a transfer or a sub-licence from the musician's initial contracting partner.

5.4.2 *Exploitation*

In accordance with the relative effect of contracts, an agreement in principle only binds the parties thereto; only the parties may insist upon its performance.[648]

[645] Art L 132-14 French IP Code.

[646] Art 36d German Copyright Act.

[647] Cf Dusollier and others, 'Contractual Arrangements Applicable to Creators' (n 17) 15; Racine, 'L'Auteur et l'Acte de Création' (n 329) 110.

[648] See (1) in Belgium: Art 1165 Belgian Civil Code; Lardinois, *Les Contrats Commentés de l'Industrie de La Musique 2.0* (n 18) 25; Claeys and Tanghe, *Algemeen Contractenrecht* (n 400) 379–428; (2) in France: Art 1199 French Civil Code; Buffelan-Lanore and Larribau-Terneyre, *Droit Civil. Les obligations* (n 400) 296, 547–51; Terré and others, *Droit Civil. Les Obligations* (n 400) 744–47; (3) in Germany: Art 311(1) German Civil Code; Markesinis and others, *The German Law of Contract* (n 240) 181–86; Medicus and Lorenz, *Schuldrecht I. Allgemeiner Teil* (n 240) 12; Fikentscher and Heinemann, *Schuldrecht* (n 240) 51–53; (4) in the Netherlands: while the old Art 1376 Dutch Civil Code was not included in the new Dutch Civil Code, the underlying principle remains applicable, see eg Dutch Supreme Court 11 July 2014, docket number 13/02493, ECLI:NL:HR:2014:1627; van Dunné, *Verbintenissenrecht*

Subject to a number of exceptions, contracts do not give rise to rights or obligations of third parties, unless a contractual arrangement to the contrary has been made.[649] If the musician is not a party to the contract with a secondary exploiter, they can in principle not force that third party to carry out certain exploitation activities. This is the case if the initial corporate partner transfers only the exploitation rights and not the corresponding obligations, or if they grant a sub-licence. In such cases, the musician is still likely to be able to have recourse to the initial corporate partner, but not to the third party. The secondary contract may expressly grant musicians the right to assert a duty to exploit vis-à-vis the third party, but this is unlikely. In case of a full contract transfer, the third party takes the place of the initial corporate partner in the initial contract and becomes subject to all the rights and obligations set out in that initial contract.[650]

If a third party is called upon to perform some or all of the exploitation activities concerning a given piece of music, musicians should be able to retain some degree of control (and thus agency) – especially in case of a transfer or an exclusive licence. Musicians should have some form of recourse vis-à-vis their initial contracting party regarding the (in)activity of the third party. There is therefore definitely an argument in favour of extending the scope of the use-it-or-lose-it clause to third parties.[651] This is the case under Dutch law.[652] Considerations that apply to initial corporate partners also ring true by analogy as to secondary relationships: music deserves to be heard – for efforts to be made for it to receive an audience.

It may be argued that the requirement for musicians' consent[653] at the moment of formation of the secondary contract suffices, and that an additional form of control would constitute a disproportionate encroachment upon both initial corporate partners' and secondary parties' freedom of contract. According to this line of argument, musicians have the possibility – and maybe even the duty – to research the identity and the characteristics of the secondary contracting party before consenting to the secondary grant. However, this is also true for the initial corporate partner, where the mere fact that consent is required at the start of the contract does

(n 400) 797–809; Carel Asser, *Verbintenissenrecht. Algemeen Overeenkomstenrecht* (Asser Serie 6. III*, 13th edn, Kluwer 2008) 435–42; Hijma and others, *Rechtshandeling en Overeenkomst* (n 500) 331–32; and (5) in the UK: Joseph Chitty and Hugh Beale, *Chitty on Contracts* (32nd edn, Sweet & Maxwell 2015) ch 18; Edwin Peel, *Treitel on the Law of Contract* (15th edn, Sweet & Maxwell 2020) ch 14; Mindy Chen-Wishart, *Contract Law* (7th edn, Oxford University Press 2022) 167–202.

649 See Valerie Withofs, *Contractsoverdracht* (Recht en Onderneming 47, die Keure 2015) 367–70.

650 See ibid 211–17, 469–505.

651 Lucas-Schloetter, 'The Remuneration of Authors and Performers in Copyright Contract Law' (n 26) 267; Ramalho and Lopez-Tarruella, 'Implementation of the Directive 2011/77/EU' (n 45) 19.

652 Art 25e(6) Dutch Copyright Act *jo* Art 2b Dutch Neighbouring Rights Act; Visser, 'Pippi Langkous en het nieuwe auteurscontractenrecht' (n 277) 1295; Houben and Visser, 'De Beëindiging van Muziekexploitatieovereenkomsten' (n 500) 142–43.

653 See Chapter 4, Section 4.5.

not release the corporate partner from the constraints of the law. Therefore, musicians should be able to reclaim their rights from secondary contracting parties that do not engage in fair exploitation, either via their initial corporate partner, or, preferably, through direct action against the secondary contracting party/parties. This is especially true where the musicians' consent was not required or was obtained in advance. In such a case, moreover, the initial corporate partner and the third party involved should remain jointly and severally liable for the fulfilment of the initial corporate partners' obligations under the initial contract, as is the case under German law.[654]

The relative effect of contracts also extends to the content of exploitation activities. While in the case of contract transfer, the initial corporate partner's obligations shift to the transferee, musicians can in principle not exert any influence vis-à-vis sub-licensees, except on the basis of moral rights protection, rules mandating good faith and/or the general prohibition on the abuse of law.[655] Given the restrictive application of these general principles, as well as the fact that these general rules are not tailored to the creative sector, this role is likely to be relegated to the background. Further obligations vis-à-vis third parties may excessively limit parties' freedom of contract. Moreover, it would not make sense to subject secondary contracting parties to stricter regulation than musicians' primary corporate partners. Much greater importance is attached to applicable obligations in terms of remuneration, which are discussed in the next subsection.

5.4.3 *Remuneration*

5.4.3.1 Fair Remuneration

In terms of remuneration, a distinction may be made between revenues arising from the secondary transaction (in case a transfer of rights is effectuated) and those arising from the exploitation activities of the third party or parties.

If a corporate partner transfers the exclusive rights of musicians to a third party, the musician cannot claim any rights on (part of) the net gains of the initial corporate partner through the sales transaction. The contract adjustment mechanism that was partially harmonised through the DSM Directive also applies to corporate partners' successors in title (so transferees, not sub-licensees) and could be invoked in such a context. However, it would be difficult to claim the existence of a manifest disproportion in the sense of this mechanism.

An option to strengthen musicians' position would be to find inspiration in the existing resale right for artworks. Subsequent to this unwaivable right, which is harmonised at the EU level, artists have a right to a percentage of the price of

[654] Art 34(4) German Copyright Act.
[655] See Withofs, *Contractsoverdracht* (n 649) 211–17, 367–70, 469–505.

public resales of their artwork following the initial sale.[656] Member States are free to operationalise the resale right through collective management, or to maintain its individual enforcement.[657] The resale right seeks to ensure that artists 'share in the economic success of their original works of art', thus contributing to a fairer balance between the interests of stakeholders.[658] The link with this book's objective of securing fair remuneration for all stakeholders in the streaming age is clear. A resale right for music could allow musicians to claim part of the profit made by their initial corporate partner through the sales transaction. This is not prohibited at the international or EU level. As to authors, Article 14*ter*(1) Berne Convention not only posits an inalienable 'right to an interest in resales' on the part of both the author of original 'works of art', but also for 'manuscripts of writers and composers', expressly acknowledging the possibility of extending the resale right to compositions. While the international framework concerning the protection of (fixations of) performances does not contain an equivalent provision, the minimum harmonising nature of the applicable EU norm implies that a resale right for performers could be envisaged. Such a right could be limited to transactions that exceed a certain monetary threshold and/or that take place after a certain minimum period following the initial transaction.[659] The specifics could be the subject of sector-specific dialogues. For the purpose of transparency and in order to allow effective monitoring, the operationalisation of such a right would greatly benefit from the establishment of an active reporting obligation for corporate partners as to relevant transactions, as well as a passive reporting obligation upon a musician's express request.[660]

However, it is difficult to say whether the establishment of a resale right for music would actually lead to increased income for musicians, given the possibility that this would result in a diminished initial transfer fee.[661] In order to establish whether or not this would be the case, further empirical research is needed.

[656] Art 1 Resale Right Directive; Thomas Dreier and P Bernt Hugenholtz (eds), *Concise European Copyright Law* (2nd edn, Kluwer Law International 2016) 491–510; Jane Ginsburg, 'Copyright' in *The Oxford Handbook of Intellectual Property Law* (Oxford Handbooks, Oxford University Press 2018) 509; Justine Pila and Paul Torremans, *European Intellectual Property Law* (2nd edn, Oxford University Press 2019) 304–05; Jens Gaster, 'The Resale Right Directive' in Irini Stamatoudi and Paul Torremans (eds), *EU Copyright Law. A Commentary* (Elgar Commentaries, Edward Elgar 2021) 255–78.

[657] Commission, 'The Implementation and Effect of the Resale Right Directive' (Report) COM (2011) 878 Final (14 December 2011) 8. See (1) in Belgium: Arts XI.173–178 *jo.* XV.110 Belgian CEL; (2) in France: Arts L122-8 and R122-2–R122-12 French IP Code; (3) in Germany: Art 26 German Copyright Act; (4) in the Netherlands: Arts 43–43g Dutch Copyright Act; and (5) in the United Kingdom: the Artist's Resale Right Regulations 2006 (SI 2016/346).

[658] Rec 3 Resale Right Directive.

[659] Cf Arts 1(3), 3 Resale Right Directive.

[660] Cf Art 9 *jo* Rec 30 Resale Right Directive.

[661] Cf Kretschmer and others, 'The Relationship between Copyright and Contract Law' (n 260) 79; Ruth Towse, *A Textbook of Cultural Economics* (2nd edn, Cambridge University Press 2019) 419–20.

In addition to the secondary transaction itself, secondary transferees' or sub-licensees' exploitation activities also garner revenues – at a rate that has been increasing significantly over the past few years.[662] The economic value of the exploitation activities carried out by DSPs under the sub-licences thus acquired from musicians' primary corporate partners is not to be underestimated. The same rings true as to their follow-on impact on the contractual relationship between musicians and their corporate partners.

On the one hand, substantive discussions concerning the activities of DSPs and their interplay with the CCIs have largely revolved around the issue of the so-called value gap. This relates to protected content that is shared on social media and online content-sharing service providers (OCSSPs) and for which the media industries seek to obtain remuneration. It refers to the significant difference that is said to exist between the economic value extracted from creative content by DSPs through exploitation, and the remuneration ultimately accruing to rightsholders.[663] The value gap issue ties in with the second dimension of the balance between copyright and other fundamental rights: the balance between rightsholders and users as well as exploiters of protected content.[664] As this book centres around the third dimension – the balance between interests within the music value chain itself – an in-depth analysis of the value gap issue is eschewed here. Instead, the analysis focuses on whether the revenues collected by secondary exploiters are subject to the protective framework for primary music contracts. Generally speaking, requirements applicable in terms of fair remuneration are not enforceable against third parties with whom musicians do not have a contractual bond, such as transferees and sublicensees.[665] Two types of exceptions apply. First, under German law, if the requisite consent of the musician(s) to the transaction was not required or was obtained in advance, the initial corporate partner and the third party involved remain jointly and severally liable for the fulfilment of the initial corporate partners' obligations under the initial contract with the musician.[666] This leads to an indirect application of the requirement of fair remuneration. Second, under Belgian law, in case the primary publishing contract is rescinded,[667] secondary (transfer or licence) contracts remain unaffected, but authors (not performers) have a direct remuneration claim vis-à-vis

[662] See Chapter 2, Section 2.3.

[663] On this topic from the perspective of the CCIs, see Paul Kempton and Massimo Travostino (eds), *Finding the Value in the Gap* (IAEL Yearbook, 2018).

[664] See Chapter 3, Section 3.2.1.

[665] Lucas-Schloetter, 'The Remuneration of Authors and Performers in Copyright Contract Law' (n 26) 258. Cf Mark Anderson, 'Assignments and Royalties Don't Mix' (2009) 4 JIPLP 283, 284–88. Under UK law, see *Barker v Stickney* [1919] 1 *KB* 121; John Adams, 'The Passing of the Burden of Royalty Payments' (2007) 4 IPQ 403; Arnold, *Performers' Rights* (n 370) 277–79.

[666] Art 34(4) *jo* 79(2a) German Copyright Act; Schricker, *Urheberrecht. Kommentar* (n 58) 736–51; Markellou, *Le Contrat d'Exploitation d'Auteur* (n 17) 232.

[667] For more detail on the termination of the contracts under review and the consequences thereof, see Chapter 6.

the third party.[668] This rule provides an opening, albeit rather limited, to an indirect application of the requirement of fair remuneration to secondary relationships in the field of copyright *sensu stricto*.

Moreover, the scope of some of the other specific rules on remuneration has been expressly extended to secondary relationships. The right to additional remuneration for emerging methods of exploitation under German and Dutch law may be directly enforced against third parties to which corporate partners have transferred (not licensed) musicians' rights.[669]

The significant economic value of secondary relationships should be coupled with additional regulatory action to ensure reciprocity in the form of a fair distribution of revenues. While an express extension of the principle of fair remuneration to such secondary relationships would be excessive, an argument may be made in favour of the application of a contract adjustment mechanism to all third-party corporate partners when an actionable disproportionality in revenue distribution arises, subject to applicable rules pertaining to prescriptive periods.[670]

As noted above, the harmonised contract adjustment mechanism also applies to transferees.[671] The German and Dutch provisions have a broader scope and allow artists to assert their rights on the basis of the contract adjustment mechanism against both transferees and sub-licensees.[672] In the Netherlands, such a direct claim is unwaivable, but subject to the conditions that the required objectionable disproportion arises subsequent to the grant of rights to the third party and that the third party acquires the exploitation revenues relating to the content.[673] In Germany, the direct claim is subject to the condition that the disproportion at issue results from proceeds or benefits enjoyed by that party.[674] This claim may not be waived in advance.[675] These jurisdictions may serve as a source of inspiration, not only in view of fairness considerations, but also given the reference to 'all the subsequent relevant revenues derived from the exploitation' in the disproportionality assessment under Article 20 DSM Directive. Indeed, 'all' revenues may be said to also include revenues accrued by third parties.[676]

668 Markellou, *Le Contrat d'Exploitation d'Auteur* (n 17) 232–34.

669 Arts 32c(2), 79b(2) German Copyright Act; Art 25c(6) Dutch Copyright Act *jo* Art 2b Dutch Neighbouring Rights Act; Visser and others, *ACR: Auteurscontractenrecht* (n 44) 141–42.

670 Cf Paramythiotis, 'Fairness in Copyright Contract Law' (n 219) 88–89.

671 Art 20(1) *jo* Rec 78 DSM Directive; Shapiro, 'Remuneration Provisions in the DSM Copyright Directive and the Audiovisual Industry in the EU' (n 38) 783.

672 Under French law, see also French Supreme Court 16 July 1998, docket number 96-10.123 <https://bit.ly/3Dn8Dfk>; Hugenholtz and Guibault, 'Auteurscontractenrecht' (n 58) 58–59.

673 Arts 25d(2) *jo* 25h(1) Dutch Copyright Act *jo* Art 2b Dutch Neighbouring Rights Act; van Gompel and others, 'Evaluatie Wet Auteurscontractenrecht: Eindrapport' (n 102) 38; Visser, 'Dutch Copyright Contract Law' (n 137) 32–33.

674 Arts 32a(2) *jo* 79(2a) German Copyright Act. See Reber, 'The "Further Fair Participation" Provision in Art 32 a (2) German Copyright Act' (n 339) 382–85.

675 Arts 32a(3) *jo* 79(2a) German Copyright Act.

676 Paramythiotis, 'Fairness in Copyright Contract Law' (n 219) 89.

It would be even more beneficial to the musician if the right to claim additional remuneration from a third-party transferee were not to exclude the possibility of claiming such remuneration from the initial corporate partner, subject to an internal regress mechanism between the initial corporate partner and the grantee.[677] However, this possibility is expressly excluded under German law: once a claim against the third party is possible, any claim vis-à-vis the initial corporate partner on that basis disappears.[678] Despite largely being modelled on its German counterpart, the corresponding provision under Dutch law does not expressly treat this hypothesis and appears to accommodate both sides of the argument.[679] In practice, contractual arrangements on this issue are likely.[680]

5.4.3.2 Transparency

Transparency is an inherent aspect of fair remuneration. However, the wealth of intermediaries in the streaming age leads to a multiplicity of contracts between primary and secondary corporate partners that is difficult, if not impossible to disentangle. While ALS data management companies and dedicated DSP artist dashboards that provide access to data analytics[681] may fulfil an important role, musicians are often unable to obtain credible data on digital use and streaming of their music in the long term.[682] By way of example, since August 2023, 'Spotify for Artists' only shows detailed streaming data for 'the past 2 years plus the year to date'.[683]

Transparency should apply throughout the entire music value chain. Given the ever-increasing economic role of DSPs, secondary relationships should not be overlooked.[684] This subsection reviews the reporting obligations that apply to secondary relationships.

677 Cf Reber, 'The "Further Fair Participation" Provision in Art 32 a (2) German Copyright Act' (n 339) 385.

678 Arts 32a(2) *jo* 79(2a), 32c(2), 79b(2) German Copyright Act.

679 Arts 25d(2), 25c(6) Dutch Copyright Act *jo* Art 2b Dutch Neighbouring Rights Act.

680 Visser, 'Pippi Langkous en het nieuwe auteurscontractenrecht' (n 277) 1295.

681 See eg Amazon Music for Artists <https://artists.amazonmusic.com>, Apple Music for Artists <https://artists.apple.com>, Deezer Backstage <https://backstage.deezer.com>, Spotify for Artists <https://artists.spotify.com>, etc.

682 See eg Giblin and Doctorow, *Chokepoint Capitalism* (n 305) 160. See eg the dispute between Dutch artist Mr Probz, his label (Left Lane Recordings), and Sony Music Entertainment, see District Court Amsterdam 10 September 2020, ECLI:NL:RBAMS:2020:4618 and, most recently at the time of writing, District Court Amsterdam 9 August 2023, ECLI:NL:RBAMS:2023:5087. See also [2021] AR 40–2.

683 <https://support.spotify.com/us/artists/article/data-retention>.

684 Cf Hilty and Moscon, 'Part D – Copyright Contract Law (Article 10 and Articles 14–16 COM (2016) 593 Final)' (n 243) 75; Aisling Quinn, 'Are Online Music Platforms Undermining the Principles of Copyright Law?' (2018) 13 JIPLP 49, 59–60; European Copyright Society, 'Comment' (n 54) 133, 143; William Deresiewicz, *The Death of the Artist. How Creators Are Struggling to Survive in the Age of Billionaires and Big Tech* (Henry Holt 2020) 318; Racine,

The reporting obligation that was harmonised by Article 19 DSM Directive also applies to third parties to which musicians' initial corporate partners have transferred their rights.[685] This proviso is also included in the UK draft mechanism.[686] Consequently, such transferees have to actively inform musicians. Whether the initial corporate partner's duty to inform lapses in such a case, is not specified at the EU level. The German regime expressly treats this hypothesis.[687] In case of a further transfer (or sub-licence), the musician also has the right to demand information and accountability from the third party/parties at issue.[688] The further transfer of rights therefore does not relieve the initial corporate partner of their obligation to provide relevant information upon request. No equivalent appears to be included under Belgian, Dutch or French copyright contract law.

The harmonised reporting obligation under EU law also applies to sub-licensees,[689] albeit only in a limited way. Instead of an active duty to inform, sub-licensees are only obliged to provide information upon request, if the initial corporate partner does not hold the necessary information.[690]

The procedure consists of several stages. First, the initial corporate partner must fulfil their own reporting obligation. Contrary to what is the case for further transfers, therefore, it is clear that a sub-licence does not exempt the initial corporate partner from the fulfilment of their reporting obligation. Second, the musician must analyse the information transferred and assess whether this information allows them to determine the economic value of their music, or whether additional information is required.[691] Third, the musician must request additional information from the initial corporate partner. In case they themselves hold additional information, such information must then be provided and, again, assessed by the musician. If only their sub-licensee(s) hold(s) the additional relevant information, the initial corporate partner must provide information on their identity.[692] Relevant sub-licensees may – and will often – be DSPs, but may also be sister companies to the initial corporate

'L'Auteur et l'Acte de Création' (n 329) 110; van Gompel and others, 'Evaluatie Wet Auteurscontractenrecht: Eindrapport' (n 102) 31.

685 See Art 19(1) DSM Directive, which refers to initial corporate partners as well as 'their successors in title'.

686 Draft Arts 93D(3), 191N(3) UK CDPA. Cf Art 5 UK Voluntary Code of Good Practice on Transparency in Music Streaming (31 January 2024) <https://bit.ly/4bbBx32>.

687 Amended Art 32e(1) *jo* 79(2a) German Copyright Act.

688 Third-party grantees fall within the scope of this right to information if they essentially economically determine the exploitation of the content at issue or if their revenues or profits lead to a disproportion in the sense of the German contract adjustment mechanism. The right of information only applies if the initial contracting partner fails to fulfil their reporting obligation within three months following the due date, or if the information that was provided falls short, see amended Art 32e(1) *jo* 79(2a) German Copyright Act.

689 Including sub-licences granted subsequent to the application of Art 17 DSM Directive, see Art 17(8) DSM Directive.

690 Art 19(2) DSM Directive. See critically Visser, 'Dutch Copyright Contract Law' (n 137) 29–30.

691 Rec 76 DSM Directive.

692 Art 19(2) DSM Directive.

partner. The multi-step approach condoned by Article 19 DSM Directive thus indirectly allows the initial corporate partner to take measures to retain certain time-sensitive information.[693] Further, as to the actual request for additional information vis-à-vis the sub-licensee, Member States may require musicians to go (directly or indirectly) through their initial corporate partner.[694] In such a case, the artist should be entitled to request information directly from the sub-licensee.[695] National regulatory approaches vary. The formulation of the Dutch provision suggests that the artist may choose to request information from either the initial corporate partner or the sub-licensee.[696] The Belgian provision goes in the same direction, but adds that a collective agreement may limit artists' choice.[697] Conversely, the new German rule provides that the sub-licensee must only provide information to artists if the musicians' initial corporate partner does not comply with their obligation to inform within three months of the due date, or if the information does not provide sufficient information about the exploitation by the third party/parties and/or the relevant revenues and profits.[698] Finally, the French regime leaves the procedure for information provision by third parties up to collective bargaining.[699]

A sub-licensee that is (finally) confronted with a request for additional information must provide it. The cooperation of unwilling sub-licensees may be secured in several different ways. A first clear incentive for sub-licensees to this end exists if the non-rendering of accounts is sanctioned by contract termination that also affects contracts further down the licensing chain.[700] Indeed, if the sub-licensee does not comply, the composer may claim termination of the initial contract, which would lead to the destruction of the chain of rights – to the disadvantage of the sub-licensee.[701] On the other hand, subsequent to the implementation of the DSM Directive, German law grants artists an injunction right if a third party systematically refuses to provide relevant information – similar to the right granted in the context of primary contractual relationships.[702] Remedies under national tort law may also apply.

If the sub-licensee cooperates, no real qualitative or quantitative benchmark appears to apply to the additional information they provide. Nor is the sub-licensee subject to any deadline to take action. It may be questioned whether many

693 Aguilar, 'The New Copyright Directive: Part 1, Articles 18 and 19' (n 549).

694 Art 19(2) DSM Directive; Fair Internet Coalition, 'Joint Guidelines' (n 54) 13.

695 Parliament, 'Report on the Proposal for a Directive of the European Parliament, A8–0245/2018 (n 205) 68.

696 Art 25ca(2) Dutch Copyright Act *jo* Art 2b Dutch Neighbouring Rights Act.

697 Arts XI.167/2(5), XI.205/2(5) Belgian CEL.

698 Amended Art 32e(1) *jo* 79(2a) German Copyright Act.

699 Arts L 131-5-1(II), L 212-3-1(II) French IP Code.

700 For publishing contracts under French law, see above, Section 5.3.3.2.2.

701 Cf Bently and others, 'Strengthening the Position' (n 199) 59. Under Belgian law, as noted above (Section 5.4.3.1), the termination of the primary publishing contract has no impact on the validity of secondary contracts. Instead, authors have a direct remuneration claim vis-à-vis the third party.

702 Art 36d German Copyright Act.

musicians will invoke this right to request information in view of both the burdensome set of steps and the lack of qualitative guarantees in terms of prospective return.[703] A more elegant and effective solution could have been to extend the reporting obligation not only to third-party transferees, but also to sub-licensees, as was done for exclusive licensees under the draft UK mechanism.[704] Moreover, if the information received from the initial corporate partner(s) falls short, a direct claim for musicians vis-à-vis both their initial corporate partner(s) and the relevant sublicensee(s) would be beneficial.

5.5 RESIDUAL REMUNERATION RIGHT FOR STREAMING

Above, focus lay on exclusive rights. However, exclusivity does not in itself equal (fair) scope, exploitation and/or remuneration. The pitfalls of contractual negotiations and the ensuing risks of unfairness remain. To avoid these pitfalls, the legislator can set in motion a shift away from exclusivity and towards remuneration – from property rule to liability rule.[705] A potential avenue presents itself in the form of an unwaivable, collectively managed remuneration right for the online use of protected music.[706] Such a right would focus on the digital sphere. It would be akin to the statutory mechanism for the rental right and has been gaining significant traction in recent years.[707]

Proponents of 'equitable remuneration' (ER) for streaming argue in favour of the combination of an exclusive right and a remuneration right for online exploitation. The initial exclusive right of musicians would still be transferable or susceptible to licensing to a corporate partner.[708] That corporate partner would then still be able to

[703] Cf Commission, SWD(2016) 301 final (n 4) 178.

[704] Draft Arts 93D(3), 191N(3) UK CDPA.

[705] Jens Schovsbo, 'The Necessity to Collectivize Copyright – and Dangers Thereof' in Jan Rosén (ed), *Individualism and Collectiveness in Intellectual Property Law* (ATRIP Intellectual Property, Edward Elgar 2012) 169, 177. Regarding the pitfalls of such an approach, see ibid 179–82.

[706] Daniel Johansson, 'Revenue Distribution from Music Streaming – A Quantitative Analysis of Swedish Artists on Spotify' (2023) 24–29; 'Information Session on the Music Streaming Market – SCCR 43 Day 4 Afternoon' (16 March 2023) <https://webcast.wipo.int/video/SCCR_43_2023-03-16_PM_118736>.

[707] Cf Art 5(1) Rental and Lending Directive; David Stopps, 'How to Make a Living from Music, Second Edition' (Creative Industries, WIPO 2014) 33–34; Europe Economics and others, 'Remuneration of Authors and Performers' (n 188) 23, 27; Tomori, 'Need and Options for Regulatory Intervention' (n 632) 400; Silke von Lewinski, 'A Model that May Indeed Help' in Silke von Lewinski (ed), *Remuneration for the Use of Works. Exclusivity vs Other Approaches* (De Gruyter 2017) 255–58; Xalabarder, 'The Principle of Appropriate and Proportionate Remuneration' (n 203) 29–31; DCMS Committee, 'Economics of Music Streaming (n 280) 34–43; Sylvie Nérisson, 'The Rental and Lending Rights Directive' in Irini Stamatoudi and Paul Torremans (eds), *EU Copyright Law. A Commentary* (Elgar Commentaries, Edward Elgar 2021) 135–36; Paramythiotis, 'Fairness in Copyright Contract Law' (n 219) 95.

[708] Xalabarder, 'The Principle of Appropriate and Proportionate Remuneration' (n 203) 25.

exploit this exclusive right, such as through the grant of (sub-)licences.[709] In other words, the corporate partner would still acquire an exclusive right in addition to their own exclusive neighbouring right, and would thus be able to maintain control in terms of exploitation.[710] Upon the grant of the musician's exclusive rights to the corporate partner, the musician(s) would retain an unwaivable, 'residual'[711] right to equitable remuneration, which would only kick in upon exploitation by the corporate partner, such as through the grant of (sub-)licences to a DSP.[712] Upon exploiting music in the context of such a secondary contractual relationship, the latter would then be liable to pay a fee to a CMO, which would distribute the ensuing revenues to musicians.[713] The amount due would be calculated on the basis of the level of exploitation of the DSP.[714] This would remove musicians' remuneration from the value chain that includes the corporate partner(s) and, by doing so, contribute to a fair return to musicians.[715] Only through (mandatory) collective management, it is argued, the playing field may be levelled in a way that fairness may be achieved in terms of remuneration.[716] Simultaneously, by allowing corporate partners to maintain control through exclusivity, positive effects may be expected in terms of efficiency.[717] The associated decrease in transaction costs would be beneficial to all stakeholders.[718]

Further theoretical support for the concept of ER arises from the substantive similarities between radio and music streaming, especially non-interactive discovery

[709] ibid 26, 37, 40, 43–44, 47.

[710] Europe Economics and others, 'Remuneration of Authors and Performers' (n 188) 154; Castle and Feijóo, 'Study on the Artists in the Digital Music Marketplace' (n 307) 6.

[711] 'Residual' refers to the fact that the remuneration right remains part of the musician's assets following the grant of rights to a corporate partner.

[712] Europe Economics and others, 'Remuneration of Authors and Performers' (n 188) 155; Raquel Xalabarder, 'Appropriate and Proportionate Remuneration' (European Copyright Society Conference – Copyright Challenges during the Pandemic (and Beyond), online, 21 May 2021); P Bernt Hugenholtz, 'Remuneration Rights and National Treatment' in Susy Frankel and others (eds), *Improving Intellectual Property* (Edward Elgar 2023) 347.

[713] Dusollier, 'An Effective and Comprehensive Contractual Protection of Creators and Performers' (n 89); Xalabarder, 'The Principle of Appropriate and Proportionate Remuneration' (n 203) 27; Castle and Feijóo, 'Study on the Artists in the Digital Music Marketplace' (n 307) 6; DCMS Committee, 'Economics of Music Streaming (n 280) 34–35.

[714] Dusollier and others, 'Contractual Arrangements Applicable to Creators' (n 17) 75.

[715] Europe Economics and others, 'Remuneration of Authors and Performers' (n 188) 119; Cooke, *Dissecting the Digital Dollar* (n 301) 96.

[716] Sylvie Nérisson, 'Collective Management and Exclusive Rights: Friends or Foes?' in Paul Torremans (ed), *Research Handbook on Copyright Law* (Research Handbooks in Intellectual Property, 2nd edn, Edward Elgar 2017) 441; von Lewinski, 'A Model that May Indeed Help' (n 707) 256–58; Malevanny, *Online Music Distribution* (n 109) 334–39, 375; European Copyright Society, 'Comment' (n 54) 142; Irina Eidsvold-Tøien, 'Remunerating Authors and Performers: Are Statutory Compensation Provisions Sufficient?' in Jens Schovsbo (ed), *The Exploitation of Intellectual Property Rights: In Search of the Right Balance* (ATRIP Intellectual Property, Edward Elgar 2023) 207–12.

[717] Cf Dusollier and others, 'Contractual Arrangements Applicable to Creators' (n 17) 75.

[718] Xalabarder, 'The Remuneration of Authors and Performers' (n 52) 142.

and recommendation mechanisms.[719] While much streaming activity has a strong likeness to radio play – and Spotify even has a feature that is expressly labelled as 'radio' – the current legal status and its ensuing administration differs widely. For radio, a 50/50 division between composition and phonogram is the norm, while the division for streaming is close to a 20/80 split.[720] As for the division of revenues between musicians and their corporate partners, again a 50/50 division for radio may be contrasted with a significantly lower proportionate return for musicians for music streaming.[721] This difference in legal and practical treatment between streaming and radio is difficult to justify, especially for non-interactive streaming.

However, the idea of ER for streaming is not at all free from criticism.[722] First, from the perspective of corporate partners, a certain mistrust towards changing the status quo may be forgiven.[723] Indeed, their fear that a redistribution of the pie may work to their commercial disadvantage may be justified. From the perspective of musicians, the shift away from exclusivity may lead to a certain loss of control regarding the exploitation of their music – and thus decreased agency.[724] However, situations where such loss of control would be the most palpable may be overcome through the application of moral rights protection. Moreover, the reality of exclusive rights is their transfer.[725] For many musicians, the idea of control is already illusory; the establishment of a statutory remuneration mechanism would not lead to any real 'loss' of control in practice.[726]

A counterargument that bears more weight is that, if effective collective bargaining mechanisms are in place and/or all record companies start paying royalties to heritage artists with unrecouped balances,[727] fair remuneration may be secured via these routes, in turn rendering ER for streaming unnecessary.[728]

719 Cf Giblin and Doctorow, *Chokepoint Capitalism* (n 305) 218.

720 See Chapter 2, Section 2.4.4.

721 Castle and Feijóo, 'Study on the Artists in the Digital Music Marketplace' (n 307) 7; DCMS Committee, 'Economics of Music Streaming' (n 280) 34–40.

722 See eg Will Page, 'Equitable Remuneration: Policy Options and Their Unintended Consequences' (2023). See however AEPO-ARTIS, 'The Music Industry Is Not Just a Label-Economy' (7 April 2023) <www.aepo-artis.org/the-music-industry-is-not-just-a-label-economy/>.

723 Cf DCMS Committee, 'Economics of Music Streaming' (n 280) 36–39. See also Giblin and Doctorow, *Chokepoint Capitalism* (n 305) 216.

724 Schovsbo, 'The Necessity to Collectivize Copyright' (n 705) 180–81; Commission, 'Report on the Responses to the Public Consultation on the Review of the EU Copyright Rules' (n 375) 80, 82; Commission, SWD(2016) 301 final (n 4) 30; Raad voor de Intellectuele Eigendom, 'Advies' (n 64) 77.

725 Raad voor de Intellectuele Eigendom, 'Advies' (n 64) 77.

726 Cf Thomas Dreier, 'Exclusive Rights' in Silke von Lewinski (ed), *Remuneration for the Use of Works. Exclusivity vs Other Approaches* (De Gruyter 2017) 15–16; AEPO-ARTIS, 'Performers' Rights in International and European Legislation: Situation and Elements for Improvement' (n 238) 9.

727 See above, Section 5.3.2.2.2.

728 Cf Commission, 'Report on the Responses to the Public Consultation on the Review of the EU Copyright Rules' (n 375) 80; Commission, SWD(2016) 301 final (n 4) 30; Brigitte Lindner, 'The Role of Collective Administration in New Business Models in the Audiovisual Sector' in Silke

However, the former primarily applies to countries with a strong collective bargaining tradition. Regardless, this may provide an alternative solution for risk-averse musicians who prefer an immediate (lump sum) return for their musical contributions.[729]

In addition, it has been argued that the redistributive effects of ER would only benefit a minority of musicians, not only because the revenue proportion accorded to (successful) featured artists would diminish, but also in view of the prospective lower flat fee for non-featured artists that this risks entailing in the long run.[730] However, a redistribution of revenues inevitably results in some stakeholders being worse off than before. While it is logical for prospective 'losers' to object to such a redistribution, we must adopt a holistic perspective and move towards a model that is as fair as possible for as many stakeholders as possible. Given the current lack of remuneration for many musicians, regulatory action is required, even if this risks leaving certain artists worse off than before.

Finally, from the perspective of users, the establishment of yet another copyright levy is likely to be a cause for concern, since a risk of increased transaction costs and double payment arises.[731] However, from a conceptual standpoint, the legal object of the potential fee payable on the basis of ER for streaming differs from the payment associated with the exploitation of an exclusive right. Nevertheless, care must be taken to avoid ER for streaming that would lead to an undue increase of total costs for music use. The removal of performers' contributions from the value chain through the establishment of ER for streaming would in itself require a downward adjustment of the fee charged by corporate partners. Indeed, the contrary could give rise to a potential abuse of dominant position through excessive pricing, as the fee charged would then not (or no longer) correspond to the economic value of the exploitation right granted.[732]

Several other practical obstacles to the implementation of ER for streaming arise, in particular as to the appropriate methods of calculation, collection and distribution.[733] As regards all three aspects, streamlining is desirable. Indeed, if ER is established in each country separately, with a vastly different set of conditions and procedures, this would lead to an increase in legal uncertainty and ensuing

von Lewinski (ed), *Remuneration for the Use of Works. Exclusivity vs Other Approaches* (De Gruyter 2017) 423–24.

729 Europe Economics and others, 'Remuneration of Authors and Performers' (n 188) 155–56.

730 Hesmondhalgh and others, 'Music Creators' Earnings in the Digital Era' (n 311) 97.

731 Cf William F Patry, *How to Fix Copyright* (Oxford University Press 2011) 486; Commission, 'Report on the Responses to the Public Consultation on the Review of the EU Copyright Rules' (n 375) 82; Commission, SWD(2016) 301 final (n 4) 31; Giblin and Doctorow, *Chokepoint Capitalism* (n 305) 216.

732 Cf above, Section 5.3.2.2.2.

733 'The Ten Things People Get Wrong about Streaming – Part Two' (n 306). Cf Sari Depreeuw, 'Mandatory Collective Management of Copyright: When the Road to Deadlock Is Paved with Good Intentions' (*Kluwer Copyright Blog*, 9 February 2022) <https://bit.ly/33emVmo>.

transaction costs, as well as a decrease in transparency.[734] The (at first) purely national nature of an ER system for streaming would lead to significant difficulties in ensuring cross-border licences.[735] Further, the most logical administration method for ER for streaming would be to have recourse to mandatory collective management. If this route is chosen, care must be taken to complete the web of reciprocity agreements between CMOs and further optimise the collective management process.[736] Moreover, due care is required for the interests of performers that are not (yet) a member of a CMO, as well as those who wish to distribute their music under an open licence.[737]

Finally, in countries with a strong collective bargaining tradition and/or a well-performing system of voluntary collective management for exclusive rights, effective recourse to such collective mechanisms should not be hindered. National legislators should have the possibility to opt for collective bargaining or voluntary collective management for digital exploitation instead of mandatory collective management through a residual remuneration right. As to the former, a legislative prerequisite should be that such collectively bargained arrangements can be made generally binding.

In order to establish ER for streaming, legislative intervention is necessary, since such a right cannot be created solely through bottom-up industry-led change. The international and EU regulatory levels neither expressly mandate nor prohibit the establishment of a statutory right to ER for streaming at the national level.[738]

Given the minimum harmonising nature of the DSM Directive, in principle nothing prevents Member States from setting up such a statutory remuneration mechanism.[739] The effective implementation of Article 18 DSM Directive requires

[734] Cf Commission, 'The Online Distribution of Audiovisual Works in the European Union: Opportunities and Challenges towards a Digital Single Market' (Green Paper) COM(2011) 427 final (13 July 2011) 16–17.

[735] Cf Commission, 'Report on the Responses to the Public Consultation on the Review of the EU Copyright Rules' (n 375) 82; Commission, SWD(2016) 301 final (n 4) 31.

[736] Europe Economics and others, 'Remuneration of Authors and Performers' (n 188) 155–56; 'The Ten Things People Get Wrong about Streaming – Part Two' (n 306).

[737] Bently and others, 'Strengthening the Position' (n 199) 51–52; 'The Ten Things People Get Wrong about Streaming – Part Two' (n 306).

[738] Cf Shapiro, 'Remuneration Provisions in the DSM Copyright Directive and the Audiovisual Industry in the EU' (n 38) 780; Xalabarder, 'The Principle of Appropriate and Proportionate Remuneration' (n 203) 28. For detail, see Christophe Geiger and Oleksandr Bulayenko, 'Creating Statutory Remuneration Rights in Copyright Law: What Policy Options under the International Legal Framework?' in Henning Grosse Ruse-Khan and Axel Metzger (eds), *Intellectual Property Ordering beyond Borders* (1st edn, Cambridge University Press 2022).

[739] Paloma López, 'The Making Available Right for Performers in Spain: A Statutory Remuneration Right Managed by Performers' Collecting Societies' in Silke von Lewinski (ed), *Remuneration for the Use of Works. Exclusivity vs Other Approaches* (De Gruyter 2017); DCMS Committee, 'Economics of Music Streaming' (n 280) 41; Frank Gotzen, 'L'approche belge de la rémunération directe des auteurs et des artistes dans les cas de transmissions par plateformes numériques' [2023] RIDA 52, 63, 65–66.

a substantive implementation that goes beyond simply pasting the principle of appropriate and proportionate remuneration into national law.[740] This includes the possibility of establishing a collectively managed remuneration right.[741] The express reference in the DSM Directive to the Member States' freedom to implement the principle of fair remuneration using 'different mechanisms' (Article 18), which 'could include collective bargaining and other mechanisms' (Recital 73), supports this position. Further, Recital 61 DSM Directive, one of the recitals accompanying Article 17, expressly notes the need to secure 'appropriate' remuneration for the use of protected content. Moreover, in the summer of 2022, European Commissioner for Internal Market Thierry Breton expressly confirmed that Member States may establish an unwaivable remuneration right when implementing the DSM Directive.[742]

While idealistic at present, a cross-border solution in tune with the global nature of the internet would be the preferred final solution. However, a global musician ER mechanism is unlikely to materialise in practice. Given the choice of the EU legislator not to require the implementation of ER in the DSM Directive, the best chances for performer ER at present reside at the national regulatory level.

The German legislator established a form of ER through the German OCSSP Act, the separate act implementing Article 17 DSM Directive.[743] The German legislator has granted artists, including both composing and performing musicians, an unwaivable right to 'appropriate' remuneration, payable by the OCSSP to the artist through collective management only.[744] This right arises for any communication to the public of the content at issue that is contractually authorised through the Article 17 licensing mechanism, provided that the artist has granted the right of communication to the public to a third party. The residual right to OCSSP remuneration does not apply if the third party having been granted the rights at issue is a CMO or a party active as a *Digitalvertrieb* – the latter being roughly translatable to a

740 See also Xalabarder, 'The Principle of Appropriate and Proportionate Remuneration' (n 203) 19; Xalabarder, 'Appropriate and Proportionate Remuneration' (n 712).

741 See Gotzen, 'L'approche belge de la rémunération directe des auteurs et des artistes dans les cas de transmissions par plateformes numériques' (n 739) 71–85.

742 Answer given by Mr Breton on behalf of the European Commission, 20 July 2022, E-001255/2022 <https://bit.ly/3CvfQei>. See also more recently Answer given by Mr Breton on behalf of the European Commission, 5 March 2024, E-000066/2024(ASW) <https://shorturl.at/fgrLP>. Cf the position of the European Parliament: 'European Parliament Resolution of 20 October 2021 on the Situation of Artists and the Cultural Recovery in the EU' (2020/2261(INI)) P9_TA (2021)0430 <https://bit.ly/3rVE78s>; Parliament, 'Report on the Proposal for a Directive of the European Parliament, A8–0245/2018 (n 205) 67; Aguilar, 'We Want Artists' (n 551) 161, 163; Xalabarder, 'The Principle of Appropriate and Proportionate Remuneration' (n 203) 11–12.

743 See above, Section 5.4.3.1.

744 Artur-Axel Wandtke and Saskia Ostendorff, *Urheberrecht* (De Gruyter Studium, 8th edn, De Gruyter 2021) 402–03; Matthias Leistner, 'The Implementation of Art 17 DSM Directive in Germany – A Primer with Some Comparative Remarks' (2022) 71 GRUR International 909, 913–14; Silke von Lewinski, 'The Implementation of the Digital Single Market Directive of 2019 in Germany' [2022] RIDA 57, 86.

'digital distributor'.[745] Truly DIY musicians therefore appear not to be covered by this collectively managed right to remuneration, allowing them instead to secure 'appropriate' remuneration through contractual means – in other words: through the exploitation of their exclusive rights.

In 2022, the Belgian legislator went even further and established ER for online exploitation by both OCSSPs and streaming services.[746] The relevant provisions establish that, if an author or performing artist has transferred their right of communication to the public in the context of the exploitation of their work and/or performance by an OCSSP and/or a streaming service, they retain an unwaivable, collectively managed right to remuneration in return for such exploitation.[747] This initiative was the subject of vehement discussion in the Belgian Parliament.[748] Several actions for annulment were filed with the Belgian Constitutional Court.[749] These cases are pending at the time of writing.

The implementation of the DSM Directive in the Netherlands did not entail the establishment of a statutory remuneration right. However, recent legislative evolutions may lead to the establishment of ER in the context of video on demand.[750] In France, no musician or performer ER has been established at the time of writing. Finally, while the Brennan Bill in the United Kingdom did propose to establish performer ER for streaming, this proposal did not make it into hard law.[751]

All things considered, and acknowledging that further empirical evidence is needed, it is submitted that ER for streaming in an ideal form may beneficial. Removing the remuneration for digital exploitation from the music value chain and subjecting it to direct payment via collective management would, at least partially,

[745] On the role of digital distributors such as DistroKid and TuneCore, see Chapter 2, Section 2.3.4.

[746] See Hendrik Vanhees, 'Twee Nieuwe Vergoedingsrechten Voor Auteurs En Uitvoerende Kunstenaars' [2022] IRDI 389; Frank Gotzen, 'The Belgian Approach to Direct Remuneration of Authors and Performers in the Case of Transmission via Digital Platforms' [2023] RIDA 163; Alain Strowel and Solène Festor de Suremain, 'The Belgian Implementation of the Rules on Copyright and Related Rights Contracts in the Digital Single Market Directive' in Simon Geiregat and Hendrik Vanhees (eds), *Copyright Contracts Tomorrow* (LeA 2023) 11–15.

[747] See Art XI.228/4 BCEL as to OCSSPs and Art XI.228/10 and XI.228/11 BCEL as to streaming services.

[748] See *Verslag van de Eerste Lezing, Wetsontwerp tot omzetting van Richtlijn (EU) 2019/790 van het Europees Parlement en de Raad van 17 april 2019 inzake auteursrechten en naburige rechten in de digitale eengemaakte markt en tot wijziging van Richtlijnen 96/9/EG en 2001/29/EG*, Parl St Kamer 21–22, nr 2608/3, 12, 22–34; *Verslag van de Tweede Lezing*, Parl St Kamer 2021–22, nr. 2608/6, 3–13.

[749] See cases with docket numbers 7922, 7924, 7926, 7927, retrieved via <www.const-court.be/nl/judgments/pending-cases>. See also Amélie Lacourt, Justine Radel-Cormann and Sophie Valais, 'Fair remuneration for creators in exploitation contracts' (European Audiovisual Observatory 2023) <https://shorturl.at/dwT68> 86–87.

[750] See draft Arts 45da, 45db Dutch Copyright Code <https://bit.ly/44o7vot>.

[751] Art 1 Copyright (Rights and Remuneration of Musicians, Etc.) HC Bill (2021–22) 19, proposing a new Art 191GA UK CDPA.

counter the existing opacity and thereby contribute to transparency and ensuing legal certainty.

An important precondition is a high-functioning system of collective management, with sustained attention to the transparency and governance of CMOs. Extensive legislative measures have already been introduced in this context.[752] Title II CRM Directive[753] was implemented into the national law of all four chosen EU jurisdictions, as well as the United Kingdom.[754] Among other things, this has led to a (maximum) cost percentage charged to members.[755] Further, there is a long line of case law regarding the application of the prohibition against abuse of a dominant position to the conduct of CMOs.[756] In addition, care must be taken to ensure that CMOs use technological advancements to render their operations leaner and more transparent, efficient and cost-effective. This may aid in bringing down the cost percentage. Furthermore, the current distribution of unallocated CMO revenue to successful members on a market-share basis deserves to be reconsidered.[757]

The appropriate formulation of a statutory right to equitable or 'fair' remuneration for performers is still open to debate. The corresponding provision of the Rental and Lending Directive may serve as a source of inspiration, as may the proposed formulation put forward by the European Parliament in the context of the DSM legislative process and the provisions of national law discussed above.[758] On this basis, the below proposal is made for a potential harmonising provision at the EU level. It outlines the essence of a right to ER while simultaneously leaving Member States the freedom to regulate its specifics, or to have recourse to collective bargaining:

Unwaivable right to fair remuneration

1. Where an author or a performer has transferred their exclusive right of making available in relation to their work or the fixation of their performance, they shall retain the right to obtain an equitable remuneration for the making available of their work or the fixation of this performance. National law shall determine from whom this remuneration may be claimed or collected.

[752] Daniel Gervais, 'General Report' in Jørgen Blomqvist (ed), *Copyright, to Be or Not to Be* (Ex Tuto 2019) 160–63.

[753] Arts 6–22 CRM Directive. The CRM Directive leads to minimum harmonisation, see Rec 9 CRM Directive. See also Recs 20–36 CRM Directive.

[754] See (1) in Belgium: Arts XI.246 through XI.283 Belgian CEL; (2) in France: Art L 321-1 through L 328-2 French IP Code; (3) in Germany: the German CMO Act; (4) in the Netherlands: the Dutch CMO Act; and (5) in the United Kingdom: the Collective Management of Copyright (EU Directive) Regulations 2016 (SI 2016/221).

[755] Art 22 CRM Directive *jo* Art 2(b)(vi) Annex CRM Directive. See eg Art XI.252(3) Belgian CEL.

[756] CMOs have eg been prevented from limiting musicians' exploitation choices (Case C-395/87 *BRT v SABAM II* [1974] ECLI:EU:C:1974:6) and have been forced to accept artists from abroad as CMO members (Case C-7/82 *GVL v Commission* [1983] ECLI:EU:C:1983:52).

[757] Aguilar, 'The Collective Management of Performers' Rights in the UK' (n 237) 26–41.

[758] See also Hilty and Moscon, 'Part F – Claims to Fair Compensation (Article 12 COM(2016) 593 Final)' (n 243) 96; Fair Internet Coalition, 'Joint Guidelines' (n 54) 8.

2. This right to obtain an equitable remuneration for making available is non-transferable and cannot be waived by authors or performers.
3. The administration of this right to fair remuneration for the making available of works or fixations of performances shall be entrusted to collective management organisations. By way of derogation, Member States may provide that, for agreements subject to or based on collective bargaining agreements having been made generally binding, the relevant collective bargaining agreements are applicable, provided that the remuneration for the making available of works or fixated performances meets the requirements of Article 18 DSM Directive.

5.6 OUTRO

This brings an end to the analysis and evaluation of the relevant legal framework as applicable to the performance phase of the music contracts under review. This chapter focused on the obligations of primary and secondary corporate partners in terms of both exploitation and remuneration. Section 5.2 argued that shortcomings in terms of fair exploitation should be sanctioned by a high-performing, unwaivable rights revocation mechanism. However, fair exploitation risks remaining rather meaningless if it is not accompanied by fair remuneration, as contended in Section 5.3. Due account must be taken of the digital environment and parties' evolving position throughout the contract. This translates into the desirability of a right to additional remuneration for emerging digital uses, as well as a contract adjustment mechanism that counters disproportionately unfair remuneration arrangements in extreme situations. Due attention must also be accorded to secondary relationships in terms of both exploitation and remuneration, as discussed in Section 5.4. Finally, Section 5.5 brought to the fore the potential establishment of a residual remuneration right for digital exploitation at the EU level.

6

Termination of the Contract

I want to break free.

—Queen[1]

6.1 INTRO

Both corporate partners and musicians may have valid reasons for wanting to terminate a contract. Forcing them to uphold the contract curbs party agency. Relevant reasons may include the aim of avoiding undue investment in an artist who has proven to be commercially unviable, the wish to escape unfair situations in terms of rights transfer, or cases of (perceived) unfairness in terms of exploitation and/or remuneration.[2] The excessive duration of a contract may in itself also give rise to problems. On a more general level, the exclusive nature of many music industry contracts sits uneasily with the vision of musicians as independent, creative actors.

This chapter reviews how the selected substantive legal regimes affect parties' possibility to terminate the contractual relationship. First, the chapter reviews potentially applicable limitations on contract duration (Section 6.2), as well as grounds for termination on the basis of breach of contract (Section 6.3). Taking a more practical view, the consequences of contract termination are then assessed, in order to gauge whether these consequences may amount to switching costs that prevent the termination of contracts in practice (Section 6.4).

6.2 LIMITATIONS ON CONTRACT DURATION

Music industry contracts usually subject musicians to an obligation of exclusivity that prevents them from seeking other prospects for a period of time. The duration of

[1] Music and lyrics by John Deacon, performance by Freddie Mercury.

[2] See Chapters 4 and 5 respectively.

exclusive exploitation contracts in the music industry has traditionally been defined by a number of albums, usually consisting of a minimum amount combined with an option clause on the part of the corporate partner for further albums, on contract terms set in advance.[3] As long as such an option is on the table, musicians' freedom to contract with another party is restricted.[4] Traditional exploitation contracts do not foresee any possibility for renegotiation or termination on the part of the musicians, while corporate partners may easily terminate the relationship by not exercising their right of first refusal.

In practice, only successful musicians are able to renegotiate the terms of their relationship with corporate partners.[5] Thus, the large majority of musicians may be locked into contracts and unable to escape some of the unfavourable terms concerning rights transfers and contract performance.[6] This primarily applies to legacy artists. In the course of recent decades, the average duration of music industry contracts has decreased. In parallel, full rights transfers have become less prevalent, as is the case for licences for life of copyright. However, this trend is not omnipresent. In addition, the techniques of cross-collateralisation, multiple rights deals and 360-degree deals lead to a longer contractual relationship in practice, in view of the enhanced degree of recoupment that such arrangements entail.[7]

3 Richard Caves, *Creative Industries. Contracts between Art and Commerce* (Harvard University Press 2002) 3, 15, 19, 62–64; Phillip W Hall Jr, 'Smells Like Slavery: Unconscionability in Recording Industry Contracts' [2002] Hastings Comm & Ent LJ 189, 216–19; Stan J Liebowitz and Richard Watt, 'How to Best Ensure Remuneration for Creators in the Market for Music? Copyright and Its Alternatives' (2006) 20 Journal of Economic Surveys 513, 535; Norbert J Michel, 'Digital File Sharing and Royalty Contracts in the Music Industry: A Theoretical Analysis' (2006) 3 Review of Economic Research on Copyright Issues 29, 37; Jean-Christophe Lardinois, *Les Contrats Commentés de l'Industrie de La Musique 2.0: Cadre Général et Pratique Contractuelle* (Création Information Communication Pratique 1, 2nd edn, Larcier 2009) 84–85; David Stopps, 'How to Make a Living from Music, Second Edition' (Creative Industries, WIPO 2014) 97; Isabelle De Voldere and others, 'Mapping the Creative Value Chains. A Study on the Economy of Culture in the Digital Age. Final Report' (Publications Office of the EU 2017) <https://op.europa.eu/s/zIa8> 137; Luc Gulinck, *Hier Tekenen! (en Let Niet op de Kleine Lettertjes…) Wegwijs in het Juridische en Zakelijke Labyrint van de Muziekwereld* (Academia Press 2019) 197, 252, 276–77, 329; Alan B Krueger, *Rockonomics* (John Murray 2019) 161–62; Donald Passman, *All You Need to Know about the Music Business* (10th edn, Simon & Schuster 2019) 108–12; DCMS Committee, 'Economics of Music Streaming. Second Report of Session 2021–22' (15 July 2021) 28.

4 Yannick H'Madoun and others, *Auteursrechten en Publishing* (Poppunt vzw 2014) 72; Jan Pauly and Yannick H'Madoun, *Poppuntgids voor muzikant en dj* (Poppunt vzw no date) 197; Passman, *All You Need to Know about the Music Business* (n 3) 110. The option structure makes perfect sense from a commercial point of view, given the inherent uncertainty of the music market; cf Caves, *Creative Industries* (n 3) 63–64.

5 Stan Soocher, *They Fought the Law. Rock Music Goes to Court* (Schirmer Books 1999) 48.

6 Séverine Dusollier and others, 'Contractual Arrangements Applicable to Creators: Law and Practice of Selected Member States' (Publications Office of the EU 2014) <https://op.europa.eu/s/zIba> 6, 7.

7 See Chapter 2, Section 2.4.5.

In some jurisdictions, rules limiting parties' contractual freedom as to the formation of the contract may lead to the (partial) nullity of the contract under certain circumstances, such as in situations where the grant of rights is restricted when it comes to future music and/or methods of exploitation, or when it is deemed unreasonable on other grounds.[8] Rights that are excessively granted to a corporate partner may be declared non-binding under certain circumstances and may, in case of non-severability, result in the termination of the contract.

Even if the grant is not considered unreasonable in the sense of the restrictions set by law, the long duration of a copyright exploitation contract may sometimes be considered unfair in the rapidly changing market environment of the music industry.[9] By way of illustration, reference may be made to singer-songwriter RAYE, who spoke out against her 2014 contract with Polydor in 2021, claiming that the label refused to support her in recording and releasing her debut album.[10] For many musicians, it is difficult to break loose from early corporate partners, both if their music proves to be commercially successful and if it does not. From the commercially inclined perspective of corporate partners, this makes sense. In case of success, corporate partners may feel that they continue to be entitled to a proportion of revenues garnered by musicians they have nurtured to fame. If the musician did not break through commercially, corporate partners may want to prevent them from seeking success elsewhere, lest another corporate partner benefit from their earlier efforts towards exploitation of the music at issue. Bearing this in mind, artists such as Prince, George Michael, Megan Thee Stallion and Ye have at various points in time described such long-term contracts as a form of professional slavery.[11]

Certain rules of copyright contract law in the chosen jurisdictions may affect the duration of the contracts under review. For example, Dutch law provides that, if the

8 See Chapter 4, Section 4.4.1.

9 Cf Dusollier and others, 'Contractual Arrangements Applicable to Creators' (n 6) 11; Giblin and Doctorow, *Chokepoint Capitalism* (n 21) 195.

10 The contract was terminated in July 2021, see 'Raye and Polydor Split after Claims Record Label Wouldn't Release Debut Album' (*BBC News*, 20 July 2021) <https://bbc.in/3aJv1mD>. See for other examples Rhian Jones, '"I Had No Confidence, No Money": The Pop Stars Kept in Limbo by Major Labels' (*The Guardian*, 11 August 2021) <https://bit.ly/3BTHcco>.

11 Prince famously branded his (second) record deal with Warner Music as slavery, see 'Top Ten Legal Battles – Prince v Warner' directed by Andy Malt and Chris Cooke (Podcast, Setlist, 16 December 2019) <https://completemusicupdate.com/article/setlist-top-ten-legal-battles-prince-v-warner/>. The same was argued by George Michael relating to his deal with Sony, see Soocher, *They Fought the Law* (n 5) 46. As to the dispute between Megan Thee Stallion and record company 1501 Certified Entertainment, see Bill Donahue, 'Megan Thee Stallion's Bitter Fight with Her Label, Explained by the Lawyers from Both Sides' (*Billboard*, 26 August 2022) <https://bit.ly/3QfcAJ3>. As to the disputes between Ye and his corporate partners, see ia Glenn Litwak, 'Legal Beat: Kanye vs. EMI Litigation' (*Music Connection Magazine*, 20 January 2020) <https://bit.ly/3jbofaW>; Rhian Jones, 'Why Kanye West's Fight for His Masters Marks a Changing Music Industry' (*The Guardian*, 9 October 2020) <https://bit.ly/3j5B4qj>; Mark Savage, 'Kanye Posts Photos of His Record Deal amid Dispute' (*BBC News*, 17 September 2020) <https://bbc.in/3paoGWN>.

contract includes a right of early termination for the corporate partner, the artist can invoke this right on the same terms[12] – a provision that may in practice have a similar result to a limitation of the duration of the contract. On a more general level, restrictions to the substantive scope of rights granted under copyright contracts on the basis of reasonableness may also lead to a termination right on the part of musicians. By way of example, the Dutch Supreme Court ruled in the case opposing rock band Golden Earring to its music publisher that the restriction of the scope of copyright contracts on the basis of reasonableness under Dutch copyright contract law may under certain circumstances give rise to a reversion right applicable to copyright exploitation contracts of indeterminate duration.[13] Sufficiently serious grounds are required, taking account of the investment made by the corporate partner at issue.[14]

Finally, the prohibition on restrictive agreements set by Article 101 TFEU and under national competition law may constitute a potential avenue for musicians to escape contracts of an excessively long duration that are deemed unreasonable, as may principles of general contract law. Several precedents are available under UK law, under the doctrines of both undue influence and restraint of trade, whereby several musicians sought to terminate a contract on this basis – albeit with varying degrees of success.[15]

[12] Art 25f(3) Dutch Copyright Act *jo* Art 2b Dutch Neighbouring Rights Act; JH Spoor and others, *Auteursrecht. Auteursrecht, portretrecht, naburige rechten en databankenrecht* (Recht en Praktijk, 4th edn, Wolters Kluwer 2019) 581–82.

[13] Dutch Supreme Court 7 July 2017, docket number 15/03787, ECLI:NL:HR:2017:1270; Stef van Gompel and others, 'Evaluatie Wet Auteurscontractenrecht: Eindrapport' (2020) <https://bit.ly/3UBZrh4> 14, 46; Iris Houben and Dirk Visser, 'De Beëindiging van Muziekexploitatieovereenkomsten' [2022] ATR 135, 144–47. An unsuccessful attempt to invoke this provision was made by Dutch rapper Ronnie Flex, see District Court Amsterdam 17 January 2024, docket number C/13/714130 HA ZA 22-167, ECLI:NL:RBAMS:2024:345.

[14] Van Gompel and others, 'Evaluatie Wet Auteurscontractenrecht' (n 13) 14, 46.

[15] On the doctrine of undue influence, see eg *John v James* [1991] *FSR* 397; Edwin Peel, *Treitel on the Law of Contract* (15th edn, Sweet & Maxwell 2020) 512–29. The existence of a restraint of trade was accepted in earlier cases, such as *Macaulay v Schroeder Music Publishing Co Ltd* [1974] 1 WLR 1308, *ZTT v Johnson* [1990] EIRP 175 (re Frankie Goes to Hollywood), *Silvertone v Mountfield* [1993] EMLR 152 (re Stone Roses), but refused in the subsequent case *Panayiotou v Sony Music* [1994] EMLR 229 (re George Michael). As to management contracts, see also *O'Sullivan v Management Agency* [1985] *QB* 428; *William Nicholl v Shaun Ryder* [2000] EMLR 632 (re Happy Mondays); *Samuel v Wadlow* [2007] *EWCA Civ* 155. See Karl Zucconi, 'Freedom: Long Term Recording Agreements and the International Music Industry' (1996) 8 Pace Int'l L Rev 161; Frank Carrigan, 'Here Comes That Rainy Day Feeling Again: Shifts in the Ideology of Contract Law from Tony Macaulay to George Michael' [1997] Law in Context 105; Andrew Evans, 'The Doctrine of Restraint of Trade in Relation to Music Industry Agreements' [2003] Music Law Updates 10; Lardinois, *Les Contrats Commentés de l'Industrie de La Musique 2.0* (n 3) 39–41; Richard Arnold, *Performers' Rights* (6th edn, Sweet & Maxwell 2021) 276, 291–93; Lionel Bently and others, *Intellectual Property Law* (6th edn, Oxford University Press 2022) 347–51.

General contract law usually also provides for a right to terminate a contract of indefinite duration upon reasonable notice.[16] Such a right is based on either the right to self-determination and the freedom of commerce and contract, the prohibition of contracts contrary to good morals, or requirements of reasonableness. Thus, music industry contracts that are entered into for an indefinite period may be cancelled by either of the parties. However, given the industry custom of coupling the grant of rights with the applicable term of protection – in combination with the legal regimes applicable to the determination of the scope of rights granted[17] – the application of this rule is bound to remain limited.

A more far-reaching option would be to establish a principled right of withdrawal on the part of musicians, similar to what is the case for CMOs. Above, reference was made to the limited moral right of withdrawal that currently exists under French and German law in case of a change of conviction on the part of the author, the exercise of which leads to the retraction of the work.[18] It may be asked whether such a right should be susceptible to use for economic reasons, too, allowing the artist to switch between potential corporate partners. Such a potential economic right of withdrawal could take the principles established in the CRM Directive as a source of inspiration. As to collective management of copyright, the CRM Directive posits a freedom of choice in CMOs on the part of rightsholders. This freedom of choice affects the type(s) of rights or protected content entrusted to collective management, as well as the relevant territories.[19] It also implies that rightsholders should be able to (partially) withdraw their rights from a CMO in order to manage them individually or to entrust another entity (including another CMO) with their management.[20] This right of withdrawal does not require a change of conviction on the part of the rightsholder, or the payment of a reasonable cost compensation, or an obligation to offer a right of first refusal to the initially chosen CMO. Its scope of application is very broad. Its application through potential legislative intervention to the contracts

[16] See (1) in Belgium: *Hof van Cassatie* (hereinafter: Belgian Supreme Court) 9 March 1973, Arr Cass 1973, 671, Pas 1973, 640; Belgian Supreme Court 22 November 1973, Arr Cass 1973, 327, Pas 1974, 312; Art 5.75(2) new Belgian Civil Code; (2) in Germany: Art 138 German CC; see also ia Art 620 German Civil Code as to services relationships and Art 624 German CC as to employment contracts in particular; (3) in France: Arts 1210–1211 French Civil Code; (4) in the Netherlands: Dutch Supreme Court 28 October 2011, docket number 10/00299, ECLI:NL:HR:2011:BQ9854; Dutch Supreme Court 14 June 2013, docket number 12/01625, ECLI:NL:HR:2013:BZ4163; and (5) in the United Kingdom: *Winter Garden Theatre (London) Ltd v Millennium Productions Ltd* [1948] AC 173; *Jackson Distribution Ltd v Tum Yeto Inc* [2009] EWHC 982 (QB), [2009] *All ER (D)* 107 (May); Joseph Chitty and Hugh Beale, *Chitty on Contracts* (32nd edn, Sweet & Maxwell 2015) 1118–19, 1668–69; Neil Andrews, *Contract Rules: Decoding English Law* (Intersentia 2016) 264–65. See also Flavie Vermander, *De opzegging van overeenkomsten* (Intersentia 2014) 461–512.

[17] See Chapter 4, Section 4.4.2.

[18] See Chapter 5, Section 5.2.3.

[19] Art 5(2), (7) *jo* Rec 19 CRM Directive. See also Rec 19 CRM Directive.

[20] Art 5(4) *jo* Rec 19 CRM Directive.

under review here would be disproportionate, given the profound encroachment that this would entail on the freedom of contract and the interests of corporate partners. A right of withdrawal as such should be restricted to exceptional situations.

A second far-reaching option would be to expressly restrict the duration of a grant of rights to a certain time period, combined with a rights reversal at the end of this set time.[21] This would allow contracting parties who are confronted with a contractual setting that they consider to be unfair to renegotiate their deal or to seek new horizons following contract expiry.[22] A limited duration of copyright exploitation contracts could serve as a complement or even an alternative to an indirect duty to exploit or a broader contract adjustment mechanism.[23] Given the shift away from albums as a benchmark for contract duration due to the rise of music streaming[24], the former option appears to be the more fruitful potential avenue.

There are precedents for the restriction of the duration of copyright exploitation contracts by law. First, the 1911 UK regime provided for an automatic rights reversion to the estate of the author twenty-five years after their death.[25] Since the term of copyright protection was, at that time, life of the author plus fifty years, this implied a final twenty-five years during which the author's heirs could freely dispose of the copyright.[26] This reversion mechanism still applies to transfer contracts concluded

[21] Martin Kretschmer and others, 'The Relationship between Copyright and Contract Law' (2010) <https://ssrn.com/abstract=2624945>14; Dusollier and others, 'Contractual Arrangements Applicable to Creators' (n 6) 11–12, 15, 77–80, 104; Séverine Dusollier, 'EU Contractual Protection of Creators: Blind Spots and Shortcomings' [2018] Colum J L & Arts 436, 449, 457; Ruth Towse, 'Copyright Reversion in the Creative Industries: Economics and Fair Remuneration' (2018) 41 Colum J L & Arts 467; European Copyright Society, 'Comment of the European Copyright Society Addressing Selected Aspects of the Implementation of Articles 18 to 22 of the Directive (EU) 2019/790 on Copyright in the Digital Single Market' [2020] JIPITEC 132, 147; Ula Furgał, 'Interpreting EU Reversion Rights: Why "Use-It-or-Lose-It" Should Be the Guiding Principle' (2021) 43 EIPR 283, 283, 287; Martin Kretschmer and Rebecca Giblin, 'Getting Creators Paid: One More Chance for Copyright Law' (2021) 43 EIPR 279, 280; Rebecca Giblin and Cory Doctorow, *Chokepoint Capitalism: How Big Tech and Big Content Captured Creative Labor Markets and How We'll Win Them Back* (Beacon Press 2022) 180–95. Cf Agnès Lucas-Schloetter, 'The Remuneration of Authors and Performers in Copyright Contract Law' in Paul Torremans (ed), *Research Handbook on Copyright Law* (Research Handbooks in Intellectual Property, 2nd edn, Edward Elgar 2017) 264–65.

[22] Cf Dusollier and others, 'Contractual Arrangements Applicable to Creators' (n 6) 73.

[23] European Copyright Society, 'Comment' (n 21) 147.

[24] Passman, *All You Need to Know about the Music Business* (n 3) 2, 108.

[25] See in more detail Elena Cooper, 'Reverting to Reversion Rights? Reflections on the Copyright Act 1911' (2021) 43 EIPR 292, 293–97; Joshua Yuvaraj, 'Copyright Reversion: Debates, Data, and Directions' in Jens Schovsbo (ed), *The Exploitation of Intellectual Property Rights: In Search of the Right Balance* (ATRIP Intellectual Property, Edward Elgar 2023) 165–67.Taking a historical perspective on the earlier regime applicable in the United Kingdom between 1710 and 1814, see also Lionel Bently and Jane Ginsburg, 'The Sole Right Shall Return to the Authors: Anglo-American Authors Reversion Rights from the Statute of Anne to Contemporary US Copyright' (2010) 25 Berkeley Tech LJ 1475, 1480–549.

[26] See Cooper, 'Reverting to Reversion Rights?' (n 25) 293–97.

before 1 June 1957.[27] The potential establishment of a right to revocation (after twenty years following a transfer or exclusive licence) re-entered the legislative agenda in the United Kingdom following the recent DCMS inquiry, but this potential legislative change did not make it into hard law (as of yet).[28]

The other chosen jurisdictions do not expressly restrict the duration of the contracts under review. Under Belgian and French law, contract parties must specify the scope of their relationship, including on a temporal level.[29] This duty to specify does not imply any substantive limitation on the duration of copyright exploitation contracts. Consequently, such contracts may grant rights to a corporate partner for the entire term of protection, provided that this is made explicit in the contract.[30] Naturally, a more limited duration may also be foreseen.[31]

Second, in 1976, the US legislator enacted an inalienable right for authors to terminate the grant of US publishing rights related to works (other than 'works for hire') for a period of five years under certain circumstances.[32] In a bid to safeguard the interests of corporate partners and not render exploitation impossible, 'derivative works' prepared under authority of the grant before its termination may continue to be exploited under the terms of the grant after its termination.[33] The termination may take place during a five-year window that starts thirty-five years following the grant of the rights, with specific rules applying in case the grant covers the right to publish the work.[34] This right entered into force for creations released from 1978 onwards, leading to the first potential application of this right in 2013.[35] To date, successful applications of this revocation right in the music industry have been

[27] Paul Torremans, 'The Duran Duran Case in Private International Law: Copyright Contracts and the Question Whether 203 US Copyright Act Involves a Form of Reversionary Copyright' [2018] RIDA 81, 85–89.

[28] Arts 2–3 Copyright (Rights and Remuneration of Musicians, Etc.) HC Bill (2021–22) 19, proposing Arts 93F, 191P UK CDPA. See also DCMS Committee, 'Economics of Music Streaming' (n 3) 3, 66–67; Richard Osborne and Hyojung Sun, 'Economics of Streaming: Contract Adjustment and Rights Reversion' (6 February 2023).

[29] See Chapter 4, Section 4.4.2.

[30] Sébastien Raimond, *La Qualification du Contrat d'Auteur* (Le Droit des Affaires. Propriété Intellectuelle 34, LexisNexis 2009) 45; Brigitte Lindner, 'European Union. Part A – Copyright and Contract Law Issues' in René Viljoen (ed), *Cross-Border Copyright Licensing Law and Practice* (Elgar Intellectual Property Law and Practice, Edward Elgar 2018) 65.

[31] As to publishing contracts of definite duration, see eg Art L 132-11 para 5 French IP Code.

[32] Section 203(a) *jo* 304 US Copyright Act; Bently and Ginsburg, 'The Sole Right Shall Return to the Authors' (n 25) 1549–64; Chase Brennick, 'Termination Rights in the Music Industry: Revolutionary or Ripe for Reform?' (2018) 93 NYU L Rev 786, 790–92; Jean-Michel Bruguière, 'La Révision de La Rémunération de l'auteur et de l'artiste-Interprète' [2021] PI 5. See also Jem Aswad, 'FAIR Act to Overturn California's "Seven-Year Statute" Fails in State Senate' (*Variety*, 29 June 2022) <https://bit.ly/3dIrHNo>.

[33] Section 203(b)(1) US Copyright Act; Justin Hughes and Robert Merges, 'Copyright and Distributive Justice' (2016) 92 Notre Dame L Rev 513, 564–65.

[34] Section 203(b)(1) US Copyright Act.

[35] Michael Karas and Roland Kirstein, 'Efficient Contracting under the US Copyright Termination Law' (2018) 54 Int Rev Law Econ 39, 39.

scant.[36] This is undoubtedly influenced by cost considerations and the fear of retaliation, which affect the application of the relevant legal framework in the chosen jurisdictions, but also by the strict conditions accompanying the application of the revocation right and its apparent restrictive interpretation in practice.[37] Among other things, the exact scope of the exceptions for 'works for hire' and 'derivative works' has provided ample food for discussion.[38] A particularly contentious issue is whether this revocation right applies to the master rights in sound recordings – the US equivalent of a phonogram, which is protected by copyright (not a neighbouring right) that is allocated to the record company at the outset.[39] While record companies argue that sound recordings qualify as a work made for hire and are thus not susceptible to revocation, musicians understandably take the diametrically opposite position. It is plausible that superstar musicians use the threat

36 See eg Dylan Gilbert and others, 'Making Sense of the Termination Right: How the System Fails Artists and How to Fix It' (2019) 20; Joshua Yuvaraj, 'Back to the Start: Re-Envisioning the Role of Copyright Reversion in Australia and Other Common Law Countries' (Monash University 2021). However, see eg *Scorpio Music v Willis* [2012] SD Cal No. 11cv1557 BTM (RBB), whereby the termination by the former lead singer of the Village People was accepted. See also Stella Brown, 'It Takes a Village to Make a Difference: Continuing the Spirit of Copyright' (2014) 12 Nw J Tech & Intell Prop 129, 138–47; Paul J Heald, 'The Impact of Implementing a 25-Year Reversion/Termination Right in Canada' (2021) 28 J Intell Prop L 63, 82–83; Joshua Yuvaraj and others, 'US Copyright Termination Notices 1977–2020: Introducing New Datasets' (2022) 19 Journal of Empirical Legal Studies 250; Mandy Dalugdug, 'Warner Music Settles Lawsuit with Rock Band the Jesus and Mary Chain over Rights Dispute' (*Music Business Worldwide*, 8 March 2023) <https://bit.ly/3Dfouey>; Yuvaraj, 'Copyright Reversion' (n 25) 170–81.

37 Hughes and Merges, 'Copyright and Distributive Justice' (n 33) 564–70; Jane C Ginsburg, 'The Role of the Author in Copyright' in Ruth L Okediji (ed), *Copyright Law in an Age of Limitations and Exceptions* (Cambridge University Press 2017) 63–64; Gilbert and others, 'Making Sense of the Termination Right' (n 36) i–ii, 12, 21–25; Yuvaraj, 'Copyright Reversion' (n 25) 182.

38 A wealth of relevant sources is available on this topic. See, by way of example, Corey Field, 'Their Master's Voice?' (2000) Journal of the Copyright Society of the USA J Copyright Soc'y USA 145; Bently and Ginsburg, 'The Sole Right Shall Return to the Authors' (n 25) 1575–80; Bob Donnelly, 'Everything You Need to Know about Copyright Reversions' (2012) 1 St John's Entertainment, Arts and Sports Law Journal 1, 3–10, 27; Guy Rub, 'Stronger than Kryptonite? Inalienable Profit Sharing Schemes in Copyright Law' (2013) 27 Harv JL & Tech 49, 62–64; Amy Gilbert, 'The Time Has Come: A Proposed Revision to 17 USC Section 203' (2016) 66 Case West Reserve Law Rev 807, 810–11, 820–26, 832–37; Brennick, 'Termination Rights in the Music Industry' (n 32) 796–806; Kike Aluko, 'Terminating the Struggle over Termination Rights' (2019) 10 Harvard JSEL 119, 121–31; Gilbert and others, 'Making Sense of the Termination Right' (n 36) 8–10, 14–18; Giblin and Doctorow, *Chokepoint Capitalism* (n 21) 184–86. An additional question is whether and how the termination right applies to 360 degree music industry contracts, see Brennick, 'Termination Rights in the Music Industry' (n 32) 813–15.

39 Jessica Johnson, 'Application of the Copyright Termination Provision to the Music Industry: Sound Recordings Should Constitute Works Made for Hire' (2013) 67 U Miami L Rev 661; Kate Darling, 'Occupy Copyright: A Law & Economic Analysis of US Author Termination Rights' (2015) 63 Buffalo Law Review 147, 158–59; Brennick, 'Termination Rights in the Music Industry' (n 32) 796–801; 'Top Ten Legal Battles – Prince v Warner' (n 11).

of commencing litigation on this issue to secure more advantageous contract terms. An example of such a situation playing out is the 2014 deal between Prince and Warner, whereby Prince successfully claimed a significant part of the US master rights, only to licence them back to Warner.[40] Thus, successful artists are able to leverage the legal uncertainty surrounding the exact scope of the revocation right to their benefit. Since the results of such negotiations are usually subject to stringent NDAs, other musicians are unlikely to benefit.[41] A clear court decision on this topic would be desirable.

The restriction of copyright exploitation contracts in time may have certain beneficial economic effects. As is the case for rights reversal mechanisms based on insufficient exploitation,[42] the restriction of contract duration coupled with rights reversion may have a positive impact in terms of accessibility of protected works, since it opens up new avenues of exploitation.[43] The restriction of contract duration may also have negative follow-on consequences for secondary relationships and lead to a less advantageous deal for musicians overall. Corporate partners that only acquire exploitation rights for a short time have fewer incentives to invest in the exploitation of the content at issue and may moreover be less inclined to support emerging, up-and-coming artists in favour of established superstars.[44] It would make sense for corporate partners to manage the risk of a lack of immediate success by offering less advantageous remuneration arrangements to artists, in effect shifting the risk of commercial failure to the artist.[45] The risk of this happening has been analysed for the US reversion regime in relatively close detail, with researchers predicting a degree of internalisation of costs by corporate partners to the disadvantage of artists that may lead to the costs of this reversion regime (as it currently stands) outweighing the distributive and societal benefits.[46]

40 Aluko, 'Terminating the Struggle over Termination Rights' (n 38) 128–29; 'Top Ten Legal Battles – Prince v Warner' (n 11).

41 Aluko, 'Terminating the Struggle over Termination Rights' (n 38) 129; Gilbert and others, 'Making Sense of the Termination Right' (n 36) 1, 21.

42 See Chapter 5, Section 5.2.2.3.

43 Kretschmer and others, 'The Relationship between Copyright and Contract Law' (n 21) 14; Abdullahi Abdullahi, 'Termination Rights in Music: A Practical Framework for Resolving Ownership Conflicts in Sound Recordings' [2012] U Ill JL Tech & Pol'y 457, 482–83; Heald, 'The Impact of Implementing a 25-Year Reversion/Termination Right in Canada' (n 36) 69–82; Giblin and Doctorow, *Chokepoint Capitalism* (n 21) 187. Cf Kristelia García and Justin McCrary, 'A Reconsideration of Copyright's Term' (2019) 71 Ala L Rev 315, 388–89.

44 Darling, 'Occupy Copyright' (n 39) 168–75; Karas and Kirstein, 'Efficient Contracting under the US Copyright Termination Law' (n 35) 46; European Copyright Society, 'Comment' (n 21) 147.

45 Rub, 'Stronger than Kryptonite?' (n 38) 96–99; Brown, 'It Takes a Village to Make a Difference' (n 36) 147; Darling, 'Occupy Copyright' (n 39) 150, 162–68, 200–03; Brennick, 'Termination Rights in the Music Industry' (n 32) 793–94; Karas and Kirstein, 'Efficient Contracting under the US Copyright Termination Law' (n 35) 40.

46 See eg Rub, 'Stronger than Kryptonite?' (n 38); Darling, 'Occupy Copyright' (n 39); Karas and Kirstein, 'Efficient Contracting under the US Copyright Termination Law' (n 35).

Similar reservations have been made concerning the right granted to authors under German law to grant an additional licence after ten years.[47] This was also the primary argument against the preliminary proposal in the Netherlands to divide the duration of copyright exploitation contracts into chunks of five years with a rights reversal after five years and ensuing renegotiation of contract terms.[48] It was argued that corporate partners would manage the risk of a lack of immediate success by offering less money.[49] Further, if success were not forthcoming in the first five years, a renegotiation of contract terms would risk leaving the musician significantly worse off. This risk may be materially mitigated by setting a longer duration, such as ten years,[50] twenty-five years,[51] or another term, taking account of the average exploitation period of content in a given sector.[52] If the temporal window of envisaged exploitation matches the duration of the grant, the restriction is unlikely to have a negative effect on the level of remuneration.[53] An important criterion in this regard is the perceived net present value of a piece of music as an asset.[54] However, if the restricted duration corresponds to the exploitation period of the content at issue, providing a termination right would not lead to an increase in musician income either.[55] Indeed, a high depreciation rate of expected revenues from exploitation limits musicians' prospective income upon reclaiming their rights after a certain period of time. In other words, musicians would not benefit from a temporal restriction of copyright exploitation contracts if the set duration is too short or too long. Pinpointing an appropriate one-size-fits-all contract duration appears rather arbitrary and may even prove to be impossible. While the economic value of much music depreciates quite rapidly, a significant number of musical works *doe* stand the test of time. In this regard, reference may be made to the classical music canon, the

47 Kirstein and Karas, 'Efficient Contracting under the US Copyright Termination Law' (n 35). See also Chapter 4, Section 4.4.1.2.

48 Martin Senftleben, 'Exportschlager Deutsches Urhebervertragsrecht? Het Voorontwerp Auteurscontractenrecht in Duits Perspectief' [2010] AMI 146, 147–49; P Bernt Hugenholtz, 'Towards Author's Paradise: The New Dutch Act on Authors' Contracts' in Gunnar Karnell and others (eds), *Liber Amicorum Jan Rosén* (eddy.se ab 2016) 400; Martin Senftleben, 'More Money for Creators and More Support for Copyright in Society – Fair Remuneration Rights in Germany and the Netherlands' (2018) 41 Colum J L & Arts 413, 432.

49 Senftleben, 'More Money for Creators and More Support for Copyright in Society' (n 48) 432; European Copyright Society, 'Comment' (n 21) 147.

50 Cf Kenneth W Barr, 'Music Copyright in the Digital Age. Creators, Commerce and Copyright. An Empirical Study of the UK Music Copyright Industries' (University of Glasgow 2016).

51 Cf Heald, 'The Impact of Implementing a 25-Year Reversion/Termination Right in Canada' (n 36) 83; Giblin and Doctorow, *Chokepoint Capitalism* (n 21) 190–91.

52 Cf Martin Kretschmer, 'Short Paper: Copyright Term Reversion and the "Use-It-or-Lose-It" Principle' (2012) 1 IJMBR 44, 44, 49–50.

53 Heald, 'The Impact of Implementing a 25-Year Reversion/Termination Right in Canada' (n 36) 83.

54 Darling, 'Occupy Copyright' (n 39) 179–80; Heald, 'The Impact of Implementing a 25-Year Reversion/Termination Right in Canada' (n 36) 83–85.

55 Rub, 'Stronger than Kryptonite?' (n 38) 107.

persisting popularity of legacy artists and classics' catalogue such as the Beatles or the Rolling Stones on music streaming services, and the ever-increasing activities of music publishing maverick Hipgnosis.[56]

The difficulties in setting an appropriate duration and the significant potential impact of getting this wrong constitute a significant practical hurdle for the implementation of a temporal restriction of the duration of copyright exploitation contracts. More importantly, such a restriction would not have a significant fairness-enhancing effect, in view of the already existing protective regimes relating to fair scope, exploitation and remuneration in the chosen jurisdictions as partially harmonised at the EU level. Indeed, in case of an excessive rights transfer, several mitigating mechanisms are available – including the German rule that allows the grant of an additional licence after a decade.[57] In terms of exploitation, the indirect duties to exploit as partially harmonised by Article 22 DSM Directive and Article 3(2a) Term Directive may be mentioned, in combination with potential recourse to moral rights protection.[58] Finally, as to the objective of securing fair remuneration over time, applicable contract adjustment mechanisms as harmonised through Article 20 DSM Directive may be mentioned.[59] Granted, these regimes are not (yet) optimal, which is why this book has advanced potential avenues for their incremental amelioration. Provided that high-performing regimes pertaining to fair scope, exploitation and remuneration may be guaranteed, the potential added value of a maximum duration of copyright exploitation contract is limited. This, in turn, may render its implementation a disproportionate encroachment upon the freedom of contract.

6.3 GROUNDS FOR CONTRACT TERMINATION

Now we again move from the formation phase of the contracts under review to their performance, this time focusing on grounds for termination. Chapter 5 analysed the parties' obligations concerning the performance of music contracts. While the primary remedy in case of contractual shortcomings on the part of either party is in principle to claim specific performance, where there is serious breach of contract a right to rescission resulting in rights reversion may be available.[60] If exploitation on the part of the corporate partner is completely lacking or deemed insufficient under the

56 See <www.hipgnosissongs.com>.

57 See Chapter 4, Section 4.4.1.2.

58 See Chapter 5, Section 5.2.2.3.

59 See Chapter 5, Section 5.3.2.3.

60 See for the law on breach of contract under national law in the chosen jurisdictions (1) in Belgium: Arts 1134–1155, 1184 Belgian Civil Code; (2) in Germany: Arts 241–292, 320–326 German Civil Code; (3) in France: Arts 1217–1231-7 French CC; (4) in the Netherlands: Arts 6:74–94, 6:265 Dutch Civil Code; and (5) in the United Kingdom: Chitty and Beale, *Chitty on Contracts* (n 16) chs 24, 26–28; Andrews, *Contract Rules* (n 16) 266–364; Peel, *Treitel on the Law of Contract* (n 15) chs 17–21; Mindy Chen-Wishart, *Contract Law* (7th edn, Oxford University Press 2022) 495–614.

applicable direct/indirect duties to exploit, rights revocation mechanisms as partially harmonised under the use-it-or-lose-it clause of Article 22 DSM Directive may apply.[61]

While available case law is limited, precedents from France and the Netherlands show that a serious breach of contract relating to exploitation and remuneration may give rise to a right of termination. Two specific examples stand out, where the musician(s) sought to terminate the contractual relationship: the case brought by French rapper MC Solaar and the more recent dispute between Dutch gothic and symphonic metal band Epica and their record company.[62]

In the former case, MC Solaar sought the termination (and the associated rights reversion) of his 1993 contract with Polydor,[63] alleging a breach of contract, due to (among other things) the non-respect of certain release commitments.[64] Siding with MC Solaar, the Court of Appeal of Paris rescinded the contract.[65] This judgment was subsequently confirmed by the French Supreme Court.[66] While the context of the MC Solaar case was still largely analogue, the Epica case shows the impact of the digital sphere on corporate partners' commitments in terms of fair remuneration and transparency. In essence, the Epica band members were deprived of revenues from digital exploitation collected via digital aggregator TuneCore for a significant period of time and a total sum exceeding €200,000. In March 2021, the District Court of Amsterdam found, ruling in the context of summary proceedings, that the corporate partner's behaviour was likely to justify termination of the contract, citing both the non-payment of remuneration and the persisting lack of transparency on the part of the corporate partner.[67] In the meantime, this case has been settled under confidential terms. Regardless, the District Court's judgment may provide a valuable precedent for musicians confronted with a corporate partner that is unwilling to fulfil its obligations in terms of exploitation and/or remuneration, especially in the Netherlands.

Musicians may also have certain obligations throughout the course of contract performance, such as the duty to cooperate with exploitation activities.[68] However, as the sanction of specific performance appears to be the more logical and constructive outcome in such a context, it is unsurprising that no relevant case law was retrieved citing musician behaviour as a ground for termination of a contract.

61 See Chapter 5, Section 5.2.2.3.

62 See also eg the dispute between Golden Earring and their music publisher, Dutch Supreme Court 7 July 2017, docket number 15/03787; ECLI:NL:HR:2017:1270; Spoor and others, *Auteursrecht* (n 12) 532–33. See also Chapter 5, Section 5.2.2.3.2.

63 Polydor is part of Universal Music Group.

64 See also Lardinois, *Les Contrats Commentés de l'Industrie de La Musique* 2.0 (n 3) 73–75.

65 Court of Appeal Paris 5 April 2002, not published.

66 French Supreme Court 21 June 2004, docket number 02-43.793 <https://bit.ly/44vD4yF>. See also 'Universal défait par MC Solaar' (*Le Monde*, 8 April 2004) <https://bit.ly/3lOXnCs>.

67 District Court Amsterdam 9 March 2021, docket number C/13/696035 / KG ZA 21-32, ECLI: NL:RBAMS:2021:1041.

68 See Chapter 5, Section 5.2.3.

The remedy of contract termination may also be an option if the circumstances surrounding the contract have changed significantly and attempts at renegotiation are unsuccessful, either in application of a contract adjustment mechanism or the doctrine of changed circumstances as applicable at the time of writing in Belgium, France, Germany and the Netherlands.[69] If all efforts at renegotiation fail, the parties may commence judicial proceedings. The judge called upon to rule on the dispute may not only have the competence to revise the contract terms in a reasonable manner, but may under certain circumstances also decide to terminate the contract.[70] Thus, the parties may avail themselves of the termination of the contract as a last resort, if the circumstances so require. Partial termination could be used to limit the termination of the contract to specific methods of exploitation, such as streaming.

In Germany, judicial intervention is not required for the remedy of termination to be available to the parties under general contract law: if contract revision is impossible or legitimately unacceptable to one of the parties, that party may terminate the contract.[71] Furthermore, also under German contract law, each party may terminate a contract that relates to a continuing obligation – such as the exploitation of protected music under a licence agreement and/or the royalty payment as remuneration – without a notice period, provided that there is a compelling reason for them to do so.[72] Such a reason is deemed to be present if continued performance cannot be legitimately expected from them.[73] This requirement is analogous to the substantive condition set by the doctrine of changed circumstances under German law.

For publishing contracts in particular, a ground of termination may arise if there are no longer any copies of the work(s) (Belgium,[74] France,[75] Germany[76]).

[69] See Chapter 5, Section 5.3.2.3.

[70] See (1) in Belgium: Art 5.74 new Belgian Civil Code; (2) in France: Art 1195 French Civil Code; and (3) in the Netherlands: Art 6:258 Dutch Civil Code.

[71] Art 313(3) German Civil Code.

[72] Art 314(1) German Civil Code; Basil S Markesinis and others, *The German Law of Contract. A Comparative Treatise* (2nd edn, Hart 2006) 436–37; Dieter Medicus and Stephan Lorenz, *Schuldrecht I. Allgemeiner Teil* (Juristische Kurz-Lehrbücher, 21st edn, CH Beck 2015) 302–04; Wolfgang Fikentscher and Andreas Heinemann, *Schuldrecht: Allgemeiner und Besonderer Teil* (De Gruyter Studium, 11th edn, De Gruyter 2017) 350–52. See in the context of copyright exploitation contracts in particular Gerhard Schricker, *Urheberrecht. Kommentar* (3rd edn, CH Beck 2006) 646–54.

[73] Markesinis and others, *The German Law of Contract* (n 72); Medicus and Lorenz, *Schuldrecht I. Allgemeiner Teil* (n 72); Fikentscher and Heinemann, *Schuldrecht* (n 72); Schricker, *Urheberrecht* (n 72).

[74] According to Art XI.199(1) Belgian CEL, the author has the right to terminate the publishing contract if the publisher destroys all the copies.

[75] According to Art L 132-17(1) French IP Code, the publishing contract expires if the publisher destroys all the copies of the work(s). See Christophe Caron, *Droit d'Auteur et Droits Voisins* (6th edn, LexisNexis 2020) 449–50. See also Code des Usages et des Bonnes Pratiques de l'Edition des Œuvres Musicales (4 October 2017) s 5.2.

[76] According to Art 29(1) German Publishing Act, if the publishing contract is limited to a certain number of editions or copies, in principle the contractual relationship terminates when the editions or copies are out of print.

Finally, a particular concern arises where the corporate partner becomes insolvent. As already detailed above in the context of the formation of secondary relationships, many copyright exploitation contracts have an *intuitu personae* or *intuitu firmae* nature.[77] In order to ensure party agency, parties have a clear interest in maintaining control over the identity of their contractual counterparties. Allowing for copyright exploitation contracts to be fully maintained throughout insolvency proceedings clearly risks thwarting this objective.

Specific rules apply where the publisher becomes insolvent (Belgium,[78] France,[79] Germany[80]), including a potential termination right on the part of the author. No equivalent rule of copyright contract law exists in the chosen jurisdictions for non-publishing contracts.[81] However, restrictions on the transfer of rights in the context of secondary relationships may provide a solution for this.[82]

6.4 CONSEQUENCES OF TERMINATION

Even if it is clear in what circumstances the contracts under review may be terminated, the potential consequences of such termination add an additional layer of complexity. Contract termination leads to issues relating to the fate of rights[83] and/or revenues[84] as well as physical copies and digital files of the music that falls within the scope of the contract, including the follow-on consequences for music added to streaming services,[85] the (continued) access to relevant audience

77 See Chapter 4, Section 4.5.

78 Art XI.200 Belgian CEL grants the author the right to terminate the publishing contract if the publisher goes bankrupt or goes into receivership. The author obtains a right of first refusal to buy all remaining copies.

79 Art L 132-15 para 4 French IP Code grants the author the right to terminate the publishing contract if the publisher ceases its activities for a period of three months or a judge pronounces its liquidation. In such a case, the author obtains a right of first refusal to buy all remaining copies, see Art L 132-15 paras 5–6 French IP Code. See also Code des Usages et des Bonnes Pratiques de l'Edition des Œuvres Musicales (n 75) s 5.2.

80 Under the regime set by Art 36 German Publishing Act, upon insolvency of the publisher, the insolvency administrator may insist upon contract performance by the author. If reproduction has yet to commence at the time insolvency proceedings are opened, the author may withdraw from the publishing contract.

81 Cf P Bernt Hugenholtz and Lucie Guibault, 'Auteurscontractenrecht: Naar Een Wettelijke Regeling?' (2004) <https://bit.ly/3UvnwGx> 72–74.

82 See Chapter 4, Section 4.5.

83 For example, in the Netherlands, as to the consequences of a successful application of the use-it-or-lose-it mechanism, see draft amendment to Art 25e Dutch Copyright Code <https://bit.ly/4407vot>.

84 For example, it may be asked whether a musician may stake a claim in a share of the revenues garnered by a corporate partner through the sale of equity in DSPs that postdates contract termination, see Cooke, *Dissecting the Digital Dollar* (n 86) 101.

85 See eg the dispute between artist Four Tet and corporate partner Domino Records in the United Kingdom, which (among other things) involved the removal by Domino Records of Four Tet's music from streaming services, see Chris Cooke, 'Four Tet Allowed to Add New Legal Claims over Album Takedowns in Domino Dispute' (*CMU*, 17 December 2021)

data,[86] and even musicians' ability to perform music that falls within the scope of the initial contract in a post-contractual context. Contract provisions risk preventing musicians from reclaiming any rights. Again, the risk of unfairness is greater for legacy artists, in view of the larger scope of rights transfers in legacy deals.[87]

A first issue is how contract termination affects the scope of rights initially granted. Regulatory approaches differ. Moreover, instances of retroactive and non-retroactive contract termination are to be distinguished. While the former – such as contract nullity and rescission – are usually associated with automatic rights reversion to the benefit of the initial rightsholder, the latter – such as contract expiry and termination in common agreement – are usually not.

The former situation arises in case of shortcomings in the formation of the contract and in the event of a serious breach of contract. An example of the latter situation is provided by the case opposing French singer Johnny Hallyday and Universal Music. The singer unsuccessfully sought to obtain the master rights to the music he recorded while the contract with Universal Music was ongoing.[88] It was held that the termination in principle only has effects for the future, unless there is a contractual provision to the contrary. Thus, the transfer of rights to the corporate partner effectuated through the contract remains valid.[89] If the musician has only granted a licence to the corporate partner, this licence no longer produces any effects following contract termination. This results in a full return of exploitation rights to the musician if the licence was exclusive.[90]

Given the importance of secondary relationships to the streaming music ecosystem, it bears relevance to ascertain the follow-on consequences of the potential termination of the primary contract.[91] Again, national regulatory approaches differ.

<https://bit.ly/3B7TzCd>. This dispute was later settled, with the label committing to pay a 50 per cent royalty rate for digital exploitation, see Laura Snapes, 'Four Tet Settles Historic Royalty Rate Dispute with Domino Records' (*The Guardian*, 20 June 2022) <https://bit.ly/3RXyULu>.

86 This refers to audience data, as well as data concerning social media, a band website and so forth, see Chris Cooke, *Dissecting the Digital Dollar* (3rd edn, Music Managers Forum and CMU Insights 2020)165.

87 See Chapter 2, Section 2.4.5.

88 See Court of Appeal Paris, 12 April 2005 <https://bit.ly/3FsfFB2>; French Supreme Court 20 December 2006, docket number 05–43.057 <https://bit.ly/4bw4giQ>. In 2008, Hallyday and Universal Music reached a settlement.

89 Caron, *Droit d'Auteur et Droits Voisins* (n 75) 640.

90 In case of a non-exclusive licence, the musician also has the right to exploit prior to the termination of the licence. Therefore, the termination of a non-exclusive licence does not really imply a 'return' of rights.

91 For detail on the legal regimes applicable to the follow-on consequences of the termination of a contract on the validity of connected contracts, see Sanne van Dongen, *Groepen van Contracten* (Onderneming en Recht 95, Wolters Kluwer 2016); Tâm Dang Vu, 'Verbonden Overeenkomsten' (KU Leuven 2017). The former volume focuses on French, German and Dutch law, while the latter also includes an analysis of Belgian law.

In principle, the retroactive termination of the primary contract negatively affects the validity of secondary contracts, since the primary corporate partner then is deemed never to have been granted any exploitation rights.[92] However, under Belgian law, the rescission of a publishing contract upon the author's request does not prejudice secondary exploitation contracts that were validly concluded by the publisher.[93] In such a case, the author may directly claim remuneration from the secondary exploiter at issue.[94] No specific corresponding provisions of copyright contract law were found in any of the other chosen jurisdictions, or as to contracts with performers under Belgian law. In the absence of applicable *leges speciales*, general contract law applies.[95] In this context, the potential incidence of the third party's good faith on the validity of the secondary contract is noted. In any case, if the termination is non-retroactive, the validity of the secondary contract remains unaffected.

The consequences of contract termination on the scope of rights granted in turn also affect the possibilities in terms of further exploitation. In case of non-retroactive termination and subject to rights reversion, the corporate partner retains exploitation rights that were transferred, but can no longer invoke any exploitation rights for the future under a terminated licence. Further, if the termination has retroactive effect, logic dictates that no further exploitation be allowed on the part of the corporate partner.

[92] Cf Alain Berenboom, *Le Nouveau Droit d'Auteur et les Droits Voisins* (Création Information Communication 1, 3rd edn, Larcier 2005) 221–22; 236; Dang Vu, 'Verbonden Overeenkomsten' (n 91) 492–95; Pierre-Yves Gautier, *Propriété Littéraire et Artistique* (11th edn, Presses Universitaires de France 2019) 573, 602–06. See under Dutch law Art 6:229 Dutch Civil Code. A contract that intends to build further upon an already existing primary contractual relationship is voidable if the primary relationship is absent, unless the nature of the contract, common practice or the circumstances dictate otherwise. See also Dang Vu, 'Verbonden Overeenkomsten' (n 91) 281–92; Jac Hijma and others, *Rechtshandeling en Overeenkomst* (Studiereeks burgerlijk recht 3, 9th edn, Kluwer 2019) 190–91.

[93] Art XI.199(3) Belgian CEL; Fernand De Visscher and Benoît Michaux, *Précis du Droit d'Auteur et des Droits Voisins* (Bruylant 2000) 352–53; Berenboom, *Le Nouveau Droit d'Auteur et les Droits Voisins* (n 92) 234; Hendrik Vanhees, *De wettelijke regeling inzake auteurscontracten* (Recht en Praktijk 69, Kluwer 2012) 44–45; Hendrik Vanhees, 'Art XI.195' in Fabienne Brison and Hendrik Vanhees (eds), *Hommage à Jan Corbet Huldeboek* (3rd edn, Larcier 2018) 319.

[94] De Visscher and Michaux, *Précis du Droit d'Auteur et des Droits Voisins* (n 93); Berenboom, *Le Nouveau Droit d'Auteur et les Droits Voisins* (n 92); Vanhees, *De wettelijke regeling inzake auteurscontracten* (n 93); Vanhees, 'Art XI.195' (n 93).

[95] See eg under German law: Silke von Lewinski, 'News from Germany. Developments in Germany from Mid-2005 until the End of 2010. Part I' [2011] RIDA 164, 213–15; Jan Bernd Nordemann, 'Die Beendigung urheberrechtlicher Verträge: Automatischer Rechterückfall? Das Urhebervertragsrecht nach BGH M2Trade, Take Five und Reifen Progressiv' in Kirsten-Inger Wöhrn and others (eds), *Festschrift für Artur-Axel Wandtke zum 70 Geburtstag am 26 März 2013* (Walter De Gruyter 2013) 187–97; Patrick Zurth, *Rechtsgeschäftliche und gesetzliche Nutzungsrechte im Urheberrecht. Eine dogmatische Analyse der Rechtsnatur und der vertraglichen Gestaltungsmöglichkeiten* (Studien zum Privatrecht 54, Mohr Siebeck 2016).

In the physical realm, specific legal arrangements have been made regarding the further sale of unsold stock in the context of publishing contracts.[96] Belgian law expressly allows the publisher to sell remaining stock at a 'normal' price in case of contract termination for a period of three years, unless the author wants to buy the stock to sell themselves.[97] A similar rule applies under French law following the expiry (that is, non-retroactive termination) of a publishing contract of definite duration.[98] Conversely, subsequent to the German Publishing Act, if the publishing contract is concluded for a definite duration, the publisher is in principle no longer entitled to distribute remaining stock after its expiry.[99]

As to digital exploitation, the main consequences of contract termination relate to secondary relationships with DSPs. If termination of the initial contract results in termination of the secondary contract, exploitation by the DSP must – in theory – cease, subject to national regimes based on good faith.[100] To the extent that this may cut musicians off from their audience, this consequence may run counter to the interests of both musicians and users. Moreover, an initial corporate partner that actively pulls music off of music streaming platforms following contract termination may be held to act counter to good faith and may therefore be estopped from doing so.[101] In any case, a full cessation of online exploitation activities following contract termination appears unlikely in practice and, moreover, unwarranted. The conclusion of a direct contractual link between musicians and DSPs, most likely through the intervention of a digital distributor and/or a publishing administrator, would arguably be a beneficial alternative in such a case.

An additional layer to this debate stems from the fact that phonogram producers also acquire a neighbouring right of their own upon taking the initiative and the

[96] Cf Brigitte Dauwe, 'Overeenkomsten in het Oude en in het Nieuwe Auteursrecht' in Frank Gotzen (ed), *Belgisch Auteursrecht van Oud naar Nieuw Le Renouveau du Droit d'Auteur en Belgique* (CIR 11, Bruylant 1996) 264.

[97] Arts XI.197 *jo* XI.199(2) Belgian CEL; Hendrik Vanhees, 'Auteurscontracten en de Problematiek inzake Werken Gemaakt in Opdracht of in Uitvoering van een Arbeidsovereenkomst of Statuut' in Frank Gotzen (ed), *Belgisch Auteursrecht van Oud naar Nieuw Le Renouveau du Droit d'Auteur en Belgique* (CIR 11, Bruylant 1996) 322; De Visscher and Michaux, *Précis du Droit d'Auteur et des Droits Voisins* (n 93) 352; Vanhees, 'Art XI.195' (n 93) 319. The possibility for authors to buy remaining stock also applies in case the publisher goes bankrupt, see Art XI.199(2) Belgian CEL.

[98] Art L 132–11 para 6 French IP Code; Alexis Boisson, *La Licence de Droit d'Auteur* (Bibliothèque de Droit de l'Entreprise 86, LexisNexis 2013) 676–77; Gautier, *Propriété Littéraire et Artistique* (n 92) 639–41.

[99] Art 29(3) German Publishing Act; Friedrich Karl Fromm and Wilhelm Nordemann, *Urheberrecht. Kommentar zum Urheberrechtsgesetz, zum Verlagsgesetz und zum Urheberrechtswahrnehmungsgesetz* (Rechtswissenschaften und Verwaltung, 10th edn, Kohlhammer 2008) 2114–15.

[100] Cf Boisson, *La Licence de Droit d'Auteur* (n 98) 676.

[101] On the principle of good faith in a post-contractual context as applicable to copyright exploitation contracts (under French law), see Julie Groffe, *La Bonne Foi en Droit d'Auteur* (Institut Universitaire Varenne Collection des Thèses 106, LGDJ – lextenso éditions 2015) 275–78.

investment for the fixation of the phonogram(s) at issue.[102] Therefore, even if the termination has a retroactive effect and thus results in a rights reversion to the benefit of the performer(s), these do not acquire full exploitation rights to the phonogram(s). An inevitable risk of stalemate ensues, with both former contract parties in principle having the right to veto further exploitation, even though neither party would benefit – and nor, for that matter, would the audience – from either the exercise of this right, or the lack of exploitation that this would entail. This risk is expressly acknowledged in the Epica decision of the District Court of Amsterdam.[103] Instead of ordering a transfer of rights from the record company to the band, as requested by Epica, the Court ordered them to cooperate with the further exploitation of the phonograms at issue via TuneCore, lest penalty payments be imposed.[104] This situation was set to continue at least until contractual negotiations led to an outcome satisfactory to both parties, or until a court decision on the merits was handed down. The Court held that a refusal by the record company to cooperate at this stage would amount to an abuse of rights.[105] This pragmatic solution takes account of the interests of all parties and deserves support. In the meantime, the parties have reached a settlement.

In any case, if further exploitation post-termination is allowed, this should be accompanied by (fair) remuneration for all parties. An express legal provision in this sense has been included in the German Publishing Act.[106] Reference may also be made to the direct claim for remuneration arising under Belgian law to the benefit of artists vis-à-vis secondary exploiters in case the primary publishing contract is rescinded.[107]

A final important aspect of the consequences of contract termination is associated with ownership and/or access to data. The transparency of data flows regarding exploitation and remuneration in the course of contract performance is often problematic. The active reporting obligation set by Article 19 DSM Directive seeks to remedy this.[108] This reporting obligation ceases when exploitation no longer takes place.

However, also at the time of contract termination, issues regarding access to relevant data arise, especially as to data that allows direct contact with listeners, such as a mailing list with fans' contact details compiled over the years, a band website filled with relevant content and aggregated audience data collected by

[102] See Chapter 2, Section 2.2.3.2.

[103] District Court Amsterdam 9 March 2021, C/13/696035 / KG ZA 21–32, ECLI:NL:RBAMS:2021:1041, paras 5.20–5.22.

[104] As long as no final decision was reached, the remuneration obtained through such exploitation was to be divided according to the original contract (namely a 40/60 division between Epica and the record company), see ibid para 5.22.

[105] ibid para 5.22.

[106] Art 36(2) German Publishing Act; Fromm and Nordemann, *Urheberrecht* (n 99) 2147–53.

[107] Art XI.199(3) Belgian CEL.

[108] See Chapter 5, Section 5.3.3.2.

platforms concerning the identity and listening behaviour of their fans.[109] The economic value of such data is undeniable and increasing. Such information is usually managed by corporate partners, save in a true DIY context. While corporate partners may also have a legitimate interest in retaining such data following contract termination, (continued) access to it on the part of the musician is vital in order to enable them to nurture and enhance their fanbase.[110]

Yet, such data is not usually causally linked with the exploitation of music and/or the ensuing remuneration. This makes it difficult to argue that it would fall within the scope of corporate partners' reporting obligations. Moreover, musicians' interest in obtaining such data only spikes after the contract has been terminated. As long as the corporate partner takes good care of the band newsletter, the band has little to gain by accessing the mailing list. An additional dimension is added by the potential qualification of audience data as trade secrets.[111]

In an ideal world, considerations pertaining to data are discussed and regulated in a balanced contractual clause.[112] However, differences in relative bargaining power may prevent full data transparency in practice. Musicians who wish to seek new horizons may understandably feel constrained by the prospect of losing direct access to their fanbase and data that may help them grow their audience. Thus, exclusive access to data risks functioning as a switching cost that may lock in musicians, leaving the promise of autonomy and musician agency to sound rather hollow. The contrast with the right to data portability under data protection law, as protected under Article 20 GDPR,[113] is remarkable. As yet, beyond the general principle of good faith in contractual situations,[114] the legal framework does little to further musicians' interests in this context.

6.5 OUTRO

This chapter analysed various issues connected with the termination of music contracts in the streaming age. In essence, it treated the issue of whether the parties to the contracts under review have the opportunity to terminate a contract if instances of unfair scope, exploitation and/or remuneration arise. Several findings are noted, such as the absence of an express restriction on the duration of copyright exploitation contracts in the chosen jurisdictions (as yet), a wide and diverging array of potential grounds for termination on the basis of breach of contract, and clear

[109] See in detail Cooke, *Dissecting the Digital Dollar* (n 86) 158–79.

[110] Stopps, 'How to Make a Living from Music' (n 3) 103, 160, 166; Cooke, *Dissecting the Digital Dollar* (n 86) 5.

[111] See Chapter 7, Section 7.3.

[112] Cf in more detail Cooke, *Dissecting the Digital Dollar* (n 86) 161–62, 165, 175, 177–78.

[113] Regulation 2016/679 of the European Parliament and of the Council of 27 April 2016 on the protection of natural persons with regard to the processing of personal data and on the free movement of such data, and repealing Directive 95/46/EC [2016] OJ L119/1.

[114] See Chapter 3, Section 3.3.1 and sources referenced there.

shortcomings of the legal framework as to the consequences of contract termination. Consequently, depending on the applicable law, musicians' theoretical rights to terminate a contract differ, with predictable negative results as to procedural fairness. Also on a substantive level, the framework pertaining to the actual possibility to terminate the contracts under review may fall short.[115]

In the context of the consequences of contract termination, the two main issues are that it is not always fully clear how this affects (1) corporate partners' right to exploitation and musicians' ensuing right to remuneration or (2) musicians' right to access audience and other relevant data. As to the former, the existing rules appear to offer a more or less satisfactory solution, provided it is accepted that the principle of good faith and the prohibition of abuse of law curb the possibility for primary corporate partners to immediately pull music off streaming platforms following contract termination. However, the follow-on effects of termination on secondary contracts as affected by general contract law regimes merit further research. In any case, further exploitation in a post-contractual context, be it by a primary or secondary corporate partner, should result in (fair) remuneration, as already expressly confirmed by under Belgian and German law for publishing contracts.

As to the latter, an extension in scope of active reporting obligations for all types of audience data, including but not limited to demographic information and mailing lists, would be desirable. The inclusion of such data within the scope of active reporting obligations would imply a continuous stream thereof throughout the course of contract performance – thus also safeguarding musicians' right to access such data in a post-contractual context.

[115] For a more general, theoretical analysis that goes into the nature of appropriate remedies for breach of contract from a Kantian and Rawlsian perspective, see Martín Hevia, *Reasonableness and Responsibility: A Theory of Contract Law*, vol 101 (Law and Philosophy Library, Springer Netherlands 2013) 83–89.

7

Application of the Legal Framework in Practice

I fought the law
and the law won.

—Bobby Fuller Four

7.1 INTRO

In practice, there are several obstacles to the application of the substantive legal framework analysed in the previous chapters. First, there is a risk of contractual provisions that deviate from the legal norm. The qualification of certain rules as mandatory law may prevent such contractual deviation (Section 7.2). Even so, effective recourse to the protective regimes throughout the course of the contract is not guaranteed. Reference may be made to the possibility for corporate partners to have recourse to trade secret protection (Section 7.3) and the apparent limited invocation of the protective legal framework (Section 7.4). Collective enforcement may contribute to enhanced transparency throughout the music value chain and counter musicians' fear of commercial retaliation. Further bolstering extra-judicial enforcement is likely to fulfil an important complementary role (Section 7.5).

7.2 RISK OF CONTRACTUAL DEVIATIONS AND QUALIFICATION AS MANDATORY LAW

The mandatory nature of the protective regimes under review in this book appears to be a precondition for the effective application of the legal framework in practice. The qualification as mandatory law has important consequences. A mandatory legal norm excludes contrary contractual terms. In the absence of such qualification, contractual deviations are to be expected, especially where unequal bargaining positions apply. Moreover, subject to several nuances under national law, the temporal scope of a mandatory legal norm – or, as is the case in France and Germany, an act of public policy – may be extended to include ongoing contracts.[1] Bar certain exceptional circumstances arising from a collective bargaining context, it should not be possible to contractually override the protection offered by the relevant legal framework.[2] Derogating contractual provisions should be sanctioned with (relative) nullity.[3] This consideration rings true as to restrictions to the grant of rights as well as to obligations arising in the course of contract performance.

Many of the provisions reviewed in previous chapters have been expressly qualified as mandatory law.[4] Regarding restrictions on the scope of rights granted, the potential sanction of invalidity of contrary contractual provisions[5] and the exclusion of advance waivers of the right to invoke such invalidity[6] point towards a qualification of a certain rule as mandatory law. Many obligations applicable to the performance phase of the contract under review have also been imbued with mandatory status.[7]

As to exploitation, the qualification of *direct* duties to exploit as mandatory law would constitute a disproportionate encroachment upon parties' freedom to act (or not act). Conversely, the mandatory nature of the *indirect* duty to exploit stemming from use-it-or-lose-it clauses is warranted, given the double objective of enhancing musician agency and countering the warehousing of rights.[8]

Obligations pertaining to fair remuneration should arguably also not be overridable by contract, despite the lack of express qualification of Article 18 DSM Directive as such.[9] Each of the chosen EU jurisdictions has excluded contractual

1 See Chapter 3, Section 3.3.2.6.

2 Gilles Vercken, 'Formalism in Authors' Contracts: An Assessment after the Court of Cassation's Decision of 21 November 2006' [2009] RIDA 4, 6–7; European Copyright Society, 'Comment of the European Copyright Society Addressing Selected Aspects of the Implementation of Articles 18 to 22 of the Directive (EU) 2019/790 on Copyright in the Digital Single Market' [2020] JIPITEC 132.

3 Lionel Bently and others, 'Strengthening the Position of Press Publishers and Authors and Performers in the Copyright Directive' (2017) 85.

4 The German Publishing Act is an exception to this, as most of its provisions are not mandatory, with the exception of Arts 36 and 39(1) German Publishing Act, see eg Wirt Soetenhorst, *De bescherming van de uitgeefprestatie* (WEJ Tjeenk Willink 1993) 102; Gerhard Schricker, 'German and Comparative Intellectual Property Law Efforts for a Better Law on Copyright Contracts in Germany – A Never-Ending Story?' [2004] IIC 850; Friedrich Karl Fromm and Wilhelm Nordemann, *Urheberrecht. Kommentar zum Urheberrechtsgesetz, zum Verlagsgesetz und zum Urheberrechtswahrnehmungsgesetz* (Rechtswissenschaften und Verwaltung, 10th edn, Kohlhammer 2008) 2026; Andreas Rahmatian, 'Dealing with Rights in Copyright-Protected Works: Assignments and Licences' in Estelle Derclaye (ed), *Research Handbook on the Future of EU Copyright* (Research Handbooks in Intellectual Property, Edward Elgar 2009) 306.

5 See eg Art XI.167(1) para 4 Belgian CEL; Art L 131–3 French IP Code.

6 See eg Art 31a(4) German Copyright Act.

7 As to German law, it should be remembered that the protective provisions of copyright contract law are subject to contractual deviations in an employment context, see Art 43 German Copyright Act.

8 See Chapter 5, Section 5.2.2.3.

9 European Copyright Society, 'Comment' (n 2) 140; Yannos Paramythiotis, 'Fairness in Copyright Contract Law: Remuneration for Authors and Performers under the Copyright in the Digital Single Market Directive' in Tatiana-Eleni Synodinou and others (eds), *EU Internet Law in the Digital Single Market* (Springer International 2021) 84.

overridability.[10] Further, the express qualification of Articles 20 and 19 DSM Directive as mandatory law means that the rights arising from both the harmonised contract adjustment mechanisms and the active reporting obligations are not waivable in advance.[11]

The framework surrounding contract termination largely lacks the elevated status of mandatory law, save the prohibition against perpetual obligations, which is widely accepted as being of a public order nature.[12]

The qualification of many aspects of the protective legal framework as mandatory mitigates the risk of contractual deviations. This approach deserves to be emulated.[13]

7.3 OBSTACLES TO TRANSPARENCY

The second set of obstacles that may hinder the application of the protective legal framework relates to the objective of securing transparency throughout the music value chain. Reporting obligations will not by themselves lead to transparency, in view of the persisting problems surrounding music metadata and rights fragmentation,[14] as well as the difficulties of enforcing reporting obligations in practice. Indeed, securing the cooperation of all parties may be problematic. Moreover, assessing whether comprehensive information is provided in a timely manner may prove impossible in practice without a full audit of the corporate partner's books. The qualification of certain data as a trade secret may negatively affect the free flow of data throughout the music value chain.

The Trade Secret Directive, as implemented,[15] provides a significant additional layer of protection for secret information that derives commercial value from its secrecy and is subject to reasonable steps on the part of the lawful controller of this information to ensure its secrecy.[16] Such information, designated as a 'trade secret', is protected against misappropriation through unlawful acquisition, use and/or

[10] See Chapter 5, Section 5.3.

[11] See Chapter 5, Section 5.3.

[12] See Flavie Vermander, *De opzegging van overeenkomsten* (Intersentia 2014) 468–72.

[13] Cf Rudolf Leška, 'Contract Law Mechanisms from a Practitioner's View' in Silke von Lewinski (ed), *Remuneration for the Use of Works. Exclusivity vs Other Approaches* (De Gruyter 2017) 267.

[14] See Chapter 2, Section 2.5.

[15] See (1) in Belgium: Arts XI.332/1–5, XI.336/1–5, XI.342/1–3, XVII.21/1–5; (2) in France: Arts L 151-1-L154-1 French Commercial Code); (3) in Germany: *Gesetz zum Schutz von Geschäftsgeheimnissen (GeschGehG)*, BGBl Part I, 466 <https://bit.ly/3AeC7tK>; (4) in the Netherlands: *Wet van 17 oktober 2018, houdende regels ter uitvoering van Richtlijn 2016/943/EU van het Europees Parlement en de Raad van 8 juni 2016 betreffende de bescherming van niet-openbaar gemaakte knowhow en bedrijfsinformatie (bedrijfsgeheimen) tegen het onrechtmatig verkrijgen, gebruiken en openbaar maken daarvan (PbEU 2016, L157) (Wet bescherming bedrijfsgeheimen)*, Stb 2018, 369 <https://bit.ly/3DjwPyT>; and (5) in the United Kingdom: The Trade Secrets (Enforcement, etc.) Regulations 2018, SI 2018/597.

[16] See for the definition of a 'trade secret' Art 2(1) Trade Secret Directive. Cf Art 39(2) TRIPS Agreement.

disclosure, subject to a number of limitations.[17] The objective is to aid businesses in recouping their investments. Corporate partners may seek to rely on trade secret protection in a bid to prevent the disclosure of information relevant to the exploitation of music and the resulting remuneration therefor.

The potential conflict with the objective of securing transparency throughout the value chain is readily apparent. Not only may problems arise as to data access, but also regarding its subsequent use and further disclosure. These issues should be expressly treated in the contract.[18] However, differences in relative bargaining power also affect the content of such specifications, leading to a significant variance in degree of transparency.[19]

The question whether audience data is susceptible to trade secret protection is therefore pertinent. For this to occur, three conditions need to be fulfilled. First, the information may not be 'generally known among or readily accessible to persons within the circles that normally deal with the kind of information in question'.[20] As for the data collected by the DSP, this first condition will often be fulfilled. While, in terms of exploitation, the total number of streams of a certain song on Spotify is publicly displayed, this is not true for the division between subscription-based and ad-based streams, between playlist and on-demand streams, between different geographical territories, between thirty-second plays and full listens, and so forth. On the revenue side, precise information regarding the calculation of remuneration is deal-specific and often secret. Corporate partners may have a legitimate interest in keeping such audience data confidential and a legitimate expectation that this confidentiality will be preserved.[21] The commercial value arising from this information[22] should require no further argument. Indeed, in the music industry, really knowing your audience may very well be the biggest potential asset in terms of both strategy and competitive edge.[23] Third, the lawful controller of the information must take reasonable steps to maintain secrecy, such as NDAs.[24] Such steps are part and parcel of corporate deals in the streaming age.

The next question is who may be considered the holder(s) of these trade secrets. The Trade Secret Directive links the identity of the holder(s) to the lawful controller (s) of the data at issue. The latter is in turn linked with the question of who developed the trade secret, among other things through 'independent discovery or

[17] Arts 3–5 Trade Secret Directive.

[18] Chris Cooke, *Dissecting the Digital Dollar* (3rd edn, Music Managers Forum and CMU Insights 2020) 161–62, 165.

[19] ibid 160.

[20] Art 2(1)(a) Trade Secret Directive.

[21] Cf Rec 14 Trade Secret Directive. See also Cooke, *Dissecting the Digital Dollar* (n 18) 106; DCMS Committee, 'Economics of Music Streaming. Second Report of Session 2021–22' (15 July 2021) 72–73.

[22] Art 2(1)(b) Trade Secret Directive.

[23] Cf Rec 14 Trade Secret Directive.

[24] Art 2(1)(c) Trade Secret Directive.

creation' or 'observation, study, disassembly or testing' of a lawfully acquired product or object.[25] In case of joint control, a situation of co-holdership may be envisaged. It is difficult to translate these principles to the streaming age. Musicians, primary corporate partners, DSPs and even users may stake a claim, since they all play a role in the creation, collection and processing of audience data. As the law remains largely silent on the issue of how control or co-control of trade secrets is actually allocated in practice, contractual solutions are likely.[26] Thus, the interests of both musicians and users risk falling by the wayside, with musicians unlikely to be included in contractual specifications between corporate partners, and users likely to have waived any rights through standard end-user agreements. Contractual arrangements are likely to result in primary corporate partners and DSPs qualifying as co-holders of trade secrets in audience data.

Trade secrets are protected against unlawful acquisition, use and/or disclosure. All three acts must take place for musicians to be able to enforce their rights: not only must they obtain access to the data at issue; the reliance upon such data in the context of either judicial or extra-judicial proceedings undeniably requires both its use and disclosure. The disclosure of relevant information to representative organisations that support musicians in the enforcement of their rights, such as trade unions or CMOs, may also prove to be vital.

Careful consideration of the interplay between trade secrets and reporting obligations is therefore merited.[27] The DSM Directive itself offers little assistance. While Recital 76 posits that artists 'should always be able to use the shared information for the purpose of exercising their rights' under the DSM Directive, the legal status of this interjection is dubious.[28] Not only is it confined to the Directive's recitals; its formulation is imprecise, since it presupposes the sharing of information by the corporate partner(s) – which is exactly where trade secrets protection comes into play.

The only other express specification in the DSM Directive relates to the (secondary) relationship between OCSSPs and rightsholders in the context of licensing activities undertaken in accordance with Article 17 DSM Directive. In particular, Recital 68 exempts OCSSPs from providing rightsholders with 'detailed and individualised information for each work or other subject matter identified', without prejudice to possible contrary contractual arrangements. Thus, OCSSPs' reporting obligations appear to be curtailed by legitimate recourse to trade secret protection.[29]

[25] Cf Arts 2(2) *jo* 3 Trade Secret Directive.

[26] Arina Gorbatyuk, 'Rethinking IP Ownership in the Context of Open Innovation' (KU Leuven 2019) 149–50, 161–62, 170–72.

[27] Cf Rec 21 Trade Secret Directive, which refers to the need to weigh the interests of the stakeholders involved.

[28] See, however, Eleonora Rosati, *Copyright in the Digital Single Market. Article-by-Article Commentary to the Provisions of Directive 2019/790* (Oxford University Press 2021) 377.

[29] Cf in the context of enforcement of IP rights Arts 6(1), 6(2), 7(1), 8(1), 8(2) IPRED, whereby the possibility to obtain certain measures is expressly made subject to the protection of confidential information.

By analogy, corporate partners' reporting obligations stemming from national implementations of Article 19 DSM Directive will also apply without prejudice to trade secret protection.[30] Reference may be made to the EU Parliament proposal regarding the applicability of active reporting obligations to secondary relationships. After confirming the extension of such obligations to secondary contractual partners such as DSPs, it was specified that information from DSPs provided to artists should be unchanged, 'except in the case of commercially sensitive information' possibly subject to an NDA.[31] This leads to clear red flags. Detailed and individualised information regarding the exploitation of each piece of music – and the ensuing remuneration for it – is exactly what is required to ensure the requisite transparency.

The Trade Secret Directive itself also contains a number of specifications meant to contribute to attaining a fair balance between the interests of all stakeholders. Particular reference may be made to the fact that the acquisition of a trade secret is considered lawful if it is acquired in the context of collective labour agreements,[32], in conformity with honest trade practices,[33] or as required or allowed by law.[34] The lawfulness of subsequent use or disclosure under this provision depends on whether this is required or allowed by law.[35] The exception allowing employees to disclose information to their representatives that is necessary for the legitimate exercise of their representative functions[36] may provide a source of inspiration for musicians seeking the assistance of trade unions, CMOs or other representative organisations that may support them. Finally, an exception applies if the acquisition, use and/or disclosure follows from the protection of a legitimate interest recognised by law.[37] Given the express, repeated legislative acknowledgement of the tenuous contractual bargaining position of artists, this latter exception may provide fruitful ground to argue in favour of a restrictive application of trade secret protection in the context of active reporting obligations.

In sum, recourse to trade secret protection by corporate partners risks negating regulatory efforts to enhance transparency in the music value chain. A balanced application of trade secrets protection that curbs excessive claims on the part of both primary and secondary corporate partners is merited. It may be beneficial to accord co-holdership of audience data to musicians. However, given the prevalence of contractual solutions, the materialisation of such co-controllership in practice

[30] Cf Explanatory Memorandum Belgian Draft DSM Implementation Act (2020) 54.

[31] Parliament, 'Report on the Proposal for a Directive of the European Parliament and of the Council on Copyright in the Digital Single Market (COM(2016)0593 – C8-0383/2016 – 2016/0280(COD)) (29 June 2018) A8-0245/2018, 68.

[32] Arts 3(1)(c) *jo* 1(2)(d) Trade Secret Directive. See also Rec 34 Trade Secret Directive.

[33] Art 3(1)(d) Trade Secret Directive.

[34] Art 3(2) Trade Secret Directive. See also Rec 18 Trade Secret Directive.

[35] Art 3(2) Trade Secret Directive. See also Rec 18 Trade Secret Directive.

[36] Art 5(c) Trade Secret Directive. See also Rec 18 Trade Secret Directive.

[37] Art 5(d) Trade Secret Directive.

appears unlikely.[38] Alternatively, inspiration may be sourced from the abovementioned balancing measures that already exist within the EU trade secret regime. While employed musicians may already benefit from specifications stemming from the collective negotiation context,[39] an express hard law provision allowing – or even mandating – the lawful acquisition, use and disclosure of relevant (audience) data by artists for the purpose of enforcing their rights against their primary contractual partners would be welcome.[40] Even so, there is a significant leap between arguing that the acquisition and subsequent use or disclosure of certain secret audience data is lawful under the trade secret regime, and successfully bringing corporate partners to fully share such data in a timely way. Musicians who acquire data that may also have an impact on other musicians are likely to be requested to sign an NDA in order to avoid setting a public precedent.[41] The complex nature of many secondary relationships with sub-licensees across the globe further exacerbates this issue.[42] Finally, musicians faced with a corporate partner that is unwilling to provide full audience data during or after the contract are unlikely to take any steps to remedy this – either because their contract does not contain an express right to audit, or because they hesitate to invoke such a right due to cost considerations or because of fear of retaliation.[43] Regardless, such a hard law measure may contribute to granting musicians and their representatives a right – to a certain extent – to obtain access to such data, as well as use and/or disclose it under certain, well-defined circumstances. Cross-border stakeholder dialogue on appropriate rules concerning confidentiality leading to soft law, such as Commission guidelines, is the preferred solution. Inspiration may be drawn from other sectors at the crossroads between transparency and trade secret protection – also outside the CCIs, such as relating to environmental information.[44] In the context of dispute resolution, a form of 'confidentiality clubs' or a filtering system may be envisaged.[45] Such a mechanism may be used to limit the dissemination of data on a need-to-know basis, while safeguarding the right

38 cf Chapter 5, Section 5.2.3.

39 As to acquisition and disclosure, see respectively Arts 3(1)(c) *jo* 1(2)(d) Trade Secret Directive and Art 5(c) Trade Secret Directive.

40 Such an express proviso under national law is possible in accordance with Art 3(2) Trade Secret Directive.

41 Cooke, *Dissecting the Digital Dollar* (n 18) 208; Rebecca Giblin and Cory Doctorow, *Chokepoint Capitalism: How Big Tech and Big Content Captured Creative Labor Markets and How We'll Win Them Back* (Beacon Press 2022) 164–65.

42 Stef van Gompel and others, 'Evaluatie Wet Auteurscontractenrecht: Eindrapport' (2020) <https://bit.ly/3UBZrh4>44.

43 Cf Cooke, *Dissecting the Digital Dollar* (n 18) 33, 206–07; DCMS Committee, 'Economics of Music Streaming' (n 21) 73.

44 See in this regard Juliana Zuluaga Madrid, 'Access to Environmental Information Held by the Private Sector under International, European and Comparative Law' (KU Leuven 2020).

45 Cf Cooke, *Dissecting the Digital Dollar* (n 18) 104–05, 120; Irini Stamatoudi and Olivier Vrins, 'The Enforcement Directive' in Irini Stamatoudi and Paul Torremans (eds), *EU Copyright Law. A Commentary* (Elgar Commentaries, Edward Elgar 2021) 413–14.

for musicians to lean on the support of representative organisations. Finally, while the prohibition on abuse of law may in theory provide a fallback solution in certain situations, this is unlikely to provide added value in practice, given the existing checks and balances within the trade secret regime. Indeed, a judge that has held none of these internal mechanisms to apply is unlikely to nevertheless label certain behaviour as abusive.

7.4 LACK OF INVOCATION IN PRACTICE

Effective challenges to the fairness of the contracts under review on the basis of the relevant legal framework remain, to date, rather scarce. This finding not only applies to the scope of rights granted,[46] but also to the exploitation of music and the ensuing remuneration. As to indirect duties to exploit, their traditionally rare application[47] has been confirmed in an EU study concerning the application of the Term Extension Directive, where no examples enforcing the indirect duty to exploit pertaining to performers were reported.[48] There is also a conspicuous lack of cases on the measures regarding remuneration. The abovementioned EU study on the implementation of the Term Extension Directive identifies no examples of any recourse to either the clean slate provision or the right to annual supplementary remuneration.[49] Empirical research conducted in the Netherlands reports only two cases in total on fair remuneration (regarding photography[50] and

46 As to restrictions pertaining to future methods of exploitation, the past few years appear to have brought few 'new' methods in the sense of this concept. This in turn partially explains the limited application of the relevant restrictions in practice. See Stef van Gompel, '"Non, Non, Rien n'a Changé": Over Vergoedingsaanspraken voor Makers uit Hoofde van Exploitatiecontracten' [2021] Auteursrecht 3, 4. See also Raad voor de Intellectuele Eigendom, 'Advies betreffende de omzetting in Belgisch recht van richtlijn 2019/790/EU van 17 april 2019 inzake auteursrechten en naburige rechten in de digitale eengemaakte markt en tot wijziging van Richtlijnen 96/9/EG en 2001/29/EG' (19 June 2020) 108.

47 See eg Rita Matulionyte, 'Empowering Authors via Fairer Copyright Contract Law' (2019) 42 UNSWLJ 681, 708–12; Raad voor de Intellectuele Eigendom, 'Advies' (n 46) 99; Ula Furgał, 'Interpreting EU Reversion Rights: Why "Use-It-or-Lose-It" Should Be the Guiding Principle' (2021) 43 EIPR 283, 290. More evidence on the application of reversion rights in the CCIs – which has traditionally been rather scarce – is being gathered at the time of writing. See in particular the Author's Interest project, led by Associate Professor Rebecca Giblin <https://authorsinterest.org>. See also Furgał, 'Interpreting EU Reversion Rights' (n 47) 284; Rebecca Giblin and Joshua Yuvaraj, 'Copyright Reversion and the Author's Interest Project' [2020] 4.

48 Ana Ramalho and Aurelio Lopez-Tarruella, 'Implementation of the Directive 2011/77/EU: Copyright Term of Protection' (2018) 26.

49 ibid 29.

50 District Court Amsterdam 1 November 2019, docket number 7329753 CV EXPL 18-24837, ECLI:NL:RBAMS:2019:8099, ordering the defendant *De Persgroep* to pay around €300, as well as the costs of the proceedings; Court of Appeal Amsterdam 19 January 2021, docket number 200.276.610/01, ECLI:NL:GHAMS:2021:80, accepting the procedural admissibility of the appeal filed by De Persgroep.

journalism,[51] respectively), with no cases on the additional right to remuneration for emerging methods of exploitation.[52] Contract adjustment mechanisms have also led to a very limited number of cases in the chosen jurisdictions.[53] More generally, empirical research in Germany and the Netherlands indicates that these measures have not improved the income of artists to a significant extent.[54]

Several factors contribute to this. A first aspect is the apparent limited interest in and/or knowledge of the ins and outs of the protective framework among musicians, combined with the limited resources that most musicians are able to devote to the legal aspects of their career.[55] Many musicians are insufficiently aware of their rights and the various options that are available.[56] This contributes to the persistence of information asymmetries between musicians and their corporate partners. Musicians who are unaware of their rights are unlikely to invoke them. Remedying this not only requires a transparent legal framework that provides the

[51] District Court Amsterdam 1 November 2019, docket number 7329738 CV EXPL 18-24835, ECLI:NL:RBAMS:2019:8119, also ordering the defendant *De Persgroep* DP to pay around €300, as well as the costs of the proceedings.

[52] Van Gompel and others, 'Evaluatie Wet Auteurscontractenrecht' (n 42) 28, 30, 35; van Gompel, 'Non, Non, Rien n'a Changé' (n 46) 3–5. See also Dirk Visser and others, *ACR: Auteurscontractenrecht* (DeLex 2016) 88.

[53] Nikolaus Reber, 'The "Further Fair Participation" Provision in Art 32 a (2) German Copyright Act – Claims against a Third-Party Exploiter of a Work' (2016) 11 Journal of Intellectual Property Law & Practice 382, 383; Bently and others, 'Strengthening the Position' (n 3) 58–59; Agnès Lucas-Schloetter, 'The Remuneration of Authors and Performers in Copyright Contract Law' in Paul Torremans (ed), *Research Handbook on Copyright Law* (Research Handbooks in Intellectual Property, 2nd edn, Edward Elgar 2017) 262; van Gompel and others, 'Evaluatie Wet Auteurscontractenrecht' (n 42) 38, 44; van Gompel, 'Non, Non, Rien n'a Changé' (n 46) 6; Richard Osborne and Hyojung Sun, 'Economics of Streaming: Contract Adjustment and Rights Reversion' (6 February 2023) s 3.3.

[54] rRegarding Germany, see the studies referred to in Martin Senftleben, 'More Money for Creators and More Support for Copyright in Society – Fair Remuneration Rights in Germany and the Netherlands' (2018) 41 Colum J L & Arts 413, 422. See also Stefanie Hubig, 'Keynote' in Silke von Lewinski (ed), *Remuneration for the Use of Works. Exclusivity vs Other Approaches* (De Gruyter 2017) 314. See regarding the Netherlands, van Gompel and others, 'Evaluatie Wet Auteurscontractenrecht' (n 42) 36.

[55] Phillip W Hall Jr, 'Smells Like Slavery: Unconscionability in Recording Industry Contracts' [2002] Hastings Comm & Ent LJ 189, 191, 221; Ananay Aguilar, 'Distributed Ownership in Music: Between Authorship and Performance' (2018) 27 Social & Legal Studies 776793; Ananay Aguilar, '"We Want Artists to Be Fully and Fairly Paid for Their Work". Discourses on Fairness in the Neoliberal European Copyright Reform' [2018] JIPITEC 160, 167; Ramalho and Lopez-Tarruella, 'Implementation of the Directive 2011/77/EU' (n 48) 25.

[56] Jason Lee Guthrie, 'Taking the Liberty: Toward a Theory of Copyright and Creativity' (2016) 16 MEIEA Journal 97, 109; Aguilar, 'Distributed Ownership in Music' (n 55) 777, 787, 792–93; Ananay Aguilar, 'The Collective Management of Performers' Rights in the UK: A Story of Competing Interests' (2019) 16 SCRIPTed 4, 48; Donald Passman, *All You Need to Know about the Music Business* (10th edn, Simon & Schuster 2019) 5–6.

requisite legal certainty, but also sustained attention to the empowerment of musicians through knowledge creation and dissemination.[57]

Sector-specific knowledge on the part of musicians – and, if applicable, their managers – such as regarding the wide array of available ALS, their rights under the protective legal framework, and their options to effectively enforce those rights in practice, both individually and collectively and in either a judicial or extra-judicial context, may enhance their bargaining power and lead to a fairer music marketplace.[58] The steep increase in the variety of choices, coupled with musicians' prospective enhanced knowledge of those choices, provides an additional opportunity; the strong competition in the music distribution sector may lead to balanced deals.

Significant efforts are ongoing. The importance of the commercial and legal literacy of musicians is widely accepted. Online portals for artists,[59] dedicated music blogs,[60] academic institutions[61] and musician and/or manager interest groups[62] conduct timely research on sector-related topics and offer relevant information on

[57] P Bernt Hugenholtz and Lucie Guibault, 'Auteurscontractenrecht: Naar Een Wettelijke Regeling?' (2004) <https://bit.ly/3UvnwGx> vii, xiii, 85; Abhinay Muthoo, 'Bargaining Theory and Royalty Contract Negotiations' (2006) 3 RERCI 19, 27; Séverine Dusollier and others, 'Contractual Arrangements Applicable to Creators: Law and Practice of Selected Member States' (Publications Office of the EU 2014) <https://op.europa.eu/s/zIba>15, 105; Europe Economics and others, 'Remuneration of Authors and Performers for the Use of Their Works and the Fixations of Their Performances. Final Report' (Publications Office of the EU 2015) <https://op.europa.eu/s/zIa9> 150; Rethink Music Initiative, 'Fair Music: Transparency and Payment Flows in the Music Industry. Recommendations to Increase Transparency, Reduce Friction, and Promote Fairness in the Music Industry' (2015) 4, 28; Brigitte Lindner, 'The Role of Collective Administration in New Business Models in the Audiovisual Sector' in Silke von Lewinski (ed), *Remuneration for the Use of Works. Exclusivity vs Other Approaches* (De Gruyter 2017) 424; Cooke, *Dissecting the Digital Dollar* (n 18) 153; Bruno Racine, 'L'Auteur et l'Acte de Création' (January 2020) 7. However, on the difficulties of knowledge transfer see eg John Williamson and others, 'Having an Impact? Academics, the Music Industries and the Problem of Knowledge' (2011) 17 IJCP 459, 459–74.

[58] Cooke, *Dissecting the Digital Dollar* (n 18) 91, 124; 'The Ten Things People Get Wrong about Streaming – Part One' directed by Andy Malt and Chris Cooke (Podcast, Setlist, 5 November 2020) <https://bit.ly/3papHkF>. Cf in the literary sector Martin Kretschmer and others, 'UK Authors' Earnings and Contracts 2018: A Survey of 50.000 Writers' (2019) 3.

[59] See eg MusicAlly <https://musically.com>, WIPO for Creators <www.wipo.int/wipoforcreators/en>.

[60] See eg Complete Music Update (CMU) <https://completemusicupdate.com>, Music Business Worldwide <www.musicbusinessworldwide.com>, RightsTech <https://rightstech.com>.

[61] See eg the Rethink Music Initiative within the Berklee College of Music in the US <www.rethink-music.com>.

[62] See eg vi.be in Belgium <http://vi.be>, CNM in France <https://cnm.fr>, Deutsche Tonkünstlerverband in Germany <www.bdmv.de>, Artiesten Belangen Centrum in the Netherlands <http://artiestenbelangen.nl>. On the international level, reference may be made to the International Federation of Musicians (Fédération Internationale des Musiciens or FIM in short <www.fim-musicians.org>. For music managers in particular, see the Music Managers Forum <https://themmf.net>.

their website. CMOs and trade unions for composers and/or performers offer similar services to their members.[63] Helpful and to-the-point books oriented towards musicians provide the essence of the legal and business framework surrounding the music industry as well as practical tips that guide musicians on the road towards (commercial) success.[64] Online simulation tools guide musicians through the complexities of the fine print of their contracts towards transparent information on the amount of remuneration that is due to them.[65]

More can be done. Scoping surveys on commercial and legal knowledge and perceived musician needs provide a clearer picture of what action may be taken to move the music industry further in the right direction. Training programmes that cover commercial and legal aspects of their career should be further developed, possibly under the auspices of musician interest groups and/or CMOs, and should obtain enhanced and sustained institutional and financial support.[66] Within advanced music schools, an argument may be made in favour of making courses on commercial and legal skills mandatory. Through knowledge creation and transfer, musicians will be empowered to make free, personal choices regarding the exploitation of their music. Not only musicians would benefit from knowledge enhancement concerning the functioning of the music marketplace. In line with society's inherent pull towards the underdog, users are likely to be more drawn towards the interests of musicians than those of their corporate partners.[67]

Taking inspiration from fair trade labels that promote sustainable and equitable trade relationships, a type of certification for 'fair music' may be envisaged. A (neutral) body could draw attention to corporate partners that adhere to certain standards in terms of fair scope, exploitation and remuneration – the latter including

[63] Europe Economics and others, 'Remuneration of Authors and Performers' (n 57) 150; Isabelle De Voldere and others, 'Mapping the Creative Value Chains. A Study on the Economy of Culture in the Digital Age. Final Report' (Publications Office of the EU 2017) <https://op.europa.eu/s/zIa8> 67; Ramalho and Lopez-Tarruella, 'Implementation of the Directive 2011/77/EU' (n 48) 34–35.

[64] See eg David Stopps, 'How to Make a Living from Music, Second Edition' (Creative Industries, WIPO 2014); Luc Gulinck, *Hier Tekenen! (en Let Niet op de Kleine Lettertjes…) Wegwijs in het Juridische en Zakelijke Labyrint van de Muziekwereld* (Academia Press 2019); Passman, *All You Need to Know about the Music Business* (n 56); Pierre-Marie Bouvery, *Les Contrats de la Musique* (7th edn, IRMA 2020); Hayleigh Bosher, *Copyright in the Music Industry. A Practical Guide to Exploiting and Enforcing Rights* (Elgar Practical Guides, Edward Elgar 2021).

[65] See for helpful simulations of artist remuneration for streaming in particular: (1) for recorded music <https://dealsim.createos.app> and (2) for music publishing: <https://pubsim.createos.app>.

[66] Cf Bhamati Viswanathan, *Cultivating Copyright: How Creators and Creative Industries Can Harness Intellectual Property to Survive the Digital Age* (Routledge 2019) 228–31; House of Lords Communications and Digital Committee, 'At Risk: Our Creative Future' (HL Paper 125, 2023).

[67] For more detail, see above Chapter 2, Section 2.2.4.

a high-performing transparency mechanism.[68] Such 'naming and faming'[69] may have a nudging effect on users. It is therefore likely to result in a competitive advantage for certified 'fair' partners.[70] A general emphasis on 'fair trade music' may also motivate musicians.[71] An incentive could be provided by making the grant of certain government subsidies dependent on the adherence to certain benchmarks as to contractual fairness, including the participation in relevant ADR mechanisms.[72] Much work has already been done to set certain minimum standards for this particular purpose. Reference may be made to industry guidelines such as the Industry Agreement on Music Streaming Metadata in the United Kingdom,[73] the Belgian 'Juist is Juist' campaign[74] and the Dutch 'Fair Practice Code'.[75] Other projects offer promise, such as the UK music industry working group on fair pay for creators[76] and the international 'Fair Trade Music' (FTM) project.[77]

A second obstacle to the invocation of the legal framework is that fear of the chilling effect of overt disputes with contractual partners on their musical career risks deterring musicians faced with unfair contracts.[78] Conducting a public feud

[68] Pierre-É Lalonde, 'Study Concerning Fair Compensation for Music Creators in the Digital Age' (2014) 2, 4, 25–26, 28; Eddie Schwartz, 'Coda: Fair Trade Music: Letting the Light Shine In' in Susy Frankel and Daniel Gervais (eds), *The Evolution and Equilibrium of Copyright in the Digital Age* (Cambridge University Press 2014) 312; Rethink Music Initiative, 'Fair Music' (n 57) 4, 25–26; Aisling Quinn, 'Are Online Music Platforms Undermining the Principles of Copyright Law?' (2018) 13 JIPLP 49, 59. See also the 'fairness score', to be developed by the Fair MusE project.

[69] As opposed to 'naming and shaming'.

[70] See also Schwartz, 'Coda' (n 68) 313, 316; Jeremy de Beer, 'Making Copyright Markets Work for Creators, Consumers and the Public Interest' in Rebecca Giblin and Kimberlee Weatherall (eds), *What If We Could Reimagine Copyright?* (ANU Press 2017) 172–75; Cooke, *Dissecting the Digital Dollar* (n 18) 112; William Deresiewicz, *The Death of the Artist. How Creators Are Struggling to Survive in the Age of Billionaires and Big Tech* (Henry Holt 2020) 316.

[71] See in this sense Stephanie Plamondon, 'Rational Faith: The Utility of Fairness in Copyright' (2017) 97 BU L Rev 1487, 1502–06.

[72] Hugenholtz and Guibault, 'Auteurscontractenrecht' (n 57) vii, xiii, 85; van Gompel and others, 'Evaluatie Wet Auteurscontractenrecht' (n 42) 66; van Gompel, 'Non, Non, Rien n'a Changé' (n 46) 8.

[73] <https://bit.ly/3EqYsZI>. On transparency, see also UK Intellectual Property Office, 'Guidance: UK Voluntary Code of Good Practice on Transparency in Music Streaming' (31 January 2024) <https://bit.ly/4bbBx32>. On the working group on fair pay, see also UK Parliament Press Release, 'Economics of music streaming: Government accepts CMS Committee recommendation on industry remuneration working group' (30 May 2023) <https://bit.ly/44SR6ch>.

[74] <www.juistisjuist.be>.

[75] <www.fairpracticecode.nl>.

[76] Andre Paine, 'UK Government to Establish Music Industry Working Group on Fair Pay for Creators' (*Music Week*, 30 May 2023) <https://bit.ly/46WICD8>. As to more recent developments in this context, see Council of Music Makers, 'Creator Remuneration Working Group: CMM Opening Statement' (18 April 2024) <https://bit.ly/3QEaS6K>.

[77] <Cwww.fairtrademusicinternational.org>.

[78] Rec 79 DSM Directive; Lionel Bently, 'Between a Rock and a Hard Place: The Problems Facing Freelance Creators in the UK Media Market-Place. A Briefing Document on Behalf of

with a corporate partner almost inevitably implies a temporary halt to a musician's career. Moreover, legal complaints voiced by musicians risk compromising their commercial future.[79] As a result, musicians tend to submit to disadvantageous contractual terms, even if their chances of success in a judicial setting would in fact be substantial. This, in turn, may incentivise corporate partners to overreach and press for contractual conditions that would not survive judicial scrutiny. Moreover, given the oversupply of musicians, corporate partners are more or less unhindered by the risk of retaliation. Therefore, they are more inclined to strategic litigation and/or settlement behaviour.

Moreover, the costs associated with the enforcement of the legal framework are significant.[80] Given that the burden of proof regarding instances of unfairness lies with the musician(s) and in view of the inherent risk of legal proceedings, such costs may have a prohibitive effect.[81] This risk is exacerbated by the use of abstract legal terms that would benefit from further concretisation, as well as the lack of specialised knowledge of the music industry on the part of judges. Since relevant case law is largely lacking, the lingering legal uncertainty may dissuade other musicians from challenging the fairness of their contracts. Moreover, when a musician eventually amasses the resources and the stamina to directly challenge a contract in court, often a confidential settlement is reached in order to avoid the lengthy, costly judicial

The Creators' Rights Alliance. Third and Final Draft' (2009) 18–19; Dusollier and others, 'Contractual Arrangements Applicable to Creators' (n 57) 23; Tristan Azzi, 'Exclusive Rights. General Report: Mechanisms to Ensure Adequate Remuneration for Creators and Performers' in Silke von Lewinski (ed), *Remuneration for the Use of Works. Exclusivity vs Other Approaches* (De Gruyter 2017) 97; Lucas-Schloetter, 'The Remuneration of Authors and Performers in Copyright Contract Law' (n 53) 270; Séverine Dusollier, 'EU Contractual Protection of Creators: Blind Spots and Shortcomings' [2018] Colum J L & Arts, 436, 447–48, 454; Senftleben, 'More Money for Creators and More Support for Copyright in Society' (n 54) 430; Dusollier, 'The 2019 Directive on Copyright in the Digital Single Market' (n 150) 1025; DCMS Committee, 'Economics of Music Streaming' (n 21) 6; van Gompel, 'Non, Non, Rien n'a Changé' (n 46) 3.

79 Hall Jr, 'Smells Like Slavery' (n 55) 191; Silke von Lewinski, 'Collectivism and Its Role in the Frame of Individual Contracts' in Jan Rosén (ed), *Individualism and Collectiveness in Intellectual Property Law* (ATRIP Intellectual Property, Edward Elgar 2012) 118; Commission, 'Impact Assessment on the Modernisation of EU Copyright Rules Accompanying the Document Proposal for a Directive of the European Parliament and of the Council on Copyright in the Digital Single Market and Proposal for a Regulation of the European Parliament and of the Council Laying Down Rules on the Exercise of Copyright and Related Rights Applicable to Certain Online Transmissions of Broadcasting Organisations and Retransmissions of Television and Radio Programmes' (Staff Working Document) SWD (2016) 301 Final (14 September 2016) 176; Aguilar, 'We Want Artists' (n 55) 167; Gulinck, *Hier Tekenen!* (n 64) 539; Nikita Malevanny, *Online Music Distribution – How Much Exclusivity Is Needed? A Study of International, European, German and US Copyright Systems and Their Objectives*, vol 12 (Munich Studies on Innovation and Competition, Springer Berlin Heidelberg 2019) 95.

80 Aguilar, 'We Want Artists' (n 55) 167.

81 Dirk Visser, 'Pippi Langkous en het nieuwe auteurscontractenrecht' [2015] NJB 1289, 1292; Senftleben, 'More Money for Creators and More Support for Copyright in Society' (n 54) 423.

process, as well as, ultimately, precedent.[82] Further, the scarce disputes that play out publicly lead to legal sagas that span several years, due to the propensity of appeal proceedings. This long duration of the judicial process constitutes another reason for musicians to avoid a courtroom.[83] The consolidation and ensuing increased concentration in the music industry is likely to increase appeals by corporate partners against negative judgments at first instance, since bigger companies have more revenues and thus a bigger budget for litigation. By way of example, the case of Jost Vacano, the director of photography of *Das Boot*, was filed in 2008 and was ultimately settled in July 2021, after three judgments of the German Supreme Court.[84]

Corporate partners are likely to think twice before entering into a contractual relationship with musicians that are known for having objected to unfavourable contract terms in the past. This attitude is understandable and, from a commercial perspective, perfectly legitimate. The risk of commercial retaliation is therefore very real.

The path towards a solution to the obstacles discussed above is likely to be illuminated by enhanced recourse to collective initiatives. In addition to knowledge creation and awareness-raising, representative groups such as CMOs, trade unions, guilds and other representative entities may play an important role in providing a collective voice for the heterogeneous groups of relevant stakeholders, with a significant margin for collective bargaining and self-regulation.[85] Both sustained public support and high-performing oversight mechanisms are merited.[86]

The interests of composers are defended by cross-border organisations such as ECSA,[87] as well as several national initiatives.[88] The heterogeneous group of

[82] Cf Hall Jr, 'Smells Like Slavery' (n 55) 191, 218, 228; Gulinck, *Hier Tekenen!* (n 64) 52; Cooke, *Dissecting the Digital Dollar* (n 18) 33. Examples of such situations include the royalty disputes between Universal Music and (1) Eminem, which was settled out of court in 2012, see Gulinck, *Hier Tekenen!* (n 64) 295; Cooke, *Dissecting the Digital Dollar* (n 18) 87 and (2) Enrique Iglesias, who filed a suit in 2018, but where no judgment is available, see DCMS Committee, 'Economics of Music Streaming' (n 21) 29.

[83] Hall Jr, 'Smells Like Slavery' (n 55) 222; Gulinck, *Hier Tekenen!* (n 64) 247.

[84] German Federal Court of Justice 22 September 2011, docket number I ZR 127/10 <https://openjur.de/u/338982.html>; German Federal Court of Justice 2 February 2020, docket number I ZR 176/18 <https://openjur.de/u/2198095.html>; German Federal Court of Justice 1 April 2021, docket number I ZR 9/18. See on the settlement eg '"Das Boot"-Kameramann: Jost Vacano im Hafen' (*faz.net*, 29 July 2021) <https://bit.ly/2WGuX3E>.

[85] Dusollier and others, 'Contractual Arrangements Applicable to Creators' (n 57) 64–65; Commission, 'Report on the Responses to the Public Consultation on the Review of the EU Copyright Rules' (July 2014) 80; Aguilar, 'We Want Artists' (n 55) 176; Jacqueline Seignette and Jørgen Blomqvist, 'A Future Proof Copyright System' in *Copyright, to Be or Not to Be* (Ex Tuto 2019) 270.

[86] Cf the governance and transparency rules applicable to CMOs.

[87] European Composer and Songwriter Alliance <https://composeralliance.org>.

[88] See (by way of non-exhaustive examples) (1) in Belgium: BSCG (Belgian Screen Composers Guild); (2) in France: UNAC (Union Nationale des Auteurs et des Compositeurs); (3) in Germany: DKV (Deutscher Komponistenverband); (4) in the Netherlands BAM! Popauteurs

performers also has several international entities that seek to further their collective interests, such as AEPO-ARTIS,[89] FAC,[90] FIM[91] and IAO.[92] Grouping composers and performers are, among others, the Artist Rights Alliance[93] and the UK Council of Music Makers.[94] Other notable musician-led initiatives include the 'Broken Record' and 'Keep Music Alive' campaigns established in 2020, which advocate for substantive changes to the distribution of revenues in the music industry – albeit primarily in the United Kingdom.[95]

The potential role of CMOs in furthering the collective interests of musicians is clear. The main CMOs in the chosen jurisdictions were already mentioned above.[96] In addition, it is noted that national CMOs have joined forces in several umbrella organisations, such as GESAC[97] and CISAC.[98] In the political sphere, musicians can count on groups such as the CCFG.[99] For managers, reference may be made to IMMF[100] and EMMA.[101]

The interests of corporate partners are also defended collectively, through a number of representative organisations. As to record companies, in addition to national associations such as the BRMA,[102] at the international level, reference may be made to IFPI, IMPALA[103] and WIN.[104] Music publishers are represented by, among others, AIMP,[105] ICMP[106] and IMPF.[107]

(Beroepsvereniging voor Auteur-Muzikanten); and (5) in the United Kingdom: the Ivors Academy.

89 Association of European Performers' Organisations <www.aepo-artis.org>.

90 Featured Artists Coalition <http://thefac.org>.

91 Fédération Internationale des Musiciens <www.fim-musicians.org>.

92 International Artists Organisation <www.iaomusic.org>. See further also at the European level (in alphabetical order of acronyms) eg ECA (European Choral Association – Europa Cantat), EFNYO (European Federation of National Youth Orchestras), EOFed (European Orchestra Federation), ELIA (Globally Connected European Network of Higher Arts Education), EMU (European Music School Union).

93 <https://artistrightsalliance.org>.

94 <https://councilmusicmakers.org>.

95 See eg John Harris, 'Musicians Call for Industry Shake-Up to Protect Artists during Lockdown' (*The Guardian*, 11 May 2020) <https://bit.ly/3viAM4m>; DCMS Committee, 'Economics of Music Streaming' (n 21) 5.

96 See Chapter 2, Section 2.2.2.2.

97 Groupement Européen des Sociétés d'Auteurs et Compositeurs <https://authorsocieties.eu>.

98 Confédération Internationale des Sociétés d'Auteurs et Compositeurs <www.cisac.org>.

99 European Cultural Creators Friendship Group, a cross-partisan coalition in the European Parliament <http://members.culturalcreators.eu>.

100 International Music Managers Forum <http://immf.com>.

101 European Music Managers Alliance <https://emma.community>.

102 Belgian Recorded Music Association <www.brma.be>.

103 Independent Music Companies Association <https://impalamusic.org>.

104 Worldwide Independent Network <https://winformusic.org>.

105 Association of Independent Music Publishers <www.aimp.org>.

106 International Confederation of Music Publishers <https://icmp-ciem.org>.

107 Independent Music Publishers International Forum <www.impforum.org>.

Finally, in the United Kingdom in particular, a collective voice for various representatives of the music industry stakeholder groups is provided through UK Music.[108]

The voice of users has traditionally had limited traction in the copyright debate. However, it is noted that BEUC,[109] the umbrella group for European consumer organisations, has registered increased interest in copyright-related matters.[110]

The groundwork for collective empowerment in the music industry has been laid. While many opportunities are already being mined, progress is possible. Collective interest groups may not only provide support for individuals, but also substantively affect copyright policy and engage in self-regulation, including through recourse to collective bargaining.

First, collective entities have a key, long-term role to play in knowledge dissemination and the reduction of information asymmetries. Reference may be made to the provision of information on average revenues, a clear overview of the ins and outs of the relevant legal framework, and/or a comparative list of typical contractual arrangements that allows interested parties to compare cross-border opportunities, accompanied by the drafting and sustained promotion of balanced model agreements that include the baselines of contractual protection.[111] CMOs may use a share of the revenues they collect for such sociocultural and educational purposes.[112] While an argument may be made in favour of a certain degree of uniformity, care must be taken to accord sufficient attention to the specificity of independent repertoire and niche genres, such as jazz and classical music – and thus contribute

[108] <www.ukmusic.org>.

[109] Bureau Européen des Unions de Consommateurs <www.beuc.eu>.

[110] See eg resources at <www.beuc.eu/digital-rights/copyright>.

[111] Europe Economics and others, 'Remuneration of Authors and Performers' (n 57) 146, 150; Lionel Bently and others, *Intellectual Property Law* (6th edn, Oxford University Press 2022) 347.

[112] Cf Rec 4 CRM Directive. See in this sense also eg Art XI.258 Belgian CEL, which allows CMOs to reserve up to 10 per cent of their revenues to this end. See also Glynn Lunney, *Copyright's Excess: Money and Music in the US Recording Industry* (1st edn, Cambridge University Press 2018) 204; Dusollier and others, 'Contractual Arrangements Applicable to Creators' (n 57) 61–65; Europe Economics and others, 'Remuneration of Authors and Performers' (n 57) 140–41, 149–51; Lucie Guibault, 'Relationship between Copyright and Contract Law' in Estelle Derclaye (ed), *Research Handbook on the Future of EU Copyright* (Research Handbooks in Intellectual Property, Edward Elgar 2009) 526–27; Ruth Towse, 'Copyright and Economic Incentives: An Application to Performers' Rights in the Music Industry' (1999) 52 Kyklos 369, 382. In the future, the budget available for such purposes may decrease in view of Case C-265/19 *Recorded Artists Actors Performers (RAAP) v Phonographic Performance (Ireland)* [2020] ECLI:EU:C:2020:677, which will lead to a decrease in non-allocable CMO income, see Ole-Andreas Rognstad, 'The RAAP Case of the CJEU – What Happened to Reciprocity?' in Morten Rosenmeier (ed), *Festskrift til Jørgen Blomqvist* (Ex Tuto 2021) 525–48; European Copyright Society, 'Comment of the European Copyright Society on the Impact and Consequences of the CJEU Decision in C-265/19 (RAAP)' (2022). See also Catarina Arnaut and others, 'Study on the International Dimension of the Single Equitable Remuneration Right for Phonogram Performers and Producers and Its Effect on the European Creative Sector. Final Report' (2023).

to enhancing the diversity of cultural expression.[113] Individual stakeholders have a responsibility to make use of the possibilities offered by such a collective platform to make their voices heard.

Another positive effect that collective organisations may have on the individual empowerment of musicians is for them to make use of the possibilities granted by the legal framework to represent individuals collectively.[114] It should be remembered that the fact-specific nature of many disputes is likely to thwart the objective of maintaining anonymity and thus indirectly quelling fears of retaliation.[115] Regardless, providing a collective backbone to the individual may contribute to the effective application of the protective legal framework.

A second strand of opportunities results from the collective representation of stakeholders at the policy level, in the debate surrounding the balance between the interests of rightsholders and users. At present, different initiatives risk remaining heterogeneous and siloed. Ideally, in the long term, all of these relatively scattered groups should be brought together in a positive industry-wide discussion on the future of the music industry, to create synergies – and, ultimately, meaningful change.

Two sources of inspiration may be referred to in this regard. First, AEPO-ARTIS, FIM and IAO joined forces in the 'Fair Internet for Performers' Campaign in the context of the legislative process of the DSM Directive, in a bid to establish a collectively managed right to equitable remuneration for performers for online exploitation.[116] While this joint initiative was not fully successful, it resulted in the inclusion of the right to appropriate and proportionate remuneration in Article 18 DSM Directive.[117] A second example is provided by the various open letters sent to the EU regulatory level regarding the effect of the COVID-19 pandemic, which were signed by a large variety of collective organisations across all CCIs.[118] In May 2021, the Creative Europe 2021–2027 programme was launched, bringing €2.44 billion to support the CCIs over the following years.[119] The unified voice of the heterogeneous group of CCI stakeholders has undoubtedly played a role in this context.

For positive change to occur, stakeholders' individual and collective voice must be harnessed. Sustained individual empowerment primarily depends on awareness-raising and knowledge-building, and mainly applies to the artistic side of the music industry equation. Further, providing a collective voice to all stakeholders in the

113 Cf Rec 4 CRM Directive.

114 Van Gompel and others, 'Evaluatie Wet Auteurscontractenrecht' (n 42) 66.

115 ibid.

116 <www.fair-internet.eu>.

117 See eg Fair Internet Coalition, 'Joint Guidelines for the Implementation of the 2019 Copyright Directive' (2019).

118 See for an overview <https://bit.ly/3Ut2AzQ>.

119 See press release at <https://ec.europa.eu/culture/news/creative-europe-2021–2027-programme-launch>.

music industry, listening to it and acting upon the results may ensure that all stakeholders can acquire that coveted seat at the table. Nurturing industry-wide dialogue may contribute to a fairer distribution of revenues in the long run. A clear opportunity for meaningful intra-industry collaboration arises. As extensively discussed in Chapter 5, collective bargaining can play an important role in this regard.[120]

Collective enforcement may also contribute to enhanced transparency in the music value chain in practice, as well as to the effective application of the protective legal framework.[121] Indeed, the prevalence of collaborations in the music sector raises the question whether the collective dimension of copyright affects – or rather, should affect – the provision of information under the applicable reporting obligations. The impact of the collective dimension of copyright on the scope of reporting obligations in the chosen jurisdictions was already briefly discussed, as was the desirability of fleshing out substantive standards for reporting obligations on a sector-specific level, potentially through the vehicle of collective agreements.[122]

The application of reporting obligations in practice usually takes place on an individual basis. This may hinder efficiency in the context of large groups, such as (chamber) orchestras. While transparency on an individual level certainly has its benefits, collective transparency could have additional advantages. Given that many musicians shy away from enforcing their rights on an individual level, representative organisations, including CMOs, should be able to obtain information for the benefit of their members through recourse to passive reporting obligations.[123] Alternatively or complementarily thereto, inspiration may be drawn from the role of group leaders and elected representatives as already exists in Belgium and Germany for live performances by large groups of performing musicians.[124] These rules, meant to allow efficient contracting in the context of large-scale live productions, may also aid in operationalising transparency requirements. Further cementing these roles would require hard law legislative intervention. Also for active reporting obligations, it makes sense to require that relevant information (only) be provided to certain representative members of the group(s) at issue. This would alleviate the administrative burden for corporate partners and contribute to legal certainty. Thus, the enhancement of the role of representatives and representative organisations in the operationalisation of transparency requirements could amplify the potential impact of collectiveness. The DSM Directive expressly refers to the potential for 'representatives' of artists to assist in the operationalisation of active reporting obligations.[125] It should be made clear that such 'representatives' include representative

[120] See Chapter 5, Section 3.2.2.3.
[121] Cf Giblin and Doctorow, *Chokepoint Capitalism* (n 41) 161–79.
[122] See Chapter 5, Section 5.3.3.
[123] Cf European Copyright Society, 'Comment' (n 2) 143.
[124] See Chapter 2, Section 2.2.2.2.
[125] Art 19(2) DSM Directive.

organisations such as CMOs, trade unions, guilds, and so forth.[126] The importance of securing a balanced trade secret protection framework also rings true here, since undue recourse to trade secret protection could prevent representative organisations from accessing and using relevant audience data, as well as from disclosing such data in a dispute resolution context.

Moreover, the potential for collectiveness as to transparency should extend to the possibility to take relevant follow-up action, such as recourse to a collective adjustment mechanism – or even judicial or extra-judicial dispute resolution – if the circumstances so require. French law already expressly notes the possibility for the contract adjustment mechanism to be invoked by representatives of artists.[127] The explicit inclusion of this possibility in the (hard) laws of the other jurisdictions is to be supported. The same is true for an additional reference to the powers of representation of representative organisations.

In terms of enforcement, a collective dimension may also be developed. Individual musicians may be supported by collective entities.[128] If the circumstances so require, representative organisations should have the possibility to file a collective complaint.[129] The concept of class actions as known in a consumer law context could serve as a source of inspiration.[130]

In order for collective organisations effectively to be able to take on their role in this regard (which would give them an identity that is similar to a consumer rights body), both qualified personnel and sufficient financial means to undertake legal action are required. While membership fees and non-allocated CMO revenue may provide some margin in this regard, additional institutional support may be warranted.[131]

[126] Fair Internet Coalition, 'Joint Guidelines' (n 118) 11–12, 19.

[127] See Chapter 5, Section 5.3.2.3.1.

[128] See eg Azzi, 'Exclusive Rights' (n 78) 97.

[129] Cf Sofie De Pourcq, *Oneerlijke Handelspraktijken en Bedingen in Contracten Tussen Ondernemingen* (Intersentia 2018) 723–25.

[130] on the various mechanisms for collective redress in the chosen (and other) jurisdictions, see <www.collectiveredress.org>. See in particular (1) in Belgium: Arts XVII.36–XVII.70 Belgian CEL; (2) in France: Arts L 621-1–L 623-32 French Consumer Code; (3) in Germany: UKlaG, Art 79(2)(3) *Zivilprozessordnung* (in English: Code of Civil Procedure), Art 8 UWG; (4) in the Netherlands: Arts 1018b–1018m *Wetboek van Burgerlijke Rechtsvordering* (in English: Code of Civil Procedure) and Art 7:907–910 Dutch Civil Code; and (5) in the United Kingdom: Civil Procedure Rule (CPR) 19.6. See also Thomas Hoeren, 'Was bleibt von §§ 32, 32a, 36 UrhG? Überlegungen zur Zukunft des Urhebervertragsrechts' in Kirsten-Inger Wöhrn and others (eds), *Festschrift für Artur-Axel Wandtke zum 70 Geburtstag am 26 März 2013* (Walter De Gruyter 2013) 186; Dusollier and others, 'Contractual Arrangements Applicable to Creators' (n 57) 61, 105; Europe Economics and others, 'Remuneration of Authors and Performers' (n 57) 151; de Beer, 'Making Copyright Markets Work' (n 70) 169–72; Frances Lewis, 'Slipping through the Cracks: How Digital Music Streaming Cuts Corners on Artists' Royalty Revenues Globally' (2017) 43 Brook J Int'l L 297, 299; Dusollier, 'EU Contractual Protection of Creators' (n 78) 457; van Gompel and others, 'Evaluatie Wet Auteurscontractenrecht' (n 42) 44; van Gompel, 'Non, Non, Rien n'a Changé' (n 46) 8.

[131] Europe Economics and others, 'Remuneration of Authors and Performers' (n 57) 151.

Several rules already allow for collective judicial enforcement of (part of) the legal framework. The DSM Directive expressly notes the potential for representative organisations in this context.[132] It does not specify anything regarding the possibility and/or desirability of granting such organisations the legal standing to commence judicial proceedings in the name of and on the account of musicians. Article 4 IPRED expressly noted the option for Member States to grant legal standing to CMOs and professional defence bodies that are regularly recognised as having authority to represent rightsholders, insofar as permitted by and in accordance with national law.[133] Both Belgium and France have made use of this possibility.[134] As a result, in those countries, such collective entities have legal standing in cases deemed of interest to their members with a view to defending the rights of those members, if this is expressly provided in those entities' statutes.[135] In the Netherlands, a foundation or association with full legal capacity may commence legal proceedings aimed at protecting similar interests of other persons, insofar as the objective of furthering these interests is included in the articles of association.[136]

In the field of copyright contract law in particular, under pre-DSM German law, trade unions and representative associations already had the right to bring legal action in their own name in order to secure injunctive relief following the breach of a joint remuneration agreement.[137] Given that only a limited number of such collective agreements have been entered into so far, this possibility remains rather theoretical at present.[138] In addition, the newly added, more general Article 32g German Copyright Act grants representative organisations the possibility to represent artists collectively when it comes to the application of Articles 32–32f German Copyright Act 'in accordance with the Act on Out-of-Court Legal Services and the procedural rules'.[139] Thus, it grants a right of action to representative

[132] Art 20(1) *jo* Rec 78 DSM Directive. See also Arts XI.167/3, XI.205/3 Belgian CEL; Art L 131-5 (III) French IP Code.

[133] Art 4(c)–(d) IPRED. See also Rec 18 IPRED.

[134] See (1) in Belgium: Art XVII.7 para 1, 3° *jo* para 2 Belgian CEL for professional organisations having legal personality and (2) in France: Art L 331-1 French IP Code; Commission, 'Guidance on Certain Aspects of Directive 2004/48/EC of the European Parliament and of the Council on the Enforcement of Intellectual Property Rights' (Communication) COM (2017) 708 final (29 November 2017) 25; André Lucas and others, *Traité de la Propriété Littéraire et Artistique* (5th edn, LexisNexis 2017) 946–847; Pierre-Yves Gautier, *Propriété Littéraire et Artistique* (11th edn, Presses Universitaires de France 2019) 803–05; Christophe Caron, *Droit d'Auteur et Droits Voisins* (6th edn, LexisNexis 2020) 574–75.

[135] Commission, 'Guidance' COM(2017) 708 final (n 135) 25.

[136] Arts 3:305a–3:305d Dutch Civil Code; Barbara Baarsma and Nicole Rosenboom, 'Oneerlijke Handelspraktijken. Voldoet Bestaande (Zelf)regulering?' (2013) 14–17.

[137] Art 36b German Copyright Act; Lucas-Schloetter, 'The Remuneration of Authors and Performers in Copyright Contract Law' (n 53) 271; Gunda Dreyer and others, *Urheberrecht* (Heidelberger Kommentar, 4th edn, CF Müller 2018) 814–15; Philipp Möhring and Käte Nicolini, *Urheberrecht* (4th edn, CH Beck 2018) 553–62.

[138] See Chapter 5, Section 5.3.2.2.3.

[139] New Arts 32g *jo* 79(2a) German Copyright Act.

organisations on both a judicial and extra-judicial level. Representative organisations also have the right to commence ADR proceedings under both French and Dutch law, while such a right remains absent under Belgian law at the time of writing.[140]

Collective enforcement also appears to be on the rise in the application of the law of unfair B2B contract terms and trade practices.[141] The legal standing of professional defence bodies under Belgian law also applies in the context of unfair B2B situations.[142] It grants the competent minister a right to obtain an injunction. The provision specific to unfair B2B contract terms and trade practices under French law also refers to a right of initiative on the part of the competent minister.[143] Finally, on unfair trade practices in particular, reference may also be made to the right of action granted to certain professional organisations with legal personality under the German Act on Unfair Competition.[144]

The fear of retaliation associated with the enforcement of the legal framework would cease to apply if the anonymity of the artist(s) involved is preserved throughout the (collective) proceedings. The DSM Directive expressly acknowledges the pertinence of protecting the anonymity of the represented artists.[145] However, it seems almost inevitable for the identity of the artist(s) involved to surface in the course of dispute resolution proceedings, in view of the specific set of facts surrounding the dispute(s) at issue and the concrete evidence.[146] In many cases, the objective of preserving anonymity is likely to remain a pipedream.[147] Consequently, it appears unproductive to focus on measures aimed at maintaining such anonymity outside the context of potential class actions[148] that transcend a specific set of facts.

[140] See respectively Art L 214-6(I) French IP Code and Art 25g(3) Dutch Copyright Act.

[141] Cf De Pourcq, *Oneerlijke Handelspraktijken* (n 130) 303–05, 486–93.

[142] Art XVII.7 Belgian CEL; De Pourcq, *Oneerlijke Handelspraktijken* (n 130) 304, 480–81; Jules Stuyck and Bert Keirsbilck, *Handels- en Economisch Recht. Deel 2. Mededingingsrecht. A. Handelspraktijken en Contracten met Consumenten* (Beginselen van Belgisch Privaatrecht XIII, 5th edn, Wolters Kluwer 2019) 127–36.

[143] Art L 442–4(I) French Commercial Code; De Pourcq, *Oneerlijke Handelspraktijken* (n 130) 306–10, 482–83.

[144] Art 8 UWG. See also Art 3 *Gesetz über Unterlassungsklagen bei Verbraucherrechts- und anderen Verstößen* (commonly abbreviated as UKlaG); De Pourcq, *Oneerlijke Handelspraktijken* (n 130) 311, 483–87.

[145] Rec 78 DSM Directive.

[146] Ananay Aguilar, 'The New Copyright Directive: Fair Remuneration in Exploitation Contracts of Authors and Performers – Part II, Articles 20–23' (*Kluwer Copyright Blog*, 1 August 2019) <https://bit.ly/3Qh8WBl>; van Gompel and others, 'Evaluatie Wet Auteurscontractenrecht' (n 42) 44; van Gompel, 'Non, Non, Rien n'a Changé' (n 46) 8.

[147] See also Baarsma and Rosenboom, 'Oneerlijke Handelspraktijken' (n 137) 19–20.

[148] See on the various mechanisms for collective redress in the chosen (and other) jurisdictions: <www.collectiveredress.org>. See in particular (1) in Belgium: Arts XVII.36–XVII.70 Belgian CEL; (2) in France: Arts L 621-1–L 623-32 French Consumer Code; (3) in Germany: UKlaG, Art 79(2)(3) *Zivilprozessordnung*, Art 8 UWG; and (4) in the Netherlands: Arts 1018b–1018m *Wetboek van Burgerlijke Rechtsvordering* (in English: 'Code of Civil Procedure') and Art 7:907–910 Dutch Civil Code.

7.5 EXTRA-JUDICIAL ENFORCEMENT

The courtroom is not the only place to settle a dispute. In addition, several alternative extra-judicial routes are available, such as negotiation, conciliation, mediation and arbitration. These are commonly grouped together under the label 'alternative dispute resolution' or 'ADR'. Proponents of ADR argue that it is quicker, less expensive and less antagonistic than litigation, all of which are considerations that may be beneficial to musicians who seek to enforce the rights drawn from Chapters 4–6.[149] This section reviews the potential of ADR in the streaming age.

While, prior to the DSM Directive, some efforts had been made towards the establishment and promotion of ADR in the CCIs in Belgium[150] and Germany,[151] the main notable initiatives in this regard may be found in France and the Netherlands.

First, in 2016, in addition to the general framework on ADR, the French legislator created the figure of a *médiateur de la musique*.[152] This mediator has jurisdiction for all disputes pertaining to the interpretation and/or performance of contracts between performing musicians and record companies.[153] Extra-judicial proceedings before the mediator may be brought by performing musicians, record companies, their representatives, any interested professional organisation and/or trade union, or even the French minister for culture.[154] If the parties cannot come to an agreement themselves, the mediator may propose a compromise.[155] Both the agreement and the proposed compromise may be published, provided that applicable trade secrets are safeguarded.[156] The mediator may also propose measures that could lead to codes of conduct regarding the behaviour of stakeholders, thus also potentially

[149] Stopps, 'How to Make a Living from Music' (n 64) 88; Séverine Dusollier, 'The 2019 Directive on Copyright in the Digital Single Market: Some Progress, a Few Bad Choices, and an Overall Failed Ambition' [2020] CML Rev 979, 1025; Dev Gangjee and others, 'Alternative Dispute Resolution Mechanisms for Business-to-Business Digital Copyright- and Content-Related Disputes: A Report on the Results of the WIPO–MCST Survey' (WIPO Publication, WIPO 2021) 21–25.

[150] See eg Marie-Christine Janssens and others, 'Boek XI. Intellectuele Eigendom' in Evelyne Terryn and Bert Keirsbilck (eds), *Het Wetboek van economisch recht: van nu en straks?* (Intersentia 2014) 271, 292–93.

[151] See eg the establishment of an arbitration board for joint remuneration agreements, see Arts 36 (3)–(4) *jo* 36a *jo* 79(2a) German Copyright Act).

[152] <http://mediateurdelamusique.fr>, in English: music mediator. See for the general framework on ADR under French law: Book V, Title I of the French *Code de procedure civile* (in English: Code of Civil Procedure).

[153] Art L 214-6 French IP Code. See also Arts R 214-8–R 214-18 French IP Code; Lucas and others, *Traité de la Propriété Littéraire et Artistique* (n 135) 1150–51; Racine, 'L'Auteur et l'Acte de Création' (n 57) 113–14; Séverine Dusollier and Léo Pascault, 'Contractual Protection of Authors and Performers in France after the CDSM Directive' in Simon Geiregat and Hendrik Vanhees (eds), *Copyright Contracts Tomorrow* (LeA 2023) 78–79.

[154] Art L 214-6(I) French IP Code.

[155] Art L 214-6(I) French IP Code.

[156] ibid.

contributing to bottom-up change within the music industry.[157] In addition to the mediator, in the music publishing sector there is the potential establishment of a conciliation commission to address contractual disputes relating to exploitation and remuneration.[158] Finally, indicating the potential value of ADR over litigation, the French IP Code expressly allows for extra-judicial arbitration of copyright disputes.[159] However, the reports published by the French music mediator show an extremely sparse utilisation of the mediation function – with a total of three cases falling within the mediator's jurisdiction between its establishment in 2017 and the second report in March 2020.[160] This limited number of cases even brought the previous music mediator to the rather discouraging conclusion that it may be best just to abolish this ADR mechanism in its entirety, or instead transfer its competence to the Centre National de la Musique (CNM), a public institution under the supervision of the French Ministry for Culture that was established in January 2020.[161]

Second, in the Netherlands, the primary entity of note is the Geschillencommissie Auteurscontractenrecht,'[162] which was established in 2015 following the overhaul of Dutch copyright contract law.[163] This committee has jurisdiction for disputes concerning the provisions of Dutch copyright contract law that regulate fair scope, fair exploitation and fair remuneration.[164] Regardless of this broad scope of jurisdiction, recourse to this dispute resolution mechanism has been scant so far. The only available cases pertain to an (albeit successful) action brought on the basis of the Dutch contract adjustment mechanism by the director and screenwriter of the Dutch film *Soof 2*.[165] One of the reasons for this apparent lack of recourse to the mechanism is that it is voluntary. Indeed, a dispute may only be submitted to the ADR proceedings if the corporate partner at issue has enlisted with the committee, and if both parties agree to submit the specific dispute to

[157] Art L 214-6(II) French IP Code.

[158] See extensively Code des Usages et des Bonnes Pratiques de l'Edition des Œuvres Musicales (4 October 2017) s 4. See also as to the literary sector <https://bit.ly/2YBqZuo>.

[159] Art L 331-1(4) French IP Code.

[160] See Denis Berthomier, 'Médiateur de la musique. Rapport d'activité 2017–2018' (2019); Denis Berthomier, 'Médiateur de la musique. Rapport annuel 2019–2020' (2020).

[161] Berthomier, 'Médiateur de la musique' (n 161) 6.

[162] <www.degeschillencommissie.nl>, in English: copyright contract law dispute resolution committee.

[163] Art 25g Dutch Copyright Act *jo* Art 2b Dutch Neighbouring Rights Act. See in detail on the legislative history and scope of this provision Visser and others, *ACR: Auteurscontractenrecht* (n 67) 209–27; JH Spoor and others, *Auteursrecht. Auteursrecht, portretrecht, naburige rechten en databankenrecht* (Recht en Praktijk, 4th edn, Wolters Kluwer 2019) 584–86; van Gompel and others, 'Evaluatie Wet Auteurscontractenrecht' (n 42) 61–62. As to ongoing legislative developments in this context, see <https://bit.ly/3Uze3Ov>.

[164] Art 25g(1) Dutch Copyright Act *jo* Art 2b Dutch Neighbouring Rights Act. See also van Gompel and others, 'Evaluatie Wet Auteurscontractenrecht' (n 42) 61–62.

[165] Geschillencie ACR 18 April 2018, docket numbers 113417 (director) and 113462 (screenwriter), <www.degeschillencommissie.nl>. This decision was rather ardently criticised by some, see eg van Gompel and others, 'Evaluatie Wet Auteurscontractenrecht' (n 42) 38–40, 62.

ADR.[166] Incentives for corporate partners to participate voluntarily are lacking at present, also in view of the currently limited number of cases and the negative reception of the *Soof 2* decisions.[167] The lengthy ADR process has also been cited as a reason for the Dutch ADR mechanism's limited success to date.[168] Artists' fear of commercial retaliation also applies here.[169] In a bid to mitigate this risk, a claim before the committee may also be introduced by representative organisations of artists.[170] Apparently, this possibility has not yet been used, as is the case for the possibility to file a complaint anonymously – the latter because of the fear of this anonymity being compromised in the course of the proceedings.[171] In parallel, a mechanism concerning the extra-judicial rescission of publishing contracts was set up in 2010 between BumaStemra, the songwriter association Professionele Auteurs Lichte Muziek (PALM)[172] and the music publishers' association Nederlandse Muziek Uitgevers Vereniging (NMUV). Authoritative research from the Netherlands has found that, between 2010 and 2015, use of the mechanism was made in a total of forty-five cases, a small minority of which was followed by judicial proceedings.[173] While these proceedings, at the time of writing, are conceptually separate from the Geschillencommissie, it has been considered to link both types of ADR proceedings in some way.[174]

Inspired by the French and Dutch examples, Article 21 DSM Directive obliges Member States to take active steps towards the establishment of a voluntary ADR mechanism for the harmonised active reporting obligations and the harmonised contract adjustment mechanism.[175] The temporal application of such ADR mechanisms to acts of exploitation after 7 June 2021 is warranted.[176] Member States may extend the scope of such an ADR mechanism to other types of disputes. The implementation leeway for Member States extends beyond the appropriate scope of the ADR mechanism and includes questions of procedure, composition and presidency of the ADR panel, as well as cost issues.[177] If an existing national ADR

[166] Spoor and others, *Auteursrecht* (n 164) 585; van Gompel and others, 'Evaluatie Wet Auteurscontractenrecht' (n 42) 62.
[167] Van Gompel and others, 'Evaluatie Wet Auteurscontractenrecht' (n 42) 62–64, 66.
[168] ibid 63.
[169] ibid.
[170] Art 25g(3) Dutch Copyright Act; Visser and others, *ACR: Auteurscontractenrecht* (n 67) 210.
[171] Van Gompel and others, 'Evaluatie Wet Auteurscontractenrecht' (n 42) 63.
[172] In 2013, PALM changed its name to Popauteurs.nl. In 2020, Popauteurs.nl merged its activities with BAM!, forming BAM! Popauteurs <www.bampopauteurs.nl>.
[173] See van Gompel and others, 'Evaluatie Wet Auteurscontractenrecht' (n 42) 47–48.
[174] ibid 52.
[175] Bently and others, 'Strengthening the Position' (n 3) 49, 67; Gangjee and others, 'Alternative Dispute Resolution Mechanisms' (n 150) 11, 29–30.
[176] Cf Rosati, *Copyright in the Digital Single Market* (n 28) 399.
[177] Aguilar, 'We Want Artists' (n 55) 168; Ted Shapiro, 'Remuneration Provisions in the DSM Copyright Directive and the Audiovisual Industry in the EU: The Elusive Quest for Fairness' (2020) 42 EIPR 778, 783.

mechanism fulfils the substantive conditions set by Article 21 DSM Directive – without any requirements as to institutional setup – the Member States need not set up a new one.[178]

Post-DSM, the ADR setup in France and the Netherlands remains essentially the same.[179] In Germany, two new provisions are of note. First, the German legislator has expressly acknowledged the possibility of voluntary mediation or another form of ADR for disputes concerning Articles 32–32e German Copyright Act.[180] The mandatory nature of this option is confirmed by the fact that corporate partners cannot invoke a clause to the disadvantage of artists.[181] Second, since the implementation of the DSM Directive, the German Copyright Act expressly provides that artists can be represented collectively in the event of disputes concerning the application of Articles 32–32f German Copyright Act 'in accordance with the Act on Out-of-Court Legal Services and the procedural rules' – thus implying the possibility of both extra-judicial and judicial collective representation.[182] The Belgian legislator decided not to actively implement Article 21 in view of detailed existing regimes for both judicial and extra-judicial mediation proceedings in the Belgian Judicial Code.[183] Contrary to what the last sentence of Article 21 DSM Directive establishes, the Belgian extra-judicial mediation mechanism requires the initiative of one of the parties to the dispute, without referring to the possible role of representative organisations. Therefore, while the general mechanisms on mediation under Belgian law may have their merits, a mere reference to these mechanisms in the context of the implementation of the DSM Directive falls short.

For the sake of completeness, it is noted that the Brennan Bill does not accord express attention to ADR. Instead, it opted to accord jurisdiction for the proposed rules to the Copyright Tribunal.[184]

Out-of-court alternatives that enhance application of the legal framework in practice, such as those outlined, deserve institutional support.[185] The slow uptake

[178] Rec 79 DSM Directive.

[179] Fabrice Siiriainen, 'L'article 21 sur le reglement des litiges: une disposition utile dont la transposition est inutile?' [2021] PI 53.

[180] Arts 32f(1) *jo* 79(2a) German Copyright Act.

[181] Arts 32b, 32f(2) *jo* 79(2a) German Copyright Act.

[182] New Arts 32g *jo* 79(2a) German Copyright Act. Excerpt in German: *nach Maßgabe des Rechtsdienstleistungsgesetzes und der Prozessordnungen*. The *Rechtsdienstleistungsgesetzes*, which pertains to out-of-court legal services, is available at <www.gesetze-im-internet.de/rdg>. Given that this provision is not included in Art 32b German Copyright Act, is does not appear to be of a(n overriding) mandatory nature. Cf Gernot Schulze, 'Das Urhebervertragsrecht nach Erlass der EU-Richtlinie über das Urheberrecht im digitalen Binnenmarkt' [2019] GRUR 682, 685.

[183] Arts 1724–1737 Belgian Judicial Code; Explanatory Memorandum Belgian Draft DSM Implementation Act (n 30) 18; Raad voor de Intellectuele Eigendom, 'Advies' (n 46) 95.

[184] Draft Art 142A UK CDPA, as introduced in Copyright (Rights and Remuneration of Musicians, Etc.) HC Bill (2021–22) 19 <www.gov.uk/government/organisations/copyright-tribunal>.

[185] Racine, 'L'Auteur et l'Acte de Création' (n 57) 5, 57–59. cf Rec 46 InfoSoc Directive; Commission, 'Impact Assessment' SWD(2016) 301 final (n 79) 189. Regarding the merits of

of ADR in practice is cause for concern. In addition to the merits of increasing awareness and allowing collective representation of musicians to counter the fear of commercial retaliation, four courses of action are suggested.

First, applicable ADR mechanisms should cover all types of disputes concerning copyright exploitation contracts, in terms of fair scope, exploitation *and* remuneration. Procedural rules by ADR mechanisms that allow them to refuse to hear a certain dispute – such as a monetary threshold – should be kept at a minimum.[186] The specification of the jurisdiction of the French *médiateur de la musique* as extending to all disputes pertaining to the interpretation and/or performance of contracts may serve as a source of inspiration. This jurisdiction should apply to both composing and performing musicians, as is the case in Germany and the Netherlands. On a substantive level, the German and Dutch alternative of expressly attaching the jurisdiction of the relevant ADR mechanism to the relevant provisions of copyright contract law may also be assessed largely positively.[187] However, it has the slight disadvantage of implicitly excluding from its scope the complementary provisions of unfair B2B contract terms and trade practices, as well as relevant principles of general contract law.

Second, in order to enhance the use of ADR mechanisms in practice, their legitimacy should be ensured, providing stakeholders with sufficient incentives to submit their dispute(s) to such a mechanism.[188] This means that available ADR mechanisms should fulfil demanding procedural and substantive requirements in terms of overall quality and, importantly, neutrality.[189] The participation of representative stakeholder organisations in the setup and functioning of ADR mechanisms is desirable.[190] Procedurally speaking, guarantees must be offered in terms of accessibility, impartiality and independence, transparency, speed and cost-effectiveness.[191] Substantive fairness requires an objective assessment that takes due account

ADR in an IP dispute resolution context, Jacques de Werra, 'Can Alternative Dispute Resolution Mechanisms Become the Default Method for Solving International Intellectual Property Disputes' (2012) 43 Cal W Int'l LJ 39.

186 Rec 25 Directive 2013/11/EU of the European Parliament and of the Council of 21 May 2013 on alternative dispute resolution for consumer disputes and amending Regulation (EC) No 2006/2004 and Directive 2009/22/EC (Directive on Consumer ADR) [2013] OJ L165/63.

187 See Art 25g Dutch Copyright Act; Art 32f(1) German Copyright Act.

188 Cf Rec 49 Consumer ADR Directive; Aguilar, 'The New Copyright Directive: Part II, Articles 20–23' (n 147).

189 Appropriate benchmarks may be shaped on the basis of the criteria set by the Directive 2008/52/EC of the European Parliament and of the Council of 21 May 2008 on certain aspects of mediation in civil and commercial matters [2008] OJ L136/3 (hereinafter 'Mediation Directive') and the Directive on Consumer ADR referenced above.

190 Cf Rec 51 Consumer ADR Directive.

191 Cf Art 4(1) Mediation Directive; Arts 1, 6–9 *jo* Recs 32–35, 39–40 Directive on Consumer ADR. The requirement of independence implies the need for rules concerning potential conflicts of interest on the part of (the panel of) adjudicators. As to the consideration of cost-effectiveness in particular, fee calculators such as those available for certain registered IPRs may provide a source of inspiration.

of the interests of all stakeholders, with a practical perspective that is grounded in the reality of the music sector.[192] To this end, the legal and music industry expertise of relevant mediators and adjudicating panels should be guaranteed.[193]

Supervisory authorities and public oversight bodies, as more frequently active in the area of consumer law and data protection, may have a complementary role to play in terms of ex post quality control – or even participate in ADR mechanisms themselves.[194] As another form of quality control, but also to further transparency and legal certainty, ADR entities should publish a periodic overview of relevant findings in specific cases that have a broader potential application, allowing for public scrutiny regarding their decisions while maintaining confidentiality and privacy where necessary.[195] This may contribute to the establishment of good practices.[196] Similarly, the exchange of such good practices between ADR entities established in different national territories is likely to be beneficial.[197]

Third, if the above safeguards prove to be insufficient to convince stakeholders to opt for ADR in times of need, it may be considered to make recourse to ADR mandatory if one of the parties to the disputes so requests.[198] The Dutch legislator has proposed to include the possibility to force publicly financed corporate partners to submit to the jurisdiction of the Geschillencommissie.[199] Reference may also be made to the rule of general Belgian procedural law established in 2018 that seeks to enhance recourse to ADR by, among other things, allowing judges to impose mediation when deemed appropriate.[200]

Article 23(1) DSM Directive expressly qualifies the possibility to have recourse to ADR as mandatory law.[201] Regardless, the mechanism is referred to as 'voluntary'. The question therefore arises whether corporate partners may avoid ADR proceedings by just refusing to submit a particular dispute to ADR. On the one hand, if a party wishes to go to court, they must arguably be free to do so.[202] The right of access

[192] Cf Rec 31 Directive on Consumer ADR.

[193] Cf Art 4(2) *jo* Rec 16 Mediation Directive; Art 6 *jo* Rec 36 Directive on Consumer ADR.

[194] Cf Arts 17–20 *jo* Rec 55 Consumer ADR Directive; Arts 51–59 GDPR.

[195] Cf Recs 29–30 Consumer ADR Directive. See as to considerations of confidentiality also Art 7 *jo* Rec 23 Mediation Directive.

[196] Cf Rec 30 Consumer ADR Directive.

[197] Cf Art 16 *jo* Rec 54 Consumer ADR Directive.

[198] Cf Raad voor de Intellectuele Eigendom, 'Advies' (n 46) 96; van Gompel and others, 'Evaluatie Wet Auteurscontractenrecht' (n 42) 64; Giblin and Doctorow, *Chokepoint Capitalism* (n 41) 167.

[199] See draft amendment to Art 25g Dutch Copyright Code <https://bit.ly/44o7vot>.. The legislative process on this as well as other amendments to the Dutch regulatory framework is ongoing at the time of writing, see <https://bit.ly/3Uze3Ov>.

[200] See Art 1734(1) Belgian Judicial Code.

[201] Art 23(1) *jo* Rec 81 DSM Directive.

[202] Rec 79 DSM Directive. See also Commission, 'Impact Assessment' SWD(2016) 301 final (n 79) 180.

to the judicial system must be safeguarded.[203] Prior recourse to ADR should not be a precondition for being allowed to commence judicial proceedings. On the other hand, if the ADR mechanism is actually purely voluntary, there is a risk that corporate partners refuse participate – even if the proceedings may be commenced by representative organisations, as is the case in the Netherlands.[204] This renders the potential intervention of representative organisations rather ineffective.[205] In turn, this supports the argument that corporate partners should not be able to avoid ADR proceedings by simply refusing to participate.[206] Another argument is the principled mandatory nature of the ADR mechanism, which renders it impervious to contractual deviation.[207] A future preliminary reference to the ECJ may be envisaged. Presumably relevant criteria will be whether the ADR proceedings lead to a binding result for the parties and whether certain procedural benchmarks are attained, such as on speed and costs, and the possibility to obtain interim measures.[208]

Fourth and finally, ADR would benefit from increased recourse to collectiveness. Article 21 DSM Directive already requires EU Member States to ensure that representative organisations of artists can initiate ADR proceedings at the specific request of one or more artists, but only for the application of contract adjustment mechanisms and active reporting obligations.[209] This possibility should be extended, as is already the case in France, Germany and the Netherlands.

7.6 OUTRO

A protective legal framework risks pointlessness if its application in practice is not secured. Precisely this application in practice leaves much to be desired at present. The express qualification of much of the relevant provisions as mandatory law is laudable. However, the limited number of cases where the legal framework is actually invoked is concerning.

This rings all the more true in view of the recurring observation that the relevant legal framework sets forth many abstract, vague concepts that would benefit from further concretisation through case law. The resulting chicken and egg situation is that stakeholders confronted with vague legal provisions are likely to shy away from taking legal action, while precisely such action could bring clarity.

[203] Joined Cases C-317/08 to C-320/08 *Rosalba Alassini and Others v Telecom Italia and Others* [2010] ECLI:EU:C:2010:146; Case C-75/16 *Livio Menini, Maria Antonia Rampanelli v Banco Popolare Società Cooperativa* [2017] ECLI:EU:C:2017:457. cf Arts 5(2), 8(1) *jo* Recs 14, 24 Mediation Directive; Arts 1, 10 *jo* Recs 43, 45, 49 Consumer ADR Directive.

[204] Van Gompel and others, 'Evaluatie Wet Auteurscontractenrecht' (n 42) 65.

[205] ibid.

[206] ibid.

[207] See above and Art 23 DSM Directive.

[208] Cf Joined Cases C-317/08 to C-320/08 *Alassini and Ors v Telecom Italia and Others* [2010] ECLI:EU:C:2010:146.

[209] Art 21 *jo* Rec 79 DSM Directive.

The limited amount of available case law does little to remedy this. This goes back to an aversity to invoking relevant legal provisions that finds its basis in a fear of retaliation. If we want to avoid the legal framework becoming an empty shell, affirmative action is required. This implies increased attention for individual and collective stakeholder empowerment, as well as regulatory intervention aimed at optimising the application of the legal framework in practice. Tentative proposals include several measures that may further boost collective enforcement, and contribute to the optimisation of judicial and extra-judicial dispute resolution.

8

Conclusions

You better start swimmin'
Or you'll sink like a stone
For the times they are a-changin'.

—Bob Dylan (1964)

This book has focused on the main contractual dynamics of music industry contracts between musicians and their primary corporate partners in the music publishing and recorded music sectors, as embedded in the age of music streaming. It has analysed how the legal framework can contribute to achieving a fair(er) balance between the interests of musicians and their main corporate partners.

Following an introductory Chapter 1 that framed the research project and explained the main methodological choices, Chapter 2 focused on the digital reality with which the music industry value chain is faced and explored several avenues for industry-led change. Particular attention was accorded to the rise of streaming and the main relevant exploitation contracts in the streaming age, as well as the concrete distribution of revenues. Among other things, an argument was made in favour of a transition from the pro rata distribution of revenues on the basis of consumption share to the UCPS method that matches users' subscription fees to the music they listen to.

The music industry is affected by a wealth of factors, such as the digital environment, the inherent complexity and opaqueness of the music value chain and the music industry's propensity towards a winner-takes-all market where luck and leverage have an important role to play. While it is undeniable that a more artist-friendly environment is emerging, with a significant increase in commercial options for musicians to bring their music to a global audience, instances of unfairness remain in practice. An unfair contract may render the (economic) situation for musicians much worse than the inherent characteristics of the music market would in themselves imply in terms of scope, exploitation and remuneration.

Therefore, acknowledging that contractual analysis is by no means a panacea, a balanced and transparent regulatory framework for music contracts would be beneficial. Bottom-up change must be intertwined with top-down regulatory efforts. A choice example is the issue of transparency within the music value chain. Indeed, solving this problem not only requires high-performing reporting obligations for corporate partners, but also an effective long-term solution for the fragmentation in music rights and the music metadata issue. Both the legal and commercial layers are necessary to attain the goal of a protective framework that may be leveraged in practice to ensure an appropriate distribution of value among stakeholders.

This book has sought to contribute to such a balanced legal framework, on the basis of an analysis and assessment of the relevant regulatory regimes in Belgium, France, Germany and the Netherlands as influenced by the EU acquis, as well as the relevant provisions in the United Kingdom. Most Member States, including the chosen jurisdictions within the EU, have laid down rules that protect the weaker party to a contract and many of these provisions directly affect the contractual bargain between musicians and their corporate partners.

Chapters 3–6 analysed in detail how the relevant legal framework in the chosen jurisdictions, consisting primarily of copyright contract law and secondarily of general contract law and the law of unfair B2B contract terms and trade practices, regulates music contracts in the streaming age. The bulk of the analysis pertained to the field of copyright contract law, with the law of unfair B2B contract terms and trade practices as well as principles of general contract law functioning as fallback mechanisms that serve a background role.

First, there are certain formal requirements, such as the need for a written document for purposes of proof or validity. Second, the legal framework results in the prohibition of clauses deemed unfair or excessive, such as restrictions relating to rights in future content and/or methods of exploitation. Third, the law imposes substantive obligations on one (or more) of the contracting parties, such as a duty to exploit and/or distribute revenues fairly. For contract performance in particular, an important move towards partial harmonisation in the field of copyright contract law was made with a dedicated chapter in the DSM Directive. In addition to setting minimum benchmarks as to exploitation, remuneration and transparency, this directive paves the way for ADR resolution in the CCIs.

In addition to analysing the law as it currently stands in the chosen jurisdictions, these chapters proposed a number of incremental amendments. Recognising the particular situation of the United Kingdom, a fine line was walked between advocating certain harmonised solutions at the EU level and simultaneously maintaining a sound regulatory basis at the national level where appropriate, as well as between the objectives of providing legal certainty through hard law and of securing a flexible framework that is fit for the streaming age.

Chapter 3 first took a step back, analysing the role of the law in achieving this book's policy objective of moving towards a fair(er) balance in the streaming age. It conceptualised the normative criterion of 'fairness' as the achievement of a fair balance between the interests of the relevant stakeholders that achieves a level playing field in the music market. This was done while duly acknowledging that fairness is always 'in the eye of the beholder' and that 'almost all possible solutions are partisan',[1] and also building upon a Rawlsian notion of egalitarian distributive justice. After having stressed the importance of freedom of contract as a central tenet of contract law in the chosen jurisdictions, this chapter then provided a typology of the selected substantive legal regimes, categorising and contrasting the different sets of relevant regulatory regimes on the basis of their substantive, geographical and temporal scope.

The further legal analysis in this book followed the 'life' of a music industry contract and analysed the rules that apply at different stages in the chosen jurisdictions. Chapter 4 analysed and evaluated the rules that bear relevance to the negotiation and formation stages of the contracts under review. First, the potential relevance of precontractual liability regimes was briefly highlighted. The other findings of Chapter 4 may be characterised as seeking to ascertain, albeit in a piecemeal way, what exactly qualifies as 'fair scope' in the particular context of music contracts in the streaming age.

Then the chapter examined both material and formal requirements pertaining to consent relating to such contracts. Starting from the basic rule of express consent by the parties, exceptions pertaining to the audio-visual industry as well as regarding music made either in an employment context or on commission were reviewed. On a formal level, the analysis focused on the requirements of a written contract that apply in some of the chosen jurisdictions, either for purposes of proof or affecting the validity of the contract. On the basis of the analysis, an argument was made in favour of a generalised requirement of express consent in the music industry, combined with a written – potentially digital – instrument for purposes of proof vis-à-vis the musician(s), similar to the regime that already exists in Belgium, France and Germany.

As to the substance of rights granted, focus lay on both theoretical limitations to the scope of transfers and/or licences and relevant rules concerning the determination of such scope in practice. The regulatory choices made by the chosen jurisdictions in this regard differ significantly. The theoretical limitations under review included the prohibition of the transfer of copyright *sensu stricto* under German law, limitations applicable to the grant of rights in future music and methods of exploitation, as well as complementary limitations based on a reasonability assessment. A full ban on the grant of rights in future music (as applicable under French law) and/or methods of exploitation (as applicable under Belgian law) was labelled as excessive. As to the determination of the scope of rights granted, the duty to specify combined with restrictive interpretation under Belgian and French law was contrasted with the purpose-limitation principle under German and Dutch

[1] Annette Kur, 'Fairness as a Legal Concept – A Guiding Principle for IP?' (Herchel Smith Lecture, online, 5 May 2021).

law. While the limited substantive effect of restrictions on the grant of rights in future content and/or methods of exploitation should be acknowledged, their applicability to option contracts should be expressly confirmed – especially under Belgian law.

The final topic of the chapter was the regulation of the formation stage of secondary relationships, whereby the rights initially granted to primary corporate partners are further transferred or sub-licensed to a third party, such as a DSP. The balanced regime on the establishment of secondary relationships (either further transfers or sub-licences) under German law deserves a wider hard law application, as it provides a comprehensive framework that also deals with problems that may arise in the context of insolvency of the corporate partner.

The regulatory regimes applicable to the substance of rights granted seek to secure informed consent on the part of the contracting parties – bar the prohibition of transfer under German law, which stems from its monist copyright tradition. However, given that many of the restrictions under review apparently lead to lengthy contractual clauses that stretch the abovementioned theoretical limitations, the substantive effect of these restrictions is limited in practice. More generally, a focus on what musicians receive in return for the grant of rights in terms of exploitation and remuneration has a greater impact on fairness as conceptualised in the context of this book than the substantive scope of rights granted. Therefore, Chapter 5 focused on the regulatory framework that applies to the performance phase of the contract, with separate substantive sections on issues pertaining to exploitation and remuneration.

Regarding the exploitation of rights in music, the extent of corporate partners' duty to exploit was analysed and assessed. The relevant sections zoomed in on applicable direct and indirect duties to exploit (recorded) music to which they have been granted certain exploitation rights. The analysis sought to combine the relevant regimes in the chosen jurisdictions with the applicable harmonising provisions of EU law, most importantly the harmonised use-it-or-lose-it clause set forth in Article 22 DSM Directive. After having reviewed the relevant provisions, a number of guiding criteria were developed that may aid stakeholders in determining whether the grant of rights in the contracts under review is met with 'fair exploitation' on the part of the corporate partner in a given contractual setting. In turn, the analysis focused on substantive, personal, geographical and temporal aspects. In terms of substance, account was taken of both the use of the musician's contribution in the music at issue, the use of the music as such and the overarching impact of digitisation. In addition, relevant sector practices and the potential contribution of collective arrangements were added to the mix. These concrete criteria may be crystallised further by way of a soft law instrument.

First, in a bid to avoid disproportionate encroachment on parties' freedom of contract, a marked preference was noted for indirect over direct duties to exploit. Instead of linking an absence of (sufficient) exploitation with breach of contract and an associated right to damages, it is deemed fairer to opt for a high-performing rights reversion mechanism with appropriate procedural and substantive safeguards. In this context, any reference to the word 'copy' or 'copies' in the relevant provisions (as is still the case under Belgian law in particular) should be removed, since this concept is ill-fitted for the streaming age. In a second stage, the perspective was broadened from the contractual relationship between musicians and their primary corporate partners to the secondary relationship with third parties such as DSPs. The inclusion of third-party transferees in the scope of the Dutch use-it-or-lose-it mechanism was evaluated positively, as was the joint and several liability arising under German copyright contract law in case the formation of a secondary contract was not expressly assented to by the musician(s) at issue.

As to the control over exploitation activities undertaken by corporate partners, the role of moral rights protection was stressed, as well as the potential fallback role of general contract law restrictions on the basis of public order and good morals. While noting the limited effect of these regimes in practice, it was considered that further regulatory action risked overly encroaching upon parties' freedom of contract, especially in the context of secondary contractual relationships.

As to matters of remuneration, the book first extensively focused on the requirement of 'fair remuneration', as provided for in the laws of the chosen jurisdictions and as harmonised by the principle of appropriate and proportionate remuneration set forth by the broadly worded Article 18 DSM Directive.

A preliminary conceptual hurdle was to determine whether a lump sum can be 'proportionate' in the sense required by Article 18, or whether this provision requires contracts to include a royalty arrangement – as under French law. Considerations of risk allocation led to the conclusion that the nature of a remuneration arrangement (either a lump sum or a royalty) does not in itself determine its fairness. Other criteria are merited.

The book then took up the challenge of establishing such criteria for stakeholders, seeking a parallel with the criteria used in the context of the determination of fair exploitation. Again, focus first lay with substantive aspects and the impact of digitisation, before bringing in personal, geographical and temporal considerations and invoking both sector practices and collectively bargained solutions as an additional guideline. The soft law harmonisation of the concept of 'fair remuneration' is advocated, again with the conceptualisation in this book as a potential source of inspiration.

A useful specific accompanying hard law measure would be to expressly grant musicians a right to additional remuneration regarding emerging methods of exploitation, as already provided under German and Dutch law. More generally, in order to make full use of the potential of collective bargaining in CCIs such as the music industry, it was proposed to expressly grant freelance musicians the right to bargain collectively, to simplify applicable proceedings and to provide the possibility to extend the mandatory nature of collectively bargained solutions to all stakeholders in a given sector.

The inherent unpredictability of commercial success in the music industry, combined with continued technological progress that opens up new avenues for digital exploitation, render it hard to establish what exactly qualifies as 'fair' remuneration in advance. Therefore, in addition to taking a static perspective that focuses on the situation at the moment of contract formation, a dynamic perspective on fair remuneration was added through the analysis of applicable contract adjustment mechanisms that allow for renegotiation in case the agreed remuneration arrangement becomes unfair over time. In this regard, both the copyright contract law mechanisms harmonised by Article 20 DSM Directive and the general contract law regimes applicable in case of changed circumstances were reviewed. An effective application of the requirement of disproportionality was said to be a prerequisite for a balanced – and fair – application of such contract adjustment mechanisms. In addition, certain ameliorations to applicable contract adjustment mechanisms were proposed.

Following the extensive analysis of the concept of 'fair remuneration' from both an ex ante and ex post perspective, this book posited the seminal importance of transparency throughout the performance of the contract for the purpose of ensuring fair remuneration. It then discussed applicable reporting obligations. Distinguishing passive reporting obligations that grant musicians a right to request and obtain relevant information from the active reporting obligations that have been harmonised by Article 19 DSM Directive. In turn, the analysis focused on the scope and content of applicable reporting obligations, delving into the information that is to be provided as well as the specific ways in which the provision of information is to take place. In view of the significant potential contribution of enhanced transparency to both procedural and substantive fairness, the key role that active reporting obligations have to play in achieving the objectives set by this book was stressed. A wait-and-see attitude concerning the active reporting obligations that entered into force in June 2022 was coupled with proactive proposals to further polish these obligations in practice, as well as further shape an effective right to audit in the context of both the primary and secondary contractual relationships under review.

Finally, as was the case for both contract formation and corporate partners' duties in terms of exploitation, the perspective was then broadened to secondary contractual relationships. As to remuneration, revenues collected through the further transfer of rights were distinguished from revenues accrued through exploitation of protected content through sub-licences. As to both strands, a significant leeway for national legislators was found, leaving a margin for improvement in terms of fairness – both fair remuneration as such and associated issues of transparency. In particular, the potential of a resale right for music in granting musicians a claim in profits made through the further sale of their rights was explored, as was the extension of contract adjustment mechanisms to secondary contracting parties.

A separate section was then devoted to the potential of a residual, collectively managed remuneration right for musicians for digital exploitation, as a complementary way to secure a fair division of revenues in the music industry. While the decision whether or not to establish such a right will ultimately be based on policy reasons, this chapter weighed the theoretical and practical arguments for and against, ultimately finding in favour of such a collectively managed solution. Theoretical support for the establishment of musician ER follows from the obvious similarities between radio and (playlist and discovery) streaming, where a 50/50 division appears to be the standard in the chosen jurisdictions. As contractual negotiations between contracting parties usually do not lead to such a result, it is hard to deny the benefits in terms of substantive fairness that a generalised move towards musician ER would bring. While the establishment of musician ER would require additional attention to the user interest in not having prices for the consumption of music increase disproportionately, as well as the interests of corporate partners that may be characterised as SMEs, the practical counterarguments are surmountable. However, countries with a strong basis for collective bargaining should be empowered to build further upon this tradition. Moreover, if the choice is made for collective management, sustained attention must be accorded to the transparency and governance of CMOs tasked with amassing and distributing the additional revenues. The ongoing review process of the CRM Directive may provide fruitful ground for debate in this regard.

Chapter 6 investigated the legal framework surrounding the end of the researched music industry contracts. It focused on parties' abilities to terminate the contractual relationships under review. First, it was found that none of the chosen jurisdictions expressly limit contract duration, bar the requirement of reasonability that exists under either copyright contract law or rules concerning unfair B2B contract terms and the principled right to terminate perpetual obligations under general contract law. Second, a brief analysis was included of potential grounds for termination of the contracts under review. Instances of serious breach of contract in case of non-respect of applicable duties of exploitation and remuneration were discussed, as well as the potential termination of the contract if renegotiations following a significant change of circumstances are unsuccessful. Again, diverging national regimes were found. Third, Chapter 5 assessed the consequences of contract termination under the laws of the chosen jurisdictions in terms of scope, exploitation and remuneration, assessing whether these consequences act as switching costs in practice. A lingering sense of legal uncertainty was uncovered, especially regarding the practical follow-on effects of termination on secondary relationships in the digital sphere and the right of musicians to access relevant data in a post-contractual context.

The chapter then assessed and discounted the potential of a more extensive right of withdrawal on the part of musicians. It also studied restrictions on the duration of copyright exploitation contracts in the United Kingdom and United States, in a bid to assess whether such restrictions may contribute to the fairness sought in the context of this book. However, the relevant legal framework in the chosen EU jurisdictions provides musicians with ample opportunities to terminate primary contractual relationships in cases of excessive scope of rights granted and/or shortcomings on the part of the corporate partner when it comes to either exploitation or remuneration. In view of this, it was argued that an additional reversion right based on the passing of time alone would not provide significant added value. Finally, regarding the consequences of contract termination, it was found that both the remuneration for potential post-contractual exploitation and musicians' post-contractual right to access relevant audience data should be secured – the latter potentially through an extension of the scope of active reporting obligations to data not directly linked with the exploitation of relevant content.

Chapter 7 discussed the tools that are available to enforce the substantive provisions discussed in Chapters 3–6. First, the chapter discussed the possibility for contracting parties to contractually deviate from the protective provisions under review. It stressed the merits of qualifying certain aspects of the protective legal framework as mandatory law, in order to prevent excessive contractual deviations under the influence of imbalances in relative bargaining power.

Second, it delved into the potential conflict between the objective of securing transparency throughout the music value chain and the qualification of relevant audience data as trade secrets. It was also found that musicians' low bargaining power is likely to translate into a lack of – material and/or moral – means to challenge the fairness of contracts, either in court or in an extra-judicial context. In addition to often not having access to the funds required to secure legal relief, the fear of retaliation and the ensuing chilling effect on their musical career is likely to deter artists faced with unfair situations. Cases that do reach the courtroom are often settled on confidential terms. The lack of case law may dissuade other musicians from challenging the fairness of their contracts.

Subsequently, opportunities for individual empowerment and the enhancement of a collective voice were put forward. First, on the individual level, the importance of knowledge creation and dissemination was highlighted as a countering force against persisting information asymmetries. Second, the potential of the collective as a positive force for change was mined. It was found that representative groups such as CMOs, trade unions, guilds and other representative entities may play an important role in providing a collective voice for the heterogeneous groups of stakeholders active in the music industry. Collective interest groups may not only provide support for individuals, but also substantively affect copyright policy and engage in self-regulation, including through recourse to collective bargaining. Moreover, collective enforcement has the potential to enhance transparency throughout the music value chain and counter musicians' fear of commercial retaliation.

The chapter then assessed the potential of ADR as an alternative avenue to settle disputes pertaining to the contracts under review – as promoted (and even required) by Article 21 DSM Directive. In the pre-DSM era, both France and the Netherlands have already taken significant steps in extra-judicial dispute resolution in the CCIs, with the appointment of the *médiateur de la musique* and the *Geschillencommissie Auteurscontractenrecht*. However, neither mechanism appears to have been widely used in practice so far. Several measures may boost the uptake of ADR mechanisms in practice. First, an expansion of its scope to all disputes relating to copyright exploitation contracts may be envisaged – with a combination of the situations in France, Germany and the Netherlands as a potentially optimal solution. In addition, sustained attention to quality control is required. Finally, it is vital to further incentivise stakeholders to participate in relevant ADR mechanisms, while safeguarding their right to submit a dispute to a judge.

The road towards a level playing field for all music industry stakeholders in the streaming age is long and somewhat rocky. While the partially harmonising provisions of the DSM Directive definitely constitute a step in the right direction, they are by no means a panacea. In this regard, several final overarching considerations may be noted.

First, the use of broad, abstract concepts – while a necessary corollary of political compromise – is not conducive to either procedural or substantive fairness, since this allows significant divergences between Member State laws to persist. Second, similar consequences stem from the fact that many aspects of the contractual relationship remain unharmonised at the EU level, such as those relating to the negotiation and formation phase of the contract, as well as its termination. Third, while the title of the DSM Directive promises a legal instrument fit for the digital age, its chapter on copyright exploitation contracts pays little to no attention to the specifics of digital exploitation of protected content – arguably a missed opportunity.[2] This book made an attempt to mitigate these three obstacles, by operationalising the broad applicable concepts using concrete criteria that take due account of the ubiquity of the digital sphere.

An equally regrettable element is the lack of full clarity on the temporal application of the harmonising rules of the DSM Directive, which seems to allow Member States to adopt a conservative application of these rules to ongoing contracts. The immediate or even retroactive effect of a progressively more protective legal framework negatively affects legal certainty and risks resulting in a chilling effect for corporate partners. Thus, if a measure results in an excessive encroachment upon the freedom of contract, considerations of fairness argue in favour of a conservative application in time. However, while the harmonising provisions on copyright exploitation contracts are not fully ideal, they have been evaluated as being both procedurally and substantively fair. Therefore, their temporal application to ongoing contracts is deemed justifiable. Any legislative choices for a conservative application in time may be considered as a missed opportunity to right past wrongs.

It can hardly be denied that the DSM Directive may be considered somewhat of a missed opportunity for a holistic approach. In the words of Professor Séverine Dusollier:

[2] Séverine Dusollier, 'An Effective and Comprehensive Contractual Protection of Creators and Performers' (Copyright in the Digital Single Market, Brussels, 30 January 2020). See also Daniel Johansson, 'Streams & Dreams: A Fair Music Economy for All, Part 2' (2024) <https://bit.ly/3Sh3D5R>.

> The Directive on copyright in the digital single market fails to deliver on its promise of a more ambitious copyright reform. Another piece of legislation was just piled up to an already entangled puzzle of legal provisions. It was time to profoundly revise the acquis. Instead, the construction of an effective single market in cultural and entertainment products and services, but equally importantly of a digital society where all have access to creative works, information and knowledge, and where artists get a fair remuneration, still relies on 27 different national copyright frameworks, partly outdated notions, intricate practical solutions, and unsolved issues.[3]

At the very end of this book, it is time to circle back to its overarching objective: to move towards a fair(er) balance in the contracts between musicians and their primary corporate partners in the streaming age. Has this goal been attained? Honesty requires us to give a nuanced answer.

On the one hand, looking at the substantive legal framework in the chosen jurisdictions in the EU in particular, the overall assessment is rather positive. The relevant regulatory regimes in Belgium, France, Germany and the Netherlands provide detailed rules on how contracting parties' freedom of contract is limited in a bid to further considerations of distributive justice. These national laws seek to work to the advantage of those 'least fortunate' in the Rawlsian sense of the word, as understood here to encapsulate a group of people (musicians) that are often at the losing end of the contracting equation and suffer from a systemic imbalance in bargaining power. While there is a clear margin for improvement, as evidenced by the proposals for incremental amelioration discussed above, the essence of the legal framework may be said to engender hopefulness. On a substantive level, therefore, we are clearly moving in the right direction, towards enhanced fairness. It is hoped that the UK legislator, too, may find inspiration in the regulatory framework offered by the continental EU jurisdictions under review in this book.

On the other hand, there is no straight line between the ideal that this book aspires to and modern-day music industry practice. Similar to the hurdles that arise in the context of the application of abstract legal theory to a specific legal field such as (copyright) contract law, the road towards actual implementation of the relevant legal framework in practice is rather bumpy. Additional ambition is therefore merited. If the application of the legal framework 'in action' is found wanting, what is the point of a balanced, well-thought-out law 'in the books'? From this perspective, further bolstering the development and application of 'fair trade' principles in music contracts and encouraging stakeholders to speak up in case of unfairness – be it on the judicial or extra-judicial stage – is key. Moreover, if efforts in this direction prove to be insufficiently fruitful, the only credible solutions left may be to further collectivise the exploitation of music through (mandatory) collective bargaining and (equally mandatory) collective management.

[3] Séverine Dusollier, 'The 2019 Directive on Copyright in the Digital Single Market: Some Progress, a Few Bad Choices, and an Overall Failed Ambition' [2020] CML Rev 979, 1029.

With some imagination, the legal framework surrounding the music industry may be likened somewhat to a mixing desk, with multiple channels and inputs, as well as filters and equalisers. There are many stakeholders whose voice deserves to be heard – and sometimes even amplified – while some influencing factors, such as the winner-takes-all nature of the music industry and its tendency towards the mainstream, should be somewhat filtered out in order for an equalised, level playing field to emerge. Just like sound engineers, we must continuously bear in mind that minor adjustments may have major consequences, as well as be weary of excessive compression of input that does not do justice to the diversity in the music industry.

Contrary to what is the case for sounds, therefore, legal 'engineering' requires a continuous feedback loop with industry stakeholders, whereby regulatory action is guided and inspired by empirical evidence. This book has identified a number of avenues for potential bottom-up initiatives as well as possible regulatory action, opting for incremental modifications to the legal framework instead of the proverbial 'mic drop'. May the analysis, assessment and proposed amelioration of the legal framework advanced by this book contribute towards a more balanced legal soundtrack for the music industry in the streaming age.

Fine

Select Bibliography

Abdullahi A, 'Termination Rights in Music: A Practical Framework for Resolving Ownership Conflicts in Sound Recordings' [2012] U Ill JL Tech & Pol'y 457.

AEPO-ARTIS, 'Performers' Rights in International and European Legislation: Situation and Elements for Improvement' (2018) <https://shorturl.at/pteRo>.

'Performers' Rights Study 2022' (2022) <https://shorturl.at/QWQ2Y>.

'The Music Industry Is Not Just a Label-Economy' (7 April 2023) <https://shorturl.at/wqiDH>.

AEPO-ARTIS, EuroFIA, FIM and IAO, 'Remuneration of Performers for Download and Streaming Services. Survey Results' (2015) <https://shorturl.at/UvD2j>.

Aguiar L and Waldfogel J, 'Streaming Reaches Flood Stage: Does Spotify Stimulate or Depress Music Sales?' (JRC Technical Reports, 2015) <www.nber.org/papers/w21653>.

'Platforms, Promotion, and Product Discovery: Evidence from Spotify Playlists' (NBER Working Paper, 2018) <www.nber.org/papers/w24713>.

Aguilar A, 'Distributed Ownership in Music: Between Authorship and Performance' (2018) 27 Social & Legal Studies 776.

'"We Want Artists to Be Fully and Fairly Paid for Their Work": Discourses on Fairness in the Neoliberal European Copyright Reform' [2018] JIPITEC 160.

'The Collective Management of Performers' Rights in the UK: A Story of Competing Interests' (2019) 16 SCRIPTed 4.

'The New Copyright Directive: Fair Remuneration in Exploitation Contracts of Authors and Performers – Part 1, Articles 18 and 19' (Kluwer Copyright Blog, 15 July 2019) <https://bit.ly/2YGtnjt>.

'The New Copyright Directive: Fair Remuneration in Exploitation Contracts of Authors and Performers – Part II, Articles 20–23' (Kluwer Copyright Blog, 1 August 2019) <https://bit.ly/2YG4a8r>.

Albinsson S, 'The Resilience of Music Copyrights: Technological Innovation, Copyright Disputes and Legal Amendments Concerning the Distribution of Music' (2013) 5 Culture Unbound 401.

Aluko K, 'Terminating the Struggle over Termination Rights' (2019) 10 Harvard JSEL 119.

Anderson M, 'Assignments and Royalties Don't Mix' (2009) 4 JIPLP 283.

Andrews N, *Contract Rules: Decoding English Law* (Intersentia 2016).

Antal D, Fletcher A and Ormosi PL, 'Music Streaming: Is It a Level Playing Field?' (2021) 2 Antitrust Chronicle 14.

Arditi D, 'iTunes: Breaking Barriers and Building Walls' (2014) 37 Popular Music and Society 408.

Getting Signed: Record Contracts, Musicians, and Power in Society (Springer International 2020).

Streaming Culture: Subscription Platforms and the Unending Consumption of Culture (Emerald 2021).

Arenal A, Armuña C, Ramos S, Feijóo C and Aguado J-M, 'Giants with Feet of Clay: The Sustainability of the Business Models in Music Streaming Services' (2022) 31 El Profesional de la información e310509.

Arnaut C, Pont M, Lanzuela M, Erol E, Koshchiyenko O, Cilli V, Quaresma H and López-Tarruella A, 'Study on the International Dimension of the Single Equitable Remuneration Right for Phonogram Performers and Producers and Its Effect on the European Creative Sector. Final Report' (Publications Office of the EU 2023) <https://data.europa.eu/doi/10.2759/207313>.

Arnold R, 'Are Performers Authors?' [1999] 21 EIPR 464.

Asser C, *Verbintenissenrecht. Algemeen Overeenkomstenrecht* (Asser Serie 6.III*, 13th edn, Kluwer 2008).

Verbintenissenrecht. De Verbintenis uit de Wet (Asser Serie 6.III*, 13th edn, Kluwer 2008).

Verbintenissenrecht. De Verbintenis in het Algemeen, Eerste Gedeelte (Asser Serie 6.I*, 14th edn, Kluwer 2012).

Axhamn J (ed), *Copyright in a Borderless Online Environment* (Nordstedts Juridik 2012).

Baaij CJW, Cabrelli D and Macgregor L (eds), *Interpretation of Commercial Contracts in European Private Law* (The Common Core of European Private Law 1, Intersentia 2020).

Baarsma B and Rosenboom N, 'Oneerlijke Handelspraktijken. Voldoet Bestaande (Zelf) regulering?' (SEO Economisch Onderzoek 2013) <https://pure.uva.nl/ws/files/1741416/139641_409699.pdf>.

Barnett JM, 'Copyright without Creators' (2014) 9 RLE 389.

Barr KW, 'Music Copyright in the Digital Age. Creators, Commerce and Copyright. An Empirical Study of the UK Music Copyright Industries' (University of Glasgow 2016) <http://theses.gla.ac.uk/7752/1/2016barrphd.pdf>.

Baym NK, *Playing to the Crowd. Musicians, Audiences, and the Intimate Work of Connection* (New York University Press 2018).

Bazinet JB, Singlehurst TA, May M, Suva J, Ezawa K and Yap A, 'Putting the Band Back Together: Remastering the World of Music' (Citi GPS 2018).

Bently L, Blakeney M, von Borries C, Chesser R, Cloonan M, Cook N, Gibson J and others, 'Creativity Stifled? A Joint Academic Statement on the Proposed Copyright Term Extension for Sound Recordings' (2008) 30 EIPR 341.

Bently L, 'Authorship of Popular Music in UK Copyright Law' (2009) 12 ICS 179.

'Between a Rock and a Hard Place: The Problems Facing Freelance Creators in the UK Media Market-Place. A Briefing Document on Behalf of The Creators' Rights Alliance. Third and Final Draft' (2009) <http://creatorsrights.org.uk/media/between.pdf>.

Bently L and Ginsburg J, 'The Sole Right Shall Return to the Authors: Anglo-American Authors Reversion Rights from the Statute of Anne to Contemporary US Copyright' (2010) 25 Berkeley Tech LJ 1475.

Bently L, Kretschmer M, Dudenbostel T, del Carmen Calatrava Moreno M and Radauer A, 'Strengthening the Position of Press Publishers and Authors and Performers in the Copyright Directive' (Publications Office of the EU 2017) <https://rb.gy/zdu7v7>.

Bently L, Sherman B, Gangjee D and Johnson P, *Intellectual Property Law* (6th edn, Oxford University Press 2022).

Berenboom A, *Le Nouveau Droit d'Auteur et les Droits Voisins* (Création Information Communication 1, 3rd edn, Larcier 2005).

Berthomier D, 'Médiateur de la musique. Rapport d'activité 2017–2018' (2019) <https://rb.gy/ku49jg>.

'Médiateur de la musique. Rapport annuel 2019–2020' (2020) <https://rb.gy/oge1ja>.

Blanc N, *Les Contrats du Droit d'Auteur à l'Epreuve de la Distinction des Contrats Nommés et Innommés* (Nouvelle Bibliothèque de Thèses 93, Dalloz 2010).

Blomqvist J (ed), *Copyright, to Be or Not to Be* (Ex Tuto 2019).

Bogre M and Wolff N (eds), *The Routledge Companion to Copyright and Creativity in the 21st Century* (Routledge Companions, Routledge 2020).

Boisson A, *La Licence de Droit d'Auteur* (Bibliothèque de Droit de l'Entreprise 86, LexisNexis 2013).

Bosher H, *Copyright in the Music Industry. A Practical Guide to Exploiting and Enforcing Rights* (Elgar Practical Guides, Edward Elgar 2021).

Bosher H and Rosati E (eds), *Developments and Directions in Intellectual Property Law* (Oxford University Press 2023).

Bostoen F and Vanherpe J, 'Competition Law in the Digitized Music Industry: The Winners Take It All – But Should They?' (2021) 2 CPI Antitrust Chronicle 30.

Bouvery P-M, *Les Contrats de la Musique* (7th edn, IRMA 2020).

Bowrey K, *Copyright, Creativity, Big Media and Cultural Value. Incorporating the Author* (Routledge 2020).

Braun I, *Grundeinkommen statt Urheberrecht? Zum kreativen Schaffen in der digitalen Welt* (transcript Verlag 2014).

Brauneis R, 'Musical Work Copyright for the Era of Digital Sound Technology: Looking Beyond Composition and Performance' (GW Law Faculty Publications & Other Works 2014 <www.ssrn.com/abstract=2400170>.

Braxton JA, 'Lost in Translation: The Obstacles of Streaming Digital Media and the Future of Transnational Licensing' (2014) 36 Hastings Comm/Ent LJ 193.

Brennick C, 'Termination Rights in the Music Industry: Revolutionary or Ripe for Reform?' (2018) 93 NYU L Rev 786.

Brereton I, 'The Beginning of a New Age: The Unconscionability of the 360-Degree Deal' (2009) 27 Cardozo Arts & Ent LJ 168.

Brison F, *Het Naburig Recht van de Uitvoerende Kunstenaar* (Creatie Informatie Communicatie 7, Larcier 2001).

Brison F and Vanhees H (eds), *Hommage à Jan Corbet Huldeboek* (4th edn, Larcier 2018).

Brown AEL and Waelde C (eds), *Research Handbook on Intellectual Property and Creative Industries* (Research Handbooks in Intellectual Property, Edward Elgar 2018).

Bruguière J-M, 'The Irresistible Rise of the Exploitation Obligation in Literary and Artistic Property Agreements' [2022] 70 RIDA 3.

Buccafusco C and García K, 'Pay-to-Playlist: The Commerce of Streaming' (2021) 12 UC Irvine L Rev 1.

Buffelan-Lanore Y and Larribau-Terneyre V, *Droit Civil. Les obligations* (16th edn, Sirey 2018).

Burkart P, 'Music in the Cloud and the Digital Sublime' (2014) 37 Popular Music and Society 393.

Burkart P and McCourt T, 'Infrastructure for the Celestial Jukebox' (2004) 23 Popular Music 349.

Digital Music Wars: Ownership and Control of the Celestial Jukebox (Rowman & Littlefield 2006).

Cabay J, Delforge V, Fossoul V and Lambrecht M (eds), *20 Ans de Nouveau Droit d'Auteur 20 Jaar Nieuw Auteursrecht* (Anthemis 2015).

Carlsson S and Leijonhufvud J, *The Spotify Play. How CEO and Founder Daniek EK Beat Apple, Google and Amazon in the Race for Audio Dominance* (Diversion Books 2021).

Carnes R, 'Developing a Copyright System that Works for Songwriters' (2015) 38 Colum JL & Arts 309.

Carre S, Le Cam S and Macrez F, 'Buyout Contracts Imposed by Platforms in the Cultural and Creative Sector' (Publications Office of the EU 2023) <https://shorturl.at/bhsNR>

Carrigan F, 'Here Comes That Rainy Day Feeling Again: Shifts in the Ideology of Contract Law from Tony Macaulay to George Michael' [1997] 15 Law in Context 105.

Caron C, *Droit d'Auteur et Droits Voisins* (6th edn, LexisNexis 2020).

Castle C, 'Record Producer Agreements, a Practical Guide' (2023) <https://bit.ly/3OdwB58>.

Castle C and Feijóo C, 'Study on the Artists in the Digital Music Marketplace: Economics and Legal Considerations' (WIPO 2021) <https://rb.gy/oh8wsg>.

Caves R, *Creative Industries. Contracts between Art and Commerce* (Harvard University Press 2002).

'Contracts between Art and Commerce' (2003) 17 Journal of Economic Perspectives 73.

Centre for Data Ethics and Innovation, 'The Impact of Recommendation Algorithms on the UK's Music Industry' (9 February 2023).

Centre National de la Musique and Deloitte, 'Étude Relative à l'Impact du Passage à l'UCPS par les Services de Musique en Ligne. Rapport Détaillé' (2021).

Centre Nationale de la Musique, 'Manipulation des écoutes en ligne' (2023).

Chen-Wishart M, *Contract Law* (7th edn, Oxford University Press 2022).

Chiou T, 'On Royalties and Transfers without (Monetary) Consideration – Looking for the "Magic Formula" for Assessing the Validity of Remuneration Clauses of Copyright Transfers under French Copyright Law' (2013) 44 IIC 585.

Chitty J and Beale H, *Chitty on Contracts* (32nd edn, Sweet & Maxwell 2015).

Chozick D, 'Help! Fixing the Problem of Copyright Termination Inconsistencies through Public and Private International Law' (2018) 49 Georget J Int Law 1461.

Claeys I and Tanghe T, *Algemeen Contractenrecht. Handboek voor Nu en Straks* (Intersentia 2021).

CMA, 'Music and Streaming: Final Report' (29 November 2022) <https://tinyurl.com/mr9fh7f2>.

CMU, 'Performer Payments from Streaming' (2021) <https://rb.gy/it4vr9>.

Commission, 'Impact Assessment Reforming Cross-Border Collective Management of Copyright and Related Rights for Legitimate Online Music Services' (Staff Working Document) SEC(2005) 1254.

'Creative Content Online in the Single Market' (Communication) COM(2007) 836 final.

'Proposal for a European Parliament and Council Directive Amending Directive 2006/116/EC of the European Parliament and of the Council on the Term of Protection of Copyright and Related Rights' COM(2008) 464 final.

'Copyright in the Knowledge Economy' (Green Paper) COM(2008) 466 final.

'Impact Assessment on the Legal and Economic Situation of Performers and Record Producers in the European Union' (Staff Working Document) SEC(2008) 2287.

'A Digital Agenda for Europe' (Communication) COM(2010) 245.

'The Online Distribution of Audiovisual Works in the European Union: Opportunities and Challenges Towards a Digital Single Market' (Green Paper) COM(2011) 427 final.

'Report on the Responses to the Public Consultation on the Review of the EU Copyright Rules' (July 2014) <https://bit.ly/3yjVQN8>.

'A Digital Single Market Strategy for Europe' (Communication) COM(2015) 192 final.

'Proposal for a Directive of the European Parliament and of the Council on Copyright in the Digital Single Market' COM(2016) 593 final.

'Impact Assessment on the Modernisation of EU Copyright Rules Accompanying the Document Proposal for a Directive of the European Parliament and of the Council on Copyright in the Digital Single Market and Proposal for a Regulation of the European Parliament and of the Council Laying Down Rules on the Exercise of Copyright and Related Rights Applicable to Certain Online Transmissions of Broadcasting Organisations and Retransmissions of Television and Radio Programmes' (Staff Working Document) SWD(2016) 301 final.

'Annexes to the Impact Assessment on the Modernisation of EU Copyright Rules' (Staff Working Document) SWD(2016) 301 final.

'Assessment of the Possible Need for an Extension of the Term of Protection of Rights of Performers and Producers in the Audiovisual Sector (Commission Staff Working Document) SWD(2020)342 final.

'Collective Bargaining Agreements for Self-Employed – Scope of Application of EU Competition Rules' (Inception Impact Assessment) Ares(2021)102652.

'Impact Assessment Report accompanying the Document Communication from the Commission, Guidelines on the Application of EU Competition Law to Collective Agreements Regarding the Working Conditions of Solo Self-Employed Persons (Commission Staff Working Document) SWD(2022)321 final.

Cook A, 'The Power of Playlisting' [2017] MBJ <https://tinyurl.com/2vym2xu2>.

Cooke C, *Dissecting the Digital Dollar* (3rd edn, Music Managers Forum and CMU Insights 2020).

Cooper E, 'Reverting to Reversion Rights? Reflections on the Copyright Act 191' (2021) 43 EIPR 292.

Corbet J, *Auteursrecht* (Algemene Praktische Rechtsverzameling, Story-Scientia 1997).

Cornfield D, *Beyond the Beat: Musicians Building Community in Nashville* (Princeton University Press 2015).

Cornu E and Meys R, 'La transposition en droit belge de la directive sur le droit d'auteur et les droits voisins dans le marché unique numérique: Une modification significative du cadre contractuel d'exploitation des droits' [2022] JT 773–88.

Council of Music Makers, 'Creator Remuneration Working Group: CMM Opening Statement' (18 April 2024) <https://bit.ly/3QEaS6K>.

Cruquenaire A, *L'Interprétation des Contrats en Droit d'Auteur* (Création Information Communication 11, Larcier 2007).

Cummings AS, *Democracy of Sound. Music Piracy and the Remaking of American Copyright in the Twentieth Century* (Oxford University Press 2013).

Cuntz A, 'Creators' Income Situation in the Digital Age' (Economic Research Working Paper, 2018).

Czychowski C, 'AGB Kontrolle von umfassenden Nutzungsrechtsklauseln, die sog. Zweckübertragungslehre und das urheberrechtliche Vergütungsrecht' in K-I Wöhrn, W Bullinger, E Grunert and C Ohst (eds), *Festschrift für Artur-Axel Wandtke zum 70 Geburtstag am 26 März 2013* (Walter De Gruyter 2013).

D'Agostino G, *Copyright, Contracts, Creators: New Media, New Rules* (Edward Elgar 2010).

'Contract Lex Rex: Towards Copyright Contract's Lex Specialis' in Graeme Dinwoodie (ed), *Intellectual Property and General Legal Principles* (Edward Elgar 2015) 4–29.

Dang Vu T, 'Verbonden Overeenkomsten' (KU Leuven 2017).

Dannen F, *Hit Men: Power Brokers and Fast Money inside the Music Business* (Vintage Books 1991).

Darling K, 'Occupy Copyright: A Law & Economic Analysis of US Author Termination Rights' (2015) 63 Buffalo Law Review 147.

Daskalova V, 'The Monopsony Paradox: Buyer Power and Enforcement of the EU Antitrust Provisions' (Tilburg University 2016).

'Regulating the New Self-Employed in the Uber Economy: What Role for EU Competition Law?' (2018) 19 Ger Law J 461.

DCMS Committee, 'Economics of Music Streaming. Second Report of Session 2021–22' (15 July 2021).

Creator Remuneration. Fifth Report of Session 2023–24 (10 April 2024) <https://shorturl.at/oFNSZ>

De Beer J, 'Making Copyright Markets Work for Creators, Consumers and the Public Interest' in R Giblin and K Weatherall (eds), *What If We Could Reimagine Copyright?* (ANU Press 2017).

De Boeck A, *Informatierechten en-plichten bij de Totstandkoming en Uitvoering van Overeenkomsten* (Intersentia 2002).

De Pourcq S, *Oneerlijke Handelspraktijken en Bedingen in Contracten Tussen Ondernemingen* (Intersentia 2018).

De Visscher F and Michaux B, *Précis du Droit d'Auteur et des Droits Voisins* (Bruylant 2000).

De Voldere I and others, 'Mapping the Creative Value Chains. A Study on the Economy of Culture in the Digital Age. Final Report' (Publications Office of the EU 2017) <https://op.europa.eu/s/zIa8>

De Werra J, 'Can Alternative Dispute Resolution Mechanisms Become the Default Method for Solving International Intellectual Property Disputes' (2012) 43 Cal W Int'l LJ 39.

(ed), *Research Handbook on Intellectual Property Licensing* (Research Handbooks in Intellectual Property, Edward Elgar 2013).

Delp L, *Der Verlagsvertrag. Handbuch für die Praxis* (8th edn, CH Beck 2008).

Depoorter B, Van Hiel A and Vanneste S, 'Copyright Backlash' (2011) 84 South Calif Law Rev 1251.

Derclaye E (ed), *Research Handbook on the Future of EU Copyright* (Research Handbooks in Intellectual Property, Edward Elgar 2009).

Deresiewicz W, *The Death of the Artist. How Creators Are Struggling to Survive in the Age of Billionaires and Big Tech* (Henry Holt 2020).

Despringre C, Taylor J and Amilhat M, 'Audiovisual Authors' Rights and Remuneration in Europe' (SAA White Paper, 2015).

DiCola PC, 'Money from Music: Survey Evidence on Musicians' Revenue and Lessons about Copyright Incentives' (2013) 55 Ariz L Rev 301.

Dietz A, 'Amendment of German Copyright Law in Order to Strengthen the Contractual Position of Authors and Performers' [2002] 33 IIC 828.

'News from Germany. Significant Legislative and Case Law Developments in Copyright Contract Law in Germany' [2003] 51 RIDA 146.

'Copyright Contract Law According to the New German Legislation and Practice' [2005] 5 AMI 20.

Dimont J, 'Royalty Inequity: Why Music Streaming Services Should Switch to a Per-Subscriber Model' (2018) 69 Hastings LJ 675.

Doctorow C, *Information Doesn't Want to Be Free: Laws for the Internet Age* (McSweeney's 2014).

Donnelly B, 'Everything You Need to Know about Copyright Reversions' (2012) 1 St John's Entertainment, Arts and Sports Law Journal 1.

Drassinower A, *What's Wrong with Copying?* (Harvard University Press 2015).

Dreier T, 'Copyright in the Times of the Internet. Overcoming the Principle of Territoriality within the EU' (2017) 18 ERA Forum 7.

Dreier T and Hugenholtz PB (eds), *Concise European Copyright Law* (2nd edn, Kluwer Law International 2016).

Dreyer G, Kotthoff J, Meckel A and Hentsch C-H, *Urheberrecht* (Heidelberger Kommentar, 4th edn, CF Müller 2018).

Dusollier S, 'The Relations between Copyright Law and Consumer's Rights from a European Perspective' (European Parliament 2010) <https://ssrn.com/abstract=2127736>.

'EU Contractual Protection of Creators: Blind Spots and Shortcomings' [2018] 41 Colum J L & Arts 435.

'The 2019 Directive on Copyright in the Digital Single Market: Some Progress, a Few Bad Choices, and an Overall Failed Ambition' [2020] 57 CML Rev 979.

and others, 'Contractual Arrangements Applicable to Creators: Law and Practice of Selected Member States' (Publications Office of the EU 2014) <https://op.europa.eu/s/zIba>.

Dysart T, 'Author-Protective Rules and Alternative Licences: A Review of the Dutch Copyright Contract Act' (2015) 37 EIPR 601.

ECSA, 'ECSA's Vision on How Europe Can Prevent Buyout Contracts. An Insight into Buyouts Affecting Audiovisual Composers and Actual Solutions to Prevent Them' (2021) <https://tinyurl.com/3r27kjcu>.

'Music Streaming and Its Impact on Music Authors: Why We Should Fix Streaming and How to Ensure a Sustainable Future for All Music Creators' (2022) <https://tinyurl.com/y5umxayj>.

EIF, 'Market Analysis of the Cultural and Creative Sectors in Europe: A Sector to Invest In' (2021) <https:/tinyurl.com/4wedksda>.

Elton S, 'Standardized Identifiers and Electronic Data Interchange Rules for Music' in SM O'Connor (ed), *The Oxford Handbook of Music Law and Policy* (Oxford University Press 2020).

Ericsson S, 'The Recorded Music Industry and the Emergence of Online Music Distribution: Innovation in the Absence of Copyright (Reform)' (2011) 79 Geo Wash L Rev 1783.

Eriksson M, Fleischer R, Johansson A, Snickars P and Vonderau P, *Spotify Teardown: Inside the Black Box of Streaming Music* (MIT Press 2019).

EUIPO, 'European Citizens and Intellectual Property: Perception, Awareness, and Behaviour' (2017) <https://tinyurl.com/y9enwpyd>.

Europe Economics and others, 'Remuneration of Authors and Performers for the Use of Their Works and the Fixations of Their Performances. Final Report' (Publications Office of the EU 2015) <https://op.europa.eu/s/zIa9>.

European Copyright Society, 'Comment of the European Copyright Society Addressing Selected Aspects of the Implementation of Articles 18 to 22 of the Directive (EU) 2019/790 on Copyright in the Digital Single Market' [2020] JIPITEC 132.

'Comment of the European Copyright Society on the Impact and Consequences of the CJEU Decision in C-265/19 (RAAP)' (2022).

European Institute for Comparative Cultural Research, Capiau S and Wiesand AJ, 'The Status of Artists in Europe' (European Parliament 2006) <https://tinyurl.com/2vjbf2n8>.

Evans A, 'The Doctrine of Restraint of Trade in Relation to Music Industry Agreements' [2003] Music Law Updates <https://tinyurl.com/22kjm438>.

Fair Internet Coalition, 'Joint Guidelines for the Implementation of the 2019 Copyright Directive' (2019) <https://tinyurl.com/2fdsceds>.

Farrand B, *Networks of Power in Digital Copyright Law and Policy. Political Salience, Expertise and the Legislative Process* (Routledge 2014).

Favale M, 'Bouncing Back from Oblivion: Can Reversionary Copyright Help Unlock Orphan Works?' (2019) 41 EIPR 339.

Ficsor M, *Collective Management of Copyright and Related Rights* (WIPO 2002).

Fikentscher W and Heinemann A, *Schuldrecht. Allgemeiner und besonderer Teil* (De Gruyter Studium, 11th edn, Walter de Gruyter 2017).

Florida RL, *The Rise of the Creative Class* (Basic Books 2012).

Foong C, *The Making Available Right. Realizing the Potential of Copyright's Dissemination Function in the Digital Age* (Elgar Law, Technology and Society series, Edward Elgar 2019).

Forde E, *The Final Days of EMI. Selling the Pig* (Omnibus 2019).

Fortunet E, 'The Author's Moral Right to Withdraw a Work (Droit de Repentir): A French Perspective' (2011) 6 JIPLP 535.

Frankel S and Gervais D (eds), *The Evolution and Equilibrium of Copyright in the Digital Age* (Cambridge Intellectual Property and Information Law, Cambridge University Press 2014).

Fraser J, 'Sharing the Spoils of a Shared Practice' (2019) 73 Tempo 51.

Free D, 'Beckingham v Hodgens: The Session Musician's Claim to Music Copyright' (2003) 13 Entertainment Law Review 93.

Freundlich K and Kaiser M, 'A View from across the Pond: Duran Duran's Termination Rights under the US Copyright Act Come Undone by British High Court Ruling' (2017) 33 Entertain Sports Lawyer 1.

Frey BS, *Economics of Art and Culture* (Springer Briefs in Economics, Springer International 2019).

Fromm FK and Nordemann W, *Urheberrecht. Kommentar zum Urheberrechtsgesetz, zum Verlagsgesetz und zum Urheberrechtswahrnehmungsgesetz* (Rechtswissenschaften und Verwaltung, 10th edn, Kohlhammer 2008).

Furgał U, 'Reversion Rights in the European Union Member States' (CREATe Working Paper, 19 November 2020).

'Interpreting EU Reversion Rights: Why "Use-It-or-Lose-It" Should Be the Guiding Principle' (2021) 43 EIPR 283.

Gangjee D, Zou M, and Bora A, 'Alternative Dispute Resolution Mechanisms for Business-to-Business Digital Copyright- and Content-Related Disputes: A Report on the Results of the WIPO–MCST Survey' (WIPO Publication, WIPO 2021).

Galuszka P, 'Music Aggregators and Intermediation of the Digital Music Market' [2015] 9 International Journal of Communication 254.

García K, 'Contracts and Copyright: Contemporary Musician Income Streams' in SM O'Connor (ed), *The Oxford Handbook of Music Law and Policy* (Oxford Handbooks, Oxford University Press 2020).

García K and McCrary J, 'A Reconsideration of Copyright's Term' (2019) 71 Ala L Rev 315.

García K, Hicks J, and McCrary J, 'Copyright and Economic Viability: Evidence from the Music Industry' (2020) 17 J Empir Leg Stud 696.

Gautier P-Y, *Propriété Littéraire et Artistique* (11th edn, Presses Universitaires de France 2019).

Geiger C (ed), *Research Handbook on Human Rights and Intellectual Property* (Research Handbooks in Intellectual Property, Edward Elgar 2016).

Geiger C and Bulayenko O, 'Creating Statutory Remuneration Rights in Copyright Law: What Policy Options under the International Legal Framework?' in H Grosse Ruse-Khan and A Metzger (eds), *Intellectual Property Ordering beyond Borders* (1st edn, Cambridge University Press 2022) 408–462.

Geiregat S, *Supplying and Reselling Digital Content: Digital Exhaustion in EU Copyright and Neighbouring Rights Law* (Edward Elgar 2022).

Geiregat S and Vanhees H (eds), *Copyright Contracts Tomorrow* (LeA 2023).

Gervais D (ed), *Collective Management of Copyright and Related Rights* (3rd edn, Kluwer Law International 2016).

Gervais D, Marcus KM and Kilgore LE, 'The Rise of 360 Deals in the Music Industry' (2011) 3 Landslide 40.

Ghestin J and Barbier H, *Traité de Droit Civil. Introduction Générale. Tome 2* (5th edn, LGDJ – lextenso éditions 2020).

Giblin G and Doctorow D, *Chokepoint Capitalism: How Big Tech and Big Content Captured Creative Labor Markets and How We'll Win Them Back* (Beacon Press 2022).

Giblin R and Weatherall K, 'A Collection of Impossible Ideas' in R Giblin and K Weatherall (eds), *What If We Could Reimagine Copyright?* (ANU Press 2017).

Gilbert A, 'The Time Has Come: A Proposed Revision to 17 USC Section 203' (2016) 66 Case West Reserve Law Rev 807.

Gilbert D, Rose M, and Valentin A, 'Making Sense of the Termination Right: How the System Fails Artists and How to Fix It' (2019) <https://tinyurl.com/58yfpstz>.

Ginsburg J, 'How Copyright Got a Bad Name for Itself' (2002) 26 Colum JL & Arts 61.

'Fair Use for Free, or Permitted-but-Paid' (2014) 29 Berkeley Tech LJ 1383.

'The Role of the Author in Copyright' in RL Okediji (ed), *Copyright Law in an Age of Limitations and Exceptions* (Cambridge University Press 2017).

'Copyright' in *The Oxford Handbook of Intellectual Property Law* (Oxford Handbooks, Oxford University Press 2018).

Goldmedia, 'Musik-Streaming in Deutschland: Erlössituation Im Deutschen Musik-Streaming-Markt 2022' (2023) <https://tinyurl.com/2s4bh9f8>.

Goldstein P, *Copyright's Highway. From Gutenberg to the Celestial Jukebox* (2nd edn, Stanford University Press 2003).

Goldstein P and Hugenholtz PB, *International Copyright. Principles, Law and Practice* (2nd edn, Oxford University Press 2010).

Gorbatyuk A, 'Rethinking IP Ownership in the Context of Open Innovation' (KU Leuven 2019).

Gordon WJ, 'The Core of Copyright: Authors, Not Publishers' (2014) 52 Hous L Rev 613.

Gorgoni A, 'The Music Modernization Act: A Songwriter's Perspective' in S O'Connor (ed), *The Oxford Handbook of Music Law and Policy* (Oxford University Press 2021).

Gotzen F, 'The Belgian Approach to Direct Remuneration of Authors and Performers in the Case of Transmission via Digital Platforms' [2023] 71 RIDA 163.

Graham G, Burnes B, Lewis GJ and Langer J, 'The Transformation of the Music Industry Supply Chain. A Major Label Perspective' (2004) 24 Int J Oper Prod Man 1087.

Groffe J, *La Bonne Foi en Droit d'Auteur* (Institut Universitaire Varenne Collection des Thèses 106, LGDJ – lextenso éditions 2015).

Gronau N and Schaefer M, 'Why Metadata Matters for the Future of Copyright' (2021) 43 EIPR 488.

Guibault L, *Copyright Limitations and Contracts: An Analysis of the Contractual Overridability of Limitations on Copyright* (Information Law Series 9, Kluwer Law International 2002).

'Relationship between Copyright and Contract Law' in E Derclaye (ed), *Research Handbook on the Future of EU Copyright* (Research Handbooks in Intellectual Property, Edward Elgar 2009).

Guibault L and Hugenholtz PB, 'Study on the Conditions Applicable to Contracts Relating to Intellectual Property in the European Union' (2002) <https://bit.ly/4bzdGud>.

Gulinck L, *Hier Tekenen! (En Let Niet op de Kleine Lettertjes...) Wegwijs in het Juridische en Zakelijke Labyrint van de Muziekwereld* (Academia Press 2019).

H'Madoun Y, Pauly J and Deneuter D, *Auteursrechten en Publishing* (Poppunt vzw 2014).

Haekens J and Vanherpe J, 'Spotlight Op Spotify: Een Analyse van de Samenstelling van Playlists Door de Lens van Het Auteurs- En Mededingingsrecht' [2023] 24 IRDI 14.

Haidinger L, *Online-Musiklizenzierung in der Europäischen Union und in den USA* (Schriften zum europäischen Urheber-, Immaterialgüter- und Informationsrecht, De Gruyter 2021).

Hall Jr PW, 'Smells Like Slavery: Unconscionability in Recording Industry Contracts' [2002] 25 Hastings Comm & Ent LJ 189.

Handke C, Balazs B and Vallbé J-J, 'Going Means Trouble and Staying Makes It Double: The Value of Licensing Recorded Music Online' (2016) 40 Journal of Cultural Economics 227.

Heald PJ, 'The Impact of Implementing a 25-Year Reversion/Termination Right in Canada' (2021) 28 J Intell Prop L 63.

Help Musicians and Musicians' Union, 'Musicians' Census. Financial Insight Report' (September 2023).

Herman A, 'You Belong with Me: Recording Artists' Fight for Ownership of Their Masters' (2021) 18 Nw J Tech & Intell Prop 239.

Hesmondhalgh D, 'Is Music Streaming Bad for Musicians? Problems of Evidence and Argument' [2021] 23 New Media & Society 3593.

'Streaming's Effects on Music Culture: Old Anxieties and New Simplifications' [2021] 16 Cultural Sociology 3.

Hesmondhalgh D, Osborne R, Sun H and Barr K, 'Music Creators' Earnings in the Digital Era' (2021) <https://tinyurl.com/ysw3was8>.

Hijma J, van Dam CC, van Schendel WAM and Valk WL, *Rechtshandeling en Overeenkomst* (Studiereeks burgerlijk recht 3, 9th edn, Kluwer 2019).

Hilty RM and Moscon V (eds), *Modernisation of the EU Copyright Rules. Position Statement of the Max Planck Institute for Innovation and Competition* (Max Planck Institute for Innovation and Competition Research Paper Series 17–12, Max Planck Institute for Innovation and Competition 2017).

Hilty RM and Nérisson S (eds), *Balancing Copyright: A Survey of National Approaches* (MPI studies on Intellectual Property and Competition Law 18, Springer 2012).

Hilty RM, Kur A, Klass N, Geiger C, Peukert A, Drexl J and Katzenberger P, 'Comment by the Max-Planck Institute on the Commission's Proposal for a Directive to Amend Directive 2006/116 Concerning the Term of Protection for Copyright and Related Rights' (2009) 31 EIPR 59.

Hoeren T, 'Was bleibt von §§ 32, 32a, 36 UrhG? Überlegungen zur Zukunft des Urhebervertragsrechts' in K-I Wöhrn, W Bullinger, E Grunert and C Ohst (eds), *Festschrift für Artur-Axel Wandtke zum 70 Geburtstag am 26 März 2013* (Walter De Gruyter 2013).

Houben I and Visser D, 'De Beëindiging van Muziekexploitatieovereenkomsten' [2022] 3 Auteursrecht 135.

House of Lords Communications and Digital Committee, 'At Risk: Our Creative Future' (HL Paper 125, 2023).

Hudson E, *Drafting Copyright Exceptions: From the Law in Books to the Law in Action* (Cambridge Intellectual Property and Information Law, Cambridge University Press 2020).

Hugenholtz PB, 'Directive 93/83/EC – on the Coordination of Certain Rules Concerning Copyright and Related Rights to Copyright Applicable to Satellite Broadcasting and Cable Retransmission (Satellite and Cable Directive)' in T Dreier and PB Hugenholtz (eds), *Concise European Copyright Law* (2nd edn, Kluwer Law International 2016).

'Towards Author's Paradise: The New Dutch Act on Authors' Contracts' in G Karnell, PJ Nordell, A Kur, D Westman, J Axhamn and S Carlsson (eds), *Liber Amicorum Jan Rosén* (eddy.se ab 2016).

(ed), *Copyright Reconstructed. Rethinking Copyright's Economic Rights in a Time of Highly Dynamic Technological and Economic Change* (Information Law Series 41, Wolters Kluwer 2018).

'Artikel 18-23 DSM-richtlijn: Exploitatiecontracten' [2020] 20 AMI 187.

'Three Cheers for the DSM Directive's Rules on Author's Contracts – and a Cautionary Note from the Netherlands' (*Kluwer Copyright Blog*, 14 June 2021) <https://bit.ly/2YEPTIX>.

'Remuneration Rights and National Treatment' in S Frankel and others (eds), *Improving Intellectual Property* (Edward Elgar 2023) 341–352.

Hugenholtz PB and Guibault L, 'Auteurscontractenrecht: Naar Een Wettelijke Regeling?' (2004) <https://Ibit.ly/3UvnwGx>.

Hugenholtz PB, van Eechoud M, van Gompel S, Guibault L and Helberger N, 'The Recasting of Copyright & Related Rights for the Knowledge Economy' (2006) <https://tinyurl.com/2k5mph3f>.

Hughes J and Merges R, 'Copyright and Distributive Justice' (2016) 92 Notre Dame L Rev 513.

Hviid M, Izquierdo-Sanchez S and Jacques S, 'Digitalisation and Intermediaries in the Music Industry: The Rise of the Entrepreneur?' (2018) 15 SCRIPTed 242.

Hviid M, Schroff S, and Street J, 'Regulating Collective Management Organisations by Competition' [2016] 7 JIPITEC 256.

IFPI, 'Global Music Report 2024 – State of the Industry' (2024) <https://globalmusicreport.ifpi.org>.

IMPALA, 'Streaming Reform Revisited – IMPALA Calls for Increased Subscription Prices, Bespoke Deals for Fans, and a Higher Share for Master Rights, among Other Proposals for a Fairer, More Dynamic Market' (27 April 2023).

Janssens M-C and Vanherpe J, 'Blockchain and Copyright. Beyond the Buzzword?' [2018] 19 IRDI 93.

Jenkins G, 'An Extended Doctrine of Implied Consent – A Digital Mediator?' [2021] 52 IIC 706.

Jensen FJ, 'Rethinking Royalties: Alternative Payment Systems on Music Streaming Platforms' [2024] J Cult Econ <https://rdcu.be/dHsmY>.

Johansson D, 'Streams & Dreams: A Fair Music Economy for All, Part 1' (2022) <https://tinyurl.com/3jskdxde> and 'Part 2' (2024) <https://bit.ly/3Sh3D5R>.

'Revenue Distribution from Music Streaming – A Quantitative Analysis of Swedish Artists on Spotify' (2023) <https://tinyurl.com/2pywf76y>.

Johnson J, 'Application of the Copyright Termination Provision to the Music Industry: Sound Recordings Should Constitute Works Made for Hire' (2013) 67 U Miami L Rev 661.

Kanellopoulou J, *Competition Policy and the Music Industries: A Business Model Perspective* (Routledge 2022).

Karapapa S, *Defences to Copyright Infringement: Creativity, Innovation and Freedom on the Internet* (Oxford University Press 2020).

Karas M and Kirstein R, 'Efficient Contracting under the US Copyright Termination Law' (2018) 54 Int Rev Law Econ 39.

Kariyawasam K and Palliyaarachchi R, 'The Song Would Be Nothing without Someone to Sing It: Copyright and Performers' Rights in Music' [2020] 35 Int Rev Law Comput Technol 1.

Karubian S, '360° Deals: An Industry Reaction to the Devaluation of Recorded Music' (2009) 18 S Cal Interdisc LJ 395.

KEA, 'The Collective Management of Rights in Europe. The Quest for Efficiency' (2006) <https://tinyurl.com/nhy62m4x>.

Kempton P and Travostino M (eds), *Finding the Value in the Gap* (IAEL Yearbook, 2018).

Keustermans J and Blomme P, *Auteursrecht. Capita Selecta* (2nd edn, Intersentia 2021).

Kirstein R and Karas M, 'More Rights, Less Income? An Economic Analysis of the New Copyright Law in Germany' (Working Paper Series, 2017).

Klingner S and Friedrich J, 'Status Quo and Perspectives of Licensing Synchronisation Rights' (2017) 6 IJMBR 69.

Klobučník L, 'Navigating the Fragmented Online Music Licensing Landscape in Europe: A Legislative Compass in Sight?' (2020) 11 JIPITEC 340.

Knopper S, *Appetite for Self-Destruction: The Spectacular Crash of the Record Industry in the Digital Age* (CreateSpace 2017).

Koo J, *The Right of Communication to the Public in EU Copyright Law* (Hart 2019).

'The EU Right of Communication to the Public – Still Looking for a Good Link' in E Rosati (ed), *Routledge Handbook of EU Copyright Law* (Routledge Handbooks, Routledge 2021).

Korsten L and Movig J, 'Belgische Wetswijziging Introduceert B2B-Bescherming; een Voorbeeld voor Nederland?' (2020) 23 M&M 68.

Kretschmer M, 'Short Paper: Copyright Term Reversion and the "Use-It-or-Lose-It" Principle' (2012) 1 IJMBR 44.

Kretschmer M and Giblin R, 'Getting Creators Paid: One More Chance for Copyright Law' (2021) 43 EIPR 279.

Kretschmer M, Derclaye E, Favale M and Watt R, 'The Relationship between Copyright and Contract Law' (2010) <https://ssrn.com/abstract=2624945>.

Kretschmer M, Gavaldon AA, Miettinen J and Singh S, 'UK Authors' Earnings and Contracts 2018: A Survey of 50.000 Writers' (2019) <https://ssrn.com/abstract=3389685>.

Kretschmer M and others, 'What Constitutes Evidence for Copyright Policy?' (CREATe Working Paper, 2013).

Krikke J, 'Directive 2006/115/EC – on Rental Right and Lending Right and on Certain Rights Related to Copyright in the Field of Intellectual Property (Rental and Lending Right Directive)' in T Dreier and PB Hugenholtz (eds), *Concise European Copyright Law* (2nd edn, Kluwer Law International 2016).

Krueger AB, *Rockonomics* (John Murray 2019).

Lacourt A, Radel-Cormann J and Valais S, 'Fair Remuneration for Creators in Exploitation Contracts' (European Audiovisual Observatory 2023) <https://shorturl.at/dwT68>

Lalonde P-É, 'Study Concerning Fair Compensation for Music Creators in the Digital Age' (2014) <https://tinyurl.com/3dh2czap>.

Landes WM and Posner RA, *The Economic Structure of Intellectual Property Law* (Belknap Press of Harvard University Press 2003).

Lardinois J-C, *Les Contrats Commentés de l'Industrie Audiovisuelle : Cadre Général et Pratique Contractuelle* (Création Information Communication Pratique 3, Larcier 2007).

Les Contrats Commentés de l'Industrie de La Musique 2.0 : Cadre Général et Pratique Contractuelle (Création Information Communication Pratique 1, 2nd edn, Larcier 2009).

Leech-Wilkinson D, *Challenging Performance: Classical Music Performance Norms and How to Escape Them* (e-book, 2020), e-book.

Leistner M, 'The Implementation of Art 17 DSM Directive in Germany – A Primer with Some Comparative Remarks' (2022) 71 GRUR International 909.

Lenaerts K and Van Nuffel P, *European Union Law* (3rd edn, Sweet & Maxwell 2011).

Lenselink BJ, *De verlening van Exploitatiebevoegdheden in het Auteursrecht. Een Rechtsvergelijkend Onderzoek naar Overdracht en Licentieverlening in Auteursrechtelijke Exploitatieverhoudingen naar Nederlands, Duits en Amerikaans Recht* (Sdu Uitgevers 2005).

Lesser B, 'Record Labels Shot the Artists, but They Did Not Share the Equity' (2018) 16 Geo JL & Pub Pol'y 289.

Levine R, *Free Ride. How Digital Parasites Are Destroying the Culture Business, and How the Culture Business Can Fight Back* (Anchor 2012).

Lewis F, 'Slipping through the Cracks: How Digital Music Streaming Cuts Corners on Artists' Royalty Revenues Globally' (2017) 43 Brook J Int'l L 297.

Liebowitz SJ and Watt R, 'How to Best Ensure Remuneration for Creators in the Market for Music? Copyright and Its Alternatives' (2006) 20 Journal of Economic Surveys 513.

Lindner B, 'The Role of Collective Administration in New Business Models in the Audiovisual Sector' in S von Lewinski (ed), *Remuneration for the Use of Works. Exclusivity vs Other Approaches* (De Gruyter 2017).

Litman J, *Digital Copyright* (Michigan Publishing, University of Michigan Library 2017).

Lobel O, *Talent Wants to Be Free. Why We Should Learn to Love Leaks, Raids, and Free Riding* (Yale University Press 2013).

Loewenheim U, 'Rückruf des Nutzungsrechts nach § 41 UrhG und Fortbestehen der Enkelrechte' in K-I Wöhrn, W Bullinger, E Grunert and C Ohst (eds), *Festschrift für Artur-Axel Wandtke zum 70 Geburtstag am 26 März 2013* (Walter De Gruyter 2013).

Lucas A, '*La transposition en France de la directive droit d'auteur dans le marché unique numérique* 2019/790' [2021] 26 AM 307.

Lucas-Schloetter A, 'Qu'y a-t-Il Dans La "Deuxième Corbeille"? La Loi Allemande Du 26 Octobre 2007 Relative Au Droit d'Auteur Dans La Société de l'Information' [2008] 28 PI 368.

'Das neue Urhebervertragsrecht' [2017] 66 GRUR 235.

'European Copyright Contract Law: A Plea for Harmonisation' (2017) 48 IIC 897.

'The Remuneration of Authors and Performers in Copyright Contract Law' in P Torremans (ed), *Research Handbook on Copyright Law* (Research Handbooks in Intellectual Property, 2nd edn, Edward Elgar 2017).

Lucas-Schloetter A and Bernault C, *Traité de la Propriété Littéraire et Artistique* (5th edn, LexisNexis 2017).

Lunney G, 'Copyright Collectives and Collecting Societies: The United States Experience' in D Gervais (ed), *Collective Management of Copyright and Related Rights* (3rd edn, Kluwer Law International 2016).

Lunney G, *Copyright's Excess: Money and Music in the US Recording Industry* (1st edn, Cambridge University Press 2018).

Lyons F, Sun H, Collopy DP, Curran K and Ohagan P, 'Music 2025 – The Music Data Dilemma: Issues Facing the Music Industry in Improving Data Management' (2019) <https://ssrn.com/abstract=3437670>.

Malevanny N, *Online Music Distribution – How Much Exclusivity Is Needed? A Study of International, European, German and US Copyright Systems and Their Objectives*, vol 12 (Munich Studies on Innovation and Competition, Springer Berlin Heidelberg 2019).

Marisi F, 'Law and Music: Copyright and Neighboring Rights' [2013] 5 Review of Artistic Education 25.
Mariuzzo F and Ormosi PL, 'Independent v Major Record Labels: Do They Compete on a Level-Playing Streaming Field?' [2020] SSRN Electronic Journal.
Markellou M, *Le Contrat d'Exploitation d'Auteur. Vers un Droit d'Auteur Contractuel Européen. Analyse Comparative des Systèmes Juridiques Allemand, Belge, Français et Hellénique* (Création Information Communication, Larcier 2012).
Markesinis BS, Unberath H and Johnston A, *The German Law of Contract. A Comparative Treatise* (2nd edn, Hart 2006).
Marshall L, 'The 360 Deal and the "New" Music Industry' (2013) 16 EJCS 77.
Marušić B, *The Autonomous Legal Concept of Communication to the Public Interpretation in EU Copyright Law* (Edward Elgar 2023).
Matulionyte R, 'Empowering Authors via Fairer Copyright Contract Law' (2019) 42 UNSWLJ 681.
Mazziotti G and Ranaivoson H, 'Can Online Music Platforms Be Fair? An Interdisciplinary Research Manifesto' [2024] 55 IIC 249.
McClean D (ed), *Artist, Authorship & Legacy: A Reader* (Ridinghouse 2019).
McDonagh L, 'Rearranging the Roles of the Performer and the Composer in the Music Industry: The Potential Significance of Fisher v Brooker' [2012] 1 IPQ 64.
McMeel G, *The Construction of Contracts: Interpretation, Implication and Rectification* (Oxford University Press 2007).
Medicus D and Lorenz S, *Schuldrecht I. Allgemeiner Teil* (Juristische Kurz-Lehrbücher, 21st edn, CH Beck 2015).
Menger P-M, 'The Market for Creative Labour: Talent and Inequalities' in C Jones, M Lorenzen and J Sapsed (eds), *The Oxford Handbook of Creative Industries* (Oxford Handbooks, Oxford University Press 2015).
Meyn J, Kandziora M, Albers S and Clement M, 'Consequences of Platforms' Remuneration Models for Digital Content: Initial Evidence and a Research Agenda for Streaming Services' (2023) 51 Journal of the Academy of Marketing Science 11.
Mezei P, *Copyright Exhaustion: Law and Policy in the United States and the European Union* (2nd edn, Cambridge University Press 2022).
Michel NJ, 'Digital File Sharing and Royalty Contracts in the Music Industry: A Theoretical Analysis' (2006) 3 Review of Economic Research on Copyright Issues 29.
MIDEM, 'Artist & Label Services: How Technology Is Energising an Artists-First Global Business' (2020).
Möhring P and Nicolini K, *Urheberrecht* (4th edn, CH Beck 2018).
Morgan G and Nelligan P, *The Creativity Hoax: Precarious Work in the Gig Economy* (Anthem Press 2018).
Muikku J, 'Pro Rata and User Centric Distribution Models: A Comparative Study' (30 November 2017).
Mulligan M, *Awakening: The Music Industry in the Digital Age* (Createspace 2015).
Musgrave G, 'Collaborating to Compete: The Role of Cultural Intermediaries in Hypercompetition' (2017) 6 IJMBR 41.
Nérisson S, *La Gestion Collective des Droits des Auteurs en France et en Allemagne: Quelle Légitimité?* (Bibliothèque de l'Institut de recherche juridique de la Sorbonne-André Tunc 49, IRJS Editions 2013).
Neu T, *Der Zwang zur angemessenen Vergütung und weiteren Beteiligung nach der Urheberrechtsreform* (Walter De Gruyter 2013).
Nordemann JB, 'Die Beendigung urheberrechtlicher Verträge: Automatischer Rechterückfall? Das Urhebervertragsrecht nach BGH M2Trade, Take Five und Reifen

Progressiv' in K-I Wöhrn, W Bullinger, E Grunert and C Ohst (eds), *Festschrift für Artur-Axel Wandtke zum 70 Geburtstag am 26 März 2013* (Walter De Gruyter 2013).
Nordemann JB, Pukas J and Waiblinger J, 'Transposition of the DSM Copyright Directive 2019/790 in Germany' [2021] 26 AM 325.
Obergfell EI (ed), *Zehn Jahre reformiertes Urhebervertragsrecht: 1. Josef Kohler-Symposion* (Josef Kohler-Symposion, Berlin/Boston, Walter De Gruyter 2013).
O'Dwyer A, 'The Artists' Resale Right Directive 2001/84/EC: A Means of Targeted Intervention for Visual Artists' (2021) 24 J World Intellect Prop 3.
Okorocha D, 'A Full 360: How the 360 Deal Challenges the Historical Resistance to Establishing a Fiduciary Duty between Artist and Label' (2010) 18 UCLA Ent L Rev 1.
OMC Working Group of Member States' Experts, 'The Status and Working Conditions of Artists and Cultural and Creative Professionals' (European Union Publications Office June 2023) <https://tinyurl.com/mtjahkv4>.
Osborne R, 'Is Equitable Remuneration Equitable? Performers' Rights in the UK' (2017) 40 Popular Music and Society 573.
Osborne R and Sun H, 'Economics of Streaming: Contract Adjustment and Rights Reversion' (6 February 2023).
Page W, *Tarzan Economics. Eight Principles for Pivoting through Disruption* (Simon & Schuster 2021).
'Equitable Remuneration: Policy Options and Their Unintended Consequences' (2023) <https://pivotaleconomics.com/undercurrents/wipo>.
Page W and Dalla Riva C, '"Glocalisation" of Music Streaming within and across Europe' (Europe in Question 2023).
Page W and Safir D, 'Money In, Money Out: Lessons from CMOs in Allocating and Distributing Licensing Revenue' [2018] Music & Copyright Newsletter 23.
Panteia and KEA, *Feasibility Study for the Establishment of a European Music Observatory: Final Report* (Publications Office of the European Union 2020).
Paramythiotis Y, 'Fairness in Copyright Contract Law: Remuneration for Authors and Performers under the Copyright in the Digital Single Market Directive' in T-E Synodinou, P Jougleux, C Markou and T Prastitou-Merdi (eds), *EU Internet Law in the Digital Single Market* (Springer International 2021).
Parliament, 'Resolution of 13 March 2007 on the Commission Recommendation of 18 October 2005 on Collective Cross-Border Management of Copyright and Related Rights for Legitimate Online Music Services (2005/737/EC)' 2006/2008(INI).
'Report on the Proposal for a Directive of the European Parliament and of the Council on Copyright in the Digital Single Market (COM(2016)0593 – C8-0383/2016 – 2016/0280 (COD))' A8-0245/2018.
'Recommendations to the Commission on an EU Framework for the Social and Professional Situation of Artists and Workers in the Cultural and Creative Sectors' (Draft Report) 2023/2051(INL).
Parliament, Committee on Culture and Education, 'Report of 4 December 2023 on Cultural Diversity and the Conditions for Authors in the European Music Streaming Market' A9-0388/2023 <https://shorturl.at/covxK>
Passman D, *All You Need to Know about the Music Business* (11th edn, Simon & Schuster 2023).
Patry WF, *How to Fix Copyright* (Oxford University Press 2011).
Pauly J and H'Madoun Y, *Poppuntgids voor Muzikant en DJ* (1.2, Poppunt vzw 2017).
Pavis M, 'The Author–Performer Divide in Intellectual Property Law: A Comparative Analysis of the American, Australian, British and French Legal Frameworks' (University of Exeter 2016).

'Is There Any-Body on Stage? A Legal (Mis)Understanding of Performances' (2016) 19 Journal of World Intellectual Property 99.
Pedersen RR, 'A Meta Study of User-Centric Distribution for Music Streaming' (2020) <https://api.semanticscholar.org/CorpusID:229196609>.
Peel E, *Treitel on the Law of Contract* (15th edn, Sweet & Maxwell 2020).
Phillips T and Street J, 'Copyright and Musicians at the Digital Margins' (2015) 37 Media, Culture & Society 342.
Pitt IL, *Direct Licensing and the Music Industry* (Springer International 2015).
Polcz S, 'Loyalties v Royalties' (2021) 74 Hastings LJ 765.
Pollicino O, Riccio GM and Bassini M (eds), *Copyright and Fundamental Rights in the Digital Age. A Comparative Analysis in Search of a Common Constitutional Ground* (Edward Elgar 2020).
Poort J and Pervaiz A, 'Survey Data Perspectives Authors and Performers' (2022) <www.ivir.nl/publications/survey-data-perspectives-authors-and-performers/>.
Poort J, Pervaiz A and Furgał U, 'Mapping Document on Income Development of Authors and Performers and Copyright Reversal in EU' (2021) <https://zenodo.org/records/5552531>.
Poort J, Quintais JP, van der Ende M, Yagafarova A and Hageraats M, 'Global Online Piracy Study' (2018) <https://ssrn.com/abstract=3224323>.
Prassl J, *Humans as a Service. The Promise and Perils of Work in the Gig Economy* (Oxford University Press 2018).
Price J, 'The Definitive Guide to Spotify Royalties' [2020] <https://shorturl.at/ADHS3>.
Priora G, 'Catching Sight of a Glimmer of Light: Fair Remuneration and the Emerging Distributive Rationale in the Reform of EU Copyright Law' [2020] 10 JIPITEC 330.
'Distributive Justice in EU Copyright Law: A Function-Based Assessment for a Sustainable Harmonization' (Sant'Anna School of Advanced Studies 2020).
Pro Musik, 'Payment Option Transparency: On the Impact of Alternative Payment Models in Music Streaming' (9 June 2023) <https://tinyurl.com/3w27jrxr>.
Quiggin J and Hunter D, 'Money Ruins Everything' (2008) 30 Hastings Comm & Ent LJ 203.
Quinn A, 'Are Online Music Platforms Undermining the Principles of Copyright Law?' (2018) 13 JIPLP 49.
Raad voor de Intellectuele Eigendom, 'Advies betreffende de omzetting in Belgisch recht van richtlijn 2019/790/EU van 17 april 2019 inzake auteursrechten en naburige rechten in de digitale eengemaakte markt en tot wijziging van Richtlijnen 96/9/EG en 2001/29/EG' (19 June 2020).
Racine B, 'L'Auteur et l'Acte de Création' (January 2020) <https://tinyurl.com/3jxmd74b>.
Rahmatian A, 'Is Copyright Good for Music?' (2010) 5 JIPLP 869.
Raimond S, *La Qualification du Contrat d'Auteur* (Le Droit des Affaires. Propriété Intellectuelle 34, LexisNexis 2009).
Ramalho A, *The Competence of the European Union in Copyright Lawmaking. A Normative Perspective of EU Powers for Copyright Harmonization* (Springer International 2016).
Ramalho A and Lopez-Tarruella A, 'Implementation of the Directive 2011/77/EU: Copyright Term of Protection' (European Parliament 2018) <https://tinyurl.com/59hw3csc>.
Reber N, 'The "Further Fair Participation" Provision in Art 32a (2) German Copyright Act – Claims against a Third-Party Exploiter of a Work' (2016) 11 JIPLP 382.
Reinbothe J and von Lewinski S, *The WIPO Treaties on Copyright. A Commentary on the WCT, the WPPT, and the BTAP* (2nd edn, Oxford University Press 2015).
Rethink Music Initiative, 'Fair Music: Transparency and Payment Flows in the Music Industry. Recommendations to Increase Transparency, Reduce Friction, and Promote Fairness in the Music Industry' (2015) <https://tinyurl.com/yc2s5yyx>.

Ricketson S and Ginsburg J, *International Copyright and Neighbouring Rights. The Berne Convention and Beyond* (2nd edn, Oxford University Press 2006).

Riemer K, Schellhammer S and Meinert M (eds), *Collaboration in the Digital Age. How Technology Enables Individuals, Teams and Businesses* (Progress in IS, Springer International 2019).

Rogers J, *The Death & Life of the Music Industry in the Digital Age* (Bloomsbury 2013).

Rombouts B, 'Ictu v. Ireland: Expanding the Scope of Self-Employed Workers Entitled to Collective Bargaining Rights in Relation to Competition Law Prohibitions' (2019) 5 ILARC 17.

Rosati E, 'When Does a Communication to the Public under EU Copyright Law Need to Be to a "New Public"?' (2020) 46 EL Rev 802.

Copyright in the Digital Single Market. Article-by-Article Commentary to the Provisions of Directive 2019/790 (Oxford University Press 2021).

'The DSM Directive Two Years On: Do Things Ever Get Easier?' [2021] 52 IIC 1139.

(ed), *The Routledge Handbook of EU Copyright Law* (Routledge Handbooks, 1st edn, Routledge 2021).

Copyright and the Court of Justice of the European Union, vol 2 (Oxford University Press 2023).

Rosén J (ed), *Individualism and Collectiveness in Intellectual Property Law* (ATRIP Intellectual Property, Edward Elgar 2012).

Rosenmeier M (ed), *Festskrift til Jørgen Blomqvist* (Ex Tuto 2021).

Rosenmeier M, Szkalej K and Wolk S, *EU Copyright Law. Subsistence, Exploitation and Protection of Rights* (Kluwer Law International 2019).

Rub G, 'Stronger than Kryptonite? Inalienable Profit Sharing Schemes in Copyright Law' (2013) 27 Harv JL & Tech 49.

Sawyer RK and Dezutter S, 'Distributed Creativity: How Collective Creations Emerge from Collaboration' (2009) 3 Psycholreatehet Creat Arts 81.

Scheuerer S, 'The Fairness Principle in Competition-Related Economic Law' [2023] 72 GRUR International 919.

Schovsbo J (ed), *The Exploitation of Intellectual Property Rights: In Search of the Right Balance* (ATRIP Intellectual Property, Edward Elgar 2023).

Schricker G, 'German and Comparative Intellectual Property Law Efforts for a Better Law on Copyright Contracts in Germany – A Never-Ending Story?' [2004] 35 IIC 850.

Urheberrecht. Kommentar (3rd edn, CH Beck 2006).

Schulze G, 'Das Urhebervertragsrecht nach Erlass der EU-Richtlinie über das Urheberrecht im digitalen Binnenmarkt' [2019] 68 GRUR 682.

Schwemer S, *Licensing and Access to Content in the European Union: Regulation between Copyright and Competition Law* (1st edn, Cambridge University Press 2019).

Senftleben M, 'Exportschlager Deutsches Urhebervertragsrecht? Het Voorontwerp Auteurscontractenrecht in Duits Perspectief' [2010] 10 AMI 146.

'More Money for Creators and More Support for Copyright in Society – Fair Remuneration Rights in Germany and the Netherlands' (2018) 41 Colum J L & Arts 413.

Senftleben M, Margoni T, Antal D, Bodó B, van Gompel S, Handke C, Kretschmer M, Poort J and Quintais JP, 'Ensuring the Visibility and Accessibility of European Creative Content on the World Market: The Need for Copyright Data Improvement in the Light of New Technologies' [2021] 13 JIPITEC 67.

Shapiro T, 'Remuneration Provisions in the DSM Copyright Directive and the Audiovisual Industry in the EU: The Elusive Quest for Fairness' (2020) 42 EIPR 778.

Silbey J, *The Eureka Myth: Creators, Innovators, and Everyday Intellectual Property* (Stanford University Press 2014).

Sinclair G and Green T, ‘Download or Stream? Steal or Buy? Developing a Typology of Today’s Music Consumer’ [2016] 15 J Consumer Behav 3.

Simone D, *Copyright and Collective Authorship: Locating the Authors of Collaborative Work* (Cambridge Intellectual Property and Information Law 50, Cambridge University Press 2019).

Skladany M, *Big Copyright versus the People: How Major Content Providers Are Destroying Creativ*^{it}*y and How to Stop Them* (1st edn, Cambridge University Press 2018).

Skopelja S, ‘The Boundaries of “Authorship” and “Performance” in Musical Copyright’ [2015] UNSWLJ Student Series No 15-04 9.

Smiers J and Schijndel M van, *Imagine There Is No Copyright and No Cultural Conglomerates Too: An Essay* (Institute of Network Cultures 2009).

Soetenhorst W, *De Bescherming van de Uitgeefprestatie* (WEJ Tjeenk Willink 1993).

Soocher S, *They Fought the Law. Rock Music Goes to Court* (Schirmer Books 1999).

Spoor J, Verkade D and Visser D, *Auteursrecht. Auteursrecht, Portretrecht, Naburige Rechten en Databanken*^{re}*cht* (Recht en Praktijk, 4th edn, Wolters Kluwer 2019).

Stamatoudi I and Torremans P (eds), *EU Copyright Law. A Commentary* (Elgar Commentaries, Edward Elgar 2021).

Stijns S, *Verbintenissenrecht. Boek 1* (die Keure 2005).

Stopps D, ‘How to Make a Living from Music, Second Edition’ (Creative Industries, WIPO 2014).

Stuyck J and Keirsbilck B, *Handels- en Economisch Recht. Deel 2. Mededingingsrecht. A. Handelspraktijken en Contracten met Consumenten* (Beginselen van Belgisch Privaatrecht XIII, 5th edn, Wolters Kluwer 2019).

Sun H, *Digital Revolution Tamed. The Case of the Recording Industry* (Springer International 2019).

‘Paradox of Celestial Jukebox: Resurgence of Market Control’ (2019) 12 Creative Industries Journal 105.

Suzor N, ‘Access, Progress, and Fairness: Rethinking Exclusivity in Copyright’ (2013) 15 Vand J Ent & Tech L 297.

Synodinou T-E (ed), *Codification of European Copyright Law. Challenges and Perspectives* (Information Law Series 29, Kluwer Law International 2012).

Terré F, Lequette Y, Simler P and Chénedé F, *Droit Civil. Les Obligations* (Précis. Droit privé, 12th edn, Dalloz 2019).

Timberg S, *Culture Crash: The Killing of the Creative Class* (Yale University Press 2015).

Tjittes RPJL, ‘De Aansprakelijkheid Voor Afgebroken Onderhandelingen – Een Kritisch Overzicht’ [2016] Rechtsgeleerd Magazijn THEMIS 237.

Tomlinson DE, ‘Everything That Glitters Is Not Gold: Songwriter-Music Publisher Agreements and Disagreements’ (1995) 18 Hastings Comm & Ent LJ 85.

Torremans P (ed), *Research Handbook on Copyright Law* (Research Handbooks in Intellectual Property, 2nd edn, Edward Elgar 2017).

‘The Duran Duran Case in Private International Law: Copyright Contracts and the Question whether 203 US Copyright Act Involves a Form of Reversionary Copyright’ [2018] 66 RIDA 81.

(ed), *Intellectual Property Law and Human Rights* (Information Law Series 34, 4th edn, Kluwer Law International 2020).

‘Transposition of the DSM Copyright Directive 2019/790 in the United Kingdom’ [2021] 26 AM 374.

Towse R, ‘Copyright and Economic Incentives: An Application to Performers’ Rights in the Music Industry’ (1999) 52 Kyklos 369.

‘Economics of Music Publishing: Copyright and the Market’ (2017) 41 J Cult Econ 403.

'Copyright Reversion in the Creative Industries: Economics and Fair Remuneration' (2018) 41 Colum J L & Arts 467.
A *Textbook of Cultural Economics* (2nd edn, Cambridge University Press 2019).
'Dealing with Digital: The Economic Organisation of Streamed Music' (2020) 42 Media, Culture & Society 1461.
Travis H, *Copyright Class Struggle: Creative Economies in a Social Media Age* (1st edn, Cambridge University Press 2018).
Tschmuck P, *Creativity and Innovation in the Music Industry* (2nd edn, Springer 2012).
UK IPO, Guidance: United Kingdom Industry Agreement on Music Streaming Metadata (31 July 2023) <https://bit.ly/3EqYsZI>.
UK Intellectual Property Office, 'Guidance: UK Voluntary Code of Good Practice on Transparency in Music Streaming' (31 January 2024) <https://bit.ly/4bbBx32>.
Ulvaeus B, 'Rebalancing the Song Economy' (TEDxSSE, April 2021).
Vaidhyanathan S, *Copyrights and Copywrongs: The Rise of Intellectual Property and How It Threatens Creativity* (New York University Press 2001).
Van Couter Y and Vanbrabant B, *Handboek Licentieovereenkomsten* (Bibliotheek Handelsrecht Larcier. Mededinging, Handelspraktijken en Intellectuele Rechten 7, Larcier 2008).
Van Dongen S, *Groepen van Contracten* (Onderneming en Recht 95, Wolters Kluwer 2016).
Van Dunné JM, *Verbintenissenrecht. Deel 1. Contractenrecht* (5th edn, Kluwer 2004).
Van Eechoud M, *Choice of Law in Copyright and Related Rights: Alternatives to the Lex Protectionis* (Universiteit van Amsterdam 2003).
Van Eechoud M, Hugenholtz PB, van Gompel S, Guibault L and Helberger N, *Harmonizing European Copyright Law: The Challenges of Better Lawmaking* (Information Law Series 19, Kluwer Law International 2009).
Van Gerven W and Van Oevelen A, *Verbintenissenrecht* (Studie Juri, 6th edn, Acco 2021).
Van Gompel S, '"Non, Non, Rien n'a Changé": Over Vergoedingsaanspraken voor Makers uit Hoofde van Exploitatiecontracten' [2021] 21 Auteursrecht 3.
'Omzetting van de DSM Auteursrecht Richtlijn 2019/790 in Nederland' [2021] 26 AM 335.
Van Gompel S, Hugenholtz PB, Poort J, Schumacher L and Visser D, 'Evaluatie Wet Auteurscontractenrecht: Eindrapport' (2020) <https://tinyurl.com/352jm6ak>.
Vanbrabant B, *La Propriété Intellectuelle. Tome 1. Nature Juridique* (Création Information Communication, Larcier 2016).
La Propriété Intellectuelle. Tome 2. Régime Patrimonial (Création Information Communication, Larcier 2018).
Vancoppernolle T, *Intertemporeel Recht* (Intersentia 2019).
Vanhees H, *Een Juridische Analyse van de Grondslagen, Inhoud en Draagwijdte van Auteursrechtelijke Exploitatiecontracten* (Maklu 1993).
'De Belgische Regeling inzake Auteurscontracten: 10 jaar later (1994-2004)' [2004] 9 AM 513.
De Wettelijke Regeling inzake Auteurscontracten (Recht en Praktijk 69, Kluwer 2012).
'Auteurscontract' [2019] OBO 1.
'Twee Nieuwe Vergoedingsrechten Voor Auteurs En Uitvoerende Kunstenaars' [2022] 23 IRDI 389.
Vanherpe J and Janssens M-C, 'Toepassingen van smart contracts in het auteursrecht: Tussen droom en daad' in P-J Aerts, F Hoogendijk and N Vandezande (eds), *Smart contracts: een overzicht vanuit juridisch perspectief* (KU Leuven Centre for IT & IP Law Series, Intersentia 2020).
Vercken G, 'Formalism in Authors' Contracts: An Assessment after the Court of Cassation's Decision of 21 November 2006' [2009] 57 RIDA 4.
Vermander F, *De Opzegging van Overeenkomsten* (Intersentia 2014).

Vetulani-Cęgiel A, 'EU Copyright Law, Lobbying and Transparency of Policy-Making' [2015] 6 JIPITEC 146.

Visser D, 'Pippi Langkous en het nieuwe auteurscontractenrecht' [2015] 90 NJB 1289.

Visser D and Terpstra S, 'De stelling van Pythagoras. De lumpsumoverdracht van muziekrechten aan investeringsmaatschappijen en het auteurscontractenrecht' [2023] 23 Auteursrecht 4.

Visser D, Schaap JA and Kreijger PJ, *ACR: Auteurscontractenrecht* (DeLex 2016).

Viswanathan B, *Cultivating Copyright: How Creators and Creative Industries Can Harness Intellectual Property to Survive the Digital Age* (Routledge 2019).

Von Lewinski S, *International Copyright Law and Policy* (Oxford University Press 2008).

'News from Germany. Developments in Germany from Mid-2005 until the End of 2010. Part I' [2011] 59 RIDA 164.

(ed), *Remuneration for the Use of Works. Exclusivity. vs Other Approaches* (De Gruyter 2017).

Vrakas GD, 'Does Copyright Support Musical Creativity in a Remix Era?' in T-E Synodinou, P Jougleux, C Markou and T Prastitou-Merdi (eds), *EU Internet Law in the Digital Single Market* (Springer International 2021).

Vučković RM, 'Remunerations for Authors and Other Creators in Collective Management of Copyright and Related Rights' (2016) 66 Zbornik PFZ 35.

Waas B and Hießl C (eds), *Collective Bargaining for Self-Employed Workers in Europe* (Bulletin of Comparative Labour Relations, Kluwer Law International 2021).

Waelkens J, *Interpretatie van Overeenkomsten en Eenzijdige Rechtshandelingen. Deel I* (Intersentia 2016).

Walter MM and von Lewinski SS (eds), *European Copyright Law. A Commentary* (Oxford University Press 2010).

Wandtke A and Ostendorff S, *Urheberrecht* (De Gruyter Studium, 8th edn, De Gruyter 2021).

Williamson J, Cloonan M and Frith S, 'Having an Impact? Academics, the Music Industries and the Problem of Knowledge' (2011) 17 IJCP 459.

WIPO, 'Guide to the Copyright and Related Rights Treaties Administered by WIPO and Glossary of Copyright and Related Rights Terms' (WIPO 2004).

The Wittem Group, 'European Copyright Code' (2011) 33 EIPR 76.

Withofs V, *Contractsoverdracht* (Recht en Onderneming 47, die Keure 2015).

Witt S, *How Music Got Free. The End of an Industry, the Turn of the Century, and the Patient Zero of Piracy* (Viking 2015).

Woodcock J and Graham M, *The Gig Economy – A Critical Introduction* (Polity Press 2020).

Wright D, 'Playwrights and Copyright' (2015) 38 Colum J L & Arts 301.

Xalabarder R, 'The Equitable Remuneration of Audiovisual Authors: A Proposal of Unwaivable Remuneration Rights under Collective Management' [2018] 66 RIDA 5.

'International Legal Study on the Implementation of an Unwaivable Right of Audiovisual Authors to Obtain Equitable Remuneration for the Exploitation of Their Works' (2018) <https://tinyurl.com/whp34h4a>.

'The Principle of Appropriate and Proportionate Remuneration for Authors and Performers in Art 18 Copyright in the Digital Single Market Directive. Statutory Residual Remuneration Rights for Its Effective National Implementation' [2020] 19(11) InDret 1.

Yuvaraj J, 'Back to the Start: Re-Envisioning the Role of Copyright Reversion in Australia and Other Common Law Countries' (Monash University 2021).

Yuvaraj J, Giblin R, Russo-Batterham D and Grant G, 'US Copyright Termination Notices 1977–2020: Introducing New Datasets' (2022) 19 Journal of Empirical Legal Studies 250.

Zemer L, *The Idea of Authorship in Copyright* (Applied Legal Philosophy, Ashgate 2007).

Zucconi K, 'Freedom: Long Term Recording Agreements and the International Music Industry' (1996) 8 Pace Int'l L Rev 161.

Index

CAMBRIDGE INTELLECTUAL PROPERTY AND INFORMATION LAW

Titles in the Series (formerly known as Cambridge Studies in Intellectual Property Rights)

Graeme W. Austin, Andrew F. Christie, Andrew T. Kenyon and Megan Richardson
Across Intellectual Property: Essays in Honour of Sam Ricketson

Brad Sherman and Lionel Bently
The Making of Modern Intellectual Property Law

Irini A. Stamatoudi
Copyright and Multimedia Products: A Comparative Analysis

Pascal Kamina
Film Copyright in the European Union

Huw Beverley-Smith
The Commercial Appropriation of Personality

Mark J. Davison
The Legal Protection of Databases

Robert Burrell and Allison Coleman
Copyright Exceptions: The Digital Impact

Huw Beverley-Smith, Ansgar Ohly and Agnès Lucas-Schloetter
Privacy, Property and Personality: Civil Law Perspectives on Commercial Appropriation

Catherine Seville
The Internationalisation of Copyright Law: Books, Buccaneers and the Black Flag in the Nineteenth Century

Philip Leith
Software and Patents in Europe

Geertrui van Overwalle
Gene Patents and Clearing Models: Patent Pools, Clearinghouses, Open Source Models and Liability Regimes

Lionel Bently, Jennifer Davis and Jane C. Ginsburg
Trade Marks and Brands: An Interdisciplinary Critique

Jonathan Curci
The Protection of Biodiversity and Traditional Knowledge in International Law of Intellectual Property

Lionel Bently, Jennifer Davis and Jane C. Ginsburg
Copyright and Piracy: An Interdisciplinary Critique

Megan Richardson and Julian Thomas
Fashioning Intellectual Property: Exhibition, Advertising and the Press, 1789–1918

Dev Gangjee
Relocating the Law of Geographical Indications

Andrew Kenyon, Megan Richardson and Ng-Loy Wee-Loon
The Law of Reputation and Brands in the Asia Pacific

Edson Beas Rodrigues, Jr
The General Exception Clauses of the TRIPS Agreement: Promoting Sustainable Development

Annabelle Lever
New Frontiers in the Philosophy of Intellectual Property

Sigrid Sterckx and Julian Cockbain
Exclusions from Patentability: How Far Has the European Patent Office Eroded Boundaries?

Sebastian Haunss
Conflicts in the Knowledge Society: The Contentious Politics of Intellectual Property

Helena R. Howe and Jonathan Griffiths
Concepts of Property in Intellectual Property Law

Rochelle Cooper Dreyfuss and Jane C. Ginsburg
Intellectual Property at the Edge: The Contested Contours of IP

Normann Witzleb, David Lindsay, Moira Paterson and Sharon Rodrick
Emerging Challenges in Privacy Law: Comparative Perspectives

Paul Bernal
Internet Privacy Rights: Rights to Protect Autonomy

Peter Drahos
Intellectual Property, Indigenous People and their Knowledge

Susy Frankel and Daniel Gervais
The Evolution and Equilibrium of Copyright in the Digital Age

Edited by Kathy Bowrey and Michael Handler
Law and Creativity in the Age of the Entertainment Franchise

Sean Bottomley
The British Patent System during the Industrial Revolution 1700–1852: From Privilege to Property

Susy Frankel
Test Tubes for Global Intellectual Property Issues: Small Market Economies

Jan Oster
Media Freedom As a Fundamental Right

Sara Bannerman
International Copyright and Access to Knowledge

Edited by Andrew T. Kenyon
Comparative Defamation and Privacy Law

Pascal Kamina
Film Copyright in the European Union (second edition)

Tim W. Dornis
Trademark and Unfair Competition Conflicts: Historical-Comparative, Doctrinal, and Economic Perspectives

Ge Chen
Copyright and International Negotiations: An Engine of Free Expression in China?

David Tan
The Commercial Appropriation of Fame: A Cultural Analysis of the Right of Publicity and Passing Off

Jay Sanderson
Plants, People and Practices: The Nature and History of the UPOV Convention

Daniel Benoliel
Patent Intensity and Economic Growth

Jeffrey A. Maine and Xuan-Thao Nguyen
The Intellectual Property Holding Company: Tax Use and Abuse from Victoria's Secret to Apple

Megan Richardson
The Right to Privacy: Origins and Influence of a Nineteenth-Century Idea

Martin Husovec
Injunctions against Intermediaries in the European Union: Accountable but Not Liable?

Estelle Derclaye
The Copyright/Design Interface: Past, Present and Future

Magdalena Kolasa
Trade Secrets and Employee Mobility: In Search of an Equilibrium

Péter Mezei
Copyright Exhaustion: Law and Policy in the United States and the European Union

Graham Greenleaf and David Lindsay
Public Rights: Copyright's Public Domains

Ole-Andreas Rognstad
Property Aspects of Intellectual Property

Elena Cooper
Art and Modern Copyright: The Contested Image

Paul Bernal
The Internet, Warts and All: Free Speech, Privacy and Truth

Sebastian Felix Schwemer
Licensing and Access to Content in the European Union: Regulation between Copyright and Competition Law

Daniela Simone
Copyright and Collective Authorship: Locating the Authors of Collaborative Work

Emily Hudson
Drafting Copyright Exceptions: From the Law in Books to the Law in Action

Graeme Gooday and Steven Wilf
Patent Cultures: Diversity and Harmonization in Historical Perspective

Mark Burdon
Digital Data Collection and Information Privacy Law

Tanya Aplin and Lionel Bently
Global Mandatory Fair Use: The Nature and Scope of the Right to Quote Copyright Works

Edited by Niklas Bruun, Graeme B. Dinwoodie, Marianne Levin and Ansgar Ohly
Transition and Coherence in Intellectual Property Law: Essays in Honour of Annette Kur

Alexander Peukert
A Critique of the Ontology of Intellectual Property Law

Brent Salter
Negotiating Copyright in the American Theatre: 1856-1951

Patrick R. Goold
IP Accidents: Negligence Liability in Intellectual Property

Péter Mezei
Copyright Exhaustion: Law and Policy in the United States and the European Union, (second edition)

Jose Bellido and Kathy Bowrey
Adventures in Childhood

Henning Grosse Ruse-Khan and Axel Metzger
Intellectual Property Ordering Beyond Borders

Brad Sherman
Intangible Intangibles: Patent Law's Engagement with Dematerialised Subject Matter

www.ingramcontent.com/pod-product-compliance
Lightning Source LLC
LaVergne TN
LVHW011703200926
848484LV00004B/1047
* 9 7 8 1 0 0 9 3 9 4 7 0 3 *